OXFORD STUDIES
IN MODERN EUROPEAN HISTORY

General Editors
SIMON DIXON, MARK MAZOWER,
and
JAMES RETALLACK

The Global Revolution

A History of International Communism
1917–1991

SILVIO PONS

Translated by
ALLAN CAMERON

OXFORD
UNIVERSITY PRESS

OXFORD
UNIVERSITY PRESS

Great Clarendon Street, Oxford, OX2 6DP,
United Kingdom

Oxford University Press is a department of the University of Oxford.
It furthers the University's objective of excellence in research, scholarship,
and education by publishing worldwide. Oxford is a registered trade mark of
Oxford University Press in the UK and in certain other countries

First published in Italian as *Stato e Rivoluzione* © Giulio Einaudi editore s.p.a., Torino 2012.

English translation © Oxford University Press 2014

The moral rights of the author have been asserted

First Edition published in 2014

Impression: 1

Published in the United States of America by Oxford University Press
198 Madison Avenue, New York, NY 10016, United States of America

British Library Cataloguing in Publication Data
Data available

Library of Congress Control Number: 2014940483

ISBN 978–0–19–965762–9

Printed and bound by
CPI Group (UK) Ltd, Croydon, CR0 4YY

Links to third party websites are provided by Oxford in good faith and
for information only. Oxford disclaims any responsibility for the materials
contained in any third party website referenced in this work.

The publication of this book was assisted by a grant made by the Fondazione Istituto Gramsci.

For Chiara

Contents

Abbreviations

ARCHIVES

APCF Archive du Parti communiste français [Archive of the French
Communist Party]

APCI Archivio del partito comunista italiano [Archive of the Italian
Communist Party]

AVPRF Arkhiv Vneshnei Politiki Rossiiskoy Federatsii [Foreign Policy Archive of the
Russian Federation)

RGANI Rossiiskii Gosudarstvennyi Arkhiv Noveishei Istorii [Russian State Archive of
Contemporary History]

RGASPI Rossiiskii Gosudarstvennyi Arkhiv Sotsial'no-Politicheskoy Istorii [Russian
State Archive of Social and Political History]

SAPMO Stiftung Archiv der Parteien und Massenorganisationen der DDR im
Bundesarchiv [Foundation Archives of Parties and Mass Organizations of the
GDR in the Federal Archives]

DOCUMENT COLLECTIONS

KIMR *Komintern i ideya mirovoy revoliutsii: dokumenty* [The Comintern and the
Idea of World Revolution: Documents], ed. J. S. Drabkin (Moscow: Nauka,
1998)

KVMV *Komintern i Vtoraya Mirovaya Voyna* [The Comintern and the Second World
War], ed. N. S. Lebedeva and M. M. Narinskii (2 vols, Moscow: Pamyatniki
Istoricheskoy Misly, 1994; 1998)

PBKI *Politburo CK Rkp(b)–Vkp(b) i Komintern 1919–1943: dokumenty*
[The Central Committee Politburo of the Rkp(b)–Vkp(b) and the
Comintern 1919–1943: documents], ed. G. M. Adibekov and K. K.
Shirinya (Moscow: Rosspen, 2004)

Prezidium *Prezidium TsK KPSS 1954–1964. Chernovye protokol' nye zapisi zasedanii.
Stenogrammy. Postanovleniya* [The Presidium of the Central Committee
of the Communist Party of the Soviet Union, 1954–1964] (3 vols,
Moscow: Rosspen, 2003–8)

SFVE *Sovetskii faktor v Vostochnoy Evrope 1944–1953: dokumenty* [The Soviet Factor
in Eastern Europe: Documents](2 vols, Moscow: Rosspen, 1999, 2002)

VEDRA *Vostochnaya Evropa v dokumentakh rossiiskikh arkhivov 1944–1953* [Eastern
Europe in the Documents of the Russian Archives] (2 vols, Moscow/
Novosibirsk: Sibirskii Khronograf, 1997–8)

INSTITUTIONS AND POLITICAL PARTIES

CCP	Chinese Communist Party
Cheka	Special Commission
Comecon	Council for Mutual Economic Assistance
Cominform	Communist Information Bureau
Comintern	Communist International
CPGB	Communist Party of Great Britain
CPSU	Communist Party of the Soviet Union
CPUSA	Communist Party of the United States of America
CSCE	Conference on Security and Cooperation in Europe
ECCI	Executive Committee of the Communist International
Gulag	Main Camp Administration
ICP	Indonesian Communist Party
KGB	Committee for State Security
KKE	Kommunistiko Komma Ellados [Greek Communist Party]
KPD	Kommunistische Partei Deutschlands [German Communist Party]
KSČ	Komunistická Strana Československá [Czechoslovak Communist Party]
MPLA	People's Movement for the Liberation of Angola
Narkomindel	People's Commissariat for External Affairs
NATO	North Atlantic Treaty Organization
NEP	New Economic Policy
NKVD	People's Commissariat for Internal Affairs
OGPU	Joint State Political Directorate
PCE	Partido comunista de España [Spanish Communist Party]
PCF	Parti communiste français [French Communist Party]
PCI	Partito comunista italiano [Italian Communist Party]
PCP	Partido comunista português [Portuguese Communist Party]
Politburo	Political Office
RCP(b)	Russian Communist Party (Bolshevik)
SED	Socialistische Einheitspartei Deutschlands [United Socialist Party of Germany]
SPD	Sozial-Demokratische Partei Deutschlands [Social Democratic Party of Germany]

Introduction

During the twentieth century, communism left its mark on the life, death, hopes, fears, dreams, nightmares, identity, and choices of a large part of humanity. It is not easy to find a single significant aspect of world history in the past century that was not in some way connected to it and did not come under its influence. Communism was many things together: a reality and a mythology, a state system and movement of parties, a closed elite and a mass politics, a progressive ideology and an imperial dominion, a project for a just society and an experiment on humanity, a pacifist rhetoric and a strategy of civil war, a liberating utopia and a system of concentration camps, an antagonist of world order and a form of anti-capitalist modernity. Communists were victims of dictatorial regimes and the creators of police states. Protagonists in social struggles, national liberation movements, and campaigns for citizens' rights, they invariably founded totalitarian, oppressive, and liberticidal regimes. Their dogmatism, discipline, leadership cults, and organization were proverbial, as was their adaptability to very different social, political, and cultural contexts. The attraction or repulsion evoked by the states, parties, and societies that grew out of the communist experience for a long time defined individual lives, intellectual orientations, and collective psychology.

Communism displayed a formidable ability to expand in the first half of the century and went into a precipitous decline in the second half. From the very beginning it presented itself as a demiurge of the modern world pursuing a rational and irreversible historical progress founded on Marxist doctrine, but it ended up emptied of meaning in relation to the tendencies and nature of modernity itself—in its institutions, customs, culture, and economy. Its collapse in Europe, Russia, and Central Asia has only left room for political heirs who have either become marginal or undergone a democratic or nationalist metamorphosis. It is remembered for some of the worst crimes against humanity in the last century. Its continuing existence in China and Vietnam has been entrusted to one-party states, which however constitute the political framework of an economic and social system turned on its head and based on the market and integrated into the capitalist world. The survival of more traditional regimes in Cuba and North Korea continues in a state of isolation without any prospects. Authors who take up the challenge of a general historical narrative have to confront the paradox of revolutionary events on a global scale that appear to have left no clear traces of themselves.[1] Communism seems to belong to a past that has been buried—plunged into a different time, distant from us and our world.

---

[1] F. Furet, *Le passé d'une illusion: essai sur l'idée communiste au XXe siècle* (Paris: Laffont/Calmann-Lévy, 1995); R. Service, *Comrades! A World History of Communism* (London: Macmillan, 2007); A. Brown, *The Rise and Fall of Communism* (New York: HarperCollins, 2010); D. Priestland, *The Red Flag: A History of Communism* (New York: Grove Press, 2009).

And yet it is precisely its impact on the development of the globalized world that represents communism's main legacy in our times. The Leninist idea of world revolution, the vision of imperialism as world system, the connection between mass society and the transnational concept of politics constituted original and founding features of communist ideology and experience. Communism was not only an internationalist ideal. For a long time it was a quintessential international phenomenon in its political culture, the geopolitical dimension of its movement, and the strategies and myths of the Soviet state. The birth of a revolutionary state was not new in European history, but its transformative power in relation to the individual and society most certainly was, as was its ability to recruit followers, organize them, and give life to a constellation of states inspired by its original model. The place occupied by the Communist Revolution as 'the culmination of modern society' proved to be central in the history of most of the century.[2]

In this way, communism generated new messianic and universalist expectations. It provided the impulse and the material for life styles, collective identities and 'imagined communities'. It fostered new forms of authoritarianism and mass violence. It applied an extreme paradigm of modernity, founded on a unilinear idea of progress, faith in the teleology of history, a classist vision of society, terror, mass pedagogy, social engineering, and planning as the regulating principle in development. After the Second World War, the expansion of the Soviet Union and communism led to a sudden leap forward in the strategies of power.[3] At the same time, to some extent it forced capitalist countries into setting up adequate welfare policies together with a solid transnational cohesion. The combination of the Soviet Union's power, the birth of new communist states, and the growth in the movement gave rise to a global antagonism with the United States and Western Europe, which influenced changes and transformations in the post-colonial world. Communist models, actions, and language became tied up with decolonization, took the Cold War outside Europe, and increased the rivalry between contrasting projects for development and modernity.

The object of this book is communism's international history, with a focus on the political, ideological, organizational, and symbolic relations between the Soviet state and the movement made up of communist parties, both in power and not. For most of the century, 'international communism' was a basic concept in the contemporary world. The main players at the time conceived it or perceived it as a fundamental force in politics, firstly in terms of the 'world party of revolution' created by the October Revolution in 1917 and identified with the Comintern, and later as a characteristic of the 'socialist camp' and mass communist parties after the Second World War. The notion of international communism referred to a political movement made up of parties deployed almost everywhere and equipped with a centralized organization that had its base in the Soviet Union until the war,

---

[2] F. Halliday, *Revolution and World Politics: The Rise and Fall of the Sixth Great Power* (Durham, N.C. Duke University Press, 1999).

[3] For the outlook and practice of war as a feature of modern revolutionary regimes, see T. Skocpol, *Social Revolutions in the Modern World* (Cambridge: Cambridge University Press, 1994), 281.

and closely linked to Moscow and its allies even after the war. But the notion also referred to a particular state, the Soviet Union, and subsequently a system of states that came into being after the war in Europe and Asia, which followed the political, economic, and social model produced by the Bolshevik Revolution and were configured as a separate world and an international community. With this double meaning, international communism was a reality and a myth both for its followers and protagonists, and for its adversaries and antagonists.

The interaction between the Soviet state and the communist movement was based on shared cultural archetypes and a reciprocal legitimization, no less than discipline and organization. The Soviet state played a constituent role as the guide for communist action and the pillar of the dichotomous structure of the world, which underpinned their culture and identity. It constituted a hierarchical apparatus of dominion, mobilization, social transformation, and police control in Russia, which was extended to followers of the revolution outside the USSR. But it also represented the fulcrum from which motivations and decisive choices for all communists emanated. While the movement could not exist without the revolutionary state, that state rested an essential part of its authority on the communist parties, as vehicles of its policies and myths. The identification between Soviet interests and the prospects of world revolution assigned a crucial significance to the international dimension, even more so for a regime that cared little about social consensus but projected itself forward to socialist modernization and building its power. This book proposes in particular to investigate the methods, limitations, and failures of the Soviet Union and international communism in their exercise of hegemony and search for legitimacy.[4]

In this sense, a large part of the historiography of the communist movement has missed its target. The tendency to see the origins of the communist parties in their respective national societies has the defect of losing the constituent link established between the revolutionary state and the communist movement. This link was a primary element for all the communist parties, which throughout their histories represented both a strength and a decisive limitation. The deep social roots, the more or less mass following, and the various cultural profiles of some communist parties in particular periods—in Germany, France, and Italy rather than Great Britain or the United States, or in China, Indonesia, and Vietnam rather than Japan, India, or Iran—have to be explained in the light of particular national realities. However, not only the praxis, finances, and organization models but also the worldviews, the political culture, and the language of communists were dependent on and moulded by the Bolshevik party-state. This does not mean that it would be useful to write the history of communism in a one-directional and mono-dimensional manner, as has often happened in the more widely used historiographical approaches

---

[4] The concept of hegemony adopted in this book is not synonymous with domination and preponderance of material resources, but refers to the ability to generate legitimacy, according the definition used by the neo-Gramscian school in the theory of international relations. See R. Cox, 'Gramsci, hegemony and international relations: an essay in method', in S. Gill (ed.), *Gramsci, Historical Materialism and International Relations* (Cambridge: Cambridge University Press, 1993).

during the Cold War and even after it ended. It means that historians should grasp the centrality of transnational relations between the revolutionary state and the movement for most of the last century, without suppressing the multidimensional nature of the history of communism.[5] Communist identity was never unambiguous, but it was unthinkable that, working within a global project, it would not assert the primacy of politics over individuals, societies, and nations.

The world revolution Lenin dreamt of was not achieved. In spite of the ideological and social radicalization instigated everywhere by the First World War, a revolution similar to the Bolshevik one was not experienced in Germany, epicentre of all hopes, or in any other European country. Contrary to their expectations, the Bolsheviks organized themselves in a militarized party-state, won the Civil War, and kept themselves in power. Revolutionary Russia was isolated and marginalized by the Treaty of Versailles. However, the project of a world revolution continued to be cultivated, although it did undergo a gradual metamorphosis. The revolutionary state and the communist movement configured a centralized and hierarchical relationship between the centre and the periphery through the Comintern. The communist parties were formed under the direction of the Bolsheviks, who forged for them an intransigent, sectarian, and anti-social-democratic identity. Stalin imposed the primacy of state-building in the Soviet Union, provoking an exodus of dissidents but also finding fertile ground. 'Building socialism' and power politics, the myth of Revolution and the myth of anti-capitalist modernity fused with each other in the Stalinist 'revolution from above'. The communists' firm conviction that they were taking part in a 'European civil war' sustained the terror in the Soviet Union. Their identification with the imperatives of the Soviet state reached its extremes in the self-annihilation during the Weimar Republic. The task of defending the USSR replaced the failed revolutionary project, particularly after Hitler's rise to power. Both the new anti-fascist policy in the mid-1930s and the Molotov–Ribbentrop Pact at the end of the decade were dictated by the primacy of the Soviet state, irrespective of the positive or negative consequences for the communist parties.[6]

The Second World War changed the destiny of the state and the movement, but confirmed their mutual relationship. The destruction of Nazism raised communism to the level of epoch-making antagonist of liberal capitalism. The USSR emerged from the war as a great power with a dual nature—a state amongst other states and the centre of world socialism. The communist movement reached its

---

[5] A paradigmatic example of the sterile historiographical opposition between mono-dimensional and mono-causal approaches in the history of communism on the one hand and 'pluralist' and sociohistorical approaches on the other is the controversy that divided French historians in the 1990s: see S. Courtois, N. Werth, et al., *Il libro nero del comunismo: crimini, terrore, repressione* (Milan: Mondadori, 1998); M. Dreyfus et al., *Le siècle des communismes* (Paris: Éditions ouvrières, 2000). Various essays in both volumes actually put forward a more refined and less unilateral approach than would appear from the presentation of the books and the debate that followed.

[6] K. McDermott and J. Agnew, *The Comintern: A History of International Communism from Lenin to Stalin* (Basingstoke: Macmillan, 1996); A. Y. Vatlin, *Komintern: idei, resheniya, sudby* (Moscow: Rosspen, 2009); S. Wolikow, *L'Internationale communiste (1919–1943): le Komintern ou le rêve déchu du parti mondial de la révolution* (Paris: Les Éditions de l'Atelier, 2010).

high point of expansion through the anti-fascist resistance in Europe and the anti-imperialist struggle in Asia. In a few years, the USSR became the second nuclear superpower in a bipolar world and constituted the epicentre of a 'revolution from above' in Europe and revolution in China. New Sovietized states were installed in Central and Eastern Europe. Communists won the Civil War in China and triggered a war in Korea. The Soviet state presided over an extended 'socialist camp' covering much of Eurasia as far as China, and ready to relaunch the original antagonism between the communist and capitalist 'worlds'. Its role was based on an inextricable combination of ideology and power politics, destined to continue for the entire period of the Cold War.[7]

The monolithic self-representation of international communism was largely accepted in the West, to the point of becoming a political and analytical norm. That image and that norm were well suited to the propagation of the idea of an antagonism between irreconcilable philosophies and alliances on a planetary scale.[8] However, although the Soviet Union and the communist movement were compact and well integrated, they also suffered from serious inconsistencies and contradictions. The connection between the interests of the Soviet state and the prospect of world revolution proved to be controversial from the 1920s onward. The dilemmas of security and revolutionary ambitions were not easy to reconcile. The identification of communists with the Soviet state's interests was not up for discussion, but their interpretation could vary considerably. The tensions between the centre and the periphery that were on the Comintern's political agenda were not removed by its dissolution in 1943, nor by the creation of a new centralized organization for international communism, the Cominform, only four years later. After the war, Stalinist communism seemed to enjoy a period of maximum unity, but the differences and latent conflicts manifested themselves in its moment of triumph. Moscow's control proved to be incompatible with both the idea of 'nationalizing' the communist parties and the radicalism resulting from the partisan struggle. The partner who most closely combined autonomy and intransigence, the Communist Party in Yugoslavia, came on a collision course with the Soviet Union. The excommunication Stalin decreed against Tito in June 1948 appeared to bring the question rapidly to an end, but the rift demonstrated that the creation of new communist states, although crucial to the Soviet Union's increasing power, created dramatic contradictions in the structure, influence, and development of international communism.

The Cold War engendered the challenge from the Soviet Union and communism for world power. However, the ideological and power struggle presented the communist world with troubling unknowns, and increased its vulnerability the

---

[7] J. Haslam, *Russia's Cold War: From the October Revolution to the Fall of the Wall* (New Haven, Conn.: Yale University Press, 2011); V. Zubok, *A Failed Empire. The Soviet Union in the Cold War from Stalin to Gorbachev* (Chapel Hill, N.C.: University of North Carolina Press, 2007).

[8] M. J. Selverstone, *Constructing the Monolith: The United States, Great Britain, and International Communism, 1945–1950* (Cambridge, Mass.: Harvard University Press, 2009); D. C. Engerman, *Know Your Enemy: The Rise and Fall of America's Soviet Experts* (Oxford: Oxford University Press, 2009).

more it became global.[9] The bipolar configuration was highly imbalanced in favour of the Western bloc, which centred on the enormous power of the United States and included the most advanced countries in the world. Moreover, American hegemony was founded not only on its industrial, financial, and military strength but also on its multiple economic and cultural instruments and resources, which sustained a multilateral international system. Apparently better equipped, with a messianic message and more capacity for ideological mobilization than liberal capitalism, Soviet communism actually expressed a much more traditional imperial model based on state centralism, systemic separation, and territorial sovereignty. Its institutions and ideology were marked by the experience of war in the first half of the century and by the idea of using force to replace capitalist 'chaos' with a unitary principle. The Sovietization of Central and Eastern Europe, which aimed to install an absolute dominion and to homogenize the Soviet Union's sphere of influence, left violence and ignominy in its wake. The limitations to the hegemony of the Soviet monocratic system would soon emerge, together with the erosion of communism as a model and actor in international politics.

After Stalin's death, the tensions that exploded in the 'socialist camp' compromised in less than a decade the tradition of the leading state and the movement that was loyal to it. Khrushchev's demolition of Stalin's reputation in 1956 heralded the decadence of the Soviet myths. The rebellions and repressions in Eastern and Central Europe from 1953 to 1956, culminating in the Soviet invasion of Hungary, revealed the instability of the 'external empire' and the lack of national legitimacy of the communist regimes created from above. The expansion of communism in the post-colonial world appeared to counterbalance the repercussions of de-Stalinization and even to readjust the balance of power with the West, opening up a favourable scenario for Soviet modernization and more radical applications of the anti-imperialist spirit. However, the communist edifice was profoundly damaged by the schism between the two main socialist powers, the Soviet Union and China, in the early 1960s. As had occurred with Tito, Mao Zedong split from Moscow because of his own autonomy and radicalism, generated by a sufficiently independent revolution. This time, however, communist unity was shattered. Historians have now uncovered reliable information on the various motives that underlay the conflict between the USSR and China, linking them to state interests, ideology, and culture.[10] This conflict would modify the strategic make-up of the Cold War, shifting the balance of power in an even more unfavourable direction for the Soviet Union.[11] But its significance and profound consequences probably become more visible in the light of the dissolution of international communism.

---

[9] O. A. Westad, 'The Cold War and the international history of the twentieth century', in M. P. Leffler and O. A. Westad (eds), *The Cambridge History of the Cold War*, vol. I: *Origins* (Cambridge: Cambridge University Press, 2010), 1–19.

[10] L. M. Lüthi, *The Sino-Soviet Split: Cold War in the Communist World* (Princeton, N.J.: Princeton University Press, 2008); S. Radchenko, *Two Suns in the Heavens: The Sino-Soviet Struggle for Supremacy, 1962–1967* (Stanford, Calif./Washington, D.C.: Stanford University Press/Woodrow Wilson Center, 2009).

[11] C. Jian, *Mao's China and the Cold War* (Chapel Hill, N.C. University of North Carolina Press, 2001).

The legacy of Sovietization in Europe and China's split from the 'socialist camp' gravely damaged the authority of the Soviet Union. The Soviet state had influenced and forged the birth of new communist states, but its system of command and its imperial behaviour created more division and tension than unity and harmony. The axiom that world revolution and Soviet interests were one and the same was challenged from inside the communist movement itself. The end of communist unity was an indicator and factor in the emerging crisis, as yet unnoticed, of the main player which had proclaimed itself the antagonist of liberal capitalism. The decline of international communism came to light in the global uprising of 1968. In different ways, the reformers in Prague, the rebellious students in the West, and the Third World revolutionaries exposed the Soviet Union's loss of relevance and that of the movement linked to it. After the invasion of Czechoslovakia, the Soviet Union preserved by inertia a symbolic and political role for most communists, but it presided over a field of unstable and centrifugal forces, for the most part in decline. On the other hand, Maoist China was not capable of replacing the USSR and creating an alternative movement in the Third World. The most lively revolutionary mythologies and realities—the Vietnamese and Cuban ones—were largely autonomous from the communist powers, and in any case would not last for long.

No longer resolvable or capable of being interpreted within a unitary paradigm, the increasing national, cultural, and geopolitical divergences opened the way for the movement's fragmentation. The Western crisis of the 1970s, linked to the American defeat in Vietnam and the global economic crisis following the Yom Kippur War, did not create any substantial advantages for international communism over the long term, because the terrain that might have sustained it had already crumbled. This reality was largely hidden due to the force of Soviet power. But the landslide of political and ideological motivations could not easily be stopped. The rise of the Soviet Union as a global power did not create a new source of legitimacy. Détente with the West and expansion into the Third World were two ways to acquire credibility in terms of power politics, but they did not produce any serious alliances or new forms of international support. At the same time, the notion of an international communist movement, by then vague and a sham, was severely undermined by the semi-heresy of Eurocommunism. At the height of the 'global Cold War', interaction between the Soviet Union and the rest of the world was becoming increasingly elusive and ineffective.[12]

Contemporaries became aware of the crisis of communism in the late 1970s and early 1980s. Many different factors were making it clear. The outbreak of wars between Vietnam, Cambodia, and China marked the definitive fragmentation of international communism. The very notion of the Third World lost its significance, together with the dream of anti-imperialist revolution. The birth of a 'Soviet Vietnam' in Afghanistan combined with the birth of a mass anti-communist opposition in Poland. The persistence of communist police states and the 'Iron

---

[12] O. A. Westad, *The Global Cold War: Third World Interventions and the Making of Our Times* (Cambridge: Cambridge University Press, 2005).

Curtain' in Europe appeared to be increasingly contested and intolerable. The visible stagnation and backwardness of Soviet-type economies and societies gave rise to unflattering comparisons with the post-industrial transformation of Western societies and their promise of prosperity and freedom. From then onwards, the crisis of communism was associated with the notion of the Soviet Union's imperial overstretch and the unsustainability of a similar transformation of the centrally planned economies of the socialist countries.[13] Hence the increasing tendency of historians to consider not only the impact of the late Cold War but also that of the global processes triggered by the West in economics and communications.

Today we consider globalization to be a decisive factor for understanding the end of the Cold War and Soviet communism, because its advance from the late 1970s modified the bipolar framework and relegated the closed system of the 'socialist camp' to the margins, rendering its antagonistic role obsolete.[14] But the destabilizing impact of globalization can be best understood in the light of the historical erosion of communist legitimacy. A deficit of hegemonic capacity, dogmatic immobility, and cultural marginality prepared the terrain for the ultimate crisis. Communism had not only changed the course of the century's history; it had also been forged by the era of world wars. Preparation for war constituted its main strategy for state-building, social integration, and foreign policy. In its essential elements, the vision of the 'international civil war' between communism and capitalism remained unaltered for decades and became the key to universal understanding. However, the fate of the movement was affected by that particular identification with the modernity of the early twentieth century. The interaction between the Soviet state and the revolutionary movement, which had presided over the life of international communism between the First and the Second World War, did not survive for long in the second post-war period.

The creation of an imperial centre that imposed its domination on a periphery of states in Eurasia and China, and on a periphery of parties right around the world, contributed decisively to the global dynamics of the Cold War. But that model proved unsuited to challenging new forms of state-building, the changing concept of war in the atomic age, formation of a polycentric socialist community, diversification of the resources of power, the interdependent and multipolar features of international order, and national, social, and cultural diversities. Before it became established that the USSR and the Soviet-type economies were not capable of keeping up with the globalizing post-Fordist capitalist economy, the communist global project had already been compromised by the absence of political and cultural resources even in its ability to maintain a unity of intents, orientations and strategies. The limitations of the Soviet Union and the 'socialist camp' were visible not only in relation to the advanced realities of Western capitalism, but also

---

[13] For a discussion on both concepts, see S. Pons and F. Romero (eds), *Reinterpreting the End of the Cold War: Issues, Interpretations, Periodizations* (London: Frank Cass, 2005). See also C. Maier, *Dissolution: The Crisis of Communism and the End of East Germany* (Princeton, N.J.: Princeton University Press, 1997).

[14] F. Romero, *Storia della Guerra Fredda: l'ultimo conflitto per l'Europa* (Turin: Einaudi, 2009).

where the economic challenge was sustainable and the application of the Soviet model appeared credible, that is, in the post-colonial world. Contained in Europe by American hegemony, the communist movement did not experience the expansion outside Europe that the Chinese Revolution had promised. The scenarios of decolonization were decisive in feeding the conflict between the Soviet Union and China. The end of unity constituted a key step towards a crisis of legitimacy for communism, because it compromised its *raison d'être* as an antagonist of world politics bearing with it its own modernizing project. The epiphany of the crisis of communism in the last decade of its existence arose from a gradual but irreparable loss of cohesion, influence, and credibility, which had its origins in a previous era.

Around the mid-1980s, the Soviet Union was not collapsing, but its attraction and relevance for world civilization were already in pieces. This was the central problem for Gorbachev, and explains why his attempts at reform not only concerned the great power rivalry with the United States but also reclaimed communism's original ideals.[15] His plan to bring the Cold War to an end was a means to free up resources for internal reforms, but also an attempt at regaining legitimacy. The revolutions of 1989 in Central and Eastern Europe showed that this attempt was illusory and destined to fail, even if it was crucial to avoid a catastrophic outcome. Amongst the historic tasks carried out by Gorbachev, there was the acknowledgement that the very concept of international communism had long since lost any meaning. Immediately afterwards, the state created by the 1917 Revolution ceased to exist. Thus communism's alternative project came to its definitive end, and Western globalization fully asserted itself, destined to leave its mark on our own times with its expansionist force and profound contradictions.

This book is based on a substantial body of sources published in the last few years, and coming out of Russian, Chinese, and Eastern European archives and the archives of Western communist parties, which have not always been fully used in spite of their richness. I have supplemented these sources with some direct references to archive documents considered to be particularly significant, partly to document the route of my own research over the last twenty years in the archives of the CPSU, the Comintern, the Cominform (Rossiiskii Gosudarstvennyi Arkhiv Sotsial'no-politicheskoy Istorii, RGASPI, Moscow; Rossiiskii Gosudarstvennyi Arkhiv Noveishei Istorii, RGANI, Moscow), and the Ministry of Foreign Affairs of the USSR (Arkhiv Vneshnei Politiki Rossiiskoy Federatsii, AVPRF Moscow), the archives and materials of some of the main communist parties in Western, Central and Eastern Europe (in particular, the Archivio del partito comunista italiano, APCI, Fondazione Istituto Gramsci, Rome; Archives du Parti communiste français, APCF, Fondation Gabriel Péri, Paris; Stiftung Archiv der Parteien und Massenorganisationen der Ddr im Bundesarchiv, Sapmo-Ddr, Berlin), and some important archives for the history of communism (Hoover Institution, Stanford; Gorbachev Foundation, Moscow; Fondazione Feltrinelli, Milan).

---

[15] S. Kotkin, *Armageddon Averted: The Soviet Collapse 1970–2000* (Oxford: Oxford University Press, 2001).

I owe an intellectual debt which is difficult to repay in relation to numerous scholars and friends, to whom I express my gratitude. Francesco Benvenuti, Andrea Graziosi, Jonathan Haslam, Federico Romero, Robert Service, and Arne Westad read the entire manuscript, making essential criticisms and comments which I often found enlightening. Gianluca Fiocco, Francesca Gori, Andrea Romano, and Carlo Spagnolo gave me important advice. A particular mention must go to Francesco Piva and Beppe Vacca, who were unstinting in reading and suggestions. A special thank you to Chiara Lucrezio Monticelli. During the long preparation and writing of the book, I drew inestimable benefit from the discussion and exchange of ideas with many others: in particular, Alessandro Brogi, Victoria de Grazia, Mario Del Pero, Leonid Gibianskii, Roberto Gualtieri, David Holloway, Stephen Kotkin, Mark Kramer, Marc Lazar, Mark Mazower, Norman Naimark, Mikhail Narinskii, Svetozar Rajak, Stephen Smith, Anders Stephanson, Molly Tambor, Luigi Tomba, Antonio Varsori, Victor Zaslavsky, and Vladislav Zubok. I had the opportunity to debate decisive aspects of my work during my stay at the Italian Academy for Advanced Studies in America, Columbia University, New York, in 2008; the workshop on Russia and China which was run by Paul Gregory at the Hoover Institution, Stanford, California, in 2010; and as visiting professor at the European University Institute of Florence in 2012–13. All responsibility for the content of this book falls exclusively on the author.

Rome, September 2013

Prologue
War and Revolution

There can be no doubt that the socialist revolution in Europe must take place and will take place. All our hopes for a final victory of socialism are grounded on this conviction and this scientific prediction.

Lenin, 21 January 1918

Twentieth-century communism was a product of the First World War. Between 1914 and 1917, as war spread devastation across Europe, small cosmopolitan groupings were developing a communist political project. It became a revolutionary regime in the Russian empire, where the social and national consequences of the war were most deeply felt, through the unforeseen seizure of power by the Bolsheviks in October 1917. As a result of the outbreak of the Russian Civil War, the fall of the Central Powers, and the upheavals of the immediate postwar period, communism came to be identified with a new state and a transnational movement intent upon triggering a pan-European revolution. It was not long before this chain of events had shaped a new reality very different from the eighteenth-century utopias that had been its precursors, and created a new player distinct from the tradition of prewar socialism, although still inspired by Marxism. Communism now had a world dimension and ambition—the necessary qualifications for leaving its mark on the century.

Such a transformation would have been inconceivable without the impact of the war. Before the world war, Bolshevism had been restricted to the particular circumstances of Tsarist Russia. Part of the Socialist International even after the split within Russian social democracy between them and the Menshevik minority became permanent in 1912, the Bolsheviks were a radical Marxist party with a conspiratorial bent. Theirs was a variant of the maximalist and anti-reformist groupings within European socialism—one that had been forged by the experience of police repression and exile. In the 1890s their leader, Lenin, had undertaken a Marxist analysis of the Russian transition to a capitalist economy, and this would lead him to formulate a political theory that contrasted with the gradualist orthodoxy of the Second International, according to which 'bourgeois democratic revolution' was a stage that had to be kept distinct from 'socialist revolution'. Following the failure of the revolution in 1905, Lenin became increasingly convinced that the working classes in Russia would carry out the progressive role that elsewhere had been the task of the middle class. This opened the way for a socialist revolution in spite of the country's backwardness. At the same time, he argued for the creation of a party made up of professional revolutionaries—trained cadres subject to a highly centralized organization. This argument brought him strong opposition from those Russian and European Marxists who were critical of its potential authoritarianism and believed that, at the very most, it would only be suitable for the Tsarist police state. In other words, Lenin stood out as an energetic radical, very much part of the political and intellectual climate of contemporary socialism, but one that emphasized the special circumstances of revolutionary activity in the Russian Empire.[1]

It was only during the First World War that Lenin and the Bolsheviks came to be seen as having a more autonomous international role. They were amongst those who challenged the policies of the main European socialist parties in favour of defending their respective nation-states in July 1914, which led to the collapse of the Second International. Lenin was the leader of the most uncompromising faction in the Zimmerwald movement, which in September 1915 brought together the minority of European socialists determined to voice their opposition to the war and salvage the internationalist tradition of socialism. Although he represented a minority faction within the movement, his break with Karl Kautsky—the 'red pope' of the German Social Democratic Party—his unfailing opposition to socialist patriotism inspired by war, and his denunciation of militarism and imperialism meant that he could justifiably claim to be a revolutionary leader on the European stage. This turned Bolshevism into a movement that, aiming to renew the existing socialist world, gave birth to a political heresy opposing the gradualist orthodoxy, and caused a schism out of the ashes of the old International in order to create a new one.

Lenin's leadership was supported by an original theory on the development of capitalism, which stood out in the debate amongst Marxists for the centrality it accorded the international nature of the phenomenon. It was a theory that could claim its origins in Marx's analysis of the global nature of the capitalist economy, but it placed much less emphasis on capitalism's dynamism and much more on its prospects of ending in catastrophe. For Lenin, advanced and monopolistic capitalism was a highly integrated world system, characterized by the incessant conquest of new markets, strategic resources, and geopolitical territory. This irrepressible imperialist mission had governed the power politics of European states to the point of causing the outbreak of world war. The link between imperialism and war was therefore not a contingent fact but the distinguishing feature of the era. The pacifism that socialists had to preach was inevitably a revolutionary pacifism, because only an anti-capitalist revolution could bring an end to the wars by removing the class-based causes of the phenomenon. This theoretical framework provided the basis for a political project that marked a radicalization of Lenin's thought compared with his prewar positions. While imperialism and war were necessarily

---

[1] For an account of Lenin's thought and political activity before Oct. 1917, see R. Service, *Lenin: A Political Life*, vol. 2: *Worlds in Collision* (London: Macmillan, 1995). For relations between Lenin and the rest of the European socialist movement, see G. Haupt, *Lenin e la Seconda Internazionale* (Rome: Samonà e Savelli, 1969).

interdependent, the war created the conditions for severing that iron logic in the only way possible: the insurrectionary overthrow of the capitalist system and the collapse of the imperial order. The link between war and revolution was not new. It had been a settled position in the Marxist tendency of socialist thought, which had often based its revolutionary expectations on the consequences of war. But Lenin translated this link into a political programme. Hence the slogan 'Turn the imperialist war into a civil war' became an important Bolshevik motif from the early months of the war.[2]

Lenin's revolutionary vision was largely influenced by the experience and psychology of war. Its strength lay not so much in his intellectual hinterland as in his own schematic approach, which strained Marxist legitimacy for the purposes of political ends. Lenin understood that the world war, which had started as a war between states, now threatened to tear apart European civil order. Moreover, he saw the potential for military mobilization and its social impact turning into a new mass politics. This intuition gave Bolshevism its particular strength. In Lenin's opinion, the bourgeois era had run its historical course. The radical response that he was putting forward fully took into account the tumultuous effects of the war— barbarization and the destruction of civilization—and was based on the perception of their absolute dominance of the historical moment. Thus the slippage into a 'European civil war' was no longer a terrifying reality but an unmistakable development that was necessary for the genesis of a new era of modern civilization. The result was an aggressive and extreme political programme, whose efficacy was equal to the simplification inherent in its peculiar mixture of voluntarism and determinism. The reduction of the era's possible alternatives and the complexity of European politics to the brutally simple norms typical of a war mentality became the new framework of Bolshevik ideology. Bolshevism put itself forward as the party of the 'European civil war', an event that Lenin called for from the outbreak of the February Revolution in Russia. The relationship of this self-portrayal and historical reality would constitute one of the fundamental problems concerning the entire communist phenomenon.[3]

Immediately after the fall of Tsarism, Lenin applied to the Russia of 1917 the ultra-radical concept he had developed during the war, and imposed it even on his most reluctant comrades, who effectively followed the same line as the Mensheviks. He subjected his entire political practice to the most paradoxical corollary of his own ideas: namely that, breaking with the established tenets of orthodox Marxism, the socialist revolution would not necessarily be unleashed in the

---

[2] R. C. Nation, *War on War: Lenin, the Zimmerwald Left, and the Origins of Communist Internationalism* (Durham, N.C. Duke University Press, 1989).

[3] The Bolsheviks' representation of themselves as the 'party of civil war' has been used by Ernst Nolte to argue that communism was a cause of a 'European civil war' between the First World War and the Second World War: see E. Nolte, *Der europäische Bürgerkrieg 1917–1945: Nationalsozialismus und Bolschewismus* (Berlin: Propyläen Verlag, 1987). In reality, the notion of a 'European civil war' does not necessarily presuppose origins in Bolshevism, and has been used with different meanings by many historians. For a critical review, see E. Traverso, *A ferro e fuoco: la guerra civile europea 1914– 1945* (Bologna: il Mulino, 2007).

high points of capitalist development—the industrially advanced countries—but quite the opposite. The possibility of breaking free of imperialism's chains was greater precisely amongst its 'weaker links'—in the countries where the capitalist system was still backward. The revolutionary schism had greater chances of success at Europe's periphery rather than its heart, even though the triumph of socialism would only be ensured by a revolution in Germany. Russia's backwardness was therefore an opportunity, rather than a delay that would have to be waited out. Indeed, it was an opportunity for all European revolutionaries. From the moment of his return to Russia in April 1917, Lenin established a close link between the February Revolution, the birth of the soviets of workers and peasants, and the 'crisis of imperialism'. The Bolsheviks' revolutionary action took place within the context of a general movement, a 'world revolution' which was producing its earliest symptoms. A little later, in the summer of 1917, Lenin set out his ideas on power in a few of his writings, in particular his pamphlet *State and Revolution*, which would become perhaps the most celebrated of the works produced by his keen political talent. He decided to reject the evolutionism shared by the Marxists of the Second International not only at a theoretical level but also in political action, commencing with the foundation of a 'dictatorship of the proletariat', a notion Marx adopted but never explained. The expression was primarily forged in his controversial analysis of the state during the French Revolution and the Paris Commune.[4] Lenin cut short the quibbling arguments over whether some theory of the state could be conjured up from Marx's thought. He defined the state and parliamentary democracy as the expression of the ruling class's interests, in line with the principal direction provided by Marxism on this question. He looked on the soviets as a new form of direct democracy, and the dictatorship of the proletariat as a necessary form of authoritarian government, albeit a transitional one on the way to the commune-state. He broke the link between socialism and political democracy, not in the name of the nation, as occurred with nationalistic socialists, but in the name of internationalism. His political model was explicitly based on Jacobinism, which Lenin identified with a universal revolutionary tradition, also valid for socialism. His appeal to revolutionary subjectivism and class violence was not restricted to Russia and its particular conditions, but embraced Europe as a whole.

Following General Kornilov's attempted coup in September 1917, and faced with the inaction of the socialist Alexander Kerensky's government, Lenin's radical theories ensured that the Petrograd and Moscow soviets came out decisively in support of the Bolsheviks' strong and solid organization. Although the majority of the country did not support the Bolsheviks, the seizure of power in October 1917 was a revolution that had been previously publicized and that enjoyed the passive support of important sections of society.[5] According to Lenin's script, this was only the first act of a play—also previously publicized—in which a dramatic liberation was

---

[4] F. Furet, *Marx and the French Revolution* (Chicago: University of Chicago Press, 1989).
[5] O. Figes, *A People's Tragedy: The Russian Revolution 1891–1924* (London: Pimlico, 1997), 474–84.

fated to find its epicentre elsewhere and to spread like wildfire throughout Europe. The Great War would end in a huge wave of revolutionary activity, turning the old continent's social, state, and geopolitical map into a relic of the past. This evolutionary upheaval would be no less cruel than the conflict that was raging at the time; it would eradicate the iniquities of the capitalist system and the disastrous consequences of its imperialism. Despite the proclamation of a republic based on soviets of workers and peasants, the power seized so audaciously and opportunistically by the Bolsheviks as post-Tsarist Russia descended into chaos was not so much the foundation of a new state as the first breach in the old order which could only collapse. Not the first brick in a new building, but the first blow of the pick-axe in the demolition of an age-old construction. The snapping of the 'weak link' would be followed by similar fractures in the links holding up the edifice. The initial steps were clear: the imposition of a class-based dictatorship and an exit from the war. The next decisions would be determined by a pan-European earthquake, whose actual form could not be predicted, but which was imminent and ineluctable. Immediately after taking power, the Bolsheviks had no other political perspective than their unshakable conviction that a world revolution was fast approaching. This was the kernel of their plans for the future; it was what gave meaning to their revolution in Russia and to their break with the tradition of European socialism.

Lenin and the Bolsheviks knew that they were capable of creating a symbolic reference point for the majority of the European working peoples who had been drawn into the tragedy of war and for the disinherited of all the world, given that their revolution offered a promise not only to the workers but also to the peasants and subject nations. The widespread feeling that the old liberal order had failed, the expectations of social improvement and national liberation, and the prospect of crisis in colonies together had an enormous potential. In the final year of the war, the whole of Europe was shaken by protests over social questions. The creation of a socialist power could not fail to make a strong impression on the collective imagination, stirring up passions and hopes and provoking fears and hatreds. Initially the Bolsheviks appeared to be trying to extend the horizons of the revolution as far as possible. Far from reflecting their extremist views, the decrees issued after they took power, giving land to the peasantry and declaring universal peace, met with a wide consensus, and not only in Russia. Above all the Decree on Peace, with its appeal to peoples for a 'just and democratic peace', was drawn up avoiding the use of classist language, and expressed a universal message that rivalled the ideas of the American president, Woodrow Wilson. For some time, Lenin and Wilson looked like the opposing heroes of two different hegemonic wills, both attempting to provide the means to create a new peaceful world order that was humanitarian and freed from the legacy of imperialism.[6]

In reality, the Bolsheviks' universalism was marked by a rigid division of societies and states according to classist criteria, revealing hegemonic principles that

---

[6] E. H. Carr, *The Russian Revolution from Lenin to Stalin 1917–1929*, 2nd edn (London: Palgrave Macmillan, 2003); A. J. Mayer, *Wilson vs Lenin: Political Origins of the New Diplomacy* (New York: World Publishing, 1964).

were more restricted and less inclusive than would appear from the democratic and humanistic rhetoric. The very logic of their revolution, which envisaged the total and violent overthrow of world order, led them to adopt a Manichaean perspective, thus polarizing the divide between those who identified with them and those who feared them. Historians have perceived this perspective either in terms of ideological traditions and systems or in terms of the impersonal dynamic inherent within Carl Schmitt's friend/enemy dissociation.[7] In any event, the international and universalist dimension was crucial to the Bolshevik Revolution and how it was perceived in the world, and was mediated through visions of an epoch-making clash between revolution and counter-revolution, between radically different and opposing civilizations, and between irreconcilable identities. Deeply marked by the link between war and revolution, the communist regime in Russia founded a state and a mythology that emphasized their impact on the whole world and their place in European revolutionary history.[8]

---

[7] See respectively F. Furet, *Le passé d'une illusion: essai sur l'idée communiste au XXᵉ siècle* (Paris: Laffont/Calmann-Lévy, 1995) and A. J. Mayer, *The Furies: Violence and Terror in the French and Russian Revolutions* (Princeton, N.J.: Princeton University Press, 2000).

[8] For the link between war and revolution, see H. Arendt, *On Revolution* (New York: Viking Press, 1963). On the centrality of the international element in the revolutions of the twentieth century, see F. Halliday, *Revolution and World Politics: The Rise and Fall of the Sixth Great Power* (Durham, N.C. Duke University Press, 1999).

1
Time of Revolution (1917–1923)

The ice has been broken. The Soviets have won all round the world. They have won first of all and above all in the sense that they have won the sympathies of the proletarian masses... The new movement advances towards the dictatorship of the proletariat... The foundation of the Third International, of the Communist International, is the prelude to an International Soviet Republic.

Lenin, 5 March 1919

Before the Revolution and even after it, we thought: if not immediately then in the worst case scenario very soon, the revolution would win in other more developed countries from a capitalist point of view; if this did not occur, we would have to succumb.... We have done all we can to preserve the Soviet system in all circumstances and at any cost, because we knew were acting not only for ourselves, but for the world revolution.... And this, in general terms, was correct. But in reality, the movement has not been as linear as we had expected.

Lenin, 5 July 1921

LENIN, THE SOVIET STATE, AND THE COMINTERN

The immediate international consequences of the October Revolution proved to be a harsh test-bed for the Bolshevik project of world revolution. The psychological impact of Russia's exit from the war was far-reaching both inside and outside the country. But the military reality was that Russia was a defeated country and incapable of defending itself. As far as its adversaries were concerned, the war on the eastern front had been won after more than three years of bloody conflict. Peace could only be obtained on conditions acceptable to the Central Powers. It was highly improbable that the generals of Kaiser Wilhelm's Reich would be influenced by the propaganda of a band of utopian revolutionaries who had taken over Petrograd by exploiting the power vacuum caused by the fall of the Tsar. This became brutally clear from the conclusion of the armistice in early December 1917. During the subsequent negotiations, held in Brest-Litovsk, the Bolsheviks' aim was simply to play for time in the hope that a popular insurrection in Germany would get them out of trouble. This delaying tactic was primarily implemented by Lev Trotsky, the most prominent Bolshevik leader after Lenin, who, as head of the delegation, exhibited all the remarkable oratorical skills of which he was capable. However, the punitive territorial claims made by the Germans left few doubts about their intentions. A separate peace was conditional on their acceptance of the amputation of the Baltic States, Finland, Poland, and the Ukraine from the body of what had been the Russian empire. Without this, the war would have continued and the Kaiser's armies would have strangled the revolution.

This dilemma divided the Bolsheviks. Some of them, the Left Communists, followed their ideology's more extreme logic: the avoidance of any agreement with the imperialists and the triggering of a 'revolutionary war' that would inflame Russian working people and provide German working people with the opportunity for their own insurrection. Such a move utterly disregarded any assessment of the balance of power or the instinct to preserve the power established in Russia. Nikolay Bukharin, the leading exponent of the theory of 'revolutionary war', effectively argued that the defence of power had to be put at risk rather than betraying internationalist ideals. The sole aim of the Bolsheviks was European revolution, and the only chance was to risk it all in the hope that a German military offensive would hasten the day. Acceptance of those conditions for peace would have weakened Soviet Russia and would not have protected it from enemy aggression. The other Bolsheviks followed Lenin's appeal to realism: acceptance of the Germans' harsh conditions in order to save Russia's new republic. According to Lenin, agreement on a separate peace would provide the essential breathing space, whereas the opposite decision would be suicide, given the absence of a military force to repel the Germans. For the moment, the primary objective of the revolution was its survival. This was the only way to keep alive the chances of a European revolution in the future. On this point, Lenin repeatedly referred to the historical model provided by the Jacobins, who in the years to come were to be the principal yardstick used by the Bolsheviks, to the point of their becoming 'fervent analogists' of the events in the French Revolution.[1]

From the beginning of January to the end of February 1918, the two factions were engaged in a bitter dispute in which Lenin held the minority position. Trotsky's delaying tactic—which, with its slogan 'No war, no peace', vacillated between the two opposing factions—could not go on indefinitely. The reckoning came when the Germans resumed military operations after having declared an ultimatum that was ignored. In the climate of panic caused by the German advance, Lenin's threat to resign from the Central Committee and Trotsky's decision to align himself with Lenin put Bukharin and the Left Communists in a minority. On 24 February the Bolshevik government unconditionally accepted the German peace proposals. The treaty was signed on 3 March 1918 at Brest-Litovsk. Soviet Russia lost a large part of the territories that had belonged to the Empire in Central and Eastern Europe, a third of the population, and half of the industrial plant. Lenin

---

[1] A. J. Mayer, *The Furies: Violence and Terror in the French and Russian Revolutions* (Princeton, N.J.: Princeton University Press, 2000), 232.

was accused of betraying national interests in anti-Bolshevik circles, and of betraying revolutionary interests amongst the Left Communists. But power remained in the hands of the Bolshevik Party.[2]

During the months that followed, the pace of domestic and international events quickened, and the critical divisions between Bolsheviks caused by the negotiations for a separate peace came to be looked on as a fleeting episode. The outbreak of the Civil War reunified the party around the much more dramatic struggle for survival. The treaty lost all its value following Germany's defeat in the world war. Nevertheless, Brest-Litovsk would long represent a harsh lesson for the Bolsheviks. Immediately afterwards, Lenin provided his own interpretation of the events and the lessons to be drawn. On 7 March 1918, in his report to the Seventh Congress of the RCP (b), he argued that the Revolution had been 'sheltered from imperialism' because of a 'special international conjuncture', in which the counter-revolutionary powers found themselves divided 'into two groups'. Thus Brest-Litovsk was not only a harsh necessity, but also an opportunity to avoid immediate conflict with 'international imperialism', which would however prove inevitable in the long run.[3] Lenin appealed to both the prospect of European revolution and a realistic assessment of the international balance of power. He did not see any contradiction between the two. The revolutionary regime's foreign policy was taking shape in a manner that the Bolsheviks had not expected. Its task was to exploit the 'contradictions' between the capitalist states. In this sense, Brest-Litovsk would not remain a straightforward event, in spite of having been imposed by circumstance. Quite the opposite: it became the archetype and cornerstone of the new revolutionary state's foreign policy.

The moment the separate peace was signed, Lenin declared that there would be a period of setbacks and difficult times. They found themselves at the beginning of an era of violence, war, and 'gigantic cataclysms'. He could not have imagined how tragically precise his prophecy would turn out to be for Russia, if not for Europe. Lenin believed that the Bolsheviks had already won the Civil War in Russia through early decisions taken by the revolutionary regime, namely the liquidation of political adversaries, the abolition of large estates in the countryside, and Russia's exit from the war. He was terribly wrong. The storm of a genuine internecine conflict was brewing. Polarization of Russian society and increasing social violence during the war had created the conditions for the success of Bolshevik radicalism; but in power, Bolshevism did not heal that wound; it opened it further. It was precisely those early decisions of the revolutionary regime that decisively contributed to widening the rift within Russian society, creating extreme tension and ultimately pushing the country into civil war: the establishment of the

---

[2] For a historical account of the negotiations that led to the Treaty of Brest-Litovsk, see R. K. Debo, *Revolution and Survival: The Foreign Policy of Soviet Russia 1917–1918* (Toronto: Toronto University Press, 1979), 45–169; R. Service, *Lenin: A Political Life*, vol. 2: *Worlds in Collision* (London: Macmillan, 1991), 318ff.; S. Cohen, *Bukharin e la rivoluzione bolscevica: biografia politica 1888–1938* (Milan: Feltrinelli, 1975), 71–7.

[3] V. I. Lenin, *Polnoe sobranie sochinenii*, 5th edn, 55 vols (Moscow: Izdatel'stvo politicheskoy literatury, Moscow 1958–75), vol. 36, pp. 3–26.

dictatorship, the dissolution of the Constituent Assembly, the invasion of Ukraine, the violent requisitions of grain in the countryside, and the Brest-Litovsk peace agreement itself, which many experienced as a national humiliation.[4]

The fuse was lit by the insubordination of the Czechoslovak Military Legion, which had fought alongside the Russians in pursuit of Czech independence from the Hapsburg Empire. This took place at the end of May 1918 in eastern Siberia. The threat from the German military presence in the Ukraine, even after the separate peace, rapidly became a secondary matter. At the beginning of the summer, clashes on Russian territory started to multiply and the forces determined to fight the Revolution were organizing themselves. The Red republic, which now governed a territory reduced to the size of medieval Muscovy, was surrounded by White counter-revolutionary armies. At the same time, the extreme tension between the Soviet government and the Western powers, who were hostile to both the revolution and the separate peace, led to the dispatch of a Franco-British expeditionary force and the opening of an international front in the Civil War. The Western counter-revolutionary intervention created a scenario that the Bolsheviks had not really considered in their calculations, but this did not shake the Bolshevik conviction that they were the epicentre of a 'European civil war'; indeed, it strengthened it. This was the political significance of Lenin's definition of the Soviet Republic as a 'besieged fortress'—a definition that was to leave a profound mark on Bolshevik psychology.

One of the lessons of Brest-Litovsk was the revolutionary regime's pragmatic need for a new army. In autumn 1918, following the declaration of a state of emergency and mass conscription, the Red Army became reality on the basis of which the state arising from the Revolution and the dissolution of the Empire would consolidate its position. According to the vision of Trotsky, its founder, the task of the new mass army was both to defend the 'socialist fatherland' and to prepare itself for armed assistance of the international revolution.[5] The Red Army would therefore constitute a strategic reserve in any future revolutions in Central Europe. Centred upon its army, the revolutionary regime demonstrated that it had now taken on the task of self-defence, but without giving up on its internationalist ambitions. The Bolsheviks were convinced that the defence of their power was a decisive element in the European revolution.

The defeat of the German empire a year after the October Revolution rendered the conditions of the separate peace a dead letter, and appeared to relaunch the internationalist perspective. Lenin repeated that the survival of the Soviet Republic in isolation had been possible because of the divisions between imperialists. But now the situation had changed, since only the victorious allies of the Entente were left standing. Lenin concluded: 'we have never been so close to the international proletarian revolution as we are now' but also: 'our situation has never been as dangerous as it is now.'[6] The great opportunity was attended by the greatest danger.

---

[4] O. Figes, *A People's Tragedy: The Russian Revolution 1891–1924* (London: Pimlico, 1997), 550, 616.

[5] F. Benvenuti, *The Bolsheviks and the Red Army* (Cambridge: Cambridge University Press, 1988).

[6] Lenin, *Polnoe sobranie sochinenii*, vol. 37, pp. 164–7.

On the one hand, the fall of the German empire and the creation of the more fluid situation in Germany that had long been anticipated and, on the other, the geopolitical vacuum had created an ideal space for counter-revolution in the Baltic and the Ukraine. This opened a new phase in the Soviet Republic's struggle for survival. What really counted for the Bolsheviks was the fact that the Russian Civil War could eventually prove to be a factor in a 'European civil war'.

This was argued eloquently by Karl Radek, one of the leading figures in the Bolshevik Party and a prominent personality in the Zimmerwald movement. He acknowledged: 'history has on several occasions taken different roads from what we had expected...it went slowly.' The policy adopted by Soviet Russia in Brest-Litovsk had so far 'intensified the global contradictions' and made it possible to manoeuvre between the two imperialist 'camps'. But the decisive moment was coming. Even if the defeat of Kaiser Wilhelm's Germany would for the moment mean only a victory for French and British imperialism, Radek predicted that 'the German revolution would develop rapidly'. After a year's existence, Soviet Russia finally found itself 'at the start of the European revolution'. The struggle between the revolution and the counter-revolution would last 'a very long time and with variable results', but it was now a struggle that would dominate world politics.[7] In other words, the fall of the German empire did not open the way to peace, but to civil war in Europe. This hope was shared by all Bolsheviks.

The first convulsions in postwar Germany appeared to meet their expectations. The extent of popular protests, the spread of strike action, and the birth of workers' councils might constitute a shock wave that would replicate the Russian events of 1917 on an even greater scale. The fall of the German empire and the proclamation of the Weimar Republic in November 1918 were welcomed, or feared, as a prelude to a more radical upheaval. The foundation in December 1918 of the German Communist Party, based on the Spartacist movement, presented a direct challenge to the newly formed Social Democratic government. The leading political and intellectual figure in German communism, Rosa Luxemburg, although a critic of the Bolshevik dictatorship, believed (just as Lenin did) that the German revolution would come in the wake of Russian one. Luxemburg took issue with Lenin's anti-democratic decisions, but she detested social democracy's moderation and reformism. Her famous formula 'Socialism or barbarism' pointed to the sole possibility for the future, and legitimized the idea of an implacable clash between the forces of reaction and those of the revolution. In spite of her democratic and humanistic sensitivities, Luxemburg 'provided the ideological and linguistic underpinning for a policy of unyielding confrontation'.[8] The confrontation was triggered immediately and its sudden outcome was tragic: the cruel suppression of the Spartacist uprising in January 1919 and the assassination of the two leaders

---

[7] K. Radek, *Vneshnyaya politika Sovetskoy Rossii* (Moscow/Petrograd: Gosudarstvennoe izdatel'stvo, 1923), 17, 21, 27–9.

[8] E. D. Weitz, *Creating German Communism, 1890–1990: From Popular Protests to Socialist State* (Princeton, N.J.: Princeton University Press, 1997), 93.

of German communism, Luxemburg herself and Karl Liebknecht, by members of extreme right-wing military corps.

This did not, however, discourage the Bolsheviks. The mobilization and level of protest of the working class in Germany gave no sign of abating. Radek, who was sent to Berlin as a Bolshevik emissary, wrote to Lenin that in his opinion the German communists would be able 'to think about taking power' within a few months.[9] In a letter to the historian N. A. Rozhkov at the end of January, Lenin asserted that the widespread collapse of bourgeois order could only lead to civil war, as was shown by the situation in Germany.[10] Lenin abandoned the idea of setting up the Third International in Berlin, but when he wrote 'to the workers of Europe and America', he stated: 'today the Third International de facto already exists.'[11] A few weeks later, from the 4th to the 6th of March 1919, a meagre group of foreign delegates undertook the hazardous journey to Moscow in order to establish the Communist International together with the Bolshevik leaders. In reality, the birth of the international communist movement was purely symbolic. Although there were a number of delegations—even from countries outside Europe—they comprised few members and were hardly representative. For this reason, the German Hugo Eberlein, the only exponent of a significant communist movement in Europe—evidently conscious of Luxemburg's strong reservations about the Bolshevik dictatorship and the possibility of an International dominated by the Russians—proposed that the establishment of the new International should be postponed. But his appeal was ignored. The Bolsheviks were keen to lessen their own isolation and exploit the Revolution's international resonance. Dominated by the Russian presence, the new International adopted Bolshevism's doctrine and analysis in full. Its founding manifesto restated that the world war, even after its conclusion, would necessarily generate a civil war in Europe, and that this was the unavoidable transition to an authentic peace.[12] Grigory Zinoviev, one of the more prominent Bolshevik leaders, became the first head of the Comintern. The new institution, which was de facto subject to the Politburo of the RCP (b) in its principal decision-making processes, was modelled on the ruling bodies of the Russian party and worked alongside the Ministry of Foreign Affairs.[13] From the very beginning, the Comintern was an integral part of the Soviet state.

[9] *Komintern i ideya mirovoy revoliutsii: dokumenty* (hereinafter: *KIMR),* ed. J. S. Drabkin (Moscow: Nauka, 1998), doc. 6, p. 93.

[10] R. Pipes (ed.), *The Unknown Lenin: From the Secret Archive* (New Haven, Conn.: Yale University Press, 1996), doc. 33, p. 62.

[11] Lenin, *Polnoe sobranie sochinenii,* vol. 37, p. 455.

[12] W. Hedeler and A. Vatlin (eds), *Die Weltpartei aus Moskau: der Gründungskongress der Kommunistischen Internationale 1919. Protokoll und neue Dokumente* (Berlin: Akademie, 2008); K. McDermott and J. Agnew, *The Comintern: A History of International Communism from Lenin to Stalin* (Basingstoke: Macmillan, 1996), 12; B. Lazitch and M. Drachkovitch, *Lenin and the Comintern* (Stanford, Calif.: Hoover Institution Press, 1972), 62–7.

[13] A. Y. Vatlin, *Komintern: idei, resheniya, sudby* (Moscow: Rosspen, 2009), 37–70; *Politburo TsK RKP(b)–VKP(b) i Komintern 1919–1943: dokumenty* (hereinafter: *PBKI*), ed. G. M. Adibekov and K. K. Shirinya (Moscow: Rosspen, 2004), doc. 1, p. 25.

The distinguishing feature of the Communist International was the link between the reality of Bolshevik power struggling for survival and its ambition to bring its transnational project to life by exploiting the Revolution's idealist and mythical driving force. Lenin never lost an opportunity to justify retrospectively his decision to reach a peace agreement in Brest-Litovsk, in the light of the fall of Kaiser Wilhelm's Reich and the transition to European revolution. At the Eighth Congress of the RCP (b) on 18 March 1919, he pointed out that every 'great revolution' was linked to the war, and proclaimed, 'the existence of the Soviet Republic alongside the imperialist states is unthinkable in the long term.'[14] The link between the Brest-Litovsk peace agreement and the birth of the Comintern has often been neglected by historians. Many have followed the mainstream view, based on E. H. Carr's judgement that the outcome of Brest-Litovsk was a combination of ideology and realism that would last until the end of the Civil War, when the drive for world revolution would give way to the pursuit of the new state's security.[15] Backdating a terminology that actually belonged to the post-Lenin period, Orlando Figes argued that in 1918 the 'permanent revolution' phase was already coming to an end and that, from that moment, the regime would aim to consolidate 'socialism in one country'.[16]

However, the lessons drawn from Lenin must have been much more ambiguous than would appear from such interpretations. The abandonment of 'world revolution' would have been an admission of failure that he simply was not willing to make. Lenin limited himself to making small adjustments to the naive and visionary forecast in which Bolsheviks—himself included—believed in 1917 in relation to the imminence of a great upheaval in Europe. He was more concerned by political efficacy than intellectual coherence. In this sense, Brest-Litovsk can be seen as 'the end of the age of innocence' amongst Bolsheviks, as Adam Ulam wrote.[17] But it did not lead to the abandonment of the European revolutionary project, which remained, as Robert Service has observed, the authentic mission of Bolshevism and regained its centrality with the fall of the German empire.[18] The new regime's mission did not change, because those who held power could not have conceived any other future for themselves. There was therefore no revision of political culture, but rather an adjustment of Bolshevism's psychology and timetable. A strategy for survival sacrificed utopian impulses on the altar of the defence of power. The most fervent expectations were not discarded but merely kept out of sight. Revolutionary Russia discovered that it was just a state amongst many others. But it had to be a state different from the others.

For Bolsheviks, the prospect of world revolution provided legitimacy for the violence they were causing on an unprecedented scale. Lenin and Trotsky justified

---

[14] Lenin, *Polnoe sobranie sochinenii*, vol. 38, p. 139.
[15] E. H. Carr, *A History of Soviet Russia*, vol. 1: *The Bolshevik Revolution*, New York: Palgrave Macmillan, 1978.
[16] Figes, *A People's Tragedy*, 550.
[17] A. B. Ulam, *Storia della politica estera sovietica (1917–1967)* (Milan: Rizzoli, 1968), 110.
[18] R. Service, *Lenin: A Political Life*, vol. 3: *The Iron Ring* (London: Macmillan, 1995), 44–6.

the Red Terror as a preventive measure to combat the counter-revolution not only in Russia but also in Europe. The revolutionary and classist violence of the Reds and the counter-revolutionary and anti-Semitic violence of the Whites fed off each other. Modelled on the Jacobin precedent that obsessed the Bolshevik mindset, the Red Terror was also sustained by the blind ideological conviction that only a civil war could open the way to a new historical era.[19] In practice, the formula 'war communism' was a hotchpotch of utopian visions and ferocious methods of government. From 1918 to 1920, the extensive use of terror, the dictatorship deployed against the dispossessed ruling classes, violent requisitions in the countryside, the abolition of market relations, primitive forms of egalitarianism, the ethos of sacrifice and organization, the passion for social and sexual emancipation, the negation of the private sphere in daily life, and the messianic faith in the advent of a just society all came together as both a tumultuous projection into the future and the result of an exceptional situation. The Revolution's strategy for retaining power fused with the revolutionary socialist and Marxist traditions of the previous century. The latter were widely refashioned in new rituals and symbols, ranging from processions to festivals and street theatre, which showed a strong tendency to sacralize politics, particularly through the celebration of the Revolution's universal mission and its leaders. The period of 'war communism' expressed, in an extreme but fairly faithful manner, the socialist model advocated by the Bolsheviks and their somewhat hazy vision of an 'alternative modernity' to that of capitalism.[20]

The manner in which reality and the Bolshevik mentality combined during the Civil War was typified by the structure of the resulting state organization, which was unprecedented in European history and unforeseen by the Marxist tradition. Lenin's concept of power provided the basis for a totalitarian response to the impact on Russian society wrought by the cycle of wars and revolutions that had commenced in 1914. Consequently it did not simply become entangled in the models for wartime authoritarianism experienced in Germany and Europe. The Soviet party-state, which emerged from the twin circumstances of the struggle for the survival of Red power and the expectation of world revolution, created a new form of authoritarian power. The command structure centred upon the army provided the Bolshevik party with the opportunity to recruit, train, and promote a mass of new cadres who could support and consolidate the state. Communists in Russia rapidly grew in number to a few hundred thousand. However, their wretchedly low level of education, their familiarity with violent methods, increasing police powers, and hierarchical principles soon alienated the working masses, particularly in the countryside. Thus the consolidation of the state apparatus was accompanied by a decline in the mass support the Bolsheviks had enjoyed in 1917.[21] The

[19] N. Werth, 'Uno stato contro il suo popolo: violenze, repressioni, terrori nell'Unione Sovietica', in S. Courtois, N. Werth, et al., *Il libro nero del comunismo: crimini, terrore, repressione* (Milan: Mondadori, 1998), 71–4.

[20] R. Stites, *Revolutionary Dreams: Utopian Vision and Experimental Life in the Russian Revolution* (Oxford: Oxford University Press, 1989).

[21] A. Graziosi, *L'URSS di Lenin e di Stalin: storia dell'Unione sovietica, 1914–1945* (Bologna: il Mulino, 2007), 113–14.

authentic base of the Soviet state was therefore neo-authoritarian, plebeian, and hostile to the peasantry.

Following a trend which had been triggered in the whole of Europe by the experience of war—albeit in a more extreme form—the political lexicon used by communists abounded with words and metaphors of military origin, and these were then transferred to communist circles elsewhere in the world.[22] Bolshevism now represented much more than a 'party of the civil war': it was the driving force behind a new state and the headquarters of world revolution. In spite of being a brutal police state, the Bolshevik regime's self-image of leading player in the social-ist and proletarian revolution spread beyond Russia's borders, partly because of apologists like the American journalist John Reed. His celebrated reportage on the 'ten days that shook the world', which naively depicted the Revolution in romantic colours, opened the way for an avalanche of similar political journalism. It would have been hard to deny the truth of this assertion. The world revolution that Lenin dreamt of did not materialize, but the Bolshevik Revolution was a global event for all to see. The Menshevik Yuli Martov very quickly understood—more lucidly than Lenin's Western adversaries—that Bolshevism was capable of becoming a global phenomenon in the wake of the disruption, social levelling, hatred, and rebelliousness generated by the disastrous Great War.[23]

The unifying factor was provided by the persistence of the revolutionary myth within the European cultural and political scene. François Furet has observed the crucial role played by the perception in the collective imagination that the Bolshevik Revolution was a continuation of the French Revolution.[24] The power of this symbol explains the fascination with the October Revolution, which was seen as the birth of a new egalitarian universalism, particularly in the world of European socialism. From the beginning, the image created by the Bolsheviks' actions and self-perception took on a life of its own and had different aspects: decision-making by popular councils, even though the regime had rejected any form of democ-racy from early 1918; equality, which 'war communism' appeared to sustain and embody; pacifism, reinterpreted as the redemptive final destination for social and political violence. The birth of the communist movement was grafted onto this stratified myth of revolution. For the Bolsheviks, the myth of the Revolutionary state became a redress outside Russia for their increasing unpopularity in Russia. At the same time, this state provided a guiding principle for the organization and membership of the new International. In its twin role as political apparatus and symbolic authority, the Soviet state inevitably became the cohesive factor in the communist movement.

---

[22] M. von Hagen, *Soldiers in the Proletarian Dictatorship: The Red Army and the Soviet Socialist State, 1917–1930* (Ithaca, N.Y.: Cornell University Press, 1990), 64–6.

[23] J. Martov, *Bolscevismo mondiale: la prima critica marxista del leninismo al potere (1919)* (Turin: Einaudi, 1980).

[24] F. Furet, *Il passato di un'illusione: l'idea comunista nel XX secolo* (Milan: Mondadori, 1995), 75ff. See also M. Flores and F. Gori (eds), *Il mito dell'URSS: la cultura occidentale e l'Unione sovietica* (Milan: FrancoAngeli, 1990).

VICTORY IN RUSSIA, DEFEAT IN EUROPE

The new International found its place within the divisions between socialists, and could count on the high standing of the Bolshevik Revolution amongst large sections of radical socialism. Criticism by reformist socialists of the abolition of political democracy in Russia did not seem to affect the Bolsheviks' prestige on the European Left, partly because the credibility of social democratic leaders had been profoundly shaken by the collapse of internationalism at the start of the Great War. The leadership of European socialism was split between fierce critics of Soviet Russia—such as Kautsky, who saw the Bolshevik dictatorship as a despotic model very distant from socialist ideals—and sympathetic critics, such as the Austrian Marxists Otto Bauer and Friedrich Adler, though all denied the universal validity of the Bolshevik example. But no one could limit the attraction exerted by the resurgence of the revolutionary myth amongst European socialists.[25] While the existence of a communist movement was still largely symbolic, the gamble that had created it suffered a harsh backlash from 1919 onwards. The first year after the war in Europe was marked by social conflict and political instability, especially in Central Europe. It was now widely believed throughout Europe that the prewar reality was gone forever, and that the upheavals and changes caused by the war would lead to new kinds of social order. In this sense, the Bolsheviks' prophecies of uprising and epoch-changing events proved to have some foundation. But their revolutionary and cataclysmic expectations proved to be unrealistic. According to Lenin's analysis, the old order was more resistant in Europe than it was in Russia, but when it came to the moment it started to give way, its collapse would set off a devastating dynamic, creating a classic domino effect. The Bolshevik conviction was that the world war had loosened the old national identities and shaped a transnational civil conflict along the divide of class membership. This was not to be. The break-up of the Central Powers and the Tsarist empire itself led to national revolutions, not social ones. The limited and fragmented nature of the revolutionary Marxist forces outside Russia soon revealed itself. The decapitation of the Spartacist movement was a sign of early defeat and impotence, and not the tragic precondition for a future resurgence.

The establishment of a Soviet republic in Hungary and subsequent revolutionary outbreaks in Bavaria and Slovakia were short-lived episodes, which did not meet expectations that soviets would spread throughout Europe; it was all over by March–August 1919. In spite of this, the Bolsheviks constantly looked towards the old continent when the fate of the Soviet Republic was most dramatically in the balance. The vicissitudes of the Hungarian Republic of Workers' Councils in particular provoked agonizing concern in Moscow. Although they were tormented by the pressing difficulties of the Civil War and their inability to adequately assist the Hungarian revolutionaries led by Béla Kun, the Russian leaders

---

[25] I. Getzler, 'Ottobre 1917: il dibattito marxista sulla rivoluzione in Russia', in *Storia del marxismo*, vol. 3.1: *Il marxismo nell'età della Terza Internazionale: dalla Rivoluzione d'ottobre alla crisi del '29* (Turin: Einaudi, 1981).

did give the latter some material support.[26] The simultaneous conquest of power by revolutionaries in Budapest and Munich so excited Zinoviev that he predicted that within a year the whole of Europe would be communist.[27] The rapid fall of the Hungarian Soviet Republic—overwhelmed by the ruthless methods adopted by Kun's government even before it was suffocated by the Romanian army at the instigation of the French—undermined such expectations.[28] As with the suppression of Spartacism in Germany, however, this event was perceived in Moscow as a temporary defeat that did not change the timetable of revolutionary struggle in Europe. The Bolsheviks nurtured the same illusions as the Hungarian communists, who perceived the nationalist sentiments of the popular masses as only the superficial manifestation of a more profound revolutionary upheaval. The establishment of the proletarian dictatorship and the indiscriminate use of violence accelerated the collapse of Soviet power in Hungary, and provoked a reaction from society that could not be attributed to domestic or international plots.[29]

Lenin and his comrades were only willing to draw lessons from the Russian Civil War. In the territory of the former Tsarist empire, now in total disarray and a thoroughfare of brutal civil conflict from the Baltic to the Ukraine and the Caucasus, social and ideological motivations appeared to fuse with national ones, and the Bolsheviks thought the greatest threat to be the potential combination of a counter-revolutionary revolt and an intervention from outside.[30] At the same time, they considered the restoration of international order that was emerging after the Great War to be negative, illusory, and infeasible, because it excluded Soviet Russia's involvement in the conclusion of a European peace agreement. In their eyes, both Wilson's plans for democracy and national self-determination and French and British ambitions to increase their power were an impediment to, and a distraction from, the advent of a socialist Europe. This interpretation remained unchanged after the British and French imposition of a 'punitive peace agreement' on Germany. For the Bolsheviks, the Treaty of Versailles was no different from the Treaty of Brest-Litovsk. They were quite right about the fragility of the postwar political order in Europe, though they certainly were not the only ones to notice it. However, the Bolsheviks were alone in mistaking this fragility for the impossibility of consolidating the postwar order in the short term. Communists in both Russia and Germany believed in the prospect of a sudden breakdown of peace in Europe.

At the end of 1919, with the turning point in the Civil War that came with the Red offensive against the White armies led by General Denikin in the south and Trotsky's victorious defence of Petrograd against the troops of Yudenich, Lenin's speeches came to be dominated by his vision of the Russian Civil War as the Soviet Republic's struggle to the last drop of blood against French and British

---

[26] *KIMR*, docs 19 and 22.   [27] *L'Internationale communiste* 2, June 1919.

[28] R. K. Debo, *Survival and Consolidation: The Foreign Policy of Soviet Russia, 1918–1921* (Montreal: McGill-Queen's University Press, 1992), 117.

[29] R. L. Tőkés, *Béla Kun and the Hungarian Soviet Republic: The Origins and Role of the Communist Party of Hungary in the Revolution of 1918–1919* (New York: Praeger, 1967).

[30] Graziosi, *L'URSS di Lenin e di Stalin*, 129–30.

imperialism, and not simply against the White armies. The significance and the vision of the original project were still there, in spite of the repression of the first attempts at revolution in Central and Eastern Europe. The Treaty of Versailles was seen as a precarious order destined to collapse under the blows of the imminent revolution in Germany. In December 1919, at the Eighth Conference of the RCP (b), Lenin demanded that the project of world revolution be implemented. In his opinion, the risk was well worth taking, because the workers of Western countries had supported the Russian revolutionaries against the Triple Entente. An 'immediate insurrection' across Europe had not happened, but Soviet power remained in place in part because of the support of the revolutionary masses in Europe.[31] It is hard to believe that such an interpretation was simply taken from their armoury of propaganda. The idea that the only ally of the Russian revolutionaries was the international proletariat arose from the isolation of the Civil War and the defeat of attempts at revolution in Central Europe, but it was also a powerful factor in mobilizing and consolidating support. The appeal to the masses in capitalist countries was founded on strong reverberations arising from the Revolution outside Russia. Even though his argument concerning the actual part played by the international proletariat was fuelled by bombast and self-delusion, Lenin consciously attracted attention to a political and symbolic resource, which the Bolsheviks would later be able to draw upon. At the same time, he recognized that the revolution in Europe would involve a much more complex scenario than the one that the Bolsheviks had believed in. This gave rise to a dilemma that would mark out the future of the Bolshevik Revolution: what was their fate to be without a revolution in Europe? But Lenin did not face up to the question; he was still searching for possible omens of a 'European civil war'.

For the Bolsheviks, General Kapp's failed coup in Germany in March 1920 immediately suggested a close analogy with their own revolution. On 17 March Lenin notified Iosif Stalin, then engaged on the Civil War's southern front, of his opinion that military operations needed to be brought to a speedy conclusion in Crimea, 'in order to have our hands entirely free, given that civil war in Germany could oblige us to move west to assist the communists'.[32] The Comintern concluded that the only possible outcomes were a military dictatorship or a dictatorship of the proletariat, and that the response from the streets, where workers mobilized against the coup, meant that civil war was inevitable in Germany.[33] On 29 March Lenin argued at the opening of the Ninth Congress of the RCP (b) that German events were developing along the same lines as the Russian ones in 1917. He now perceived the Russian experience as a 'world-historical phenomenon' and the international scene as divided into 'two camps' clashing with each other. The archetypal value of the Bolshevik experience of power constituted a solid foundation for his vision of the revolutionary project during the aftermath of the civil war. It was a matter of 'awaiting the world revolution'.[34]

---

[31] Lenin, *Polnoe sobranie sochinenii*, vol. 39, p. 346.   [32] *PBKI*, doc. 15, p. 39.
[33] *KIMR*, doc. 29.   [34] Lenin, *Polnoe sobranie sochinenij*, vol. 40, pp. 242–5.

How long they would have to wait was not clear. However, Lenin was convinced that the situation would be full of surprises and that they were in a state 'of neither peace nor war' with the Entente powers and Poland. From his point of view, the defeat of the Whites, which by then was clear to everyone, was not the endgame and could not lead to genuine peace. Shortly afterwards, the Polish offensive into the Ukraine led by Józef Piłsudski, resulting from a long series of sporadic military actions, provided further confirmation of this argument. Lenin disregarded the nationalistic motivation behind Piłsudski's action, and interpreted it as part of a wider international context—an attempt to prevent the development of a European revolution by breaking all channels of communication between Moscow and Berlin.[35] The Bolshevik reaction was not purely military: inspired by unprecedented patriotic rhetoric, they drove the Poles from Kiev in the space of a few weeks. The Polish offensive in the Ukraine, following hard on the heels of the attempted coup in Germany, appeared to prove that the fluid situation in Central Europe was not yet over. The sense of danger and the feeling that great opportunities existed continued to feed off each other. This transformed the defensive war with Poland into an offensive one in July 1920, after Moscow had rejected British Foreign secretary George Curzon's offer of mediation through the League of Nations.[36]

The high point of the Bolshevik counter-offensive and Lenin's decision to drive the Red Army onwards towards Warsaw coincided with the Second Congress of the Comintern. However accidental the timing, it took on a highly symbolic significance. The Congress was called on to ratify the effective birth of the communist movement as an antagonist of the old socialist one—a movement now capable of gathering sufficient consensus, particularly in Germany and France. This time the foreign delegations were substantial, a group of about 200 delegates from more than thirty countries. The draconian conditions for parties joining the Comintern, which were dictated in twenty-one points by Zinoviev, set out a strict separation from the traditional forces of socialism without any possibility of appeal. This was the moment in which European communism came into existence. The rigid discipline demanded by the Bolsheviks as the essential element of the new parties consisted of subordination to the decisions of the International, the principle of 'democratic centralism', unconditional support for Soviet Russia, aversion to reformist compromise, and sectarianism perceived as a positive attitude.[37]

Conscious of the real possibilities created by the movement that started in the Russian October, the delegates to the Second Congress worked in a climate of excitement and fervour as the Red Army appeared to be on the point of exporting the revolution to Poland. Unlike the period of Brest-Litovsk, the Revolution could now rely on a powerful military force. Unlike the period in which the Comintern was set up, the communist option appeared to be attracting substantial sections of European socialism. Seen from Moscow, the European revolution appeared to

---

[35] Service, *Lenin: A Political Life*, vol. 3, p. 118.
[36] Pipes, *The Unknown Lenin*, doc. 53.
[37] F. Claudin, *La crisi del movimento comunista : dal Comintern al Cominform* (Milan: Feltrinelli, 1975), 87.

be developing the necessary momentum. On 16 July 1920 Lenin presented the Plenum of the RCP (b) with the political proposals for supporting the Red Army's offensive, in which he assumed there would be a Soviet rebellion in Poland.[38] In his speech to the Congress on 19 July, Lenin once again declared that the Treaty of Versailles was unsustainable and would soon meet the same end as the Treaty of Brest-Litovsk. This was not a new idea. But this time he was putting the argument at the time when Poland, the bastion of the new postwar settlement in Central and Eastern Europe, appeared to be on the point of collapsing under the force of the Red Army. Lenin quoted John Maynard Keynes's pessimistic predictions concerning the 'economic consequences of the peace', never failing to supplement the arguments of the liberal economist with the doctrine of 'capitalist contradictions'. As they had allowed the Soviet Republic to survive in a weak and backward country like Russia, the end of the war would not mean the disappearance of such contradictions; indeed, it would exacerbate them.[39]

In reality, Lenin had just made the riskiest move of his political career in power. The decision to cross the Polish border had not gone unchallenged. Trotsky and Radek were reluctant and sceptical about the idea of a mass insurrection in Poland to support the invading army.[40] As on other occasions, Lenin forced other people's hands, but this time he came down on the more radical side. Compared with the Brest-Litovsk Treaty, the alignments within the Bolshevik ruling group had now inverted their positions. Lenin saw victory in the Russian Civil War, the advance of the Red Army into Polish territory, and the continuing crisis in some European countries as the supreme opportunity for acting upon his original revolutionary project. Back in June he had already been proposing the 'Sovietization of Lithuania'.[41] But his fanciful ambitions went far beyond that. On 23 July, he sent Stalin a telegram whose feverish tone revealed his extraordinarily ambitious aims: 'Zinoviev, Bukharin and I think that we need to promote revolution in Italy without further delay. My personal opinion is that to do this we need to sovietize Hungary and possibly also Czechoslovakia and Romania.'[42]

The Red Army's offensive in Poland was therefore part of an attempt to relaunch the European revolution. Only in this light can we understand the logic behind such a dangerous gamble as marching on Warsaw. Lenin and Stalin went so far as to discuss the future Soviet republics in Europe, which the former saw as a union and the latter as separate republics based on nationality, to take into consideration the irreducible historical characteristics of the nations of Central and Eastern Europe.[43] In other words, Stalin seemed more inclined to acknowledge the obdurate national identities of Europe, which Lenin largely failed to take into account. Their shared vision was, however, the product of wishful thinking. The revolutionary prospects of the movement behind the factory occupations in Italy would soon prove to

[38] *PBKI*, doc. 23, p. 53.   [39] Lenin, *Polnoe sobranie sočinenij*, vol. 41, 219, 225.
[40] Service, *Lenin: A Political Life*, vol. 3, p. 120.
[41] Pipes, *The Unknown Lenin*, doc. 51.   [42] *KIMR*, doc. 39.
[43] J. Smith, *The Bolsheviks and the National Question 1917–1923* (London: Macmillan, 1999), 176–7.

have been grossly overestimated and those of Hungary nonexistent following the disaster of the previous year, not to speak of the other countries in Central Europe. The idea that the Red Army would have been greeted enthusiastically in Poland was equally unfounded. Quite the opposite: the popular mobilization against the Russian invasion prevented the fall of Warsaw and reversed the fortunes of the war. By the end of August the conflict had ended in a Soviet defeat.[44]

On 22 September 1920, Lenin presented his own review of these events to the Ninth Conference of the RCP (b). In the part of his speech that was made public, he acknowledged that the military campaign in July and August had created 'a difficult situation'; but he did not admit that there had been a defeat. In his judgement, the decision to launch an offensive in Poland had had 'an enormous influence on Western Europe', given Warsaw's proximity to the 'centre of the entire system of world imperialism', and had turned the Soviet Republic into 'a player of primary significance in global politics'. According to Lenin, revolutionary prospects were still alive, particularly in Germany but even in Great Britain. His outlook had not changed. Even after the conclusion of the Polish–Soviet War, he was not expecting a genuine peace. He predicted that 'a probable new period of war' was imminent.[45] In the part of his speech that was kept secret, Lenin explicated the strategy for Soviet power in the light of this prediction. The decision to shift from the 'period of defensive war with global imperialism' to an 'offensive war' in order 'to favour the Sovietization of Poland' had served as a deterrent against the repetition of foreign intervention to strangle revolutionary power in Russia. Now the Westerners had been warned that the consequence could be the expansion of the Soviet Republic. Even if this had not happened on this occasion, Lenin declared that recent events represented 'an extremely important turning point not only in the policy of Soviet Russia, but also in world politics'.[46]

Victory in the Civil War, the strength of the Red Army, and the birth of the communist movement now provided greater confidence in the ability of Soviet power to survive and even play an international role. But these factors did not in any way justify the idea that it could threaten to attack the settlement put in place by Versailles. The end of the Polish–Soviet War quite possibly led to the stabilization of Central and Eastern Europe. It was up to Radek to sound the note of realism which was lacking in Lenin's speech. Radek reasserted his opinion, which he had expressed two months earlier, that 'the conditions for revolution in Central Europe were not yet in place', and that the conquest of Warsaw would not have created them. He therefore distanced himself from Lenin's pronouncement on the new inspiration for Bolshevik policy, and invited delegates to reject 'the method of sounding out the international situation with the assistance of bayonets'. The

---

[44] Debo, *Survival and Consolidation*, 213–26, 231–47; N. Davies, *White Eagle, Red Star: The Polish–Soviet War, 1919–1920* (London: Pimlico, 1972). On revolutionary illusions in Italy during the summer and autumn of 1920, see P. Spriano, *Storia del Partito comunista italiano*, vol. 1: *Da Bordiga a Gramsci* (Turin: Einaudi, 1967), 82–3.
[45] Lenin, *Polnoe sobranie sochinenii*, vol. 41, 281–5.　　　[46] *KIMR*, doc. 47.

only reassuring factor was the strength of the Red Army, which had now become a 'decisive element in world politics'.[47]

This plea for self-criticism was not taken up by other Bolshevik leaders. Putting aside his initial doubts, Trotsky declared that the final victory in the Civil War would make it possible to establish the 'national power' of the Russian proletariat and 'free' the Red Army as a 'force for international action'. Diplomacy could therefore negotiate peace with Poland in Riga, but the objective of marching on Warsaw remained unchanged.[48] According to Bukharin, the offensive in Poland would in any event take the European revolutionary movement to 'a higher level of development', and, basing his argument on events in Italy, he rejected the idea that there had been a slowdown in the Western revolution.[49] In fact Lenin had done more than just evaluate revolutionary prospects in Europe; he had decided to rely on the use of the Red Army to implement the original Bolshevik project of European revolution. For the first time, revolutionary expansionism was combined with the prospect of Soviet Russia exercising the role of a world power.[50] Hence we can better understand the patriotic language that the Bolsheviks were using for the first time in an attempt to fuse class mobilization with an appeal to the defence of the fatherland—albeit an appeal that was being exploited for the purposes of the revolution outside Russia.

It is unlikely that, as Richard Pipes has argued, Lenin intended to sovietize Poland as the first stage in a plan to export revolution to the West exclusively through the bayonets of the Red Army.[51] It would be more sensible to accept his confidential arguments developed after the defeat. Lenin had not abandoned the idea of insurrection. For him, the military constituted a possible trigger for social revolution. His aim was to test the relative strength of the Soviet Republic, bring about the collapse of the existing regime in Poland, terrorize the Polish ruling classes, and foster the insurrectional mood of the working masses in Central Europe. But the Bolsheviks had to experience first-hand the limitations on their ability to expand and the deafness of the European masses to their appeal. The example of the French Revolution encountered its limit here. The precedent of a national and revolutionary war was not repeatable, because revolutionary power in Russia did not have sufficient impetus and its universalist ambitions did not accord with European social reality. The obstinacy of Lenin and the majority of Bolsheviks in pursuing a revolutionary war only revealed their inability to understand this reality. Even after the failure of the Red Army, Lenin refused to acknowledge that the war in Poland had been a defeat with many very serious implications, dismissing it instead as 'a provisional historical event'.[52] The Ninth Conference called for

[47] *KIMR*, doc. 48.
[48] *Devyataya Konferentsiya Rkp(b). Sentyabr' 1920 goda. Protokoly* (Moscow: Izdatel'stvo politicheskoy literatury, 1972), 78.
[49] Ibid. 59.
[50] A. Di Biagio, *Coesistenza e isolazionismo: Mosca, il Comintern e l'Europa di Versailles (1918–1928)* (Rome: Carocci, 2004), 53.
[51] R. Pipes, *Il regime bolscevico: dal terrore rosso alla morte di Lenin* (Milan: Mondadori, 1999), 209.
[52] *KIMR*, doc. 50.

a transition from 'passive pacifist support' for the working masses to 'an offensive tactic in defence of the first proletarian republic and for the extension of the territory over which workers' power has triumphed'.[53]

All this threw light on the ambivalence of the 'lessons' of Brest-Litovsk. Lenin had not only kept his faith in the European revolution as the necessary outcome of the Bolshevik one; it now emerged that he was deeply attached to that expectation and its underlying logic. Although he often acknowledged that the timing of the future revolutions was not as unrelenting as he had hoped, Lenin could not resign himself to the idea that in future Europe would be immune to the tidal wave set in motion by the Bolsheviks in Russia. In other words, he could not accept that the prospects of international revolution that had inspired his entire political activity were fading. It was this that drove him to take the adventurist decision to launch the offensive on Poland, with no serious assessment of the Soviet state's security. This decision was more an act of desperation than of conviction: the drastic attempt to light a fuse that refused to catch alight. This would leave its mark on subsequent Bolshevik policy, because it linked the world revolution and the communist movement to the role and strength of the Soviet state.

Thus the end of the Russian Civil War created a paradox. Of all the Revolution's possible outcomes, the one that the Bolsheviks had considered the most improbable had prevailed: the survival of their state in international isolation. Throughout 1920, they refused to accept that this unforeseen reality could continue for very long. Any revision of their political axioms having been precluded, they found themselves obliged to respond in two different ways: to consider the possibility of coming to agreements with other states, and to rely exclusively on themselves by modelling the communist movement in their own image. The first of these two orientations was purely pragmatic. The treaties signed with Estonia in February, Lithuania in July, and Latvia in August of 1920, and the armistice with Finland in that same month, signified a truce on the Baltic borders. The treaty signed in Riga in October was the necessary conclusion to the defeat in the war with Poland.[54] However, no stable agreement with the capitalist countries was in sight. The second orientations followed the logic of the political primacy assumed by the Bolsheviks in the new International, but also reflected the largely self-referential nature of their perception of reality. In Lenin's speeches, a proliferation of events occurring in European countries were interpreted as replicas of various stages in the Russian Revolution and codified as unavoidable transitions. While Kapp was the German Kornilov, Great Britain, following the strikes, was moving towards a situation of dual power typical of February 1917. Everywhere there would be the same polarization, between the forces of reaction and those of the revolution, which had distinguished the Russian situation. As the prospects of insurrection outside Russia became less likely, so the Bolshevik model acquired greater centrality. In April 1920, Lenin declared in his pamphlet 'Left-wing communism, an infantile disorder'—which aimed to define the communist identity in relation to

[53] *PBKI*, doc. 31, pp. 66–7.   [54] Debo, *Survival and Consolidation*, 144, 227–9, 282.

spontaneous extremism and to argue against the rejection of parliamentary practices that was widespread in radical socialist circles particularly in Germany and Italy—that 'some fundamental aspects of our revolution have a significance that is not only local or specifically Russian, but also international'. This amounted to no less than 'the international validity, or the historical inevitability of repetition on an international scale, of what has taken place in our country'.[55]

In the light of this, it was somewhat paradoxical to argue a rejection of 'extremism'. If anything, the Bolshevik model of 1917 referred back to a radical view of how to use institutional spaces in a pragmatic way before seizing power. The call for realism and tactical flexibility for communists was thus based on an invented tradition. Lenin was more concerned about reformists than he was about extremists. Hence the obsessive demarcation line between the parties adhering to the Comintern and the great majority of the tendencies belonging to the old socialist world. At the Second Congress of the Comintern, Zinoviev chose the adoption of the centralized and sectarian model of the Bolsheviks as the only reliable method for distinguishing between communism and reformism. The communist movement came into being under the rigid discipline replicated by the Bolsheviks from their own experience, with the intention of creating a single party of world revolution. The question on the agenda did not simply concern the Social Democrats' nationalistic 'betrayal'. Social democracy played an essential role in holding the European order together in the postwar period, especially in Germany. Instead of acknowledging that the failure of the First World War to generate a widespread civil war challenged the very premise of their political project, the Bolsheviks blamed a vague grouping of forces for the non-fulfilment of their prediction. Foremost amongst these forces were the social democrats. Clearly this attitude arose from the Bolsheviks' defensiveness about their own *raison d'être* and their need to consolidate an identity that was in danger of failing in spite of the enormous impact of the October Revolution on the collective imagination of the time. The denial of any legitimacy for the social democratic parties became even more intransigent—to the point that, in their search for allies hostile to the new settlement, the Bolsheviks even started to look favourably on the extreme Right. Thus opposition to social democracy became a founding characteristic of communist political culture.

THE BIRTH OF THE COMMUNIST PARTIES

At the end of 1920 and start of 1921 mass communist parties were created in Germany and France as the result of significant splits from the socialist parties. Uniquely in France, the majority of the Socialist Party went over to communism.[56] In Germany, the unification of communists and independent socialists produced a sizeable communist party, albeit smaller than the social democratic one.[57] These

---

[55] Lenin, *Polnoe sobranie sochinenii*, vol. 41, p. 3.
[56] For the birth of the Communist Party in France, see S. Courtois and M. Lazar, *Histoire du Parti communiste français* (Paris: PUF, 2000), 50–67.
[57] For the birth of the Communist Party in Germany, see Weitz, *Creating German Communism*, 95–9.

were reassuring events for the Bolshevik strategy of building communist parties for the purpose of fomenting revolution in Western Europe and contributing to the defence of the Soviet republic.[58] But the pan-European revolutionary project was clearly at a standstill. Defeat in Poland was probably providential for the security of the Soviet state, which might otherwise have been drawn into a conflict with the Western powers the outcome of which would have been unpredictable.[59] Following the Polish–Soviet War, Lenin's predictions of an imminent resumption of warfare in Eastern Europe seemed much less convincing. The communist movement only began to gather strength once the crisis and conflict that had justified the new International had started to recede. The new European communist parties were the product of a defeat, not a victory.

Although the resilience of bourgeois Europe and, in some cases, the counter-revolutionary reaction had frustrated their hopes everywhere, the Bolsheviks perceived this as confirmation of the epoch-changing nature of the Civil War—an obligatory stage in the socialist revolution. This was the principal message in Zinoviev's speech to the Halle Congress in October 1920, which saw the German Independent Social Democratic Party join Comintern.[60] At the same time, Lenin reasserted in Moscow that the Bolshevik Revolution was only 'one link in the chain of international revolution', and that the settlement established by the Treaty of Versailles was founded 'on a volcano' both inside and outside Europe. Similar statements had been made on several occasions in the period 1918–19. What was new in 1920 was that Lenin pointed to Soviet Russia as the power capable of destroying the Versailles settlement—a role that in his opinion had been demonstrated by the war in Poland.[61] This assertion was not just an attempt to justify the risky decisions taken in the summer; it also defined the nature of the Soviet state. Lenin's initial portrayal of the international reality following the Civil War was of an unstable balance of power between opposing forces that were destined sooner or later to enter into conflict, although the timing was difficult to predict. Bukharin had this interpretation propagated in the Comintern press.[62]

So the Bolsheviks adopted the idea of a transition from a 'war of movement' to a 'war of position', without, however, sensing that the latter might require them to rethink their strategy. The revolutionary delusions dating from the war with Poland were put aside in favour of more prudent positions that took into account the less favourable balance of power. But this did not interfere with the overall continuity in how the role of the Soviet state was perceived, which Lenin backed precisely in these circumstances. Awareness that the world revolution was not just around the corner, in spite of the Comintern's more solid foundations, struggled to make headway. Lenin revived a note of pragmatism, as he had done at the time of the Brest-Litovsk agreement. It was still a valid example, because revolutionary Russia always had to exploit divisions amongst its enemies. The method of economic concessions now became the principal tool for setting up useful relations

[58] *KIMR*, doc. 51.   [59] Ulam, *Storia della politica estera sovietica*, 158.
[60] *KIMR*, doc. 53.   [61] Lenin, *Polnoe sobranie sochinenii*, vol. 41, pp. 356–7.
[62] *KIMR*, doc. 60, p. 227.

with capitalist countries. However, Lenin failed to criticize his own reckless adventure in the summer of 1920. He argued that there was no need to make any substantial changes to strategy. The era of a 'war of movement' had come to a close, but the notion of a permanent conflict between the Soviet state and all the others was still pivotal. In December 1920, Lenin paraphrased Clausewitz when arguing that, if war was the pursuance of politics by other means, concessions to capitalist countries were in turn 'the continuance of war and not peace'. In his opinion, Soviet Russia's existence was guaranteed by 'the radical split between imperialist powers' sanctioned by the Treaty of Versailles, which would make life impossible for the German nation. The revolutionary state's foreign policy had to exploit this division in the knowledge that 'the experience of the history of revolutions and great conflicts teaches that wars—a series of wars—are inevitable'.[63]

At the end of the Civil War the idea of the inevitability of war, which Lenin had developed much earlier, became an essential element in the political culture of the Soviet state's elite. Its significance was that it rationalized the experience of war and violence unconsciously assimilated by the new regime, and provided the basis for the prediction of a long haul that previously would have been unthinkable. The totally unforeseen reality of the survival of the revolutionary state in Russia was reinterpreted as merely a change in the chronology that glossed over the failure of the original project of pan-European revolution. Lenin's apparent conversion to gradualism at the end of the Civil War did not provide Bolshevism with new strategic tools. The transition from wartime to peacetime was taking place in a country that had experienced unheard-of devastation long after the end of the First World War and was going through dramatic economic and cultural decline. Russia had lost much of its human and productive resources, was disrupted by famines and endemic peasant revolts, and the pillars of civilized life had all but rotted away.[64] This meant that the state had to adjust to unexpected conditions, which were once again the result of Lenin's improvisation: the break with 'war communism', the introduction of market relations in the countryside and the launch of the New Economic Policy (NEP), the related clampdown and ban on 'factionalism' in the party, the recognition of state interests in foreign policy and the notion of 'peaceful coexistence' with other states, which was symbolized by the treaty signed with Great Britain.[65]

Lenin did not put too much emphasis on the failed insurrection by German communists in March 1921, at the time of a miners' strike. He agreed with Clara Zetkin and Paul Levi when they condemned the adventurism of the Comintern's emissary, Béla Kun, who fomented the putsch which was inevitably suppressed.[66] But the other leaders of the Russian party were not on the same wavelength. In a

[63] Lenin, *Polnoe sobranie sochinenii*, vol. 42, p. 101.

[64] Graziosi, *L'URSS di Lenin e Stalin*, 172–3.

[65] Di Biagio, *Coesistenza e isolazionismo*, 63. For the notion of 'peaceful coexistence', see G. Procacci, 'La coesistenza pacifica: appunti per la storia di un concetto', in L. Sestan (ed.), *La politica estera della perestrojka: L'URSS di fronte al mondo da Breznev a Gorbaciov* (Rome: Editori Riuniti, 1988).

[66] Lenin, *Polnoe sobranie sochinenii*, vol. 52, pp. 149–50.

note to Lenin dated 18 April, Trotsky rejected Levi's criticisms because, in his opinion, the 'March action' was 'the first autonomous act of the German Communist Party' and demonstrated the 'treachery' of the social democrats.[67] The Comintern followed the same path and defended the leadership of the German Communist Party, supporting Béla Kun even though he was now the symbol of the failed communist revolutions in Central Europe. The moderate German leader was expelled from the party, and shortly afterwards from the International.[68] But the 'Levi affair' was something more than an internal dispute within German communism. The arguments over the attempted insurrection in Germany went to the heart of a question that was difficult to evade. Was it not time to redefine the political prospects of the communist movement, given that the project of world revolution had met with no success, and that the idea itself was increasingly associated with the longer term? From this angle, was it still possible to argue the universal relevance of the Bolshevik Revolution and its role as a model? These seemed perfectly legitimate questions after the Russian Civil War and in the third year since the end of the European war. However, these questions would have quickly challenged the very idea of the communist international. Lenin refused to pose them. Having devoted his remaining energies to the introduction of the New Economic Policy as a long-term strategy, he concluded instead that Soviet Russia could have an influence on world events primarily by its own gradual economic recovery. Lenin pursued this theme in his reports to the Third Congress of the Comintern on 13 June 1921. As far as international politics was concerned, the Soviet Republic was destined 'to coexist' with a 'capitalist encirclement' albeit for a period that would 'not be long'.[69] Consequently Lenin criticized the radicalism of Radek's arguments, which did not abandon the idea of an imminent 'breakthrough against the counter-revolutionary front', if not in Germany then in southeastern Europe or Italy.[70]

In his main speech to the congress on 5 July, Lenin acknowledged that 'the development of world revolution' had not been 'as straightforward as we had expected'. On the basis of this statement, he called on communists to undertake 'thorough preparation for revolution' and an 'in-depth analysis of its actual development' in the advanced capitalist countries. The more immediate prospects would have to be modified, but the main objective would not differ from the programme set out a year earlier to the newly formed communist parties—to challenge the influence of the socialist parties on European workers, because they were the 'principal foundation' that held capitalism in place.[71] Lenin defended the policy of the previous years in its entirety. His words encouraged greater realism, but not a review of the communists' culture and strategy. Trotsky argued along the same lines. In 1918–19 it had, in his opinion, been 'historically justified' to believe that the 'disorganization of the bourgeoisie' and 'the impetus' of the working class would lead without difficulty to the latter seizing control of state power. This scenario did not take place,

[67] *KIMR*, doc. 68, pp. 257–61.   [68] *KIMR*, doc. 82, pp. 290–93.
[69] Lenin, *Polnoe sobranie sochinenii*, vol. 44, p. 4.   [70] *KIMR*, doc. 77, pp. 282–5.
[71] Lenin, *Polnoe sobranie sochinenii*, vol. 44, pp. 36–7.

but this was not a reason to conclude that the position on world revolution had been mistaken. Trotsky believed that the resilience of the European bourgeoisie was largely due to chance. The argument that belief in the proximity of revolution was the only factor dividing communists and social democrats had to be rejected, because the latter had effectively contributed to the defence of bourgeois power. The Bolsheviks may have been guilty of naivety, but on the whole they had got it right ('In 1919 we used to say: it's a matter of months; now we say: it's perhaps a matter of years. We don't know with any certainty, but have all the more reason to believe that development is in this direction and in the meantime we have become much stronger throughout the world').[72]

The limitations of Lenin's and Trotsky's view of the past left plenty of room for the continuance of radicalism amongst communist ruling groups, including the Bolshevik one. None of the leaders Lenin accused of 'leftism' before the congress seemed ready retract anything. Zinoviev proclaimed that the 'March action' had not been a putsch but 'a revolutionary episode along the troubled road followed by the German working class'.[73] Radek rejected the very notion of a 'war of position', and expressed the political language that would typify the Bolsheviks for some time: 'We're not living through a period of transformation from 'war of movement' to trench warfare,' he pronounced, 'but rather a period in which the great armies of the proletariat shall be formed.'[74] Even Lenin stopped short of talk of a transition towards 'trench warfare'. Although he doubted the advisability of formulating 'a theory of the revolutionary offensive' in Germany, he argued that the 'March action' had been 'an enormous achievement, in spite of the errors its leaders made'. Thus he approved Levi's expulsion as a 'necessary' act. Given the disciplinary measure already in force in organized international communism, he considered the German leader's insubordination to be a more serious matter than the stubborn extremism of the German Communist Party and many of the Comintern's leaders. Lenin's condemnation of 'leftism' was measured, and ultimately came down to criticism of insufficient preparation for revolutionary offensive.[75]

There would be no NEP for international communism. Lenin believed that the establishment of communist parties in Germany, France, and even Italy was a historic event capable of strengthening the movement and inflicting defeat on the social democracies. In September 1921 he wrote a letter to the Soviet representative in Italy, Vatslav Vorovsky, in which he intensified his attack on extremism and the insubordination of Italian communist leaders, who had already been criticized at the Comintern's congress.[76] They were asked to be realistic, but also to firm up their identity based on implacable antagonism. Lenin acknowledged that the birth of the communist movement had not ousted social democracy, and that the balance of power was clearly in the latter's favour. However, he set the target of overthrowing them in the longer term. The tactic of a 'united front'

---

[72] *Protokoll des III Kongresses der Kommunistischen Internationale (Moskau, 22 Juni bis 12 Juli 1921)* (Hamburg, 1921), 87–90.
[73] Ibid. 184.　　　[74] Ibid. 438.
[75] Lenin, *Polnoe sobranie sochinenii*, vol. 44, pp. 28–9.　　　[76] *PBKI*, doc. 56, p. 96.

developed as a result of the Third Congress was consequently open to very different interpretations: an attempt at alliances with the social democrats and an tactic for destroying their grip on the European proletariat; a plan to increase gradually the mass base of the new parties and a purely propagandistic instrument while awaiting the next revolutionary opportunity. The proposals for the 'united front' submitted by Presidium of ECCI (the Executive Committee of the Communist International) in December 1921 fully reflected this contradictory line.[77] Lenin and the Bolsheviks continued to apply to postwar Europe the same rigid and simplistic ways of thinking that had been used in wartime. Thus social democracy became for them merely an expression of the bourgeois world, the division in the working-class movement came to be identified with class divisions, and the existence of the Soviet state itself was seen as an epoch-making reflection of these divisions.

The European communist parties in the first year of their existence fell well short of the Bolsheviks' expectations, but were nevertheless the result of Bolshevik decisions and dictates. The Comintern acted upon its global vocation, creating communist parties not only in Europe but beyond it. From 1920 to 1921, when the main European parties were founded, the first communist parties were set up outside Europe by Comintern plenipotentiaries, most notably in China, India, and Iran. But the greater geopolitical reach did not correspond to a numerical strength. Mass communist parties only existed in Germany and Czechoslovakia, where they had a few hundred thousand members, and in France, where the party reached about 100,000 members. In Italy, Yugoslavia, and Bulgaria, the parties had recruited some tens of thousands of activists, but they were soon outlawed or reduced to a state of semi-legality. In the rest of Western and Eastern Europe and in the whole of Northern Europe, they were either weak or insignificant. On the whole, social democrats were overwhelmingly in the majority. The communist parties brought together the fringes of European socialism that had been radicalized during the war and the postwar crisis. The internationalist and anti-revisionist group during the war had been enlarged by the support of anarcho-syndicalist organizations, and above all by socialists of a maximalist orientation. All members of the communist parties had been influenced to a greater or lesser extent by the experience of grass-roots councils—a model based on the working-class counter-power that emerged in Russia in 1917 and also in Germany in 1918–19. The common features would leave a deep impression, even though national and social particularities make simplistic generalizations impossible.[78] The generational rift was even more important than proletarian roots. The leaderships and cadres of the new parties were primarily made up of young people who did not have a long experience of politics and who were recruited by their opposition to the war. They were impatient of gradualism and inclined to voluntarism; they were attracted to

---

[77] Vatlin, *Komintern: idei, resheniya, sudby*, 80–85. See M. Hájek, *Storia dell'Internazionale comunista (1921–1935): la politica del fronte unico* (Rome: Editori Riuniti, 1969).

[78] A. Agosti, 'La famiglia politica comunista negli anni Venti: spunti per una storia comparative', in A. Agosti., *Il partito mondiale della rivoluzione: saggi sul comunismo e l'Internazionale* (Milan: Unicopli, 2009).

a new kind of combative militancy. For many young intellectuals, the Bolshevik Revolution represented the primacy of politics and the discovery of new human capabilities. However, the generational rift did not imply the creation of a new political culture. Although experienced as the start of a new era, communist sectarianism also perpetuated the marginal, anti-establishment, self-referential, and subversive mentalities and subcultures typical of the prewar socialist world. On the other hand, the political features of communism were mainly the result of its structural link with the Soviet state—a significant fact that has been ignored by most of the historiography of the Comintern and its communist parties.[79]

Communists were not necessarily 'agents of Moscow', as anti-communist propaganda described them, although the distinction between devoting oneself to the revolutionary cause and serving the Soviet regime could become blurred.[80] Their political faith drew considerable sustenance from the experience of war, and from the social and ideological radicalization of the masses after the war. It was, however, the Bolsheviks who provided their language and identity, along with generous financial support. The perception of civil war as a political aim, the image of the class adversary as an enemy, the elitist concept of the relationship between the party and the masses, authoritarian practices in relation to organization and discipline, and unconditional loyalty to Soviet Russia all separated the destinies of communists and socialists. The authority of the new International was founded on the revolutionary state, which also redefined and repositioned affiliations and symbols, and provided a stronger reference point and identity than any institution that had previously existed in the history of socialism. Lenin was rapidly becoming a charismatic figure outside Soviet Russia as well. Although European communists frequently took decisions independently from the Bolsheviks, this was a consequence of the fluid and volatile situation the new parties found themselves in, even when it came to the composition of their ruling groups, and they were almost always confident that they were following the authentic Bolshevik teachings and precepts.

The new International was firmly under the control of the Soviet leadership, and few challenged the rightfulness of this situation. Its apparatus, set up by the Second Congress in the summer of 1920, was cosmopolitan even at the highest levels: the ECCI, its presidium and secretariat, and its working groups and parallel organizations (Workers' International Relief, Red International of Labour Unions or Profintern, Young Communist International). However, the Comintern organization was from its inception intertwined with the Soviet Communist Party and the Narkomindel (People's Commissariat for Foreign Affairs). A chain of command made up of Comintern emissaries secured information channels and the organizational and financial assistance required for the survival of the parties, and this

---

[79] An example of a history of the European communist parties that omits the central question of relations with the USSR is A. Agosti, *Bandiere rosse: un profilo storico dei comunismi europei* (Rome: Editori Riuniti, 1999).

[80] E. K. Poretsky, *Our Own People: A Memoir of 'Ignace Reiss' and His Friends* (London: Oxford University Press, 1969).

operated alongside the Soviet embassies.[81] The semi-conspiratorial organizations created in Germany and other European countries had their central command in Moscow in a secret section of the Comintern, the Department of International Communications, under the direction of Osip Pyatnitsky. From the very beginning, this department had a special status and was linked to the Soviet police (Cheka).[82]

Victory in the Civil War and the transition to peacetime in Russia in 1921 did not constitute a break in revolutionary power. The suppression of the rebel sailors of Kronstadt—the final episode for the libertarian variant of the Revolution's council-based democracy, which never really established itself as a political actor— was the most revealing sign that the party-state created by the Bolsheviks since 1918 would continue to exercise a monopoly on power with great ferocity.[83] Founded in the social and institutional vacuum left by the devastation of war, revolution, and civil war between 1914 and 1921, the Soviet party-state was a bureaucratic and highly centralized organism that was militarized in its organization and spirit, largely isolated from society, and opposed by the hostile peasant masses. The Bolsheviks were completely aware of these realities; tellingly, they defined themselves as a military corps. The most incisive expression was used by Stalin, who spoke of an 'order of sword-bearers', referring to the precedent of a medieval chivalric order.[84] The Bolshevik state carried through the methods of mass mobilization from wartime to peacetime, and thus established its distinctiveness in relation to other European states.[85] The paradigm of the final conflict between revolution and counter-revolution that had dominated the preceding years was steadfastly preserved. Every political revision was conceived from the restricted perspective of a 'withdrawal' in expectation of better times.

Lenin repeated this notion untiringly. In December 1921, he acknowledged that the revolutionary outcome of the imperialist war had been perceived in 1917 as a much simpler development than it had proved to be outside Russia. 'How can it be,' Lenin asked, that they had created a Soviet Socialist Republic isolated 'within an encirclement of a whole series of imperial powers hostile to it?' His reply was, 'This has occurred because our understanding of the events was fundamentally correct.' The essential fact was that although there had been no 'direct support' from the popular masses in other countries, their 'indirect support' had indeed prevented the imperial powers from strangling the revolution in Russia. The survival of revolutionary Russia had to be seen as confirmation of predictions

---

[81] RGASPI, fo. 17, op. 2, d. 15. G. M. Adibekov, E. N. Shakhnazarova, and K. K. Shirinya, *Organizatsionnaya struktura Kominterna 1919–1943* (Moscow: Rosspen, 1997). Moscow's practice of funding groups and communist parties goes back to 1919: see *PBKI*, doc. 3, pp. 27–8.

[82] N. E. Rosenfeldt, *The 'Special' World: Stalin's Power Apparatus and the Soviet System's Secret Structures of Communication* (Copenhagen: Museum Tusculanum Press, University of Copenhagen, 2009), vol. 2, pp. 220–3; V. I. Piatnitskii, *Osip Piatnitskii i Komintern na vesakh istorii* (Minsk: Kharvest, 2004).

[83] I. Getzler, *L'epopea di Kronštadt 1917–1921* (Turin: Einaudi, 1982).

[84] Graziosi, *L'URSS di Lenin e Stalin*, 150.

[85] P. Holquist, *Making War, Forging Revolution: Russia's Continuum of Crisis, 1914–1921* (Cambridge, Mass.: Harvard University Press, 2002), 286–7.

that 'capitalism is in decay'.[86] As he had already done in the summer of 1920 at the time of the offensive in Poland, Lenin was emboldened by Keynes's pessimism over economic prospects in the postwar period.

Many things had changed since then. The immediate expectation of pan-European conflagration had been put aside, and methods of government in Russia had been mitigated by the adoption of the NEP. Yet when he referred to his project of world revolution and attempted to give it meaning, Lenin spoke the same language as he had a year earlier, because the world, in his eyes, had been divided into 'two worlds': the old capitalist one and the 'new world' represented by Soviet Russia. This metaphor was to legitimize the centrality of the Soviet state. At the Eleventh Congress of the RCP (b) on 27 March 1922, he stressed once again that the 'revolutionary road' was the only way to get out of the war, that 'reactionary imperialist wars' in the contemporary world were 'inevitable', and that the foundation of the Soviet state constituted 'a world-historic victory'.[87]

Lenin said these words when the Soviet state's interest in international relations had already emerged in the run-up to the Genoa Conference on European Reconstruction. After the end of the Civil War, the requirements of reconstruction had in fact dictated the desire to establish relations with the principal European states, including the protagonists of Versailles, Great Britain and France. The Genoa Conference was the high point in this process. However, the Soviet reluctance to negotiate a general agreement was made very clear. In spite of pleas for realism from the head of Soviet diplomacy, Gyorgy Chicherin, the Bolsheviks took care to circumscribe participation in the conference by means of a tactical manoeuvre. Zinoviev asked Lenin to instruct him and Trotsky how to explain to the communist parties 'the "pacifist" part of our tactics' without triggering a 'Babylon'.[88] Lenin shared these concerns. The Genoa Conference produced nothing concrete. In April 1922, Soviet Russia entered into a separate agreement with Germany, the Treaty of Rapallo, something it had been pursuing since before the conference.[89] The Bolshevik leadership extolled the failure in Genoa while playing up the anti-Western political significance of Rapallo. The possibility of Russia being accepted back into the international system was set aside in favour of a rapprochement between the two powers humiliated by and excluded from the Treaty of Versailles.[90]

Rapallo was the second decisive move in revolutionary Russia's foreign policy after Brest-Litovsk. While the latter had been necessary for survival—although retrospectively ennobled as a strategy—Rapallo really was the birth a foreign policy. Revolutionary Russia was effectively proving to be a state intent upon defending its interests, obtaining specific economic advantages and at the same time appearing on the European stage with a coherent aim and its own disposition: the desire to create an alliance against the Versailles establishment. The agreement with

---

[86] Lenin, *Polnoe sobranie sochinenii*, vol. 44, pp. 291–5.   [87] Ibid. vol. 45, p. 108.
[88] *KIMR*, doc. 98, pp. 351–2.   [89] *KIMR*, doc. 93.
[90] J. Jacobson, *When the Soviet Union Entered World Politics* (Berkeley, Calif.: University of California Press, 1994), 96–101.

Germany consolidated the statist dimension of the revolution, and positioned the Soviet state amongst those antagonistic to the post-war status quo. As in the case of Brest-Litovsk, Rapallo appeared to reconcile the interests of the state with those of the world revolution. Unlike Brest-Litovsk, however, Rapallo had some policy features that would prove to be lasting and that therefore opened the way to conflicting scenarios. The absolute centrality of Germany in the Bolshevik outlook was strengthened, but it had a split identity: that of the key to European revolution and that of the Soviet state's principal partner. Thus the twin nature of Bolshevik foreign policy emerged fully formed, and this was expressed institutionally by the overlapping positions of the Narkomindel and the Comintern. Relations between the two organizations became very strained following the Civil War.[91] These tensions would be constantly reproduced in various European countries, such as Italy under Benito Mussolini, where the communists' anti-fascism clashed with Moscow's interest in establishing diplomatic relations.[92]

Lenin left a political legacy whose principal features were the reaffirmation of the original project of world revolution, the notion of the 'withdrawal' into domestic and international politics, and the idea of a mutual siege and 'war of position' between the Soviet state and the capitalist states. In late 1922 and early 1923, while his physical strength was declining, he struggled to define and refine his thinking on these matters. At the Fourth Congress of the Comintern in November 1922, Lenin was lavish in his reassuring assessments of world revolution's prospects. At the same time, he displayed a degree of self-criticism over the methods used to build the communist parties, which had conformed too closely to the 'Russian situation'.[93] For the first time, he appeared to acknowledge that the birth of the communist movement had been excessively influenced by a rigid model. But he did not clarify what should be done to remedy this error; nor did he suspect that it was actually the result of the Bolsheviks' political culture. At the end of his life, Lenin's dominant concerns were the isolation of Soviet power in the country and the world, his awareness of Russia's backwardness, and the need to change the culture of the country, but this did not lead him to rethink the original revolutionary project.[94] Rather than drawing on analogies with past European revolutions, Lenin now dwelt upon the special conditions pertaining in Russia. He continued proudly to reassert the Bolsheviks' revolutionary voluntarism, summed up in the Napoleonic motto 'On s'engage et puis on voit'. He did, however, concern himself with the defence of Soviet Russia against the threat of Western European states, and this did not allow him to delude himself over an inevitable final victory of socialism. At this stage it was clear that Soviet Russia could no longer rely exclusively on the world revolution for protection from external threats. The need for

[91] In August 1921, Zinoviev and Chicherin each accused the other of interfering in his jurisdiction: see *PBKI*, doc. 54, pp. 92–4.

[92] RGASPI, fo. 17, op. 84, d. 594; ibid. fo. 495, op. 19, dd. 106–9; AVPRF, fo. 098, op. 6, d. 46, p. 103.

[93] Lenin, *Polnoe sobranie sochinenii*, vol. 45, p. 292.

[94] M. Lewin, *Lenin's Last Struggle* (Ann Arbor: University of Michigan Press, 2005).

national security was now compelling, and required a clearer definition of state's interests. But on this crucial point, Lenin did not leave clear instructions, and did not transform the international socialist prospects into national ones. His real testament was much more limited. It came down to the idea that the Soviet state was the pivot of world revolution, and that the latter would deliver and save the Russian Revolution.

The birth of the communist parties in the principal European countries had come on the crest of a wave of social and political conflicts following the war, but also following a series of setbacks when the cycle of instability was coming to an end almost everywhere. Their relatively stronger position had not made their prospects any the less uncertain and nebulous. The 'united front' was met with more incomprehension than favour amongst German, French, and Italian communists. Having been urged to challenge the social democrats' majority in the trade unions but also to proclaim their commitment to unity, the national communist parties reacted unenthusiastically to the urgings of the Comintern, or even rejected them. In Germany, the 'Levi affair' had split the leadership and increased the drift towards the radicalism of Heinrich Brandler, who, together with August Thalheimer, fought against Levi with the support of the Comintern. For Amadeo Bordiga, who had already been the target of Lenin's anger because of his unbending anti-parliamentarianism in Italy, it was a matter of pride to oppose any compromise with Giacinto Serrati, even after the Socialist Party split between reformists and maximalists. In France, the Communist Party was going through a veritable crisis and split; within a short time it had lost its majority in the trade unions.[95] Difficult relations between the Comintern and the main European communist parties was entirely comprehensible, given the clear contradictions between the directives coming out of Moscow, which asked them to break off the remaining links with the socialists and at the same time to find common ground for their activities. The Russian leaders were themselves desperately searching for premonitory signs of revolution in the larger European nations—a revolution that, according to their own teachings, imposed the virtue of purity and the vice of sectarianism.

The report on the prospects of 'world revolution' read by Trotsky to the Fourth Congress of the Comintern acknowledged the existence of a stalemate, but he rejected the need for a reappraisal. According to Trotsky, capitalism was experiencing a historical crisis, but the working class was not yet ready to resolve it. He defended the line followed in the previous year of a 'withdrawal' parallel to that of the NEP. He admitted that the Western communist parties were facing difficulties 'incomparably greater' than those faced by Russian revolutionaries. He went no further than to put them on their guard against the 'pacifist and reformist delusions' that were emerging in the uncertain international situation they were entering.[96] Lacking Trotsky's brilliant rhetoric, Zinoviev argued inconsistently that

---

[95] L. Trotsky, *La crise du parti communiste français* (Paris: Librairie de l'Humanité, 1922).
[96] *Protokoll des Vierten Kongresses der Kommunistischen Internationale: Petrograd–Moskau vom 5 November bis 5 Dezember 1922* (Hamburg, 1923), 292–4.

it had been wise to avoid a revolution in Italy in the autumn of 1920, because it would have ended up as a second Hungary, but he claimed to be convinced that a 'decisive event' would soon occur in Germany. He argued that fascism taking power in Italy was not a local difficulty, and that 'similar phenomena' would soon occur in Germany and the rest of Central Europe, but declared that this would not mean a set-back for world revolution. He praised the 'united front', but reminded the delegates that in countries with 'a highly developed bourgeoisie' it would not be possible to take power 'other than with a civil war'.[97]

Given this situation, even Bukharin's judicious lecture to the Italian communists on how to interpret fascism appeared to have no practical results for anyone. Bukharin criticized Bordiga for his narrow understanding of fascism as an authoritarian variant of bourgeois domination, when it was actually 'an entirely new form suited to a new movement capable of attracting the masses' and fulfilling the historical needs of a 'mass party' for the bourgeoisie. After the Fourth Congress, the extremism of Italian and French communists came under criticism from the Comintern, without producing any appreciable results.[98] In June 1923, the Italian communist Antonio Gramsci observed that the tactic of a 'united front' had not been taken up 'in any country [by] a party or members capable of implementing it'.[99] Bukharin's interpretation of fascism did not help to distinguish between political regimes. The motions for the Fourth Congress presented fascism as in the same category as any other authoritarian government.[100] The idea that 'fascism' might spread across Europe led all communists—in Moscow, Berlin, or elsewhere—to see the drift towards authoritarianism, real or imaginary, as a sign that the era of the bourgeoisie was coming to an end and that revolution could be predicted.

THE END OF EUROPEAN REVOLUTION

The plan to gather forces and carefully prepare for revolution foundered on the German crisis that followed the French occupation of the Ruhr in January 1923 as a reprisal for failure to pay war reparations. This created a serious dilemma for Soviet Russia: whether to give priority to national security, which was threatened by a possible armed conflict between France and Germany with which Russia had agreed to military cooperation through the Treaty of Rapallo, or to rekindle a revolutionary situation in Germany, which had always been pivotal to Bolshevik hopes. In the first case, it would have been necessary to employ the instruments of diplomacy and force the German communists to support the 'bourgeois government'. In the second case, they would have had to gamble on the insurrectionary option, which was favoured by the German government's serious domestic and international problems. The Bolshevik ruling group was divided, but it was the second scenario that prevailed. The 'offensive theory' was soon back in fashion;

---

[97] Ibid. 193.   [98] *PBKI*, doc. 94, p. 148.
[99] A. Gramsci, *La costruzione del Partito comunista 1923–1926* (Turin: Einaudi, 1971), 457.
[100] *Komintern protiv fashizma: dokumenty* (Moscow: Nauka, 1999), doc. 9, pp. 72–3.

it had been criticized by Lenin but never entirely eliminated. Having to develop policy in the absence of Lenin for the first time at their Twelfth Congress of the RCP (b) in April 1923, the Bolsheviks attempted to follow his teachings. Zinoviev predicted a cycle of wars, which would have taken the form of 'a national war of the defeated countries against the currently victorious imperialist countries'. He rejected the idea of a NEP 'in foreign policy', which would have meant an abolition of the state monopoly over foreign trade and a greater integration of Soviet Russia into the international economy. Here too the authority was Lenin's teaching on the antagonistic nature of the Soviet state and the limitations of any possible 'withdrawals'.[101] Bukharin called on the German communists to stand up in defence of their nation, which in his opinion had been betrayed by the bourgeoisie—a position that had been suggested by the Comintern and adopted by the KPD shortly after the start of the German crisis.[102] The Bolshevik leaders appeared to be more concerned with loyalty to Lenin than with the formulation of a cogent policy. The ground was being prepared for the struggle for the succession soon to break out. The truth was that Lenin could be invoked in support of differing political decisions. His legacy did not provide a key to resolve the contradictions in communist foreign policy.

Radek, once more the Comintern emissary in Germany, was responsible for the most unscrupulous attempt to resolve these problems. In June 1923 he put forward a possible strategy that had been suggested several times without ever being fully developed: to rely as much on nationalist forces as on class forces for revolutionary ends. He gave the funeral oration for Schlageter, an activist of the extreme right who became a hero for German nationalists, and asserted that 'the great majority of the masses identified in the nation belong to the world of labour and not of capital'. He proposed a form of 'national Bolshevism' which would have squared the circle of a Russian alliance with Germany, support for the German government on a nationalist basis, and the idea of a future German national and social revolution on an anti-imperialist basis.[103] An indicator of their hatred of social democracy rather than a conversion to nationalism, this 'national Bolshevik' temptation would not prevail, though it would re-emerge later in communist history. In the immediate future, the crisis in Germany—where passive resistance to the occupation of the Ruhr produced disastrous economic consequences and a tidal wave of strikes—would lead the Bolsheviks to adopt policies more congenial to their ideological tradition.

At the end of July 1923, Zinoviev and Bukharin supported the leaders of the KPD, Brandler and Thalheimer, whom Radek had criticized for having announced an anti-fascist demonstration (later cancelled) which could have degenerated into

---

[101] *Dvenadtsatii s'ezd Rkp(b) 17–25 aprel'ya 1923 goda: stenograficheskii otchet* (Moscow: Gosudarstvennoye izdatel'stvo politicheskoy literatury, 1958).

[102] Ibid. 285–92.

[103] *Rasshchirennii plenum Ispolnitelnogo Komiteta Kommunisticheskogo Internatsionala 12–23 iunya 1923g. Otchet* (Moscow, 1923), 239–41. Radek's speech in June 1923 was circulated widely and supported in the KPD press: see H. Weber, *La trasformazione del comunismo tedesco: la stalinizzazione della KPD nella Repubblica di Weimar* (Milan: Feltrinelli, 1979), 53–54.

a clash between communists and the government. The argument was that the principal danger was the risk of replicating the passivity that opened the way to Mussolini taking power in Italy in October 1922 and to the right-wing coup in Bulgaria in June 1923.[104] In the Bolshevik ruling group, only Stalin shared Radek's opinions. Having been invested a year before with the powers of the party's general secretary at Lenin's behest, Stalin for the first time adopted a significant foreign policy position during the German crisis of 1923. In an exchange of letters with Zinoviev, he rejected the advisability of pushing the German communists to take power, arguing that any comparison with the Russian situation in 1917 was ill-founded.[105] However, the radical position held by the Comintern's leader, shared by the German communists and emboldened by the governmental crisis in Germany, would win through.[106] Stalin supported Zinoviev's arguments, shifting his reservations from the question of taking power to that of 'maintaining power'. A revolution in Germany, observed Stalin, would have very probably caused a war with France and Poland, and would have drawn Russia into the conflict. It had to be realized that a revolution in Germany would have put the security of the Soviet State at risk, and Russian involvement would have meant preparation for war.[107] Zinoviev declared the disagreements within the ruling group to be a thing of the past, as it was no longer the case that a German revolution would be inadvisable because it would have caused a war. Using the temptations of the German crisis, the leader of the Comintern reintroduced the 'theory of the offensive' under false colours.[108]

The entire ruling group agreed that the aim should be to take power in Germany, with the sole precaution (proposed by Trotsky and Stalin) of doing so in a conspiratorial manner that kept secret the role of the RCP (b) and the Comintern. On 22 August, the Politburo opined that 'the German proletariat finds itself on the verge of decisive struggle for power'.[109] This analysis only apparently overturned the 'united front' line and Lenin's pleas for moderation at the end of his life. It had always been obvious that the 'united front' was no more than a means to an end. The radicalism of the German communists, substantially unchanged due to the unresolved contradictions in Bolshevik international instructions, interacted with the decisions of the Russian leadership. Faced with unexpected opportunities provided by the German crisis, the Bolshevik ruling group's reflex action was to relaunch the same expectations of revolution in Central Europe that had motivated Lenin's decisions at the end of the Civil War at the time of the war with Poland. Concerns over the security of the Soviet state were relegated to second place and linked to the success of the European revolution. On 25 August Trotsky wrote to E. Sklyansky his deputy in the Directory of the Revolutionary Military Council, and revealed both his awareness of the danger and his resolve. The revolution in

---

[104] *PBKI*, doc. 103, pp. 157–8. [105] *PBKI*, docs 104 and 107.

[106] *Rkp(b). Vnutripartiinaya bor'ba v dvadtsatye gody: dokumenty i materialy 1923 g.* (Moscow: Rosspen, 2004), 140–2.

[107] *Istochnik* 5 (1995), 117–18. [108] RGASPI, fo. 324, op. 2, dd. 5, 6, 11.

[109] *PBKI*, doc. 111, p. 167.

Germany could persuade the European bourgeoisie 'to drown communism in a river of blood' and take action against Soviet Russia. It was necessary to prepare for the worst and for 'an attack against us'.[110]

No one in the Bolshevik ruling group broke ranks on this line, and no one argued that this scenario was to be avoided even at the cost of giving up on the German revolution. On 20 September, Stalin wrote to Thalheimer that the next revolution in Germany would have 'even greater significance' for the international proletariat than the Russian Revolution. It would have shifted 'the centre of world revolution from Moscow to Berlin'.[111] On 23 September, the Politburo approved Zinoviev's report on the 'future revolution in Germany and the tasks of the KPD' in its final version.[112] Faith in the imminence of the German revolution was professed unconditionally. The scenario was that of a victorious revolution and the unification of 'Soviet Germany' to Soviet Russia or, alternatively, that of a war triggered by the counter-revolution.[113] The Comintern was apparently not in any way discouraged by the disastrous example of the Bulgarian communists sent off to certain defeat in September 1923 during an attempt to take power that ended with the dictatorship inflicting bloody repression.[114] In the last ten days of September and in early October, there was a prolonged debate at the ECCI between Russian representatives and those of the main European parties—the Germans, the French, and the Czechoslovaks. As it was taken for granted that the revolutionary uprising in Germany was imminent, the central question became one of technical and organizational preparation for armed struggle, in accordance with the classical conspiratorial paradigm. The Russians were responsible for dispelling any of the Germans' remaining uncertainties. Zinoviev emphatically declared that it was not simply a matter of German revolution but 'the start of world revolution'.[115] Trotsky put the emphasis on the seizure of power, and demanded no more shilly-shallying over other questions. 'If politically the necessary preconditions exist,' he announced in an unmistakably military manner, 'then the revolution becomes a technical and organisational task, and consequently you have to fix the time, prepare it and strike.'[116] On 4 October Zinoviev made public the decision to set 9 November as the date for the German revolution; this was not only an obvious symbolic reference to the birth of the Weimar Republic, but also a desperate attempt to reproduce the October Revolution in Russia.[117]

The 'German October' was a total failure. The Comintern emissaries, starting with Radek, vacillated between unfounded optimism and belated afterthoughts.[118] After having ascertained the disorganization of German communists and recorded the collapse of the insurrection in Hamburg on 23 October, Radek sent Moscow pessimistic reports in which he judged any attempt at revolution to be premature.[119] On 3 November, the Politburo decided to convene in Moscow the emissaries sent to

---

[110] *PBKI*, doc. 112, pp. 168–9.   [111] *PBKI*, doc. 114, pp. 169–70.
[112] RGASPI, fo. 17, op. 2, d. 101.   [113] *PBKI*, doc. 118, pp. 185–203.
[114] *PBKI*, doc. 99, 152–3; doc. 119, pp. 203–4.   [115] *PBKI*, doc. 117, 175.
[116] *PBKI*, 177.   [117] *PBKI*, 179–82.   [118] RGASPI, fo. 326, op. 2, d. 21.
[119] *PBKI*, doc. 123, pp. 209–13; *KIMR*, doc. 115, pp. 428–35.

Germany.[120] But this did not happen. The decision to seize power was not counter-manded; German communists were encouraged by Comintern emissaries to press on. However, Saxony and Thuringia, both communist strongholds, were compromised and firmly under the control of the police and the army. On 4 November the KPD issued a document that decreed the end of the Weimar Republic and the victory of 'fascism'.[121] Moscow reacted with fury. The Politburo sent an open letter to German communists criticizing them for their lack of resolve.[122] The attempted revolution had ended in a fiasco and had been snuffed out before the first spark could catch. German communists would be censured by the Comintern. Zinoviev held them and Radek accountable for the defeat.[123] However, the real blame lay with those who had succumbed to their fanciful beliefs and launched the operation: namely, the Bolshevik leadership.

The failure of the 'German October' could not be dismissed as a minor incident. It marked the end of the project for world revolution, as it had been conceived in 1917. Six years after the October Revolution, the Bolsheviks continued to see the mission of their power and the communist movement through the prism of their original expectations. It was precisely their obstinacy that laid bare the delusions that had sustained them. They took their desires to be realities, because their vision of a breakthrough on the European front modelled on the Bolshevik Revolution remained the genuine red thread running through their perceptions. This vision had undergone various mutations: the immediate expectation of a spontaneous wave of mass rebellions as a result of the war, the export of revolution by means of the Red Army, the postponement of the revolutionary period to the long term, and the preparation for an insurrection by the communist parties. There had been a transition from the idea of the European revolution as a natural and redemptive event driven by momentum to the idea that Bolshevik power would play a decisive role in its explosion. But the paradigm of the revolution's imminence and the irreversible crisis of capitalism had not undergone any revision, and represented a distinguishing feature of communist identity. Thus there was an abiding conviction that the collapse of social democracy was also imminent, in spite of its considerable staying power in the face of a communist challenge. In 1923 the intermediate space occupied by dissident socialist forces unwilling to be drawn into the Comintern's draconian discipline was reabsorbed by the creation of a new Socialist International, which revealed the barriers to the communists' attractive capacity.[124] The communist movement was war-hardened, but its minority status was becoming its enduring feature. The main post-revolutionary transformation was the primacy of the Soviet state as an international factor and bastion of world revolution. As late as 1923, Bolshevik leaders were willing to risk

---

[120] *PBKI*, doc. 126, p. 216.   [121] *Komintern protiv fashizma*, doc. 24, pp. 114–22.
[122] *PBKI*, doc. 127, pp. 218–20.
[123] Vatlin, *Komintern: idei, resheniya, sudby*, 120ff.; Weber, *La trasformazione del comunismo tedesco*, 56–7.
[124] L. Rapone, *La socialdemocrazia europea tra le due guerre: dall'organizzazione della pace alla resistenza al fascismo* (Rome: Carocci, 1999).

the survival of their state at the altar of world revolution. But this would be the last time. It was also the last time that a communist party attempted to take power in one of the main European countries following the model of the Bolshevik Revolution. The Bolsheviks would not renounce world revolution, but they would increasingly identify it with a process that depended on a growth in the power of the Soviet state.

The impact of the Bolshevik Revolution on world politics was nevertheless confirmed by the revolutionary state's ability to consolidate its position, the spread of communist parties to the whole of Europe and the principal countries elsewhere, and the pull of the myth of the Revolution even amongst workers and intellectuals who were not members of the communist movement.[125] Further evidence of the international impact of the Bolshevik Revolution was provided by increasing anti-communism in Europe. In the first few years after the European war, anti-Bolshevik political writing was as widespread as the groundswell of opinion favourable to the revolution.[126] Social and cultural fear of communism led many forces to take on a deliberate counter-revolutionary role even though they represented differing political tendencies: it was a social democratic government that repressed the Spartacist movement in Germany; it was Hungarian nationalists who inflicted White Terror on their country in retaliation for the Red Terror; it was Winston Churchill, a leading figure in British liberalism, who planned the suppression of revolutionary power in Russia, even at the cost of installing a no less brutal regime, as long as it was of the opposing ideological persuasion.[127] The ferocity of the Bolshevik exercise of power, the news of the Red Terror and anti-religious persecutions, the birth of communist parties, and the revolutionary impulses in Europe consolidated and legitimized European anti-Bolshevism, albeit as a composite and uneven tendency. Once the existence of the revolutionary state in Russia was no longer up for discussion, European governments' hostility was increasingly directed against their national communist parties. The example of Béla Kun in Hungary suggested that should the communists take power in another European country, they would replicate his establishment of a bloody dictatorship and would probably, in a situation different from that of 1919, rely on the intervention of the Red Army. The Treaty of Versailles was taking on a counter-revolutionary hue, and this new order was sustained by the buffer states of Poland and Romania. For many, this justified the treaty's unbalanced and pointlessly punitive nature, particularly after the Bolshevik offensive on Warsaw in the summer of 1920. Even in Germany, the country humiliated by Versailles, fear of communism would encourage strategies for consolidating state authority and containing social conflict that favoured the survival of traditionalist forces.[128] In the United States, workers' strikes in the

---

[125] R. Service, *Comrades! A World History of Communism* (London: Macmillan, 2007), 130–7.

[126] For the typical example provided by France, see S. Coeuré, *La grande lueur à l'Est: les Français et l'Union soviétique 1917–1939* (Paris: Seuil, 1999), 42ff.

[127] D. Carlton, *Churchill and the Soviet Union* (Manchester: Manchester University Press, 2000), 9–26.

[128] Weitz, *Creating German Communism*, 129.

first year after the war were suppressed on the pretext of a 'red peril', despite the complete absence of a genuine revolutionary threat.[129]

Mutual conspiratorial obsessions played a decisive role, mixing reality with fantasy and fuelling theories of revolutionary and counter-revolutionary plots. The Bolshevik conviction that the enemy within and enemy abroad were one and the same, and answered to imperialism's premeditated plan, was the mirror image of the red threat. Although their principal ideological and cultural roots were buried in a more distant past, the radical nationalist movements generated by the world war defined their identity in a similar context. Italian fascism could claim that one of its motivations for violence and barbarism was its drive to restore order. This partly explains why its actions had a mass following and were tolerated or indulged in liberal circles around Europe. Communism was not the cause of fascism, which was itself an expression of the brutality of the world war and a factor in civil war.[130] However, fascists adopted methods for annihilating their adversaries analogous to those of the Bolsheviks, and they harboured inverse conspiracy theories. The shared aversion to liberal society, the convergence of political forms, and similar techniques of mass manipulation had to coexist with their permanent ideological conflict and the promise of each to annihilate the other, which sustained the idea of the 'European civil war' in time of peace. From the early 1920s, Adolf Hitler cherished the dream of destroying Bolshevism, which in his mind was the expression of a Jewish plot to take over the world.[131]

Was all this sufficient to justify an interpretation of the postwar period as a bipolar conflict between revolution and counter-revolution, between communism and capitalism, and between two worlds divided by the chasm of class struggle, as the Bolsheviks would have it? In reality, the postwar landscape did not resemble the 'European civil war' imagined by Lenin and his followers. The collapse of the imperial states did not open the way to social revolution. The bonds of class did not replace loyalties to the state and national identities. Liberal capitalism was undergoing a profound crisis, but it was threatened more by political polarization and nationalistic snares. The elements of civil war were overlaid with continuing traditional forms of politics and the emergence of new democratic forms. For years Europe had been going through unrest, strikes, and insurrections, but no social revolution had actually been achieved. At the heart of the old continent, the reality that would prevail was the expansion of civil liberties, parliamentary rule, political and trade union associations, and the public sphere, whereas reactionary

---

[129] M. P. Leffler, *The Specter of Communism: The United States and the Origins of the Cold War, 1917–1953* (New York: Hill and Wang, 1994), 14–15; L. Ceplair, *Anti-Communism in Twentieth Century America: A Critical History* (Santa Barbara, Calif.: ABC-Clio, 2011), 20–2.

[130] On the ideological theory of the 'causal link' between communism and fascism, see E. Nolte, *Der europäische Bürgerkrieg 1917–1945: Nationalsozialismus und Bolschewismus* (Berlin: Propyläen Verlag, 1987); For a similar interpretation, see Pipes, *Il regime bolscevico*.

[131] L. Waddington, *Hitler's Crusade: Bolshevism and the Myth of the International Jewish Conspiracy* (London: I. B. Tauris, 2007). Cf. I. Kershaw, *Hitler 1889–1936: Hubris* (London: Penguin, revised 2001).

counter-revolution and fascism only triumphed at the periphery.[132] In Western, Northern, and Central Europe, where the idea of nation and collectivity based on citizenship was established, the social democratic parties took over government without losing their influence over the great majority of the working classes. In Eastern and Southeastern Europe, the definition of the national communities and the new states organized mainly along ethnic and cultural lines did not favour socialist movements, and still less identification with Russian Bolshevism introduced by the communists. The case of Poland, where communists were marked out as traitors to their nation—given their rejection of the very foundation of a Polish state and their support for the Red Army in the war of 1920—was an extreme example, but also a symbolic one.[133] Communists were not capable of blending nationalism into their classist arguments even in Germany, the country most suited to reconciling the two themes. They believed that they could make use of radical nationalists for their own purposes, but in the years that followed, if anything, the opposite occurred. The new mass politics that emerged from the disastrous Great War did not conform to simplistic borrowings from the Marxist tradition.[134]

The Great War broke the barriers holding back ideological radicalization and the use of violence against civilians as a political tool. However, the Leninist project of world revolution failed. In the period after its foundation, the communist movement had not realized any of its objectives, which appeared to be further and further away as time elapsed after the end of the world war. The main achievement of the Bolshevik Revolution was not the destruction of the European bourgeoisie, but the foundation of a state. At the same time, the nature of this state appeared difficult to reconcile with that of the other states, even taking into account the authoritarian and bureaucratic tendencies generated by the First World War in the institutions and state apparatuses of all European countries. This new state was distinguished by its peculiar combination of classist authoritarianism wholly based on the methods of total war transferred into peacetime; a position antagonistic to the international system equally founded on class archetypes; a vague project capable of mobilizing an 'alternative modernity' based on a collectivist and socialist predisposition; a following of converts to its civil religiosity centrally organized in Europe and throughout the world; and a progressive and militarist image that evoked ferocious and diametrically opposed passions. Lenin's prophesy of an era of 'gigantic cataclysms', which he made immediately after the October Revolution, had proved to be a mirage. However, that scenario, projected into the long term, was still required to legitimize the new state and maintain the movement's identity. The catastrophist vision on which Bolshevism was founded had to survive as a dogma that moulded Soviet Russia's strategies and the principal instruments of communist political culture.

[132] G. Eley, *Forging Democracy: The History of the Left in Europe, 1850–2000* (Oxford: Oxford University Press, 2002), 153.

[133] G. Simoncini, *The Communist Party of Poland 1918–1929: A Study in Political Ideology* (New York: Mellon Press, 1993).

[134] D. Diner, *Raccontare il Novecento: una storia politica* (Milan: Garzanti, 2001), 28–30.

2

Time of the State (1924–1939)

The world has been divided into two camps: the imperialist camp and the camp of those who struggle against imperialism...England and America are leading the capitalist countries...The Soviet Union is leading those who oppose and fight to the death against imperialism.

Stalin, 18 December 1925

An internationalist is someone who is willing to defend the USSR without any reservations, without any hesitations and without making any conditions, because the USSR is the foundation of the world revolutionary movement.

Stalin, 1 August 1927

The world revolution as a single act is a folly. It takes place in different times and in different countries. The behaviour of the Red Army is also something that concerns the world revolution.

Stalin to Dimitrov, 21 January 1940

WORLD REVOLUTION AND 'SOCIALISM IN ONE COUNTRY'

Lenin's death left its mark on all communists. His embalmed corpse, wrapped in the flag of the Paris Commune and placed in a mausoleum in Moscow's Red Square, became part of their symbolism. At his funeral on 27 January 1924, Zinoviev and Stalin were the principal celebrants at the birth of this cult, in the absence of Trotsky. The oath recited by Stalin in tones of religious devotion probably represented the most significant moment of that transition, although not many people realized it at the time. The cult had to act as the key element in the regime's new forms to sacralize politics. Lenin's personality cult and the codification of Marxism-Leninism were the two foundations of the transition from the utopianism of the early post-revolutionary years to organized messianism, along with its ideological dogmas and canonical rites.[1] Loyalty to Lenin's precepts became

---

[1] N. Tumarkin, *Lenin Lives! The Lenin Cult in Soviet Russia* (Cambridge, Mass.: Harvard University Press, 1997).

from that moment a source of unassailable legitimacy. The unity of the Soviet ruling group and the party of world revolution was increasingly an unchallengeable axiom. In reality, this supposed unity was largely fictitious, and the underlying principle turned out to be a perverse repressive mechanism within the political elites themselves. Only the charismatic figure of Lenin could have settled the numerous conflicts that had arisen since the time of the October Revolution. But over that period, Lenin had revealed facets of his thought and actions too different from each other to allow a purely political synthesis of his legacy, which contained more uncertainties than certainties. His successors contested it, provoking a classic power struggle that would reverberate throughout the entire communist movement.

Neither the decision to adopt the NEP nor the party's rigid internal regime was capable of unifying the Bolsheviks. In 1923 Trotsky, always restless, had already commenced hostilities on both questions by denouncing the 'bureaucratization' caused by the overlap of the party and the state, proposing democracy limited to the party organs, and demanding a greater concentration on the country's industrialization. But the question that more than any other undermined the very meaning of the revolution inherited from Lenin was the fiasco of the 'German October', an unequivocal indicator of the failure of his global revolutionary project. This failure could have been acknowledged much earlier than 1923. Lenin had gone, leaving the hot potato in his successors' hands. On the first occasion in Germany, they had pursued his pipe-dreams with the greater conspiratorial skill provided by the presence of a strong communist party, but with the same tendency to mistake their illusions for reality. The umpteenth failure of revolutionary forces in Germany posed increasingly pressing questions, but the ruling Bolshevik group refused to examine them.

From December 1923 Zinoviev and Trotsky clashed over the 'lessons of the German events'. But the conflict between the two keenest supporters of insurrection did not involve any self-criticism or revision.[2] Zinoviev cynically placed the blame for the defeat on the German leaders' lack of resolution, whereas Trotsky defended them and accused his rival of bureaucracy. Both believed that they had let slip a real chance of revolution.[3] To varying degrees, the entire Bolshevik leadership had been involved in the decision to support the insurrection. For the moment, no one was willing to draw the more serious lessons of the 'German October'. Thus the tensions already troubling the Bolshevik leadership became more acute, and gave rise to a misleading debate on tactics rather than genuine scrutiny of what had occurred. The emphasis was on the lost opportunity and the need to follow the Bolshevik example more strictly. The critical voices, such as Radek in the Soviet

---

[2] The interaction between German and Soviet affairs is outside the remit of the classic work by E. H. Carr, *The Interregnum, 1923–1924* (London: Macmillan, 1965). See also R. V. Daniels, *The Conscience of the Revolution: The Communist Opposition in the Soviet Union* (Cambridge, Mass.: Harvard University Press, 1960), 323ff. For a historical account based on archive documents, see A. Di Biagio, *Coesistenza e isolazionismo: Mosca, il Comintern e l'Europa di Versailles (1918–1928)* (Rome: Carocci, 2004), esp. 123–6.

[3] PBKI, doc. 133, pp. 227–9; doc. 134, pp. 229–30; doc. 135, pp. 231–3.

party and Wilhelm Pieck in the German one, were silenced. Indeed, extremist tendencies in the KPD were encouraged, with the promotion of Ruth Fischer and Arkady Maslow, the 'left' adversaries of Brandler and Thalheimer.[4]

The Thirteenth Congress of the RCP(b) in May 1924 appeared to bring to an end the first period of conflict, which had started with Trotsky, and stabilize the command of the 'triumvirate' of Zinoviev, Kamenev, and Stalin. The motives for this consolidation were significant. The NEP had created the basis for economic recovery and a relatively stable relationship between the city and the countryside. The constitution of the federal state had completed the process of regaining control over most of the territory which had once been part of the Tsarist empire, and the final embers of national resistance in the Ukraine and elsewhere had been extinguished. Diplomatic recognition of the Soviet Union by the main European countries, starting with Great Britain, appeared to constitute a stabilizing factor. However, there was clearly an absence of strategic thinking and a vision of the international situation in line with this new stability in Germany and Europe. Only Bukharin, who had now shifted from his previous lapses into left-wing extremism to a more moderate position, provided an interpretation of Lenin's legacy different from that of the principal pretenders to the succession, Zinoviev and Trotsky, and invited his Bolshevik colleagues to acknowledge the end of their revolutionary delusions. In his opinion, the capitalist economy was undergoing 'a kind of stabilization' underwritten by American capital, even though the Western world continued to suffer from the absence of a political role for the United States that reflected its economic one. Ideologically this new situation tended towards 'pacifism' in the Western bourgeoisie, and this manifested itself in the diplomatic recognition of the USSR and the growth in the role of social democratic governments. Consequently they needed to jettison the Bolshevik scenario adopted in October 1917, according to which their experiences would be repeated elsewhere in the same pattern.[5] In other words, Bukharin was suggesting that they renounce the universality of the Bolshevik revolutionary model and abandon the more extreme catastrophist concepts that had held sway in the communist movement. He was the only Bolshevik leader to go down this road and draw lessons from the failure of the German insurrection. His proposed review was an isolated incident, and was not followed up.

The Comintern's leftward drift was confirmed by the Fifth Congress in June–July 1924. The main slogan urged the 'Bolshevization' of the communist parties. Vague like all the many other slogans Moscow issued, 'Bolshevization' required both a stricter alignment to the Russian model and more expression of nationalist sentiments from the communist parties.[6] It responded to a need for discipline that

---

[4] PBKI, doc. 144, pp. 251–2. See also H. Weber, *La trasformazione del comunismo tedesco: la stalinizzazione della KPD nella Repubblica di Weimar* (Milan: Feltrinelli, 1979), 80ff.

[5] *Trinadtsatii s'ezd Rkp(b). Mai 1924 goda. Stenograficheskii otchet* (Moscow: Gosudarstvennoe izdatel'stvo politicheskoy literatury, 1963), 307, 311, 315.

[6] K. McDermott and J. Agnew, *The Comintern: A History of International Communism from Lenin to Stalin* (Basingstoke: Macmillan, 1996), 44–6; S. Wolikow, *L'Internationale communiste (1919–1943): le Komintern ou le rêve déchu du parti mondial de la révolution* (Paris: Éditions de l'Atelier, 2010), 76–7.

went back to the famous 'twenty-one conditions', but now took on the function of relaunching the movement's identity in a time of crisis. The 'Bolshevization' of communist parties and the sacralization of 'Leninism' occurred in the context of a catastrophist reading of the postwar crisis of capitalism and a resumption of the anti-social-democratic polemic. Zinoviev invented the formula whereby social democracy became 'the left wing' of fascism—the high point of Bolshevik Manichaeism.[7] The Russian ruling group still could not come to terms with the failure of the 'German October'. At the Comintern, Bukharin did not repeat the ideas he had been developing and had expressed at the congress of the Soviet party. Stalin remained aloof from international questions, leaving the stage free for Zinoviev, his ally in the conflict with Trotsky. Stalin's behaviour reflected his unfamiliarity with international affairs. Even greater problems were created for him by Lenin's harsh personal criticism in his 'testament', although this document also provided dismissive assessments of all his possible heirs. However, the silences and uncertainties of the Bolshevik ruling group reflected their disorientation. At the same time, the contribution of European communists to the definition of a political strategy for the movement after the 'German October' was irrelevant. From the French Albert Treint to the German Fischer, their political discourse revolved around 'Bolshevization' and the fight against 'deviationism', which could be interpreted in many different ways but which united their mental outlook. Under the direction of the Politburo, the Comintern after Lenin once more recalled the communist parties to universal value of the Russian experience.

The launch of the Dawes Plan and the American contribution to European reconstruction, which commenced in the summer of 1924, provoked a debate amongst Lenin's successors over the relationship between world revolution and the domestic and international stabilization of states, including Soviet Russia. The positions that emerged in the second half of 1924 did not follow the usual divisions within the Politburo. In fact, they emerged as two different visions that cut across each other, and both could claim Leninist antecedents. On the one hand, there was the contention that American intervention in Europe would not produce a genuine stabilization and would, if anything, aggravate the contradictions between capitalist countries; on the other hand, there was the proposition that stabilization was the prevailing reality but under a new Anglo-American hegemony. With differing slants, the first interpretation was adopted by Zinoviev, Trotsky, and Stalin, with a strong emphasis on the continuity of Bolshevism's traditional catastrophist concept; the second was put forward by Bukharin and Radek, with an implicit invitation to revise old convictions.[8] Trotsky's challenge to the revolutionary credibility of the other Bolshevik leaders in his *Lessons of October*, published in the autumn of 1924, exacerbated the personal rivalries and the doctrinaire nature of the clash. Trotsky focused the debate on the legacy of the revolutionary

[7] *V Congrès de l'Internationale Communiste (17 juin–8 juillet 1924): compte rendu analytique* (Paris: Librairie de l'Humanité, 1924), 31. See M. Hájek, *Storia dell'Internazionale comunista (1921–1935): la politica del fronte unico* (Rome: Editori Riuniti, 1969), 104ff.

[8] Di Biagio, *Coesistenza e isolazionismo*, 155ff.

spirit, which he claimed for himself. The real political and strategic kernel of the expression 'socialism in one country', which was coined by Stalin and Bukharin, was circumvented. This expression implied acknowledgement of the failure of the European revolution. But no one would go that far, not even Bukharin, the only one who believed that Europe had entered a period of stability which was hard to define with the analytical categories the Bolsheviks had been using up to that time.[9]

The Bolshevik leaders' view of their revolution recalled Lenin's attitude after the Polish–Soviet War. The main concern was not to review some of the fundamentals of their political culture in the light of its inadequacies, but rather to prevent such a review happening. Thus even the majority of the leadership avoided the term 'war of position', which de facto they supported, and instead devoted their energies to the elimination of 'Trotskyism'. The campaign against 'Trotskyism', viewed as an extremist and anti-Leninist tendency, was exported to the communist parties in late 1924 and early 1925, thus increasing the dependency of their ruling groups on the majority of the Communist Party of the USSR. In March and April 1925, following an agreement between Zinoviev, Bukharin, and Stalin, the Fifth Plenum of ECCI stated that the 'Bolshevization' of the communist parties was a requirement of the 'relative stability' of European capitalism.[10] However, the emphasis was much more on the adjective than on the noun, and so it would be in the future.[11] It is revealing that the three individuals held responsible for the 'German October' fiasco in 1923—Radek, Brandler, and Thalheimer—did not obtain a pardon from the Politburo and the ECCI.[12] The link between 'socialism in one country' and 'capitalist stabilization' was not explicitly admitted or shared.

At this stage, Stalin came up with a specific point of view that separated the current viability of the revolution from capitalism's catastrophic prospects. From the moment of his first sortie into international politics in September 1924, he had argued that Europe was not experiencing any kind of stability, and indeed that the appearance of the United States on the scene created a new source of conflict with Great Britain.[13] Shortly afterwards, in January 1925, Stalin stressed the risks inherent in the international situation and put everyone on their guard against 'the preconditions for war' that were destined in a few years to become 'an inevitable fact'. This meant being 'ready for anything' and banking on the military factor to save the revolutionary movement in the West, which otherwise would be unable to maintain power. More prudent than Lenin in 1920 and mindful of the teachings of Brest-Litovsk, Stalin made it clear that in any war Soviet Russia would be the last to intervene 'in order to throw its decisive weight onto the scales'. His

---

[9] N. I. Bukharin, *Put' k sotsializmu i raboche-krestyanskii soyuz* (1925), in *Izbrannie proizvedeniya* (Moscow: Politizdat, 1988).

[10] PBKI, doc. 182, pp. 307–8.

[11] *Exécutif élargi de l'Internationale communiste: compte rendu analytique de la session du 21 mars au 6 avril 1925* (Paris: Librairie de l'Humanité, 1925), 171–88.

[12] PBKI, doc. 183, pp. 308–10.

[13] I. V. Stalin, *Sochineniya* (13 vols, Moscow: Gosudarstvennoe izdatel'stvo politicheskoy literatury, 1946–1951), vol. 6, pp. 280–301.

obvious reference was still the idea of the centrality of state power for the purposes of world revolution, which had emerged at the time of the war with Poland.[14] The context of Stalin's speech was in fact the resumption of hostility towards Poland arising from the rapprochement between Warsaw and the Baltic states at the beginning of 1925, which was seen by the Politburo as a prelude to the formation of a new anti-Soviet bloc fostered by Great Britain.[15] In a speech made on 9 May 1925, Stalin argued that the world was now divided into two antagonistic camps. The existing balance of power between the two would therefore be decisive. The 'ebb' of revolutionary forces offered a momentary advantage to the capitalist camp that encircled the socialist one. But in the longer term, the capitalist camp was undermined by profound contradictions, starting with those between the victorious nations and Germany, which had prevented an alliance against the Soviet Union. Soviet economic development, the consolidation of the socialist state, and the 'Bolshevization' of the communist parties were interdependent elements in the same strategy, which aimed to reverse the balance of power between the 'two camps' in the future.[16]

Stalin's dichotomous vision did not just follow in the steps of his ally Bukharin. Stalin's outlook was not based so much on the 'peaceful construction' in the USSR and the 'party of world revolution', which were Bukharin's principal concepts, as on the inevitability of war and the state as the central factor in the mutual encirclement of communism and capitalism. Far from the established opinion of a long historiographical tradition, Stalin's version of 'socialism in one country' was not simply an appeal to Russian national pride and a 'declaration of independence from the West', but also a strategic reassessment of world revolution centred on the role of the Soviet state.[17] For the moment, this duplicity in Stalin's thought had to stay on the back burner while prominence was given to the theories bound up in the struggle between Lenin's successors. Once again Trotsky attacked the ruling group in the summer of 1925, using a particularly insidious argument. In his opinion, the creation of a 'backward socialism' theorized by Bukharin would place Soviet Russia in a state of economic dependence on the West and expose it to the dangers of international crises. Only the elimination of the autarkic regime and speedier economic development could have allowed Russia to face up to its global challenges.[18] Trotsky's accusation of counter-revolution aimed at the leaders of the majority persisted unaltered, but his criticism pointed to a real dilemma of which the governmental establishment and the managers of the economic bureaucracies were well aware.

[14] Ibid. vol. 7, pp. 11–14.

[15] G. Adibekov et al. (eds), *Politburo TsK Rkp(b)–Vkp(b) i Evropa: resheniya 'Osoboy Papki' 1923–1939* (Moscow: Rosspen, 2001), doc. 34, pp. 75–7.

[16] Stalin, *Sochineniya*, vol. 7, pp. 90–101. See R. C. Tucker, *Stalin in Power: The Revolution from Above, 1928–1941* (New York: Norton, 1990), 44–50.

[17] E. H. Carr, *Il socialismo in un solo paese*, vol. 1: *La politica interna, 1924–1926* (Turin: Einaudi, 1968), 551.

[18] L. Trotsky, *Towards Socialism or Capitalism?* (London: Methuen, 1926; repr. Abingdon: Routledge, 2012).

The principal response was provided by Stalin at the Fourteenth Party Congress in December 1925. He acknowledged the need to accelerate the rate of industrial development to avoid the transformation of Soviet Russia into 'an appendage' of world capitalism, but refused to abandon the autarkic regime. This decision was based on a precise vision of the international situation. Stalin reasserted the official doctrine of 'partial or temporary stabilization' of capitalism, and declared that 'the question of taking power... is not on the agenda today in Europe'.[19] He insisted, however, on the 'contradictions' within the capitalist system. In the preceding months, the impossibility of genuine stability in Europe had been stressed by the Bolshevik leaders in their assessment of the Locarno Treaties between Stresemann's Germany and the victorious powers, which guaranteed Germany's western borders and provided for the demilitarization of the Rhineland. Both the majority and minority of the leadership rejected Chicherin's judgement that the treaties were a sign of increasing stability in Europe, and rejected the concern that Berlin was now outside the sphere of Rapallo agreements with Moscow. They argued that Locarno was simply a vain attempt to maintain the Versailles settlement, which was destined to fail. But this attempt could create the conditions for an anti-Soviet coalition that included Germany.[20] Stalin privately expressed his contempt for Chicherin, asserting that the latter found it easy to forget 'the interests of his own state'.[21]

In Stalin's vision, America's economic power, the divisions between the victors and the vanquished of the First World War, the latent tensions between the victors themselves, the conflicts outside Europe, and the existence of the Soviet Union were all factors that created uncontrollable breeding grounds for conflict. The 'peaceful coexistence' between the Soviet world and the capitalist one would not therefore constitute a long-lasting reality. He proclaimed the existence of a 'state of armed peace', which followed the same pattern as the one leading up to 1914, and argued that there was an inherent incompatibility 'between the world of capitalism and the world of the Soviets', and between 'the imperialist camp' and 'the struggle against imperialism'. The economic consolidation of the USSR and the 'struggle for peace' that made it possible were consequently two interdependent strategic tasks. Such considerations had specific implications for relations between the Soviet state and the communist movement. Stalin asserted the primacy of the Soviet state, and declared that 'the revolutionary sections of the proletariat in Europe, which have adopted our state and consider it to be their own creation' were ready 'to defend it and fight for it if necessary'.[22]

The Fifteenth Congress of the Soviet party ratified the condemnation of 'Trotskyism' and the triumph of 'socialism in one country', but it did not resolve— indeed, it aggravated—the internal divisions within the Bolshevik ruling group, causing a break in the alliance between Stalin and Zinoviev. The new opposition

---

[19] Stalin, *Sochineniya*, vol. 7, p. 265.
[20] Di Biagio, *Coesistenza e isolazionismo*, 207–8; J. Jacobson, *When the Soviet Union Entered World Politics* (Berkeley, Calif.: University of California Press, 1994), 174–6.
[21] PBKI, doc. 194, p. 325.   [22] Stalin, *Sochineniya*, vol. 7, pp. 274, 280–5.

group formed by Zinoviev and Kamenev would eventually come closer to Trotsky, shifting in favour of his objections to the New Economic Policy. The creation of a stronger opposition also had repercussions for the headquarters of the world revolution. Meeting together for the last time in a gesture of goodwill, all the Soviet leaders decided to send the communist parties a letter in which they declared it would be inopportune to transfer the 'Russian question' to the ranks of the communist movement.[23] But the impact of the 'Russian question' was inevitable. The subjugation of the communist parties to Moscow exposed them to the same logic of internal divisions that affected Lenin's successors. The case of the German party seems typical. Since the summer of 1925, the ultra-radical ruling group installed by Zinoviev following the failed insurrection in Germany was attacked by Bukharin and Stalin, who agreed to promote Ernst Thälmann to the leadership of the KPD.[24] The operation was concluded at the Sixth Plenum of the ECCI in February and March of 1926. Fischer and Maslow were accused of having set up an opposition group within the Comintern, and of negating the primacy of the USSR's interests.[25] The decision to avoid a link between the internal struggles of the Soviet ruling group and the communist movement immediately proved impossible to implement.

Stalin himself undertook to assert the positions of the Comintern's new majority. At a meeting of Italian communists, he accused Trotsky of nurturing an 'old conviction' that without a revolution in Europe it would not be possible to develop the revolution in Russia. This had in fact been the original Bolshevik view on the matter, and Stalin's criticism showed just how much priorities had changed in Soviet Russia. At the same time, he reasserted the existing hierarchy of the party of the USSR and the others, speaking of a 'privilege' that placed special 'responsibilities' on the Bolshevik leadership. Very significant was his reaction to the provocative question asked of him by Bordiga, then an ally of Trotsky's: 'Does comrade Stalin think that the development of the Russian situation and the internal problems of the Russian party are linked to the development of the international proletarian movement?' Stalin indignantly replied, 'This question has never been asked of me. I would never have thought that a communist could have asked it of me. God forgive you for having done so.'[26] Stalin reacted to what he considered a violation of all the revolution held to be sacred. For him, identifying 'socialism in one country' with the cause of world revolution was not a cynical act, but a political faith.

The crisis in Great Britain brought about by the miners constituted the principal international flashpoint in the reawakened conflict within the Soviet party. Since the beginning of March 1926, Trotsky had been warning the Politburo that they should not lose another revolutionary opportunity, as had happened three years earlier in Germany.[27] The British general strike on 1 May 1926 apparently

---

[23] PBKI, doc. 209, pp. 342–6.   [24] PBKI, docs 192, 193, 194, 195, pp. 320–7.
[25] Weber, *La trasformazione del comunismo tedesco*, 152–4.
[26] C. Daniele (ed.), *Gramsci a Roma, Togliatti a Mosca: il carteggio del 1926*, with an essay by G. *Vacca* (Turin: Einaudi, 1999), doc. 1, pp. 165, 168–70.
[27] PBKI, doc. 214, pp. 350–1.

reinvigorated the opposition. Zinoviev sent the Communist Party of Great Britain a secret letter that suggested suspending the traditional line of communists participating in trade union organizations.[28] However the Comintern's organizational and financial assistance to the combative but small CPGB—counting just a few thousand members—was not provided in time to reproduce the events of three years earlier in Germany.[29] The strike was called off without a genuine workers' insurrection, and debate on the British question reopened fierce divisions in the Politburo. On 3 June 1926 Zinoviev and Trotsky fulminated against the majority, which they accused of giving everything up for lost before it was necessary.[30] Bukharin replied that the oppositionists did not understand the peculiarities of the British trade unions and their deep roots in the workers' movement. Stalin did not take part in the debate, but wrote from Tbilisi to Molotov demanding that Bukharin's report include specific accusations against Zinoviev.[31] The majority of the Politburo rejected Zinoviev's and approved Bukharin's argument, which was then ratified by the Comintern.[32] By this time, the transfer of control of the Comintern to Bukharin and Stalin was more or less complete.[33]

The conflict then became public. Zinoviev and Trotsky accused the majority of having accepted the 'capitulation' of the British working class. Stalin argued that the British events demonstrated the impossibility of 'lasting stabilization' of capitalism, but that it would be wrong to proclaim the commencement of 'new period of great revolutionary upsurge'.[34] This clash sealed Zinoviev's fate. By the end of July Stalin had prepared his removal from the office at the head of the Comintern, which was sanctioned by the Plenum of the Central Committee of the Soviet party and immediately approved by the ECCI.[35] In the following months the clashes in the Politburo escalated uncontrollably and led to police measures being taken against the opposition. This culminated in the Fifteenth Conference of the party in November 1926, at which Stalin launched into a lengthy tirade against the opposition, accusing it of spreading pessimism about the possibility of 'building socialism' in the USSR and sapping the hopes the 'international proletariat' placed in it. In reply to Trotsky's accusation that he had given up on world revolution, Stalin proclaimed that the majority saw the Russian Revolution 'as a revolution that represented an autonomous force capable of entering the struggle

---

[28] PBKI, doc. 222, p. 365.
[29] A. Thorpe, *The British Communist Party and Moscow, 1920–1943* (Manchester: Manchester University Press, 2000), 91–4.
[30] RGASPI, fo. 324, op. 2, d. 67.   [31] PBKI, doc. 229, pp. 377–8.
[32] *Stenogrammy zasedanii Politburo TsK Rkp(b)-Vkp(b) 1923–1938gg. V trekh tomakh*, vol. 1: *1923–1926gg.* (Moscow: Rosspen, 2007), 743–827; PBKI, doc. 226, pp. 371–4; doc. 228, pp. 376–7; doc. 230, pp. 379–82. A. Vatlin, '"Class brothers unite"! The British General Strike and the formation of the "United Opposition"', in P. R. Gregory and N. M. Naimark (eds), *The Lost Politburo Transcripts: From Collective Rule to Stalin's Dictatorship* (New Haven, Conn.: Yale University Press, 2008), 57–77.
[33] RGASPI, fo. 17, op. 85, d. 670.
[34] Stalin, *Sochineniya*, vol. 8, p. 166. See A. Y. Vatlin, *Komintern: pervye desyat let* (Moscow: Rossiya Molodaya, 1993), 60–2; *Rossiya nepovskaya* (Moscow: Novyi Khronograf, 2002), 355–7.
[35] *Pis'ma I. V. Stalina V. M. Molotovu 1925–1936 gg: sbornik dokumentov* (Moscow: Rossiya Molodaya, 1995), 72–4. See Vatlin, *Komintern: pervye desyat let*, 65–6.

against world capitalism', whereas the opposition considered it 'an appendage to the future revolution in the West'.[36] Thus he alluded yet again to the central role of the Soviet state in world revolution.

Immediately afterwards, at the Seventh Plenum of the Comintern, Bukharin aimed to acknowledge finally that the 'imminent revolutionary situation' Lenin had detected in the capitalist countries just after the world war no longer existed, without this sounding like a call to the communist movement to break ranks. He provided the opposition and their followers on the extreme left of European communism with a lesson in realism, and put forward a 'differentiated' reading of the international situation that identified the strongholds of capitalist stability in the United States, Germany, France, and Italy and the more vulnerable areas in the decline of the British empire and China. Although he could see some sense in the theory of 'ultra-imperialism', discussed by Kautsky and revived by Rudolf Hilferding, who speculated about how the great capitalist powers might avoid the conflicts of the past,[37] Bukharin denounced 'pacifist and pan-European utopias' as counter-revolutionary, and fully endorsed the theory of the inevitability of war.[38] In effect, he rejected any revision of Lenin's theory of imperialism, even though his own analysis raised serious questions about its validity, in light of the world order that had emerged from the convulsions of the early postwar years. This behaviour demonstrated that he had reached the Pillars of Hercules beyond which no communist was willing to go.

In other words, Lenin's successors in the main continued to share a common political culture in spite of the conflict that was tearing them apart—a political culture based on a catastrophist vision of capitalist modernity and the axioms that resulted from this. More than anything else, the spectre of a war directed against the USSR, which harked back to the period of the Russian Civil War, had never faded from their minds, and engendered their vision of a 'European civil war' now becoming an 'international civil war'. On this point, it is worth recalling Theda Skocpol's distinction between ideologies—political tendencies consciously expressed by identifiable players—and 'cultural idioms'—shared codes with deeper and more extended roots that are used in different ways according to which players are involved and the historical circumstances.[39] The Bolshevik leaders took different paths in their political orientations, but their codes and parlance were not so distant as might have appeared to their contemporaries. The Leninist theory of imperialism was their compass, and constituted a share basis for their identity.

The dramatic split in the Russian ruling group provoked bewilderment and anxiety for the very reason that shared values could not prevent disruptive conflict. An example of this was the letter sent by Gramsci, the secretary of the Italian

---

[36] Stalin, *Sochineniya*, vol. 8, pp. 263, 280–1, 348.

[37] L. Rapone, *La socialdemocrazia europea tra le due guerre: dall'organizzazione della pace alla resistenza al fascismo* (Rome: Carocci, 1999), 65–9.

[38] *Protokoll: Erweiterte Exekutive der Kommunistischen Internationale. Moskau, 22 November–16 Dezember 1926* (Hamburg/Berlin, 1927), 25–38, 88–130.

[39] T. Skocpol, *Social Revolutions in the Modern World* (Cambridge: Cambridge University Press, 1994), 204.

Communist Party, to the leaders of the Soviet Communist Party in October 1926. He performed the duties Stalin and Bukharin assigned to all the communist leaders, that of supporting the positions of the majority. But he did not restrict himself to this, and attributed an essential part of the blame to the majority, not just to the opposition. He sent them the most severe warning conceivable: in his judgement, they risked 'nullifying the leading role' of the Soviet party in the 'world party' and 'losing sight of the international aspects of Russian affairs'.[40] Gramsci shared a mythical concept of the Bolshevik dictatorship, which was widespread in the communist movement. An essential part of this myth was the idea that the unity of the 'old guard' of Leninism was a supreme principle, and the idea that the politics of Bolshevism in power coincided with an effective realization of freedom, consensus, and socialization, rather than reflecting a diametrically opposed reality. The unity of the Bolshevik ruling group was in fact shattered, and the very logic of Lenin's unitary principle was producing a repressive clampdown even on the political elites of the USSR. Nevertheless, Gramsci's conviction that the revolutionary state constituted a symbolic resource pinpointed a crucial question. The credibility of 'building socialism' in the USSR represented a decisive element in its attraction to the working masses in Europe and elsewhere. Without that strategic resource, even the most sophisticated revolutionary concept in the West was destined to be marginal. But Bolshevik leaders appeared to have little awareness of the exercise of political and cultural hegemony, which they reduced to power struggles and forms of military command.

Although symbolic for the questions it raised, Gramsci's letter was a unique case, linked as it was to the personality of its author, an exponent of a ruling group made up of intellectuals and not typical of European communism. Angelo Tasca and Palmiro Togliatti were also members of this group. The question posed by Gramsci would remain unanswered. It was put aside by Togliatti, then the PCI's representative in Moscow, who sided unconditionally with Stalin and Bukharin, and a month later Gramsci was arrested and imprisoned by the fascists. The reaction of the great majority of the communist movement was that of a supine and pragmatic acceptance of Stalin's and Bukharin's harsh decisions. Being part of an international organization conceived and structured as a politico-military order, the ruling groups of the communist parties did not have the independence to take an active role in the dispute that was lacerating Lenin's successors. The main European parties were directed from abroad through emissaries of the Comintern, and moreover were dependent on financial support from Moscow. Having joined the party to spread the Bolshevik gospel, communists found themselves dealing with a situation that from the very beginning kept the revolution distant from their political prospects.

Thus the constitutive link to the Soviet state was not loosened; rather, it was tautened with the passage of time. The progressive strengthening of the state in accordance with a logic dictated by the civil war and its legacy coexisted with

---

[40] Daniele, *Gramsci a Roma, Togliatti a Mosca*, doc. 42, p. 408.

sectarian parties incapable of acquiring majority consent in the trade unions and of putting down roots in their national societies. Seen in this light, 'Bolshevization' appears to have been not only a process of regimentation of post-Lenin communism from above but also the consequence of subordination, accepted out of necessity or conviction, that acknowledged the primogeniture of the Bolsheviks and their role as rulers of the revolutionary state. The state's interests risked coming into conflict with those of the movement, as Trotsky and his followers rightly argued; but without the influence of the former the very existence of the latter would have been in doubt.

BETWEEN EAST AND WEST

The European scenario continued to play a central role in the conflict between Lenin's successors and in their view of the world revolution, but the Asian scenario was also making itself felt. The Bolsheviks had on several occasions considered the possibility of shifting the fire of revolutionary expectations outside Europe, as Lenin himself had suggested in his essay on imperialism; but invariably they ended up shelving it. As far as we know, Trotsky was the first to assess this possibility immediately after the defeat of the revolutionary movements in Hungary and Bavaria in the summer of 1919. He submitted a rationale which would reappear periodically in the years to come. If the revolution was impeded in the West, its centre of gravity had to be shifted to the anti-imperialist East, because 'our Red Army constitutes an incomparably more potent force on the Asian political terrain than on the European one', and because 'the road to Paris and London passes through the cities of Afghanistan, the Punjab and Bengal'.[41] A similar option did not emerge even after the Red Army's defeat in Poland a year later. The Bolsheviks did, however, set the target of a revolutionary alliance with anti-imperialist nationalism outside Europe. This line was proposed by Lenin at the Second Congress of the Comintern, when he criticized the ideas of the Indian communist Manabendra Nath Roy, who denied that the national bourgeoisies of countries like India and China would take on a revolutionary role.[42] In September 1920 the Bolsheviks convened in Baku a 'Congress of Peoples of the East', which recorded the presence of 2,000 European and Asian representatives, both communists and nationalists. Zinoviev and Radek preached heartfelt sermons against British imperialism—an example of the rhetoric of national self-determination that Soviet power exploited uniformly from Turkey to Central Asia and from Persia to India and China.[43] Zinoviev reported to Moscow that the congress had been a further step along the

[41] J. M. Meijer (ed.), *The Trotsky Papers 1917–1922* (The Hague: Mouton, 1964), vol. 1, pp. 623–5.
[42] B. Lazitch and M. Drachkovitch, *Lenin and the Comintern* (Stanford, Calif.: Hoover Institution Press, 1972), 386–7.
[43] J. Riddell (ed.), *To See the Dawn. Baku, 1920: First Congress of the Peoples of the East* (New York: Pathfinder, 1993).

road to world revolution.[44] The failed attempt to create a revolutionary army in northern India, a task entrusted to Roy in late 1920, curbed Bolshevik enthusiasm. The alliance with anti-imperialist nationalism became an objective to be pursued gradually.[45]

Only at the end of his life did Lenin appear to become more aware of Asia's revolutionary potential. In his last work, written in March 1923, he portrayed the East as 'dragged into the general mayhem of the world revolutionary movement' and destined to ensure the victory of socialism. Bukharin was immediately inspired, and suggested the forceful image of a capitalist metropolis besieged by the unending countryside of the global periphery.[46] However, the Bolsheviks' tendency to propose their own revolution—or, to be more precise, its proletarian mythology—as the universal model did not assist the development of the 'colonial question' in a manner suited to the enormous political and social diversity of the world outside Europe. At the time of the Fifth Congress of the Comintern, Stalin argued that the time had come to pose 'the question of the proletariat's hegemony' in the liberation struggle in colonial countries like India.[47] The same idea was applied to China. A year later, he came up with a tripartite division of countries outside Europe. According to Stalin, they had to distinguish between countries that did not have an industrial proletariat, such as Morocco, countries that had been slightly developed, such as China and Egypt, and countries that had a 'national proletariat', such as India.[48] Stalin's categorization was superficial and unable to distinguish different policies towards nationalist forces outside Europe. The same limitation afflicted all the Comintern leaders, Roy included, in spite of their differences in emphasis over the nature of the anti-colonial revolution. They employed generic and often untranslatable classist concepts, which betrayed an underestimation of the prospects of decolonization and its future impact on world politics.[49]

Moscow aimed to establish agreements with national bourgeoisies imbued with hostile attitudes to British imperialism. The model from 1921 was Kemal Atatürk's Turkey, in spite of the ferocious anti-communist repression triggered by his regime.[50] But the country that presented the combination of nationalism and revolution that most closely corresponded to Bolshevik expectations was China. Controlled by Comintern emissaries, one of the most prominent being the Dutch communist Henk Sneevliet (Maring), the Chinese Communist Party was an example of the application of the 'united front' tactic, with nationalist forces that fought the 'warlords' and opposed British imperialism.[51] The CCP was obliged by Moscow

---

[44] *Devyataya Konferentsiya Rkp(b). Sentyabr' 1920 goda. Protokoly* (Moscow: Izdatel'stvo politicheskoy literatury, 1972), 221.

[45] Jacobson, *When the Soviet Union Entered World Politics*, 77–80.

[46] S. Cohen, *Bukharin e la rivoluzione bolscevica: biografia politica 1888–1938* (Milan: Feltrinelli, 1975), 254.

[47] PBKI, doc. 157, p. 271.   [48] Stalin, *Sochineniya*, vol. 7, p. 146.

[49] J. Derrick, *Africa's 'Agitators': Militant Anti-Colonialism in Africa and the West, 1918–1939* (New York: Columbia University Press, 2008); S. D. Gupta, *Comintern and the Destiny of Communism in India, 1919-1943* (Calcutta: Seribaan, 2006), 110–15.

[50] Jacobson, *When the Soviet Union Entered World Politics*, 117–18.

[51] A. V. Pantsov, *Tainaya istoriya sovetsko-kitayskikh otnoshenii: bol'sheviki i kitayskikaya revoliutsiya (1919–1927)* (Moscow: Muravey-Gayd, 2001); T. Saich, *The Origins of the First United Front in China: The Role of Sneevliet (Alias Maring)* (2 vols, Leiden: E. J. Brill, 1991).

to join the Guomindang, the nationalist grouping founded by Sun Yat-sen, with whom Soviet diplomacy had established permanent relations.[52] Following Sun's death, his successor, Chiang Kai-shek, initially strengthened the alliance between Moscow and the nationalist government in Canton. In the mid-1920s there were 'two semi-Bolshevized movements' in China: the communists and the nationalists.[53] The development of the national liberation movement in 1925, the so-called '30 May movement', led to a considerable increase in the Soviet presence.[54]

The involvement of the Comintern and the Red Army in China became massive. The Chinese Communist Party grew dramatically to several tens of thousands of activists, mainly in the large cities. However, relations between communists and nationalists were far from harmonious. Their coexistence had always been difficult, and gave rise to tensions and clashes over the control of territory, increasingly so as the prospects of reunifying the country and eliminating the 'warlords' became more likely. Like their comrades in Europe, Chinese communists only reluctantly accepted the 'united front', which in this specific case left the monopoly of military force in nationalist hands. On the other hand, Moscow's instructions were often inconsistent, fostering both communist assimilation into the Guomindang and political autonomy with the intention of gradually taking over. In February 1926, they even examined the possibility of inviting the Guomindang to join the Comintern. The Politburo ruled this out on the grounds that such a move would have mobilized the imperialists against the Chinese national liberation movement. However, the proposal was left open to future developments.[55]

The tensions turned into open conflict in March 1926, when, in response to the reverses suffered by the nationalist armies, Chiang ordered the arrest of communist political commissars. Although the conflict was difficult to settle, Moscow continued to impose prudence on the Chinese communists. On 1 April the Politburo ruled that the Chinese Revolution was not capable of resisting an imperialist intervention. The shared objective of the USSR and the Chinese revolutionaries was that of 'winning a truce', and Moscow's task was to enter an agreement with Japan on an anti-British basis.[56] On 29 April the Politburo declared any rift between the CCP and the Guomindang to be inadmissible.[57] The prudent line adopted by Moscow exacerbated the clash between the majority, led by Stalin and Bukharin, and the 'new opposition' of Trotsky and Zinoviev, which proposed that the CCP should leave the Guomindang. Stalin accused them of committing an 'error' no less serious than that of calling on British communists to act independently of the trade unions.[58]

[52] Vkp(b), *Komintern i natsional'no-revolyutsionnoe dvizhenie v Kitae: dokumenty,* vol. 1: *1920–1925* (Moscow: Institut Dalnego Vostoka Ran, 1994), docs 60 and 61.

[53] McDermott and Agnew, *The Comintern,* 169.   [54] PBKI, doc. 191, pp. 318–19.

[55] Vkp(b), *Komintern i natsional'no-revolyutsionnoe dvizhenie v Kitae: dokumenty,* vol. 2: *1926–1927 gg.* (Moscow: Institut Dalnego Vostoka Ran, 1996), docs 23 and 24. See Pantsov, *Taynaya istoriya sovetsko-kitayskikh otnoshenii,* 134.

[56] Vkp(b), *Komintern i natsional'no-revolyutsionnoe dvizhenie v Kitae,* vol. 2, doc. 36.

[57] PBKI, doc. 220, pp. 358–9.   [58] PBKI, doc. 229, p. 378.

The link established between the British question and the Chinese question dominated the conflict between Lenin's successors. In reality, all Bolsheviks placed their hopes in the Chinese Revolution. Putting aside his previous caution, Stalin wrote to Molotov in September 1926 criticizing a high-level diplomat, former people's vice-commissar of foreign affairs and now ambassador in Peking, Lev Karakhan because the latter did not appear to understand that, in Stalin's opinion, the city of Hangzhou would soon become the 'Chinese Moscow'.[59] The majority of the Politburo supported the moderate positions of ECCI's representative in Canton, Mikhail Borodin, against the more radical ones of the head of the Office of the Far East, Grigory Voytinsky, who was working in Shanghai.[60] However, at the Seventh Plenum of the ECCI, Stalin and Bukharin, under pressure from the opposition, proposed a radicalization of the policy for China.[61] Bukharin spoke of a future Chinese state of an unusual nature, a 'dictatorship of the proletariat and peasantry with an anti-imperialist content' that would be built through the gradual acquisition of power in the army and the apparatus controlled by the Guomindang.[62] In his opinion, the 'anti-imperialist national revolution' would have made it possible for China 'to avoid the capitalist phase'. Bukharin was not thinking of an immediate revolutionary prospect, but he predicted that world capitalism would not have been up to the enormous effort of encircling the USSR and containing the revolution in China.

The decision to rely on a strategy of cooperation and attrition with the nationalists did not ensure that the truce between communists and nationalists would last very long. The main tensions were in Shanghai, where the communists attempted several times to trigger a popular uprising. Although Chiang Kai-shek openly threatened to force a rift in the Guomindang, Moscow's policy did not change. Once again, on 10 March 1927, Bukharin sent Borodin a telegram requesting the Chinese communists to continue cooperating closely with the Guomindang.[63] Bukharin was right in rejecting the idea of a simple repetition of 1917, but the pragmatic relationship with nationalism proved no more effective than the doctrinaire arguments of the opposition. On 12 April 1927, thousands of communists were massacred by Chiang's men, once he had decided to take full personal control of the Guomindang. On Stalin's instructions, the Politburo decided not to react or to modify the Comintern's political line.[64] As had already occurred with the German communists, the Chinese communists found that they were blamed for their own defeat. The main scapegoats were CCP secretary Chen Duxiu and the Comintern emissaries Roy and Borodin. But the attempt to minimize this episode was not credible. The opposition went on the attack, accusing the majority of having pursued a mistaken policy that was damaging the prospects of world revolution. Trotsky gave stirring speeches proposing the creation of 'soviets' of soldiers

[59] *Pisma Stalina Molotovu*, doc. 28, p. 94.
[60] Vkp(b), *Komintern i natsional'no-revolyutsionnoe dvizhenie v Kitae*, vol. 2, doc. 117.
[61] Pantsov, *Taynaya istoriya sovetsko-kitayskikh otnoshenii*, 145–6.
[62] PBKI, doc. 253, pp. 417–22.   [63] PBKI, doc. 263, pp. 436–7.
[64] PBKI, doc. 268, pp. 442–3.

and peasants in China. The Politburo defended the Comintern's policy on China, condemned the opposition's arguments as a violation of the directives of the Soviet party, and censured their articles in the press.[65] The political situation in Moscow became even more inflammatory when, a few days later, the disaster for communists in China was followed by a serious international crisis caused by a breakdown in diplomatic relations between Great Britain and the USSR.

The crisis with Great Britain marked the end of the USSR's consolidation of its diplomatic position, and was the definitive proof that the duplicity of Soviet international policy, which both pursued 'peaceful coexistence' with Western countries and organized a revolutionary movement in those same countries, created as many problems as it resolved. Only in its relations with Germany did Soviet duplicity make any sense, given the considerable convergence of interests between the two partners of Rapallo. Berlin had avoided a rift following the communist insurrection of October 1923, while Moscow had been able to stomach the Locarno accords and had accepted the German membership of the League of Nations.[66] In April 1926 a new treaty ratified the preferential relationship between the two countries. The management of relations with Great Britain were decidedly more difficult. London proved to be much less disposed to turn a blind eye since 1924, when a letter, which was probably false and appeared to be from Zinoviev inciting British communists to insurrection, provoked a serious diplomatic incident. The British were no less intransigent in 1926, when the Soviets supported the miners' strike. The possibility of establishing normal diplomatic relations was further compromised by the anti-British policy Moscow pursued in China. London's decision to break off relations came at the end of May 1927, as the culmination of incidents and tensions that the Soviet leaders did nothing to rein in and that thwarted Chicherin's best efforts at mediation.[67]

The crisis with Great Britain was not a passing episode. It revealed a fundamental mismatch between the Soviet leaders' policies. On the one hand, the majority led by Stalin and Bukharin acknowledged the existence of a 'relative stabilization' in Europe and wished to consolidate the USSR's position by creating a network of relations that guaranteed its security and obtained the capital and technologies necessary for industrialization. On the other hand, the same leaders did not think through their ideas on 'stabilization' when they analysed the international situation and issued their directives to the communist movement, demonstrating their lack of confidence in diplomacy's ability to safeguard the interests of the state. The dualism of the Narkomindel and the Comintern confirmed the existence of an

---

[65] PBKI, doc. 270, pp. 444–57; doc. 272, pp. 459–61. On the disputes over the Chinese question in Moscow and on the relations between the Comintern and the Chinese Communist party, see Pantsov, *Taynaya istoriya sovetsko-kitayskikh otnoshenii*, 181–213; S. A. Smith, *A Road is Made: Communism in Shanghai, 1920–1927* (Honolulu: University of Hawai'i Press, 2000), 168–208. On relations between the Chinese Communist Party and the Guomindang in the 1920s, see T. Saich (ed.), *The Rise to Power of the Chinese Communist Party: Documents and Analysis* (Armonk, N.Y.: M. E. Sharpe, 1996), section B.

[66] Adibekov et al., *Politburo TsK Rkp(b)–Vkp(b) i Evropa*, docs 54, 55, 56, pp. 122–5.

[67] Di Biagio, *Coesistenza e isolazionismo*, 268–9.

institutional reflex arising from an unresolved contradiction in the 'actual constitution' of the Soviet state. It could be said that Narkomindel worked for stabilization, the Comintern for destabilization, and the Politburo both at the same time. The opposition of Trotsky and Zinoviev, fiercely antagonistic to the combination of 'socialism in one country' and 'capitalist stabilization', influenced the vacillations of the majority, which in some cases accepted the opposition's arguments fearing they could otherwise be delegitimized.

Alarmism over the possibility of war, which emerged in Europe, was echoed in the East. Since 1925, the idea that Great Britain was considering the option of attacking the Soviet Union through Poland had been associated with the birth of the national liberation movement in China. In a letter to Bukharin written in the summer of 1925, Stalin argued that the British conservatives were preparing for war against the USSR in response to the Chinese events.[68] During 1926, the intensification of internal political conflict and its interaction with international tensions encouraged references to the war scenario. This was particularly true after General Piłsudski's coup in Poland in May 1926, which appeared to bring new threats along the most insecure border of the USSR.[69] In reality, the judgements of the Soviet leaders vacillated. In the second half of the year, Stalin, Bukharin, and Trotsky avoided the use of overly alarmist rhetoric. But the war scenario still overshadowed their thinking. Given these circumstances, it is not surprising that the twin crises in China and Great Britain during the spring of 1927 caused Moscow to suffer a veritable war psychosis, in spite of the absence of any real danger. The alarm over 'the danger of war' triggered a campaign that would have a decisive effect on the future of the USSR and the communist movement.[70]

The Eighth Plenum of the ECCI at the end of May 1927 was entirely devoted to the 'danger of war'. The Comintern launched a campaign 'in defence of the Russian and Chinese Revolution', which no longer called on communist parties 'to defend the peace' but to disseminate philo-Soviet propaganda, almost as though war were imminent. All the Bolsheviks, in spite of their fierce divisions, were agreed on the risk of a Western attack on the USSR. During the escalation that followed, it became difficult to distinguish between manipulative talking-up of the outside threat for domestic political reasons and a paranoid perception of the danger. The leaders privately spoke the same language they spoke in public. Profound convictions and the magnifying of an invented danger became a heady mix, which makes it impossible to separate the truth from fiction. In a letter to Molotov dated 8 June, Stalin argued that the assassination of the Soviet consul in Warsaw, which had occurred the previous day, demonstrated that the British were preparing another Sarajevo.[71] In July 1927, at Bukharin's suggestion, the Politburo sent a directive

---

[68] PBKI, doc. 194, p. 325.   [69] PBKI, doc. 223, p. 366.

[70] On the war scare of 1927, see A. Di Biagio, 'Moscow, The Comintern and the war scare, 1926–1928', in S. Pons and A. Romano (eds), *Russia in the Age of Wars 1914–1945* (Milan: Feltrinelli, 2000).

[71] *Lubyanka: Stalin   i   VCK-GPU-OGPU-Nkvd.   Yanvar'   1922–Dekabr,   1936* (Moscow: Mezhdunarodnyi Fond 'Demokratiya', 2003), doc. 153, p. 133.

to the Soviet press to denounce the threatened 'preparation for war against the USSR'.[72] Shortly afterwards, Stalin publicly sounded the alarm for war.[73]

This was the context in which Trotsky and Zinoviev lost their last battle. They contributed to the campaign to heighten anxieties over the 'danger of war' by establishing the connection between the defeat in China and the current danger to the USSR, in an attempt to demonstrate the inadequacy of the majority's policy of reconciling the interests of the Soviet state with those of the world revolution. But this campaign backfired on the opposition. Their analysis of the Chinese situation was in part accepted by the majority, which following the repression in Shanghai radicalized their directives to the point of calling for an 'agrarian revolution'.[74] The majority finally put the opposition with its back against the wall, by accusing them of defeatism and treachery during a serious emergency for the 'socialist fatherland'. Stalin decreed that whoever thought of defending the world revolutionary movement 'without the USSR or against the USSR', would end up 'unfailingly in the camp of the revolution's enemies'.[75] The campaign on the 'danger of war' thus revealed its most manipulative feature concerning the domestic political struggle. Above all, it demonstrated the persistence of mindsets and concepts that would also influence crucial political decisions in the future.

The suppression of the communists in China in the spring of 1927 brought to an end the hopes of shifting the axis of world revolution to the East and striking at British imperialism in the wake of the failure of the revolution in the West. The scenario of an 'east Asian revolution', which made it possible to keep faith with the decline of capitalism, relaunch the role of the communist movement, and provide indirect reassurance to the Soviet state, faded before it could even take shape. In July 1927, in a letter to Bukharin and Molotov, Stalin expressed the disenchanted view that they could not exclude the possibility of an 'interval' between the 'bourgeois revolution' that had just occurred in China and a future second 'bourgeois revolution' on a par with the one that occurred in Russia in 1905 and 1917.[76] This tendency to establish an analogy with the Russian experience was proving to be stubborn, but the prediction this time revealed pessimism about the last remaining breeding ground for revolution in the world. Stalin and Bukharin nevertheless adopted a revolutionary rhetoric for China, borrowed from Trotsky, in order to conduct the final phase of their campaign against the opposition.[77] But the harsh blow inflicted on the movement in China once again laid the bare the dilemma facing the isolated revolutionary state. Up to that moment, the response of Lenin's successors had been centred upon the alternatives provided by world revolution, in light of current events or reinterpreted as part of a process, but in any case perceived as the only authentic solution to the risks being run by the revolutionary state within the 'capitalist encirclement'. Given this priority, diplomacy had always

---

[72] PBKI, doc. 277, pp. 473–5.   [73] Stalin, *Sochineniya*, vol. 9, pp. 322–30.
[74] RGASPI, fo. 17, op. 2, dd. 282, 317; Pantsov, *Taynaya istoriya sovetsko-kitayskikh otnoshenii*, 208.
[75] Stalin, *Sochineniya*, vol. 10, p. 51.   [76] *Pis'ma Stalina Molotovu*, doc. 36, p. 111.
[77] Pantsov, *Taynaya istoriya sovetsko-kitayskikh otnoshenii*, 219.

been understood as a necessary but not decisive instrument. So it would be in the future too. None of the Soviet leaders could allow themselves to 'normalize' the state and abolish its constitutional duplicity, as expressed by the existence of the Narkomindel and the Comintern. But the collapse of every last prospect of revolution in both the West and the East just ten years after the October Revolution meant that they had to confront problems Lenin had failed to resolve.

Of his heirs, Stalin proved to be the one most suited to carrying out this task. This clearly emerged from the Politburo meeting of 8 September 1927, when the verbal conflict between the Bolshevik leaders passed the point of no return. Stalin freed himself of the spectre of Lenin's 'testament' by declaring that in reality it discredited the leaders of the opposition and threw back the accusation of 'Bonapartism' at Trotsky. His profile as the dominant figure in the party was definitively confirmed by this performance.[78] Stalin's plan was presented on the occasion of the Fifteenth Congress of the party in December 1927, by which time the opposition had been demonized and expelled from the party as extraneous elements. Stalin's speech made short work of the problem of reconciling the interests of the USSR and those of the world revolution. In his opinion, they were two sides of the same coin. He selected a few concepts that had typified Bolshevik terminology for international politics, and emphasized 'capitalist encirclement', 'the unequal development' of capitalism, and the 'contradictions' between imperialist states. Translated into a political vision, they signified prioritizing the defence of the USSR and predicting war. Stalin announced that they should imminently expect 'a very deep and serious crisis of world capitalism, which brings new wars with it'. At the same time there would be 'a gradual fascistization of bourgeois governments'. For this reason, the term 'peaceful coexistence' was now obsolete. In appearance, this interpretation contrasted with that of Trotsky and the opposition, but in reality, Stalin was subverting the prospect outlined by his ally Bukharin only a year earlier. This swept away the previous framework of European and American stability challenged by national liberation movements outside Europe, an 'organized capitalism' forged by social democracy, and a role both 'peaceful' and revolutionary for the communist movement. The only element Stalin retained was the idea that the USSR was the principal factor 'in the break-up of world imperialism'. On the other hand, Stalin did not pose the question of how to develop the communist movement, in spite of his own prediction of a new period of revolutions. Instead he cited Lenin's teachings on how to 'delay war with the capitalist world' by exploiting conflicts between imperialist powers.[79]

Historians have traditionally restricted their explanations of the conflict between Stalin and Bukharin to the question of whether or not the NEP had to be kept in

---

[78] *Stenogrammy zasedanii Politburo TsK Rkp(b)-Vkp(b) 1923–1938gg. V trekh tomakh*, vol. 2: *1926–1927* (Moscow: Rosspen, 2007), 595–7; R. Service, 'The way they talked then: the discourse of politics in the Soviet Party Politburo in the late 1920s', in Gregory and Naimark (eds), *The Lost Politburo Transcripts*, 121–34.

[79] Stalin, *Sochineniya*, vol. 10, pp. 274, 285–9.

place to industrialize Russia, while omitting the question of how domestic policy interacted with international politics.[80] However, Stalin launched his offensive on domestic policy only after he produced his own international policy for the USSR, which differed from that of the majority of the party until the summer of 1927. Impatient of the restrictions imposed by the NEP, Stalin could at this stage pursue his idea of an attack on the countryside. In the early months of 1928, the adoption of 'exceptional methods' and violent requisitions as a response to the agrarian crisis marked the final emergence of the Politburo's Stalinist nucleus. The decision to return to the method of 'war communism' led to the rapid marginalization of Bukharin's 'moderates', which was made that much easier by the fact that political rivalry no longer took place in public following the demonization of the opposition. Stalin's methods would prove to be the point of no return for a second revolution, which would violently transform relations between the state and society. During 1928 and 1929, economic and social problems were at the centre of another conflict within the party's ruling group.[81] During the crisis of 1928, Stalin made use of agitation against domestic rivals portrayed as instruments of 'international capital'—a link established at the time of the supposed sabotage by technicians and specialists in the Donbass, who included some German and British citizens prominent in the 'Shakhty affair' in March 1928. On this occasion, the Politburo decided to meet representatives of the communist parties in Moscow to promote a propaganda campaign against the suspect activities of 'foreign powers and embassies'.[82] A little later, in July, Stalin declared that the balance between the 'two worlds', the Soviet one and the capitalist one, had by then been broken.[83] Thus he evoked the Bolsheviks' worst nightmare, a combination between the enemy within and foreign intervention, and proposed an undifferentiated view of capitalism as the principal compass by which to confront the challenges facing the USSR.

Bukharin's opposition was weak and inadequate. Indeed he contributed to the radicalization of international policy. His leadership of the Comintern had been shifting unmistakably to the left since the summer of 1927, while he called on the communist parties to mobilize against the supposed threats of war against the USSR.[84] In response to the suppression of the workers' revolt in Vienna on 15 July 1927, he proposed that the European communist movement turn against social democracy.[85] Thus he accepted de facto Stalin's claim that 'capitalist stabilization' had come to an end, even if his language was more moderate.[86] The drafting of the Comintern's new programme demonstrated that Stalin had taken the upper

---

[80] M. Reiman, *The Birth of Stalinism: The USSR on the Eve of the Second Revolution* (London: I. B. Tauris, 1987); M. Lewin, *The Making of the Soviet System: Essays in the Social History of Inter-War Russia* (New York: New Press, 1994).

[81] *Kak lomali Nep: stenogrammy plenumov TsK Vkp(b) 1928–1929* (5 vols, Moscow: Mezhdunarodnyi Fond 'Demokratiya', 2000).

[82] *Lubyanka*, doc. 186, p. 163.   [83] Stalin, *Sochineniya*, vol. 11, p. 200.

[84] McDermott and Agnew, *The Comintern*, pp. 74–5; *Kak lomali Nep*, vol. 2, pp. 100, 105.

[85] A. Y. Vatlin, *Komintern: idei, resheniya, sudby* (Moscow: Rosspen, 2009), 199.

[86] *Pyatnadtsatii s'ezd Vkp(b), Dekabr' 1927 goda: stenograficheskii otchet* (Moscow: Gosudarstvennoe izdatel'stvo politicheskoy literatury, 1961), vol. 1, pp. 623–58.

hand.[87] At the Sixth Congress of the Comintern in July 1928, Bukharin continued to appeal for a more nuanced analysis of the capitalist world and argued against the tendency to consider 'any reaction' to be fascism, reminding his audience that, during the struggle to come, communists would always be able to appeal to social democratic workers, whereas this was not the case for fascist organizations. But the prevailing theme was intransigence towards social democracy and the imminence of new wars.[88] Bukharin believed mistakenly that the political line he had endorsed at the Sixth Congress was a compromise with Stalin.[89] Instead, Stalin banked the radicalization of the Comintern and then relaunched it in even more intransigent terms.

Stalin's defence of Thälmann against the 'right wing' of the KPD, delivered at the Presidium of the ECCI in December 1928, was a decisive moment in changing the course of the Comintern. Stalin denounced the German 'right-wingers' as the negative example of a 'deviation' that existed in the communist movement.[90] The result was a purge of the Comintern and a revival of verbal extremism—sectarian and catastrophist declarations on the continuing significance of 'world revolution', which actually aimed at expelling those linked to Bukharin from the communist parties. At the party Plenum of April 1929, Stalin railed against Bukharin and accused him of not understanding 'the intensification of the class struggle' both domestically and internationally, as well as overestimating the 'stabilization of capitalism'.[91] In May and June Bukharin was expelled from the Presidium of ECCI and the political secretariat of the Comintern.[92] His elimination was confirmed at the Tenth Plenum of ECCI in July 1929, when he was accused of having capitulated to the 'class enemy' and to social democracy.[93] In November 1929 Bukharin was expelled from the Politburo. From this moment onwards there would never again be any challenge to Stalin's leadership of the USSR and the communist movement.

In many ways, Stalin's ultimate success and turn towards the 'revolution from above' was a response to the collapse of the latest revolutionary scenarios in the West and the East in 1926 and 1927. Even after the 'German October', Bolsheviks had continued to nurture expectations of new waves of revolutions, albeit with a different understanding. The combination of workers' strikes in Great Britain and the national liberation movement in China had been emphasized and interpreted by Zinoviev and Trotsky as mere reruns of the Soviet experience, but Bukharin and Stalin had also hoped to destabilize the British empire. Now the drive for industrialization, which had commenced in 1925, was reinforced by the definitive

---

[87] RGASPI, fo. 558, op. 11, dd. 136, 137.

[88] *VI Congrès de l'Internationale Communiste, 17 juillet–1er septembre 1928: compte rendu sténographique* (Milan: Feltrinelli, 1967), 10–13; *Komintern protiv fashizma: dokumenty* (Moscow: Nauka, 1999), doc. 53, pp. 207–13.

[89] N. I. Bukharin, *Problemy teorii i praktiki sotsializma* (Moscow: Izdatel'stvo politicheskoy literatury, 1989), 298.

[90] A. Y. Vatlin and J. T. Tutochkina (eds), *'Pravyi uklon' v KPG i stalinizatsiya Kominterna: stenogramma zasedaniya Prezidiuma EKKI po germanskomu voprosu 19 dekabrya 1928g* (Moscow: Airo-XX, 1996), 120; PBKI, doc. 347, pp. 571–3.

[91] Stalin, *Sochineniya*, vol. 12, pp. 20–1.   [92] PBKI, doc. 363, p. 595.

[93] PBKI, doc. 367, pp. 597–601.

collapse of such expectations, opening the way for an entirely Stalinist version of 'socialism in one country'. Stalin's response would only in part follow the ideological and political paths set out by Lenin's successors in their implacable struggle. Trotsky had left the scene at the end of a gruelling battle. He had not provided convincing plans for dealing with the dilemmas posed by the link between the USSR and the world revolution, but merely an appeal to voluntarism and the 'heroic revolutionary' tradition. His role as the merciless leader of the Red Army had caused the analogies with the French Revolution—which he, more than any-one else, had deployed to justify the Red Terror—to backfire on him, and had caused many to suspect him of embodying a Russian Bonaparte. His ideas on the question of fast-tracked industrialization ended up providing an unwitting contri-bution to Stalin's 'revolution from above'. Sent into internal exile in Alma-Ata in 1928 and expelled from the USSR in 1929, he would doggedly continue his battle against Stalinist 'degeneration' in exile, but would never establish a strong political following.[94]

Bukharin had been as zealous in fighting the opposition as he would be inef-fectual when it came to resisting Stalin. His ideas on building socialism 'at a snail's pace' and on the world revolution as a process were devoid of an inspiring message. His faith in the rise of a revolutionary movement outside Europe capable of taking on the imperialist metropolises would turn out to be intuitive in the long term, but in the politics of the 1920s it proved to be unrealistic. The call for a nuanced analy-sis of the capitalist world and his theories of 'organized capitalism' exposed him to the accusation of deviating towards social democracy. His discovery that Stalin was 'a new Genghis Khan'—as Bukharin put it in the summer of 1928 during a secret meeting with ex-oppositionists—came when the game was already over. He was reduced to a marginal role.[95]

Too late Trotsky and Bukharin understood the unscrupulousness of Stalin's management of power, but they also underestimated his persuasiveness and politi-cal intuition. His scholastic interpretation of politics was striking clear to his adver-saries, but much less so to the functionaries recruited by party-state during the civil war or to those communist party leaders co-opted on the basis of personal loyalty. Stalin appropriated the sacrality the Bolsheviks had cultivated around Lenin's uni-tary principle and set himself up as the defender of the state constructed by the Revolution.[96] The refusal to distinguish between the interests of the Soviet state and those of the world revolution, between conservative Europe and liberal Europe, and between the stable and unstable elements of capitalism allowed him to increase his credibility amongst Bolshevik cadres, whose principal motivation was to feel they were engaged in a struggle against the 'capitalist world'. At the same time, he

---

[94] R. Service, *Trotsky: A Biography* (London: Macmillan, 2009), part 4; B. Knei-Paz, *The Social and Political Thought of Leon Trotsky* (Oxford: Clarendon Press, 2001), 337–66.

[95] Cohen, *Bukharin e la rivoluzione bolscevica*, 276–334.

[96] H. Kuromiya, 'Stalin in the light of the Politburo transcripts', in Gregory and Naimark (eds), *The Lost Politburo Transcripts*, 49.

did not hesitate to select the Bolshevik concepts most suited to the creation of state power as the mobilizing force. In spite of the opposition's accusations against him, Stalin followed a path of sufficiently precise continuity with an essential part of Lenin's legacy: the concept of the state as an instrument used by revolutionaries in the 'international civil war'. This was the red thread that asserted the self-referential context of all Bolshevik politics, as it rejected any genuine cultural innovation in the light of the changes that had occurred in Europe and the rest of the world after the war. The 'war of position' predicted by Lenin and undertaken by Stalin did not imply a revision of conceptual tools and language but rather their selection, codification, and continued existence in a different historical time.

STALIN, THE 'REVOLUTION FROM ABOVE', AND THE PSYCHOSIS OF WAR

The extraordinary measures introduced in the campaigns quickly led to pressure from the Soviet state for an end to market relations. The offensive against the peasants revived amongst Bolshevik cadres the class hatred that had never been assuaged. Thus many oppositionists repented and supported Stalin's leadership, perceiving his decisions to be the long-awaited end to the 'withdrawal' that came at the end of the Civil War. At the same time, an extremely ambitious plan for modernization of the country was put in place. Stalin adopted the industrialization plan supported by the opposition, but in an extreme form that ended up creating an overgrown, primitive, and brutal chain of command rather than economic planning. The autarkic orientation of the USSR was able to found itself on its immense energy reserves, but demanded an enormous transfer of resources from consumption to investment, which became an intolerable burden for the population. This was the prelude for a radical, violent, and unprecedented transformation that attacked the very foundations of society in an inhuman drive to tear down the wall of backwardness. This 'revolution from above' had an eclectic and impromptu nature, but conformed to the power-building tradition of the Bolsheviks after the Revolution. The state that emerged from the devastating cycle of war, revolution, and civil war ten years earlier was the protagonist of yet another devastation of society, this time perpetrated in time of peace. The class war against the peasantry was to all intents and purposes a second civil war in which there could only be one victor. In a short time, the detention camps for political prisoners created by the Bolsheviks during the Civil War of 1918–21 were populated by a multitude of deportees from the countryside, and many more were set up in the Siberian east, creating an infamous system of detention and forced labour known to all by the acronym Gulag. The height of state terrorism was reached in 1932 and 1933, when Stalin resorted to the use of hunger and starvation, caused by collectivization, to break the peasantry's resistance. The mass extermination of millions of people was inflicted on rural society on a scale that dwarfed even the consequences of the famine in 1921. In the Ukraine, the nature and proportions of the tragedy could only be defined as genocide. From all this, a state emerged that was even more powerful and oppressive.[97]

The essential premise of the 'revolution from above' was a clear vision of relations between the Soviet Union and the other states. Stalin's central objective was the construction of a state based on a real economic and military force capable of facing up to the challenges of world politics and leaving behind, in a single leap, the vulnerability and marginality that had constricted Russia before and just after the Revolution. Hence his famous prophecy in 1931: 'We are fifty to a hundred years behind the advanced countries. We must make up for this backwardness in ten years. We shall either do it or be crushed.'[98] In November 1932, he declared to the Politburo that without rapid industrialization the USSR would be 'disarmed' by 'a capitalist encirclement armed to the teeth' and would become a subject territory like China.[99] This was not the Soviet Thermidor on which Trotsky reflected from exile—the umpteenth reference to the French Revolution.[100] It was, however, a decisive shift away from the original Bolshevik project, which Lenin himself had predicted at the end of the Civil War. Stalin was not renouncing world revolution; he was replacing the movement with the state as the revolutionary actor. He offered an alternative perspective of the original project for world revolution, a 'second revolution' in Russia which, like the first, would have an international dimension, but defined this time by power and the conflict between states. Bolsheviks believed, on the basis of their experience of power, that the process of state-building constituted the primary response to the 'international civil war' they considered the central feature of the period. The 'revolution from above' took place in the shadow of warfare, all the more so after the Japanese invasion of Manchuria in September 1931.[101] This was how Stalin expressed a central element of Bolshevik political culture and stirred up their 'animal spirits', indelibly marked by the Russian Civil War, which they saw as the archetypal conflict against imperialism.

The 'revolution from above' relaunched the myth of the USSR as a new civilization and a form of anti-capitalist modernity.[102] Still more than after the 1917 revolution, the regime's self-image asserted itself as the basis for the myth. The standardization of communist jargon speeded up, thus increasing the gulf between image and reality. The propaganda machine depicted, in ever more garish colours, the stereotype of a capitalist world in decline and a socialist world on the rise. The faded and frustrating image of the NEP and 'backward socialism' was swept away

---

[97] N. Werth, 'Uno stato contro il suo popolo', in S. Courtois, N. Werth, et al., *Il libro nero del comunismo: crimini, terrore, repressione* (Milan: Mondadori, 1998), 136–56. See also A. Graziosi, *L'URSS di Lenin e di Stalin: storia dell'Unione sovietica, 1914–1945* (Bologna: il Mulino, 2007), 362.

[98] Stalin, *Sochineniya*, vol. 13, p. 39.

[99] *Stenogrammy zasedanii Politburo*, vol. 3: *1928–1938*, 584.

[100] L. Trotsky, *La mia vita* (Milan: Mondadori, 1930), 489.

[101] PBKI, doc. 404, pp. 645–6; L. Samuelson, 'Wartime perspectives and economic planning: Tukhachevsky and the military-industrial complex, 1925–1937', in Pons and Romano, *Russia in the Age of Wars*.

[102] S. Kotkin, 'Modern times: the Soviet Union and the interwar conjuncture', *Kritika: Explorations in Russian and Eurasian History* 1.2 (2001).

by the inspiring and promising one of rapidly building a socialist society without compromises. The mass mobilization for the purpose of industrialization and the promotion of young people in the party-state apparatus were part of a 'cultural revolution' that restored egalitarianism, collectivism, and heroism. The utopia of 'new man', which went back to the early years of the Revolution, became state policy that aimed at the authoritarian construction of social conscience using the instruments of political pedagogy and self-criticism.

For all communists both in the USSR and outside, the events of the early 1920s constituted a stirring confirmation of an unchallengeable truth: reeling from the crisis of 1929, capitalism was destined to sink further into chaos and mass pauperisation, whereas the 'construction of socialism' in the USSR offered the only credible alternative. The contemporary 'collapse' of the capitalist economy heralded revolutionary opportunities in the West, just as the growth of the planned economy would turn the USSR into the powerful midwife of a new era. This reproduced a mechanism that went right back of the origins of the revolutionary state: the lack of domestic consensus was compensated for by the spread of the myth outside Soviet Russia. Driven by political commitment but also swept along by the great Soviet transformation, intellectuals of such calibre as Paul Nizan and Bertolt Brecht supported communism in the shared opinion that above all it constituted an existential dimension and a vision of the world. Brecht perhaps provided the popular exposition of the communist ethos by presenting it as the conscious and painful acceptance of harshness and mercilessness that would open the way to a new humanism: a vision on which the generation of post-revolutionary communists modelled themselves.[103]

In 1932, Arthur Rosenberg, one of the first historians of Bolshevism and a former German communist in the tradition of Luxemburg, noted that the 'secret force' of the link between the Soviet Union and the communist movement consisted in the 'proletarian socialist mythology' and the support this ensured abroad.[104] Rosenberg wrongly believed that this 'mythology' had run its course and would go into rapid decline. The profound connection between the socialist state and the spread of the Soviet myth beyond its borders, which was generated by the international ambitions of the Bolsheviks, would soon have a new lease of life. Unlike what had happened in Europe ten years earlier, the Soviet myth was more organized and less spontaneous. The task of influencing international public opinion and moulding a positive image of the Soviet Union abroad was systematically implemented, and created an unequalled cultural diplomacy by instituting a system of encounters with observers and Western visitors.[105] Partly because of this, the Soviet myth proved to have an attraction that went beyond the communist movement, which was its principal vehicle. For some, the expectation of a 'normalization' of the Soviet state, already encouraged by the introduction of the NEP, was once more

---

[103] E. J. Hobsbawm, *Anni interessanti: autobiografia di uno storico* (Milan: Rizzoli, 2002), 159–60.
[104] A. Rosenberg, *Storia del bolscevismo* (Florence: Sansoni, 1969).
[105] M. David-Fox, *Showcasing the Great Experiment: Cultural Diplomacy and Western Visitors to the Soviet Union, 1921–1941* (Oxford: Oxford University Press, 2012).

confirmed by the image of a regime dedicated to the concrete tasks of economic development and no longer motivated by subversive ambitions, although not yet on the road to restoring the primacy of traditional imperial views. For others, the 'alternative modernity' of Bolshevism was acquiring credibility in view of the hardships and pessimism caused by the grave depression of the world economy. The breakthrough in overcoming backwardness, the planned economy, and the aim of social modernization were for Western public opinion more reassuring features than the evocation of Jacobinism.

The idea that this opened the way to a 'new civilization'—the expression used by the Fabian socialists Sidney and Beatrice Webb—was not the product of particularly naive intellects.[106] It captured the imagination of many intellectuals, seduced not by Bolshevism's radical solutions to the consequences of the First World War but by its simplistic interpretation of the postwar period focused upon the division between bourgeois society—in decay or even anti-modern in its fascistic forms—and a new socialist society—an alternative civilization. Indeed, Stalinism proved capable of expanding the potential audience for Soviet mythology and convincing European intellectuals who were strangers to the Marxist tradition but susceptible to the idea of actually building a socialist society.[107] This empathy gave rise to the so-called 'fellow travellers'.[108] The separateness of the Soviet world helped to strengthen the mythologies, even though the information on what was really happening in the USSR was circulating in Europe and was much more detailed than it had been in the Civil War. The persistence of the myth revealed a willingness to give credence to the USSR, which was deeply rooted in another stubborn idea—the belief that the Great War had caused a crisis of civilization that was destined to bring unpredictable outcomes. This fostered a basic psychological mechanism: the propensity to believe in the possibility of creating a society that was the reverse of those characteristics considered, rightly or wrongly, the most intolerable of the capitalist societies of the time. The convergence between the propensity and the seductive attraction of the privileged relationship with the USSR blinded many travellers, although their motivations and political orientations differed considerably.[109] Thus the Soviet myth could hide and even overturn the reality of mass violence inflicted in time of peace.

In the context of the Soviet 'revolution from above' and its mythic influences on the West, the Comintern moved on to ultra-radical positions because the economic crisis of capitalism appeared to be promising new opportunities for revolutionaries.

---

[106] S. Webb and B. Webb, *Soviet Communism: A New Civilization?* (London: Longman, 1935). See K. Morgan, *The Webbs and Soviet Communism*, vol. 2: *Bolshevism and the British Left* (London: Lawrence & Wishart, 2006).

[107] F. Furet, *Il passato di un'illusione: l'idea comunista nel XX secolo* (Milan: Mondadori, 1995), 177–84.

[108] M. Flores, *L'immagine dell'URSS: l'occidente e la Russia di Stalin (1927–1956)* (Milan: il Saggiatore, 1990), 147–51.

[109] David-Fox, *Showcasing the Great Experiment*, ch. 6. See also P. Hollander, *Pellegrini politici: intellettuali occidentali in Unione Sovietica, Cina e Cuba* (Bologna: il Mulino, 1988), ch. 4; R. Mazuy, *Croire plutôt que voir? Voyages en Russie soviétique* (Paris: Odile Jacob, 2002).

The clash of 'class against class' was at the centre of the directives sent out to the communist parties. Social democracy was labelled 'social fascism'. Following the phase of movement and the phase of stabilization in postwar Europe, there came a 'third period' which would be typified by crisis and revolutions. In reality, the solution based on continuity with the previous political line was not so clear and obvious. The vocabulary that accompanied the radical shift in the communist movement's policy had been formulated previously, and was linked to the very definition of communist identity. The association of social democracy with fascism went back to the phraseology used by Zinoviev and Stalin in 1924. The intensification of class conflict in the capitalist world had been theorized by Bukharin in 1926. The slogan 'class against class' had been coined by Jules Humbert-Droz, one of Bukharin's closest collaborators in the Comintern in 1927.[110] Leaving aside the language used, the 'Bolshevization' of the communist parties had come to mean enforcing discipline and loyalty to their leaderships, which were largely dependent on the alignment within Moscow's political struggles. This had not always prevented the extremist and sectarian drift that had been the original trademark of the communist parties. The conflict with the opposition had the paradoxical effect of shifting the majority to more radical positions for fear of being delegitimized. When Stalin decided to assume control of the Comintern and remove Bukharin, his orientation followed this logic.

Ten years after their creation, the European communist parties were still struggling to become political entities capable of putting down roots in their national realities. Their financial and organizational dependency on the Muscovite headquarters was the premise that determined their activity.[111] Leading party cadres were mainly trained and indoctrinated in Moscow, where they learnt propaganda methods, mass mobilization techniques, and ideological fundamentals. Their attendance at meetings of the Comintern's central bodies was an important distinction in their curricula vitae. They were monitored by records held in Moscow. Their autobiographies in particular were an instrument for identification and uniformity, edifying and bureaucratic texts modelled on increasingly standardized parameters.[112] From the early 1930s, cadres in the Comintern and its national sections were widely subject to institutionalized practices of a pedagogic and normative nature, which were parallel to and replaced those implemented in their respective national communities. Such practices extended to invasive forms of constructing a person's identity, especially through the precept of self-criticism.[113]

No less 'international' were the political culture, terminologies, and networks that defined the political spaces and distinctions on which a communist's identity and sense of belonging were based. For communists, the mass politics that

[110] McDermott and Agnew, *The Comintern*, 73.

[111] Vatlin, *Komintern: idei, resheniya, sudby*, 134–5.

[112] C. Pennetier and B. Pudal (eds), *Autobiographies, autocritiques, aveux dans le monde communiste* (Paris: Belin, 2002).

[113] B. Studer, 'Liquidate the errors or liquidate the person? Stalinist Party practices as techniques of the self', in B. Studer and H. Haumann (eds), *Stalinist Subjects: Individual and System in the Soviet Union and the Comintern, 1929–1953* (Zurich: Chronos, 2006), 197–216.

emerged from the First World War signified above all the discovery of a transnational dimension. Their vocabulary and their idea of modernity presupposed this dimension. The 'party of world revolution' emerged to all intents and purposes as an 'international community', a network of relations which could count on only limited numbers but which covered the globe. Not surprisingly, more discerning communists in the 1920s posed the problem of a national 'translation' of their political language. However, this path was taken by very few. One example was the ruling group of the Italian Communist Party centred on Gramsci; they attempted to graft the idea Lenin developed late in life of an 'alliance' between workers and peasants onto the historical dualism of the Italian nation, divided between the industrial north and the rural south. Italians communists were imbued with a degree of sensitivity towards a nation's specificity by the very fact that they had to deal with the fascist regime then being put in place, but their political practice continued to be largely informed by the extremism and sectarianism that typified all European communists.[114] Besides, when the Italian Communist Party was forced underground in 1926, its influence became negligible in the context of the communist movement.

The German Communist Party was in fact the model mass party that acted as the main conduit of the communist 'international community'—a bridge between Moscow and the rest of Europe. Following the insurrectionist period, 1919–23, German communism had not consolidated its foundations among working people in employment, the great majority of whom remained loyal to social democracy. Its mass base was recruited amongst the unemployed and the marginalized, and its theatre of action was in the streets rather than the factories. Participation in electoral campaigns was perceived more as an opportunity to mobilize support than to open up a political space in the republic. Luxemburg's original classist and anti-bourgeois vocation had been superimposed with a Soviet imprint that forged a militarist, elitist, and voluntarist ethos.[115] German communists constituted an 'imagined community' that felt excluded from the body of the German nation, and produced its own subculture made up of its own rituals and symbols, largely imitating the Soviet ones.[116] The German Communist Party thus represented the first model of communism in a European democracy. It was a Bolshevized model that managed to keep in tune with both social malcontent and nationalist sentiment against the system of Versailles, and fostered an anti-institutional outlook, while failing to penetrate society.

The German national context appeared to strengthen the original vocation of the German Communist Party, whose radicalism was constantly nurtured by a situation in which social democracy took the majority position in parliament and

[114] G. Berti, *I primi dieci anni di vita del Pci: documenti inediti dell'archivio Angelo Tasca* (Milan: Feltrinelli, 1967).

[115] E. D. Weitz, *Creating German Communism, 1890–1990: From Popular Protests to Socialist State* (Princeton, N.J.: Princeton University Press, 1997), 159.

[116] C. Epstein, *The Last Revolutionaries: German Communists and Their Century* (Cambridge, Mass.: Harvard University Press, 2003), 42–3. For French communism, see S. Coeuré, *La grande lueur à l'Est: les Français et l'Union soviétique 1917–1939* (Paris: Seuil, 1999), 113–19.

the trade unions, as well as having governmental functions and being identified with the defence of the state. Hostility towards the policies of order and security adopted by the social democrats since the birth of the Weimar Republic ended up affecting welfare policies, thus pushing the communists into extremist positions.[117] However, interpretations based exclusively on national sociopolitical matters are decidedly restricted. German communism was in fact distinguished, more than anything else, by the aspiration to become the successor to Russian Bolshevism. In this sense, there was continuity between the Spartacist uprising of 1919 and the attempted coup of 1923, even though the former was organized autonomously and the latter by Moscow. The failed insurrections of the early 1920s left an indelible mark of political radicalism and subversion. At the same time, they accentuated the dependency of the German communists on Moscow. Their demands for autonomy were always accompanied by a revival of internationalist positions, and not by decisions of a national character. The group led by Fischer and Maslow, which attracted the most intransigent left, was fostered by Zinoviev rather than even entertaining the possibility of an international opposition and an attack on the bureaucratization of the Comintern. Thälmann's leadership was even more dependent on Moscow. When Stalin orchestrated an attack on the German 'right' in his conflict with Bukharin, the party found itself in the eye of a storm of purges. Its cadres experienced alternation of policies. The launch of the 'social fascist' label and the split from the reformist trade unions exalted the traditional anti-social-democratic radicalism of the German Communist Party, and constituted in many ways its high point by predicting the impact of the economic crisis that affected Germany with particular virulence. The contrast between the KPD and SPD was further fuelled by the increasing gap between the world of the trade unions and the social democratic workers on the one hand and the communist unemployed on the other.[118] While radicalization fed off demands triggered in Berlin, its primary source was Moscow. If anything, the KPD acted as an outrider.

The elimination of the opposition in USSR provoked a spiral of conformism and falling back in line. At the end of the 1920s, the era of critical communists, such as Luxemburg and her followers, or the philosophers Karl Korsch and György Lukács, both intent upon stemming the drift towards the positivism and dogmatism of Soviet Marxism, was over, never to return. The fall of Bukharin completed the process. The ultra-radical change of tack imposed by Stalin disoriented many communists moulded by 'Bolshevization' and loyal to the majority of the Soviet party. Removal and expulsion of leaders charged with 'right-wing deviation' were the order of the day, and brought to a close the purges that for some time had been directed against the opponents on the left. Amongst the well-known victims this time were such figures as the German Heinrich Brandler, the Indian M. N. Roy, the Americans Jay Lovestone and Bertram Wolfe, and the Argentine José Penelón. A new generation of young leaders and functionaries were promoted into

---

[117] Weitz, *Creating German Communism*, 130.
[118] Weber, *La trasformazione del comunismo tedesco*, 228–32, 295.

the governing bodies of the Comintern and its national sections on the basis of blind loyalty to Moscow. Ironically, it was precisely through this changeover of personnel that 'Bolshevization' was successfully completed, if it is seen as a process of rendering the leading groups totally loyal and erasing the social democratic memory of single individuals.[119]

All the communist parties adapted. Even the most reluctant leaders had to bow their heads. Gramsci's successor at the head of the Italian Communist Party, Togliatti, was one of these. He busied himself with the expulsion of 'right-wing' elements, including Tasca, who along with Humbert-Droz had drawn a personal attack from Stalin for having denounced the latter's monopoly of power as a 'counter-revolution'.[120] Togliatti did however invoke the right to a mental reservation over the 'social fascism' line, which was particularly incongruous for a party struggling against Mussolini's regime.[121] His attitude demonstrated how open dissent had disappeared in the communist world, and had been replaced by oppressive conformism or, at the most, dissembling more suited to members of a religious order. The primacy of loyalty to the Soviet state took precedence over judgements concerning the appropriateness of political decisions—a transformation that emerged in the 1920s and was now complete.

Stalin had often proved unwilling to support communists' revolutionary dreams, and was sceptical of the results of their actions. He considered the communist movement to be a political instrument, but doubted its efficacy in supporting the interests of the Soviet state, which he saw as better defended by the propagation of its myth. Consequently he separated the catastrophist vision of capitalism, with which he had held trust even during the period of the so-called 'stabilization', from faith in the revolutionary movement. He never gave any sign of harbouring such faith in a measure comparable to that of Lenin's other successors. His scepticism brought about political change following the defeat of the Chinese communists. In his vision, the revolutionary state, rather than the movement, would be the instigator and beneficiary of the future collapse of the capitalist system. At the end of the 1920s, this distinction became crucial. It gave rise to an ultra-radical rhetoric prophesying the imminent collapse of capitalism. But what actually happened was a downgrading of the Comintern's role in the political priorities of the USSR. It is revealing that Stalin never became the head of the Comintern, leaving this task to Molotov. The era in which all the principal Bolshevik leaders took part in the International's activities and the supervision of the communist parties was now definitively over. The Russian leadership of the Comintern grouped around Molotov was considerably different. The figures who emerged or acquired greater

---

[119] M. Worley (ed.), *In Search of Revolution: International Communist Parties in the Third Period* (London: I. B. Tauris, 2004); N. Laporte, K. Morgan, and M. Worley (eds), *Bolshevism, Stalinism and the Comintern: Perspectives on Stalinization, 1917–53* (Basingstoke: Palgrave Macmillan, 2008).

[120] Vatlin, *Komintern: idei, resheniya, sudby*, 243–45; J. Humbert-Droz, *L'Internazionale comunista tra Lenin and Stalin: memorie di un protagonista 1891–1941* (Milan: Feltrinelli, 1974), 226–56; J. Humbert-Droz, *Il contrasto tra l'Internazionale e il PCI 1922–1928: documenti inediti dell'archivio di Jules Humbert-Droz, segretario dell'Internazionale comunista* (Milan: Feltrinelli, 1969).

[121] A. Agosti, *Palmiro Togliatti* (Turin: Utet, 1996), 126–9.

power had previously carried out primarily organizational roles, such as Pyatnitsky, Dmitry Manuilsky, Otto Kuusinen, and Solomon Lozovsky.[122]

The Comintern's activities took on an even more conspiratorial flavour. The directives aimed at restricting the prerogative of the Comintern's emissaries in their relations with the Soviet embassies became more severe. In April 1928, leaders of the party and Soviet diplomats were prohibited from appearing in the activities of foreign communist parties.[123] Consequences of the domestic crisis in 1928 included a substantial curtailing of political initiatives abroad and the decision to pursue self-isolation. Chicherin's repeated remonstrances against the campaigns over the 'threat of war', which weakened the USSR's international role, were ignored.[124] The traditional dualism between the Narkomindel and the Comintern was therefore resolved by Stalin, in that he lessened the importance of both institutions in defining the interests of the state. There perhaps emerged a similarity in the decision-making processes on domestic issues and those on international ones. Just as the gigantic and violent socio-economic modernization was launched without taking into consideration the needs of the population and the resources of the country in pursuance of visionary and teleological aims, so also the interests of the state were defined by Stalin through a combination of realism and ideology, the primacy of power politics, and the myth of 'socialist power'.

Seen in this light, the radical drive forced on the communist movement was deceitful and misleading. It was not in fact a relaunch of the world revolution, but a footnote in the struggle for succession in the USSR and a consequence of the same apocalyptic predictions that accompanied the emergence of Stalin's statism. The main test-bed of Stalin's policy was supposed to be Germany, and it turned out to be a complete disaster. The impact of the economic depression produced a considerable increase in membership for the German Communist Party. Alone amongst the European communist parties, the KPD could count on about 300,000 activists and in 1932 reached almost 6 million votes, corresponding to 17 per cent of the electorate. This success was believed to result from their anti-social-democratic line, which was maintained in spite of the spread of radical nationalism. The political line of the KPD and the Comintern determined a fundamental underestimation of the National-Socialist threat. Thälmann's political discourse from 1929 established a link between 'social fascism' and preparation for a war against the USSR.[125] Moscow's directives vacillated between two options. In July 1930 the Soviet leaders asked the German communists to fight energetically against the National Socialists.[126] A year later however, the Comintern inspired the

---

[122] McDermott and Agnew, *The Comintern*, 90–4.

[123] G. M. Adibekov, E. N. Shakhnazarova, and K. K. Shirinya, *Organizatsionnaya struktura Kominterna 1919–1943* (Moscow: Rosspen, 1997), 133–4. On the organization of the conspiratorial section of the Komintern, see N. E. Rosenfeldt, *The 'Special' World: Stalin's Power Apparatus and the Soviet System's Secret Structures of Communication* (Copenhagen: Museum Tusculanum Press, University of Copenhagen, 2009), vol. 2, pp. 234ff.

[124] Di Biagio, *Coesistenza e isolazionismo*, 282–3.

[125] Weber, *La trasformazione del comunismo tedesco*, 236.

[126] PBKI, doc. 388, pp. 626–9.

communists' decision to support a referendum moved by the National Socialists against the social democratic government in Prussia.[127] In reality, as had occurred a decade earlier, the behaviour of the German communists was not entirely determined by directives from the centre. Many cases of anti-fascist unity did occur at local level. Disapproval of directives from above was not new in the lower echelons of the KPD, nor in other European communist parties, although the political implications could differ. But the conflict with the social democrats ended up taking precedence over resistance to the impetuous rise of the radical right, because the rejection of Weimar was stronger than the will to stem nationalism, and because it was believed that the collapse of the precarious equilibrium of the republic would open the way to a new revolutionary period. The German communists were pioneers in the application of the axiom that the worse things go, the more favourable the situation. Since 1930 they had been branding Weimar governments 'fascist', and by so doing they obscured the very real threat of National Socialism.[128]

Once again, the 'national Bolshevism' imagined by Radek years earlier found no real outlet and remained subordinate to the classist perspective.[129] But the fracture between communists and social democrats was sufficient to aggravate irreparably the division in the German workers' movement, and this would favour Hitler. Unlike 1923, however, the German communists did not even play the insurrection card. In spite of all the revolutionary rhetoric of the Comintern, such a decision was not in the interests of the USSR, which wanted to avoid war in Central Europe, as Manuilsky explicitly asserted at the Tenth Plenum of ECCI in March 1931.[130] The paramilitary organization in the KPD had its plans ready to assist the USSR in the event of war, but not for taking power.[131] There was no genuine rethinking of the theory of 'social fascism' in Moscow or Berlin even after Hitler's advent to power in March 1933. German communists distinguished themselves by becoming the first victims of the Nazi regime. The Soviets watched as the principal European communist party was destroyed without changing a comma of their own assertions. In December 1933, the Thirteenth Plenum of ECCI pointed once again to both fascism and social democracy as the enemies they had to fight against, and announced new revolutionary crises.[132]

Trotsky raised his voice from exile to rightly denounce the blindness of the theory of 'social fascism'.[133] He glossed over the fact that this theory was the product of the anti-reformist mentality nurtured by all Bolsheviks, himself included, but he hit the mark when he claimed that in the order of Stalin's priorities the revolutionary movement had been moved down a step or two. The point is not

[127] *Komintern protiv fashizma: dokumenty* (Moscow: Nauka, 1999), doc. 70, p. 272.
[128] PBKI, doc. 412, pp. 666–7; N. Laporte, 'Presenting a crisis as an oppportunity: the KPD and the Third Period, 1929–1933', in Worley, *In Search of Revolution*.
[129] Weitz, *Creating German Communism*, 249.
[130] McDermott and Agnew, *The Comintern*, 97.
[131] Weber, *La trasformazione del comunismo tedesco*, 356ff.
[132] *Komintern protiv fashizma*, doc. 87, pp. 309–20.
[133] L. Trotsky, *Scritti 1929–1936* (Milan: Mondadori, 1968), 337–43.

simply that the Stalinist leadership imposed its own interests on the communist movement without thinking too much about the consequences; the disastrous German experience reveals a more subtle interaction, at least in Europe. For the KPD, the connection with the USSR was an insurmountable restriction on the consensus it could win, but also its strong point. This was what made it formidable and important, even if it was marginalized from the political game. Communist leaders turned the interests of the Soviet state into their own, believing that they could combine and adapt the requirements implicit in the line dictated by Moscow with their own vision of national politics. The myth of the revolutionary state had always occupied their minds, but whereas ten years earlier their fixed idea was to replicate the Bolshevik assault on the fortress of bourgeois power, now it was to take part in the USSR's 'war of position' with the capitalist world.

Basically German communists went towards their tragic destiny never doubting they were doing the right thing for themselves and the USSR, even if they were heading to a terrible defeat, as was probable. As Eric Hobsbawm, then a young activist in Berlin, recalls, the line taken by the KPD was 'a suicidal idiocy' but it was not only dictated by a lack of awareness. German communists did not realize that 'in 1932 the international communist movement was reduced to its historical low since the foundation of the Comintern', but they understood that they were in for a defeat: 'What we expected was not the drama of an insurrection, but that of a persecution', knowing that 'behind us stood the triumphant Soviet Union of the first five-year plan'.[134] Except in isolated cases, no profound doubts would surface in the communist movement for years to come. The primacy of the state over the movement was expressed not only through imposition of a political line but also through the introduction of the notion of the USSR's interests in the individual parties. This culture would survive the destruction of German communism.

COMMUNISTS AND ANTI-FASCISM

At the end of 1933, it was not difficult to draw up a balance sheet for the ultra-radical line that had distinguished Stalin's leadership. In Germany, the Communist Party no longer existed, and was no more than a miserable group of political refugees in Moscow. In the rest of Europe, anti-trade-union and anti-social-democratic policy had marginalized communists and exacerbated their minority status. In 1929, ten years after the foundation of the Comintern, communists outside the USSR counted half a million, but four years later their number had been drastically reduced (whereas the Soviet party was undergoing huge growth, doubling during the 'revolution from above' the 1.5 million members recorded at the end of the previous decade). In Czechoslovakia, the Communist Party lost a third of its members and its votes, although it had now become, following the collapse of the KPD, the largest of the European communist parties with almost 100,000 members. It

---

[134] Hobsbawm, *Anni interessanti*, 88–9.

was also the only party in Central and Eastern Europe that was operating legally. In France, the party fell to its lowest level of influence in the trade unions and lost half its members. In Great Britain, where it had always been marginal to national politics, it lost the relative strength it had gained amongst the miners, especially during the strike of 1926. Communist parties were well organized but they constituted a ghetto in the European political panorama, in spite of the parallel crisis of social democratic parties which culminated in the destruction of the SPD.[135] The legitimization of communism in Europe was entirely entrusted to the myth of the 'construction of socialism' in the USSR. It would be the development of anti-fascism on an international scale, in response to the rise of Hitler, that would give a new lease of life to the movement. The discipline, the cult of organization, and the propensity for conspiracy provided communists with the particular skills of adaptability and combativeness required to face the growing fascist-inspired forces in Europe.

This development, however, took place in relation to the interests of the Soviet state. At the end of the 'revolution from above', the USSR had constructed the industrial and military foundations for it to take on the role of a great power. But the illusion that it could isolate itself from the rest of the world and proceed with the 'construction of socialism' unaffected by the great crisis of the 1930s faded. Hitler's arrival on the scene constituted a challenge of such magnitude that it marked a sudden change in the way the external threat was perceived. The Bolshevik vision of the 'European civil war' had now become a reality, but the gravity of the threat cast doubt on the suitability of the isolationism pursued in previous years to ensure the security of the USSR. For about a year, Stalin did not appear particularly concerned about the change to European politics brought about by Hitler. In his speech to the Seventeenth Congress of the Soviet party in January 1934, he limited himself to dramatizing the traditional prediction of war as the inevitable result of the capitalist crisis. In his opinion, another 1914 was imminent. The war would once more trigger revolution, this time putting at risk 'the very existence of capitalism', particularly if it were to be directed against the USSR, because it would then be fought 'not only on the fronts, but also behind the enemy's lines'.[136] The warning was principally a rhetorical one which did not provide a precise scenario for the world revolution. Stalin grandiloquently reasserted the autarkic concept of state security: 'We were not oriented towards Germany, nor are we today towards Poland and towards France. In the past we were oriented and currently we are still oriented towards the USSR and solely towards the USSR.'[137] Bukharin was the only Bolshevik leader who genuinely pointed out the danger threatened by Nazism, but by then he was completely marginalized.[138]

---

[135] For an overview of the various parties, see Worley, *In Search of Revolution*. For the crisis of social democracy, see Rapone, *La socialdemocrazia europea tra le due guerre*, 233ff.

[136] Stalin, *Sochineniya*, vol. 13, p. 297.   [137] Ibid. p. 302.

[138] *XVII s'ezd vsesoyuznoy kommunisticheskoy partii (b) 26 yanvarya–10 fevralya 1934 g. Stenograficheskii otchet* (Moscow: Partizdat, 1934), 127–8.

Nevertheless the USSR shifted its foreign policy in an attempt at an agreement with the Western powers in the name of 'collective security', and this led within a few months to its joining the League of Nations in September 1934. Maxim Litvinov, Chicherin's successor, outlined the abandonment of traditional isolationism and adoption of an idea of security based on the political distinction between different states. A parallel reorientation took place in the communist movement. The first real lessons were drawn from the European events after February 1934, as a result of the bloody suppression inflicted by the authoritarian Dollfuss regime on social democratic workers in Vienna, and the united strike action to protest against the attempted coup by the fascist right in Paris. A policy review then made slow headway and was fostered by Georgi Dimitrov, the Bulgarian leader who emigrated after the failed insurrection of 1923 and the Comintern's emissary to Germany, who sought refuge in Moscow after having been tried for burning down the Reichstag in March 1933—an act probably perpetrated by the Nazis themselves. Dimitrov's energetic defence at the trial in Leipzig had turned him into a symbolic figure denouncing Hitler's regime. Stalin saw him as the personality who could tap into growing anti-fascist sentiments in European public opinion. He asked Dimitrov to take charge of the ruling group at their first meeting on 7 April 1934.[139] Shortly afterwards, Dimitrov joined the political secretariat and Presidium of ECCI. On 26 May, at Stalin's suggestion, the Politburo agreed an agenda for the next congress of the Comintern, in which the two main reports, one on fascism and one on the war, were entrusted to Dimitrov and Togliatti, relegating Manuilsky and Pyatnitsky to a secondary role.[140]

On 1 July 1934 Dimitrov sent Stalin a letter with the outline of the report to the Seventh Congress. This outline implied a criticism of the strategy followed in Weimar Germany, alluding to the fact that the interests of the communist movement should now be identified with the defence of democracy and not its subversion. However, this kind of self-criticism could never be uttered. Stalin imposed specific restrictions on the rapprochement with social democracy.[141] Within these restrictions, Dimitrov was encouraged to continue his work. In October, the Political Commission of ECCI invited French communists to build on their own unitary policies, which had been launched in the summer, and to create an anti-fascist 'workers' coalition'.[142] In reality, the affirmation of the new anti-fascist line did not come smoothly, and was challenged by part of the leading group of the Comintern in late 1934 and early 1935, using the argument that the connection between war and revolution should remain the watershed between communism and social democracy.[143] In spite of this, Stalin proposed the appointment

---

[139] G. Dimitrov, *Diario: gli anni di Mosca (1934–1945)*, ed. S. Pons (Turin: Einaudi, 2002), 11–14.

[140] PBKI, doc. 438, pp. 701–3.

[141] A. Dallin and F. I. Firsov (eds), *Dimitrov and Stalin 1934–1943: Letters from the Soviet Archives* (New Haven, Conn.: Yale University Press, 2000), doc. 1, pp. 13–14.

[142] KIMR, doc. 209, pp. 848–51.

[143] RGASPI, fo. 495, op. 4, d. 384: E. H. Carr, *The Twilight of the Komintern, 1930–1935* (London: Macmillan, 1982), 403–27.

of Dimitrov to secretary general of the Comintern.[144] Thus there appeared to be a genuine attempt to expunge the sectarianism that had been the distinguishing feature of communist parties not only after 1929 but throughout their history. The Manichean reading of the postwar situation gave way to a search for social and political alliances. Educated by Bolsheviks to indifference to or contempt for liberal democracy, communists ended up being called on to defend it. Anti-fascism opened up an inconsistency within communist political culture, even though this was not immediately obvious.

Dimitrov's report to the Seventh Congress provided a view of the 'capitalist world' that emphasized, rather than denied, how different fascism's state structure and mass was from 'bourgeois democracy'. The 'principal enemy' was fascism and no longer social democracy. The task for communists became the creation of 'popular fronts' and the unity of anti-fascist forces to constitute a government 'before the Soviet Revolution'. Dimitrov appealed for the communist parties to become 'a political factor in the life of their countries'.[145] He implicitly acknowledged that this had not been the experience of the communist movement until the mid-1930s. The 'turning point' thus postulated contained two strategic elements: the formulation of the communist movement's transitional political objectives, and the definition of the Comintern not simply as a propaganda tool for the defence of the USSR, but also as an organization promoting an active policy in support of 'collective security'. The association of fascism with the danger of war put aside, at least potentially, the idea of an undifferentiated imperialism.

Dimitrov's review had very few precedents in the history of the Comintern. Bukharin's intuitions on fascism as a mass phenomenon had never really been developed, with the exception of the Italian communists in the second half of the 1920s. Togliatti in particular had attempted to formulate a more sophisticated analysis than the prescribed interpretation that simply identified fascism as a form of bourgeois government, suggesting that the mass authoritarian regime in Italy could constitute a model for the most advanced capitalist countries in Europe as well.[146] Now these ideas were emerging from the marginal circles to which they had been relegated, and were combining with the political decision to resist the expansion of fascism. The 'struggle for peace' was back at the centre of communist policy, after having been eliminated for many years. The difference from the previous decade was that the anti-fascist option strengthened the objective of preventing war. If the fascistization of Europe was not inevitable, as Dimitrov argued, then neither was the success of the Hitler's plans for war. Togliatti's report also rejected the fatalism and passivity associated with classist determinism. In other words, Dimitrov and Togliatti presented anti-fascism as a form of political realism that did not pose the immediate objective of the 'dictatorship of the proletariat', and

[144] Dallin and Firsov, *Dimitrov and Stalin 1934–1943*, 23; PBKI, doc. 454, pp. 722–3.
[145] F. De Felice, *Fascismo, democrazia, fronte popolare: il movimento comunista alla svolta del VII Congresso dell'Internazionale* (Bari: De Donato, 1973).
[146] Togliatti, *Sul fascismo*.

rejected the idea that international crisis triggered by Nazi Germany was necessarily the prelude to a repeat of 1914.

The slogans of the 'struggle for peace' and the 'popular front' could undermine the theory that war was inevitable and the idea of the uniqueness of the state created by Bolshevism. Yet from the very beginning neither review would be properly implemented. The contradictions within Dimitrov's and Togliatti's political discourse were very clear and irresolvable. The distinction between fascism and capitalism did not disprove classist axioms, and the slogan 'struggle for peace' did not challenge the doctrine of imperialism. The analysis of the international situation, based on 'capitalist contradictions', left little room for the objective of containing the risk of war, entrusted to the temporary convergence of the USSR's interests with those of a few capitalist states such as France. The idea that the future would lead ineluctably to a second cycle of revolutions and wars remained a constraint incompatible with the possibility of presenting the 'struggle for peace' as a prospect suited to revolutionaries.[147] Consequently, the possibility of formulating democratic objectives in a manner that did not involve orchestration was very limited. As had occurred with Bukharin a decade earlier, the ideas of political revision in international communism were conditioned by Lenin's doctrine of imperialism. The dramatic change called for by Dimitrov and Togliatti revealed insuperable restrictions on the decisive questions of state, war, and peace.

Dimitrov's and Togliatti's reports were viewed favourably by Stalin in a letter to Molotov.[148] It was clear, however, that this judgement meant approval not only of the anti-fascist line but also of the restrictions on what it could say. Stalin approved the decision to limit the new strategy to a change in tactics, thus avoiding emphasis on breaks with the past. His political horizons were dominated not so much by strategic imperatives as by short-term ones, such as the need for allies in Western countries and the postponement of war for as long as possible. On 1 March 1936 he publicly declared that the 'enemies of peace' in Europe were capable of starting a war.[149] Immediately afterwards, the crisis provoked by the Nazi remilitarization of the Rhineland could have demonstrated that his words contained a sudden injection of political realism, but equally they could have favoured the opposite, the persistence of an orthodox mentality. At ECCI, Dimitrov and Togliatti appealed for political realism, arguing that the role of the Comintern could not be restricted to propaganda to defend the USSR from the Nazi threat, and that communists had to mobilize for peace in Europe. But the debate in the ruling group revealed the influence of more traditionalist positions and the fragility of the changes introduced by the Seventh Congress, concluding with a vague warning of the 'danger of war'.[150]

---

[147] G. Procacci, 'La "lotta per la pace" nel socialismo internazionale alla vigilia della Seconda guerra mondiale', in *Storia del marxismo*, vol. 3, part 2 (Turin: Einaudi, 1981), pp. 578–82.

[148] *Pis'ma Stalina Molotovu*, 252.

[149] I. V. Stalin, *Works [Sochineniya]*, ed. R. McNeal (3 vols, Stanford, Calif.: Hoover Institution, 1967), vol. 1 [14], pp. 118–19.

[150] RGASPI, fo. 495, op. 73, d. 12; fo. 495, op. 60, d. 216.

By adopting the anti-fascist option, the Comintern was in step with the foreign policy of the USSR. The communist movement's search for political allies accompanied the creation of new relations with the Western democracies, such as the agreements between the USSR and France and the USSR and Czechoslovakia in May 1935. A year later, when the Popular Front triumphed at the elections and the government presided over by Léon Blum was established in Paris with the support of the communist deputies in Parliament, the joint action of the Comintern and Narkomindel appeared to crown with success the change in Moscow's foreign policy. Whereas no synergy between Moscow's alliance with Berlin and the KPD's policy was ever achieved in Germany in the 1920s, in the late 1930s in France there appeared to be a new consistency between the USSR's foreign policy and the PCF's national conversion. However, as Jonathan Haslam has noted, the pact with France did not fully replace the tradition that went back to Rapallo.[151] In the international situation in the second half of the 1930s, the dogma that war was inevitable kept open the alternative to the combination between anti-fascism and 'collective security'—an alternative based on the association between anti-imperialism and unilateral security. The traditional Bolshevik hostility to the Versailles settlement and the undifferentiated view of capitalist countries had never gone away. The 'struggle for peace' related to the defence of the USSR and the necessity of deflecting the threat of a new widespread conflict, destined soon or later to flare up. It would be the principal compass by which Stalin planned his route in the years to come.[152]

The true test-bed of anti-fascism was the war in Spain. The outbreak of the Civil War in July 1936 was immediately seen as the opportunity for a mass anti-fascist mobilization, which up to that point had never really been promoted, merely invoked. For about two years, the Comintern put Spain at the centre of its own initiatives. When the International Brigades—the voluntary anti-fascist formations that rushed to defend the republic against the nationalist rebellion—were set up, the link between communism and anti-fascism appeared to become so strong that it constituted a new identity: of course one could be anti-fascist without being a communist, but it was difficult to see how the two could be inverted. At the same time, Moscow, overturning its policy in Germany at the beginning of the decade, called on Spanish communists to moderate their social and political aims, and identify them with the defence of the democratic republic. A few days after the beginning of the nationalist sedition against the legitimate government born of the electoral victory of the Popular Front, Dimitrov submitted to Stalin the directives to be sent to Spanish communists, which appealed to the task of 'not going beyond the struggle for a democratic republic', and received his approval.[153] On the same day, he declared to the secretariat of ECCI: 'in this phase we cannot put forward the task of creating soviets and establishing the dictatorship of the proletariat in Spain.'[154]

[151] J. Haslam, 'Litvinov, Stalin, and the road not taken', in G. Gorodetsky (ed.), *Soviet Foreign Policy 1917–1991* (London: Macmillan, 1994).

[152] S. Pons, *Stalin and the Inevitable War* (London: Frank Cass, 2002).

[153] Dallin and Firsov, *Dimitrov and Stalin 1934–1943*, doc. 8, p. 46.

[154] *Komintern i grazhdanskaya voyna v Ispanii* (Moscow: Nauka, 2001), doc. 30, pp. 110–13.

This orientation would be a foundation stone of communist policy. In September and October 1936 Dimitrov and Togliatti proposed the idea of an 'anti-fascist state' and 'a new kind of democracy' as a transitional regime towards socialism in an attempt to underpin communist anti-fascism.[155] This idea would not last long, but it would resurface at the end of the Second World War. However innovative it sounded, it was also vague, and its actual meaning was never clarified. Anti-fascist democracy never took on the mantle of an alternative to the Soviet model. Indeed, it was perceived by communists as a transitional regime towards that model, implicitly taken as the final objective. Anti-fascist tendencies emerged as a political change lacking any basis for a genuine conceptual and cultural revision. An indicative case was that of Pieck, who followed in the wake of Dimitrov and Togliatti on the distinction between fascism and capitalism. In February 1937, while arguing with the Comintern's official economist, Yevgeny Varga, Pieck claimed in the ECCI secretariat that Nazism was 'a force independent of' German financial capital and that the persistent portrayal of Hitler as 'an element lacking responsibility' would make it impossible to promote real anti-fascist movement.[156] This declaration was by no means taken for granted, in spite of developments over the last two years, all the more so given that it was made when German communists were in the eye of the storm of Stalinist purges. But basing communist policy on such a view would have meant revising doctrine, which was something impossible and intolerable in Stalin's USSR.

Anti-fascism modified the old unresolved problem of the 'translatability' of terminology and experience from Russia to Europe, because it presented a different paradigm—an adjustment that required drawing on cultures and language largely repressed and demonized. As Geoff Eley has observed, the Popular Front redefined socialism as the highest form of old progressive traditions and not as their implacable opponent.[157] The criticism of determinism that equated class politics with war contained an allusion to the Marxist tradition, which tended to explain away the original polarization between Wilsonism and Leninism. That allusion was not articulated in a coherent manner capable of modifying the dominant paradigms and conventions. These were overlaid with statements made by Stalin and others close to him. In this sense, the role of Dimitrov and other communists committed to anti-fascism has been exaggerated by many historians.[158] Not only was their position subordinate to the international communist hierarchy, but their arguments never involved a fundamental innovation of the existing political culture. Thus communist anti-fascism ended up with a schizophrenic disposition: on the one hand, a new political vocation and even a new identity superimposed on the old one, and on the other, a manipulative concept that did not redefine the original identity.

---

[155] RGASPI, fo. 495, op. 18, d. 1135.

[156] *Komintern protiv fashizma*, doc. 114, p. 445.

[157] G. Eley, *Forging Democracy: The History of the Left in Europe, 1850–2000* (Oxford: Oxford University Press, 2002), 266.

[158] See the critical assessment in McDermott and Agnew, *The Comintern*, 132–3.

The war in Spain broke the apparent harmony between the policy of popular fronts and that of 'collective security'. In spite of the instructions regarding a moderate line issued to the communist parties, the Comintern and the Narkomindel found themselves once more on a collision course, just as they had in the 1920s. The Comintern prioritized the anti-fascist mass mobilization, which presupposed a refusal to sacrifice the Spanish struggle at the altar of diplomatic agreements, particularly in the light of the 'non-intervention' pact signed by the European powers and the USSR. The Narkomindel went down the road of consolidating international alliances, which presupposed the search for an agreement with Great Britain and France over what should be done with Spain. Both orientations had to give some ground. Stalin decided to commence an undeclared intervention in Spain in support of the republic through the dispatch of arms and military advisers in order to thwart the open support of the fascist powers, without however abandoning the non-intervention pact. This was a twin policy, dictated by a desire to keep his hands free and not to bind himself to onerous commitments in terms either of his agreements with the Western democracies or of international ideological challenges. It was precisely this attitude that appears to have weakened communist anti-fascism—a process which rapidly became irreversible. As late as the end of 1936 and mid-1937, in the wake of the Soviet decision to intervene in the war, Dimitrov aimed to obtain recognition of the international nature of the conflict in Spain, as he was convinced that a republican victory would enhance the prestige of communists and anti-fascist forces in Europe. This position contrasted with that of Litvinov, who believed the intervention had to be terminated in order to re-establish the conditions for a credible diplomatic initiative by the USSR.[159]

As he had done in the 1920s, Stalin would not fully back either the Narkomindel or the Comintern. He chose a third option, which avoided prioritizing the Spanish question one way or the other: to maintain the regional nature of the conflict and avoid it coming to a rapid and unfavourable conclusion, which would have shifted the epicentre of the international crisis to a part of Europe more crucial to Moscow's interests. An early signal of this orientation appears in a conversation he had with Dimitrov, André Marty, and Togliatti in March 1937. Stalin considered the possibility of disbanding the International Brigades in the event of an agreement with the European powers on the withdrawal of foreign forces from Spain.[160] This increased his opinion that he had to maintain his initial cautious rejection of any kind of radicalization of the conflict in Spain. The aim of Spanish communists was to be that of increasing their influence over government bodies and the army, especially after the fall of Largo Caballero and his replacement by Juan Negrín in May 1937. Thus conflict with the radical elements of the republican alignment became inevitable, while the republic's international isolation continued.[161]

The Spanish Communist Party was the linchpin of the armed republic and became a mass party during the Civil War. In spite of Stalin's deviousness, this

---

[159] Pons, *Stalin and the Inevitable War*, 57, 62, 70.   [160] Dimitrov, *Diario*, 72.
[161] G. Ranzato, *L'eclissi della democrazia: la guerra civile spagnola e le sue origini 1931–1939* (Turin: Bollati Boringhieri, 2004), 467–70.

brought about a process of 'Sovietization' of the republic's institutions. Although it is not clear whether there was a clear intention of creating a Soviet-type regime, the constant endeavours by communists to take control of the republic's destiny, which they saw as the only guarantee of victory, were in some ways a precursor of what would happen in the 'people's democracies' after the Second World War.[162] In the short term, this undoubtedly helped to divide and weaken the anti-fascist camp. In July 1937, Togliatti was sent to Spain as a Comintern plenipotentiary with a mandate to rein in the radical urges and consolidate the position of the Spanish Communist Party in the republic's state apparatus and army. He became the principal political adviser to the Spanish communists and came into conflict with other Comintern emissaries, primarily Codovilla, who were considered abrupt and unwilling to uphold the image of a communist party dedicated to alliances in keeping with the popular front policy.[163] Soviet disengagement from Spain started in the second half of 1937, and this would inevitably compromise the republic's solidarity campaign and the Comintern's appeal to internationalist militancy.[164] Dimitrov never ceased to press for aid and military assistance.[165] But the USSR was not willing to expose itself in the Spanish theatre of war as it had in the early months of the Civil War, and certainly not more than that.

The gradual Soviet disengagement from Spain was probably linked to the alarm provoked by the Japanese invasion of China in the summer of 1937. Here, the popular front policy was much more controversial than in Europe and the tension between the centre and the periphery was more evident. Following the ruinous defeat of 1927, Chinese communists had followed a strategy of military consolidation and building up their base among the peasantry, particularly in the south of the country. This unusual combination turned them into a communist organization *sui generis*. At the same time, the conflict with the nationalists had never ceased and had in fact reignited to the point that in the autumn of 1934, the communists were obliged to abandon their main territorial stronghold, the Soviet established in the southern region of Jiangxi. This led to the emergence of the leadership of Mao Zedong, a provincial intellectual of humble origins who had distinguished himself as a political and military commander by reorganizing their forces for rural guerrilla warfare. Under his guidance, over 100,000 Chinese communists undertook the Long March, which made it possible for the survivors—fewer than 10,000—to move to the safer territories in the northwest of the country and there consolidate the uniquely rural nature of the party. Mao asserted his own line by defeating the leaders more closely tied to Comintern orthodoxy and the 'urban

---

[162] For the transformation of the PCE during the Civil War, see T. Rees, 'The highpoint of Comintern influence? The Communist Party and the Civil War in Spain', in T. Rees and A. Thorpe (eds), *International Communism and the Communist International* (Manchester: Manchester University Press, 1998).

[163] RGASPI, fo. 495, op. 74, d. 201. *Komintern i grazhdanskaya voyna v Ispanii*, doc. 53, p. 305. See A. Elorza and M. Bizcarrondo, *Queridos camaradas: la Internacional Comunista y España, 1919–1939* (Barcelona: Planeta, 1999), 398.

[164] E. H. Carr, *The Comintern and the Spanish Civil War* (London: Macmillan, 1984), 50.

[165] Dallin and Firsov, *Dimitrov and Stalin 1934–1943*, docs. 11, 12, 13, 14, pp. 73ff.

strategy', and benefited from the setbacks suffered by his main rival over military strategy, Zhang Guotao. The Chinese Communist Party was able to push through its organization and military plan in time to confront the twin struggle against the Japanese and the Nationalists.[166] The only communist party provided with a direct link to Dimitrov's secretariat, the CCP, together with the Spanish Communist Party, would receive the greatest attention from Moscow.

Very soon, however, a disagreement arose between the Comintern and the CCP concerning the application of the popular front policy. The Chinese communists wished to fight the nationalist forces of Chiang Kai-shek no less than the Japanese invaders. Dimitrov judged this tendency to be politically mistaken, and demanded that they collaborate with the Guomindang. On 27 July 1936, he prepared a directive on the application of the anti-Japanese 'national front' and submitted it to Stalin, who ruled in its favour.[167] Mao yielded to the ECCI directive, which was issued on 15 August.[168] On various other occasions, Dimitrov requested Stalin's intervention to consolidate the policy of national unity in China.[169] In effect, the Chinese communists followed the moderate line suggested by Moscow when it came to economic and social policy, and this allowed them to gain ground in rural society without making any decisive move towards an alliance with the nationalists. The question was never really resolved even after the Japanese invasion. In November 1937, when there was a real danger of conflict between the USSR and the Japanese armies, Stalin stated the tasks of Chinese communists in the 'national revolution'—not the social revolution—and in the war against the Japanese side by side with the other national forces.[170] Mao came into line and thus managed to marginalize his main challenger, Wang Ming, who had been sent back to China by the Comintern after a long stay in the USSR.[171] However Moscow's exhortations did not entirely convince the Chinese communists. All the protagonists remembered all too clearly the Shanghai massacre in 1927. The mutual distrust between communists and nationalists had not been rectified, but Stalin had never declared any regrets about his decisions at the time, and continued to consider them fundamentally correct. He would have relied much more on the Red Army than on the role of deterrence played by Chinese communists to contain Japanese aggression along the eastern borders of the USSR in 1938 and 1939.[172]

Stalin was sceptical about the prospects of the communist movement. The position of the Comintern within the Soviet system had been devalued, in spite of the

---

[166] Saich, *The Rise to Power of the Chinese Communist Party*, section E.

[167] Dallin and Firsov, *Dimitrov and Stalin 1934–1943*, doc. 18, pp. 101–5.

[168] *Vkp(b), Komintern i Kitay: dokumenty*, vol. 4, part 2 (Moscow: Rosspen, 2003), doc. 380, pp. 1067–71; M. M. Sheng, *Battling Western Imperialism: Mao, Stalin, and the United States* (Princeton, N.J.: Princeton University Press, 1997), 34–5.

[169] Dimitrov, *Diario*, 56, 64 (16 Dec. 1936, 19 Jan. 1937); *Vkp(b), Komintern i Kitay*, vol. 4, part 2, doc. 386, pp. 1084–5.

[170] Dimitrov, *Diario*, 82–4.

[171] F. C. Teiwes, *The Formation of the Maoist Leadership* (London: Contemporary China Institute, 1994); *Vkp(b), Komintern i Kitay: dokumenty*, vol. 5 (Moscow: Rosspen, 2007), doc. 25.

[172] J. Haslam, *The Soviet Union and the Threat from the East, 1933–1941: Moscow, Tokyo and the Prelude to the Pacific War* (London: Macmillan, 1992).

political relaunch at the Seventh Congress. Its ruling group was no longer identified with the highest levels of power. The leaders of the ECCI were, as they always
had been, a centralized oligarchy in charge of the directives governing international
communism through its own bodies. But the substance of these ruling bodies
would progressively weaken after 1936, particularly in the case of the Executive
Committee. The ECCI constituted a section, which had permanent contacts with
the other branches of the Soviet bureaucracy only at executive level, particularly
with the political police. On the other hand, it had only an intermittent channel of communication with the central core of power, in which Stalin exerted his
personal authority in an absolute manner, depriving even the Politburo of most of
its power. In the Stalinist regime, decisions were made more on the basis of infor-
mal encounters and personal relations than through the exercise of institutional
procedures. There was no genuine mediation between the operational experience
of the state apparatus and the policy making process, except perhaps through the
personal whim of the leaders and the unfathomable sphere of their relationships.[173]

The Comintern's apparatus was a machine of huge dimensions, which for over
a decade extended its activity and its tentacles over a geopolitical scenario that was
more or less global. The network of emissaries unleashed almost everywhere, financial and organizational support for national parties, links and exchanges of cadres
and militants between the centre and the periphery, between European parties and
those of the colonial empires, constituted an enviable global reach for any other
political movement of the time. The Comintern bureaucracy reflected this dimension in its internal bodies, with departments for different parts of the world and
for the national 'sections'. The reorganization that followed the Seventh Congress
enlarged the territorial model adopted in the mid-1920s, and set up ten secretari-
ats whose activities ranged from Europe to Latin America, from the Far East to
Southeast Asia, and from the Middle East to South Africa, which led to even closer
links between the ECCI leadership and the leaderships of the individual parties.[174]
However, this landscape of very different communist parties was typified more
by limitations and fragility than by strongholds, particularly outside Europe, but
even more so in the old continent after the destruction of the KPD. The parties
expanded their memberships with anti-fascist recruits, but their capabilities for
mass mobilizations were not commensurate with the ambitions of their political
rhetoric. Moreover, as demonstrated by the Chinese example, the disagreements,
tensions, and interactions between the directives from the centre and the orientations of the periphery remained an unresolved problem, which occasionally spilled
over into hidden conflicts. The hierarchical chain of command and the discipline
of local communists were unarguable, but the relationship between the centre and
periphery did not correspond to the image of a pyramid.[175]

---

[173] O. Khlevniuk, *Master of the House: Stalin and his Inner Circle* (Stanford, Calif./New Haven,
Conn.: Hoover Institution, Stanford University/Yale University Press, 2009).

[174] Adibekov et al., *Organizatsionnaya struktura Kominterna*, 189–90.

[175] M. Narinsky and J. Rojahn (eds), *Centre and Periphery: The History of the Comintern in the Light
of New Documents* (Amsterdam: International Institute of Social History, 1996).

THE TOTAL-SECURITY STATE

Stalin had not waited for the alarming international scenario that emerged in the summer of 1937, which was much more serious than the 'danger of war' a decade earlier, before manifesting his own manic insecurity. The consequences of the war in Spain were already considerable. He perceived Franco's rebellion and the military intervention by the fascist powers as a model of aggression that could strike at the USSR as well, or even as a test run for an attack on the Soviet Union. The spectre that the Bolsheviks had always feared, and which Stalin had talked up at the end of the 1920s—the combination of an internal uprising and an armed intervention from abroad was now even more threatening. For the despot, the annihilation of the peasantry carried through by collectivization had not eliminated this scenario. The social isolation of the regime was in fact making it more probable. The difficulties in stabilizing the system were exacerbated by the assassination of Sergey Kirov, the party leader in Leningrad, on 1 December 1934. Perhaps driven by emulation of Hitler and his 'night of the long knives', Stalin exploited this event to launch the first campaign to persecute the opposition. However, it was the war in Spain that evoked the threat of a 'fifth column' that could subvert the regime from inside by preparing or favouring an international intervention. Stalin both suffered from this phantasm and exploited it by triggering the terror that struck the Soviet elites in the summer of 1936. This attack on the elites culminated in May and June 1937 with the liquidation of Marshal Tukhachevsky and the most important leaders of the Red Army. Immediately afterwards—commencing in July 1937, while the international situation continued to deteriorate—the Terror spread and became a mass phenomenon that affected society and many of the national minorities.[176] While 'collective security' and anti-fascism appeared to be bringing about a revision of isolationism and sectarianism, the perceived threat was in fact translating into a further exacerbation of the police state and a new wave of violence.

The anti-fascist conversion of the communist movement corresponded to a change in the domestic climate in the USSR. As the gigantic and violent transformation, the 'revolution from above', had now been completed, the ideological mobilization of the militant, working-class nucleus of the 'socialist offensive' could disappear definitively from the scene. The trajectory of Bolshevism's original drive to power changed direction, but it did not vanish. The regime's official propaganda started to exalt patriotic, puritanical, and sexist values, and at the same time made a great play of the myth of social unity and the end of class divisions as the fulfilment of the revolution. A selective re-evaluation of Russia's past, a manipulation of nationalism, and a decline in the internationalist ethic came to the fore. Family values were revived to promote demographic policies and impose social discipline. The transformative power of the state continued to be exalted, along with its role

---

[176] O. Khlevniuk, 'The reasons for the Great Terror: the foreign-political aspect', in Pons and Romano, *Russia in the Age of Wars*, 159–69.

in purifying the body politic of alien elements on the road to a harmonious society. The Soviet state retained its ambition to remould society and provide a modern response to mass politics, but it redirected its work decisively towards preparation for war and the unification of the social conscience.[177]

The cult of power became the key factor. Stalin indirectly but eloquently proposed that members of the Politburo should rehabilitate Russia's power politics. On 19 July 1934, he sent them a document in which he criticized Engels for his tendency to distinguish between Tsarist Russia and bourgeois Germany.[178] He reasserted the validity of the Leninist theory of imperialism and the undifferentiated view of capitalist powers, while also revealing his own conversion to the idea of a rebirth of Russian power. State idolatry and a vision of the world inherited from Lenin were combined. With the proclamation of 'socialism achieved', the old distinction between 'two worlds' had to be conserved in a new form. From the regime's point of view, the socialist state was founded on the 'political and moral unity' of society, whereas capitalist states continued to act under the impulse of 'class interests'. The regime amplified as much as it could the traditional agitation concerning the external threat, using this as a form of blackmail to consolidate the 'total-security state' and mobilize society, thus obscuring the fragility of the system, as even the political elites were aware. In accordance with a mechanism already experienced in the past, the image of the USSR evolved in a manner entirely different from that of its internal reality. The universalist rhetoric of the Soviet state was relaunched when the 1936 Constitution came into force, and presented the USSR as a bulwark of peace and Enlightenment values threatened by fascism and irredeemably lost by bourgeois and liberal civilization. This image asserted itself very effectively in line with the inability of the Western democracies to challenge the rise of Hitler with any vitality. Soviet propaganda obscured the substantial difference between the struggle against Hitler based on irreconcilable principles and opposition to the Nazi totalitarian regime based on a mirror image of the physiognomy of power. However, in the climate of suspicion, violence, and xenophobia of the great purges, anti-fascism came increasingly to be seen as a sin rather than a virtue, or even as an insidious agent of democratic contamination. Thus the anti-fascist image of the USSR contrasted with its internal political evolution.

Along with other institutions, the Comintern was fully involved in the Terror. Its leaders were both complicit in the repression and potential victims, exposed at all times to the mortal danger of falling into disgrace. Dimitrov was involved from the outset in the campaign begun in January 1935 on the lessons of vigilance to be drawn in the wake of the Kirov assassination.[179] The suspicion that the circles of political émigrés in the USSR were a pool for recruitment by foreign secret

---

[177] D. L. Hoffman, *Stalinist Values: The Cultural Norms of Soviet Modernity* (Ithaca, N.Y.: Cornell University Press, 2003).

[178] Stalin, *Works*, vol. 1, pp. 2–10.

[179] W. J. Chase, *Enemies within the Gates? The Comintern and the Stalinist Repression, 1934–1939* (New Haven, Conn.: Yale University Press, 2001), doc. 5, pp. 96–8.

services gradually but inevitably made the Comintern a target for purges. The deadly inquiries by the NKVD were initiated in the first half of 1936, primarily with the support of Manuilsky.[180] The first threatening accusation against a whole community of political émigrés would strike at the German Communist Party in September 1936, immediately after the first Moscow trial against Zinoviev and Kamenev.[181] In December 1936, the head of the NKVD, Nikolay Yezhov, presented a secret Plenum of the party with the results of their 'investigations', which led to the second trial and the indictment of Bukharin and Rykov.[182] The ECCI secretariat issued a directive for communist parties on the results of the trial, which invited them to continue the anti-Trotskyist campaign.[183] But Stalin censured the resolution, calling it 'a piece of nonsense', because it did not adhere to the letter of the acts of the trial, and he accused the Comintern leaders of working 'in the enemy's interests'.[184] At the Plenum of the party in February and March of 1937, Stalin presented his dire assessment of the 'capitalist encirclement' as a virtual state of war.[185] At the same time, the persecutions took on an international dimension in Spain. The Comintern's campaign of repression against 'Trotskyist' organizations quickly intensified the divisions within the republican camp, which soon after culminated in a bloody suppression of the anarcho-syndicalist uprising in Barcelona and the assassination of Andrés Nin.[186]

The 'struggle against Trotskyism' soon affected the Comintern's headquarters. At one of his meetings with Yezhov, Dimitrov noted down that 'the worst spies have worked for the Communist International'.[187] The organization was affected so deeply that in October 1937, Dimitrov and Manuilsky complained in a letter to Andrey Zhdanov about their lack of cadres, who could no longer be recruited, as they had in the past, from among the political émigrés.[188] In November 1937, Stalin personally listed for Dimitrov the 'spies' in the ruling group of the Comintern, who included long-term leaders such as Pyatnitsky, Knorin, and Kun. On the same occasion, Stalin celebrated the continuity between the Tsarist state and the Soviet one by threatening that anyone who challenged the unity of the state was an enemy to be annihilated in accordance with a veritable process of extermination: 'We will destroy every enemy of this kind, even if he is an old Bolshevik; we will destroy his breed, his family. We will pitilessly destroy whoever it is with his actions and his thoughts (yes, even his thoughts) in our care for the unity of the socialist state.'[189] In a conversation with Dimitrov held a few days later, Stalin revealed that he was convinced of the existence of a plot hatched at the time of the collectivization of

[180] PBKI, doc. 460, pp. 728–31.
[181] Chase, *Enemies within the Gates?*, doc. 17, pp. 163–74.　　　[182] Dimitrov, *Diario*, 53.
[183] Chase, *Enemies within the Gates?*, doc. 26, pp. 202–3.　　　[184] Dimitrov, *Diario*, 67.
[185] Stalin, *Works*, vol. 1, pp. 194–5, 210.
[186] Elorza and Bizcarrondo, *Queridos camaradas*, 351ff.; S. Payne, *The Spanish Civil War, the Soviet Union, and Communism* (New Haven, Conn.: Yale University Press, 2004), 228–30; R. Radosh, M. R. Habeck, and G. Sevostianov (eds), *Spain Betrayed: The Soviet Union in the Spanish Civil War* (New Haven, Conn.: Yale University Press, 2001), docs 41, 42, 43, 44.
[187] Dimitrov, *Diario*, 77.　　　[188] Chase, *Enemies Within the Gates?*, doc. 36, pp. 283–4.
[189] Dimitrov, *Diario*, 80–2. See also V. A. Nevezhin, *Zastol'nye rechi Stalina: dokumenty i materialy* (Moscow: Airo-XX, 2003), 151.

the countryside, which aimed to overthrow the regime by exploiting a war between Germany and the USSR.[190]

Repression within the Comintern reached its peak with the purging of the entire leadership of the Polish Communist Party, which in reality was only the most visible provision of the physical liquidation of the tens of thousand of members of the Polish community in the USSR. On 28 November 1937, Dimitrov sent Stalin the secret ECCI resolution that disbanded the party, drawn up a few days earlier to ratify the NKVD purge. Stalin merely commented that 'the resolution was two years late'.[191] The dissolution of the Polish party was only formalized in August 1938. Dimitrov, Togliatti, and the other members of the ruling group of the Comintern took on the heavy responsibility for the mass purges—a fatal involvement, given that any other behaviour might have exposed them to the danger of being indicted as well, but revealed at the same time they broadly agreed with the logic of repression. It is probable that Dimitrov and others shared the cautious objections raised by Varga in a letter to Stalin after the third Moscow trial in March 1938, at which the accused were Bukharin and Rykov, on the counterproductive effects of the terror in international communist circles.[192] However, Dimitrov and the other Comintern leaders agreed with the basic motivations provided by Stalinist power to justify the terror: the threat of a war against the USSR and the need to destroy a 'fifth column' in the country. This psychosis was directed against many who had shared it and cultivated it.

While the purges were raging, the perceived decline of the Spanish Republic as Franco's armies advanced and the crisis of the Popular Front in France were a decisive blow to communist anti-fascism. Stalin suggested that Dimitrov withdraw communist participation in the Spanish government in order to weaken 'the international position of the Spanish republic' and to maintain the same position in France, where the communists had never joined the government.[193] The directive was not applied in Spain, where Togliatti's position prevailed. He did not think it opportune to force communists to neglect their responsibilities.[194] On 20 March 1938, after having consulted Stalin, Dimitrov notified French communists that Moscow was against their participation in the government of national unity, unless there was 'a state of war against fascist aggression'.[195] The strategy of anti-fascist alliances no longer appeared to be a decisive aspect of communist policy. Stalin's allusion to the need to improve relations with Great Britain by abandoning the inclusion of communists in the Spanish republican government put a realistic assessment of the international situation before any other consideration. The paradox was that Litvinov, the exponent of dialogue with London, found himself in

---

[190] Dimitrov, *Diario*, 85.

[191] Ibid. 87; Dallin and Firsov, *Dimitrov and Stalin 1934–1943*, doc. 4, pp. 28–31.

[192] PBKI, doc. 486, pp. 766–9. For the repressive measures taken against the community of political émigrés, see E. Dundovich, F. Gori, and E. Guercetti (eds), *Reflections on the Gulag* (Milan: Feltrinelli, 2003).

[193] Dimitrov, *Diario*, 89 (17 Feb. 1938).

[194] F. I. Firsov, *Sekretnye kody istorii Kominterna 1919–1943* (Moscow: Airo-XXI, 2007), 251–5.

[195] PBKI, doc. 485, pp. 765–6. Dallin and Firsov, *Dimitrov and Stalin 1934–1943*, 36–8.

a position of increasing political impotence. His foreign policy was considerably compromised by the USSR's withdrawal into isolationism. At the beginning of January 1938, he wrote his letter of resignation to Stalin, although the matter was not pursued.[196]

The USSR's passivity and self-marginalization from the turbulent European scene must have been confirmed by the outbreak of an even more dangerous crisis, caused by the Hitler's aggression against Czechoslovakia. Litvinov's appeals for 'collective security' were ignored by Western appeasers, but it is reasonable to doubt that Stalin was ready to adopt measures to deter Hitler. The Soviet military mobilization was real enough, but Litvinov himself complained that it wasn't backed up by an adequate warning to Hitler. The official Soviet position was still dependent on French intervention, as provided for in the agreements signed in 1935.[197] Even Dimitrov's anti-fascist appeals were shattered against the wall of Soviet passivity in August and September of 1938. His pleas were both numerous and ineffectual in achieving a mobilization in support of Czechoslovakia.[198] The USSR did not launch a mobilization comparable with the one two years earlier for Spain. The Munich agreement between Great Britain, France, Germany, and Italy over the break-up of Czechoslovakia was the definitive blow to any hopes of an anti-fascist mobilization in peacetime. In Moscow they predicted the formation of an alliance of fascist powers and Western powers—the 'united front' of capitalist countries that had always been the principal bugbear of the USSR and the communist movement.[199] Manuilsky proposed that they dump the policy of popular fronts and related 'pacifist delusions', and replace them by relaunching an ambivalent nationalist propaganda. Dimitrov, on the other hand, sent the Czechoslovak Communist Party a directive to maintain their links with democratic and socialist forces.[200] But the Czechoslovak Communist Party was by then a clandestine organization. In effect, Dimitrov was obliged to lower the flag of militant anti-fascism.

The Munich Conference was a crucial turning-point for Stalin's policy. The USSR's international isolation increased its sense of danger and fed the obsession that the Western powers had given Hitler a free hand in the east. It is probable that the decision to end the mass terror, which was taken by Stalin in the autumn of 1938, resulted from the Munich Conference and the need to close ranks now that war was imminent. For the despot and his purgers, terror was a preventative for war. This was the significance of the decision to destroy a potential 'fifth column' nesting within the state and to carry out ethnic-cleansing operations amongst entire national groups settled on the USSR's borders, because they were seen as a possible reservoir of infiltrations and espionage.[201] Terror was therefore linked for the entire period of its implementation to Stalin's notion of security, which was

---

[196] RGASPI, fo. 82, op. 2, d. 1036.
[197] Adibekov et al., *Politburo TsK Rkp(b)–Vkp(b) i Evropa*, doc. 271, p. 363.
[198] Dimitrov, *Diario*, 100–1, 108–9.
[199] Pons, *Stalin and the Inevitable War*, 227–8.   [200] Dimitrov, *Diario*, 133–7.
[201] T. Martin, *An Affirmative Action Empire: Nations and Nationalism in the Soviet Union, 1923–1939* (Ithaca, N.Y.: Cornell University Press, 2001), 335–41.

very closely associated with his perception of the international situation. Its end signified that it was no longer a matter of preparing for war but of confronting it.

THE MOLOTOV–RIBBENTROP PACT

In March 1939, the simultaneous fall of Madrid and Prague signified the disappearance of two democratic republics, while fascism expanded across Europe, and the end of the final hopes for anti-fascist mobilization. There were increasing signals of the Comintern's disorientation and irrelevance. Stalin expressed his barbed criticisms of Spanish communists and the Comintern leaders most directly involved in the Spanish struggle, whom he judged incapable of explaining to the masses the reality and reasons for the defeat.[202] On 20 April 1939, Dimitrov and Manuilsky sent him a letter asking whether or not French communists should maintain the line of 'collective security' and the Franco-Soviet Pact.[203] Only three days earlier, Litvinov had presented, with Stalin's consent, the Soviet proposal for an alliance between the USSR, Great Britain, and France, which appeared to mark the end of the divisions created by the Munich Conference, following the German invasion of Czechoslovakia and London's decision to offer its guarantees to Poland. Stalin sent Dimitrov to take a decision alone on the matter, demonstrating his disregard for the conduct of European communists.[204] But even Litvinov's diplomatic initiative, which the West treated with condescension, would be short-lived. On 3 May 1939, he was dismissed and replaced by Molotov at the head of the Narkomindel. This succession did not bring to an end negotiations between the USSR and France and Britain, but it certainly opened the way to negotiations with Germany, which were destined to result in the Molotov–Ribbentrop Pact in August 1939.

In the Stalinist ruling group, Molotov represented a foreign-policy position that had not given up on the idea of an agreement with Germany in the tradition of the relations between the two countries dating from the 1920s, in spite of the Nazi regime's anti-communism.[205] The British guarantee to Poland, which Litvinov had interpreted as a possible prelude to a tripartite alliance with the Western powers, was perceived by Stalin as an opportunity to drive a wedge between London and Berlin, and reach an agreement with Hitler. Shortly afterwards, actual negotiations were commenced with Nazi Germany in parallel with those ongoing with Great Britain and France. Stalin formulated a strategic vision that for the first time revealed the USSR's expansionist geopolitical objectives in Central and Eastern Europe. These objectives were up for discussion in Berlin, but not in London. The secret protocols of the non-aggression pact concluded between Stalin and Hitler on 23 August 1939 effectively provided for the partition of Poland and a Soviet sphere of influence in the Baltic. A week later Hitler could attack Poland and set

---

[202] Dimitrov, *Diario*, 166–7.
[203] Dallin and Firsov, *Dimitrov and Stalin 1934–1943*, doc. 7, pp. 40–3.
[204] Dimitrov, *Diario*, 171.   [205] Ibid. 179.

off the Second World War. On 17 September, while the German military machine was overrunning Poland's defences, the USSR invaded the eastern part of the country, as agreed in the pact. On 28 September, the USSR and Germany signed a Treaty of Friendship which sanctioned the partition of Poland and provided for a new partition of the spheres of influence, assigning Lithuania to Moscow, as well as Latvia and Estonia.

The object of interminable political and historiographical polemics, the pact was in fact the result of the political conduct that Stalin had been following for some years. It was not a foregone conclusion, but nor was it entirely unpredictable. Contrary to what has long been argued, the option of an alliance with Hitler was not the result of improvisation and necessity, after the Western powers had the USSR with its back to the wall through the Munich Agreement and after their lukewarm reaction to the Soviet proposal for a tripartite alliance in the spring of 1939.[206] This option had in fact been there as an alternative since 1936, and emerged as a concrete possibility only in May and June 1939, when the British guarantee to Poland was accompanied by the first real manifestation of Hitler's willingness to engage, now that he had decided to go to war with the Western powers. But it also appears unfounded to argue that Stalin saw the alliance with Germany as the principal objective of his foreign policy, and that the pact was the realization of this constant aim.[207] He chose instead to keep his hands free, keep the USSR out of involvement in the war, and ward off a combined military attack from Germany in the west and Japan in the east.

Munich reinforced his suspicion that a policy of firmness could prove risky and dangerous, by making the USSR a target for Hitler. The idea of 'collective security' was increasingly giving way to the idea of unilateral security, which had its roots in the psychosis of encirclement. The propensity to put all the capitalist powers on the same level did the rest. When the moment came for decision, Stalin was predisposed to one or other of the possible scenarios on the international chessboard, and in the end went for the more hazardous but also more remunerative solution in the geopolitical sense, because it guaranteed a space of territorial security considered crucial, should it come to future involvement in the war. Thus the idea emerged that an agreement with Hitler could constitute a strategic instrument for encouraging the mutual attrition of the imperialist powers and extending the USSR's influence in Eastern Europe.[208] In this sense the pact marked the beginning of a new phase in the history of the Soviet state and its international role.

Kept in the dark about the real direction of Soviet foreign policy, the Comintern's ruling group suddenly found itself having to deal with the abandonment of the anti-fascist line. Dimitrov submitted to the change out of a sense of discipline, after having futilely attempted to argue that the pact between the USSR and Nazi Germany did not mean a change of direction for the Comintern. However, the new Comintern line caused dismay and confusion even in the ruling group, as well

---

[206] G. Roberts, *The Soviet Union and the Origins of the Second World War: Russo-German Relations and the Road to War, 1933–1941* (London: Macmillan, 1995).
[207] Tucker, *Stalin in Power.*   [208] Pons, *Stalin and the Inevitable War.*

as in the European communist parties, as was entirely predictable. On 27 August, Dimitrov and Manuilsky asked Stalin directly for advice on the line to be taken, expressing their conviction that the French communists would have to maintain their own position of 'resistance to fascist Germany's aggression', while also defending the Russo-German Pact as 'an act of peace'.[209] Evidently their request was not granted. Immediately after the outbreak of war in Europe, Dimitrov wrote to Zhdanov to request a meeting with Stalin in order to resolve the 'exceptional difficulties' that the communist movement was encountering.[210] On 7 September, Stalin received Dimitrov at the Kremlin along with Molotov and Zhdanov, and outlined the new strategic direction in the light of the 'imperialist' nature of the war. Stalin explained that the prewar distinction between democracy and fascism was now a thing of the past, because the war was between two groups of imperialist countries, and therefore 'to remain today on yesterday's positions (unitary popular front, national unity) would signify slipping into bourgeois thinking'. Stalin confessed that he would have preferred an alliance with the British and the French, and chose the new strategy not for the alliance with Hitler as such, but because of the possibility of creating the conditions for a 'war of attrition' between capitalist states: 'It's not a bad thing if Germany is the means of shaking up the position of the richest capitalist countries (England in particular). Hitler is, unwittingly and without wanting it himself, upsetting and undermining the foundations of the capitalist system.'[211]

The next day, the secretariat of the Comintern issued a resolution that declared that there was no longer a distinction between democratic and fascist capitalist states.[212] Dimitrov sent a telegram to the leaders of the French Communist Party demanding that they reverse the line they had been following up to that moment.[213] However, the full conversion to the communist policy required time, and was carried out under the strict supervision of Stalin and his lieutenants. Only on 26 September did Dimitrov submit to Stalin, Molotov, and Zhdanov a plan for the war and for tasks to be carried out by the communists.[214] But on 17 October, Dimitrov was still writing to Stalin that 'confusion' reigned in the communist parties over 'the nature and the causes of the war'.[215] The ECCI Presidium discussed the 'errors' committed by parties arising from their tendency to denounce Hitler, and requested the purging of leaders and cadres who were responsible for this.[216] On 25 October Dimitrov met Stalin, who asked him to raise his voice against 'social democratic leaders' and declared that they needed to censure governments that were 'for the war' and not the governments that were 'for peace'—by

---

[209] Dallin and Firsov, *Dimitrov and Stalin 1934–1943*, doc. 27, p. 150.

[210] N. S. Lebedeva and M. M. Narinskii (eds), *Komintern i Vtoraya Mirovaya Voyna* (hereinafter KVMV) (2 vols, Moscow: Pamyatniki Istoricheskoy Misly, 1994–8), vol. 1, doc. 8, p. 88.

[211] Dimitrov, *Diario*, 194–5.   [212] Ibid. 195–6; KVMV, vol. 1, doc. 9, p. 89.

[213] B. H. Bayerlein et al., *Moscou–Paris–Berlin: télégrammes chiffrés du Komintern (1939–1941)* (Paris: Tallandier, 2003), doc. 12, pp. 74–5.

[214] KVMV, vol. 1, doc. 17, pp. 108–20.

[215] Dallin and Firsov, *Dimitrov and Stalin 1934–1943*, doc. 29, p. 164.

[216] KVMV, vol. 1, doc. 24, pp. 141–3.

which he meant Nazi Germany, which had launched a propaganda campaign for a peace agreement.[217] The text of Dimitrov's public declaration to clarify the situation was worked on until the end of October under the supervision of Stalin and Zhdanov.[218] Published at the beginning of November, the article decried the 'myth' of the anti-fascist nature of the war, which was attributed to the social democrats.[219]

The change of direction provoked bafflement and unease amongst European communists. French and British communists voted at the beginning of September in favour of war credits, but they soon had to adapt to the consequences of the new line, which put them on a collision course with the requirements of national defence.[220] However, the disorientation was not purely political. Deprived at a stroke of their anti-fascist identity, European communists were much more bewildered by the agreement with Hitler than by the Great Terror, which was much easier to justify in terms of revolutionary tradition and mythology. Cases of dissent within the communist rank and file during the Stalin's terror were very limited. The most notable episode was the defection of Willi Münzenberg—the architect of the Comintern's propaganda in Germany during the 1920s and the instigator of the anti-fascist myth of the USSR in France during the Popular Front period. In 1937, he abandoned the KPD and after the pact became a lone voice denouncing Stalin until he met his tragic end in the summer of 1940, in all probability at the hands of assassins working for the Soviet secret services.[221] The pact caused very serious disorientation. Humbert-Droz recalls that initially, many experienced it as a genuine betrayal.[222] In France, as Koestler observed at the time, communist militants were literally stunned for a period of time, and only pulled themselves together under pressure of the police measures taken against them by the government.[223]

If we consider the devastating impact of the event, what appears most significant is not so much the cases of perplexity and dissent as the restricted nature of their consequences. Of the more prominent members of European parties, dissidents like Gabriel Péri can be counted on the fingers of one hand. Even more exceptional was the case of Harry Pollitt, the general secretary of the Communist Party of Great Britain, who continued to invoke the anti-fascist line and was deposed by more orthodox exponents of his party, led by the Marxist theoretician R. Palme Dutt.[224] Communist loyalty to the USSR proved to be strong enough to take the blow. The appeal to anti-imperialism was sufficiently powerful, as it drew on a

---

[217] Dimitrov, *Diario*, 200–1.

[218] KVMV, vol. 1, doc. 31, p. 171; Dimitrov, *Diario*, 202.

[219] G. Dimitrov, 'Voyna i rabochii klass kapitalisticheskikh stran', *Kommunisticheskii Internatsional*, 1939, nn. 8 and 9.

[220] S. Courtois and M. Lazar, *Histoire du Parti communiste français* (Paris: PUF, 2000), 167–9; Thorpe, *The British Communist Party and Moscow*, 256–7.

[221] S. McMeekin, *The Red Millionaire: A Political Biography of Willi Münzenberg, Moscow's Secret Propaganda Tsar in the West 1917–1940* (New Haven, Conn.: Yale University Press, 2003), 295–307; S. Koch, *Double Lives: Stalin, Willi Münzenberg and the Seduction of the Intellectuals* (New York: Enigma Books, 2004).

[222] Humbert-Droz, *L'Internazionale comunista tra Lenin e Stalin*.

[223] A. Koestler, *Schiuma della terra* (Bologna: il Mulino, 1989), 70–1.

[224] Thorpe, *The British Communist Party and Moscow*, 260–1.

strong tradition, in spite of the fact that the change to an anti-Western line after the pact with Hitler left no credible path open to the communist movement. Its most conspicuous result was that it compromised all action by the leading communist party in Europe, the PCF, which the French government banned for its defeatist positions in September 1939. A few years after having set German communism on the path to destruction by Hitler, the policy of the Soviet state caused a rift in the only remaining European communist party of any importance.

Both laboratories of the popular-front policy were swept away in a matter of months—between March and September 1939. The Spanish Communist Party was the protagonist of anti-fascist militancy, but the French Communist Party was no less powerful. The main beneficiary of the change of direction towards anti-fascism in the middle of the decade, French communism had acquired a mass base, taking 15 per cent of the votes in May 1936 and with over 300,000 members in 1938, with a different line from that of the KPD during the Weimar Republic. It had not only been a force when it came to street agitation and militancy, but also in parliament, where it provided disciplined support for the Popular Front government. Of the European communist leaders, Maurice Thorez was the one who went furthest in the deployment of rhetoric modelled on national traditions but who was quite capable, at the same time, of exploiting the USSR's anti-fascist and progressive image.[225] Its deep working-class roots—both in the trade unions and in town councils—must have been the distinguishing feature of French communism, although the difficult balancing act between social demands and the pro-governmental orientation was shattered by the crisis of the Popular Front and the wave of strikes that followed.[226] In many ways, the PCF and the PCE had constituted two variants of a new model of European communism, following the demise of the KPD. An anti-fascist model was expressed in various ways: the PCF was identified with moderate national anti-fascism that aimed to build a mass base in society, and the PCE with internationalist, combatant anti-fascism that aimed at taking over the levers of power. Both the Spanish and the French experience provided an example for European communism after the Second World War, although only the French party would flourish again. By autumn 1939 nothing of those experiences remained. Defeat in the Civil War reduced Spanish communists to a flow of political refugees who mainly ended up in Moscow, where they were greeted with marginalization and suspicion. Their illegal status forced French communists to abandon their discovery of the nation, and they would soon number just a few thousand. From that moment until the end of the Second World War, the communist movement in Europe was largely made up of clandestine parties, whose leaders lived in the USSR or took part in illegal networks which two years later would merge into the resistance movements against Nazism.

Peacetime anti-fascism had foundered. Its emotional and militant motivation was not sufficient to create alternative traditions, values, and experiences, and to

---

[225] M. Lazar, *Le communisme: une passion française* (Paris: Perrin, 2005), 72; Coeuré, *La grande lueur à l'Est*, 264.

[226] Courtois and Lazar, *Histoire du Parti communiste français*, 135–61.

prevent the survival of stronger identities. The International Brigades for a while constituted the enthralling example of anti-fascist struggle, made up of romantic urges, transnational unity, and progressive and universalist symbols contrasting with the obscurantist night of clerical and fascist reaction. While the war in Spain did give a considerable impetus to unify anti-fascists, it did not eliminate their divisions. The export of Stalin's witch-hunts weakened the republican camp and communist credibility. The distinction between 'professional revolutionaries' and the plenipotentiaries sent by Soviet secret services turned out to be nonexistent— as demonstrated by the example of the Italian Vittorio Vidali, the 'Commander Carlos' of the Fifth Regiment of the International Brigades and a member of the Soviet Party who went to Spain after years of exile in the USSR and clandestine activities in the United States and Mexico.[227] The notion of unity with the other anti-fascist forces could never be fully accepted, as it risked unmasking the elitist and sectarian nature of the movement—forged in the climate of the Russian Revolution and the counter-revolution in Europe—which was no longer suited to the time and perhaps never had been. Stalin never gave any indication that anti-fascism was the mainstay of his politics. From the mid-1930s, he limited himself to abandoning the previous ultra-radical line and checking communist urges for social revolution. The pact with Hitler showed that Stalin had conceived anti-fascism as a tactical decision, taken because it served the interests of the Soviet state at a given historical moment, and abandoned in the light of those same interests a few years later.

During the Stalinist era, the communist political culture developed a combination of discipline, loyalty, and self-control which was much stricter than it had been in the previous decade, and impeded them from defining distinct and ultimately alternative viewpoints. Conflict followed more tortuous paths, often giving the appearance of tension between the periphery's tendency to interpret the centre's diktats with a margin of autonomy. It is not difficult to sense the recurring presence of this tension between the centre and the periphery over adherence by individual parties to Comintern directives, which were perceived as demonstrating insufficient understanding of the local reality.[228] Communists did not always follow requests from Moscow to show moderation. This was possibly because such requests were never presented as the consequence of a new strategy, but instead as a mere tactical opportunity. Moscow's change of attitude was not an insignificant matter, given that it was upheld in the face of the wars in Spain and China. Bolsheviks had held that civil wars were the natural terrain for revolution. Now Stalin was distinguishing between victory in the civil war and social revolution. This manifested a tendency towards the 'deradicalization' of communist policy, which was destined to assert itself more clearly during the Second World War. It made sense in the light of the existence of the Soviet state, but the interests of the state could be interpreted in different ways. The 'international civil war' was the

---

[227] D. Cattell, *Communism and the Spanish Civil War* (Berkeley, Calif.: University of California Press, 1955), 130–1; Radosh et al., *Spain Betrayed*, doc. 60.
[228] Dallin and Firsov, *Dimitrov and Stalin 1934–1943*, 61, 71–2.

principal concept governing the communist understanding of world politics. The 'deradicalization' of the movement would therefore remain a highly ambiguous tendency.

The communist movement might well have been an army racked with reluctance to show restraint, but nevertheless it was still an army. The Soviet state laid down for communists a line that was based not on any revolutionary prospect, but on the compatibility of their actions and the interests of the USSR. This outlook became the very nucleus of communist political culture. Immediately after the pact with Hitler, there was no change of direction towards revolutionary radicalism, even in their rhetoric. In November 1939, Stalin privately engaged in an impromptu critique of the Leninist slogan on the transformation of the world war into a civil war, arguing that this was relevant to Russia, but not to European countries, 'given that there the workers have obtained a few democratic reforms from the bourgeoisie to which they cling, and are therefore not prepared to go into a civil war (revolution) against the bourgeoisie'.[229] If the Bolsheviks' old revolutionary slogans were in any case unsuited to the First World War, this was all the more true of the Second World War. Stalin defined his own thoughts on world revolution in terms of his manipulation of the Bolshevik legacy and its role in Soviet power politics: 'World revolution as a single act is nonsense. It is taking place in different time and in different countries. The actions of the Red Army are also something that concerns world revolution.'[230]

The pact with Hitler was the international expression of the cult of power and state idolatry in the USSR. In 1937 and 1938, Stalin had declared his defence of the heritage of the Russian state against all the 'enemies of the people', intent upon destroying 'the power of the Soviet Union' by involving the country in a war and transforming it into a 'protectorate' subject to the great powers.[231] In March 1939, at the Eighteenth Party Congress, he publicly revised Marxist orthodoxy for his own purposes. In spite of the doctrines of Marx and Engels on its 'withering away', the consolidation of the state in the USSR was justified by the existence of a hostile 'capitalist encirclement'.[232] In the eyes of the Stalinist leadership, the Soviet state had by then acquired one feature that was impossible to express in the terminology of Marxist radicalism and the model of the 'dictatorship of the proletariat' adopted by the Bolsheviks. The culture and terminology most suited to identifying the characteristics of the new statism and patriotism were more easily defined in 'national Bolshevism'.[233] This invented tradition contained curious echoes of and analogies with modern European 'national socialism' going back to the beginning of the century: to extend socialism to an entire people as a community with the aim of suppressing social contradictions; exploiting nationalism as a method of creating social unity and a myth to mobilize society, which was capable

[229] Dimitrov, *Diario*, 203.   [230] Ibid. 212.

[231] RGASPI, fo. 558, op. 11, d. 1122; Dimitrov, *Diario*, 81.

[232] Stalin, *Works*, vol. 1, p. 395.

[233] D. Brandenberger, *National Bolshevism: Stalinist Mass Culture and the Formation of Modern Russian National Identity, 1931–1956* (Cambridge, Mass.: Harvard University Press, 2002).

of replacing the ideals of socialist transformation; and to transfer the class struggle from the social sphere to that of relations between national communities.[234]

These elements were not however assimilated to the point of determining a revision of communist identity. The external threat that Stalin invoked to justify the Soviet Leviathan was still perceived in class terms and under the lens of the Leninist theory of imperialism.[235] The regime's political culture was distilled into Stalin's handbook on the party's history published in 1938, the *Short Course* on the history of the Soviet party, a model of Marxist-Leninist orthodoxy, historical falsification, and the construction of Soviet mythologies, which was printed in millions of copies in all the principal languages of the world.[236] The censorship and selectivity of revolutionary history, which had long before emerged under the Stalinist regime, came together in what amounted to a standard procedure for the mutilation of memory. In the long term, this would rebound on future generations of communists, making it difficult for them to provide a credible narrative of themselves. But for the moment, Stalin's propaganda was effective. Up to his death, the *Short Course* would remain a fundamental teaching tool no less for communists outside the USSR than for those inside. In spite of the regime's patriotic rhetoric and xenophobia, the basic text for training communists was still addressed to an 'international community' rather than a national one, however that was defined.

The development of the USSR remained a process of state-building without nation-building. As had occurred in Tsarist Russia, the modernization of the Soviet Union did not favour—and in fact obstructed—the creation of a Russian national identity.[237] The Soviet state was not dedicated to the formation of a political community, but only to a hierarchical system of local, national, and imperial elites that were organized through the channels of a single party, personal and family ties, and networks of communist parties abroad. Stalinist political symbolism created an even wider chasm between the myth of the state and its 'actual constitution'. On the one hand, there was the rhetoric of social unity and socialist patriotism, and the cult of leadership and power.[238] On the other, there was a party-state that had developed organically since the Civil War into a bureaucratic monster dominated by administrative apparatus, propaganda, and security. It was a caricature of a political and governmental system lacking a recognizable structure and institutional framework, oppressive and arbitrary in the way it operated, unstable and riven by self-destructive tendencies.

At the end of the decade, Stalin's personality cult had reached its zenith in both the USSR and international communism. Within the restricted political elites that

---

[234] Z. Sternhell, *Nascita dell'ideologia fascista* (Milan: Baldini & Castoldi, 1993).

[235] For the continued presence of Marxism-Leninism in Stalin's thought, as a kind of 'revolutionary patriotism', see E. Van Ree, *The Political Thought of Joseph Stalin: A Study in Twentieth-Century Revolutionary Patriotism* (London: Routledge Curzon, 2002).

[236] F. Bettanin, *La fabbrica del mito: storia and politica nell'URSS staliniana* (Naples: Edizioni scientifiche italiane, 1996).

[237] G. Hosking, 'The state and Russian national identity', in L. Scales and O. Zimmer (eds), *Power and the Nation in European History* (Cambridge: Cambridge University Press, 2005).

[238] M. Y. Gefter, *Iz tekh i etikh let* (Moscow: Progress, 1991), 235–64.

surrounded him, he represented a supreme authority against which there was no appeal, and was by then identified with the state. To the wider mass of officials, militants, and followers, he appeared as the builder of socialist power and an infallible prophet. Was it not Stalin who had foreseen the devastating crisis of capitalism and the tendency of European bourgeois civilization to give increasing support to fascism? Had he not predicted the outbreak of a new war caused by the very contradictions within the capitalist world, and long prepared the Soviet Union to confront this threat by establishing the required military bases and eliminating potential traitors? Moreover, what could Stalin have done on the eve of the war, if not safeguard the Soviet state from the danger of a joint attack by imperialist states by exploiting their divisions, even at the cost of entering an agreement with the worst of his enemies? The reality was very different. Stalin's leadership had produced disastrous results. His coarse and dogmatic Marxism was based on a mechanistic and teleological vision of history that he had accentuated by eliminating any appeal to the subjective element in the original Bolshevik ideology. Stalin had raised expectations of a collapse of capitalism and a fatal degeneration of its structures—expectations that had proved to be fallacious and meaningless. He only perceived Nazism as an extreme manifestation of imperialist capitalism and a model of the decline of Western democracy. For him, the drift towards a new war was the inexorable result of blind forces that could be contained but never impeded. The fact was that the new war arose from the plans and actions of Hitler and Nazism, a phenomenon that Marxist-Leninists had neither predicted nor understood. Stalin had not realized that Hitler's anti-communism, which was based on a radical racist ideology and planned annihilation, had no place in the Bolshevik notion of the 'European civil war' as a political and class-based conflict.

At the end of the 1930s, the existence of a world hostile to the USSR was not the product of their imagination. Hitler's Germany dominated the European scene threateningly and had entered into an alliance with Fascist Italy. Anti-communist proclamations were an inherent part of Nazi politics and ideology. In the authoritarian states of Eastern and Central Europe, particularly Poland, Hungary, and Romania, anti-Soviet ideology was now part of the baggage of national identity.[239] British anti-communism had resulted in the appeasement of Hitler and thrived on the reports of terror in the USSR. In France, the Popular Front had constituted a brief exception, whereas in Spain communism together with the republic had been swept away by pro-fascist nationalism. The Catholic Church had blessed the revolt and Francoist violence as a just war. Japanese imperial expansion had provoked serious military clashes along the Soviet border. Anti-fascism was a minority phenomenon in European public opinion, which was influenced by the radical right of fascist inspiration. The war in Spain now constituted the main symbol of an 'international civil war'.[240] Seen from Moscow, anti-communism was showing a more extreme and threatening expression than it had done twenty years earlier

---

[239] For the Polish case, see B. Szlachta (ed.), *Polish Perspectives on Communism: An Anthology* (Lanham, Md.: Lexington Books, 2004).

[240] D. Diner, *Raccontare il Novecento: una storia politica* (Milan: Garzanti, 2001), 59–60.

at the end of the First World War. The Leninist concept of imperialism prevented communists from analysing the trends of the postwar years and formulating appropriate policies. The prophecy of war bolstered a syndrome of insecurity that would prove decisive in the development of the totalitarian state, which compromised the basis for national security with mass purges and favoured the delusion that new revolutionary crises were imminent.

At the same time, the protective shield of revolutionary myth had been weakened. Anti-fascism consolidated the prestige of the USSR, but the Terror tested it to the extreme. Even the intellectual advantage of anti-fascism, which had been consolidated around such figures as Henri Barbusse, Romain Rolland, André Malraux, and André Gide, was experiencing deep divisions in spite of the heroism of the war in Spain. In the second half of the 1930s, the first to be disappointed by communism withdrew their membership or support. Of the voices leaving the choir, the most important was probably that of Gide, who in November 1936 published a bitter and disillusioned account of his trip to the USSR, calling on others to distinguish between its image and its reality.[241] The influence of communist dissidents was widened by anti-Stalinism. Trotsky continued his lonely battle, and in particular denounced the grotesque fabrications of the Stalinist trials.[242] The purges of his and Bukharin's followers in the USSR and the communist parties had, however, created a considerable diaspora of left-wing dissidents, who knew the communist world from the inside and provided a particularly acute and devastating historical and intellectual critique of it, particularly when compared to the shameless lies of the *Short Course*. Rosenberg opened the way, and was followed by others, from the ex-Trotskyist Boris Souvarine, author in 1935 of the first biography of Stalin, and the German ex-communist Franz Borkenau, author of a merciless account of the Comintern's failures.[243] The pact could only open the eyes of many others and raise fundamental questions about the nature of the Stalinist regime.[244] After the summer of 1939, the authority and international legitimacy of the USSR, which was based on 'building socialism' and its anti-fascist arguments, risked disintegration.

Communists did not perceive the gravity of this danger. For them, the pact was explained by a vital necessity, the defence of the USSR. They saw the threat of Nazism and the war in Spain as a continuation of the 'European civil war', which found its most vivid expression in the atrocities on both war fronts. The idea that the conjunction of civil and inter-state conflicts and of national and social conflicts heralded another world war twenty years after the first one was widely held in anti-fascist circles. Otto Bauer, a leading European socialist leader, and

---

[241] A. Gide, *Ritorno dall'URSS seguito da Postille al mio ritorno dall'URSS (1936–1937)* (Turin: Bollati Boringhieri, 1988); Flores, *L'immagine dell'URSS*, 284–91.

[242] L. Trotsky, *The Revolution Betrayed* (New York: Doubleday, Doran, 1937).

[243] B. Souvarine, *Staline: aperçu historique du bolchévisme* (Paris: Plon, 1935); F. Borkenau, *The Communist International* (London: Faber and Faber, 1938).

[244] A. Koestler, *La scrittura invisibile: autobiografia 1932–1940* (Bologna: il Mulino, 1991), 457–9; W. D. Jones, *The Lost Debate: German Socialist Intellectuals and Totalitarianism* (Urbana: University of Illinois Press, 1999).

Karl Polanyi, a socialist intellectual, amongst many others, held this opinion.[245] Communists made this idea their own, adding the dogmatism of which they were capable. Even though their predictions of upheavals and collapse in the capitalist world proved to be profoundly mistaken, they were the prophets of doom par excellence in an era that it was difficult not to define as ill-starred and catastrophic. This contributed decisively to the preservation of their political culture. The outbreak of a new war in Europe retrospectively justified Stalin's response to their original revolutionary expectations, which was the construction of USSR as a great power. The Soviet state was no longer the protagonist of social change capable of catching imaginations and motivating minds, but it reigned over a society without class, while the capitalist world descended once more into chaos. Now that war was no longer a prophecy but a reality, the imperative of defending the USSR was sufficient to keep the movement alive, even if the resources thrown into the anti-fascist struggle had been wasted. The alliance with Hitler was a bitter pill to swallow, but the imminence of war cemented communist identification with the Soviet state. The very fact that the pact gave new life to the image of communists as 'agents of Moscow' was yet another cause for pride and loyalty.[246]

Communists were not aware of the tragedy and infamy that would be their destiny. Many had lost their lives as victims of Hitler, Franco, and the Japanese, while they associated their heroic dedication with the causes of liberty and liberation that continued the humanist and universalist ideals attributed to the October Revolution. But their sacrifice was above all made at the altar of another cause, that of a regime that had sullied itself with even worse crimes and concealed behind its myth a reality no less oppressive than that of Nazi Germany. Yet this painful reality affected few consciences. In the USSR, communists took on the twin role of persecutor and victim. In spite of this, many of those who suffered torture under the NKVD or experienced the Gulag maintained their own blind faith in revolution up to the very end, as Bukharin did in prison. The link with the USSR and the image of the 'international civil war' appeared to be stronger than any tragedy, because to their eyes these things expressed the realization and the guarantee of the project of a just society against an implacable enemy. This pivotal fact was all that remained after two decades of mass campaigns and terror, delusions and crimes, defeats and self-destruction.

[245] O. Bauer, *Tra due guerre mondiali? La crisi dell'economia mondiale, della democrazia e del socialismo* (Turin: Einaudi, 1979); K. Polanyi, *Europa 1937: guerre esterne e guerre civili* (Rome: Donzelli, 1995).

[246] Hobsbawm, *Anni interessanti*, 174–5.

3

Time of War (1939–1945)

We overestimated our forces when we set up the CI [Comintern] and we thought we could direct the movement in all countries. That was our mistake. The continued existence of the CI would discredit the idea of the international, something we don't want.... the communist parties that are members of the CI are falsely accused of being some kind of agents of a foreign state, and this impedes their work amongst the masses. With the dissolution of the CI, we take this card away from our enemies' hands.

Stalin to Dimitrov, 21 May 1943

The crisis of capitalism has manifested itself through the division of capitalists into two factions: the fascist one and the democratic one. There has been an alliance between us and the democratic faction of capitalists, because it was in the latter's interests not to allow Hitler's domination, given that this harsh domination would have led the working class to extreme solutions and the overthrow of capitalism itself. Now we are with one faction against the other, but in the future we will also be against this faction of capitalists.

Stalin to Dimitrov, January 1945

THE ALLIANCE WITH HITLER

Having been predicted in vain by the Bolsheviks since 1919, the collapse of the Treaty of Versailles came too late for their revolutionary dreams, but in time to exalt the Soviet state's role as a great power. This historic moment brought the birth of Stalin's power politics in the international arena. From the summer of 1939, he took on a visible role in foreign policy for the first time and formulated a doctrine of the USSR's interests based on the undifferentiated concept of the 'capitalist world' and the prospect of an 'international civil war'. Stalin's directives to his aides at the outbreak of the Second World War reveal that his pact with Nazi Germany was part of his own vision and a continuation of the 'war of position' that he had pragmatically embraced in the 1920s. His strategy was mainly based on the USSR's territorial security and the 'war of attrition' between capitalist powers. Stalin's appeasement of Hitler corresponded to the return of the orthodox anti-imperialist concept: the aim of avoiding involvement in the war and the attempt to gain the greatest possible advantage from the conflict between capitalist powers.

The pact also meant the mutual recognition of the Soviet and Nazi regimes. This bolstered interpretations aimed at putting the Soviet dictatorship on a par with the Nazi one, which had been previously developed by such figures of a liberal mindset as Simone Weil, Élie Halévy, Bertrand Russell, or such figures of a social-democratic one as Kautsky and Hilferding, but also by former communists, like Victor Serge. Analysis of the analogies between the two regimes made use of the concept of totalitarianism, which focused on the authoritarianism founded on the party-state, the organization of the masses, the systematic use of terror, and the role of the leader. Many took the alliance between the USSR and Nazi Germany to be a natural and revelatory development that demanded a judgement of the USSR that no longer feared compromising the anti-fascist struggle. Communist dissidents continued to exercise a leading role. It was in this climate of the pact that the Hungarian former communist Arthur Koestler published his novel *Darkness at Noon*, a denunciation of the blindly repressive and self-censuring mechanisms of the communist mentality, which would have an enormous success after the war. Borkenau, another former communist, was amongst the first to use the concept of totalitarianism as the key to comparing the two regimes and identifying them with each other.[1]

Since then, two different perceptions have underlain this concept: on the one hand, the comparison of two regimes that differed in their cultural and ideological roots, distinguished by a shared aversion to liberal society and by their dictatorial response to mass society; on the other, the definition of an increasingly uniform phenomenon capable of cancelling out ideological antagonism, now sealed by a plan for world domination. In reality, the idea that the Second World War was a conflict between liberalism and totalitarianism would prove illusory. The common foundation of the pact between Stalin and Hitler was not the plan for a systematic alliance, given that for both parties it was based on a pragmatic assessment of their own interests; what they shared was the idea that for the moment those interests had converged significantly. Stalin's guiding principles remained the inevitability of war, a principle which he had inherited from Lenin, and the antagonism between the Soviet Union and the capitalist powers. From this point of view, Nazi Germany represented the spearhead of a hostile world.[2] It was precisely this concept, fixated on imperialist motives behind German policy, that prevented him from comprehending Nazism's radical racial ideology and the unprecedented nature of National Socialism in Germany's history. This laid the foundations for a fatal misunderstanding of Hitler's behaviour and objectives.

Even in this more limited sense, the pact was destined to leave a considerable legacy. The latent conflict between the two regimes and between the

---

[1] F. Borkenau, *The Totalitarian Enemy* (London: Faber and Faber, 1940). See W. D. Jones, *The Lost Debate: German Socialist Intellectuals and Totalitarianism* (Urbana: University of Illinois Press, 1999), 118–23.

[2] S. Pons, *Stalin and the Inevitable War* (London: Frank Cass, 2002), 180–1. For the continuity of Hitler's anti-communist motivations, even after the pact, see L. Waddington, *Hitler's Crusade: Bolshevism and the Myth of the International Jewish Conspiracy* (London: I. B. Tauris, 2007), 156–72.

different ideologies that motivated them could not be resolved. But their similarities were undeniable, not only in terms of their political structures. The dictatorships of Stalin and Hitler both presented themselves as models for an anti-liberal modernity, bearers of new political religions, and projects for warfare based on the metaphor of the permanent conflict and the prospect of total war.[3] Some commentators on the period experienced first-hand the terrible affinities between the machinery of oppression and the concentration camps used by the Stalinist regime and those used by the Nazi one. One of these was the German communist Margarete Buber-Neumann—wife of the KPD leader Hans Neumann who was arrested in 1937—as she and many others lived through the devastating experience of being delivered by the NKVD to the SS and transferred from the Gulag to the Nazi lager in 1940.[4] The shared aversion to liberal democratic capitalism and the claim to represent a different and successful response to the challenge of mass politics produced a series of mirror images.[5] In the USSR, the emulation of the Nazi capacity for absolute command, assertion of power, and organization of the masses had emerged some time previously. It now appeared that, by entering into armed conflict with the Western democracies, Hitler would in the long term trigger an anti-bourgeois and socialist trend in Germany, in conjunction with the clash between capitalist states which would favour Soviet power.

For the moment, an alliance was established between Moscow and Berlin, which was made concrete by the USSR providing substantial economic assistance and fuel supplies for the Nazi war effort. Moscow denounced the Western powers as those mainly responsible for the war, placed the Baltic states under its protection, and in return profited from German acceptance of its invasion of Finland at the end of November 1939. However, the Winter War produced more difficulties than advantages. It was a military fiasco, which revealed the Red Army's deficiency's following the purges of the previous years, showed that Moscow was not really neutral, and exacerbated the tensions with the Western powers caused by the Molotov–Ribbentrop Pact. The purpose of the attack on Finland, which came at a high price, was the territorial security that appeared to be Stalin's main objective. The peace signed in March 1940 granted the USSR the annexation of a strip of territory bordering the city of Leningrad. The occupation of eastern Poland resulted in a Soviet security policy previously implemented on the eve of the war: repressive measures and mass deportations. The policies of violent Sovietization and ethnic cleansing in the occupied regions, to the detriment of entire sections of the population deemed to be hostile, were enacted systematically

[3] R. Overy, *The Dictators: Hitler's Germany, Stalin's Russia* (London: Penguin, 2005), 297–9, 457–67.

[4] M. Buber-Neumann, *Under Two Dictators: Prisoner of Stalin and Hitler* (London: Pimlico, 2009).

[5] K. Clark and K. Schlögel, 'Mutual perceptions and projections: Stalin's Russia in Nazi Germany—Nazi Germany in the Soviet Union', in M. Geyer and S. Fitzpatrick (eds), *Beyond Totalitarianism: Stalinism and Nazism Compared* (Cambridge: Cambridge University Press, 2009), 396–441.

and in successive waves from the autumn of 1939 and throughout 1940.[6] They brought about summary executions and massacres, such as the annihilation of thousands of Polish officers at Katyń in the spring of 1940, which would become an affair of international importance following the war.[7] In the brutal logic of the Soviet regime, this represented a guarantee of security against a possible attack on its western border. It is doubtful that the repressive measures taken by the Red Army and the Soviet security services in the occupied regions actually increased security along the borders. They may well have had exactly the opposite effect, by nurturing effective popular resistance.[8]

The primary condition for Soviet security was in any case that Hitler kept faith with his intentions to prosecute the war in the west. The Nazi offensive in April and May 1940, first to the north against Denmark and Norway and then to the west against Belgium and France, bore out the theory of a 'war of attrition' and the illusion that the USSR would enjoy a sufficiently long period in which to recover an appropriate state of military preparedness to confront tired and weakened enemies. This hope would not last long. The ruinous defeat and collapse of France in June 1940 dramatically disproved the prediction of a long war in the west. As Khrushchev reported in his memoirs, the reaction in Moscow was one of bewilderment and alarm.[9] This destroyed Stalin's cherished hope that Germany would be worn down by the war, leading to a subsequent destabilization of the Nazi regime.[10] However, he did not reconsider his decisions, and refused the offers of talks from London, declaring to the British diplomat Stafford Cripps that the USSR rejected any possibility of defending the 'old order' in Europe.[11] Stalin continued to maintain that the alliance with Germany was the best way to guarantee the interests of Soviet power, which he identified as a revision of the postwar order and the creation of a Soviet sphere of influence in Eastern Europe. He probably feared that any other course of action would have led to an anti-Soviet agreement between the Germans and British, the phantasm of Munich. Certainly, after the fall of France, he decided to guarantee greater security on the northern borders by annexing the Baltic states, and on the southwestern borders by annexing Bessarabia and Bukovina. The first tensions between the USSR, Germany, and Italy emerged in the Balkans and the region of the Danube, but did not undermine his conviction that Soviet interests in Southeastern Europe and the Turkish straits could be resolved by negotiation.

[6] J. T. Gross, *Revolution from Abroad: The Soviet Conquest of Poland's Western Ukraine and Western Belorussia* (Princeton, N.J.: Princeton University Press, 1988); T. Snyder, *Bloodlands: Europe Between Stalin and Hitler* (New York: Basic Books, 2010).

[7] V. Zaslavsky, *Class Cleansing: The Massacre at Katyn* (Candor, N.Y.: Telos Press, 2008); N. S. Lebedeva (ed.), *Katyn Mart' 1940 g.–Sentyabr' 2000 g. Rasstrel. Sudby zhivykh. Ekho Katyni. Dokumenty* (Moscow: Ves' Mir, 2001).

[8] R. D. Petersen, *Resistance and Rebellion: Lessons from Eastern Europe* (Cambridge: Cambridge University Press, 2001), 88ff.

[9] S. Khrushchev (ed.), *Memoirs of Nikita Khrushchev* (3 vols, Pennsylvania, Pa.: Pennsylvania State University Press, 2004–7), vol. 1: *Commissar (1918–1945)*, 265–6.

[10] G. Dimitrov, *Diario: gli anni di Mosca (1934–1945)*, ed. S. Pons (Turin: Einaudi, 2002), 203.

[11] *1941 god* (Moscow: Mezhdunarodnyi Fond 'Demokratiya', 1998), vol. 1, doc. 37, pp. 76–80.

Stalin was even willing to discuss the USSR's admission to the tripartite agreement between Germany, Italy, and Japan in September 1940. The openly anti-American tone of the agreement appeared to provide the glue between the fascist regimes and the Soviet one, but the division of influence constituted an insoluble problem. Stalin's instructions to Molotov on the eve of the talks in Berlin in November 1940 were entirely concerned with the division of spheres of influence as a guarantee of security, especially in Central, Eastern, and Southeastern Europe.[12] The Soviet objective was that of reviving the entente between the two powers, but the meeting proved to be a dialogue of the deaf: Hitler had no intention of granting concessions in Europe and, besides, had already decided to attack the USSR. The failure of the negotiations was clear even to the Soviets.[13] Nevertheless they continued to delude themselves that a conciliatory policy towards Germany could lead to an agreement in the Balkans. In the following months, the German invasion of Bulgaria in February 1941 and then of Yugoslavia at the beginning of April 1941 destroyed any possibility of agreement. The scenario of a war with Nazi Germany loomed definitively. In spite of this, the neutrality pact signed with Japan in April fuelled new false hopes. Stalin continued to believe that Hitler would not go to war on two fronts without being sure that the USSR was in a similar situation, and he was tied to the vain quest for détente in order to gain time after having gained territory.[14]

Consequently the communist movement, already much reduced in size, did not lift a finger against Hitler's conquest of continental Europe. In the sphere of Soviet influence, communists devoted themselves to simply supporting the policy of Sovietization. It was not a decisive task. The 'popular government' of Kuusinen set up in Finnish territory at the end of 1939 did not last long, because it was clear to everyone that it was a puppet government and a caricature of revolutionary power, in spite of an attempt by the Comintern to run a campaign in its favour.[15] After this, the Comintern's activities in the occupied territories were mainly in support of the Soviet security services. Its propaganda in Europe was reduced almost entirely to an anti-Western orientation, even though there was still much distrust of Nazi Germany. In a document on the line adopted by the German Communist Party sent by Dimitrov to Molotov at the beginning of 1940, it was argued that Hitler's regime would not 'necessarily continue to follow a policy of friendliness' towards the USSR, and that Germany might even violate the pact and start a war against the USSR.[16] The reality was that the communist movement was largely in a state of chaos and lacked political direction.

---

[12] 'Direktivy I. V. Stalina V. M. Molotovu pered poezdkoy v Berlin v noyabre 1940 g', *Novaya i noveishaya istoriya* 4 (1995).

[13] *Sto sorok besed s Molotovym. Iz dnevnika F. Chueva* (Moscow: Terra-Terra, 1991), 23.

[14] G. Gorodetsky, *Grand Delusion: Stalin and the German Invasion of Russia* (New Haven, Conn.: Yale University Press, 1999).

[15] *Komintern i Finlandiya, 1919–1943* (Moscow: Nauka, 2003), docs 116, 117, 118; B. H. Bayerlein, M. M. Narinsky, B. Studer, and S. Wolikow, *Moscou–Paris–Berlin: télégrammes chiffrés du Komintern (1939–1941)* (Paris: Tallandier, 2003), doc. 51, pp. 130–1.

[16] N. S. Lebedeva and M. M. Narinskii (eds), *Komintern i Vtoraya Mirovaya Voyna (KVMV)* (2 vols, Moscow: Pamyatniki Istoricheskoy Misly, 1994, 1998), vol. 1, doc. 52, pp. 237–9.

The day of reckoning came with the fall of France under the impact of the Nazi attack. On 10 June 1940 Dimitrov and Manuilsky wrote to Stalin asking advice on how they should instruct French communists to behave, and this revealed their own state of confusion. They judged as 'not incorrect' the decision by the French Communist Party to denounce 'French imperialism' while the German troops were rapidly advancing towards Paris.[17] Stalin brought about a change to this suicidal stance. On 16 June after the Nazis had entered Paris, Dimitrov questioned Stalin once more, this time to obtain his approval for another declaration in which the 'French bourgeoisie' was condemned, but also the threat to France's national independence and its subjugation to Germany.[18] The French leaders quickly fell into line, and put the accent on the threat of 'German imperialism'.[19] On 22 June, the day France signed the armistice, Dimitrov and Thorez sent Eugen Fried—a Slovak emissary of the Comintern and for a decade an *éminence grise* of French communism—a detailed directive on the prospects of resistance to the occupation forces.[20] But the torment was not over. During the summer of 1940, the Comintern secretariat first encouraged and then censured the ambiguous tendency of French communists to establish contacts with the German forces of occupation, in order to obtain a semi-legal leeway and permission to publish their daily paper, *L'Humanité*.[21] On 3 August 1940, Dimitrov wrote to Stalin submitting for his perusal a directive that warned of the dangers of such behaviour and the possibility of it being exploited by the Nazis.[22] Immediately afterwards Dimitrov and Thorez sent Fried a directive to end all contacts with the occupation authorities.[23] French communists backtracked, but it would be some time before they could take an active part in the national resistance.[24]

The Comintern regained the initiative only when the first disagreements started to appear in the alliance between the USSR and Nazi Germany, particularly after the deterioration in relations in the Balkan theatre at the end of 1940 and the beginning of 1941. Any action to hinder the Nazi penetration of Bulgaria and Yugoslavia was, however, thwarted by the Soviet leaders. Immediately after the non-event at the Berlin negotiations, Dimitrov asked Molotov whether 'the line on disrupting German troops in various countries', followed by the Comintern's clandestine network since the fall of France, might constitute an element of friction. Molotov advised him to be prudent: 'we wouldn't be communists if we didn't follow that

[17] A. Dallin and F. I . Firsov (eds), *Dimitrov and Stalin 1934–1943: Letters from the Soviet Archives* (New Haven, Conn.: Yale University Press, 2000), doc. 30, pp. 167–8. See also Bayerlein et al., *Moscou–Paris–Berlin*, 199.

[18] Dallin and Firsov, *Dimitrov and Stalin 1934–1943*, 170–4.

[19] Bayerlein et al., *Moscou–Paris–Berlin*, 200.

[20] Ibid. doc. 134, pp. 240–42. For Fried's role, see A. Kriegel and S. Courtois, *Eugen Fried: le grand secret du PCF* (Paris: Éditions du Seuil, 1997).

[21] *KVMV*, vol. 1, docs 110 and 113, pp. 401–7.

[22] Dallin and Firsov, *Dimitrov and Stalin 1934–1943*, doc. 32, pp. 175–81.

[23] Bayerlein et al., *Moscou–Paris–Berlin*, docs 160 and 161, pp. 277–81.

[24] *KVMV*, vol. 1, doc. 116, pp. 421–2. See also S. Courtois, *Le bolchévisme à la française* (Paris: Fayard, 2010), 134–74: S. Wolikow, *L'Internationale communiste (1919–1943): le Komintern ou le rêve déchu du parti mondial de la révolution* (Paris: Éditions de l'Atelier, 2010), 122–9.

line. Only it must be done without too much rumpus.'[25] Stalin explained his reason for so much caution to Dimitrov. The USSR was proposing a pact for mutual assistance to Bulgaria in order to defend its own security interests, but with the prospect of a renewed agreement with Germany.[26] The failure to reach an agreement with Bulgaria and the evident unwillingness of Hitler to pursue negotiations with the USSR did not make him desist. Consequently the Comintern's role continued to be secondary. Dimitrov stressed the need to consider the 'German question' and the 'Italian question' jointly, associating the two allies in the European war on the basis of the political nature of their regimes. However, the communist movement's policy was still tied to a generic anti-imperialist rhetoric.[27] The Soviet leaders' instructions did not change even when the tension between the USSR and Germany reached its height, due to the Yugoslav crisis at the end of March and beginning of April in 1941. Stalin decided not to react when the Nazi invasion swept away the government which was pro-British but also pro-Soviet, and had been installed on 27 March by a coup directed against Yugoslavia's decision to join the pact between fascist powers. The revolutionary ambitions of Josip Broz Tito, the Yugoslav leader who had returned to his country at the beginning of 1940 with instructions from the Comintern to rebuild the party devastated by purges, after he himself had been accused of 'Trotskyism', were countermanded before they could get off the ground.[28] Molotov suggested to Dimitrov that he send the Yugoslav communists a directive 'not to cause a rumpus, not to shout, but to hold firmly to their positions', ceasing all demonstrations in the streets.[29] The directive came from Stalin.[30]

Immediately after the German invasion of Yugoslavia, Zhdanov confirmed to Dimitrov the absolute continuity of the USSR's policy towards Germany ('We do not approve of the German expansion into the Balkans. But this does not mean that we are abandoning our pact with Germany and going over to England's side. Those of our people who think along those lines underestimate the Soviet Union's power and autonomous role').[31] On 17 April, Dimitrov sent Stalin the directives to the communist parties with a view to the First of May celebration, which contained a cautious proposal for mobilizing against the regimes in occupied Europe.[32] Stalin reasserted the imperialist nature of the war.[33] Thus Hitler's European empire was shaped without encountering any genuine resistance from the communists. The possibility of reversing this policy was only conceivable in the event of the alliance

---

[25] Dimitrov, *Diario*, 245.
[26] V. K. Volkov and L. Y. Gibiansky (eds), *Vostochnaya Evropa mezhdu Gitlerom i Stalinym 1939–1941 gg.* (Moscow: Indrik, 1999), 288–92.
[27] *KVMV*, vol. 1, doc. 161, pp. 514–15.
[28] G. Swain, 'Tito and the twilight of the Komintern', in T. Rees and A. Thorpe (eds), *International Communism and the Communist International* (Manchester: Manchester University Press, 1998).
[29] Dimitrov, *Diario*, 291; *KVMV*, vol. 1, doc. 166, pp. 519–20.
[30] Volkov and Gibiansky, *Vostochnaya Evropa mezhdu Gitlerom i Stalinym*, 472.
[31] Dimitrov, *Diario*, 297–8.
[32] Dallin and Firsov, *Dimitrov and Stalin 1934–1943*, doc. 34, pp. 185–7.
[33] Dimitrov, *Diario*, 300.

between the two states being broken, which Stalin was not willing to entertain in the immediate future.

The plan under consideration was that of attempt to 'nationalize' the parties for a role in the predicted war against the USSR, which they held to be not imminent but inevitable in the medium term. In line with Stalin's assessment of the future since 1939, Zhdanov made the following very clear at a meeting on training communist cadres in Slavic countries held in February 1941: 'We haven't paid sufficient attention to the national aspects. Combining proletarian internationalism with the healthy national sentiments of any determined people. We need to prepare our "nationalists".'[34] It was in this context that Stalin, at the end of April, mentioned for the first time that the Comintern constituted 'an unsettling element' in relation to the development of the individual communist parties, and questioned its future existence. In his opinion, the communist parties needed to become 'national parties', capable of putting down roots among 'their own people.'[35]

The matter had immediate results. Dimitrov met Zhdanov to examine the political and organizational implications of dissolving the Comintern. Echoing the xenophobic climate of the Terror rather than the experience of anti-fascism, Zhdanov explained to Dimitrov that 'there is not and could not be any contradiction between nationalism as it is correctly understood and proletarian internationalism'. Instead, it was 'cosmopolitanism without fatherland, which denies national feelings and the idea of the fatherland' which had to be rejected, because it prepared the ground 'for the recruitment of spies and enemy agents'. Although the decision was not considered urgent, the end of the International was now taken for granted.[36] For the moment this did not occur, probably because of the German invasion of the USSR. However the theme of appropriating national identity was now an integral part of communist political strategy in time of war. The main example of the ongoing reconversion was that of the French communists. On 26 April 1941, Dimitrov and Thorez sent Fried a directive calling on the PCF to join the 'struggle for national liberation' and to avoid conflicts with General de Gaulle's partisans, thus bringing to an end generic anti-imperialist propaganda.[37]

In the spring of 1941, the perception that war was imminent had become acute in Moscow, as appears evident from a note written by Dimitrov at the end of April: 'The flames of war are coming closer and closer to the Soviet Union, which must prepare with all its forces against any "surprise".'[38] At a meeting held on 5 May 1941 at the military academy in Moscow, which the press reported without referring to the content, Stalin alluded to the possibility of war with Germany and even a preventive Soviet attack. He argued that Germany could have counted at the beginning of the war on the 'understanding of the peoples damaged by the Treaty of Versailles', but that now it was presenting itself as the oppressor that conducted war with the 'intention of hegemony', and that this represented 'a great handicap for the German army'. Immediately afterwards, he declared: 'our policy

---

[34] Ibid. 278.   [35] Ibid. 302.   [36] Ibid. 314.
[37] Bayerlein et al., *Moscou–Paris–Berlin*, doc. 243, pp. 402–4.
[38] Dimitrov, *Diario*, 304.

of peace and security is at the same time a policy of preparedness for war. There is no defence without attack. We need to educate the army to the spirit of attack. We need to prepare for war.'[39] Historians are divided over whether or not to interpret this speech by Stalin as the announcement of the imminent 'preventive war' against Hitler. The USSR's strategic military plans had a noticeable leaning towards the offensive, but did not necessarily outline the scenario for a preventive attack.[40] Stalin's words reveal that he considered it very probable that the USSR would be going to war, and looked on the alliance with Germany as a temporary affair. But his main aim was to gain more time, while failing to see that war was at the gate.[41] Thus the German attack came as a genuine surprise.[42]

Stalin closed his eyes to a spectacular quantity of information on the German military build-up, which was pouring into Moscow from various different sources. His limited room for manoeuvre in 1941 was clear and the possibilities of post-poning the war minimal, given the power of the German war machine and the USSR's isolation. But it had largely been Stalin's own decision over the preceding years that had reduced his range of choices. The dramatic scenario of June 1941 arose from Hitler's plans for conquest, but also from the irrational enfeeblement of the USSR's security resulting from repression in the country and in the army. The evident relaxation of the USSR's defences had increased Western scepticism and encouraged Hitler's ambitions. The renunciation of deterrence against Hitler through an agreement with Western governments and the decision to make an alliance with Nazi Germany had prevented an unlikely conflict in 1939 in order to favour a real one less than two years later—a period of time sufficient for Hitler's conquest of the European continent, but insufficient to remedy the blows Stalin himself had inflicted on the USSR's defensive capability. As Ian Kershaw has observed, the pact was more beneficial to Germany than it was to the USSR.[43] The annexation of the territories in Northern, Eastern, and Southeastern Europe would prove to be irrelevant for the purposes of military defence, and their Sovietization counterproductive for the consolidation of the borders. Stalin's bet on a 'war of attrition' in the West was lost. The search for détente with Berlin at any cost iso-lated Moscow. Hitler's threat grew immeasurably without the USSR and the com-munist movement being able to react.

---

[39] *Istochnik*, 1995, n. 2, pp. 29–30. See also Dimitrov, *Diario*, 309–10; V. A. Nevezhin, *Zastol' nye rechi Stalina: dokumenty i materialy* (Moscow: Airo-XX, 2003), 279–93.

[40] See V. A. Nevezhin, *Sindrom nastupatelnoy voiny: sovetskaya propaganda v preddverii 'sviashchen-nykh boyev' 1939–1941 gg.* (Moscow: Airo-XX, 1997); Gorodetsky, *Grand Delusion*, 208–9, 239; E. Mawdsley, *Thunder in the East: The Nazi-Soviet War 1941–1945* (London: Hodder Arnold, 2005), 37–41.

[41] C. Pleshakov, *Stalin's Folly: The Secret History of the German Invasion of Russia, June 1941* (London Weidenfeld & Nicolson, 2005), 77.

[42] Khrushchev, *Memoirs of Nikita Khrushchev*, vol. 1, p. 304; A. Mikoyan, *Tak bylo: Razmyshleniya o minuvshem* (Moscow: Vagrius, 1999), 388–93.

[43] I. Kershaw, *Fateful Choices: Ten Decisions that Changed the World 1940–1941* (London: Penguin, 2008), 293.

Stalin did not understand the gravity of the danger, even when its presence became undeniable. The dictatorship's self-referential mechanisms, the paranoid psychology incapable of distinguishing between a genuine threat and a virtual one, and the short-circuit between awareness of military unpreparedness and the decision to seek unilateral security contributed to the most unlikely of blunders. The German attack of 22 June 1941 marked the disastrous failure of the strategy based on a 'war of attrition', territorial security and détente with Nazi Germany. The unilateral concept of security was, however, destined to leave its fundamental mark, and would prove to be the conceptual and political compass for defining the interests of the Soviet state. Molotov would retrospectively congratulate himself for having successfully fulfilled his task as foreign minister, that of 'extending as far as possible the borders of our fatherland' and 'strengthening the Soviet state'.[44] The ambition to exercise decisive influence in Eastern Europe, nurtured and developed during the alliance with Hitler, would remain at the heart of Stalin's thinking and constitute the central plank of Soviet plans for the postwar period.

THE PATRIOTIC WAR AND THE END OF THE COMINTERN

Stalin's political response to the Nazi attack was an appeal to patriotism in the USSR and a return to anti-fascism in the communist movement. In spite of this evident improvisation, this twin discourse would prove extraordinarily effective, bringing very different motivations together in a single cause. While the great majority of Soviet citizens, including many party members, were fighting in the name of the country and the hope of a regime different from that of the past, militant communists in the USSR and beyond rescued a mission and revived their political faith. The former fought and made sacrifices for a national ideal to protect their land and their dear ones and, at the most, for a socialism with a more human face than the one they had previously experienced. The latter fought and made sacrifices to destroy fascism, defend the Soviet state, and create a socialist future combined with national identity. From the beginning, the regime's rhetoric principally aimed at the defence of the country and the salvation of the Russian nation, soft-pedalling the militant and internationalist message. This laid the foundations for the myth of the Great Patriotic War, which in the USSR would replace the myth of the Revolution. The basis for the new Soviet myth was on the whole alien to both its revolutionary calling and the ideas of anti-fascism. Fascism was identified with the German invader and the Western threat to Russia, which could be traced back to the Napoleonic Wars. Communism, as an ideology and a system, was passed over in silence for the simple reason that an appeal to its defence would not have mobilized sufficient forces and would indeed have disincentivized them. But the myth of the Great Patriotic War did not herald the elimination of the

---

[44] *Sto sorok besed s Molotovym*, 14, 78.

Soviet Union's revolutionary legacy. It was not the expression of a Thermidor in the Russian Revolution. In fact the cataclysm of war restored the vision of a hostile and aggressive war, which guaranteed continuity with the past and remembrance of the Civil War. The construction of revolutionary identities that survived the worst years of Stalinist terror would not simply be erased by the impact of the war.[45]

In spite of the dismay caused by the terrifying reverses suffered by the Red Army and the apparently unstoppable Nazi advance, the state's central and regional bodies revealed an unexpected backbone and ability to react. The rapid and easy penetration of the armies of the Axis into the territory of the USSR laid bare the unpopularity and lack of preparation of the Soviet regime. The political and military disaster appeared irreparable throughout the summer of 1941. In September, Leningrad was under siege with little hope of resistance, while Moscow was not far off. The spontaneous and unexpected response of the people against the invader in the heart of Russia, together with the sense of not having anything to lose, provided the Stalinist regime with the resources to hold firm. The war on the eastern front acquired features of unheard-of ferocity and barbarity, which left no escape for anyone, whether civilian or soldier. The Nazi capacity and desire for annihilation was soon clear to all, and created an awareness of an extreme life-or-death struggle. Soviet power did not possess genuine moral and civil resources to oppose the German advance, but it did have at its disposal tried and tested techniques for organization, propaganda, and mobilization. It could also count on the people's inurement to the rigours of war in peacetime, cruelty, and sacrifice. But above all, the regime was able to appeal to patriotism and the national salvation of Russia, by using motivations that Nazi ferocity made credible and well-founded. The defence of Moscow was the first success of the resistance to the Nazi attack, whose significance went far beyond the purely military one. Although the defeats suffered by the Red Army were the direct consequence of Stalin's alliance with Hitler and his inability to understand Nazi aggression, he managed to establish a new image of himself, which took on an aura of national and international significance. The war of annihilation determined the way the regime would evolve. The appeal to mythologies and symbols of Russian tradition won for Soviet power a large consensus in society for the first time.[46]

However, the radical change in the situation brought about by the outbreak of war did not alter the features of Stalin's power politics, as defined by the alliance with Hitler. There was continuity between the Soviet geopolitical objectives in the first phase of the war, as displayed in the negotiations with Hitler of November 1940, and the requests made at the meeting with Anthony Eden in Moscow in

---

[45] A. Weiner, *Making Sense of War: The Second World War and the Fate of the Bolshevik Revolution* (Princeton, N.J.: Princeton University Press, 2001). For utopian fervour and revolutionary self-transformation under Stalin, see J. Hellbeck, *Revolution on My Mind: Writing a Diary under Stalin* (Cambridge, Mass.: Harvard University Press, 2006).

[46] D. Volkogonov, *Triumf i tragediya: politicheskii portret I.V. Stalina* (Moscow: APN, 1989), book 2, part 1, pp. 151–261; B. Bellamy, *Absolute War: Soviet Russia in the Second World War* (London: Pan, 2010); D. Brandenberger, *National Bolshevism: Stalinist Mass Culture and the Formation of Modern Russian National Identity, 1931–1956* (Cambridge, Mass.: Harvard University Press, 2002), 144–59.

December 1941, revolving around the territorial claims on the USSR's western borders made in June 1941 just before the Nazi invasion and the recognition of Soviet influence in the eastern part of Europe.[47] When the Nazi armies were at the gates of Moscow and they had encountered their first setback only a few days earlier, Stalin affected calm and sangfroid. He was ready to start negotiations on future arrangements in Europe on the basis of concepts of security he had previously formulated. The territorial claims of June 1941 demonstrated that Moscow perceived the expansion brought about during the alliance with Hitler to be an imperial acquisition and not a passing episode. The Soviet leadership was still concerned with Eastern and Southeastern Europe, now in a context that presupposed a defeat of Germany. For a period, Stalin did not bet all his postwar cards on the prospect of an agreement with the Western powers, but kept open the possibility of a unilateral settlement. He did not exclude the possibility of reaching a separate peace agreement with Hitler modelled on Brest-Litovsk, which would have led to the loss of the territories annexed in 1939–40. The chances of a separate peace were not, however, very high.[48] The political turning point came with the Battle of Stalingrad, the military and symbolic event destined to reverse the fortunes of war on the eastern front from the beginning of 1943. From that time on, the option for a unilateral exit from the war disappeared, and Soviet ambition to exercise influence over Central and Eastern Europe became a key and achievable objective.

Even the Comintern was involved in the war effort, albeit invisibly. It provided a considerable contribution to the mobilization, in the form of massive propaganda activity and organization of conspiratorial networks and resistance measures in many of the parts of Europe occupied by Nazi-Fascism, as well as political agitation among prisoners of war in close collaboration with the Soviet espionage bodies.[49] At the time of the Nazi invasion of the USSR, Dimitrov immediately agreed with Stalin on a new direction for the communist movement: 'The parties develop in their area a movement in defence of the USSR. Do not pose the question of the socialist revolution. The Soviet people are fighting a patriotic war against Fascist Germany. The aim is the destruction of fascism, which has subjugated a number of peoples and is attempting to subjugate other peoples.'[50] Dimitrov revived anti-fascist discourse, declaring to the secretariat of the ECCI that 'the fact that the aggression is coming from Germany appears to be a positive factor for us', and that 'in this stage, we will not make any appeals to the overthrow of capitalism in individual countries or to world revolution'.[51] During the following days, the head of the Comintern sent directives to various European communist parties requesting that they avoid defining the war 'as a war between the capitalist system and

---

[47] O. A. Rzheshevskii, 'Vizit A. Idena v Moskvu v dekabre 1941 g. Peregovory s I. V. Stalinym i V. M. Molotovym', *Novaya i noveishaya istoriya* 2 (1994), 98–100.

[48] Mawdsley, *Thunder in the East*, 247–8.

[49] F. I. Firsov, *Sekretnye kody istorii Kominterna 1919–1943* (Moscow: Airo-XXI, 2007), 434–78; N. E. Rosenfeldt, *The 'Special' World: Stalin's Power Apparatus and the Soviet System's Secret Structures of Communication* (Copenhagen: Museum Tusculanum Press, University of Copenhagen, 2009), vol. 2, p. 249.

[50] Dimitrov, *Diario*, 320.   [51] *KVMV*, vol. 2, doc. 2, 93–5.

the socialist system'.[52] On 1 July he wrote to Molotov that in countries occupied by Germany, communists should contact all the forces wishing to join a 'national united front' and avoid 'raising the question of their hegemony'.[53] This expression, which had already emerged two months earlier in France, now took on a universal significance. On 7 July, the secretariat of the Comintern issued a directive inspired by the line on the 'national fronts'.[54]

In this context, one of the most significant decisions was to rebuild the Polish Communist Party, which had been destroyed during the Great Terror—a measure Dimitrov agreed directly with Stalin. Revealingly, the new party was called the Polish Workers' Party at the request of Stalin himself, who was persuaded that 'the name "communist" terrifies not only alien elements but even some of our own people'.[55] The words Dimitrov wrote after having renounced being present at the military parade of 7 November 1941 should not come as any surprise—'No point in putting the Comintern on display'—just at the time when Stalin's presence in Red Square gave the signal for a spirit of resistance capable of taking on the terrible impact of the German advance.[56] The secrecy maintained by Comintern activity increased further after the main leaders (Florin, Gottwald, Ibárruri, Marty, Pieck, and Togliatti) and the ECCI staff were evacuated to Ufa in Bashkiria for security reasons. The strategy of the communist movement concentrated on the relative instability of the collaborationist regimes and the objective of weakening the Nazi 'new order', in part through armed guerrilla attacks that were of symbolic rather than military significance.[57] At the same time, there was persistent emphasis on the 'national' character of the propaganda in Europe, and on calling to order those who continued to use slogans of a class nature. Thus the outbreak of war between Nazi Germany and the USSR resulted in a review by the European communist parties of their relationship with the nation, which was more far-reaching than had ever occurred in the past, and in their cultivation of a national image in the style of Soviet 'socialist patriotism'.[58]

In reality, this did not prove to be an easy road to travel, both because many communists could not swallow the new national recipe and because the Soviet manipulation of nationalism turned out to be a difficult product to export. The Soviet model of 'nationalization' had serious drawbacks. In the USSR, the new patriotic rhetoric had been deployed in the mid-1930s in a manner unrelated to anti-fascist discourse and, if anything, emulating fascist and Nazi nationalism. This rhetoric exalted the cult of the state and power, together with social unity and suppression of 'enemies of the people'. When communists were inspired by that

---

[52] Dimitrov, *Diario*, 321–2.　　[53] *KVMV*, vol. 2, doc. 12, pp. 109–11.

[54] Ibid. doc. 15, pp. 114–15. See Wolikow, *L'Internationale communiste (1919–1943)*, 136–7.

[55] Dimitrov, *Diario*, 349.　　[56] Ibid. 384.

[57] *KVMV*, vol. 2, doc. 74, pp. 226–30. On the PCF question, see also Bayerlein et al., *Moscou–Paris–Berlin*, 432–5.

[58] Of the case studies on the behaviour of European communists, see esp. M. Mevius, *Agents of Moscow: The Hungarian Communist Party and the Origins of Socialist Patriotism, 1941–1953* (Oxford: Oxford University Press, 2005).

model outside the USSR, they only managed to express ambiguous and tenuous intentions of brotherhood with the fascistized masses, as in Italy and Germany before the war, or undifferentiated anti-bourgeois messages, as in France after September 1939. Only anti-fascist discourse had provided a foundation for the claims to national identity made by European communists. However, the revival of that discourse did not eliminate the evidence of its uncertainty. The requirements of the Soviet state could change once again: the scenario of the 'international civil war' had not disappeared; communists could see themselves as 'national' even in the fight to the death with the class enemy, as the experience of the USSR showed. In this sense, the 'nationalization' of communists would remain a distinct process, separate from that of European socialism.[59]

During 1942, communist participation in the resistance to occupation was mainly concentrated in the western regions of Russia, Byelorussia, and the Balkans, where the liberation movements managed to survive the massive campaigns of repression carried out by the Nazis. The political line of the communist parties in Europe became clear only at the end of the year, after the start of the Red Army's counteroffensive in Stalingrad, the allied landing in northwest Africa, the elimination of Vichy France, and the Nazi occupation of the whole of France. The ECCI secretariat suggested that 'the new situation in the West' could be better exploited.[60] The countries most immediately affected were France and Italy, but the Comintern committed itself to a more general mobilization in the critical areas of Nazi-dominated Europe. On 19 November, Dimitrov called on Tito to create a popular committee for the liberation of Yugoslavia with a national and anti-fascist nature, while avoiding clashes with Mihajlović's Četnik partisans and adopting harmful positions against the monarchy.[61] Moscow insisted on the need to prevent conflict between the Committee of Liberation and the Yugoslav government in exile with an explicit foreign-policy motivation: to look to the future 'not only from a national point of view, but also the international one—from the point of view of the Anglo-Soviet-American coalition'.[62] Immediately afterwards, on 3 December 1942, Dimitrov, Togliatti, Thorez, and Marty prepared a directive to the French and Italian communists adopting the same line and emphasizing the proposal of 'national fronts', which de facto revived the idea of popular fronts and embraced all forces opposed to fascism.[63] Dimitrov sent the document to Stalin with a note clarifying that it was a necessary development in the light of the Red Army's offensive and also the allied offensive in North Africa.[64] Two days later, in record time, Dimitrov received Stalin's approval.[65] On 5 January 1943, the Czechoslovak party also received similar instructions.[66]

[59] M. Cattaruzza (ed.), *La nazione in rosso: socialismo, comunismo e 'questione nazionale'*, 1889–1953 (Soveria Mannelli: Rubbettino, 2005).

[60] *KVMV*, vol. 2, doc. 97, pp. 265–6.   [61] Ibid. doc. 98, pp. 267–68.

[62] Dimitrov, *Diario*, p. 541.   [63] *KVMV*, II, docs 101, 110.

[64] Dallin and Firsov, *Dimitrov and Stalin 1934–1943*, doc. 40, p. 200.

[65] Dimitrov, *Diario*, p. 548.   [66] *KVMV*, vol. 2, doc. 110, pp. 286–99.

The turning point in the war after Stalingrad and the adoption of the line on 'national fronts' heralded the decision to dissolve the Comintern in May 1943. The institution's survival for two years after Stalin's first mention of his desire to end its existence, back in April 1941, was a transition imposed by the contingencies of war. On 8 May 1943, Dimitrov and Manuilsky were summoned by Molotov and agreed with him that 'the Comintern, as a centre directing the communist parties, is in the current circumstances an obstacle to the autonomous development of communist parties and the fulfilment of their specific tasks'.[67] Within three days, the resolution on the dissolution of the Comintern was ready and approved by Stalin.[68] Immediately afterwards, the members of the ECCI Presidium were consulted, and without raising any objections they approved the proposal. There was no debate on strategy. Even the key idea of a national identity for the parties encountered only mild reactions from the communist leaders. Only Thorez and Ján Šverma of the Czechoslovak party accepted the proposal with conviction. Others, like the Hungarian Rákosi, had concerns and wanted the door left open for the re-establishment of a central body of international communism. Dimitrov argued, however, that it would be unlikely that after the war there would be any need for a new Comintern.[69]

On 21 May 1943, the Politburo approved the draft resolution on the dissolution of the Comintern, which was made public the following day.[70] At the Politburo meeting, Stalin explained the decision with a retrospective critique of the original profile of the Comintern, and reasserted the need for a national structure for the communist parties. He declared that the claim 'to be able to direct the movement in all countries' had been a mistake. Moreover, he added, the dissolution would prevent their enemies from arguing that the communist parties were 'some kind of agency of a foreign state', which had impeded their growth. The parties would be strengthened as 'national workers' parties', and this would equally strengthen 'the internationalism of the popular masses, whose base is the Soviet Union'.[71] His public reasons were no different in substance.[72] On 5 June, Dimitrov notified Molotov of the results of the consultations with the leaders of individual communist parties, specifying that he had received consent to the dissolution from twenty-nine of the forty-one parties in the Comintern.[73] The last meeting of the Presidium of ECCI was held on 8 June.[74]

Stalin attributed real political significance to the idea of the increasingly national character of the communist parties.[75] The continuity of this reasoning from 1941

[67] Dimitrov, *Diario*, 611–12.

[68] Dallin and Firsov, *Dimitrov and Stalin 1934–1943*, doc. 50, pp. 229–32.

[69] *KVMV*, vol. 2, docs 134, 136, 137; Dallin and Firsov, *Dimitrov and Stalin 1934–1943*, docs 51, 52, 53, pp. 233–50.

[70] Dimitrov, *Diario*, 618.　　　[71] Ibid. 618.

[72] J. V. Stalin, *Works* [*Sochineniya*], ed. R. McNeal (3 vols, Stanford, Calif.: Hoover Institution, 1967), vol. 2 [15], pp. 104–5.

[73] *KVMV*, vol. 2, doc. 142, pp. 377–8.

[74] Dimitrov, *Diario*, 629; *KVMV*, vol. 2, doc. 143, pp. 378–9.

[75] M. Djilas, *Conversations with Stalin* (London: Hart-Davis, 1962), 88–9.

to 1943 demonstrates that the dissolution of the Comintern was not mere improvisation. That the International represented an obstacle to the establishment of communist parties had been his thinking for some time. The need to free communists from the uncomfortable label of 'Moscow's agents' had already been apparent, although only now was something being done about it. On the other hand, Stalin had always seen the Comintern as an awkward institution for the Soviet state. In a state of war, he decided that the time had come for the radical solution of eliminating the duality of the USSR's foreign-policy institutions. The end of world communism's centralized organization would remove the spanner that kept on getting into the works of the USSR's diplomatic relations, without depriving it of the strategic resource provided by the communist parties. The management of the communist movement could in fact become more effective through a network of bilateral relations between the Soviet state and the individual parties. Development of the national dimension would increase their ability to exercise influence in post-war Europe. In other words, the dissolution of the Comintern did not herald the 'normalization' of the Soviet state they paraded before the West, but nor was it a merely cosmetic operation. Stalin really did want to modify the modus operandi of the communist movement and find a way to consolidate the parties' place within their own national societies. The problem was the actual ability to pursue this route both in Moscow and outside the USSR.

The dissolution of the Comintern did not bring about the abolition of the institutional channels between Moscow and the individual communist parties. Its bureaucratic apparatus was kept alive through a series of 'special agencies' that continued to ensure relations between the parties. In June 1943, it was decided to set up a new international information section under the administration of the Soviet party; this would inherit the organizational functions of the Comintern. At the beginning of 1944, Dimitrov was nominated the head of this department, responsible to Molotov.[76] The tasks allocated to this new body involved propaganda, the training of cadres, clandestine contacts, and information from abroad.[77] Even the financial support Moscow gave to all the parties was never interrupted. The USSR's policy after 1943 therefore maintained influence over the communist parties that was no less direct than it had been in the past, but the Stalinist leadership was not bound by overly demanding political declarations. For the first time, the orientations of the communist parties could be different and modulated according to the national and geopolitical context, in accordance with the interests of Moscow. Stalin's newly acquired international prestige, the authority of the Soviet Union, and the loyalty of the communist leaders made this calculated move much easier. The paradox of the dissolution of the Comintern is that it appeared to celebrate the triumph of the communist monolith built around Stalin the figurehead. The Terror of the late 1930s had brought to completion the cruel and systematic homogenization that had lasted a decade. The death of Trotsky,

---

[76] Dimitrov, *Diario*, 637, 675.
[77] G. M. Adibekov, E. N. Shakhnazarova, and K. K. Shirinya, *Organizatsionnaya struktura Kominterna* (Moscow: Rosspen, 1997), 228–41.

at the hands of Stalin's assassin in Mexico in July 1940, had eliminated the most troublesome symbolic figure.[78] The diaspora of dissidents could now be considered a problem that was fading after the outbreak of war. The communist leaders and cadres who had survived the purges and whose experience went back to the 1920s had been Stalin's followers since those times. The others had been trained in the cult of Stalin. Identification with the Soviet state and loyalty to Stalin could not be separated. The experience of war, in appearance, constituted the culmination of the construction of the communist monolith, in accordance with the canons of sacralized unity established particularly after Lenin's death.

The Comintern's balance sheet was not flattering. Its legacy was a movement spread around the world, although there were marked imbalances and an uncertain future. It had clandestine networks in Nazi-occupied Europe and some of the Asian regions occupied by the Japanese, and a political and military force in Northern China; and links with the USSR would prove to be a formidable resource in the final stage of the war. But the 'party of world revolution' could not boast a single victorious revolution in its history of more than two decades. Its original ambitions were revised following the failure of the revolutions in Germany and China during the 1920s. The main battle of the 1930s was fought in Spain in defence of a democratic republic and with the aim of establishing the control of the communist party at its heart. But that too was a lost battle. What remained of communist presence in Europe was soon destabilized by the pact between Stalin and Hitler. Nevertheless, the strategic turning point of the war in 1943 heralded a new season, irrespective of whether or not the Comintern existed. In the Balkans, an important European laboratory of resistance was being tested out in a movement under communist leadership. The Yugoslav communists led by Tito and his closest aides, Edvard Kardelj, Milovan Djilas, and Aleksandar Ranković, were the model for the others to follow, as explicitly instructed by Moscow.[79] After the winter of 1942–3, the growth of communist partisan forces in Yugoslavia and Greece, together with Soviet partisans, became a serious thorn in the side of Hitler's empire in continental Europe. The south of Europe constituted Nazis' most exposed position, and the situation would deteriorate further with the fall of Mussolini regime's in Italy.[80] The other communist parties of Western, Central, and Eastern Europe were for a variety of reasons backward in the organization of effective action against the Nazis, while joining with the emerging liberation movements, as in France and Poland. In spite of this, the final stage of the war provided real opportunities for improvement and recovery, especially in Southern Europe.

Outside Europe, communist parties generally found themselves in a weak and precarious situation, despite the considerable organization and financial resources invested by Moscow, or they had suffered blows from which they were struggling

---

[78] B. M. Patenaude, *Trotsky: Downfall of a Revolutionary* (New York: HarperCollins, 2009).

[79] G. Swain, 'The Comintern and Southern Europe, 1938–1943', in T. Judt (ed.), *Resistance and Revolution in Mediterranean Europe 1939–1948* (London: Routledge, 1989).

[80] M. Mazower, *Hitler's Empire: How the Nazis Ruled Europe* (New York: Penguin Press, 2008), 482–91, 496ff.

to recover. A singular case was that of the People's Republic in Mongolia, which was established in the mid-1920s following the occupation by the Red Army and subsequently became a kind of protectorate of the USSR. Mongolian nomadic society was an early test bed for the export of the Stalinist model, but the significance of this experience was marginal for the communist movement.[81] Attempts to coordinate a common policy for communism outside Europe were sporadic, for example the congress of the Anti-Imperialist League held in Brussels in 1927 and organized by Münzenberg.[82] The policy of popular fronts evidently fostered a Eurocentric perspective, and the 'colonial revolutions' called for by the Chinese delegate Wang Ming were a secondary feature of the Seventh Congress of the Comintern. The parties outside Europe were much more likely to have been built 'from above'—at the initiative of some plenipotentiary of the Comintern and the communist parties of European countries with a colonial empire—and until the war, they were a scattered assortment of organizations.

Clearly the Chinese communists were the strong point of the movement outside Europe. They consolidated their stronghold in the region of Yan'an during the war, having saved themselves almost miraculously by means of an adventurous geographical relocation from the south to the northwest of the country, which had never had much to do with the Comintern's strategies. The party created much larger mass followings than it had in the past, and now had hundreds of thousands of activists. Mao Zedong firmly imposed his leadership with his brusque methods. He eliminated his rival Wang Ming, cemented his partnership with Liu Shaoqi, the party's main organizer, who had been trained in Russia, and subdued Zhou Enlai, an intellectual who had been educated in Europe and represented the Chinese Communist Party at the Guomindang. The two latter were destined to form the central nucleus of the revolution's ruling group.[83] However, Chinese communism was an exception, linked to the permanent state of armed struggle which had brought the communists since the 1930s to control a vast territory under their own authority. China was, in fact, at the heart of a great Asiatic war which had started before the Second World War with the Japanese invasion in 1937, and extended by Japanese imperialism to the entire southeast of the continent in 1942. It would continue after 1945 in a succession of civil wars and anti-colonial, anti-imperialist, and post-colonial conflicts.[84] Communists found fertile terrain for their original vocation, inspired by the link between war and revolution. They appeared to be capable of exploiting the crisis of the European empires and the

[81] I. Y. Morozova, *The Comintern and Revolution in Mongolia* (Cambridge: White Horse Press, 2002).

[82] J. Derrick, *Africa's 'Agitators': Militant Anti-Colonialism in Africa and the West, 1918–1939* (New York: Columbia University Press, 2008), 172–82. See also Wolikow, *L'Internationale communiste (1919–1943)*, 222–3.

[83] F. C. Teiwes, *The Formation of the Maoist Leadership* (London: Contemporary China Institute, 1994); T. Saich (ed.), *The Rise to Power of the Chinese Communist Party: Documents and Analysis* (Armonk, N.Y.: M. E. Sharpe, 1996), section G.

[84] C. Bayly and T. Harper, *Forgotten Wars: Freedom and Revolution in Southeast Asia* (Cambridge, Mass.: Harvard University Press, 2006).

demise of Japanese imperialism only where there was Chinese influence. This influence made possible the formation of large organized groups that extended from Korea to Indochina. Korean communists campaigned in exile under Chinese protection, in the partisan movement in Manchuria, and in the Soviet Far East.[85] In North Vietnam, communists followed the Chinese example and created the Viet Minh alliance which struggled against both the Japanese invader and the French imperial administration.[86]

Elsewhere, however, the communist parties were decidedly smaller and faced uncertain futures. In Japan, the communists had been devoured by factional infighting until the end of the 1920s, even though the Bolshevik idea had been that the country would be the Asian equivalent of Germany. Police repression in the early 1930s and a lack of interest in Moscow, which could not see the communists representing any kind of deterrent to Japanese imperialism, reduced the party to insignificance. After the Hitler–Stalin Pact, the Japanese ruling communist group, led by an intellectual educated at the London School of Economics, Sanzō Nosaka, was transferred to Northern China under the protection of the CCP.[87] In Indonesia, the Communist Party recovered only during the war from the harsh repression suffered at the time of the failed insurrections of 1926–7. Its clandestine guerrilla war was inspired by the Chinese example against the Japanese occupation, and the same occurred in Malaysia with British support.[88] In India, unlike China, the communists had not established a link with the national liberation movements, nor had they tried to penetrate peasant society, with the result that by the mid-1930s the party had no genuine social base. Its close relations with Moscow and the CPGB did not help the situation, and exposed it to repression by the British imperial authorities.[89] Only when they established relations with the Congress Party and the Socialists, as part of the Popular Front under the leadership of Puran C. Joshi, did they review their opposition to Gandhi. The adoption of the 'national unity' line from 1942 made it possible to increase the communist presence in the trade unions and to exert a limited influence in the army, although Indian communism continued to be on the margins of the national liberation movement.[90] In Iran, the communist movement had been suffocated at birth, just as in Turkey during the Kemalist Revolution. As the country came partly under Soviet occupation, the Iranian Communist Party (Tudeh) underwent considerable growth during the war, reaching a membership of about 20,000, which turned it

---

[85] *Vkp(b), Komintern i Koreya 1918–1941* (Moscow: Rosspen, 2007).

[86] W. J. Duiker, *The Communist Road to Power in Vietnam*, 2nd edn (Boulder, Colo.: Westview Press, 1996), 69–73.

[87] *Vkp(b), Komintern i Japoniya 1917–1941* (Moscow: Rosspen, 2001). See also S. Wilson, 'The Komintern and the Japanese Communist Party', in Rees and Thorpe, *International Communism and the Communist International*.

[88] Bayly and Harper, *Forgotten Wars*, 30, 161.

[89] W. Singer, 'Peasants and the peoples of the East: Indians and the rhetoric of the Komintern', in Rees and Thorpe, *International Communism and the Communist International*. See also S. D. Gupta, *Comintern and the Destiny of Communism in India, 1919–1943* (Calcutta: Seribaan, 2006).

[90] D. N. Gupta, *Communism and Nationalism in Colonial India, 1939–45* (New Delhi: Sage, 2008), 211–37; S. R. Chowdhuri, *Leftism in India, 1917–1947* (London: Palgrave, 2007), 101–7.

into one of the principal national political forces.[91] Soviet influence was also felt in the Arab world, but this did not translate into an increase in the movement. The Comintern's activities from above turned out to be particularly ineffective there. In the main Arab countries, the communist groups, which almost always grew within intellectual circles and were distinguished by strong Jewish components, as in Egypt, had a precarious and marginal existence, which revealed their subordination to nationalist forces.[92] In Africa, the activism of Comintern emissaries had not translated into creation of genuine parties, and failed to act as a bridge between pan-African movements.[93]

The non-European communist parties, with all their limitations, had by the end of the Second World War shaped some influential personalities and ruling groups, often distinguished by long and obscure vicissitudes in exile, conspiracy, and clandestine activities. They were destined to play a role in the process of decolonization. This was particularly true in Asia. In Indochina, there was the prominent leadership of the Vietnamese communist Ho Chi Minh. An intellectual in exile in the United States during the First World War and in Paris in the 1920s, he was a member of the French Communist Party, later a Comintern representative in China and Malaysia, and a founder of the Communist Party of Vietnam in 1930. He had around him and sometimes against him a leadership made up of men who had emerged from the underground anti-colonial struggle, who would hold important positions in North Vietnam and would take part in anti-imperialist struggle, such as Truong Chinh, Le Duan, Pham Van Dong, and Vo Nguyen Giap.[94] In Korea, leaders such as Kim Il-sung and Pak Hon-yong were products of the armed struggle in China and underground activities, later taking refuge in the USSR during the war.[95] In Indonesia, the leading figures were Tan Malaka, member of the Dutch Communist Party, Comintern agent, and nationalist theoretician of a fusion between Islam and communism, and Musso, a strict observer of Stalinism. They left the scene tragically after the failed insurrection that followed independence, and their place was taken by a new generation led by Dipa N. Aidit.[96] In Malaysia, the youthful personality of Chin Peng had distinguished

[91] M. Behrooz, *Rebels with a Cause: The Failure of the Left in Iran* (London: I. B. Tauris, 1999), 4–5, 22–3; C. Chaqueri (ed.), *The Left in Iran 1941–1957* (London: Merlin Press, 2011), 387.

[92] R. Ginat, *A History of Egyptian Communism. Jews and Their Compatriots in Quest of Revolution* (Boulder, Colo.: Lynne Rienner, 2011); T. Y. Ismael, *The Communist Movement in the Arab World* (London: Routledge Curzon, 2005); G. G. Kosats, *Krasnii flag nad Blizhnim Vostokom? Kompartii Egipta, Palestiny, Sirii i Livana v 20-30-e gody* (Moscow, 2001).

[93] Derrick, *Africa's 'Agitators'*; for the situation in South Africa, see A. Drew, *Discordant Comrades: Identities and Loyalties on the South African Left* (Aldershot: Ashgate, 2000), ch. 11. See also A. Davidson et al. (eds), *South Africa and the Communist International: A Documentary History* (2 vols, London: Frank Cass, 2003).

[94] S. Quinn-Judge, *Ho Chi Minh: The Missing Years* (London: Hurst, 2003); C. Marangé, *Le communisme vietnamien (1919–1991): construction d'un état-nation entre Moscou et Pékin* (Paris: Presses de la Fondation Nationale des Sciences Politiques, 2012).

[95] B. K. Martin, *Under the Loving Care of the Fatherly Leader: North Korea and the Kim Dynasty* (New York: St. Martin's Press, 2004).

[96] R. McVey, *The Rise of Indonesian Communism* (Ithaca, N.Y.: Cornell University Press, 1965); T. Malaka, *From Jail to Jail* (Athens: Ohio University Press, 1991).

himself, and after the war he would lead the armed anti-colonial rebellion.[97] In India, several leaders were destined to play a significant role after independence, such as Bhalchandra T. Ranadive, Ajoy Ghosh, and Jyoti Basu.[98] Even in the Arab world, some leading protagonists of decolonization were moulded by the experience of the 1930s and the war. The most charismatic of these were the Egyptian communist Henri Curiel, founder of the National Liberation Movement in 1943, the Syrian Khalid Bakdash, and the Iraqi Yusuf Salman (Fahd), who created a centralized party that would constitute the model for Arab socialism in the postwar period.[99]

The fact was that, until the war, the use of anti-imperialist nationalism for the purposes of strengthening the communist movement in countries outside Europe produced disappointing results. Communists were almost always in an inferior position to nationalist forces or had stirred up conflicts that ended up damaging them. The final years of the war appeared to modify or even reverse this reality, but the change would not turn out to be widespread and was restricted to particular war conditions and the Asian conflicts. The relationship between communism and nationalism also turned out to be squaring the circle in Latin America. Just as in other parts of the world, party-building in the principal countries of Latin America was carried out by emissaries of the Comintern. A typical case was Mexico, where the prospects of anti-imperialist nationalism appeared promising and the Communist Party was set up by the Indian emissary, Roy, and a Russian one, Borodin, and then led, albeit with little success, by the American communist Charles Phillips and the Japanese Sen Katayama.[100] Only in the second half of the 1920s did leading Latin American cadres start to emerge under the direction of the Italo-Argentinean Victorio Codovilla. Although Marxist intellectuals such as the Peruvian José Carlos Mariátegui developed ideas about the particular nature of peasant society on the continent, none of the communist parties adopted them. The anti-imperialist approach applied in Asia against the British and the French was unthinkingly applied against the United States, but with little success.[101] The strikes that broke out in Cuba in the summer of 1933 led to the overthrow of the Machado dictatorship, and revealed a Comintern presence that was as meddling as it was ineffectual. Its sectarian impulses prevented the communists from

[97] C. Peng, *My Side of History* (Singapore: Media Masters, 2003); C. C. Chin and K. Hack (eds), *Dialogues with Chin Peng: New Light on the Malayan Communist Party* (Singapore: Singapore University Press, 2004).

[98] Gupta, *Communism and Nationalism in Colonial India, 1939–45.*

[99] Ginat, *A History of Egyptian Communism*, 254–65; J. Franzen, *Red Star Over Iraq: Iraqi Communism Before Saddam* (London: Hurst, 2011), 39–42.

[100] D. Spenser, *The Impossible Triangle: Mexico, Soviet Russia, and the United States in the 1920s* (Durham, N.C. Duke University Press, 1999), 39–49; S. Roy, *M. N. Roy: A Political Biography* (New Delhi: Orient Longman, 1997), 22ff.

[101] M. Caballero, *Latin America and the Comintern, 1919–1943* (Cambridge: Cambridge University Press, 2002); M. Becker, *Mariategui and Latin American Marxist Theory* (Athens: Ohio University Press, 1993).

grasping the opportunity to establish new alliances.[102] Things went no better in Brazil, in spite of the communists being joined by Luís Carlos Prestes, the legendary captain who had led military guerrillas against the oligarchic republic in the 1920s. The attempted insurrection launched by the communists in November 1935 was easily quashed by the Vargas government. Subsequent repression severely affected Brazilian communism, though at the end of the Second World War it was the main party in Latin America.[103] At the time of the war in Spain, the fight against 'Trotskyism' became an imperative that kept Latin American communists busy until the end of the 1930s, when Trotsky and his followers in the Fourth International were active in the region.[104]

The only communist party on the American continent that enjoyed relative success before the war and after its outbreak was the one in the United States. After a good ten years of difficulties caused by police repression in the early interwar period but also by its own radicalism and sectarianism, the CPUSA had convinced certain sections of intellectual and trade union opinion during the years of the New Deal, by supporting President Franklin D. Roosevelt. Its leader, Earl Browder, translated the Popular Front line into a policy of 'Americanization' of the party, making it a bearer of an anti-fascist message even among Latin American communists. During the period of the Hitler–Stalin Pact, Browder safeguarded the image of his party better than others did. Moscow even conceded formal autonomy from the Comintern to the CPUSA, implicitly acknowledging its principal role as a pressure group rather than a political party.[105] This role was increased by the relaunch of the 'Americanization' policy after the USSR and the United States entered the war.[106]

The last phase of the war proved a significant turning point for many communist parties, including those outside Europe. The significance of anti-fascism in many European nations and the development of national liberation movements in the non-Western world, especially Asia, created favourable conditions that had never previously existed in the history of international communism. For some time the new prestige of the USSR and the alliance with the Western powers provided communists with a political space that had never before been enjoyed in the societies and public spheres of their own countries. However, this phenomenon only had a truly transnational character in Europe, where the advance of the Red Army, the anti-fascist resistance, and the outbreak of civil wars in the central, eastern and southern parts of the continent brought about a leap forward for the movement. The expansion of international communism at the end of the Second World War thus preserved its deeply Eurocentric character.

---

[102] B. Carr, 'From Caribbean backwater to revolutionary opportunity: Cuba's evolving relationship with the Komintern, 1925–34', in Rees and Thorpe, *International Communism and the Communist International*.

[103] Caballero, *Latin America and the Comintern, 1919–1943*, 109–20.

[104] *Komintern i Latinskaya Amerika: sbornik dokumentov* (Moscow: Nauka, 1998), docs 50, 52, 53, 54.

[105] Dimitrov, *Diario*, 243.

[106] F. M. Ottanelli, *The Communist Party of the United States: From Depression to World War II* (New Brunswick, N.J.: Rutgers University Press, 1991), 197–208.

SPHERES OF INFLUENCE, NATIONAL FRONTS, AND 'PEOPLE'S DEMOCRACY'

The Comintern's dissolution gave out a reassuring message for the Western powers, and brought to an end the institutional duality of Soviet foreign policy, creating the image of a 'normalization' of the USSR's conduct of international relations. After the turning point on the eastern front in the winter of 1942–3, the Stalinist regime emerged from the harshest phase of the war to consolidate new forms of national support. Stalin became the figure of a military and imperial leader, even though this meant justifying *a posteriori* the 'revolution from above', the state of total security, and the Terror. Stalin acquired international prestige, which was sanctioned at the Conference of the Big Three held in Teheran in November and December 1943. However, the final phase of the war not only announced a new dimension to Soviet power and its pre-eminent role in Europe, but also a much more complex scenario to be managed within the architecture of international relations. For the first time, the USSR would find itself exercising influence over sovereign states in Europe in a prospective peace very different from those of Brest-Litovsk and Versailles, because the Soviet state would dictate the conditions. But the USSR would also have to take into account the interests of the other victorious powers. This would require it to moderate—to a degree yet to be verified—the concept of security and state interests hitherto adopted by Stalin. In 1943–4, the Soviet approach was mainly to extend as far as possible the Big Three's joint supervision of all the occupied countries, whether they were defeated or liberated from the Nazi–Fascist yoke.[107] It cannot be said that this approach corresponded to a genuine model for negotiations with the allies over the definition of European order. The capacity and willingness of the Stalinist leadership to adapt to the necessary compromises for the establishment of a new international system on a consensual basis would reveal itself to be very limited.

The plans for the postwar period drawn up by diplomats reflected this approach and its limitations.[108] Immediately after Teheran on 11 January 1944, Maysky sent Molotov a memorandum on the 'desirable bases for a future peace'. The draft plan provided a long-term guarantee of security for the USSR and peace in Europe and Asia, over a period of two generations. Maysky insisted on the democratization of the defeated countries and those occupied by the Nazis 'in the spirit of the ideas of the Popular Front', and its postwar cooperation with the Western allies, also seen as a condition for the economic reconstruction of the USSR. At the same time, it proposed a redefinition of American policy as an expansionism 'of a new kind', no longer based on territorial interests and therefore different from

---

[107] V. Mastny, *Russia's Road to the Cold War: Diplomacy, Warfare, and the Politics of Communism, 1941–1945* (New York: Columbia University Press, 1979), 107.

[108] S. Pons, 'In the aftermath of the age of wars', in S. Pons and A. Romano (eds), *Russia in the Age of Wars, 1914–1945* (Milan: Feltrinelli, 2000); V. O. Pechatnov, *The Big Three after World War II: New Documents on Soviet Thinking about Post War Relations with the United States and Great Britain* (Washington, D.C.: Woodrow Wilson Center, 1995); G. Roberts, *Stalin's Wars: From World War to Cold War, 1939–1953* (New Haven, Conn.: Yale University Press, 2006), 228–32.

the traditional tendencies of imperialism. The memorandum lacked any concept of security rigidly based on spheres of influence. The prevailing vision was one of influence over Europe exercised by a common agreement between Great Britain and the Soviet Union. The author listed among Soviet interests exploitation of the tensions between the United States and Great Britain, but no return to the traditional isolationism of the USSR and, while taking into account the eventual formation of hostile international configurations, no return to predictions of new wars.[109] Litvinov's view was more pessimistic. He doubted that there could be a lasting détente between the Big Three over the German question, and considered it necessary to divide the world into spheres of influence. Litvinov associated himself with views of authoritative Western opinion-makers, such as E. H. Carr and Walter Lippmann.[110] A different point of view was submitted by Lozovsky, according to whom relations between the two hegemonic powers on the European continent, the USSR and Great Britain, were destined to deteriorate, and the task for Soviet foreign policy was to prevent the formation of an anti-Soviet bloc by the British and the Americans.[111] The options for Moscow's foreign policy appeared to vacillate between a definition of its interests in Europe that was consensual as far as possible and one that was unilateral.

Soviet policy shifted noticeably towards the assessment of spheres of influence, after the opening of the second front in the west and after the Red Army crossed the western borders of the USSR in the summer of 1944. The military campaign in Central and Eastern Europe definitively established the USSR as a great power.[112] The revival of the notion of Russian power was by then part of the Stalinist ideological baggage. But it could not be presented separately from the Soviet model without the risk of delegitimizing the regime. In their public discourse, the Soviet political authorities continued to represent the Second World War principally as a 'patriotic war'. Nevertheless, they also gave credence to an 'international civil war', as part of a cycle that had started in 1914–21. The definition of the war in terms of class constituted a key element for the revival of political propaganda within the country. The main concern was to snuff out in time the Western contamination of soldiers in the Red Army who crossed the borders of the 'socialist fatherland' into Europe in the summer of 1944, discovering a different reality from the one portrayed in Soviet propaganda.[113] An essential feature of the ideological campaign was the assumption that, with the removal of the common enemy, relations between the USSR and the Western powers would return to the path of conflict between 'systems'. The emphasis on the geopolitical positions attained by the USSR through the war combined with the idea that the future Soviet sphere of influence in Central and Eastern Europe would not only be distinguished by

[109] *Sovetskii faktor v Vostochnoy Evrope 1944–1953: dokumenty (SFVE)* (2 vols, Moscow: Rosspen, 1999, 2002), vol. 1, doc. 1, pp. 23–48.

[110] J. Haslam, *The Vices of Integrity: E. H. Carr 1892–1982* (London: Verso, 1999), 107–8.

[111] Pons, 'In the aftermath of the age of wars', 286–8.

[112] Mawdsley, *Thunder in the East*, 359.

[113] A. Werth, *Russia at War 1941–1945* (New York: Carroll & Graf, 1996), 944ff.

friendly governments but also by sociopolitical regimes half-way between the capitalist model and the Soviet one.[114]

The USSR's first political move after the opening of the second front was the
establishment of a philo-Soviet Polish government in Lublin in July 1944.[115] Talks
between Churchill and Stalin in October 1944 are the most significant episode
generally referred to when it comes to the spheres of influence, approximately
defined by setting the 'percentages' of the respective Soviet and British interests in
Southeastern Europe.[116] But the Soviet postwar plans were suddenly and significantly changed. In November 1944, Litvinov wrote a document on Anglo-Soviet
relations which foresaw the possibility of establishing lasting relations with the
other principal European power on the basis of their respective spheres, suggesting the creation of a third category of neutral countries (including Italy, Austria,
Germany, Denmark, and Norway).[117] The memorandum did not refer to the
themes of democratization and international organization, but only to the problem
of the balance of power and security zones in Europe. The Soviet strategy outside
Eastern Europe was directed towards a more targeted foreign-policy objective—
that of avoiding the formation of a Western bloc. The policy towards France and
the signing of a treaty with it in December 1944 were conceived by the Soviets for
this purpose, which foresaw a role for French power as a counterweight to Great
Britain.[118] In a memorandum of January 1945 on the eve of the Yalta Conference,
Litvinov confirmed the idea of dividing the zones of influence in Europe into three,
while stressing the advantages of establishing a privileged relationship between the
USSR and Great Britain.[119]

It is clear the proposal of 'three spheres' provided the USSR with an enormous
geopolitical space, which would be disproportionate compared with the one
reserved for Great Britain, even though neither Litvinov nor Maysky thought it
possible to define the Soviet sphere unilaterally. The two diplomats did not propose
a revision of the concept of Soviet security. Their reports reflected a traditional geopolitical vision of a nineteenth-century kind and foreshadowed the preponderance
of Soviet power in postwar Europe. The limitations of their work were evidently
not just subjective but also imposed by the decision-makers. Litvinov and Maysky
had carried out important diplomatic roles in Washington and London in the early
part of the war, but were recalled almost simultaneously to Moscow in June 1943.
Their role in the commissions on postwar structures was a demotion and of merely
consultative importance. As the most pro-Western representatives of Soviet diplomacy, both were placed under surveillance. The judgements formulated by Litvinov
in his private conversations were diligently recorded by Beria's spies and reported

---

[114] RGASPI, fo. 77, op. 4, d. 14; Pons, 'In the aftermath of the age of wars', 296–8.
[115] Mastny, *Russia's Road to the Cold War*, 167.   [116] *Istochnik* 4 (1995), 144–52.
[117] AVPRF, fo. 06, op. 6, p. 14, d. 143, ll. 31–88.
[118] G.-H. Soutou, 'General de Gaulle and the Soviet Union, 1943–5: ideology or European
equilibrium', in F. Gori and S. Pons (eds), *The Soviet Union and Europe in the Cold War, 1943–53*
(London: Macmillan, 1996), 318–25; *Istochnik* 5 (1996), 105–7.
[119] G. P. Kynin and J. Laufer (eds), *SSSR i Germanskii Vopros 1941–1949* (3 vols,
Moscow: Mezhdunarodnye otnosheniya, 1996–2003), vol. 1, doc. 140, pp. 595–7.

to Molotov.[120] The possibility of Litvinov and Maysky exercising any influence over Stalin's decisions was extremely slim. It is however admissible to think that reports approximated to the prevailing approach to foreign policy under Stalin, based as it was on spheres of influence as the essential instrument for postwar structures.

A realistic cooperation between the great powers was still an option at the end of 1944.[121] Stalin appeared to be inspired by the idea that European hegemony in world politics and the role of the British empire were not yet coming to an end, whereas the United States would represent a more important player in world affairs than in the past, while remaining distant and lacking a genuine geopolitical impact in the foreseeable future. The Yugoslav leader Kardelj recalls that in November 1944 he expressed the idea that the capitalist world was about to come under a new American supremacy, and got the following comment from Lozovsky: 'I don't know what the old man would say, given that he's convinced that England is still the centre of world imperialism and the proletariat's number one enemy, whereas he considers the role of America to be secondary.' In the same circumstance, Maysky would declare that he was in agreement with Kardelj.[122] The different opinions among the communist elites over the role of the United States had serious political implications. The Yugoslavs' assessment of the United States as the new hegemonic power of the capitalist world was in fact connected to the radically conflictual vision of relations between the capitalist world and the communist one, which inspired Tito's politics and was a division that cut across international communism.[123] The 'underestimation' of America and the 'overestimation' of Great Britain in Stalin's thought probably derived from his tendency to reject an overly conflictual scenario in the short term and to analyse the international situations in a more reassuring manner—from his point of view—and more firmly as part of a continuity of ideas concerning the conflicts between imperialist powers as the key to Soviet security. In any event, all the opinions on the table expressed reservations about the political foundations of the postwar period, which undoubtedly emanated from Stalin.

In November 1944, Stalin declared that it was the 'socialist system' that constituted the strength of the USSR, and contrasted the 'political and moral' authority of socialism with the 'politics of race hatred' of Nazism, which was 'a source of internal weakness and isolation in the foreign policy of the German fascist state'.[124] What in 1941 had been open to doubt, namely the credibility of the Soviet system, now became an axiom and retrospective justification of all past decisions. First among these was the one to build Soviet power and identify it with the socialist cause. However, Stalin did not provide his own contemporaries with a manifesto for the postwar period comparable to the Atlantic Charter, nor did he offer them any grand design comparable with that of Roosevelt. The dichotomy between Lenin and Wilson, which had attracted hopes of peace in the last year of the First

---

[120] RGASPI, fo. 82, op. 2, d. 1036.   [121] Stalin, *Works*, vol. 3 [16], p. 165.
[122] E. Kardelj, *Memorie degli anni di ferro* (Rome: Editori Riuniti, 1980), 68.
[123] G. Swain, 'The Cominform: Tito's International?', *Historical Journal* 35 (1992), n. 3.
[124] Stalin, *Works*, vol. 3, pp. 159, 162.

World War, was not repeated in the Second World War. Paradoxically, the power that failed to respond to the appeal was the heir to the socialist revolution that had claimed and petitioned to be identified with a cause concerned with the fate of all humanity. Stalin put his trust in the implicit message behind the rise of the socialist state to the position of European and world power, the only guarantee of a progressive transformation capable of uprooting fascism. That startling vacuum of ideas for the future laid bare the limitations of Soviet universalism, even in relation to its origins. The Soviet participation in the Yalta Conference, the second meeting of the Big Three in January and February 1945, did not substantially modify things. The conference's ideal was the fruit of Roosevelt's thinking. Stalin went along with it and signed the Declaration of the Denazification of Europe without providing his own contribution. He was primarily concerned with Soviet influence in Central and Eastern Europe. In his memoirs, Molotov confirmed that the Soviet leaders then saw the maintenance of the alliance as an aim that was in their interests.[125] But the very definition of Soviet interests was linked to a long isolationist and antagonistic tradition, which implied reticence over the basis for peace. The communist movement had to reflect fully on that ambivalence.

The end of the Comintern was not a traumatic event for communists, because the priority of the interests of the Soviet state was beyond dispute, at least as much as the conviction that it could not be put on a par with other states. Nevertheless the dissolution of the International had another significance, which was more difficult to absorb. Seen from Moscow, the Second World War was destined to expand socialism together with the power of the USSR, but it was not a mere rerun of the First World War. The link between war and revolution had changed. The idea of the pan-European revolution that had motivated the utopian drive of the Bolsheviks in the First World War was now a relic of the past. The fire of the revolutionary advance was concentrated in the territorial conquests of the Red Army. The communists' task was not to light the fuse of insurrection but to support and facilitate the rise of the USSR as a world power, starting in Europe. A few years later, Stalin indulged in a look at the past and told Thorez that 'if Churchill had delayed the opening of the second front in northern France for another year, the Red Army would have got to France.... We had the idea of reaching Paris.'[126]

These words appear to indicate Stalin's awareness of the USSR's new imperial force and the prospect of continental domination, glimpsed at the moment of Germany's fall. If, however, Stalin had toyed with the idea of getting to Paris, this objective was not a genuine political option in 1944. He himself had repeatedly urged the opening of the second front in Europe, and the Red Army flooded into Eastern and Central Europe only after the Anglo-American forces had reached Normandy. In reality, the Soviets gave no sign of harbouring plans for the conquest of the whole of Europe. Soviet expansionism must have been more contained than is suggested by Stalin's words to Thorez after the fact. It is probable that the

---

[125] *Sto sorok besed s Molotovym*, 76.   [126] *Istoricheskii Arkhiv* 1 (1996), 13.

memory of the summer of 1920 and the war with Poland affected Stalin's view of the past. That precedent remained valid in relation to the importance of the force of the Soviet state for the purposes of revolutionary expansion, which was invoked by Lenin in spite of the defeat. However, Stalin rejected the idea of relying on the revolutionary potential of the European masses and putting at risk the security of the USSR. The occupation of Poland was no longer an expedient for lighting the fuse of European revolution, but a decisive move to strengthen Soviet bridgeheads and with them the presence of communism in Europe.

Although the dissolution of the Comintern had eliminated the old practice of formulating a single general line for the communist parties, the policy of the 'national fronts' was applied to the whole European theatre, displaying evident links with the USSR's foreign policy. The first country in which the theory was put into practice was Italy. After the Anglo-American landing in Sicily in July 1943, the fall of Mussolini's regime, and the armistice agreement between the Allies and the military government led by Marshal Badoglio on 8 September 1943, the problem of how the forces that made up the anti-Hitler coalition and the political movements behind them were to behave towards each other had become a real one. Up to that point the 'national fronts' had been limited to resistance forces in occupied Europe, and its translation into the reality of national liberation proved more difficult and painful than it had appeared on paper. There was in fact a marked vacillation between two divergent options: the intransigent one, which rejected any form of cooperation by the resistance forces with the post-fascist regime and the monarchy in the south of the country, supported by anti-fascists and local communists, and the moderate one, which provided for communist participation in a national coalition government. In Moscow, evident uncertainty reigned for many months concerning the appropriateness of accepting or rejecting the demands for intransigence. This depended principally on foreign-policy decisions to be taken by the USSR.

Marginalized by the armistice regime which was under the control of the Anglo-Americans, the Soviets considered the possibility of exacerbating the elements of conflict with the Allies by supporting the drive towards radicalization of the sociopolitical clash in Italy, which was emerging in the north under the impact of the resistance to the Nazi occupiers and the fascists who had remained loyal to Mussolini. The alternative was to conclude diplomatic agreement with the Badoglio government, located in the southern, liberated part of the country, which would oblige the communists to cooperate and shifted the situation from conflict to political rivalry. The two alternatives and their likely repercussions were formulated by Togliatti at the end of 1943 and the beginning of 1944. It appeared that the more radical one would be chosen with the consent of Dimitrov and Molotov. But Stalin decided on the more moderate option. The essential features of the subsequent 'Salerno turning point' and the policy Togliatti, the leader of the Italian Communist Party, would pursue on return to his homeland were determined at a meeting between him and Stalin on the eve of his departure from Moscow on 4 March 1944. This provided for the abandonment of the anti-monarchical stance and opened the way for communists to join the Badoglio government, while adopting the formula of 'national unity' as the only way to avoid civil war and as a means to containing British influence.[127]

Stalin's decision did not bring to an end the previous controversies. Even after Togliatti's return to Italy, there was disagreement over whether or not to adopt the insurrectionary option. The Italian leader had to face the criticisms of the PCI's more intransigent representatives, supported by the authoritative figure of Aleksandr Bogomolov, the Soviet representative to the allied governments. Clearly this problem did not only concern the Italian situation. Italy was one of the countries where the social tensions generated by the war could easily have spilled over into revolution. For this precise reason, it was a crucial test run. Bogomolov was echoing the opinions of those who, in Moscow and Belgrade, argued that conflict between the USSR and the Western powers was inevitable or just as likely as Togliatti's interpretation of the line based on the USSR's interest in continued cooperation with the great powers even after the war.[128] The famous agreement between Stalin and Churchill in October 1944 established not only the first boundaries of the spheres of influence but also the restrictions on communist activities in the Western sphere of interest, most particularly Greece and Italy. Stalin pretended that he could exert little influence over the Italian communists, given that he could not impose directives on them through Soviet armed forces as he could in Bulgaria. Playing a part he had rehearsed too often, he argued that if he handed out orders to the Italian Communist Party, Togliatti would have been able to 'send him to the devil'. In the end he provided Churchill with the necessary assurances, suggesting that Togliatti was an intelligent person who would not embark on any 'adventures'.[129] At the same time Togliatti reasserted his leadership over the PCI, and forced its more intransigent members to hold back.[130]

The policy of the Italian Communist Party thus constituted a precedent to be followed by nearly all the European parties, and was based on three main principles: abandonment of the prospect of civil war, the decision to take part in national coalition governments, and the investiture of leaders returning from exile in Moscow and their pre-eminence over those who were participating directly in the resistance movements. On leaving Moscow to follow the political line decided on at the meeting with Stalin on 4 March 1944, Togliatti was also instructed by Dimitrov to notify the French communists of the need 'to act as a leading force in the nation' and 'as a party with respect for the state'.[131] The PCF was obliged to follow the Italian precedent, even though France was in a highly conflictual situation

---

[127] Dimitrov, *Diario*, 691–3; *KVMV*, vol. 2, docs 168, 174. See also S. Pons, *L'impossibile egemonia: l'URSS, il PCI e le origini della guerra fredda (1943–1948)* (Rome: Carocci, 1999), 145–55; E. Aga Rossi and V. Zaslavsky, *Togliatti e Stalin: Il PCI e la politica estera italiana negli archivi di Moscow*, 2nd edn (Bologna: il Mulino, 2007), 67–74.

[128] Pons, 'In the aftermath of the age of wars', 290.

[129] O. A. Rzheshevskii, *Stalin i Cherchill. Vstrechi. Besedy. Diskussii. Dokumenty, kommentarii 1941–1945* (Moscow: Nauka, 2004), 426.

[130] Pons, *L'impossibile egemonia*, 166–70.   [131] Dimitrov, *Diario*, 694.

and local communists, who were now much stronger militarily and organization-ally, were predicting a showdown with General de Gaulle.[132]

The change came with the meeting between Stalin and Thorez in November 1944, on the eve of the latter's return to France, which followed the same pattern as the one between Stalin and Togliatti six months earlier. Once again, there was an imminent and significant foreign-policy initiative: the signing of the Franco-Soviet Pact. Stalin was very insistent about the need to avoid isolation of the communists and to make political alliances, and asked Thorez to acknowledge 'that the govern-ment in France is currently recognized by the allied powers'. In such a situation, it was advisable to transform the armed organization controlled by communists 'into another organization, a political organization, while the arms need to be hidden'. He even suggested abandoning the term 'popular front', which evoked another period now passed and sounded limiting in relation to the communists' current objectives.[133]

Stalin was not interested in dividing Europe.[134] The line taken by the commu-nists did not distinguish between Western and Eastern Europe, but stressed the importance of 'nationalizing' the parties in coordination with the USSR's foreign policy. In the autumn of 1944, the line on 'national fronts' passed from theory to practice in Central and Eastern Europe, where the advance of the Red Army and the fall of the pro-Hitlerite regimes put the re-establishment of states and the creation of coalition governments on the agenda. The difference from countries in the Western sphere, like France and Italy, was that attempts to assert communist influence could count on the Soviet military presence and therefore aim for con-trol of the decisive levers of power. But the political line was formulated in almost identical terms.[135] Czechoslovak communists were the only ones to have all the requirements for 'national fronts', and could boast communist primogeniture in Central and Eastern Europe, which had been consolidated since the agreements between Stalin and Beneš in December 1943 and were based on their role in the resistance movement.[136] All the others had to adjust with difficulty and take imme-diate remedial action.

Already in Moscow's sights for having ignored the 'national fronts' line and evoked the prospect of the Sovietization of the country, the Polish communists could not even boast a significant role in the resistance movement. They were called on to forge the image of the national party to represent an alternative power to the government in exile in London since the period of the Molotov–Ribbentrop

[132] For the PCF's strategy in 1944, see P. Buton, *Les lendemains qui déchantent: le Parti communiste français à la Libération* (Paris: Presses de la Fondation Nationale des Sciences Politiques, 1993).

[133] Dimitrov, *Diario*, pp. 769–70. For the minutes of the meeting between Stalin and Thorez, see *Istochnik* 4 (1995), 152–8.

[134] N. M. Naimark, 'Stalin and Europe in the postwar period, 1945–53: issues and problems', *Journal of Modern European History* 2.1 (2004).

[135] E. Mark, *Revolution by Degrees: Stalin's National-Front Strategy for Europe, 1941–1947* (Washington, D.C.: Woodrow Wilson Center, 2001).

[136] Mastny, *Russia's Road to the Cold War*, 143.

Pact.[137] Stalin personally dictated a moderate line to the Hungarian communists, starting with the composition and programme of the new government of national unity. On receiving Moscow's directives, the Hungarian leaders adopted the French communists' model for their national party.[138] The Bulgarian communists had played their own part in the anti-Nazi resistance and, with Moscow's consent, had imposed their powerful representation on the Committee of National Liberation. However, Dimitrov asked them to consolidate their own positions without thinking of consti-tuting 'the only decisive factor in the country and dictating our will to the allies', and to remember that without the Red Army 'we would already have a civil war'.[139] The Romanian communists received instructions along similar lines.[140]

However the implications the 'national fronts' were not accepted by all com-munists. The black sheep were the Chinese in Asia and the Yugoslavs in Europe. In the case of China, the appeal to national unity was superimposed on the pol-icy of popular fronts and went back to the time of the Japanese invasion in the summer of 1937. Since then a subtle dialectic had developed between Dimitrov and Mao Zedong, who accepted all the principal slogans instructed by Moscow but twisted them into a highly daring tactic that was open to the possibility of a showdown with the nationalists. While relations between Moscow and the Guomindang in the 1930s were no longer the very close ones they had been in the previous decade, Stalin continued to provide assistance to Chiang Kai-shek, whom he considered to be the person most suited to unite the anti-Japanese front. The Molotov–Ribbentrop Pact and the attempt at détente with Japan did not modify Stalin's Chinese policy, which was governed by the priority of avoiding the scenario of a war on two fronts and therefore aimed at consolidating anti-Japanese resistance through cooperation between nationalists and communists. For his part, Mao saw the détente between the USSR and the Axis powers as another window of opportunity for conducting a struggle on two fronts: the domestic one and the anti-Japanese one. It is telling that in late 1940 and early 1941, following yet another crisis between the CCP and the Guomindang, which gave rise to a series of armed clashes, Mao argued that military mobilization and a conflict with Chiang were inevitable.[141] However, Dimitrov disapproved of Mao's position and argued that the conflict was undesirable.[142] Mao came into line with evident reluctance, declaring that the conflict would in any case be necessary in the future.[143]

---

[137] K. Kersten, *The Establishment of Communist Rule in Poland, 1943–1948* (Berkeley: University of California Press, 1991); *KVMV*, vol. 2, doc. 175.

[138] Mevius, *Agents of Moscow*, 54, 73; P. Kenez, *Hungary from the Nazis to the Soviets: The Establishment of the Communist Regime in Hungary, 1944–1948* (New York: Cambridge University Press, 2006), 25–7.

[139] Dimitrov, *Diario*, 778 (13 Dec. 1944). See also V. Dimitrov, *Stalin's Cold War: Soviet Foreign Policy, Democracy and Communism in Bulgaria 1941–48* (London: Palgrave Macmillan, 2008), 89ff.

[140] Mark, *Revolution by Degrees*; Dimitrov, *Diario*, 790 (4 Jan. 1945).

[141] Mao's communications with Dimitrov between Nov. 1940 and the beginning of Feb. 1941 can be found in *Vkp(b), Komintern i Kitay*, vol. 5, esp. docs. 135, 139, 142, 144, 151, and 152. See also Haslam, *The Soviet Union and the Threat from the East, 1933–1941*, 153–4.

[142] Dallin and Firsov, *Dimitrov and Stalin 1934–1943*, doc. 23, pp. 135–7; *Vkp(b), Komintern i Kitay*, vol. 5, doc. 153, p. 485.

[143] Ibid. doc. 24, pp. 137–41.

The outbreak of war between Germany and USSR only temporarily reduced the frictions between the unitary line dictated by Moscow and the tendency of the CCP to see the anti-Japanese struggle as a precarious armed truce with the nationalists. The question re-emerged after the start of the Pacific war in December 1941 had made a Japanese attack on the USSR less likely. By April 1942, Mao was asking Dimitrov whether it would not be advisable to react to Chiang's 'anti-communist campaign'.[144] Dimitrov replied that, in spite of Chiang's 'provocations', the CCP should do all it could to strengthen 'the united front of China in the struggle against the Japanese'.[145] After a period of apparent truce, the conflict between communists and nationalists flared up once more in the summer of 1943. In December 1943, Dimitrov wrote to Mao renewing his concerns over the CCP's 'break' with the policy of the 'national united front' and marginalization from the party of the men who has supported it, Zhou Enlai and Wang Ming.[146] Mao replied that the CCP line was 'unchanged' in spite of the risks of armed conflict with the nationalists, considered significant now the end of the war was in view. He confirmed his distrust of Wang Ming and declared his loyalty to Stalin.[147] In effect, the anti-imperialist struggle, from Mao's point of view, did not preclude civil war. At the same time, his devotion to the USSR was beyond doubt, although this did not mean blind obedience.[148]

In European communism, radical tendencies cut across all the parties. Even the Soviet representatives in Europe did not always obstruct them. These tendencies were strong and well organized among the partisans, but also had important links with the ruling groups. Yugoslav communists more than any others distinguished themselves for their reluctance to embrace the discourse of national unity, and their inclination to develop their own political and military strategy without listening too much to the advice coming from Moscow. They could carry out their role of protagonists because they had set up a strategic outpost in the Balkans through their ability to control significant portions of territory. They were therefore at the centre of the USSR's attentions. Even though the Comintern press applauded the heroic achievements of communist partisans in Yugoslavia, there was a degree of irritation in Moscow over Tito's evident propensity for acting independently. More pragmatist than theoretician, Tito had fought in the Red Army at the time of the Civil War and had lived in Moscow for much of the late 1930s. He had therefore left the USSR some time before the national wartime philosophy. He conceived the liberation struggle as the conquest of military supremacy by the communists.[149]

---

[144] Ibid. doc. 230, pp. 595–6.   [145] Ibid. doc. 235, pp. 605–6.
[146] Ibid. doc. 298, pp. 686–7.   [147] Ibid. doc. 299, p. 688.
[148] Historians are divided over the degree of Mao's independence from Stalin. For an emphasis on Mao's autonomy, see D. Heinzig, *The Soviet Union and Communist China 1945–1950: The Arduous Road to the Alliance* (Armonk, N.Y.: M. E. Sharpe, 2004). For the opposing view, see M. M. Sheng, *Battling Western Imperialism: Mao, Stalin, and the United States* (Princeton, N.J.: Princeton University Press, 1997).
[149] M. Djilas, *Wartime* (New York: Harcourt Brace, 1980), 59; G. Swain, 'Tito and the twilight of the Komintern', in Rees and Thorpe, *International Communism and the Communist International*. G. Swain, *Tito: A Biography* (London: I. B. Tauris, 2010).

Since 1942 Dimitrov had been criticizing the absence of a 'general national character' to Tito's political propaganda and the insufficient attention Yugoslav communists were paying to the creation of a 'national front'.[150] He addressed Tito in a decidedly polemical tone, which revealed the importance Moscow attributed to the new line ('You conduct a popular war of liberation with the forces of workers, peasants and intellectuals linked to the people and other patriots, and not with the proletarian struggle. You must start from this premise. Stop this—you're playing into the hands of the people's enemies, who maliciously exploit every such error on your part').[151] The question of the amount of assistance to the partisan struggle guaranteed by Moscow and the supplies demanded in vain by the Yugoslavs increased the tension.[152] In April 1944 Molotov explained to Djilas Moscow's rejection of the Sovietization of Yugoslavia, and set out the national-unity line chosen for Italy—a political lesson the Yugoslav communists would ignore.[153] In the meantime, the political and organizational model of the Yugoslav liberation movement had spread to Albania, Greece, and Bulgaria. It would shortly become clear that the intransigence of the Yugoslavs reflected a widespread sentiment throughout European communist parties—restrained but not eliminated by the tactical moderation suggested by Moscow since the time of the popular fronts.

Deaf to the lessons on pragmatism coming from Stalin and Dimitrov, the Yugoslav communist leadership had an unusual profile. Almost all the leaders of the main European communist parties who emerged after the dissolution of the Comintern had spent the first years of the war, and sometimes a much longer period, in the USSR: this was the case with Togliatti and Thorez, as with the Germans Pieck and Walter Ulbricht, the Poles Bolesław Bierut and Jakub Berman, the Hungarian Mátyás Rákosi, the Czechoslovaks Klement Gottwald e Rudolf Slánský, the Romanian Ana Pauker, and Dimitrov himself. They acted as Stalin's fiduciaries in applying the line on 'national fronts', and also as guarantors of the socialist potential inherent in the 'national roads' with the cadres and activists. Among the exceptions was the Polish leader Władisław Gomułka, who had been in prison and had then gone underground after the Molotov–Ribbentrop Pact. But the main exception was Tito, who from the beginning was the leader of the communist armed resistance and of a new ruling group. His trip to Moscow in September 1944 marked the seal of approval for his leadership, which was based on his role in the liberation movement. The subsequent offensive of the Red Army in Serbia favoured the establishment of a government of the forces of national liberation. But the status of Yugoslav communists was different from those of all other countries in the East and the West. Yugoslavia was the only country in Eastern Europe in which the communists had decided the outcome of the liberation struggle in their favour before the Red Army could become a decisive factor. They were already the dominant force in power in Belgrade, while Moscow

---

[150] *KVMV*, vol. 2, doc. 68, pp. 216–17; Dimitrov, *Diario*, 422.   [151] Ibid. 494–5.
[152] Ibid. 572–3, 594–5.
[153] *Vostochnaya Evropa v dokumentakh rossiiskikh arkhivov 1944–1953* (*VEDRA*) (2 vols, Moscow/ Novosibirsk: Sibirskii Khronograf, 1997–8), vol. 1, doc. 2, pp. 28–35.

was still instructing the European communist parties on the spirit of the 'national fronts' and while the Big Three were meeting in Yalta. In a speech delivered in Moscow on 5 February 1945, Kardelj declared that the Communist Party had taken power and that, although the international situation advised that form be respected, Yugoslavia would not be 'a half-way house'.[154] Driven by the euphoria of victory, Tito and his comrades believed that they represented the advance guard of the socialist world in expansion. They embodied a new pride instilled in communists by the success of the anti-fascist struggle, following the defeats and terror of the prewar years. The Yugoslavs fanned the flames of civil war in Greece and fomented its outbreak in Italy, as well as planning their dominance of a future confederation of Balkan states.[155]

The most startling case of insubordination was that of Greece, which revealed the limitations on Moscow's control. Having become a mass party with around 200,000 activists through the liberation struggle, the KKE behaved in the opposite manner to the PCI, by taking up arms against the alliance between London and the monarchy. The Greek communists led by Georgios Siantos played out a comedy of errors with Moscow, repeatedly requesting support that was ignored or dampened by the Soviets. Back in August 1944, Molotov had made it clear to Dimitrov that the Greeks would have to 'resolve the question they're raising on their own'.[156] In October, after the Red Army moved on Belgrade but stopped at the Greek border, Dimitrov admitted in a letter to Molotov that material assistance to Greek communists was impossible, although 'moral support' was desirable.[157] In fact, Moscow avoided taking a position. In spite of this, the Greek communists went ahead with their own plans in a country that the agreements between Stalin and Churchill had assigned to Great Britain. In December 1944, in spite of warnings from Dimitrov that Moscow would not provide any assistance, the partisan movement under communist leadership launched a mass mobilization that swiftly turned into an armed insurrection in Athens.[158]

Stalin was faced with a fait accompli, and his disapproval was total. 'I advised that this struggle would not take place in Greece,' he confided to Dimitrov, and decreed that the Greek communists had committed 'a folly' in counting on the Red Army's intervention in their country.[159] Moscow was indifferent to the bloody repression carried out with the support of the British, with the obvious intention of keeping its hands free in the Balkan countries that were part of its own sphere of influence. Shortly after the Greek communists' failed insurrection, Stalin expressed

---

[154] *SFVE*, vol. 1, doc. 35, p. 136.

[155] A. S. Anikeev, *Kak Tito ot Stalina ushel: Yugoslaviya, SSSR i SShA v nachalnii period 'kholodnoy voiny' (1945–1957)* (Moscow: Is Ran, 2002), 86ff.

[156] Dimitrov, *Diario*, 739 (15 Aug. 1944).   [157] *KVMV*, vol. 2, doc. 198, p. 474.

[158] Dimitrov, *Diario*, 776. See P. J. Stavrakis, *Moscow and Greek Communism, 1944–1949* (Ithaca, N.Y.: Cornell University Press, 1989), 35–42; A. Gerolymatos, *Red Acropolis, Black Terror: The Greek Civil War and the Origins of Soviet–American Rivalry, 1943–1949* (New York: Basic Books, 2004), 122–8; J. O. Iatrides, 'Revolution or self-defense? Communist goals, strategy, and tactics in the Greek Civil War', *Journal of Cold War Studies* 7.3 (2005), 15–18.

[159] Dimitrov, *Diario*, 794 (10 Jan. 1945).

his extreme irritation to the Yugoslav communist Andrija Hebrang over the hubris of the leaders in Belgrade. In Stalin's opinion, 'a situation is being created in which you will end up with hostile relations with Romania, Hungary and Greece. You aspire to fight the whole world; there is no sense in creating such a situation.'[160] At the time of Tito's trip to Moscow in April 1945, Dimitrov observed that the Yugoslav leader was affected by the 'vertigo of success', particularly in relation to his idea of a federation that included Bulgaria in the Yugoslav state.[161] The meeting between Tito and Stalin took up the matter of a federation to be gradually built up in stages.[162] But in practice the question was postponed *sine die*. Stalin believed that the creation of federations based on strong regional foundations would put Soviet influence at risk as well as relations with the Western powers.[163] His policy was instead the use of nationalism in Central and Eastern Europe as an instrument of imperial domination, by exploiting ethnic and national divisions to exercise control from the centre.

The tensions between the USSR and Yugoslavia culminated in the question of Trieste. In the early months of 1945, Moscow decided to support the Yugoslav claim over the city and called the Italian communists to order, as they were worried about the negative repercussions the Yugoslav annexation of the city would have on their own national image. It was probably the meeting between Stalin and Tito in April 1945 that produced this policy. Immediately afterwards, Dimitrov issued a statement on the Yugoslav annexation of Trieste, having received Stalin's consent.[164] But the arrival of Yugoslav troops in Trieste provoked a serious international crisis that Stalin had perhaps not foreseen. The Soviet decision was immediately withdrawn. Tito protested against the impositions of the great powers, but had to go into reverse.[165] The Yugoslav occupation of the city would leave a trail of violence that culminated in the killing of a few thousand people thrown into sinkholes. It was revenge for the fascist occupation, but it revealed a face similar to that of the defeated enemy.[166]

The author of this repression was no longer an armed movement carrying out a revolution but a nascent communist state, which was revealing its nature and its ambitions. The appearance of the Yugoslav communist state on the international scene heralded new political dynamics affecting the image of communism as much as threatening relations with the Soviet state. The tangle of two controversies—the territorial one that culminated in the Trieste question and the federal one concerning Belgrade and Sofia—demonstrated that the tendency to extend the borders of the eastern 'sphere' and the tendency to create a cluster around a regional pole produced the disagreeable impression in Moscow of a loss of control over the actions

---

[160] *VEDRA*, vol. 1, doc. 37, p. 130.　　　[161] Dimitrov, *Diario*, 823.　　　[162] Ibid. 824.

[163] R. C. Nation, 'A Balkan union? Southeastern Europe in Soviet security policy, 1944–8', in Gori and Pons, *The Soviet Union and Europe in the Cold War*, 125–32.

[164] Dimitrov, *Diario*, 834, 838; F. Gori and S. Pons (eds), *Dagli archivi di Mosca: l'URSS, il Cominform e il PCI* (Rome: Carocci, 1998), docs 10 and 11.

[165] M. Djilas, *Se la memoria non m'inganna: ricordi di un uomo scomodo 1943–1962* (Bologna: il Mulino, 1987), 105–8.

[166] R. Pupo, *Trieste '45* (Rome: Laterza, 2010).

of Yugoslav communists. This matter had much more serious implications than a territorial dispute or an argument between representatives of different communist parties. For the first time, there emerged the problem of reconciling the superior interests of the Soviet state not simply with those of a party that was to a great or lesser extent disobedient but with those of a new communist state, which at the same time was part of a group of forces led by the USSR and as such an agent of the movement's expansion.

VICTORY WITHOUT REVOLUTION

During the final months of the war, Moscow worked hard to create new preferential diplomatic relations with the governments of the countries in Eastern and Central Europe, starting with Poland and Yugoslavia, and to rein in the radicalism that was spreading through the European communist parties. The doctrine of the 'peaceful road' to socialism in the countries within the Soviet sphere of influence, which would become the basis for the so-called 'people's democracies', was adopted as an alternative to revolutionary insurrection.[167] In Eastern and Central Europe this idea had particular significance, given that communists were called on to play a decisive role in the formation of the social and political structures in the USSR's sphere of influence. A clear link was established between the idea of anti-fascist democracy, the search for a national dimension to the communist parties, and the USSR's foreign-policy interests. The war was not being seen as an opportunity to overthrow the economic and political basis of society, partly because they were already sufficiently disrupted. The monopoly of force won by the USSR in the eastern part of Europe could be used to strengthen the power of the new ruling classes formed by progressive forces and communists. In January 1945, Stalin told Dimitrov and Yugoslav and Bulgarian leaders, 'perhaps we were wrong in thinking that the Soviet model was the only way to socialism. It has turned out in practice that the Soviet form is the best, but it is not absolutely the only one.'[168] In April 1945 Stalin expressed this concept to Tito, who was one of the communist leaders most reluctant to listen ('Today socialism is possible even under the English monarch; the revolution is no longer necessary anywhere').[169] One of the most significant events concerning the imposition of the doctrine of 'people's democracies' in Central and Eastern Europe was the opposition of the generation of Hungarian communists who were veterans of the Soviet Republic of 1919, which they looked back on with nostalgia. They were marginalized.[170]

---

[167] G. P. Murashko and A. F. Noskova, 'Sovetskii faktor v poslevoennoy Vostochnoy Evrope (1945–1948)', in *Sovetskaya vneshnyaya politika v gody 'Kholodnoy voyny' (1945–1985): novoe prochtenie* (Moscow: Mezhdunarodnye otnosheniya, 1995), 90.

[168] Dimitrov, *Diario*, 802.

[169] Djilas, *Conversations with Stalin*, 120.

[170] Mevius, *Agents of Moscow*, 82–6.

The same policy was advised for German communists. Unlike other European communist parties, the KPD had no experience of resistance and had to rely principally on the Soviet presence in the eastern part of Germany. Immediately after the start of the occupation in early June 1945, the German leaders met Stalin, Molotov, and Zhdanov. The question on the agenda was the German communists' political programme and how to restore the KPD as a mass party. In these circumstances, Stalin declared it inappropriate to establish the Soviet system in Germany and suggested the prospect of an 'anti-fascist, parliamentary, democratic regime'.[171] According to Pieck's notes, the discussions between the Germans and Soviets revealed uncertainty over whether to pursue the prospect of 'two Germanies' or the idea that German communists should struggle for a united Germany. What was agreed, however, was the line of broad political alliances bringing in both social democrats and Catholics, as well as neutralizing the radical influence of the local anti-fascist committees that has sprung up spontaneously at the end of the war.[172] In Germany, as in Hungary, activists of the communist left who conserved the memory of the period just after the First World War and yearned for revolutionary action of the 'Bolshevik' kind were swept aside by the occupation authorities and the leaders returning from exile in Moscow.[173]

Out of the Red Army's range, the leaderships of the Italian and French parties were on the same wavelength. In both cases, strong insurrectionist minorities, made up of young people enrolled in the partisan formations and older cadres, were reined in and made to see the reason of more moderate thinking. Togliatti publicly announced that the 'Greek prospect' was a danger that had to be averted.[174] Once in the final phase of the war, the question of whether Italy and France should become a second Greece became a point of strategic disagreement both inside the PCI and the PCF, and between the Western communist leaderships and the Yugoslav one. The legacy of the main resistance movements with strong communist components was thus divided in two: on the one hand, national revolution was identified with social revolution in Yugoslavia and Greece, where engagement in the armed struggle had preceded the 'national fronts' line; on the other, the automatic transition from national liberation to revolution was contained and then blocked in France and Italy, where, on the whole, the opposite had happened.[175]

In the light of Soviet interests, Moscow held up anti-fascist democracy as the model for all European communist parties. Not only the parties operating in the Soviet 'sphere of influence' but also those in countries in the Anglo-American sphere of interest had to follow its inspiration and adapt it to the very different conditions of Western Europe, where the consequences of war were less destructive

---

[171] Dimitrov, *Diario*, 841.

[172] W. Loth, *Figliastri di Stalin: Mosca, Berlino e la formazione della RDT* (Urbino: QuattroVenti, 1997), 26–2.

[173] N. M. Naimark, *The Russians in Germany: A History of the Soviet Zone of Occupation, 1945–1949* (Cambridge, Mass.: Harvard University Press, 1995), 257–8, 271.

[174] P. Spriano, *I comunisti europei e Stalin* (Turin: Einaudi, 1982), 214–15.

[175] For an overview of the resistance movements in France, Italy, Yugoslavia, and Greece, see T. Judt (ed.), *Resistance and Revolution in Mediterranean Europe 1939–1948* (London: Routledge, 1989).

and traumatic. Although nebulous and transitory, this model did however pose a crucial question for communist history and identity. Was a civil war of the kind experienced in the Second World War the end of an era to be buried alongside fascism, or did it proclaim the continuity of the 'international civil war'? Did the catastrophist perspective of civil conflict remain the ideal condition for communist action, or should it, quite to the contrary, be avoided because experience showed that the forces of the radical right profited from it, and the strength of the USSR and the communist movement made it possible to impose a peaceful transition to socialism? Stalin did not in fact provide any real answer to these questions. The pragmatism preached by Moscow was not a clear decision to revise cultural and political thinking, as had already occurred before the war. In Eastern and Central Europe, the objective of Sovietization was discouraged through a language of tactics and opportunism, because it would have provoked a reaction from enemy forces internationally and from within. In Western Europe, the prospect of insurrection was obstructed by invoking the supreme interests of the USSR's foreign policy. But the ideological surveillance against any possible revisionism was not relaxed.

A very instructive signal, partly because of its timing, was the affair of the American leader Browder. At the beginning of 1944, he proposed the dissolution of the CPUSA and its transformation into a current of opinion that aimed to consolidate the not insignificant presence of communists, in a manner more suited to the structure of the American political system and modelled on the prospect of a postwar alliance between Moscow and Washington. In a letter to Molotov in March 1944, Dimitrov suggested inviting Browder not to go 'too far in adapting to the changing international situation, to the point of negating the theory and practice of the class struggle'.[176] Dimitrov's statement constituted a serious warning. However, Browder continued along his own path without Moscow's permission, believing that he was following the 'principles' expressed by the Big Three in Tehran. In May 1944 he formally launched the proposal of a new communist 'association' which would replace the party, and immediately afterwards enthusiastically supported Roosevelt's third re-election. Signals of a cold or even a hostile reception appeared from several quarters. In April 1945, Browder was publicly attacked by the French communist Jacques Duclos in an article prompted by the Soviets, using the same arguments Dimitrov had used a year earlier. Browder vainly attempted to defend himself while relations between Moscow and Washington deteriorated after Roosevelt's death. A few months later he was removed from the leadership of the new movement and the CPUSA was reconstituted. Within a few years it had become an irrelevant sect.[177] The Browder affair demonstrated the limited leeway for innovation and the continued existence of a shared cultural base for the various tendencies that emerged in international communism during the

---

[176] *KVMV*, vol. 2, doc. 176, p. 437. See also Dimitrov, *Diario*, 696.
[177] J. G. Ryan, *Earl Browder: The Failure of American Communism* (Tuscaloosa: University of Alabama Press, 1997), 230–45, 246ff. For the Soviet prompting of the article against Browder, see H. Klehr, J. E. Haynes, and K. M. Anderson, *The Soviet World of American Communism* (New Haven, Conn.: Yale University Press, 1998), docs 18, 19, 20, pp. 100–5.

Second World War. No other communist official would have Browder's courage to bring about change. The divisions within the political and diplomatic world of European and Soviet communism were restricted, although not lacking importance. The idea of using the opportunity provided by the war for the purposes of social revolution in Europe, and in view of the imminent conflict between the socialist world and the capitalist one, coexisted with that of a peaceful transition and cooperation with the West even after the war. All communist leaders believed they were acting in the interests of the USSR. No one even thought, as far as we know, of withdrawing their loyalty or challenging the movement's unitary basis by opening a political conflict. Every one perceived Stalin's authority as beyond debate. Stalin interpreted the change of European and international structures produced by the war as the consequence—favourable to the USSR and international communism—of a historic upheaval which only had to be supported and did not impose any political or cultural reform.

The idea of promoting anti-fascist democracy was in many ways an attempt to provide a response to the question of European order in the postwar period. But it was a temporary and reversible response. In Stalinist political discourse, there was an argument that the time had come to leave behind the era of tears and blood. But this discourse was never really followed through, and it did not subvert radically opposing convictions that had deep roots. If anything, Stalin argued that it was necessary to launch a transitional model in the Soviet sphere of influence, given that a social revolution risked provoking undesirable international reactions and that the export of the Soviet model was unpopular in Europe. The experience of the second half of the 1930s provided a useful precedent, partly because of its vagueness. Arising out of the terrain of the Spanish Civil War for the purpose of moderating revolutionary trends in order to concentrate on the war effort, the idea of anti-fascist democracy could now be applied to a very different situation, that of the peaceful reconstruction of Eastern and Central Europe under the aegis of the USSR. The 'people's democracy' had the advantage of providing an alternative both to the more radical tendencies in communist parties and to liberal democracy in Western Europe. This would be a less cruel transition than the one experienced in the Soviet Union, but destined to create a political and social structure irreversibly oriented towards future socialist transformation, thanks to the central role assigned to the communists under the USSR's influence, interpreting the popular masses' need for change.[178]

Yet Stalin took the spheres of influence more seriously than he did anti-fascist democracy. The Soviets did not see anti-fascist democracy as a political paradigm capable of influencing or even modifying the dominant role of their model of the state and society. They were, on the other hand, sufficiently aware that in Eastern and Central Europe the devastating consequences of the war were carrying out a fundamental revolutionary task: the liquidation of the old ruling classes. The

---

[178] F. Bettanin, *Stalin e l'Europa: la formazione dell'impero esterno sovietico (1941–1953)* (Rome: Carocci, 2006).

destruction of European Jews by the Nazis had opened the way to a structural change in the urban social classes in the East. The collapse of the new Nazi order left the USSR with the legacy of societies whose upper class had been decapitated and which were on their knees or complicit in the endemic violence and deprived of a clear notion of legality and political legitimacy. With the exception of Czechoslovakia, the prewar regimes had cultivated nationalism but not democracy, and their passing was not widely regretted, particularly where, as in Hungary and Romania, they had been guilty of active collaboration with the Nazis. Immediately after the war, the forced transfer of millions of Germans to the west completed the social earthquake—a cultural levelling out and ethnic and national homogenization. All this opened up space for transformative policies and practices introduced from above and destined to follow the route traced out by Soviet interests.[179] From this point of view, the 'people's democracy' alluded to the drive to homogenize politics and society in Eastern and Central Europe.

While the war created structural conditions particularly favourable to communists in the eastern part of Europe, their attraction increased in an unprecedented manner in the whole continent. It had appeared that the Molotov–Ribbentrop Pact destroyed the credibility of the communist movement in Europe. Hitler's attack on the USSR revived it. Through the armed struggle against fascism in Europe, communists gained new members as never before. Unlike the First World War, the Second World War triggered a series of civil wars, generated by the conflict between partisan movements and fascist or collaborationist regimes, but also by conflicts within the resistance itself, which in different periods involved a long front of countries from the Baltic to Byelorussia, the Ukraine to Poland, and the Balkans to Italy.[180] The transformation of the communist parties from cadre parties into mass parties took place in some of the more important cases, such as the Yugoslav Party and the Italian Party, in the context of civil war generated by world war. The characteristics of intransigence, discipline, organization, and the willingness to sacrifice themselves and others allowed communists to exploit the extreme situation of civil war, even though they did not refer to it as a political objective but rather presented themselves, except in Yugoslavia and Greece, as the exponents of national reconciliation.

In the final phase of the war it was still difficult to measure accurately the expansion of the communist parties in terms of activists, let alone in terms of votes. But it was already clear that, when they ceased to be underground organizations, many European communist parties were gaining mass followings. The most startling cases were those of parties that had lacked any significant presence between the wars, and had emerged from what had been underground organizations since long before the war. In Yugoslavia, the Communist party was a party of elitist cadres, but it had almost a million partisans under its command. In Italy, the

---

[179] J. T. Gross, 'War as revolution', in N. M. Naimark and L. Gibianskii (eds), *The Establishment of Communist Regimes in Eastern Europe, 1944–1949* (Boulder, Colo.: Westview Press, 1997).

[180] Mazower, *Hitler's Empire*, 502–7; A. J. Rieber, 'Civil wars in the Soviet Union', *Kritika: Explorations in Russian and Eurasian History* 6.1 (2003).

Communist Party had reached an unprecedented level of half a million members. In the final months of the war, there was a considerable rise in the number of registered Communist Party members in Hungary, Romania, and even Poland, from a few thousand to several hundred thousand. To complete the picture, the same occurred in countries where communists had been a significant political and social force before the war: France, where the party returned to its previous level of about 300,000 members, Czechoslovakia, and also Germany.[181] Communist ambition to mobilize a critical mass of working people and replace social democracy, which had been frustrated after the First World War, seemed to be within reach after the Second World War.

Europe in 1945 was no more revolutionary than Europe in 1918, but it was more willing to bury its recent past—just as, a quarter of a century earlier, the war had brought into play simplistic and schematic views of politics and society that promised immediate change without compromise. The communist mindset was well suited to this, just as their ethos of builders of progress in modern mass society gained credibility from denouncing the failure of liberal capitalism between the wars. They were no less favoured by the disappearance of radical nationalists, who after the First World War had been the main beneficiaries of the crisis of liberal civilization. The communists tapped into a need for renewal and a break with the Nazi nightmare, which was widespread among the young, including those who had more or less consciously followed fascist ideology. They could be admired for their self-abnegation and heroism, or feared for their mercilessness and use of violence, but it was difficult to deny their role in Europe's liberation from Nazism. In this sense, anti-fascist credentials were a resource and not a limitation for the conquest of sectors of society beyond those that identified with the Resistance. Contrary to Furet's argument, communism did not create the anti-fascist political space, but occupied it for political and cultural reasons.[182] Communists did not invent anti-fascism, but they knew how to develop its potential influence. Nazi Germany's hegemony of anti-communist ideology during wartime favoured the affirmation of communism as a European political culture on a par with liberal, socialist, and democratic Catholic political cultures, a development that could not be taken for granted in the 1920s and 1930s. Unlike the prewar years, anti-fascism did not just define a movement confined to forces of the left, but connoted the image and profile of the allied states against Hitler, apparently overcoming the international isolation of the USSR. Being part of anti-fascism facilitated the creation or relaunch of the national image of the communist parties, especially in countries that the Red Army could not occupy, in spite of the disastrous precedent of the Hitler–Stalin Pact. Anti-fascism was thus a vehicle for the legitimization of the communist movement. It was not a mask or pretence, but an identity superimposed on the original revolutionary calling.

---

[181] For an overview, see A. Agosti, *Bandiere rosse: un profilo storico dei comunismi europei* (Rome: Editori Riuniti, 1999), 132–41.

[182] F. Furet, *Il passato di un'illusione: l'idea comunista nel XX secolo* (Milan: Mondadori, 1995), 399–403.

However, anti-fascism was not the communists' only identity, nor was it the principal one. The growth of the communist parties in the final phase of the war demonstrated that they had something in which significant layers of European society could identify and disproved the idea that their strength was based exclusively on Moscow's financial and organizational support. Even in the case of the CPUSA, a party that owed its survival in the past to Soviet finances, it was the war that created the conditions for increased influence, which then faded in spite of the enormous resources Moscow poured into the United States in the years to come. But the ideological and psychological dependency of communists on the USSR would not slacken. The new anti-fascist spirit did not free the movement from the original primacy of the state. The victory appeared to minimize the crimes and tragedies of the prewar years and send them into oblivion—including those crimes that had been directed at communists themselves. The same could be said of the pact with Hitler. The myth of the patriotic war and the personal prestige acquired by Stalin brought together the threads of previous mythologies, in spite of the ambivalence displayed at the beginning of the war.

Outside the USSR, revolution, planned economy, collectivization, military-industrial power, and victory in war could appear to be the links in a continuum based on historical rationalism, as well as on a civil religion. Within the USSR, the myth of patriotic war tended to replace and obscure the previous stratifications, portraying a nationalist and militarist image, which relegated the original internationalism to the background. Stalin avoided founding a universalist discourse on the USSR's military triumph. The authority assured by victory, the revival of the Soviet myth, and the growth of the communist movement were considered more than sufficient to establish the influence of the Soviet state in the postwar world. Although the USSR, together with Poland and Yugoslavia, was the country most affected by the terrifying consequences of the Nazis' war of subjugation in the East, and was in need of a huge reconstruction programme, what mattered more was the new military, patriotic, and imperial spirit of its elites. The principal objective had to be establishing Soviet domination over Eastern and Central Europe, but this obscured the other side of the coin: while the expansion of the influence and power of the USSR was—in communist eyes and for many anti-fascists—a form of deliverance and a guarantee of progress, the great majority of Europeans perceived it as another yoke and another threat.

4
Time of Empire (1945–1953)

'This war... differs from all those in the past: whoever occupies a territory also imposes his social system on it. Each one imposes his social system, wherever his army can go.'... At this point he stood up, pulled up his trousers as if preparing himself for a fight or boxing match, and shouted as though out of his mind: 'The war will soon finish. In fifteen or twenty years we'll have built up our strength, and then we'll give them another blast.'

Stalin to Djilas, April 1945

The atomic bomb is a paper tiger that the American reactionaries use to terrorise people. They seem fearsome but in reality they are not so powerful.

Mao Zedong, August 1946

The military defeat of the bloc of fascist states, the war's nature of anti-fascist liberation, the decisive role of the Soviet Union... have radically changed the balance of power between the two systems, the socialist one and the capitalist, in favour of socialism.

Andrei Zhdanov, 25 September 1947

THE BIRTH OF THE 'EXTERNAL EMPIRE'

In 1945 the destiny of the Soviet state and the movement linked to it appeared to have been overturned in relation to five years earlier. The conflict had been an earthquake that had created a vacuum of power in the heart of Europe, which was destined to be filled primarily by the USSR. The way had been opened for radical transformation in many European societies, which offered communists a new role. The restructuring of world power posed completely different challenges from those experienced in the previous decade, which could be dealt with by deploying the enormous capital of prestige acquired by the victory over Nazism. In spite of this, Stalin did not formulate any change in policy, and stuck to the established framework of the past. The options he took into consideration included neither an alliance with the West, with a view to creating a new international order after the war, nor its liquidation for the purposes of the pure and simple occupation of the geopolitical vacuum at the centre of the continent. In the world as it was seen from Moscow, it was not desirable to trigger crises and uncontrollable revolutions, particularly in relation to the security of the Soviet state, but nor was it conceivable to expect a lasting peace between socialist and capitalist powers, which were incompatible in the long term. Thus the foundations of Stalin's policies after the Second World War had to be based on an ambivalent notion of the USSR's interests. The security of the state took priority over revolutionary prospects, but the policy of Soviet power was based on a persistent ideological view of the world.

Stalin held firm to his belief in a 'war of position' over the long term—one between the capitalist West and the Soviet state with the forces under its control. At the time of giving his lesson on political behaviour to the Yugoslavs in January 1945, he launched into a eulogy of himself, and provided a key to his thoughts on foreign policy that revealed the connection between his ideological dogmatism and unscrupulous pragmatism:

> In his time, Lenin never dreamt of the balance of power we have achieved in this war. Lenin thought that everyone would attack us and that it would be good if even one distant country, for example America, stayed neutral. But now what has happened is that one group of the bourgeoisie has lined up against us and the other with us. Lenin never thought that we could unite in alliance with one wing of the bourgeoisie and fight another. We managed to do this. We don't let ourselves be guided by our emotions, but by reason, analysis and calculation.[1]

Shortly afterwards, in his speech in the presence of Yugoslav and Bulgarian delegations at the end of February, Stalin went so far as to make a prediction. He referred back to the Bolshevik tradition of the 'international civil war' with the precision of someone expressing a key feature of their own thought. In his opinion, 'the democratic current of capitalists' had allied itself with the USSR to obstruct the domination of Hitler would lead 'to the overthrow of capitalism itself', but in the future communists would fight 'also against this current of capitalists'.[2] The famous politico-territorial formula expressed shortly afterwards to the Yugoslav leader Djilas produced a complementary principle, by which the real change brought about by the Second World War was that 'whoever occupies a territory also imposes their social system on it'.[3] This formula implied a clear distinction between the two parts of Europe, Western and Eastern. Although all communists followed the same line on 'national unity', the Western ones had to adapt to the realities dictated by the Western sphere, whereas the Eastern ones had much more room for manoeuvre in the Soviet sphere. Stalin did not allude to an immediate programme of Sovietization, but did predict the notion of 'two worlds' each opposed to the other. In this vision, the 'people's democracy' and the Soviet system were placed on the same side of a world divided between two antagonistic systems. This created the premises for a policy of homogenization of the sphere of influence and the suppression of political and social diversity in the countries of Eastern and Central Europe as a result of the changes brought about by the war.[4]

---

[1] *VEDRA*, vol. 1, doc. 37, pp. 132–3.
[2] G. Dimitrov, *Diario: gli anni di Mosca (1934–1945)*, ed. S. Pons (Turin: Einaudi, 2002), 802 (28 Jan. 1945).
[3] M. Djilas, *Conversations with Stalin* (London: Hart-Davis, 1962), 121.
[4] N. M. Naimark and L. Gibianskii (eds), *The Establishment of Communist Regimes in Eastern Europe, 1944–1949* (Boulder, Colo.: Westview Press, 1997); V. Tismaneanu (ed.), *Stalinism*

After Yalta, Moscow's tendency to consolidate its influence over Eastern and Central Europe became increasingly clear. Stalin maintained that the *de facto* recognition of the Soviet sphere of influence by Roosevelt and Churchill allowed for the adoption of resolute methods without provoking too much scandal. Roosevelt's death in April 1945 did not modify this concept. In Stalin's view, it would be enough to proceed gradually and with circumspection to avoid upsetting Western sensibilities, but guaranteeing the objective of exercising the high degree of control and subjugation considered necessary in the light of the USSR's interests. At the same time, he had no trust in a lasting partnership with the Western powers and was unwilling to sacrifice Soviet security requirements beyond a certain threshold, which were to transform the countries belonging in the past to the buffer zone into an area of allied and aligned countries. This threshold was very low indeed. To our knowledge, Stalin had no plan for the Sovietization of Eastern and Central Europe.[5] As Norman Naimark observed, the preconditions for this consisted more in a political culture that acknowledged a single model of socialist society, and was incapable of conceiving the exercise of power other than through domination and total security.[6] The advance of the Red Army created conditions for the construction of new communist states. The interaction between the Soviet state and the communist movement was at the centre of the dynamic that would establish the Soviet 'external empire'.

Even before the end of the war, Soviet policies in Eastern and Central Europe had displayed highly repressive tendencies, particularly in Poland. The prelude was the Red Army's decision to halt at the gates of Warsaw in the summer of 1944, while the Nazis bloodily suppressed the uprising by the national liberation movement and thus annihilated the anti-Soviet forces of the Polish resistance.[7] In a dramatic historical paradox, the liberation of the country from the barbaric Nazi yoke brought the return of the deportations and internments that, on a smaller scale, recalled the brutal regime of Soviet occupation of 1939–41.[8] Although claiming to avoid civil war as they did in other European countries, the Soviets supported the communists through the armed forces and the security services in what was a drawn-out civil war with the anti-communist forces of the liberation movement which opposed the government in Lublin—a war whose after-effects would long

---

Revisited: The Establishment of Communist Regimes in East-Central Europe (Budapest: Central European University Press, 2009); Z. Brzezinski, *The Soviet Bloc: Unity and Conflict* (Cambridge, Mass.: Harvard University Press, 1967).

[5] F. Fejtö and M. Serra, *Il passeggero del secolo: guerre, rivoluzioni, Europe* (Palermo: Sellerio, 2001), 229.

[6] N. M. Naimark, 'The Sovietization of Eastern Europe, 1944–1953', in M. P. Leffler and O. A. Westad (eds), *The Cambridge History of the Cold War* , vol. 1: *Origins* (Cambridge: Cambridge University Press, 2010), 175–97; N. M. Naimark, 'Stalin and Europe in the postwar period, 1945–53: issues and problems', *Journal of Modern European History* 2.1 (2004), 36.

[7] N. Davies, *Rising '44: The Battle for Warsaw* (London: Macmillan, 2003).

[8] A. Paczkowski, 'Polonia, la "nazione nemica"', in S. N. Courtois, N. Werth, et al., *Il libro nero del comunismo: crimini, terrore, repressione* (Milan: Mondadori, 1998), pp. 348–50.

be felt.[9] In this context, the efforts of Polish communists to present themselves as a national party, following an already steep path, were in any case frustrated by the violent conduct of Soviet military and administrative bodies, which Moscow was unwilling to discourage.

In May 1945 Gomułka presented Moscow with an alarming portrayal of his party's weakness in society and a veiled protest against the behaviour of the Soviet authorities, but obtained only a scolding from Dimitrov, who accused him of presenting the Red Army as 'an obstacle' instead of 'the liberator' of Poland.[10] Moscow censured Gomułka's requests to curb the escalation of repression by Soviet security bodies.[11] On the other hand, the Polish communists were aware that, without the support of the Red Army and the NKVD, they would not have been able to maintain their grip on power. There was no solution to the dilemma. Given the historical precedents of the war of 1920 and the Molotov–Ribbentrop Pact, it was not surprising that the Soviets adopted preventive policies of repression without too much concern for their effects on the popularity of the USSR and local communists. In Poland, the presence of anti-Russian and anti-Soviet sentiments was taken for granted, as was the weakness of the Communist Party in society. From mid-1945, the existence of the opposition was hanging by a thread, even though the moderate forces grouped around Stanisław Mikołajczyk appeared to be maintaining a presence. In November 1945, Stalin reminded Gomułka that a party 200,000 strong, as the Polish party now was, should be able to control the country and establish its monopoly of power.[12]

However, Poland was not entirely an exception. Once the war in Europe was over, the interference of Soviet bodies and the tendency of local communists to put up with it or even request it increased rather than decreased, demonstrating that the 'people's democracies' were going to become authoritarian political systems because of their very structures. This was first manifested in Romania and Bulgaria. At the famous meeting of the 'percentages', Churchill had acknowledged Stalin's overriding Soviet interests in both countries. The processes of interaction were different, but the results were similar. In Romania, a country where communists had always been weak and which had been a close ally of Nazi Germany, the Soviet intervention was immediately on a massive scale. The political alliances suggested by Moscow to the Romanian communists were short-lived. Faced with a political crisis in the country in March 1945, the Red Army intervened and imposed the

---

[9] K. Kersten, *The Establishment of Communist Rule in Poland, 1943–1948* (Berkeley: University of California Press, 1991), 102–3. See also A. J. Prazmowska, *Civil War in Poland, 1942–1948* (London: Macmillan, 2004).

[10] *SSSR-Polsha. Mekhanizmy podchineniya. 1944–1949 gg: sbornik dokumentov* (Moscow: Airo-XX, 1995), doc. 30, p. 120.

[11] I. Iazhborovskaia, 'The Gomułka alternative: the untravelled road', in Naimark and Gibianskii, *The Establishment of Communist Regimes in Eastern Europe, 1944–1949*, 135. See also Kersten, *The Establishment of Communist Rule in Poland*, 137.

[12] 'New evidence on Poland in the early Cold War', *Cold War International History Project Bulletin* 11 (1998), 135.

creation of a new government controlled by communists in Bucharest. From that moment, there was a clear development towards authoritarianism.[13]

In Bulgaria, a country less resistant to the communist tradition and which did not go to war against the USSR, in spite of its participation in the Hitlerite coalition, the Soviets were more willing to let things take their course gradually. The national communists had a leading role in the creation of the regime. On the eve of Potsdam, Stalin even expressed his perplexity over the 'sectarian approach' of the Bulgarian communists towards the non-communists in the government.[14] In Moscow, they continued to think that the 'national unity' line was necessary in the light of relations with the Western powers, and the elections planned for August 1945 were postponed. In the following months, the Bulgarian communists obtained consent from Moscow for their measures against the opposition. Dimitrov's return to the country on the eve of the elections in November 1945 was confirmation of this. The elections were not a conclusive transition, as the opposition candidates withdrew. The affair dragged on for some time, but the route to the communists' firm control of government had been mapped out. The Bulgarian affair throws light on the role played by a communist party stronger than the others in determining an authoritarian solution, by exerting pressure on Moscow rather than submitting to it.[15]

The Potsdam Conference, the third meeting of the Big Three in July–August 1945, did not therefore have any moderating influence on the behaviour of the USSR or the communists in Poland, Romania, and Bulgaria. Dimitrov noted that they were opening the prospect of a consolidation of the Soviet 'sphere of influence' in the Balkans.[16] Elsewhere, the definition of the USSR's interests appeared increasingly vague and uncertain. Yet the dynamics of interaction between Soviet bodies and local communist bodies was leaving its mark on all the countries in Eastern and Central Europe. In Hungary, the country that had been most closely linked to Nazi Germany, the conduct of the Red Army was particularly vindictive and unrestrained. The Soviets showed themselves to be indifferent to the damage inflicted by their repressive actions on the national communists. As in the case of Poland, Moscow ignored the concerns raised by the Hungarian communist leader Rákosi.[17] In Soviet strategy, the two countries were at opposite poles: Poland constituted an absolute priority, while Hungary was of secondary interest. The gradualist line Moscow followed towards Hungary might even have constituted a counterweight to mitigate Western concerns over the destiny of Poland. The dynamics triggered by the main players were not, however, dissimilar.

---

[13] E. Mark, *Revolution by Degrees: Stalin's National-Front Strategy for Europe, 1941–1947* (Washington, D.C.: Woodrow Wilson Center, 2001), 24–5.

[14] Dimitrov, *Diario*, 853.

[15] V. Dimitrov, *Stalin's Cold War: Soviet Foreign Policy, Democracy and Communism in Bulgaria 1941–48* (Basingstoke: Palgrave Macmillan, 2008).

[16] Dimitrov, *Diario*, 863 (6 Aug. 1945).

[17] *SFVE*, vol. 1, doc. 57, pp. 195–204; M. Mevius, *Agents of Moscow: The Hungarian Communist Party and the Origins of Socialist Patriotism, 1941–1953* (Oxford: Oxford University Press, 2005), 64–8.

Except in the case of Bulgaria, where the communists had an active role, the fragility of the communist presence and the perception of a strong anti-communist tradition drove the Soviets to adopt easier methods of preventive repression, which would leave their mark. Although they raised objections and reservations, the local communists fell into line. They looked on the Soviet bodies as the institutions they referred to for the refoundation of their own states and national governments. Soviet guardianship was for them quite acceptable and a guarantee of privileged access to power, even when they were in a minority. The alienation of large sectors of society was considered inevitable in a process experienced as a revolution, as they were persuaded that agrarian reforms and nationalizations would structurally modify the social dynamics. The dependency on Soviet bodies was an insoluble contradiction for communists when it came to winning national consensus, but it was a constituent of their political culture. This induced them to support the conduct of the Soviets even when its rationality was highly questionable, or to play the role of zealous pupils by anticipating the Soviets' real or assumed intentions. It was not so much a well-thought-out strategy as a culturally motivated practice tending towards the destruction of the democratic public sphere.[18]

Yugoslavia completed this panorama by putting itself forward as the principal bulwark of the new system, and as the pacemaker for the others. Yugoslav communists set themselves up in power without any decisive intervention from Soviet bodies, although the Red Army behaved no differently from how it did elsewhere. They believed themselves to be a revolutionary power and did not identify with the formula of 'people's democracies'. The elections of November 1945 were carried out in a situation of effective political monopoly, which produced a plebiscitary result. From that moment on, they set about the construction of a Soviet-type regime.[19] Under the massive influence of Belgrade, Albania went down the same route. There remained the unique case of Czechoslovakia, the only country in Eastern and Central Europe in which communists, having been dominant in the resistance, could boast not only an increase in membership but also a significant social consensus in circumstances of political pluralism. The Communist Party was increasing its membership, particularly among the younger generations, by exploiting the memory of Munich in an anti-Western sense, the promise of moral renewal, and the widespread expectations of profound changes in society and the economy. The government led by Gottwald was a genuine coalition with a gradualist programme, although it relied on a precarious balancing act.[20]

In Germany, the dynamics of and interactions between Soviet bodies and national communists followed a similar path to other countries in Eastern and Central Europe more subject to intervention by the USSR. However much Germany was

---

[18] J. T. Gross, 'War as revolution', in Naimark and Gibianskii, *The Establishment of Communist Regimes in Eastern Europe, 1944–1949*, 31–3.

[19] J. R. Lampe, *Yugoslavia as History: Twice There Was a Country* (Cambridge: Cambridge University Press, 1996), 225–6.

[20] B. F. Abrams, *The Struggle for the Soul of the Nation: Czech Culture and the Rise of Communism* (Lanham: Rowman & Littlefield, 2004), 139–55; I. Lukes, 'The Czech road to communism', in Naimark and Gibianskii, *The Establishment of Communist Regimes in Eastern Europe*, 249.

the central country in the restructuring of postwar Europe, the Soviets pursued no coherent objectives for the long term from the moment of their occupation. Stalin did not make any clear decision concerning the maintenance of the country's unity or its division, although it is likely that he considered the second possibility right from the beginning. The Red Army and the NKVD treated the population, and in particular women, with brutal and gratuitous violence. The bodies set up by the Soviets adopted a punitive attitude aimed at a policy of requisitions, the dismantling of assets, and reparations, for the purpose of facilitating the reconstruction of the economy in the USSR and weakening German productive capacity. Thus communists were unpopular for being identified with the interests of the occupying power instead of the interest of the nation. Having noted the relative weakness of the KPD, which did have a mass following but not one comparable with that of the SPD, Moscow decided at the end of 1945 to force through the unification of social democrats and communists. The idea of unification could have inspired the unitary tendencies that were already followed by communist and socialist activists, but in reality it was a decision imposed by the Soviets and their German partners. They were not unaware of the first electoral results in Hungary and Austria in November 1945, which recorded a very modest performance by the communists, far below expectations. The prospect of a similar result in Germany persuaded Stalin that he had to request the unification of the two parties, in spite of resistance from the socialist leaders.[21]

The creation of the new unified party, the SED (Socialist Unity Party of Germany), was pushed through by April 1946 and was clearly placed under the guardianship of the Soviet authorities. This decision clearly restricted political pluralism, and aimed at avoiding the risk of losing control of the occupied zone, but it also widened the rift between the Soviet zone and the others.[22] The interaction between Moscow and the communist parties of Eastern and Central Europe had visibly produced a spiral of events even before international tensions went beyond the point of no return. As the first year after the war was coming to an end, the USSR's 'sphere of influence' had not yet been sovietized, but it was characterized by a range of authoritarian and semi-authoritarian regimes under the decisive influence of the occupation forces. This obviously influenced the creation of blocs in a bipolar world.

Stalin had long been vacillating between two different visions of the postwar world: one was the idea of the USSR as a third pole in an international system divided by imperialist interests, as in his opinion had been the case in the interwar years; the other was a form of bipolarism which had the advantage of upgrading the USSR as a world power but the drawback of reawakening a threat that had always been considered ruinous for the USSR—that of having a united capitalist

[21] *Istoricheskii Arkhiv* 4 (1996), 117.

[22] G. P. Kynin and J. Laufer (eds), *SSSR i Germanskii Vopros 1941–1949* (3 vols, Moscow: Mezhdunarodnye otnosheniya, 1996–2003), vol. 2, pp. 26–8, and doc. 91, pp. 379–82; N. M. Naimark, *The Russians in Germany: A History of the Soviet Zone of Occupation, 1945–1949* (Cambridge, Mass.: Harvard University Press, 1995), 283.

world brought together by its anti-communist hatred. He probably modified his perception of the United States at the time of the Yalta Conference, when he sensed their hegemonic role.[23] However, the decisive shift to a bipolar concept in Moscow came as a reaction to the dropping of atomic bombs on Japan by America in August 1945. In the months that followed, the Soviets embarked on a massive programme to develop atomic weapons, which was supervised by a special committee chaired by the chief of the NKVD, Lavrentiy Beria, and was the origin of the Soviet military-industrial complex.[24] Stalin understood the potential threat and political force of the bomb in postwar international politics, which nullified most of the significance of the scenario of American isolationism. At the same time, this apprehension was translated into the perception of a real threat. In his memoirs, Molotov argued that 'the bombs were certainly not directed against Japan, but against the Soviet Union', and summarized the meaning of America's 'atomic diplomacy': 'You don't have an atomic bomb, whereas we do: here are the possible consequences of any false move on your part.'[25] The Stalinist perception of the political use of the bomb diminished the security benefits for the USSR, which had been brought about by the war and were evident in Yalta.

From the summer of 1945, the Soviets believed that there had been a serious change in the balance of power that had emerged from the war.[26] Stalin's plan to occupy northern Japan militarily and establish Soviet influence as he had done in Germany was thwarted.[27] The first signs of an increasing chill in relations came in the autumn of 1945, when Stalin accused the loyal Molotov of being overly accommodating to the West, particularly on the German question.[28] Stalin's thinking became clear in his first speech of political significance after the war, which he gave on 9 February 1946. He interpreted the Second World War as 'the inevitable result' of the development of economic and political forces based on monopolistic capitalism. In his opinion, the settlement of conflicting interests between the imperialist powers could not be achieved peacefully.[29] Lenin's teaching on the causes of war was still valid. Less than a year after Hitler's fall, Stalin was expressing the fairly explicit prophecy of another future world conflict. Thus the foundations were laid for building the Soviet superpower and setting out the USSR's global

[23] J. Haslam, *Russia's Cold War: From the October Revolution to the Fall of the Wall* (New Haven, Conn.: Yale University Press, 2011), 33.

[24] D. Holloway, *Stalin and the Bomb: The Soviet Union and Atomic Energy, 1939–1956* (New Haven, Conn.: Yale University Press, 1994), 134ff. See also M. Kramer, 'Research note: documenting the early Soviet nuclear weapons program', *Cold War International History Project Bulletin* 6 and 7 (1995–6), doc. 1, pp. 269–70.

[25] *Sto sorok besed s Molotovym. Iz dnevnika F. Chueva* (Moscow: Terra-Terra, 1991).

[26] V. O. Pechatnov, 'The Soviet Union and the outside world, 1944–1953', in Leffler and Westad, *The Cambridge History of the Cold War*, vol. 1: *Origins*, 97–8; A. Gromyko, *Memorie* (Milan: Rizzoli, 1989), 102–7.

[27] Haslam, *Russia's Cold War*, 63–4.

[28] A. O. Chubaryan and V. O. Pechatnov, 'Molotov "the Liberal": Stalin's 1945 criticism of his deputy', *Cold War History* 1.1 (2000).

[29] I. V. Stalin, *Works [Sochineniya]*, ed. R. McNeal (3 vols, Stanford, Calif.: Hoover Institution, 1967), vol. 3, pp. 2–3.

role, in spite of the destruction suffered during the war and the state of exhaustion and demoralization in which Soviet society found itself.[30]

The escalation of tensions between the Soviets and the West during 1946 was a gradual but inexorable reality, a dynamic that the main protagonists could not control.[31] The exchange of invective between Churchill and Stalin was only the prelude. In Fulton, the British statesman declared that an 'iron Curtain' had come down in Eastern Europe; the Soviet leader replied by claiming that Moscow had legitimate security interests and expressing his fear of a single power dominating the world in the postwar period.[32] At the same time, international tensions, already deteriorating because of Soviet behaviour in Eastern and Central Europe, were exacerbated by the crisis in Turkey and Iran, where Stalin was testing the ground for further expansion of the Soviet geopolitical sphere of influence.[33] For the remainder of 1946, Stalin maintained his polemical approach to the Truman administration but remained cautious about the development of international politics. On 4 September 1946, Zhdanov confided to Dimitrov that Stalin did not think another war possible in the short term. Stalin's thinking was that the 'clamour' provoked by the Anglo-Americans over the possibility of a war was 'nothing more than blackmail', and that 'the contradictions between England and America' would soon become apparent. Moscow's assessment was that communist influence in the world was on the increase.[34] Neither 'atomic diplomacy' nor the United States' abandonment of isolationism appeared to have brought about any substantial change in the fundamental concepts of Stalin's foreign policy. But these concepts hid a sense of vulnerability that in the past had already intensified the all-consuming imperatives of security, and now had to face up to America's military, economic, and military potential. Thus developments in Moscow were cautious and took place backstage, reflecting those occurring in Washington following George F. Kennan's 'long telegram' in February 1946, which pressed for the adoption of a policy of containment against the threat he identified in Soviet communism.

In the summer of 1946, the principal strategic decisions for the USSR's reconstruction were taken on the basis of autarky and rearmament. Foreign policy was moulded by the perceived American threat. The increasing level of international conflict interacted with the increasing rigidity of the Soviet regime's ideological stance. The decision to give priority to the reconstruction of Soviet power to resist the Anglo-Americans meant further austerity, which frustrated the hopes for change running through Soviet society following the terrible suffering of the

---

[30] V. Zubok and C. Pleshakov, *Inside the Kremlin's Cold War: From Stalin to Khrushchev* (Cambridge, Mass.: Harvard University Press, 1996), 34–5.

[31] M. P. Leffler, *For the Soul of Mankind: The United States, the Soviet Union, and the Cold War* (New York: Hill and Wang, 2007), 57–8.

[32] Stalin, *Works*, vol. 3, pp. 35–43.

[33] V. Zubok, *A Failed Empire: The Soviet Union from Stalin to Gorbachev* (Chapel Hill, N.C.: University of North Carolina Press, 2007), 36–45.

[34] G. Dimitrov, *Dnevnik 9 mart 1933–6 februari 1949* (Sofia: Universitetsko izdatel'stvo 'Sv. Kliment Okhridski', 1997), 535.

war. In the spring and summer of 1946, a plan for economic reconstruction was drawn up, prioritizing heavy industry and atomic weapons. There was a return to the political propaganda and censorship of the prewar period. In August, a violent domestic campaign was started against the 'cosmopolitanism' of intellectuals, and Soviet propaganda abroad also accelerated sharply. The objective was to fight the influences that might have affected not only prisoners of war but also soldiers in the Red Army, whose advance into Europe had constituted the first break with Soviet isolationism and was considered a possible source of contamination in the highest political circles.[35] The first turning point in the USSR's foreign policy came on 27 September 1946, when Nikolai Novikov, the Soviet ambassador in Washington, gave a speech under Molotov's direction in which his main argument was that the United States' foreign policy in the postwar period was now distinguished 'by a tendency towards world domination' in response to the 'USSR factor'.[36] This bipolar perception echoed the theories of the influential economist Varga on the predominant role of the United States in the economics and politics of the postwar period.[37] While Varga suggested that the fundamental characteristics of capitalism and imperialism had changed, and emphasized the regulatory function of the state, Novikov and Molotov insisted exclusively on the expansionism of the United States and the threat this constituted to the USSR. This viewpoint was clearly reflected in Molotov's public statement, even though Stalin asked him to avoid the expression 'Anglo-American bloc'.[38] On the whole, Moscow viewed the deterioration in the international situation as inevitable long before the pronouncement of the 'Truman doctrine'.

Stalin continued for some time to support the principal arguments concerning party organization in the Soviet sphere of influence as established after the dissolution of Comintern—namely the link between the 'national roads to socialism' and anti-fascist democracy. As he had already done on several occasions since the end of the war, he explained to Walter Ulbricht, the German communist leader, the essential elements of the 'democratic road' to socialism.[39] In talks with a Polish delegation, he stressed that the dictatorship of the proletariat and Sovietization of the country were not necessary, because the traditional ruling class had been discredited and the presence of the Red Army guaranteed against any return to the past. In his opinion, Poland was 'a democracy of a new kind' destined to constitute a model even for the Western democracies.[40] In a meeting with Polish socialist leaders on 19

[35] A. Graziosi, *L'URSS dal trionfo al degrado: storia dell'Unione sovietica, 1945–1991* (Bologna: il Mulino, 2008), 62.

[36] *Mezhdunarodnaya Zhzn'* 1(1990), 148–54. According to Novikov's memoirs, Molotov himself took part in drafting the document: see N. V. Novikov, *Vospominaniya diplomata: Zapiski 1938–1947* (Moscow: Izdatel'stvo politicheskoy literatury, 1989), 352–3.

[37] R. B. Day, *Cold War Capitalism: The View from Moscow 1945–1975* (Armonk, N.Y.: M. E. Sharpe, 1995), 36–9.

[38] *Vneshnyaya politika Sovetskogo Sojuza, 1946 god* (Moscow, 1952), 378–7; V. O. Pechatnov, '"Strel'ba kholostymi": sovetskaya propaganda na Zapad v nachale kholodnoy voyny, 1945–1947', in *Stalin i kholodnaya voyna* (Moscow: Ivi Ran, 1998), 192.

[39] W. Loth, 'Stalin's plans for post-war Germany', in F. Gori and S. Pons (eds), *The Soviet Union and Europe in the Cold War, 1943–53* (London: Macmillan, 1996), 26.

[40] *VEDRA*, vol. 1, doc. 151, p. 457.

August 1946, he declared that in the countries of Eastern and Central Europe the war had opened up 'a different and easier method of development that demands less blood—the method of socio-economic reforms'—and had given rise to a 'new democracy', a 'more complex' democracy compared with the prewar experiences.[41] He said much the same to a British Labour Party delegation and the Czechoslovak communist Gottwald ('Our road was much shorter and rapid, and it cost many lives and much blood. If you can avoid this, then get on with it. The price of victims and blood needed to be paid, and it has already been paid by the Red Army').[42] Even Bulgarian communists, by then already in power, were instructed to put to one side the aim of setting up the dictatorship of the proletariat.[43] Stalin's assertions appeared to authorize the continuation of the politics introduced in the final period of the war. The formula of the 'national roads to socialism' was echoed in the political discourse of the main European communist leaders in both the East and the West during 1946.[44]

However, the language of gradualism and reconciliation with democratic institutions did not obliterate the language of intransigence, classism, and anti-imperialism. This was particularly evident in Germany, but also elsewhere.[45] The policy of national integration of the communist parties in Eastern and Central Europe had already been modified in most cases by the experience of being in power. Given the pressure brought to bear by the USSR, the objective of installing a system of 'people's democracies' based on the centrality of the communists proved incompatible with the creation of a credible national image. Stalin modified the strategy of purging nationalities that had distinguished his prewar imperial expansion in order to pander to nationalism and ethnic homogeneity, as in Poland.[46] In particular, the communists' nationalist discourse exploited anti-German resentment and supported the expulsion of Germans from regions of Eastern Europe. But this manipulation only created a short-term consensus.[47] Even the agrarian reforms and nationalizations, which were also supported by socialists and other political forces, did not redress the communists' minority status. Their only prospect remained the installation of a 'dictatorship of the proletariat', as Rákosi argued after his meeting with Stalin in April 1946.[48]

[41] Ibid. doc. 169, p. 511.

[42] Dimitrov, *Dnevnik*, 535; G. P. Murashko and A. F. Noskova, 'Sovetskii faktor v poslevoennoy Vostochnoy Evrope (1945–1948)', in *Sovetskaya vneshnyaya politika v gody 'Kholodnoy voyny' (1945–1985): novoe prochtenie* (Moscow: Mezhdunarodnye otnosheniya, 1995), 90.

[43] V. Dimitrov, 'Revolution released: Stalin, the Bulgarian Communist Party and the establishment of the Cominform', in Gori and Pons, *The Soviet Union and Europe in the Cold War*, 284.

[44] P. Spriano, *I comunisti europei e Stalin* (Turin: Einaudi, 1982), 264–5.

[45] E. D. Weitz, *Creating German Communism, 1890–1990: From Popular Protests to Socialist State* (Princeton, N.J.: Princeton University Press, 1997), 313–21.

[46] T. Snyder, *The Reconstruction of Nations: Poland, Ukraine, Lithuania, Belarus, 1569–1999* (New Haven, Conn.: Yale University Press, 2003), 184–7.

[47] W. A. Kemp, *Nationalism and Communism in Eastern Europe and the Soviet Union: A Basic Contradiction?* (London: Macmillan, 1999), 100–1; N. M. Naimark, *Fires of Hatred: Ethnic Cleansing in the Twentieth Century* (Cambridge, Mass.: Harvard University Press, 2001), 109–11.

[48] C. Békés, 'Soviet plans to establish the Cominform in early 1946: new evidence from the Hungarian archives', *Cold War International History Project Bulletin* 10 (1998).

In early September 1946, Stalin stated in a conversation recorded by Dimitrov that the 'people's democracy' was a 'convenient mask' which would be replaced by a 'maximalist programme', thus revealing his duplicity.[49] Running in parallel with the increasing rigidity of Soviet domestic and foreign policy between mid-1946 and early 1947, there were further repressive measures to introduce uniformity across Eastern and Central Europe.[50] The strict control exercised by communists over the key ministries, the police, and other agencies, the enforced merger with the socialists along the model already adopted in Germany, the elections carried out in a climate of police harassment, and the persecution, intimidation, and arrest of the principal anti-communist exponents definitively set in place authoritarian regimes in Poland and Romania, which thus joined Bulgaria and Yugoslavia.[51] Only in Czechoslovakia did they organize regular elections in May 1946, in which the KSČ emerged as the party with a relative majority, winning almost 40 per cent of the votes—a unique event in the whole of Europe. In the rest of Eastern and Central Europe—including Hungary, the network of local communists and Soviet administrative, police, and military agencies constituted the central nucleus of the new power.[52] The communists of Eastern and Central Europe were beginning to resemble governors of the Soviet empire. Unsurprisingly, Stalin continued to treat them as subordinates and party functionaries rather than fellow statesmen.[53]

THE FOUNDING OF THE COMINFORM

The growth of the communist parties, which was already clear at the end of the war, was consolidated during the first year of peace. For the first time in their history, communists outside the USSR were more numerous than those within it. In Europe they now numbered 6 million, as against the figure of barely a million before the war, and in China there were more than a million (while in the USSR, the party had grown from 2.5 million, following the purges of the late 1930s, to 5.5 million members, following the recruitment during the Great Patriotic War). Communist parties participated in government in the majority of European countries, including many Western ones.[54] These apparently triumphal statistics obscured areas of darkness. Above all, the number of activists was certainly inflated

[49] Dimitrov, *Dnevnik*, 535.

[50] M. Kramer, 'Stalin, Soviet policy, and the consolidation of a Communist bloc in Eastern Europe', in V. Tismaneanu (ed.), *Stalinism Revisited: The Establishment of Communist Regimes in East-Central Europe* (Budapest: Central European University Press, 2009), 72–3.

[51] Kersten, *The Establishment of Communist Rule in Poland*, 315–41; V. Tismaneanu, *Stalinism for All Seasons: A Political History of Romanian Communism* (Berkeley: University of California Press, 2003), 90–3.

[52] P. Kenez, *Hungary from the Nazis to the Soviets: The Establishment of the Communist Regime in Hungary, 1944–1948* (New York: Cambridge University Press, 2006), 135–40.

[53] F. Bettanin, *Stalin e l'Europa: la formazione dell'impero esterno sovietico (1941–1953)* (Rome: Carocci, 2006), 201.

[54] A. Agosti, *Bandiere rosse: un profilo storico dei comunismi europei* (Rome: Editori Riuniti, 1999), 146.

(where communists were in power or looked as though they were about to be) by memberships motivated by opportunism and careerism rather than by genuine support. Becoming a communist during the war meant risking your life, but after the war, in countries occupied by the Red Army, it guaranteed a future. The weakness of the past persisted in vast areas of Europe, particularly Northern Europe, which remained large impervious to communist influence, with the exception of Iceland and Finland. Even in most of Eastern and Central Europe, the communist advance was by no means overwhelming. Compared with the interwar period, the Czechoslovak and French communist parties had revived their previous support, in spite of the heavy blows inflicted on them in the late 1930s, but this was not true of the German Communist party in the zones of Western occupation, and seemed increasingly unlikely in the future.[55] A genuine leap forward, also clear by the end of the war, had been achieved by previously weak parties such as those in Yugoslavia and Italy, which now represented new strongholds for European communism. In spite of this, they were destined in different ways to constitute the exception and not the rule.

The generational turnover in communist party cadres was significant, although not as traumatic as it had been in the late 1920s and the years of the Terror. Communist politics did not just involve officials who had experienced prison or exile, working in clandestine networks or living at the Hotel Lux in Moscow. Throughout Europe a new wave of communists, coming from the middle class as much as the working class, rapidly achieved positions of responsibility, which bolstered the movement and gave it renewed vitality and hopes for a new beginning. Moulded by the experience of anti-fascism, their ethos did not differ from that of the previous generations in terms of their discipline and spirit of sacrifice. But their memories were different: they did not go back to the Revolution and the political battles of the 1920s, but were based on more recent Soviet myths, 'real existing socialism' and the 'patriotic war', which would prove formative for the generation recruited around the time of the war and its aftermath.[56]

This generational turnover brought about a greater female presence, favoured by universal suffrage, and a capacity for widening the parties' social base, although the working-class component remained fundamental. Where the parties were more successful in extending their membership amongst the middle classes and women, as in Italy, their penetration and influence increased massively compared with the interwar period. The growth in women's participation in the parties and unions, favoured by the considerably increased presence of women in the public sphere during the war, played a decisive role in the struggle for civil and social rights in Western Europe. Even in terms of social and gender issues, however, the communist expansion was patchy and had areas of weakness. The interclass and often prevalently rural membership reflected the backward nature of some countries rather than a genuine capacity for expansion, particularly in Eastern and Central Europe.

---

[55] P. Major, *The Death of KPD: Communism and Anti-Communism in West Germany* (Oxford: Clarendon Press, 1997).
[56] R. Samuel, *The Lost World of British Communism* (London: Verso, 2006).

The sexist tradition of the KPD of the Weimar days was not just a memory of the past, and female representation amongst the leadership and cadres was minimal, even in Western Europe. The start of the Cold War would compromise—though not eliminate—the changing gender relations created by the war.[57]

The difference between the two parts of Europe would increase. Whereas the communist parties of Eastern and Central Europe could largely ignore the question of legitimacy, since their access to power was guaranteed by Soviet influence, those in Western Europe were obliged to give it serious consideration. Their credibility could not rely solely on the Soviet myth revived by its victory over Nazism, the experience of the resistance and their profile as progressive forces. These were necessary conditions, but not sufficient for significant expansion into Western societies. In a pluralist, competitive political and social environment, anti-fascist discourse and national identity needed to be refined and expanded upon. In Western Europe, the war had not erased all the political institutions, the ruling class, and prewar social relations. In different ways, the communists had the task of emphasizing a recent past without too much reference to the more distant one, and had to be able to recite their own classist credo with a new sense of national belonging. In France, they had to erase the memory of their less flattering episodes, such as their defeatism at the time of the war with Nazi Germany. In Italy, they had to deal with the long process of mass indoctrination carried out by the fascist regime. Both the PCF, which obtained 26 per cent of the vote in the elections to the Constituent Assembly in October 1945 and over 28 per cent in general election a year later, making it the largest party in France, and the PCI, which obtained 19 per cent in the election to the Constituent Assembly in June 1946, won over a much larger section of society than the parties in Eastern Europe, with the exception of the KSČ. Both could compete on equal terms with their country's socialist parties. For the PCF, this success returned the party to its significance during the years of the Popular Front, whereas for the PCI this was an absolutely new reality. However, it was Togliatti's 'new party' that displayed the greater capacity for avoiding political isolation, not only because it entered into an alliance with a pro-Soviet socialist party of a similar size, but also because it cleverly adapted itself to the institutions of the newly formed republic. The PCI played a significant role in the Constituent Assembly and opened the door to an unprecedented mass recruitment, which by 1946 had already created a membership of almost 2 million activists, more than twice the already considerable membership achieved by the PCF.[58]

Compared with the interwar period, European communism was proving capable of developing its own political models. The anti-institutional model of the Weimar KPD was now a thing of the past. The anti-fascist model, which came into existence in the second half of the 1930s, had now been regenerated but was also,

[57] G. Eley, *Forging Democracy: The History of the Left in Europe, 1850–2000* (Oxford: Oxford University Press, 2002), 32ff.

[58] S. Courtois and M. Lazar, *Histoire du parti communiste français* (Paris: PUF, 2000), 238–9; R. Martinelli, *Storia del Partito comunista italiano*, vol. 6: *Il 'partito nuovo' dalla Liberazione al 18 aprile* (Turin: Einaudi, 1995), 174–5.

much more than before, a source of several variants. The tradition of combative anti-fascism, which had been identified with the Spanish Communist party before the war, was now living on primarily in the Yugoslav and Greek parties. Its distinguishing features were based on the link between civil war and power, military organization, and the cadre party. In the 'people's democracies' the same tradition was carried over into the control of the levers of power rather than a genuine spirit of activism. In the Soviet zone of occupation in Germany, the communist party converted the intransigence of its tradition from the Weimar days into a strategy of order and discipline in the construction of a socialist regime.[59] The tradition of legalistic anti-fascism re-emerged where it was born—in the French and Czech parties—and established itself in the Italian one. Its main features were parliamentarianism, roots within society, and the mass party. In each of these variants, the link with the USSR was strong but articulated through different visions of how to balance the party's interests with those of the Soviet state. The link with Moscow guaranteed material assistance and privileged access to power in the Soviet sphere of influence, but much less political support for communists engaged in a civil war outside it, given that this could be entail a collision course with the security interests of the USSR. On the other hand, that link guaranteed the use of the myth and Soviet resources for the purpose of putting down roots in society, but could also be an impediment to a party's national credibility, particularly when international relations deteriorated.

The unified and disciplined nature of the movement appeared to have kept at bay challenges to orthodoxy. Stalin's personality cult was at its height. The metamorphosis of the parties into authoritarian regimes in Eastern Europe led to homogenization. And yet the USSR's authority and the enlargement of international communism were not immune to contradictions. The world of European communism was less monolithic than it appeared, even though it continued to rotate around the Soviet state. Participation in the resistance had created a sense of pride and party patriotism that was previously unknown. All communists pretended to follow the interests of the USSR as their lodestar, but each one put forward their own interpretation. The differentiation between moderates and radicals, which clearly emerged from the end of the war, ran through all parties and considerably complicated relations between the centre and the periphery. The division of Europe into spheres of influence created different behaviour patterns. The contexts and tasks of postwar reconstruction made the situation even more complicated. The legacy of the Second World War was as much diversity as it was uniformity.[60]

The domestic and international tensions of 1946 had a significant effect on relations between the Soviet state and the communist movement. Since the end of 1945 there had been a new foreign-policy department in the Soviet party under the direction of Mikhail Suslov and the supervision of Zhdanov, who had taken

---

[59] Weitz, *Creating German Communism*, 313, 356.
[60] S. Pons, 'Stalin and the European communists after World War Two (1943–1948)', in M. Mazower, J. Reinisch, and D. Feldman (eds), *Postwar Reconstruction in Europe: International Perspectives, 1945–1949* (New York: Oxford University Press, 2011).

over management in the Politburo of ideology and relations with the communist parties. The new department included the bureaucratic structures that survived the demise of the Comintern, which up till then had been under Dimitrov's direction.[61] Shortly afterwards there was talk of a new body for the European communist parties. The matter was brought up in a few meetings attended by Stalin, Tito, Rákosi, and Dimitrov. After the meeting between Stalin and Molotov on 1 April 1946, the Hungarian leader reported to his party on the need to set up 'a new International', different from the Comintern and fulfilling no organizational functions. Rákosi made clear that the time had not yet come, and that before taking this step they would have to deal with the elections in France, Czechoslovakia, and Romania, as well as the conclusion of the peace treaties.[62] At the end of May, Stalin rejected Tito's enquiry into the matter, declaring that the re-establishment of the Comintern was not 'even up for discussion'.[63] In spite of this, Stalin shortly afterwards discussed the possibility of creating a new body for international communism that would carry out the function of exchanging information between parties, at a meeting organized by the Yugoslav and Bulgarians, while pointing out that closing down the Comintern had been a sensible decision, as it had 'untied the hands' of the communist parties.[64] The reinstatement of an international body for communist parties was therefore on the agenda at the highest levels of the communist leadership. In particular, the British leader, Harry Pollitt, and the Italian, Pietro Secchia, expressed their unhappiness with the lack of such a body as a riposte to the Socialist International.[65] The idea of reinstating an international communist body was probably just a few of the more radical leading communists in Europe flying a kite—particularly the Yugoslavs. In any event, the project lay dormant until mid 1947.

The proclamation of the 'Truman Doctrine' in March 1947 did not alarm the Soviets. The accusation of being a totalitarian power on a par with Germany was for them defamatory but entirely expected. American intentions to replace Great Britain as the guarantors of Greece and Turkey were also predictable and did not upset Stalin's geopolitical realism too much. It was the expulsion of Western communist parties from government coalitions and the announcement in May and June 1947 of plans for American assistance in the reconstruction of Europe that provoked a reaction from the USSR. Moscow started to see the policy of establishing communist parties nationally as a source of weakness and an unacceptable dissipation of energy. On 2 June 1947—three days before George Marshall's

---

[61] RGASPI, fo. 17, op. 128, d. 846; G. Adibekov, *Kominform i poslevoennaya Evropa* (Moscow: Rossiya Molodaya, 1994), 15 ff.

[62] Békés, 'Soviet plans to establish the Cominform in early 1946', 135–6.

[63] *Istoricheskii Arkhiv* 2 (1993), 28.

[64] L. Gibianskii, 'The Soviet bloc and the initial stage of the Cold War: archival documents on Stalin's meetings with communist leaders of Yugoslavia and Bulgaria, 1946–1948', *Cold War International History Project Bulletin* 10 (1998), 113–15, 127.

[65] R. Martinelli and M. L. Righi (eds), *La politica del Partito comunista italiano nel periodo costituente: i verbali della direzione tra il V e il VI Congresso, 1946–1948* (Rome: Editori Riuniti, 1992), 573.

speech at Harvard announcing the plan that would bear his name—Zhdanov told Thorez of Soviet concerns over the exclusion of French communists from the government and his evident irritation with the lack of adequate information. He harshly declared that 'many people think that the French communists agreed their actions' with the Soviet party. 'You know very well that this isn't true, that the steps you took were totally unexpected', Molotov appraised the Eastern European communist leaders, as well as Pollitt, of the content of Zhdanov's letter to Thorez.[66] Two days later, on 4 June, there was a meeting between Stalin and Gomułka in which they discussed convening a conference of communist parties.[67] Stalin appeared to revive the project suggested by Rákosi and Tito the year before, albeit in rather vague terms without specifying the creation of a genuine political organization.

Moscow sent a delegation to the Paris Conference that launched the Marshall Plan, a decision that probably arose from a belief in their own ability to influence Western policy.[68] However, Molotov realized that the Marshall Plan was unlike the aid programmes during the war, and they could no longer exploit divisions between Western powers. Stalin and Molotov were wrong-footed by America's willingness to finance German recovery, as they had been expecting the West to be interested in keeping Germany weak, and intended to make themselves the standard-bearer of a strong and united Germany.[69] They found themselves being driven into the scenario of dividing the country. As soon as it was clear that America's aid plan provided for German recovery in the context of the reconstruction of Western Europe, Moscow's priority became the maintenance of control over their own sphere of influence.

The resilience and cohesion of the Soviet sphere could not be taken for granted. Domestic conflicts were appearing in some Eastern and Central European countries that had the potential for creating international repercussions. At the end of April 1947, shortly before the crisis of the multi-party government, Rákosi set out for Molotov the scenario for a 'power struggle' in Budapest and requested Soviet support. The Hungarian leader praised the Yugoslavs, famously hostile to the very idea of 'people's democracies', and criticized the Czechoslovaks.[70] The Soviets also considered Czechoslovakia to be the weakest link. In June, Moscow received unsettling information about the Communist Party's behaviour, which was seen as being governed by parliamentary activity and unable to strengthen its positions in the state apparatus and the army.[71] At the same time, the Soviets were preparing to repudiate the theory of 'people's democracies'. In reality, the drive for uniformity with the Soviet model was not only a product of Moscow's making; it was being encouraged

[66] RGASPI, fo. 77, op. 3, d. 89.
[67] Adibekov, *Kominform i poslevoennaya Evropa*, 23–4.
[68] *Sto sorok besed s Molotovym*, 88.
[69] N. M. Naimark, *The Russians in Germany: A History of the Soviet Zone of Occupation, 1945–1949* (Cambridge, Mass.: Harvard University Press, 1995), 299–301.
[70] *VEDRA*, vol. 1, doc. 209, pp. 616–18.
[71] Ibid. doc. 219, pp. 649–55; doc. 222, pp. 661–4.

by the more radical elements of international communism. In May 1947 the economist Varga was heavily criticized, as he had gone out on a limb boldly examining the particularities of 'people's democracies' as transitional regimes, particularly the Yugoslavs, who claimed that they were the model for the other Eastern European parties.[72] The rejection of the doctrine of 'people's democracies' sounded like the proclamation of the return to the imperatives of Soviet security. The last remnants of pluralism in the countries of the Soviet sphere of influence could be interpreted as a possible breach for the West to exploit. In the summer of 1947, Zhdanov rejected any possibility of modifying the traditional concepts of Soviet security. In his opinion, the changes in the balance of power brought about by the Second World War were not sufficient to nullify the notion of 'capitalist encirclement' on which the definition of Soviet security was based. Zhdanov reaffirmed the centrality of the 'Soviet Factor' in world politics, just as Stalin had done twenty years earlier, and pre-emptively disowned any return to Bukharin's 'revisionist' concepts.[73]

Stalin's decision to reject the Marshall Plan provided the fundamental political push to recover control of the communist parties. Moscow decided not only to reject any involvement in the aid programme, but also to obstruct the participation of countries in Eastern and Central Europe. Serious rifts between these parties soon appeared. The keenest to lend their support for this decision were the Yugoslavs, who immediately asserted their interpretation of the American plan as interference in the internal affairs of European countries.[74] Very different was the reaction from other parties, particular the Czechoslovaks, who were preparing to take part, as they saw the American plan as necessary to the reconstruction of their country.[75] On 9 July, Stalin told Gottwald and Jan Masaryk that he had made his mind up when information he had obtained persuaded him that 'in the guise of assistance with extended credit to Europe a Western bloc is being organized against the Soviet Union', and argued threateningly that Czech participation would be tantamount 'to isolating the Soviet Union'.[76] Stalin stressed the geopolitical importance of Czechoslovakia in relation to Germany, which he now considered to be a threat that would return sooner or later.[77] Molotov recalled the decision to reject the Marshall Plan: 'We wanted to ask all the socialist countries to participate, but we soon realised that this was mistaken. They [the Americans] wanted to draw us into their team, but in a subordinate position. We would have been dependent on them, without receiving anything in return; without doubt we would have been subservient, particularly the Czechs and the Poles, who were in a

---

[72] Murashko and Noskova, 'Sovetskii faktor v poslevoennoy Vostochnoy Evrope (1945–1948)', 94; A. B. Ulam, *Titoism and the Cominform* (Cambridge, Mass.: Harvard University Press, 1952), 69–95.

[73] RGASPI, fo. 77, op. 4, d. 18.   [74] *VEDRA*, vol. 1, doc. 224, pp. 668–9.

[75] Lukes, 'The Czech road to communism', 250–1.

[76] *VEDRA*, vol. 1, doc. 227, p. 673.

[77] Murashko and Noskova, 'Sovetskii faktor v poslevoennoy Vostochnoy Evrope (1945–1948)', 93.

difficult position.'[78] The Soviets perceived the Marshall Plan as a geostrategic threat in the entire European theatre, particularly in view of its attractiveness to the more unstable countries of Eastern and Central Europe. This laid the foundations for a response involving a political mobilization.

Once the danger of opening the floodgates to American interference had been overcome in Eastern and Central Europe, the next steps were the consolidation of the sphere of influence and the deployment of the strong following enjoyed by the major Western communist parties to weaken the Western 'bloc'. The Soviet expectation was that it would be torn apart by internal contradictions which would not be resolved but exacerbated by the American plan. Dissatisfaction with the behaviour of Western communists was becoming acute. As early as the Paris Conference, Molotov and Djilas shared their disapproval. Djilas criticized the French communists because, in his opinion, they were deluding themselves 'that American imperialism would not be able to prevent their return to government' and because 'they were too involved in national politics'. Molotov corrected Djilas on the question of national politics, but complained forcefully about the relations between the Western communists and Moscow ('It's good that they have a national policy; the problem is that this policy is not co-ordinated with that of the peoples' democracies and the USSR').[79] In the meantime, Zhdanov forced the Finnish communists to reject the strategic alliances they had previously been developing.[80] At a meeting with Dimitrov on 8 August 1947, Stalin confirmed his considerable unhappiness with the way the French communists were behaving; as he saw it, they were victims 'of the fear that without American loans, France would be ruined', and he extended his negative opinion to include the Italians.[81] Moscow speeded up the process of convening the communist parties and creating a new organ of international communism. By the end of August, Zhdanov had sent Stalin a memorandum on the conference that allocated the task of assessing the international situation to the Soviet delegation and criticized the Western and Czechoslovak communists.[82] At this stage, the Soviets' initial uncertainties about the nature of the new body had been overcome. Stalin's decision was to turn the event into something much more tightly coordinated, thus failing to comply with what he had already agreed with Gomułka. For this reason, the conference script was kept very secret to avoid provoking any reservations about the establishment of the Cominform.

The conference convened the backbone of European communism, with the participation of delegations from all the parties in Eastern and Central Europe, as well as from France and Italy. Initially only the Czechs and the Yugoslavs were in favour of creating the Cominform and providing it with the role of coordinating

---

[78] *Sto sorok besed s Molotovym*, 88–9.

[79] M. Djilas, *Se la memoria non m'inganna: ricordi di un uomo scomodo 1943–1962* (Bologna: il Mulino, 1987), 144.

[80] K. Rentola, 'The Soviet leadership and Finnish communism', in J. Nevakivi (ed.), *Finnish–Soviet Relations 1944–1948* (Helsinki: Dept of Political History, University of Helsinki, 1994), 233.

[81] Dimitrov, *Dnevnik*, 556.

[82] L. Y. Gibianskii, 'Kak voznik Kominform: po novym arkhivnym materyalam', *Novaya i noveishaya istoriya* 4 (1993), 131–52. Cf. *SFVE*, vol. 1, doc. 177, pp. 496–503.

activities.[83] But the Soviet delegates, Zhdanov and Georgii Malenkov, managed to impose Moscow's plan on everyone. Zhdanov introduced himself to the delegates as a plenipotentiary, and identified himself with the new radical and centralizing policy of the international communist movement. He acted on a mandate from Stalin, who was kept informed of the proceedings on a daily basis and carried out the role of the hidden puppeteer. The *coup de théâtre* orchestrated by the Soviets came when the conference proceedings had already started, and was based on reports from individual parties. On 25 September Zhdanov presented his report on the international situation, which he had prepared in close collaboration with Stalin and Molotov. The report declared that the world had been divided into 'two camps': the 'anti-imperialistic and democratic' one under the leadership of the USSR, and the 'imperialist and reactionary' one under the leadership of the United States, emphasizing the 'radical changes' of the 'entire political physiognomy of the world' and the international 'balance of power' following the war.[84] This dichotomy was nothing new, and went all the way back to Lenin. But now it was being passed off as an analysis of the second postwar period, and an argument for the USSR to have a more important role than it had played in the interwar period. The Soviet Union became one of the poles in a bipolar system. The formula of 'two camps' would take on the significance of a duel, and as such it became part of the terminology current in the Cold War.

However, reality was not so simple. Even Zhdanov's report was a less coherent and sententious document than suggested by the theory of 'two camps'. Although he insisted on the decline of British imperialism, he held out the slight possibility of an international situation that was not entirely bipolar by bringing back into play the 'contradictions' between the United States and Great Britain, a theory that also went back to the 1920s. According to Zhdanov, even Germany would produce contradictions within the 'anti-Soviet bloc'.[85] At the same time, he avoided any commitments concerning the situation in the Balkans and Greece—or, outside Europe, the situation in China. The speaker's heated arguments hid a very modest content. The theory of 'two camps' did not involve any genuine change in thinking. It aimed to bring together the forces that had gathered around the USSR in Europe, without proposing to the communist movement any more than a return to the sectarian strategies that had preceded the policy of anti-fascism and replaced it during the period of the pact with Hitler.

There is reason to doubt the idea of a mutual siege between capitalism and socialism, as put forward by Zhdanov, was the unwavering inspiration for a militant policy. This interpretation coexisted with a more cautious approach: a policy of withdrawal based on the conviction that the emerging bipolar structure of the postwar world was unstable and perhaps transitional. Malenkov's report to

[83] G. Adibekov et al. (eds), *Soveshchaniya Kominforma 1947/1948/1949* (Moscow: Rosspen, 1998), 326.
[84] G. Procacci et al. (eds), *The Cominform: Minutes of the Three Conferences 1947/1948/1949* (Milan: Feltrinelli, 1994), 219.
[85] Ibid. 243.

the conference, although lower down the hierarchy, was significant in this sense. Indeed, Malenkov provided a much less bombastic version of the tasks facing the USSR, without putting too much emphasis on the changes brought about by the war. He restricted himself to noting the importance of the incipient Cold War, asserting: 'As the antagonistic classes have been eliminated in the USSR and the political and moral unity of Soviet society has been achieved, all the harshness of the class struggle has, for the USSR, been shifted to the international arena.'[86] This very clearly expressed the antagonistic nature of the Soviet state and alluded to the problem of its security, without any doctrine that revealed new ambitions for a world revolution. It may be that the different emphases of Zhdanov and Malenkov reflected their rivalry, which Stalin fostered in order to divide and control his subordinates.[87] However, they demonstrated the range of opinions within the single Stalinist outlook.

It was the realism of the line Moscow gave out to European communists at the end of the war, more than the political and conceptual basis of the USSR's foreign policy, that was being challenged, although the ritual practices of the communist movement precluded the proclamation of an explicit discontinuity in policy decisions. As always happened when it came to learning hard lessons or making sudden policy changes, the responsibility for what had gone wrong was entirely attributed to individual communist parties. The Zhdanov report censured the French and Italian communists for their reaction to their exclusion from government and the Marshall Plan, which was considered weak and inappropriate. He accused Italian communists of being 'more parliamentarian that the parliamentarians'.[88] All the other delegates of the Eastern and Central European parties came together in chorus, while the Yugoslavs were the fiercest in their criticisms. The criticisms did not take the Western communists entirely by surprise. When the Italian delegates, Luigi Longo and Eugenio Reale, were leaving for Poland, Togliatti, who had sensed the political climate that awaited them, prophesied the outcome and suggested what their defence should be: 'If they reproach you because we haven't taken power or because we have let ourselves be driven out of government,... well, tell them that we couldn't turn Italy into a second Greece. And that was not only in our interest, but also in the interest of the Soviets themselves.'[89] However, the position of the Italian and French delegates was extremely weak. They lowered their heads, after having attempted a half-hearted defence of their parties' actions, while asking for their domestic and international problems since the war to be taken into consideration. The Soviet delegates reported Duclos's and Longo's self-criticisms to Stalin in detail.[90]

---

[86] Ibid. 91.
[87] Y. Gorlizki and O. Khlevniuk, *Cold Peace: Stalin and the Soviet Ruling Circle* (New York: Oxford University Press, 2005), 51–8.
[88] Procacci, *The Cominform: Minutes of the Three Conferences*, 194.
[89] E. Reale, *Nascita del Cominform* (Milan: Mondadori, 1958), 17.
[90] Adibekov et al., *Soveshchaniya Kominforma*, 327–32.

Zhdanov's report had clear parallels with the speeches given by the Yugoslavs emphasizing the rupture brought about by the Second World War, which they considered a decisive shift in the international balance of power in favour of international communism. The Soviet delegates sent Stalin favourable reports on Kardelj and Djilas.[91] But it was also clear that there was a difference between Zhdanov's criticisms of the Western parties, with his appeal for a mass mobilization, and the more radical ones coming from the Yugoslavs, who perceived civil war as the most authentic model for communist parties. Kardelj accused Togliatti of having failed to make use of the revolutionary opportunity in northen Italy at the end of the war and embracing the delusion that in capitalist countries there was 'a legal road for communists to take power and consequently also a peaceful transition from capitalism to socialism'. The Yugoslav delegate believed that the 'Greek situation' should be considered 'an incomparably better situation than the one prevailing in France and Italy', and even that a civil war in these countries would mean 'a very serious blow against imperialism'.[92] The different emphases of the two Soviet spokesmen and the Yugoslav one probably concealed a carefully planned allocation of different roles. This theory was corroborated by the memoirs of both Kardelj and Djilas.[93] The Soviets and Yugoslavs were in agreement on the theory of the 'two camps'. The challenge to the Western 'bloc' and the United States led to the conclusion that the outcome in France and Italy was 'in a sense, the decisive factor in the current phase of the struggle against imperialism', as Kardelj had asserted.[94] On the other hand, Zhdanov could hardly have criticized the PCI for the 'missed opportunity for revolution', as Kardelj did insouciantly, without challenging Stalin's policy of the previous years.

If the Soviets and Yugoslavs were in fact playing games, they did so within certain restrictions. Stalin's leadership would never have unconditionally underwritten Djilas's assertion that the armed struggle in Yugoslavia and Greece had 'strengthened the USSR's position as the bastion of revolutionary forces in the world'.[95] When it came to the consequences of the Civil War in Greece, the Soviet attitude was cautious in spite of the rhetoric coming from the Cominform. Greece continued to be an unresolved problem for the communist movement. The return to Athens of the one-time Comintern official Nikos Zachariadis, who had survived the Nazi concentration camps, had not reasserted Moscow's full control over the actions of the KKE following the disaster in December 1944. Ignoring Soviet instructions to avoid a British military intervention by seeking a compromise solution, he decided to boycott the general election in March 1946. From that moment, the communists resumed the armed struggle and Greece slipped back into civil war. The Greek communists' decision was influenced by the Yugoslavs, whereas the Soviets remained prudent. Tito supported the armed struggle in the north of the country in words and deeds, as the north had its strategic hinterland

---

[91] Ibid. 323.   [92] Procacci, *The Cominform: Minutes of the Three Conferences*, 299–301.
[93] E. Kardelj, *Memorie degli anni di ferro* (Rome: Editori Riuniti, 1980), 111–12; Djilas, *Se la memoria non m'inganna*, 153.
[94] Procacci, *The Cominform: Minutes of the Three Conferences*, 303. [95] Ibid. 257.

in Yugoslavian territory. In May 1947, after the proclamation of the 'Truman doctrine', Stalin was more willing to offer aid from the Soviet Union, and promised Zachariadis that he would provide arms and supplies. However, the Soviets were very careful not to take risks with overt support.[96] Zhdanov praised Zachariadis because the armed struggle in Greece had 'broken the English teeth' and turned 'the world against Truman', but pointed out: 'not everyone understands that we have to choose our moment when it comes to committing the USSR with all its forces.' The Soviet position on Greece was therefore decided before the creation of the Cominform: assistance for communist armed struggle without, however, offering open political support.[97] The Soviet delegation in Poland maintained a conspicuous silence over the Yugoslav's enthusiastic praise, and firmly rejected the possibility of admitting the Greek Communist party to the Cominform.[98] The Soviets' argument was that by their participation the Greeks would be exposed to the accusation of being 'agents of communist parties in other countries'. Zhdanov did not even accept Kardelj's emphatic appeal to the conference for militant and internationalist solidarity with Greece.[99] Moscow was no longer putting the brake on the Greek communists' revolutionary struggle, as had occurred at the end of the war, but nor did it commit itself to active engagement.

In the absence of clear strategic directives from Moscow, it was left to communists themselves to interpret Soviet interests and implement the subsequent actions. When Djilas accused the French communists of being 'poor interpreters of Soviet foreign policy' since the war, he was playing the same game that Togliatti had suggested to Longo, but for the opposite reason.[100] The reality was that since the war there had been tensions between the various interpretations of how Soviet interests and the communist movement's prospects had to be combined. The establishment of the Cominform appeared to signal a clear propensity for the more intransigent direction over the more moderate one. But it is more likely that the Yugoslavs were being overly confident in putting themselves forwards as the authentic interpreters of Soviet policy. In his final speech to the conference, Zhdanov did not even refer to the civil wars in Greece and China, and avoided any comment on the prospects of insurrection anywhere. The only indication from Moscow was that this prospect could not be rejected in principle, given that it was not valid in that moment, but could change in the future, even the near future. Only Stalin could work this out and pronounce the final word.

A few weeks after the conference, the publication of Zhdanov's report, after deleting the harsher comments on the Western communists, publicly ratified the creation of the Informburo. The new body had a significant impact on Western public opinion, which was ready to rename it the Cominform to associate it with the

---

[96] A. A. Ulunian, 'The Soviet Union and the Greek Question, 1946–53: problems and appraisals', in Gori and Pons, *The Soviet Union and Europe in the Cold War*, 150; J. O. Iatrides, 'Revolution or self-defense? Communist goals, strategy, and tactics in the Greek Civil War', *Journal of Cold War Studies* 7.3 (2005), 24–5.

[97] RGASPI, fo. 17, op. 128, d. 1019.   [98] Gibianskii, *Kak voznik Kominform*, 143.

[99] Procacci, *The Cominform: Minutes of the Three Conferences*, 303.[100] Ibid. 257.

Comintern. This impact was certainly part of Stalin's expectations. In particular, the theory of the 'two camps' needed to be launched publicly, because its appeal for a popular mobilization was an attempt to fill the vacuum left by the absence of a universalist political message coming from Stalin's USSR during the war. It was the first time since the 1920s that a Soviet leader had made a significant speech on the USSR's foreign policy from the tribune of an assembly of communist parties. But the revival of a militant line, in response to the perception of an increasing American commitment to Europe, continued to encounter its limitations in the demands of the USSR's security policy. Stalin had not repudiated his negative opinion on the Communist International, which had been demonstrated many times in the past. It soon became clear that the creation of the Cominform was perceived in Moscow more as a necessary step to recover its leadership over the European communist parties rather than being a clearly defined proclamation of an offensive plan against the West. The plan to put pressure on the two large Western communist parties—the French and the Italian—to become a thorn in the flesh of the Western 'bloc' was linked to the more repressive stance in relations between Moscow and the parties of countries in the Soviet sphere of influence. The strategy of greater discipline had to take precedence over the strategy of mobilization.

THE BREAK BETWEEN THE USSR AND YUGOSLAVIA

The Cold War revived the sense of vulnerability and fragility that weighed on the Soviet leaders during the 1920s, which the cruel domestic conflicts of the 1930s had perpetuated and which not even the new patriotism and international prestige of the Soviet Union appeared capable of affecting. Stalin did not seize the opportunity for a less obsessive definition of state security in the light of the expansion of Soviet power in Europe. The vulnerability syndrome was exacerbated by their awareness of the Soviet Union's economic and technological inferiority, which had increased as a result of the destruction wrought by war, and by the tendency to consider it nevertheless necessary to take on the role of counterweight to the American empire, with the subsequent over-commitment of the country's actual resources. This was a repetition of Russia's imperial dilemma, a historic competition with wealthier and more powerful Western rivals.[101] The decision to mobilize resources earmarked for the construction of the USSR as a superpower had been clear since the summer of 1945, when they received the shock of American atomic weapons. The decision to engage in nuclear competition with the United States would have fatal consequences in the long term, creating a gap that was never overcome between the magnitude of the challenge and the actual resources of Soviet power.[102]

---

[101] D. Lieven, *Empire: The Russian Empire and Its Rivals* (London: John Murray, 2000), 298.
[102] Holloway, *Stalin and the Bomb*, 365.

At the same time, the American initiative exposed the limits of the USSR's hegemonic capacity. The launch of the Marshall Plan forced Moscow on to the defensive by choosing the economic reconstruction of Europe as the terrain on which to compete, as this revealed the multiplicity of the resources at the United States' disposal and was disagreeable to the Soviet mentality. The Soviets could not understand the compromise between national interests and hegemonic power that lay at the foundation of the Western bloc. Stalin's reaction demonstrated his inability to take up the challenge from the West. As he thought that the very basis of Soviet influence on the European continent was in danger, his response was the imposition of imperial command. Molotov's memory of this was as follows:

> They hardened their line against us, and we had to consolidate what we had conquered. We created our socialist Germany in part of Germany, and in Czechoslovakia, Poland, Hungary and Yugoslavia, where the situation was fluid, we needed to restore order. Suppress capitalist order. This was the Cold War. Of course, you had to know the right measure. I believe that in this sense Stalin kept himself well within the limits.[103]

One limit was in fact observed—that of the territorial borders de facto created between two Europes as a result of the war—but this did not imply moderation in Moscow's exercise of influence in its own zone.

The Cominform affair was typical. It would become the symbolic institution of the Soviet bloc, rather than an instrument of revolutionary challenge in the West. Zhdanov's criticisms of the Western communists revealed his marked lack of interest in democratic institutions as a theatre of political action in Europe, as Soviet leaders expected crises and upheavals in capitalist societies, which would provide the terrain for extraparliamentary mass action. The Cominform had thus launched a fundamentalist appeal that certainly struck the right chords for communist activists and their culture. But between the end of 1947 and the beginning of 1948, Stalin reduced the impact of radicalism on the Western parties. The apparent harmony between Soviets and Yugoslavs rapidly dissolved, and the old rancours between Moscow and Belgrade re-emerged. Stalin poured oil on troubled waters during talks with the leaders of Western communist parties visiting Moscow in search of clarifications following the criticisms against them in Poland. At a meeting with Thorez on 18 November 1947, Stalin distanced himself decisively from the harsher imputations expressed two months earlier and made a great show of his sympathy for the French leader's protests against 'unjust' accusations concerning the PCF's inability 'to guarantee the power of the people' at the end of the war. Undermining the Yugoslav criticisms, he acknowledged that the French communists 'could not have taken power into their own hands. Even if they had, they would have lost it later, given that there were Anglo-American forces in the country.' At the same time, he requested information on the PCF's state of preparedness for armed struggle, should they be attacked by the enemy.[104] Stalin's attitude was no different when he met with Secchia, the second in command in

---

[103] *Sto sorok besed s Molotovym*, 86.   [104] *Istoricheskii Arkhiv* 1 (1996), 9–10, 14.

the PCI, a month later. Stalin agreed with Togliatti's position, as reported to him by Secchia, on the inappropriateness of putting civil war in Italy on the agenda. This was in spite of Secchia himself resorting to some double-dealing and informing the Soviets of the willingness of a large contingent of the PCI to choose the path of insurrection. Moscow seemed satisfied with the mass actions organized by French and Italian communists, such as the strikes against the Marshall Plan. The question of whether there should be legal activity or insurrection was not clarified, but clearly the brakes were being applied. Stalin did not exclude the possibility of things going as far as civil war in France and Italy, but unlike the Yugoslavs he did not push the Western parties to take initiatives that could have produced such consequences.[105]

A genuine conflict arose between Moscow and Belgrade concerning the Balkan theatre. On 10 February 1948, Stalin met the Yugoslav and Bulgarian leaders in Moscow, to discuss the questions of the Balkan Federation, Albania, and Greece. In the first case, the problem went back to the agreement signed in Bled by the Bulgarians and Yugoslavs in August 1947, ignoring Moscow's instruction to await the conclusion of the peace treaty with Bulgaria. In the second case, the problem was Belgrade's decision to deploy troops to Albania, taken in January 1948 without consulting Moscow. But the principal cause was the interview given by Dimitrov on 17 January 1948, in which he called for a confederation of Eastern and Southeastern European countries, including Greece, where a civil war was taking place. Thus the scenario of a regional grouping under Belgrade's direction and insufficiently controlled by Moscow was linked to a dangerous source of international conflict. Stalin and Molotov were profligate in their warnings about the risks of such foreign-policy moves, which could provoke a reaction from the United States and Great Britain that would be unfavourable to the interests of the USSR and the 'people's democracies'.[106] For this reason Stalin lashed out at Dimitrov and pointed out that the West 'wants a Europe without Russia, and "without" means "against"'. In spite of the material support for the communist armed struggle in Greece, he confirmed both his considerable pessimism about the outcome and his determination to avoid an internationalization of the civil war and a dangerous involvement of the USSR. When Kardelj said that he could see no difference between Yugoslavia and the USSR in foreign policy, Stalin interrupted him and declared that differences existed and that to deny this was a form of 'opportunism'.[107]

---

[105] F. Gori and S. Pons (eds), *Dagli archivi di Mosca: l'URSS, il Cominform e il PCI (1943–1951)* (Rome: Carocci, 1998), docs 20 and 21; and *Archivio Pietro Secchia 1945–1973* (Milan: Feltrinelli, 1979), 211, 446, 611–27. On the pressure the Yugoslavs exerted on the PCI to support insurrection, see Djilas, *Se la memoria non m'inganna*, 154.

[106] 'Na poroge pervogo raskola v "sotsialisticheskom lagere": peregovory rukovodyashchikh deyateley SSSR, Bolgarii i Jugoslavii, 1948', *Istoricheskii Arkhiv* 4 (1998), 92–123. See also L. Gibianskii, 'The Soviet bloc and the initial stage of the Cold War: archival documents on Stalin's meetings with Communist leaders of Yugoslavia and Bulgaria, 1946–1948', *Cold War International History Project Bulletin* 10 (1998), 115–17, 128–34; Dimitrov, *Dnevnik*, 596–603; Djilas, *Se la memoria non m'inganna*, 182–3.

[107] 'Na poroge pervogo raskola v "sotsialisticheskom lagere"', 104–7.

Stalin's intention was clearly to bring the situation under the Soviet Union's control and avoid a breeding ground for conflict with the Western powers. His plan was to proceed with the creation of several federal unions between various groups of countries in Eastern Europe, including one for Yugoslavia, Bulgaria, and Albania. This was probably a method to maintain specific divisions in the Soviet sphere of influence and avoiding the formation of a single pole, potentially autonomous, in the shape of the USSR.[108]

The concerns Stalin expressed to the Yugoslavs and Bulgarians over the West's possible reactions do not appear to have been a simple pretext, used to call back into line a troublesome ally. They arose from a foreign policy that since the war had pursued the aim of a strict security belt around the USSR in Eastern and Central Europe. This aim had been made all the more urgent by the perceived formation of a Western bloc. Stalin believed that the sudden break with the West that occurred at the London Conference in December 1947 made the division of Germany a fait accompli. On 10 January 1948 he confided to Djilas: 'the West will take over West Germany, and we will create our state in East Germany.'[109] Stalin had been vacillating wildly on the German question since the war, because of his obsession with the possible revival of a threat, which made any policy orientation problematic: a united Germany could once again be dangerous in the event of a break with the Western allies, and a divided Germany might tend to marginalize communist influence and let the pulsing heart of German industrial power drift to the West. The Soviets could not resolve this dilemma in their policy to Germany between 1945 and 1947. They ended up being obliged to follow decisions made in Washington and London, which were alarmed by Soviet behaviour in its occupation zone and, more generally, in its sphere of influence, and decided to move towards the constitution of a West German state.[110]

On the one hand, Stalin insisted on the need to avoid an open conflict with the West, and went so far as to censure the link expressed a few months earlier between the Soviet Union's foreign policy and the birth of the Cominform. On the other, he proceeded with consolidation of the Eastern bloc using methods that provoked international outcry, as in the case of Czechoslovakia. Molotov rejected the request, formulated by Czech communists, for support from the USSR with demonstrative military action on the Austrian frontier. But Soviet apprehension over the weakest link in the Eastern bloc inspired V. Zorin's mission to Prague, which was the origin of the coup in Czechoslovakia at the end of February. The Soviet envoy had the mandate to put an end to the legalistic vacillations attributed to Gottwald and Slánský, and to eliminate the coalition government.[111] Because

---

[108] L. Y. Gibianskii, 'Kominform v deistvii. 1947–1948 gg: po arkhivnym dokumentam', *Novaya i noveishaya istoriya* 1–2 (1996); A. S. Anikeev, *Kak Tito ot Stalina ushel: Yugoslaviya, SSSR i SShA v nachalnii period 'kholodnoy voyny' (1945–1957)* (Moscow: Is Ran, 2002), 125–37.

[109] M. Djilas, *Conversazioni con Stalin* (Milan: Feltrinelli, 1962), 158.

[110] Leffler, *For the Soul of Mankind*, 68–9; C. S. Maier, 'Who divided Germany?', *Diplomatic History* 3 (1998).

[111] G. P. Murashko, 'Fevral'skii krizis 1948g. v Chekhoslovakii i sovetskoe rukovodstvo: po novym materyalam rossiiskikh arkhivov', *Novaya i noveishaya istoriya* 3 (1998), 50–63.

of their policies, the Soviets contributed to a succession of events they had been trying to prevent. The Prague coup, in particular, would accentuate the European perception of the Soviet Union as an expansionist power, and favoured Western military cooperation. In its wake came the complete reunification of the Western zones in Germany and the signing of the Treaty of Brussels which founded the Western European Union. The events in turn intensified the Soviet perception of a Western threat.[112] From March, the Soviets had been considering the idea of blockading Berlin in response to the Western moves, a countermeasure that would exacerbate the 'war of nerves'.[113] Stalin appeared to think that the deterioration in the international situation was inevitable; his only concerns were holding the United States responsible and avoiding scenarios that could be even more damaging to the Soviet Union's security.

The proliferation of sources of international tension in the early months of 1948 finally persuaded Moscow that prudence in politics would be prescribed for Western communists. The most difficult case was Italy. After the coalition governments, competition between the forces of the left, united in the 'Popular Front', and the moderate forces, united around the Christian Democrats, became increasingly bitter during the election campaign and threatened to trigger civil war. Each side feared violence from the other, with the aim of preventing or overturning the electoral response. Both Moscow and Washington found the scenario of an armed conflict in Italy much worse than the one currently being played out in Greece, because its internationalization would have been inevitable. Although the United States were convinced, quite rightly, that Stalin would not have risked a war to support the Italian left, the situation could have slipped out of the protagonists' control. At the end of March, Togliatti secretly contacted Moscow to find out the Soviet opinion on the possibility of a communist insurrection in the country. At the same time, he notified them that should their reply be affirmative, the PCI would only take action in extreme circumstances. Togliatti reminded the Soviets that such action might provoke another world war. The reply from Stalin and Molotov was unequivocal. Moscow would not advise acts of force, unless Italian communists were being attacked by the enemy.[114] The conviction that a civil war in a key strategic Western country like Italy was not in the interests of the USSR was once more asserted in 1948, just as it had been in 1945, albeit in a different international situation. Togliatti did not consider this scenario to be in the interests of the PCI either, continuing the political line adopted at the end of the war. Shortly afterwards, when the Italian left suffered a crushing defeat in the general election, neither Moscow nor Rome changed its opinion. The Italian elections had a clear international significance, because they demonstrated the resilience of the Western

---

[112] V. Mastny, *The Cold War and Soviet Insecurity: The Stalin Years* (Oxford: Oxford University Press, 1996).

[113] M. M. Narinskii, 'The Soviet Union and the Berlin Crisis 1948–9', in Gori and Pons, *The Soviet Union and Europe in the Cold War*, 62.

[114] S. Pons, *L'impossibile egemonia: l'URSS, il PCI e le origini della guerra fredda (1943–1948)* (Rome: Carocci, 1999), 222–3.

sphere and eliminated the plan to manage a gradual shift in Italy towards the 'socialist camp', as Togliatti had hoped. Indirectly, the Italian lesson confirmed the appropriateness of a redirection of Soviet objectives towards Eastern and Central Europe. Now it was the turn of Yugoslavia, apparently the most loyal ally but in reality the most awkward.

On 27 March 1948 Stalin and Molotov sent Tito a letter that accused the Yugoslav communists of the most serious error in the ritual of communist behaviour, that of deviating from Marxist ideology. On 4 May, the Soviet leaders provided an entire sample of the offences of the Yugoslav leaders, quoting the demonic precedents of Trotsky and Bukharin. The Yugoslavs replied with prudence but also firmness, clarifying that they would not carry out the acts of submission and self-confession requested of them. On 22 May, Stalin and Molotov notified Tito that the second conference of the Cominform would discuss the 'Yugoslav question' even in the absence of the delegates from Belgrade, taking the decisive step towards a split. The Soviets avoided any significant reference to questions of foreign policy, even though these were of central importance.[115] In Moscow, the first criticisms against the Yugoslavs—who were accused of having ignored Soviet interests from the period of the Trieste crisis, when they harboured senseless ambitions of territorial expansion and wanted to play the role of a 'third force' between the USSR and the Western powers—went as far back as the summer of 1947, on the eve of the founding conference of the Cominform.[116] These complaints remained confidential, but only for a few months. The motives behind the conflict, which emerged at the meeting on 10 February 1948 between Stalin and Bulgarian and Yugoslavian officials, were most obviously a prelude for the accusations made in the letters sent by Soviet leaders between March and May 1948. At the end of March, Moscow was also urging Togliatti to ignore the advice of the Yugoslavs, who were continuing to support the Greek partisans and putting pressure on Italian communists to follow their example.[117] Stalin preferred to avoid taking this stance in public. The accusation against the Yugoslavs was the tried and tested one of 'deviationism', even though they were more coherent supporters of Sovietization than Stalin himself. The fact was that their radicalism was spreading independent thinking and insubordination. In this sense, Yugoslavia was the reference point for other countries in Eastern Europe, because its foreign policy created a distinct regional pole, even though up till then it had been closely integrated into the Soviet sphere. By choosing the terrain of doctrinal orthodoxy, Stalin hoped to avoid the risk of the other communist parties' latent solidarity with Tito becoming something firmer and more enduring. The implicit message was that foreign-policy questions and decisions were Moscow's exclusive remit.

The second conference of the Cominform, held in Bucharest on 19–23 June 1948, was the court in which to implement the excommunication. The verdict was to be pronounced by Zhdanov, the Soviet leader who had gone furthest out

---

[115] J. Perović, 'The Tito–Stalin split: a reassessment in light of new evidence', *Journal of Cold War Studies* 9.2 (2007).

[116] *VEDRA*, vol. 1, doc. 240, pp. 704–9.   [117] Pons, *L'impossibile egemonia*, 223.

on a limb to follow the Yugoslavs' radical impulses.[118] His report was greeted with the unconditional support of all the delegates. The ritual and public excommunication of the Yugoslavs was enacted by conference resolution and approved in the version prepared by the Soviet leadership, more or less without amendments. These documents added very little to the letters from Stalin and Molotov to Tito over the preceding months, which officials of the communist parties of Eastern Europe, the PCF, and the PCI had been able to examine and approve. Zhdanov's report lacked any reference to the political significance of the first conference of the Cominform. This curtain of silence appears so impenetrable that it raises questions about whether Moscow was by then wondering if it had made a false move in 1947 by establishing a link between the foundation of the new body for international communism and the Soviet Union's foreign policy. Stalin's approach in the first half of 1948 was very different. The Soviet response to the formation of a Western bloc appeared to be directed less at the political mobilization of the communist parties and much more at an ideological and police crackdown considered necessary to the Soviet Union's security zone.

The only European leader to play a significant role in the second conference of the Cominform was Togliatti. For some time he had been in disagreement with Tito's radical positions in the international communist movement. The Yugoslav leader's disgrace reflected well on Togliatti, and raised his authority further to a level no other communist leader in Bucharest possessed. Exploiting his critique of Tito, Togliatti praised the 'people's democracies' as transitional regimes, criticized the idea of the inevitability of war, which the Yugoslavs had resurrected in the communist movement, and defended the decision to build mass parties in the West.[119] But he was preaching in the desert. The delegates from Eastern and Central Europe, intimidated by the obvious implications of the ruling against Tito, kept a low profile when it came to the very notion of the 'people's democracies'. The French delegate, Duclos, did not follow the Italian leader's line. There was no room for a strategic debate. Stalin had not made his choice of the various tendencies that had been running through international communism during and after the Second World War. This was not the meaning of the break with Tito.

In 1948, it was still possible to identify Togliatti and Tito as the two figures most representative of the different tendencies in European communism. Both the Italian leader and the Yugoslav one had put themselves forward as interpreters of the Soviet Union's interests and protagonists in the positions to be taken up against the incipient logic of the blocs, but with opposing motivations. After his return to Italy, Togliatti had always shown that he agreed with the realism fostered by Stalin, and had no apparent conflict with the Soviet leader even after the creation of the Cominform. On the other hand, Tito was the protagonist of a militant orientation, which was hardly in line with the actions Stalin was instructing the movement to carry out—and indeed a source of considerable tensions since 1945. But Stalin was an ambiguous arbiter, who retained the power to support now one, now the other

---

[118] *Procacci, The Cominform: Minutes of the Three Conferences*, 523–41.   [119] Ibid. 581, 585.

option as the circumstances dictated. His temperament was in many ways closer to Tito's than to Togliatti's, although this did not prevent the Yugoslav's disgrace.[120] The difference between the two leaders never provoked a debate between divided positions. It could not have been otherwise, as the bond of loyalty to the USSR was the unifying element and the Soviet ruling group was not differentiated in the same way, or at least did not reveal that it was.

The final text of the Cominform resolution was published on 29 June 1948. The Cominform was expelling the second most important of its founding members less than a year after it was founded as an ambitious organization. By this stage, communism's new international organization could be seen as a caricature of the Comintern. In a letter to Gottwald sent on 14 July 1948, Stalin declared himself to be satisfied, arguing that 'the purpose of isolating the Yugoslav leaders from the sight of other communist parties' had been successfully achieved. There could be no doubt about the future 'victory of Marxism-Leninism in Yugoslavia'. In reality, Stalin's declaration was one of anger, which would lead to the Cominform's anti-Tito campaigns.[121] For the communist movement, the break between Stalin and Tito had a twin significance: the end of the 'national roads' in the East and the abandonment of militant protest in the West. The Cominform had not turned away from Stalin's concepts of foreign policy, which for twenty years had been constraining militancy within the confines of the Soviet state's interests. It was not an organization for expanding European communism, but rather a mechanism for the definitive formation of a Soviet bloc through the instalment of single-party dictatorships in Eastern Europe and commencement of the large-scale export of the Soviet model. The Soviet Union's imperial role resulted in rigid interdependence between Soviet foreign policy and the domestic policy of the countries in Eastern and Central Europe. The elimination of political and social pluralism was the prelude to the creation of a bloc based on a monocratic concept of international government. Thus a gap opened up between the doctrine and practice of Eastern and Central European parties and those of West European parties. The defence of national sovereignty was allowable for parties operating outside the Soviet sphere of influence, but not within it. Whereas Western communists defined their role through their anti-American campaigns, Eastern communists expunged the very concept of sovereignty from their vocabulary.

At the time of Tito's excommunication, Stalin provoked the blockade of Berlin with the aim of preventing the birth of a West German state, after having realized that the campaign against the Marshall Plan had broadly speaking been a failure. Being the first nuclear crisis of the Cold War, the blockade took the war of nerves to its highest point.[122] The result must have been the opposite of what Stalin had intended, as it helped to consolidate the Western alliance. From the summer of 1947, in fact, Soviet responses to actions taken by the United States proved to be inadequate. The challenge from the Cominform never went very far.

---

[120] 'Poslednii vizit I. Broza Tito k I. V. Stalinu', *Istoricheskii Arkhiv* 2 (1993), 27–8.
[121] APCI, 'Materiali Cominform 1947–1950', 14 July 1948.
[122] Haslam, *Russia's Cold War*, 106–7; Holloway, *Stalin and the Bomb*, 258.

The Prague coup, the split with Belgrade, the crisis in Berlin formed a chain of events that did not add up to a coherent strategic design, but were instead products of America's 'containment' strategy. The Soviet Union's behaviour was fuelled by uncertainties over the permanence of its own sphere of influence and an obsessive perception of the American threat. Thus Stalin's strategies had the opposite effect of the desired one. The conclusion of the Berlin crisis demonstrated that the initiative was firmly in the West's hands. In April 1949, the birth of the Atlantic Alliance institutionalized an American military presence in Europe. Immediately afterwards, the formation of the German Federal Republic completed the creation of the bloc and a Western community equipped with its own principles antithetical to those of communism. With the creation of two German states, the stabilization of a divided Europe became a reality. The communists' appeal for a mass campaign against American imperialism sounded like an expedient mainly aimed at consolidating the Soviet sphere of influence and contrasting an adversary better equipped with resources to impose hegemony of a multilateral nature and a capacity for inclusiveness.[123]

REVOLUTION IN CHINA AND WAR IN KOREA

The real challenge to the West came not from the Cominform but from the communist victory in China and the proclamation of the People's Republic in Peking in October 1949, an event that was not part of Stalin's strategy and predictions. Moscow's support for the Chinese communists had always been lukewarm and restricted by the policy of 'national fronts', which Stalin had applied both to Europe under the Nazi yoke and to Asia under Japanese domination. At the end of the Second World War, Stalin formulated the Soviet Union's objectives in China in terms of geopolitical influence, and entered an agreement in August 1945 with the Guomindang in order to guarantee Soviet interests in Manchuria and Outer Mongolia.[124] He replicated in Asia the model of the spheres of influence that had inspired his policy in Europe, as was demonstrated by his abortive attempt to extend the Soviet presence to part of Japan. Immediately after the Sino-Soviet Pact, Stalin asked Mao Zedong to avoid civil war and open negotiations with Chiang Kai-shek. The Soviet leader very probably intended to use the Chinese communists as a means of bringing pressure on the nationalist government. The scenario of a Chinese Civil War and its international consequences was no less dangerous than it would have been in southern Europe, because it risked provoking a reaction from the United States. Stalin's decision to discourage communists to use civil war for political purposes anywhere it might damage Soviet interests was as valid in Asia as it was in Europe.

---

[123] F. Romero, *Storia della Guerra Fredda: l'ultimo conflitto per l'Europa* (Turin: Einaudi, 2009), 65–6.
[124] D. Heinzig, *The Soviet Union and Communist China 1945–1950: The Arduous Road to the Alliance* (Armonk, N.Y.: M. E. Sharpe, 2004), 52–5.

Mao reluctantly took cognizance of the fact he would not be receiving the support from Stalin that he would have hoped for, realized that in the postwar geopolitical carve-up China found itself in a position quite similar to that of Greece, and acknowledged that they could not risk the outbreak of a third world war. But Mao perceived Stalin's policy as something very close to a betrayal of the Chinese Revolution.[125] Without doubt, the Chinese leader's enigmatic character was different from Stalin's, particularly when it came to his intuition of the insurrectionary potential of the peasant masses. More than fifteen years younger than Stalin and the same age as Tito and Togliatti, Mao was a particular mix of anti-colonial sentiment, fascination with the Russian Revolution, and the communist activism that had spread outside Europe between the two wars. His personal charisma had emerged under fire in an armed struggle, and his cult was that of a revolutionary leader. The emphasis on the revolutionary voluntarism and the 'Sinization' of Marxism-Leninism, which he had expounded in a series of writings at the end of the 1930s, revealed a powerful character in the cultural context of communism at the time.[126] However, it was precisely his twenty-year experience of semi-clandestine armed struggle that forged in him such a solid link with the communist tradition. In the mentality and collective memory of the Chinese communists, the experience and psychology of the war carried a weight just as heavy as that of Soviet communists, while the Leninist doctrine of imperialism and the image of the Soviet Union as the bulwark of socialism were no less important than for European communists. Most importantly, he had imposed a harsh centralist regime on the CCP during the Second World War, as well as extreme ideological conformism based on reading the *Short Course*. The very style of his political discourse became increasingly similar to Stalin's.[127] The bond Mao felt for Stalin must have reflected his mixed feelings of loyalty and irritation, even after the Soviet leader's death.

In any event, the Chinese situation was not easy for anyone to control, and not unfavourable to the communists. Very conscious of the disaster in 1927, Mao kept open the possibility of subverting and destroying the power of the Guomindang, repeating in Asia the Yugoslav radicalism in Europe. He wanted to present Moscow with a fait accompli, given that Western intervention in China appeared improbable and that nationalist control of the country's decisive areas was far from established. On the other hand, the CCP's organizational cohesion was the ace up its sleeve, and the communists' anti-imperialist message enhanced their national

---

[125] C. Jian, *Mao's China and the Cold War* (Chapel Hill, N.C.: University of North Carolina Press, 2001), 27–8; M. M. Sheng, *Battling Western Imperialism: Mao, Stalin, and the United States* (Princeton, N.J.: Princeton University Press, 1997), 103–4. After Stalin's death, Mao criticized the Soviet leader for having obstructed the revolution in China in August 1945: see Heinzig, *The Soviet Union and Communist China 1945–1950*, 74.

[126] S. Schram, *Il pensiero politico di Mao Tse-Tung* (Florence: Vallecchi, 1971), 75, 193–6; N. Knight, *Rethinking Mao: Explorations in Mao Zedong's Thought* (Lanham, Md.: Lexington Books, 2007), ch. 7.

[127] O. A. Westad, *Decisive Encounters: The Chinese Civil War, 1946–1950* (Stanford, Calif.: Stanford University Press, 2003), 120.

credibility. The experience of resistance during the war had been decisive in forging their anti-colonial and national identity.[128] In the spring and summer of 1946, Civil War broke out in Manchuria following the failure of negotiations between the CCP and the Guomindang, in spite of suggestions from Stalin and attempts at mediation from the United States. Predictably, the Soviet Union provided Chinese communists with funding, technical assistance, and arms, in particular the decisive military hardware confiscated from the Japanese army. But it was decidedly unenthusiastic about the political plan. For over two years, while the Cold War was developing in Europe, Stalin did not alter his stance and avoided coming out in favour of the Chinese Revolution. Besides, he had refused to meet Mao in spite of repeated requests from the latter dating from the summer of 1947.[129] Thus Stalin ignored the Chinese leader's appeals for a decisive push for the conquest of power and a discussion on the revolutionary future of Asia. The foundation of the Cominform sounded to Mao like encouragement to relaunch a militant and combative vision of the role of international communism.[130] But even regarding this plan he would be disillusioned.

Stalin had a very gradualist idea of the Chinese Revolution, and one that was at odds with Mao's. The Chinese leader wrote to him in November 1947 of his plans to eliminate the opposing political parties 'following the example of the USSR and Yugoslavia'; Stalin replied only on 20 April 1948 to suggest the model of the 'people's democracies', which implied a longer period before the installation of a communist monopoly.[131] Mao replied that he was in full agreement, again keeping quiet about their potential differences.[132] Stalin's behaviour did not change even in the autumn of 1948, when the Civil War shifted in favour of the communists in northern China. Very probably, the simultaneous occurrence of the Chinese events and the Berlin crisis created more apprehension than enthusiasm in Moscow. The re-election of Truman was a further reason for dissatisfaction and prudence. Not of least importance was Stalin's fear that Mao might prove to be another Tito, given his independent character and his radicalism, even though the Chinese leader had joined in the condemnation of the Yugoslav heresy.

Even after the People's Liberation Army started to storm out into the centre and south of the country at the beginning of 1949, Stalin showed little enthusiasm, as he was particularly concerned about the American nuclear threat. Moscow's willingness to open international negotiations on China, accepting a proposal from the nationalists to the Western powers and the USSR, met with an impatient

---

[128] M. Selden, *China in Revolution: The Yenan Way Revisited* (Armonk, N.Y.: M. E. Sharpe, 1995).

[129] *Russko-kitayskie otnosheniya v XX veke: materialy i dokumenty*, ed. S. L. Tikhvinskii (5 vols, Moscow: Pamyatniki Istoricheskoy Mysli, 2000), vol. 5, section 1, docs 219, 224, 261, 262, 296, 300, 303, 306, 308, 329, 331, 332, 333, 337, 353, 360, 361, 377, 378. For communications and relations between Stalin and Mao Zedong before the revolution, see the documents coming out of the ex-Soviet archives and the Chinese ones in the Virtual Archive of the Cold War International History Project (www.wilsoncenter.org).

[130] Westad, *Decisive Encounters*, 167–8.

[131] *Russko-kitayskie otnosheniya*, vol. 5, section 1, doc. 295, pp. 411–12; Heinzig, *The Soviet Union and Communist China 1945–1950*, 140–1.

[132] *Russko-kitayskie otnosheniya*, vol. 5, section 1, doc. 300, p. 415.

reaction from Mao, who for the first time openly expressed his disagreement with the Soviet position. He feared, probably quite reasonably, that Stalin was considering the division of China into two parts, as was happening in Germany.[133] Using language that betrayed his irritation, Mao wrote to Stalin that 'the balance of power between the classes in China has undergone a fundamental shift', and that therefore 'we no longer need to engage yet again in evasive political manoeuvring'.[134] In reply, Stalin presented the Soviet willingness to negotiate as a mere tactical expedient to shift blame for the probable failure onto their adversaries, and made it clear that 'the rejection of our advice will not affect relations between us'.[135]

Stalin's attitude to the Civil War in China has to be seen in the context of Europe's centrality. Indeed, it is the link between the European and Asian scenarios that reveals most about his policy. He was clearly hoping not to accelerate events in Asia while the 1948 crises were occurring in Europe. The Berlin blockade and the increasing Sovietization of Eastern and Central Europe, following the rift with Yugoslavia, had created a series of conflicts that had to be kept under control without opening new fronts. The very fact that Stalin had advised Mao to follow the model of the 'people's democracy' at the very time that Moscow was preparing to ditch it, together with the 'national roads to socialism' in Eastern and Central Europe, demonstrated his idea of the revolution in China as still linked to the notion of a historical transition in alliance with the 'national bourgeoisie', and also his strategic caution over the incipient Cold War. Since the end of the war, Stalin's policy had aimed to contain the risks arising from the revolutionary impulses among communists outside Europe and not just in China. In particular, he had blocked the aspirations of Iranian communists to take power, while aiming to divide the country and set up a pro-Soviet state in the north of Iran. Once this attempt to extend Soviet geopolitical influence had failed, Stalin nevertheless refused to sanction an insurrection. In May 1946 he wrote to the Azerbaijani leader Jafar Pishevari that the Iranian situation was unlike the one in Russia in 1917, and that the assistance of Soviet troops would have provided a pretext for the British and Americans, obstructing national liberation movements in the world.[136]

Stalin was also lukewarm about the proliferation of anti-imperialist flashpoints after the war in Southeast Asia. Vietnamese communists, well established in the north of the country and engaged in the struggle against French colonialism, were treated no better by Moscow than the Chinese had been. Initially the lack of Soviet support could be explained by the fact that their struggle risked complicating relations between Moscow and Paris, where communists were in government until May 1947. But Soviet behaviour did not change after the PCF had been expelled from the government.[137] The Soviet Union did not even play a role in the

---

[133] Heinzig, *The Soviet Union and Communist China 1945–1950*, 170–4.

[134] *Russko-kitayskie otnosheniya*, vol. 5, section 2, doc. 407, p. 20.

[135] Ibid. doc. 409, p. 22.

[136] N. I. Egorova, *The Iran Crisis of 1945–46: A View from the Russian Archives* (Washington, D.C.: Cold War International History Project, working paper n. 15, 1996); M. Behrooz, *Rebels with a Cause: The Failure of the Left in Iran* (London: I. B. Tauris, 1999), 29.

[137] C. Marangé, *Le communisme vietnamien (1919–1991): construction d'un état-nation entre Moscou et Pékin* (Paris: Presses de la Fondation Nationale des Sciences Politiques, 2012), 172–5.

communist insurrections that took place in Indonesia and Malaysia in 1948 and were bloodily suppressed by the British and the Dutch. Inspired by the example of Maoist guerrilla warfare and mainly based in the ethnic Chinese population, the rebels had links with Indian and Burmese communists that made up a sort of regional internationalism, perceived as a subversive threat not only to the West but also to nationalist and independence leaders, in particular Nehru and Sukarno. Immediately after independence, the Indian Communist Party put itself forward as the main pole of attraction over the entire region, and convened representatives of other parties in Calcutta at the beginning of 1948 for a series of meetings that seemed to promise revolutionary activity. American and British observers established a link between the revolts in Southeast Asia and the Berlin blockade, arguing that there was a world conspiracy orchestrated by Moscow; but that was not happening.[138] Stalin was not pursuing a revolutionary plan for the colonial and postcolonial world, because he considered this to be secondary and instrumental to the European theatre.

The strained relations between Stalin and Mao were partly overcome by the Chinese leader's talks with Moscow's envoy in China, Anastas Mikoyan, in February 1949. Once the Soviet idea of international negotiations had been dropped, an agreement was reached that now planned for taking power in the principal cities and the formation of revolutionary government. This was the point where the Soviets suggested the coordination of Asian communist parties along the lines of the Cominform. The proposal from Mikoyan as instructed by Stalin had no provision for the CCP to join Cominform, but rather for the foundation of a new Asian information bureau, led by the Chinese and initially including the Japanese and Korean parties. Moscow thus demonstrated that it had abandoned its previous reservations, but also showed that it aimed to exercise control, albeit indirectly. Mao replied that such a move would be 'premature', and undertook to do this only once communist power had been firmly established in the south of the country.[139] Evidently he wanted to be sure he could complete his revolution before helping to set up a channel of Soviet influence in Asia. The years of misunderstandings had clearly left their mark. A few more months would go by before there would be the basis for an alliance between the Soviets and the Chinese communists. This happened during the Moscow visit of Liu Shaoqi, the second in command in the CCP, in the summer of 1949.

Liu came with a declaration of the imminent establishment of communist power in China, proclaimed their absolute loyalty to the USSR, and pressed for a close relationship with Moscow on the principal questions facing the new Chinese state. Although their revolution was successful in spite of Stalin's scepticism, the Chinese

[138] C. Bayly and T. Harper, *Forgotten Wars: Freedom and Revolution in Southeast Asia* (Cambridge, Mass.: Harvard University Press, 2006), 384–5, 405, 436, 462; S. K. Gupta, *Stalin's Policy Towards India, 1946–1953* (New Delhi: South Asian Publishers, 1988), 99–100; A. Swift, *The Road to Madiun: The Indonesian Communist Uprising of 1948* (Ithaca, N.Y.: Cornell University Press, 1989); D. Mackay, *The Malayan Emergency 1948-60: The Domino that Stood* (London: Brassey's, 1997).

[139] *Russko-kitayskie otnosheniya*, vol. 5, section 2, doc. 432, p. 63. For Mikoyan's mission to China in Feb. 1949, see Heinzig, *The Soviet Union and Communist China 1945–1950*, 135–56.

communists paid homage to the primacy of the Soviet state and continued to think of themselves as a detachment of an internationalist army. They probably wanted to put their disagreements in the past, but there is no reason to doubt the sincerity of their profession of loyalty. Stalin rejected the Chinese offer to accept a subordinate role, pretending that theirs should be a relationship between equals— but that too was a ritual pretence. He promised Moscow's recognition of the 'people's democratic dictatorship'. In reality, Stalin continued to perceive the Chinese revolution as a 'national and democratic' event, rather than a socialist one, but it was obvious that the birth of a state under the guidance of Chinese communists constituted a huge advantage for the Soviet Union's international positions. The two parties to the agreement established not only the essential terms of Moscow's economic, technical, and organizational assistance for the new power but also international perspectives, particularly those of Asian communism. A master of the enigmatic, Stalin came up with a vague prediction of war, declared himself ready to take on a thermonuclear conflict, and asserted that the Marshall Plan had already failed. Liu sounded out Stalin on the matter of the information bureau and pointed to support for the Vietnamese communists as the revolutionary priority in Asia. Stalin discouraged the CCP's membership of the Cominform, but alluded to the creation of a similar organization in Asia and a sharing out of responsibilities between the Soviet Union in Europe and the People's China in Asia.[140] Having received Stalin's benediction, Mao proclaimed the birth of the People's Republic on 1 October 1949 in Peking.

Mao finally met Stalin immediately afterwards in December 1949. The occasion could hardly have been more formal and solemn. All the principal communist leaders were in Moscow to celebrate Stalin's 70th birthday. The simultaneous proclamation of the Chinese People's Republic added considerably to the significance of the event. But Stalin was not profligate with praise and acknowledgements. He addressed Mao as though dealing with a subordinate partner rather than a head of state, not even honouring him with the title of 'comrade'.[141] The Chinese leader accepted this reality, perhaps because he needed Soviet aid, but possibly also because he was willing to acknowledge Stalin's authority. In other words, the hierarchical tradition of the communist movement imposed its continuity. At the first meeting between the two leaders, which took place on 16 December, Stalin agreed to Chinese requests for economic and military assistance, but held firm to the exorbitant options the Soviet wanted in Manchuria and Northeastern China, without modifying the principal items in his agreements with the nationalists. Indeed, he revealed his intention to honour the treaty that went back to 1945, to avoid an American reaction demanding changes to the Yalta Accords, while Mao let it be known that he intended to conclude a new treaty.[142] At a second meeting, on 24

---

[140] S. Radchenko and D. Wolff, 'To the summit via proxy-summits: new evidence from Soviet and Chinese archives on Mao's Long March to Moscow, 1949', *Cold War International History Project Bulletin* 16 (2007–8), doc. 49, pp. 175–6. For Liu Shaoqi's mission to Moscow in summer 1949, see Heinzig, *The Soviet Union and Communist China 1945–1950*, 177–221.

[141] J. Chang and J. Halliday, *Mao: The Unknown History* (London: Jonathan Cape, 2005), 364–70.

[142] *Russko-kitayskie otnosheniya*, vol. 5, section 2, doc. 544, pp. 229–33.

December, Stalin unenthusiastically accepted Mao's ambition to support the anti-colonial struggle of the Vietnamese communists, but discouraged a military invasion of Taiwan, where Chiang Kai-shek's men had taken refuge, and advised prudence towards the United States.[143] The two leaders probably also re-examined the question of an information bureau for Asian communist parties, but without reaching a decision because of Mao's opposition.[144] At the third meeting, on 22 January 1950, Stalin changed his attitude, perhaps because he realized that the United States had finally accepted the existence of Communist China as a fait accompli.[145] Mao achieved this main objective: a treaty that placed the Chinese People's Republic under the protection of the USSR, which was signed on the 14th of February 1950. If Stalin's behaviour before and after the Chinese communists took power left a bad taste in the mouth, for the moment the Chinese kept it to themselves. China's membership of the 'socialist camp' had been an important ambition, for which Mao was willing to sacrifice national interests and differences of opinion. The minor disagreements and disappointments over the cautious Soviet policy on China since 1945 might have created a few suspicions, but had not weakened Mao's loyalty to the communist movement. The Chinese communist leaders unreservedly shared the concept of the world divided into 'two camps'.[146]

However, the discord between Stalin's caution and Mao's radicalism very closely resembled those between Stalin and Tito. The two leaders were in agreement that south-east Asia was a bridgehead for Western imperialism, but came to opposite conclusions. Not only had Stalin shown little interest in the cause of the Vietnamese communists, but also the People's Republic of Vietnam, which was proclaimed by Ho Chi Minh in the north of the country in August-September of 1945 had not yet been recognized by Moscow. Ho's *curriculum vitae* was certainly not the most suited to find favour with Stalin. He had been accused of 'nationalism' following the Comintern's policy change in 1929, and had to pass the next few years in Moscow in the shadows, having been barred from all responsible positions.[147] At the end of the 1930s he had established a personal relationship with Mao, which was consolidated by the years of war against Japan. The friendship between the two Asian leaders created a special relationship between Chinese communism and Vietnamese communism that would last three decades. The Vietnamese ruling group had embraced the Maoist doctrine, particularly when it came to the writings of their main ideologue, Truong Chinh.[148] Only pressure from Mao persuaded Stalin to recognise the People's Republic of Vietnam in January 1950. Under the auspices of the Chinese, Ho was immediately invited to Moscow, where he met

---

[143] Heinzig, *The Soviet Union and Communist China 1945–1950*, 285.

[144] APCI, 'Palmiro Togliatti, Carte della scrivania', 26 Dec.1949.

[145] *Russko-kitayskie otnosheniya*, vol. 5, section 2, doc. 564, pp. 267–71. See also Heinzig, *The Soviet Union and Communist China 1945–1950*, 292–3.

[146] Jian, *Mao's China and the Cold War*, 50.

[147] S. Quinn-Judge, *Ho Chi Minh: The Missing Years* (London: Hurst, 2003), 191ff.

[148] W. J. Duiker, *The Communist Road to Power in Vietnam*, 2nd edn (Boulder, Colo.: Westview Press, 1996), 134–7.

Stalin, Mao, and Zhou Enlai.[149] The Chinese went overboard with offers of military assistance, believing they had obtained tacit permission from Stalin. On their return from Moscow, Mao and Ho went to Peking together and in the following months the aid the Chinese provided to the Vietnamese underwent a considerable increase.[150] From that moment on, the Chinese had a vision of spreading their revolution to the rest of the world by providing an example to national liberation struggles in countries outside Europe.

This militant internationalism did not strike a chord with Stalin. Far from wanting to encourage revolution in Asia, he believed that it was the right moment for a strategic initiative to take advantage of the birth of the People's Republic of China and inflict a blow on the influence of the United States. At the same time, he was meditating on how to reassert the Soviet Union's leadership and tighten the bonds that held China to the alliance. This was supposedly to prevent Mao from following an independent course that would be difficult to control. The pawn Stalin used was Kim Il-Sung, the North Korean leader the Soviets had installed as head of a communist regime after the division of Korea into two parts after the defeat of Japan. As far back as March 1949, Kim expressed his desire to conquer the south of the country, but the Soviet leader had dissuaded him. In April 1950 at another meeting with the Korean leader, Stalin revealed that he was now willing to back Kim's bellicose intentions, as long as Mao guaranteed his cooperation. Kim went to Peking, where, strengthened by Stalin's support, he was able to push Mao into agreement. The Chinese leader agreed more out of internationalist discipline than any strategic conviction. For some time, he had been making it clear to the Soviets that the American presence in Korea could become a serious threat to the security of the People's Republic, given the country's closeness to Peking and China's principal industrial cities. But the pressure Stalin cunningly brought to bear won out. Contrary to Chinese expectations, the main front in the anti-imperialist struggle in Asia was to be Korea and not Vietnam. Thus Stalin obtained his objective of challenging the United States without exposing the Soviet Union to excessive risks, but leaving the Chinese communists on the stage. He told Mao that he expected a rapid victory that would seriously damage the prestige of the United States.[151]

With China's technical and military assistance, the North Koreans started the war in June 1950. But Stalin's prediction soon proved to be mistaken. The American intervention in September 1950 quickly reversed the fortunes in the conflict and threatened to overthrow communist power in the north of the country. Stalin put pressure on Mao for direct intervention by the Chinese. Mao expressed his concerns over China's full military involvement which could compromise the country's economic reconstruction. But it was not a decisive argument. Careless of

---

[149] W. J. Duiker, *Ho Chi Minh: A Life* (New York: Hyperion, 2000), 418–23; *Istoricheskii Arkhiv* 2 (2008), 88.

[150] Heinzig, *The Soviet Union and Communist China 1945–1950*, 306; Chang and Halliday, *Mao: The Unknown History*, 372.

[151] K. Weathersby, *Should We Fear This? Stalin and the Danger of War with America* (Washington, D.C.: Cold War International History Project, working paper no. 39, July 2002). See also A. Lankov, *From Stalin to Kim Il Sung: The Formation of North Korea 1945–1960* (London: Hurst, 2002).

the human cost of an armed conflict, the two dictators ended up agreeing, albeit with a different outlook: Stalin's was a strategic game on the international chessboard, while Mao's was the furtherance of the anti-imperialist revolution. Stalin's insistence and the threat that the American counter-offensive meant for China convinced Mao to send his troops in.[152] Before the end of October, China found itself in the Korean conflict with military support from the USSR. The escalation of the conflict caused it to stall and presented the parties with a scenario of prolonged hostilities that would be difficult to resolve. This scenario was not part of Stalin's plans, but seemingly it did not displease him. The United States were now tied down in a serious armed conflict. On the other hand, the responsibility for prosecuting the war fell to the Chinese. The military commitment cemented the Sino-Soviet alliance, and provided the Chinese with a prominent mission in the international communist movement, which they were proud to call their own. At the same time, Moscow's leadership in the alliance was beyond discussion.[153]

Unlike Mao, Stalin did not however see any connection between decolonization and world revolution, nor did he attribute such significance to the war in Korea. Indeed he did his best to extinguish the fire of revolutionary ambitions amongst Indian and Indonesian communists in late 1950 and early 1951, inspired by the Maoist example. The anti-insurrectionist repression against the revolutionary violence that broke out in Indonesia and Malaysia two years earlier had left a continuing situation of guerrilla war and terrorism. Stalin rejected the idea of relaunching the armed struggle arguing that both countries were not ready for social revolution. He asserted that the Chinese Revolution had benefitted from an exceptional situation, the proximity of the Soviet Union as a strategic hinterland. He insisted instead on the prospect of gradually preparing for an agrarian and bourgeois revolution, which would carry out an anti-imperialist role as well.[154] His international strategy was looking in a different direction.

Whereas the initiative had broadly been with the Americans during the early years of the postwar period, the decision to foment conflict in Korea marked a change in Stalin's behaviour. From his point of view, the construction of a Soviet atomic bomb and the advent of communist power in China in 1949 had created the conditions to test out the United States' capacity to respond in Asia. He could now even up the score after the success of America's 'containment' in Europe and hope to induce Washington to reopen the German question. The United States had militarized the doctrine of 'containment', even before the outbreak of the Korean War. Now the antagonism between the two great powers was determining

---

[152] Jian, *Mao's China and the Cold War*, 54–8.

[153] O. A. Westad (ed.), *Brothers in Arms: The Rise and Fall of the Sino-Soviet Alliance* (Stanford, Calif./Washington, D.C.: Stanford University Press/Woodrow Wilson Center, 1998), 12–15; N. Jun, 'The birth of the People's Republic of China and the road to the Korean War', in Leffler and Westad, *The Cambridge History of the Cold War*, vol. 1: *Origins*, 221–41.

[154] I. V. Gaiduk, 'Soviet Cold War strategy and prospects of revolution in South and Southeast Asia', in C. E. Goscha and C. F. Ostermann (eds), *Connecting Histories: Decolonization and the Cold War in Southeast Asia, 1945–1962* (Washington, DC/Stanford, Calif.: Woodrow Wilson Center/Stanford University Press, 2009).

military escalation and raising the Cold War to a global phenomenon. The Soviet Union was pulling the strings and guaranteeing its own security. Under the influence of a conflict that he had helped to trigger, Stalin argued that the time was ripe to prepare for another world war. In his dark and repetitive vision of history, the early 1950s increasingly resembled the late 1930s. In October 1950, Stalin came up with his prediction of a widespread war in order to convince Mao to enter the conflict; he argued that the Sino-Soviet alliance was stronger than the Atlantic one, and that 'if war is inevitable, it's better to fight it now than in a few years time'—in other words, before Japanese 'militarism' recovered.[155] In January 1951, at a meeting held in the presence of party leaders and military chiefs from Soviet bloc countries, he set out the scenario for a war with the West in a few years and a massive rearmament plan.[156] Stalin wanted to exacerbate the militarization brought about by the Korean War and with it yet another round of repressive measures in the countries of Eastern and Central Europe, where the Soviet model had been exported.

THE 'REVOLUTION FROM ABOVE' IN EASTERN AND CENTRAL EUROPE AND THE PACIFIST MOBILIZATION

As had occurred twenty years earlier in a very different context, the new psychosis of war was linked to a 'revolution from above': this time it was the international scenario of the definitive Sovietization of Eastern and Central Europe.[157] The stabilization of the Cold War in Europe meant the return to a 'war of position', increasingly interpreted in terms of military and power politics. The era of activism generated by the Second World War was definitively over. Even the last conflict on the continent, the Greek Civil War, had ended with a melancholy defeat for the communists. Besides, the Cominform had never embraced the Greek cause, not even when relations between the Soviets and Yugoslavs were apparently at their most harmonious. At the time of the second conference, membership of the Greek and Albanian communist parties still looked highly improbable, in spite of their decision to side with the Soviets against Tito. Under instructions from Stalin, Malenkov justified this rejection by arguing that the 'Greek and Anglo-American reaction' would have branded the Greek communists as 'agents of Moscow'.[158]

---

[155] A. Y. Mansourov, 'Stalin, Mao, Kim, and China's decision to enter the Korean War, September 16– October 15, 1950: new evidence from the Russian archives', *Cold War International History Project Bulletin* 6 and 7 (1995–6), doc. 13, pp. 116–17.

[156] Mastny, *The Cold War and Soviet Insecurity*, 113–15.

[157] For a panorama of the definitive creation from above of Soviet-style regimes in Eastern and Central Europe during Stalin's final years, see T. V. Volokitina, G. P. Murashko, A. F. Noskova, and T. A. Pokivailova, *Moskva i vostochnaya Evropa: Stanovlenie politicheskikh rezhimov sovetskogo tipa 1949–1953. Ocherki istorii* (Moscow: Rosspen, 2002).

[158] *Procacci, The Cominform: Minutes of the Three Conferences*, 601; Adibekov et al., *Soveshchaniya Kominforma*, 494.

Tito's excommunication meant that the Greek communists were left to their own devices. Their loyalty to Moscow prevented assistance from the Yugoslavs and deprived them of a vital resource. The Civil War carried on until the late summer of 1949, but without any hope of victory for the KKE, despite Soviet assistance and encouragement from Dimitrov.[159] The end of radical challenges left room for further establishment of the blocs. In this sense, Stalin's actions appeared to be much more consistent and in line with past experience.

For some time a link had been emerging between the condemnation of the Yugoslav leadership and the formation of a uniform and disciplined bloc. Only Finland remained an exception. Here Stalin accepted the exclusion of communists from government in exchange for a neutralist compromise that promised a less oppressive influence.[160] Following the liquidation of anti-communist forces throughout Eastern and Central Europe, repression continued to strike at society and was extended to the communist parties. This time the terror took on a highly anti-Semitic hue. Going back at least to the war years and the punitive deportations of numerous ethnic groups accused of collaboration with the Nazis, anti-Semitism had come to provide the USSR with a vehicle in the xenophobic campaign against 'cosmopolitanism' in the period 1946–8. At the end of 1948, the suppression of the Jewish Anti-Fascist Committee provided a sinister foretaste of how the Stalinist regime was evolving. At the same time and in the wake of Tito's excommunication, Stalin imposed a blanket repression that was increasingly random and struck at the communists of Eastern Europe. The fear that, in spite of official condemnation, the widespread sympathy for Tito could associate itself with active or passive forms of resistance against Moscow's influence proved to be decisive.[161] Since April 1948, the Soviets had been prepared to attack leadership groups other than the Yugoslav one. The Bulgarians, who were suspected of genuine complicity with Belgrade, were not alone in the firing line; there were also the Czechs and the Poles. In particular, a dossier had been drawn up against Gomułka, the leader in the East most linked to what remained of the of the 'national roads to socialism'.[162] He was removed from the post of general secretary of the Polish party in September 1948, accused of 'revisionism', and replaced by Bierut. In accordance with communist custom, Gomułka engaged in self-criticism, but defended himself against the more defamatory accusations.[163]

From that moment on, any reference to the 'national roads' in Eastern and Central Europe would be treated as an offence and a crime, along with the

---

[159] Iatrides, 'Revolution or self-defense?', 30–3; I. Papathanasiou, 'The Cominform and the Greek Civil War, 1947–49', in P. Carabott and T. D. Sfikas (eds), *The Greek Civil War* (London: Ashgate, 2004).

[160] K. Rentola, 'Finnish Communism, O. W. Kuusinen, and their two native countries', in T. Saarela and K. Rentola (eds), *Communism National and International* (Helsinki: SHS, 1998), 170–4; M. Majander, 'Post-Cold War historiography in Finland', in T. B. Olesen (ed), *The Cold War and the Nordic Countries* (Odense: University Press of South Denmark, 2004), 47–51.

[161] Volokitina et al., *Moskva i vostochnaya Evropa*, 500–1.

[162] *SSSR-Polsha*, doc. 46, pp. 229–47.

[163] Ibid. doc. 50, pp. 271–7. See also Kersten, *The Establishment of Communist Rule in Poland, 1943–1948*, 448–57.

accusation of Titoism. The Cold War was proving to be an ideal environment not only for exporting the Soviet model but also for the psychology of suspicions and conspiracy typical of Stalinism. The communist leaderships Stalin considered untrustworthy became the victims of a new wave of trials, following those of the anti-communist opposition and anti-religious persecutions. These trials were along the same lines as the show trials in Moscow during the period 1936–8, which consisted of absurd accusations and confessions extorted under torture. Similarly, their symbolic use fostered intolerance of any form of dissent, and police surveillance of any potential enemy. Likewise, the mechanisms of complicity turned communist leaders in the East into active collaborators in order to deflect suspicions away from themselves, eliminate adversaries at home, and prove themselves as loyal servants of Moscow. The first trial took place in Albania against Koçi Xoxe, a former foreign minister with Titoist sympathies, in May 1949. It was followed by the one against László Rajk, the Hungarian foreign minister, who was arrested in May and tried in September of the same year under Rákosi's direction and with Stalin's approval. Traikho Kostov, the second in command of the Bulgarian Communist Party, was tried and condemned to death in December 1949, after Stalin in person had accused him of being a spy linked to the West and Tito.[164] The script was the same everywhere. Charges of nationalistic deviation mixed with those of collusion with the Yugoslavs and their 'Trotskyist' conspiracies, along with the usual accusations of spying. The same accusations were made against thousands of communist cadres, including a number of Western communists, leading to arrest and often execution.[165] At the same time, repression was carried out in Yugoslavia for the opposite reasons; the methods were similar, though less theatrical.[166]

The third conference of the Cominform, which gathered in Budapest in November 1949, was preoccupied with a witch-hunt against Titoists, as well as anti-militarist and anti-imperialist propaganda, which had been increasing for a few months as a response to the foundation of NATO. Clearly the purpose was to highlight the symbolism of aligning all the European parties, both in the East and in the Wes t; Suslov's report was between those of Togliatti and the Romanian Gheorghiu-Dej. Everyone used the same schematic and stereotyped language, even more than at the second conference. The most important thing was to relaunch the campaign against the Western bloc, along with the one against Tito: two carefully prepared messages in which there was yet again that implicit call to order of both the Western communist parties and the Eastern ones.[167] The Soviet Union's new imperial dimension meant that it could organize a similar campaign to the one before the war, but mobilizing many more pro-Soviet forces in the West.

---

[164] *VEDRA*, vol. 2, doc. 60, p. 194.

[165] On the fabrication and management of the trials, see Volokitina et al., *Moskva i vostochnaya Evropa*, 514ff.

[166] I. Banac, *With Stalin against Tito: Cominformist Splits in Yugoslavian Communism* (Ithaca, N.Y.: Cornell University Press, 1988).

[167] L. Gibianskii, 'The last conference of the Cominform', in Procacci, *The Cominform: Minutes of the Three Conferences*, 645–67.

The Western communist parties had for some time been playing the part of outposts in enemy territory. The launch of American containment, the birth of the Cominform, and the division of Europe had taken away their legitimacy to rule, but they preserved solid roots in French and Italian society. Stalin had repudiated the realism of previous years, but also impeded any revolutionary impulses. The ruling groups in the West exercised a kind of self-containment when it came to the more evident insurrectional tendencies among their cadres and activists. The most dramatic and symbolic moment came with the attempted assassination of Togliatti in Rome on 14 July 1948, which brought Italy to the brink of civil war. Following advice from the Soviet Union and taking the warnings Togliatti himself had been giving them over the preceding months, the ruling group of the PCI and the communist trade union leaders chose, after some vacillation, to contain spontaneous reaction from the masses which could have easily degenerated into violence.[168] The attempt on Togliatti's life and the averted civil war were the watershed. The dream of social revolution receded. The excommunication of the Yugoslavs blocked the principal source of communist radicalism. Far from stimulating revolution from below in Western Europe, the 'revolution from above' in Eastern and Central Europe discouraged it.

The American 'containment' and the Soviet responses to it had confined Western communists to an opposing trench from which there was little hope of finding a way out. Nevertheless their capacity for adaptation to the Cold War was remarkable, and they followed the objective of becoming a thorn in the side of some key countries in the Western bloc. In 1949 and 1950, the French and Italian communists launched a series of campaigns against the dominance of the United States, which combined the anti-imperialist motif and a new 'struggle for peace', even through sabotage of American military supplies. Anti-Americanism was a method for increasing the cohesion of parties and their electorate, by using nationalism against American influence.[169] It had no difficulty in opening a breach where there was a national tradition already predisposed to accepting it, as in France. Here more than anywhere else, the communists were successful in combining the idea of defence of national sovereignty and resistance to an invasion of commodified mass culture, which intellectuals in particular perceived as a threat.[170] Even in Italy, the campaigns against the country's membership of NATO received widespread support, more because of the neutralist sentiments in Catholic culture than assertive nationalism—albeit without any concrete results. Consequently the myth of the Soviet Union's 'peaceful' role, which went back to before the war, gained further traction. The peace campaign orchestrated by Stalin, who had been developing very clear plans for this since early 1949,[171] would prove effective in the short term,

---

[168] E. Aga Rossi and V. Zaslavsky, *Togliatti e Stalin: il PCI e la politica estera italiana negli archivi di Mosca*, 2nd edn (Bologna: il Mulino, 2007), 253–4.

[169] A. Brogi, *Confronting America: The Cold War between the United States and the Communists in France and Italy* (Chapel Hill, N.C.: University of North Carolina Press, 2011), 122–36.

[170] P. Roger, *The American Enemy: The History of French Anti-Americanism* (Chicago: University of Chicago Press, 2005), 430–5.

[171] Archives of the Hoover Institution, Dmitrii A. Volkogonov papers, box 27, reel 18, 6 Jan. 1949.

and it attracted and exploited those large sections of European public opinion who abhorred warfare, as unease about a possible atomic holocaust began to grow. The Stockholm Appeal for the banning of atomic weapons, launched in March 1950, gathered millions of supporters in Europe and involved such leading personalities of international culture as Pablo Picasso, Pablo Neruda, and Paul Éluard. French and Italian communists promoted the 'partisans of peace' along similar lines to the campaigns in the 1930s, but this time the nuclear threat, the prestige of the USSR, and its much greater influence made it much more significant. In France, pacifism combined with the anti-imperialist motif through support for the anti-colonial struggle in Indochina. In both countries the pacifist movement became a mass phenomenon and spread through wide sections of society, particularly women and young people.[172] Thorez and Togliatti could present themselves as leaders of an alternative international movement to the Europeanist one led by Jean Monnet, Robert Schuman, and Alcide De Gasperi, and put themselves forward as the defenders of national prestige. The strength of Western communists, in spite of their marginalization from power, was a cause for concern in the United States, which increased their pressure on governments to restrict the communists with either reforms or repression.[173]

The pacifist campaign in Europe revealed the communists' ability to tune into the fears and hopes of European societies, along with their well-tested organizational abilities and propaganda. As occurred with anti-fascism in the mid-1930s, they successfully took over a political space and identified themselves with a cause that was not really theirs. The grass roots, branch structure, and didactic nature of the pacifist campaign in Italy increased their penetration into society and highlighted their attempt to speak to the nation as a whole, albeit through a Manichaean vision of the world. However, the political impact of the 1949–50 campaign was not what the Western governments feared. The pacifist movement would never again have such a significant following, even after Stalin's death.[174] The communists' reaction to their marginalization from government circles, which involved mass action and culminated in the pacifist campaign, would only ever be an incomplete and unfinished project. Their formidable ability to mobilize the masses was a tool in the domestic and international war of nerves, but proved to be a blunt weapon when it came to increasing their public support and tipping the balance of power away from the pro-Western establishment and in their favour. The PCI's failure to stop Italy's membership of NATO, in spite of the country being the weak link in the Western bloc, was a demonstration of the limits imposed on Western communism. The real problem for Italian and French communists was to consolidate

---

[172] Y. Santamaria, *Le parti de l'ennemi? Le parti communiste français dans la lutte pour la paix (1947–1958)* (Paris: Armand Colin, 2006); A. Guiso, *La colomba e la spada: 'lotta per la pace' e antiamericanismo nella politica del Partito comunista italiano (1949–1954)* (Soveria Mannelli: Rubbettino, 2006).

[173] A. Brogi, *A Question of Self-Esteem: The United States and the Cold War Choices in France and Italy, 1944–1958* (Westport, Conn.: Praeger, 2002), 139–44.

[174] Y. Santamaria, *Le pacifisme, une passion française* (Paris: Armand Colin, 2005).

their existing influence and mass base. The Cold War created a space for their social integration, but it had also hemmed them in.

Apart from the pacifist campaign, Stalin had no specific strategic plan to offer Western communists. When Togliatti met him in December 1949, the conversation revolved around the 'national roads to socialism', an argument censured in the East but tolerated in the West. The Soviet leader did nothing but confirm his ambiguity. He was not inclined to encourage a violent conflict in Italy, because of the dangerous international implications, and declared that a 'bourgeois government' with communist involvement might still be possible, in spite of all the evidence to the contrary. He insisted on the importance of unlawful activity as an instrument for preparing the party for future battles, even if insurrection was not yet on the cards.[175] More acutely since the foundation of the Cominform, vacillation between lawful and unlawful activity continued to distinguish the strategy and even the language of Western communists. Even though the Cominform's militancy had long since been quashed, Stalin did not give up the centralized organization of the international communist movement during the tensest period of the Cold War. As appears clear from his proposal to Mao to extend the Cominform to Asia, Stalin considered it important to have such an organization even after the birth of a system of communist states running from Eastern and Central Europe to China.

At the end of 1950 and beginning of 1951, while a rearmament plan was being launched in the countries of the Soviet bloc, he decided to strengthen the Cominform, even though the idea of creating its twin in Asia had not been put into action. Up to that time, the Cominform had had its secretariat based in Bucharest under the de facto direction of Suslov, who was the Soviet party official responsible for foreign affairs. It was now supposed to establish an operational unit capable of rigorous inspection and supervision of the communist parties that were its members.[176] This plan was clearly linked to the war scenario which was considered imminent. The Cominform's control over the communist parties in power and the Western ones was already a reality, but its bureaucratic apparatus remained weak and inadequate. The clandestine anti-Titoist struggle had not borne the expected fruits, but the scenario of a new war would provide an opportunity to settle a few scores with Belgrade, possibly involving a military attack. Stalin believed it was now necessary to form a central administration for a clandestine communist network made up of all the communist parties in Western Europe, as they would be outlawed when the international situation blew up. No prospects of an insurrection in the region were foreseeable, but the option of unlawful action was very much there, just as had happened in the late 1930s.

This was the context in which Stalin asked Togliatti to take on the leadership of Cominform. Togliatti refused, questioning the usefulness of a 'clandestine organization' when a mass movement had been generated by the 'partisans of peace'. He argued that the PCI had not yet exhausted all the existing legal channels.[177] He

---

[175] APCI, 'Palmiro Togliatti, Carte della scrivania', 26 Dec. 1949.
[176] Adibekov, *Kominform i poslevoennaya Evropa*, 205ff.
[177] Gori and Pons, *Dagli archivi di Mosca*, doc. 39.

appealed to a robust tradition in communist history: 'the struggle for peace' and the defence of the USSR. After all, the Western communist parties owed their social and political muscle to the 'deradicalization' Stalin had wanted during the Second World War, no less than to Togliatti's political skills or Thorez's popularity. It was legitimate to assume that the aims of a mass party like the PCI could better conform to the interests of the USSR, unless there really was an outbreak of war, although it is doubtful that all Western communists would have reasoned in this manner. The opposite is more likely, given that in Rome the PCI ruling group almost unanimously supported Stalin's proposal.[178] In all probability, Togliatti's opinion prevailed because Stalin had not yet made his final decision. However, the importance of Togliatti's rejection of Stalin's wishes in 1951 should not be underestimated, precisely because the Italian leader's loyalty had been tested but never wavered.

Since the end of the war, the bond between Togliatti and Stalin had been put sorely to the test, because of the former's shrewd and measured behaviour in dealing with the national and international contexts.[179] During the first two years after the war, Togliatti had fully exploited the room for manoeuvre provided by the alliance of the Big Three and committed himself, much more than Thorez, to a political discourse based on mass democracy which was destined to become a key element in the culture of the Italian party.[180] After 1947, Togliatti from time to time spoke the language of 'progressive democracy' or of civil war without ever going past the point of no return. He had not been reluctant in giving his support to and being complicit in repression in Eastern and Central Europe or the fight against Tito, using all the stereotypes of the Cominform's propaganda. At the same time, he had built a party that was socially and institutionally more integrated than the other Western communist parties. His act of disobedience to Stalin in 1951 was unique. Before the war, such an act would have been inconceivable for any European communist leader. It was now possible because of the need to adapt to the nation and to democratic legality. The episode adds a new element to the differentiation within the communist movement caused by the war, although its hierarchical nature was beyond doubt. Togliatti's refusal helped to have the plan to strengthen the Cominform dropped; it was lost in the fog of the final years of the Stalinist era. The Western communist parties remained in place and would follow a shared history, albeit with differences between them.

In the 'socialist camp', the possibility of repeating the 1930s—the main spectre in Stalinist psychology—appeared to be increasingly taking shape during Stalin's final years. The expectation of war was heavily affecting the climate of international communism. The Great Terror had been conceived fifteen years earlier as

---

[178] G. Gozzini and R. Martinelli, *Storia del Partito comunista italiano*, vol. 7: *Dall'attentato a Togliatti all'VIII Congresso* (Turin: Einaudi, 1998), 193–4.

[179] S. Pons, 'Stalin, Togliatti, and the origins of the Cold War in Europe', *Journal of Cold War Studies* 3.2 (2001).

[180] M. Lazar, 'La strategia del PCF e del PCI dal 1944 al 1947: acquisizioni della ricerca e problemi irrisolti', in E. Aga-Rossi and G. Quagliariello (eds), *L'altra faccia della luna: i rapporti tra PCI, PCF e Unione sovietica* (Bologna: il Mulino, 1997), 98.

a method for annihilating the fifth column as war came close, and now its infernal mechanism was being triggered again.[181] The most notable difference was the emergence of anti-Semitism, which marked the end of the association of Jews with communism which went back to the Russian Revolution (but elsewhere too; for instance Hungary), and was reasserted at the end of the war in Eastern and Central Europe.[182] This was the most eloquent sign of how far the regime had moved from the universalism of its origins, and established another element of affinity between the Stalinist regime and the Nazi one, a few years after the Holocaust in Europe. In the USSR, the downward spiral towards a new purge and anti-Jewish repression was halted only by Stalin's death.[183]

In Eastern and Central Europe, a red thread linked the new wave of repressions with the trials of 1949. Rákosi, the leader of the country that found itself on the front line against Titoism, made a great play of exporting the methods of the 'Rajk affair' to Poland, Romania, and Czechoslovakia, and planting the suspicion amongst the Soviets that the leaders of those parties were not genuinely trying to root out supposed Titoist and Western spies.[184] Thus the 'battle against Titoism' proved to be a destabilizing factor for the European communist regimes, while the Cominform had now become a support apparatus for the espionage and counter-espionage agencies of the Soviet Union and other countries in Eastern and Central Europe. Anti-Semitism reached its acme in Czechoslovakia with the Slánský affair. Perhaps distracted by preparations for further repressive measures in the Soviet Union, Stalin did not appear as determined as he had been in other circumstances; in a letter to Gottwald dated July 1951 he even advised prudence, suggesting that Slánský should only be removed from the post of party general secretary.[185] However Slánský was arrested in November 1951 with Moscow's approval, and then tried and executed a year later.[186] Staged in November 1952, his trial followed the same surreal script heard on many previous occasions, but was characterized by its highly anti-Semitic tones. Massive purges were carried out, with arrests of cadres and ordinary members in all the communist parties of the Soviet bloc with large Jewish memberships just after the war. The comparison with the 1930s did not end here. The purges of the communist elites were only one aspect of a more general spread of police methods and purges in society, although on a smaller scale than the one that had affected Soviet society in the prewar period.

The export of terrorist methods to Eastern and Central Europe warded off the danger of Western contamination, undermined the very sense of a unitary

[181] Kramer, 'Stalin, Soviet policy, and the consolidation of a communist bloc in Eastern Europe', 100.

[182] Y. Slezkine, *The Jewish Century* (Princeton, N.J.: Princeton University Press, 2004), 308–15; J. Frankel (ed.), *Dark Times, Dire Decisions: Jews and Communism* (Oxford: Oxford University Press, 2004).

[183] Graziosi, *L'URSS dal trionfo al degrado*, 134–5.

[184] Volokitina et al., *Moskva i vostochnaya Evropa*, 530.

[185] *VEDRA*, vol. 2, doc. 207, p. 580.

[186] Volokitina et al., *Moskva i vostochnaya Evropa*, 559–61. See also *SFVE*, vol. 2, p. 556.

European civilization, and led to the introduction of nothing less than the Soviet model under the surveillance of political, technical, and police personnel from the Soviet Union. The propaganda and administrative functions of the party-state, the collectivization of the countryside, and the workerist and productivity myths were copied widely. Deportees, political prisoners, and forced labour were the harsh reality of social existence, just as they were in the Soviet Union. Budapest, Prague, and Warsaw became provinces of an empire that exploited their resources and dominated their ruling classes, now reduced to the role of local governors subject to the wishes of the centre and deprived of any notion of national sovereignty. The 'external empire' constituted a particular form of colonial power exercised by a centre that was more backward than the periphery.[187] In many ways, the Sovietization of Eastern and Central Europe was a prolongation of the civil conflicts that occurred at the end of the war, a failed pacification that would be a source of instability and delegitimization in the communist regimes. While this reality would have decisive consequences in the long term, the immediate impact of Sovietization was to present the image of a compact system of states closely linked to Moscow, which was capable of achieving postwar reconstruction on the basis of a planned economy, and of extending anti-capitalist modernization to European societies more advanced than the Soviet one. At the same time, the new communist power in China was unreservedly committed to replicating the Soviet model of state-building as the antidote to backwardness. The Chinese party now numbered more than 4 million members and was ready to take on the mantle of elitist party-state, as in the USSR. In the bellicose climate caused by the Korean War, the Chinese regime proved to be even more radical than the Soviets would have hoped. It triggered a massive campaign to purge the country of 'enemies of the people', and reinforced its control over society with violent methods.[188]

Stalin's last international measures were mere propaganda, such as the proposal in March 1952 to the Western powers to discuss the reunification of Germany as a neutral and demilitarized zone. The Soviet dictator reacted to the predictable Western refusal by launching a plan to consolidate and militarize the East German state, which would thus be united with the communist regimes in preparation for another war.[189] His assessment of the Korean War, in a conversation with Zhou Enlai in August 1952, was that the United States had proved incapable of conducting a large-scale war.[190] It is difficult to say whether for Stalin this meant that another world war was less likely or that he should be more optimistic about the outcome of an armed conflict. In any event, his underlying thought process was not unfathomable even if his policy appeared puzzling in many ways. In the final

[187] T. Judt, *Postwar: A History of Europe since 1945* (New York: Penguin Press, 2005).

[188] Westad, *Decisive Encounters*, 282.

[189] Zubok, *A Failed Empire*, 83–5.

[190] 'Stalin's conversations with Chinese leaders: talks with Mao Zedong, December 1949–January 1950, and with Zhou Enlai, August–September 1952', *Cold War International History Project Bulletin* 6 and 7 (1995–96), doc. 3, p. 13.

years of his life, Stalin perceived the new processes of communist state-building, both in Eastern and Central Europe and in China, exclusively as elements of warfare waged from Moscow in the name of the 'socialist camp'. The construction of new communist states was being carried out in a time of peace, but involved a mobilization that heralded war and moulded the very nature of the state, which was characterized by the dominant apparatuses of command, propaganda, and security. Once again, the myth of an 'alternative modernity' was founded on the scenario of war. Once again, Stalin's political horizon was entirely governed by the Soviet experience and was a prisoner of the past—a mentality rendered increasingly obsessive and paranoid by the despot's physical and mental decline.

Stalin's main legacy was the psychology of war and the total-security state, symbolized by the thousands of miles of barbed wire that marked the Soviet Union's frontiers and those of other communist countries. Although separate territorial entities, the 'socialist camp' was configured as a unitary empire interconnected by economic, cultural, military, and police practices that crossed state borders. The monocratic exercise of central power, the invasive nature of the Soviet presence, the dense network of transnational exchanges lessened the significance of the borders between individual states in relation to the demarcation between the 'socialist camp' and the rest of the world.[191] However, the Soviet Union's imperial reach, brought about by the Second World War, contradicted the tradition of isolation and separateness. The 'external empire' and the 'socialist camp' were not only conquered territories closed within the framework of the totalitarian state, but also places of potential contamination, conflict, and destabilization.

COMMUNISTS AND THE COLD WAR

Following the Second World War, international communism had experienced two methods of expansion. The first came through the advance of the Red Army and under the direct intervention of the Soviet Union in Eastern and Central Europe; the second came through autonomous revolutions that differed from each other—the anti-fascist revolution in Yugoslavia and the anti-imperialist one in China. Stalin only perceived the first of these two processes—'revolution from above', not planned but achieved with increasing resolution. The second method unfolded in many ways outside his control, or even against his wishes. However, even in this case the Soviet state played an essential role. It is not easy to see how the Yugoslav and Chinese communists could have taken power and maintained it without Soviet aid and without the presence of the USSR as a deterrent against any

---

[191] N. Egorova, 'La formation du bloc de l'Est comme frontière occidentale du système communiste (1947–1955)', in S. Coeuré and S. Dullin (eds), *Frontières du communisme: mythologies et réalités de la division de l'Europe de la Révolution d'Octobre au mur de Berlin* (Paris: La Découverte, 2007); N. Bystrova, *SSSR i formirovanie voenno-blokovogo protivostoyaniya v Evrope (1945–1955gg.)* (Moscow: Institut Rossiiskoy Istorii, 2005); A. Jersild, 'The Soviet state as imperial scavenger: "catch up and surpass" in the transnational socialist bloc, 1950–1960', *American Historical Review* 116.1 (2011).

counter-revolutionary intervention. In this light, the prospect of world revolution continued to have its centre of gravity in Moscow, and the creation of a system of communist states did not modify that original reality. From Stalin's point of view, the symbolic meaning of Tito's excommunication, which displayed the principle of Moscow's primacy, was more important than the political meaning of his losing his main ally in Europe.[192] Another symbolic meaning emerged from his cold and distant manner towards Mao. But even Tito and Mao, after having taken power, acknowledged Moscow's supremacy, in spite of the evident home-grown legitimacy their revolutions enjoyed and in spite of their disappointment and irritation over Stalin's behaviour. The primacy of the Soviet state remained the movement's guiding star. Communist leaders, whether or not they were in power, followed the interests of the Soviet Union, or their idea of such interests, from the moment they started to define their own political direction.

The break between Stalin and Tito did not destroy international communism's image of unity. In the West, the idea that the Titoist schism might constitute the first sign of a wider decomposition was soon discarded. Precisely because it appeared to be an isolated incident, albeit a startling one in the context of the Cold War, the Yugoslav question ended up strengthening the opposing convictions. The Korean War helped to re-establish the image of a cohesive and aggressive force that was difficult to contain. The paradigm of a monolithic power would thus prevail in the Western perception of communism.[193] This perceived monolith was the mirror image of communist self-representation. The movement's unitary nature was a resource that could never be relinquished, as confirmed by the excommunication itself. The 'world party' of revolution was a past memory, but international communism continued to be the principal vehicle for expressing the interests of the Soviet Union and spreading the myth of the USSR. When it came to responding to the American initiative in Europe, Stalin set up an organization for communist parties, the Cominform, before he set up an alliance of states. In spite of everything, the relationship with the communist movement remained—even for Stalin, the victor of the Great Patriotic War—the only stable element in the Soviet Union's foreign policy. After the victory of the Chinese Revolution and the conflagration of the Korean War, Stalin put his energies into strengthening the Cominform, even though its performance was miserable, as he could plainly see. In other words, the symbiosis between the state and the movement was reproduced and consolidated after the Second World War. The Soviet state offered the communist movement mythologies and resources, but also grounded its interests and authority in the reality and image of international communism.

However, the war created new divisions and contradictions, exactly when communist unity appeared to have been achieved through terror, resistance, and victory. Loyalty to the USSR seemed strong enough to endure the tensions between

---

[192] A. B. Ulam, *The Communists: The Story of Power and Lost Illusions 1948–1991* (New York: Scribner, 1992), 19–20.

[193] M. J. Selverstone, *Constructing the Monolith: The United States, Great Britain, and International Communism, 1945–1950* (Cambridge, Mass.: Harvard University Press, 2009).

the centre and the periphery, and to contain the opposition between moderate and radical tendencies. No one would have dared to deny the need for the movement to sacrifice its aims to the superior demands of the Soviet state, where necessary. The case of Yugoslavia demonstrated, however, the limits of this axiom. The minority status of new regimes created by the 'revolution from above' in Eastern and Central Europe could not be imposed on a regime created by a genuine revolution. Exploiting his own revolutionary prestige, Tito found the strength to stand up to Stalin. The excommunication was an exhibition of Stalin's sacral power, but the unheard-of ability to resist the hostility of the supreme Soviet power demonstrated Tito's strength as a head of state. A restriction on the Soviet Union's leadership was emerging from the state and nation, and could put at risk the unitary nature of the movement just when other communist parties, apart from the Russian one, were fulfilling their mission to dissolve the capitalist state and install revolutionary power.

At the same time, the changing scenario brought about by the division of Europe had profound implications, even though it was difficult to understand that then. The bipolar order was evidently asymmetric, even after the Chinese Revolution, given that the communist camp did not include any of the main industrial centres in the world and the most advanced countries had coalesced in the Western bloc. The drive for political and social change generated by the war ran out of steam within a few years. The Cold War caused communist positions to freeze, although in some cases it led to their defeat and in others stopped them from declining more rapidly. But in Eastern and Central Europe, the social base that supported the communist governments, which had always been in a minority, was reduced rather than increased by the violence and Sovietization, although it could not be measured under the heel of Stalinist oppression. In Western Europe, the social democratic and moderate forces of liberal or Catholic inspiration had largely prevailed by making use of the transition from anti-fascism to anti-communism fostered by the Americans. Moreover, the geography of European communism confirmed its limits. The communist parties constituted a substantial force only in France and Italy, while they had no influence in Germany, Great Britain, and most of Northern Europe. The ambition to replace the social democratic parties once again proved to be unfounded. The expansion and influence of the communist parties from 1943 to 1947 would never be repeated in Europe.[194] In different ways, the refounding of European nation-states would provide new reasons for social democratic policies, which would experience an even greater expansion than the one that occurred after the First World War, thanks to the increase in democratic citizenship brought about by the Second World War.[195] Very probably, this occurred in spite of the Cold War and not because of it. Even if the Soviet threat favoured the adoption of welfare policies and Western European economic

---

[194] D. Sassoon, *One Hundred Years of Socialism: The West European Left in the Twentieth Century* (London: I. B. Tauris, 1996), 56.

[195] G. Eley, *Forging Democracy: The History of the Left in Europe, 1850–2000* (Oxford: Oxford University Press, 2002), 298, 312–13.

integration, the Cold War provided a climate more suited to Stalinist communism than to the European democratic left. In the wake of the Second World War, the birth of the Soviet superpower and a system of communist states in a bipolar world gave new grounds for communist membership, recreating the conditions for a conflict with the Western left.

Western communists adhered unreservedly to the use of anti-fascism in the Soviet Union and the regimes of Eastern Europe as a rhetorical weapon in the anti-Western Cold War, continuing however to exploit it as political and symbolic resource. Unlike most of the East, anti-fascism in the West was capable as a body of values of generating a conspicuous cultural and intellectual following for communists, a deterrent against a return to the past, and a restraining factor for those tendencies that most openly called for a restoration of previous values in labour relations and in relations between the sexes.[196] It was in the name of the anti-fascist legacy that activists learnt a lesson they had previously failed to learn: that they had to defend social rights in practical ways and acknowledge the institutions of citizenship. At the same time, the Soviet myth allowed them to cultivate the residual sociocultural legacy of communism between the wars, namely the creation of a societal dimension and a 'state within the state' with a popular and working-class base that the ideological polarization of the Cold War favoured and fomented. The twin symbolism of the anti-fascist identity and the Soviet myth was an indivisible resource for communists in France and Italy. The contradiction between the Soviet Union's totalitarian model on the one hand and the democratic kernel of the anti-fascist paradigm on the other was constantly disguised and concealed.

The tasks of legitimization, which the Eastern communists ignored, caused the Western ones to adapt to the society in which they lived. Their demand for 'genuine' anti-fascism would make use of the concepts of nation and citizenship, and not simply anti-capitalist discourse. Much more than in their past history, the structural bond with Moscow had to reconcile itself to a language not entirely derived from Soviet political culture, giving rise to strata of propaganda and political discourse according to the social groups and functions for which it was intended. In France and Italy, communists talked of the nation more assiduously and with more conviction than their partners in Eastern and Central Europe, although their need to gather support drove them to adopt an outdated nationalist rhetoric as their own.[197] In spite of this, they demonstrated that they could build a force capable of influencing the national society and driven by a vivacious popular spirit. Their ability to compete with the socialists in the trade unions was greatly increased compared with the interwar years. Their women's organizations consolidated their positions with clear and practical aims that contrasted with the

---

[196] C. S. Maier, 'I fondamenti politici del dopoguerra', in P. Anderson et al. (eds), *Storia d'Europa*, vol. 1: *L'Europa oggi* (Turin: Einaudi, 1993), 311–72.

[197] For the combination of Stalinism and nationalism in France, see I. Wall, *French Communism in the Era of Stalin: The Quest for Unity and Integration, 1945–1962* (Westport, Conn.: Greenwood, 1983). For the situation in Italy, see M. Flores and N. Gallerano, *Sul PCI: un'interpretazione storica* (Bologna: il Mulino, 1992).

increasing restoration of traditional gender roles linked to the climate of the Cold War. Their mass pedagogy went beyond activism in order to educate new generations of workers and peasants, and did so in the spirit of defending their own dignity. In France, the strikes organized by communist organizations in 1947 and 1948 reflected the Cold War and heralded their social influence. In the following years, the PCF remained the largest French party, bolstered by its deep grass-roots organization whilst remaining politically isolated. Its model was already a compromise between a mass party and a cadre party, before the ideological conformity of the Cominform halved its membership in a few years.[198] In Italy, the PCI was a mass party with a significant following in all classes—a striking anomaly among the parties of international communism—and characterized by its recurrent appeals to the Constitution, the fruit of the anti-fascist unity that existed before the Cold War got the upper hand.[199] Thus Italian communism gained its strength from the country's peculiarities in the European context: the mass politics inherited from the fascist regime, convergence and osmosis with essential elements of the dominant Catholic culture and morality, and limitations on the national ruling class's willingness to reform, it being incapable of creating a welfare state comparable to the other large European states.[200]

At the same time, the strength of Italian communism was not only in its attractiveness to intellectuals, who were followers of French communism as well, but also the intellectual profile of its original leadership, something not to be found in any of the other European parties, except the Russian one at the time of the Revolution. The intellectual standing of Thorez, Duclos, or Marty was not comparable with that of Gramsci and Togliatti. Both parties appointed leading intellectuals to responsible positions, as in the case of Louis Aragon and Emilio Sereni. But there were no political figures of a different social extraction and cultural prominence at Thorez's side. Even in the new generation of PCI leaders that emerged from the war and were cultivated by Togliatti, there were very cultured people such as Giorgio Amendola, a genuine example of a national communist.[201] Moreover, Gramsci's prison notebooks, published by Togliatti in the late 1940s and early 1950s, immediately proved to be a formidable strategic resource for the PCI, because they were deeply rooted in Italy's historical and philosophical culture, and as such provided a source of national legitimization. Although based on a conceptual orchestration that went back to the distant 1920s and politically belonged to the Leninist tradition, they constituted an invaluable legacy in the intellectual desert of Stalinist communism. Gramsci's thought could not be tied to

---

[198] Courtois and Lazar, *Histoire du parti communiste français*, 261.

[199] Gozzini and Martinelli, *Storia del Partito comunista italiano*, vol. 7, pp. 254–5. For a comparison between the PCF and the PCI after the Second World War, see M. Lazar, *Maisons rouges: les partis communistes français et italien de la Libération à nos jours* (Paris: Aubier, 1992).

[200] R. Gualtieri (ed.), *Il PCI nell'Italia repubblicana* (Rome: Carocci, 2001).

[201] G. Amendola, *Una scelta di vita* (Milan: Rizzoli, 1976); G. Amendola, *Lettere a Milano* (Rome: Editori Riuniti, 1973). See also G. Cerchia, *Giorgio Amendola: un comunista nazionale* (Soveria Mannelli: Rubbettino, 2004).

the Bolsheviks' schematic reading of the era as purely a clash between revolution and counter-revolution. It provided communists after the Second World War with a more complex vision of capitalist society. During the crisis that followed the First World War, Gramsci had not only grasped the signs of bourgeois decadence but also the resilience and transformative dynamic of Western societies, which led to reflections on the reason for the failed European revolution and linked the revolution to the conquest of political and intellectual hegemony rather than a strategy of force. To some degree, Italian communists gained from his posthumous lesson, even if it was still flanked by orthodox Stalinist literature, and they attracted a strong following amongst intellectuals.[202] Other Western communists ignored it, with the exception of a few Western Marxist intellectuals who had little influence over their parties.

Whatever their intellectual traditions and their political and institutional discourse, the twin nature of the Western parties, both lawful and anti-establishment, was a permanent feature for them all, defining their political culture and the limitations on their ability to penetrate their national societies. They renounced revolutionary violence, but did not reject the principle that such violence might become a historical necessity. They created mass parties that adapted to the shape of their society, but kept the concept of the cadre party ready to struggle for power. The Cold War accentuated their material and ideological dependency on the Soviet Union and the 'socialist camp'. The financial and organizational links with Moscow revealed continuity with the prewar years and increased in the final years of Stalin's life, when China also provided Western communists with financial support.[203] Following the creation of the Cominform, the PCI and the PCF set in place secret paramilitary structures that exacerbated the dangerous conspiratorial plots that typified the Cold War, although it is not clear whether they had any real capability.[204] Even sensitive documents in the party archives were sent to Moscow and other capitals in Eastern Europe for security reasons, following a practice introduced by the Comintern. The training of cadres continued to be carried out largely by Soviet political and ideological agencies, helping to instil into new recruits behavioural patterns and state identity different from the national ones. The life and activities of leaders, cadres, and activists was still full of symbolism that emphasized the primacy of loyalty to the USSR.[205]

---

[202] F. Chiarotto, *Operazione Gramsci: alla conquista degli intellettuali nell'Italia del dopoguerra* (Milan: Bruno Mondadori, 2010). For a lively record of the intellectual impact of Gramsci's writings on Italian and Western communists, see R. Rossanda, *La ragazza del secolo scorso* (Turin: Einaudi, 2005), 159–60.

[203] V. Riva, *Oro da Mosca: i finanziamenti sovietici al PCI dalla Rivoluzione d'ottobre al crollo dell'URSS* (Milan: Mondadori, 1999), docs 2–7, pp. 643–53; D. Volkogonov, *The Rise and Fall of the Soviet Empire: Political Leaders from Lenin to Gorbachev* (London: HarperCollins, 1998), 144–5.

[204] RGASPI, fo. 77, op. 3, d. 98; *Istoricheskii Arkhiv* 1 (1996), 13–14; Reale, *Nascita del Cominform*, 32–3. On the situation in Italy, see V. Zaslavsky, 'L'apparato paramilitare comunista nell'Italia del dopoguerra (1945–1955)', in *Lo stalinismo e la sinistra italiana: dal mito dell'URSS alla fine del comunismo* (Milan: Mondadori, 2004).

[205] F. Andreucci, *Falce e martello: identità e linguaggi dei comunisti italiani tra stalinismo e guerra fredda* (Bologna: Bononia University Press, 2005).

Communist political culture was firmly bound up with an international out-look. 'We no longer invoked the world revolution,' wrote Raphael Samuel, 'but we believed that socialism was a cosmic process, and even if we acknowledged the existence of national characteristics,... we thought that the transition from capitalism to socialism was identical everywhere.... Internationalism was not an option but a necessity for our political essence, the touchstone of our honour and our values.'[206] The possibility of fighting against the Soviet Union in the event of war was repeatedly and explicitly ruled out. When a high-ranking communist like Umberto Terracini, president of the Italian Constituent Assembly, hinted at this possibility in October 1947, he was forced into self-criticism.[207] In his conversa-tion with Stalin in November 1947, Thorez confessed that he felt more a citizen of the USSR than of France, and the Soviet leader commented laconically, 'We're all communists, and this tells us everything.'[208] The 'twin loyalty' of Western com-munists had its inconveniences, however. The link with the Soviet Union was a strong point, but would also be a considerable impediment to gathering further consensus. The contradiction between loyalty to the Soviet Union and the claim to a national identity was too obvious not to be a potent influence. However much the communists set about building a national identity, they were not capable of formulating a credible notion of national interest in their own countries. At the end of the war, Yugoslav ambitions to annex Trieste and Macedonia could not have demonstrated the problem more clearly, as they forced Italian and Greek commu-nists to attempt to square the circle between the primacy of the 'socialist camp' and the search for national credibility. At the same time, the anti-American discourse revealed the limitations and aporias of the communist vision of modernity, based on Soviet 'alternative modernity' and all kinds of prejudice against Western mass societies. The resources of the anti-fascist legacy and the Soviet myth proved, in practice, to be barely sufficient for Western communists to establish a bridgehead in the 'war of position' in Europe. The grim consequences of Sovietization in the eastern part of the continent did not improve their situation.

Besides, the fortunes of the European left were not Stalin's primary concern. He was neither a romantic governed by ideological maxims nor a realist intent upon implementing an ideology as an *a posteriori* justification.[209] Realism and the link with Marxism-Leninism were inseparable elements in his political culture. After the Second World War, Stalin revived the combination between Realpolitik and an ideological vision of the external world that had already been adopted in the prewar period. This cultural mix produced specific plans and objectives or illu-sory ambitions, which did not however include a project for asserting communist hegemony over Europe. In his memoirs, Molotov claimed that the Soviet Union's

---

[206] Samuel, *The Lost World of British Communism*, 47–8.
[207] Pons, *L'impossibile egemonia*, 207–11.   [208] *Istoricheskii Arkhiv* 1 (1996), p. 14.
[209] For the two opposing depictions of Stalin as either a 'romantic' or a 'realist', neither of them adequate for an understanding of his political culture, see respectively J. L. Gaddis, *We Now Know: Rethinking Cold War History* (Oxford: Oxford University Press, 1997), 289, and H. Kissinger, *Diplomacy* (New York: Simon & Schuster, 1994), 232.

foreign policy after the Second World War successfully achieved most of its objectives ('Stalin said more than once that Russia wins wars, but doesn't enjoy the fruits of victory. Russians fight in a remarkable manner, but don't know how to negotiate peace treaties; they are duped and get too little out of it. But what we've done as a result of this war was, I believe, well done; we have strengthened the Soviet state').[210] At the time, Litvinov expressed the opposite opinion. Since the first year after the war, by then relieved all official positions, he had argued that the Soviet Union, having won the war, was at risk of losing the peace. In his judgement, Stalin had not understood that the Soviet Union was more secure after the defeat of Nazi Germany and, convinced that a conflict between the communist world and the West was inevitable, had revived the ideological concept of security, which in reality weakened the positions established by the military victory.[211] Stalin's decisions displayed a jumble of strategies based on force and an awareness of the Soviet Union's vulnerability to the Western powers, which went back to the origins of the Soviet state. He drew up plans for another 'war of position'. The centre was Europe, in the mistaken belief that the Marshall Plan was another Dawes Plan, which would be followed by another of capitalism's great depressions. The 'war of movement' that commenced in Asia after the victory of the Chinese communists was subordinate to the scenario in Europe. Stalin's strategy was based on the idea that the 'international civil war' thought up by the Bolsheviks at the time of the First World War was unchanged in its constituent features, excepting the rising power of the USSR. But it was precisely this rise to power that heralded the future clash between two opposing scenarios of the globalized world.

Now that Nazism had left the stage, the stand-off between communism and anti-communism became paramount. On the communist side, it was easier to establish a monopoly over the combination of class and nation as the engine of progress, presenting the Soviet model as the only alternative to capitalist modernity. On the other side, anti-communism—once freed from fascist claims—could display an intolerant and reactionary physiognomy, as in the case of the Catholic Church in Italy, but on the whole it established itself much more solidly than in the interwar years on the side of liberal-democratic principles and the promise of prosperity. The denunciation of communism as a form of totalitarianism served to consolidate this position, because it put anti-communism on a par with anti-fascism. The notion of totalitarianism could support very different political and intellectual concepts. Even the father of 'containment', Kennan, developed his ideas further after having formulated the bases for the doctrine in his famous 'long telegram' published under a pseudonym in July 1947. In that document, Kennan produced an analysis and a prophecy. In his opinion, the Soviet Union was an expansionist power dominated by an acute sense of insecurity that made it aggressive and impervious to outside stimuli. Although he accepted the monolithic depiction of communism, he did perceive its fragility. His prophecy was that 'the

---

[210] *Sto sorok besed s Molotovym*, 78.
[211] RGASPI, fo. 82, op. 2, d. 1036; A. Werth, *Russia at War: 1941–1945* (New York: Carroll & Graf, 1996), 938.

powerful light still emanated by the Kremlin over the dissatisfied peoples of the Western world' could constitute 'the last powerful rays of constellation that is in fact fading', because Soviet power, 'like the capitalist world as it perceives it', carried within it 'the seeds of its own decay'.[212] The question of whether the Soviet Union and international communism were to be seen as powerful and stable, or intrinsically vulnerable in spite of rising to the status of world power, would remain a central one for many years to come. The division of Europe and the Korean War shifted the centre of gravity of American and Western perceptions towards the question of military force. Kennan was one of those opposed to this development, as he was now convinced that communism did not constitute a monolithic bloc, and a purely military response would assist the Soviet hold on Eastern and Central Europe.[213] He was then marginalized, but the question would recur with all its force after Stalin's death.

The clash between liberal democratic capitalism and communism preoccupied almost the entire panorama of world politics, and appeared to encapsulate the dilemmas and prospects facing humanity, now that the third alternative, fascism, had been annihilated. Following the uncertainties of the early postwar period, the power struggle and ideological conflict could not be disentangled from each other, and lay at the heart of the Cold War. The conflict defined and invaded most collective identities, dividing the political world, public opinion, and intellectuals in democratic societies, especially in Europe. In the anti-communist camp, dissident former communists of the previous decade still enjoyed a significant role, but soon gave way to liberal hegemony. Republished in France in 1946, Koestler's *Darkness at Noon* was a huge success, demonstrating that his distinctive challenge to the Soviet myth remained topical even after the war.[214] Two years later, George Orwell spread the concept of totalitarianism to mass opinion with his world-famous novel, *1984*, which in part resulted from an exchange of ideas with Borkenau. At the height of the anti-communist cultural campaign, the Congress for Cultural Freedom gathered in Berlin in June 1950 was primarily the creation of communist dissidents such as Sidney Hook, James Burnham, Ruth Fischer, Ignazio Silone, and again Borkenau and Koestler. In spite of Hannah Arendt's irritation at the self-publicism of some ex-communists, her book *The Origins of Totalitarianism*, published in 1951, was to some extent indebted to them, although she gave the concept of totalitarianism a new dignity by linking it to the notion of mass society and modernity.[215]

---

[212] G. F. Kennan, 'The sources of Soviet conduct', in F. J. Fleron, E. P. Hoffmann, and R. F. Laird (eds), *Classic Issues in Soviet Foreign Policy* (New York: de Gruyter, 1991), 322–4.

[213] Selverstone, *Constructing the Monolith*, 36–7, 215–16; A. Stephanson, *Kennan and the Art of Foreign Policy* (Cambridge, Mass.: Harvard University Press, 1989), 144–56; J. L. Gaddis, *George F. Kennan: An American Life* (New York: Penguin, 2011), ch. 16.

[214] T. Judt, 'Arthur Koestler, the exemplary intellectual', in *Reappraisals: Reflections of the Forgotten Twentieth Century* (New York: Penguin Press, 2008), 38–41.

[215] W. D. Jones, *The Lost Debate: German Socialist Intellectuals and Totalitarianism* (Urbana: University of Illinois Press, 1999), 124, 202–3; A. Gleason, *Totalitarianism: The Inner History of the Cold War* (Oxford: Oxford University Press, 1995), 109.

However, the role of ex-communists in the definition of anti-communism as anti-totalitarianism was now over. Western 'cold warriors', such as the French philosopher Raymond Aron, fully identified with liberalism and opposed 'fellow travellers' such as Jean-Paul Sartre. At the same time, the cultural Cold War took on more clearly the features of a propaganda and media campaign that transcended the role of individual intellectuals. The totalitarian nightmare described by Orwell hit the target and influenced entire generations of Western readers because of its lucidity and atmosphere, but also because after the author's early death in 1950, *1984* became the object of one of the most bitter propaganda struggles of the Cold War.[216] Washington promoted and funded the activities of the Congress for Cultural Freedom, together with various other initiatives—most notably Radio Free Europe—in a complex relationship with European intellectuals.[217] The resources deployed by Moscow were channelled through the communist parties in an untiring work of propaganda and counter-propaganda. One of the more famous episodes was the 'Kravchenko affair', which occurred in France in 1949, and found the PCF attempting to deny the Soviet defector's story about repression and forced labour in the Soviet Union.[218]

Political propaganda, perceived threats, and spy agencies were all features of a struggle in which no one pulled their punches. In the Western world, the image of communists as 'agents of Moscow' came back with a vengeance, after Stalin had spent the war trying to play this down, only to relaunch it through the conspiratorial activities of the Cominform. Particularly in Great Britain and the United States, this definition was not just fantasy. The restricted social base of the parties caused activism to be seen as service to the Soviet Union, particularly amongst intellectuals and professionals. It was a short step to passing on intelligence information. In the 1930s this was done in Great Britain by young intellectuals like Kim Philby and the other four members of the 'Cambridge group', who would follow a long career of spying for the Soviet Union which turned them into mythical figures of the Cold War. The principal theme around which postwar espionage revolved was the attainment of atomic weapons, which combined ideological faith and service to the Soviet Union. Typical cases were those of the physicist Klaus Fuchs, who in 1950 confessed to having been a Soviet spy at Los Alamos at the end of the war for strictly political and ideological reasons, and of the Rosenbergs, man and wife, who were tried and condemned to death in 1953 for having worked for the KGB out of their communist ideals, although in a minor role that was not commensurate with the sentence passed on them.[219]

---

[216] R. Mitter and P. Major (eds), *Across the Blocs: Cold War Cultural and Social History* (London: Frank Cass, 2004).

[217] V. R. Berghahn, *America and the Intellectual Cold Wars in Europe* (Princeton, N.J.: Princeton University Press, 2001).

[218] Judt, *Postwar*, 222–5.

[219] P. Deery and M. Del Pero, *Spiare e tradire: dietro le quinte della guerra fredda* (Milan: Feltrinelli, 2011); J. E. Haynes, H. Klehr, and A. Vassiliev, *Spies: The Rise and Fall of the KGB in America* (New Haven, Conn.: Yale University Press, 2009).

However, fantasy played an essential part and in some ways mirrored the theories of reactionary and anti-Soviet plots thought up by the communists. While a dogmatic and paranoid vision of imperialism formulated many years earlier was dominant in the USSR and the communist world, stereotypes and obsessions abounded on the other side too. Thirty years earlier, the 'Red scare' had already been a significant phenomenon in the United States. Now it risked becoming a mass psychosis, influencing the entire Western world. From 1950 to 1953 the campaigns launched by Senator McCarthy came close to transforming anti-communism into widespread hysteria and a witch-hunt which tended to condemn progressive and anti-fascist opinions indiscriminately.[220] The idea of a communist plot capable of attacking the vital nerve centres of free society gained more currency in America than in Europe. In France and Italy, paradoxically, it was the presence of strong communist parties that provided a more realistic perception of communism away from the worst conspiratorial imaginings, although extreme forms of police repression were adopted, particularly against the trade unions. In any event, the fits of obscurantist anti-communism provoked a reaction in democratic societies that was destined to neutralize them. None of this was comparable to the repression in the USSR and Eastern and Central Europe. The Western communists' denunciation of the McCarthyist persecutions was an example of double standards, because they followed the wave of democratic indignation but orchestrated it while remaining silent about what was happening in the East or, at best, establishing an unjustifiable parallel.

The Cold War did not take the communists too much by surprise. Stalin was not alone in expecting a new phase in the 'international civil war', now reduced exclusively to the antagonism between Soviet communism and liberal democratic capitalism. The birth of the bipolar world, divided into 'two camps', appeared perfectly suited to the simplification of political, social, and national realities that had always distinguished the communist mentality. The Manichaeanism of the two alignments was a way of thinking and a language that put the communist at their ease. The Cold War raised the significance of their mass political acculturation. The more intransigent anti-communist messages held the stage, the more the communist faith found opportunities to continue its existence.[221] While the Western campaigns exploited the rejection of totalitarian projects at opposite poles, which had left their mark on recent European history, the communist campaign exploited pacifism and anti-Americanism in order to revive the spectre and the concept itself of fascism in the postwar world.

It was this very rigid continuity with the past that revealed the link between the communist political culture and a world that by then had been buried. The conceptual armoury adopted by the communist ruling class went back to the 1920s, and even then it had demonstrated its limitations. The main paradox of the 1930s

---

[220] E. Schrecker, *Many Are the Crimes: McCarthyism in America* (Princeton, N.J.: Princeton University Press, 1998); L. Ceplair, *Anti-Communism in Twentieth Century America: A Critical History* (Santa Barbara, Calif.: ABC-Clio, 2011).
[221] E. J. Hobsbawm, *Interesting Times: A Twentieth-Century Life* (London: Allen Lane, 2002), 203.

and the Second World War had not been resolved: politically, following the alliance during the war, anti-fascism tended to include liberal capitalism, but structurally this included fascism, as it was seen as a phenomenon produced by the inherent mechanisms of the capitalist system. This paradox lies at the root of the difficulties they had in understanding the post-Nazi world, and provides a clue to an unresolved dilemma. Instead of projecting them into the future, the contribution of the communists to the elimination of Nazism made them prisoners of the past. They read postwar capitalism and the hegemony of the United States through the lens of economic" collapse, fascistization, and war, while precluding the possibility that liberal and capitalist democracy might encounter a new lease of life and take on a different quality. The idea that the totalitarian response provided by Bolshevism to the emergence of mass politics in the First World War could constitute even more than before the winning solution for the second postwar period was an act of faith. Anti-fascist ideas, promotion of peace, the entanglement of the concepts of class and nation had not undermined the cultural certitude that saw capitalist modernity as destined for catastrophe. Marxist political leaders and thinkers in the West made every effort to establish a more constructive perspective, but that vision remained fixed in the heart of communist political culture, although their language was ambiguously used to cover different meanings.[222]

Once the idea of the revolution's topicality had gone, the implacable antagonism cultivated since 1917 remained the basis for Soviet and communist identity. The showdown with capitalism was entrusted to the prophecy of more inevitable conflicts, the scenario of the long march of communism even after the Second World War. The Soviet Union's political and military influence along with imperial conquests from the war constituted a demarcation line and a trench to be defended. The original revolutionary utopia had taken on the features of a state mission, sustained by faith in the 'superiority' of the Soviet system over the capitalist one and by the conviction that a shift in the 'balance of power' in favour of the 'socialist camp' was inevitable. Stalinist culture combined the cult of power, a siege mentality, a catastrophist vision of capitalism, the expectation of war, and the mythology of an 'alternative modernity'. Heir to a universalism apparently more outgoing and inspiring than that of the United States, the Soviet state power suggested a more traditional concept of empire. Once the Second World War was over, Stalin did not formulate a single universalist project, nor did he come up with a global concept of national security comparable with Roosevelt's. Instead he adapted to the global nature of American power, deciding to attribute to the Soviet Union and the 'socialist camp' the role of antagonist to the 'imperialist camp'. So he drew up a Soviet strategy of containment, which mirrored the Western one. This strategy provided the potential for a global challenge, even though this was more a scenario for the future than a reality in the present. Soviet resources and

[222] M. Thing, 'The signs of communism, signs of ambiguity: language and communism', in Saarela and Rentola, *Communism National and International*; S. Pons, 'Stalinismo, antifascismo e "guerra civile europea"', in F. De Felice (ed.), *Antifascismi e resistenze* (Rome: La Nuova Italia Scientifica, 1997), 291–313.

outlook proved to be much more limited than American 'containment' as they were centred upon dominion and systematic separation. The Chinese Revolution marked a leap forward in terms of global antagonism and chances of expansion for international communism. But rather than seeking hegemony, Stalin looked at the prospects for catastrophe. The only mobilization he suggested for the communist movement in Europe and Asia was preparation for another war. In Eastern and Central Europe, Sovietization imposed the most extreme demands on the state of total security. In China, the first steps towards the construction of a new revolutionary state were carried out in the furnace of armed conflict. In the Western world, the phase of mass communist parties appeared to be coming to an end. The Stalinist era was ending with this shadow across it.

5

Time of Decline (1953–1968)

If we leave Hungary, this will strengthen the American, British and French imperialists. They will interpret it as a weakness and attack us.... Our party would not understand. Hungary will be added to Egypt. We don't have a choice.

Khrushchev to the Presidium of the CPSU, 31 October 1956

To my way of seeing things, the imperialists are like the sun at six in the evening; we are like the sun at six in the morning.... Western countries have been left behind and we have taken the lead. The west wind no longer prevails over the east wind, because the west wind is weaker. It is the east wind that will prevail over the west wind.

Mao Zedong, 18 November 1957

One thing that worries us and which we cannot fully explain is the occurrence of a centrifugal tendency amongst socialist countries. This is clearly a serious danger, which, we believe, the Soviet comrades should be concerned about.

Palmiro Togliatti, August 1964

THE CRISIS IN CENTRAL AND EASTERN EUROPE

When Stalin died, international communism was at its height. The USSR was now a nuclear superpower, although at a lower level than the United States. A system of satellite states revolved around it, and replicated the Soviet model. Contained in Europe, communism was in power in China and was showing its teeth in Korea and Vietnam. Moscow was leading one of the poles of world power, and was dominant in Eurasia and the Far East. The movement's transnational calling was suddenly achieving results. The Cold War might have imposed the rate and the method, but the result appeared to transcend the contingencies of international politics. For communists and also for many anti-communists, the Second World War had brought about the systematic geopolitical rise of the USSR and communism, which would become the distinguishing feature of the era. In spite of the United States' economic and military power, it felt as though an irrepressible force had relaunched the hopes and fears of the October Revolution on a global scale.[1]

In the face of this spectacular rise to prominence, little importance was attached to the troubling questions that needed to be put on the other side of the scales, such as the repression and Sovietization of Central and Eastern Europe, the separation of Yugoslavia from the Soviet bloc, and the setbacks suffered by the main communist parties in Western Europe. The purges and the export of the Soviet model could be seen as necessary transitions for the purpose of consolidating the bloc, a sign of strength and not of vulnerability, the split between Moscow and Belgrade as a minor drawback, and the containment of Western communism as a reversible situation. Communist China was much more significant for the consolidation of the 'socialist camp', and it also provided an example to non-European peoples as the definitive break-up of Western empires began to materialize. The prophecy Bukharin had made many years before that the capitalist system would not be able to sustain the effort of encircling the Soviet Union and containing the Chinese Revolution now appeared close to coming true. The communist world constituted a system that was closed and impermeable to outside influence and the world economy, but it still interacted with the West and the colonial and post-colonial world on the political, military, ideological, and symbolic level. International communism, which centred around the Soviet state in its twin status of state system extending across Eurasian territory as far as China and of a political movement deployed across the globe, appeared to be a decisive actor in world politics at the time. It was the presence of international communism that provided the impulse to develop the American ideal of creating a liberal, democratic, and capitalist world order into a hegemonic project and a transatlantic alliance.[2]

However, Stalin's legacy more than anything else offered a self-destructive prospect. The domestic and international foundations of the Soviet empire revealed themselves to be unmanageable immediately after the despot's death, which came on 5 March 1953. The psychology of inevitable war, which was a tool for justifying the imperial system, was also a source of instability. The tensions with the West were so extreme as to weaken the Soviet Union's security, rather than serve as a form of defence. The use of terror as a method of government was in danger of becoming counterproductive. Social repression and forced mobilization had exceeded the danger point, both in the Soviet Union and in Central and Eastern Europe.[3] Whereas Lenin's successors fought each other for the mantle of his legacy, Stalin's mainly fought each other to distance themselves from his legacy and thus avoid being dragged down with it.

[1] H. Seton-Watson, *From Lenin to Malenkov: The History of World Communism* (New York: Praeger, 1953).

[2] C. S. Maier, *Among Empires: American Ascendancy and Its Predecessors* (Cambridge, Mass.: Harvard University Press, 2006), 154–6; M. P. Leffler, 'The emergence of an American grand strategy, 1945–1952', in M. P. Leffler and O. A. Westad (eds), *The Cambridge History of the Cold War*, vol. 1: *Origins* (Cambridge: Cambridge University Press, 2010).

[3] A. Graziosi, *L'URSS dal trionfo al degrado: storia dell'Unione sovietica, 1945–1991* (Bologna: il Mulino, 2008), 141–2.

From the early months after his death, the problem facing the three main protagonists—Malenkov, Beria, and Nikita Khrushchev—was how to keep the system
on track. After a short period, the political agenda of Stalin's successors, irrespective
of their divisions, demonstrated the urgent need to slacken the international tension, reach a peaceful solution for Korea, reduce the pressure on the member states
of the Soviet bloc by mitigating the more extreme consequences of its militarization, and relax the Soviet Union's domestic regime by commencing the rehabilita-
tion of the purged and the slow dismantlement of the Gulag. This policy direction
was agreed upon by the principal players, with the exception of ultra-conservatives
like Molotov, but it was also an ill-defined plan. The most serious attempt at intro-
ducing a few radical measures came from Beria and Malenkov, who were apparently willing to dismantle the collectivized structures in the Eastern European
countryside, and even to negotiate the very existence of the West German state
on the basis of a united and neutral Germany. The two leaders proposed to revive
the distinction between Central and Eastern Europe as a vital area of conquered
territory vital for the Soviet Union's security, and Germany as a territory on the
border of the West—once a concept held by Stalin. Although it is not clear what
the real reasons for this reforming attitude were, a project of this kind clearly aimed
at easing the division of Europe. In any event, the struggle for the succession took
a different course due to the unreliability of Beria, a man who most symbolized
the Terror even to the oligarchs themselves, and the first mass revolt in one of the
satellite countries, which broke out in East Berlin on 17 June 1953 and was put
down by Soviet armed forces with hundreds of deaths.[4] The Berlin rising, preceded by stirrings of protest in Czechoslovakia and Bulgaria, sounded alarm bells
in Moscow not only over the stability of the communist regimes, but also over the
risks of liberalization. The elimination of Beria, who was arrested at the end of June
and executed at the end of the year without a trial, probably put the brakes on
possible reforms. However, the configuration of power in the international system
made it highly improbable that an agreement between the East and the West over
Germany could be reached.[5] The Soviet need for stability had to be implemented
in a strictly bipolar fashion, which meant conceiving all of Central and Eastern
Europe, including East Germany, as integral parts of the 'socialist camp'.[6]

Khrushchev's policy was both founded on and restricted by this vision. Of the
post-Stalinist oligarchs, Khrushchev was the least experienced on international
matters. The same age as Tito and Mao, his political career had developed through
the ranks of the Ukrainian party and in Moscow, without ever encountering the
circles of international communism. By the time he was appointed to the Politburo
in 1949, Stalin's tendency to undermine the authority of the main body of the

---

[4] C. Ostermann (ed.), *Uprising in East Germany 1953* (Budapest: Central European University
Press, 2001).
[5] M. P. Leffler, *For the Soul of Mankind: The United States, the Soviet Union, and the Cold War*
(New York: Hill and Wang, 2007), 129; J. L. Gaddis, *We Now Know: Rethinking Cold War History*
(Oxford: Oxford University Press, 1997), 135–6.
[6] M. Kramer, 'The early post-Stalin succession struggle and upheavals in East-Central
Europe: internal-external linkages in Soviet policy making', *Journal of Cold War Studies* 1.1–3 (1999).

party-state, by turning it into an instrument of his own personal power, had been most extreme in foreign policy.[7] In reality, Stalin had always marginalized all members of the Soviet ruling group from such decisions, with the exceptions of Molotov until 1949 and Zhdanov, who died in the summer of 1948. Malenkov could however boast a limited curriculum vitae in this field, including his participation in two Cominform conferences, whereas Anastas Mikoyan and Kliment Voroshilov had some experience in their favour. The first steps towards resolving the main sources of tension bequeathed by Stalin were carried out by the collective leadership. The signing of the armistice in Korea, which took place in July 1953, was followed by the treaty on the neutrality of Austria and the reconciliation with Yugoslavia in 1955. At the same time, the constitution of the Warsaw Pact as a response to the German Federal Republic's membership of NATO contributed to the institutionalization of the bipolar order in the international system.[8] In spite of his role as general secretary of the party, which he took on in September 1953, Khrushchev did not distinguish himself when it came to international affairs. Indeed, the rivalry with Malenkov pushed him into conservative positions, particularly over the question of military spending. He opposed the innovative thinking suggested by Malenkov in March 1954, when the latter argued that thermonuclear warfare would mean the end of human civilization rather than decree the end of capitalism, as maintained by Stalinist orthodoxy. Immediately afterwards Malenkov was forced into self-criticism by the other oligarchs, facing the accusation of having betrayed the spirit of classism and of having given in to Western blackmail. His rapid decline could only favour the rise of Khrushchev.[9]

However, Khrushchev's foreign-policy initiative was more significant than was acknowledged at the time and would appear from historiography. He personally commenced the reconciliation with Tito through an exchange of letters in the summer of 1954, before leading a Soviet delegation to Belgrade in May 1955.[10] This reconciliation provided clear evidence of a break with Stalin. His trips to China in October 1954 and India in November 1955 would herald significant innovations and rethinking concerning relations between the Soviet Union and the world outside Europe.[11] Khrushchev became aware that the question raised by Malenkov over nuclear war could not be ignored. Only by challenging the idea of the inevitability of war could he create the basis for a *modus vivendi* with the West, which was not so much a programme as a necessity, and for the idea of 'a peaceful transition' to socialism, a condition of the very existence of the communist movement in Europe. Having eliminated his rival and taken over the role of

[7] Y. Gorlizki and O. Khlevniuk, *Cold Peace: Stalin and the Soviet Ruling Circle, 1945–1953* (Oxford: Oxford University Press, 2004), 45–52.

[8] V. Mastny and M. Byrne (eds), *A Cardboard Castle? An Inside History of the Warsaw Pact, 1955–1991* (Budapest: Central European University Press, 2005).

[9] W. Taubman, *Khrushchev: The Man and His Era* (London: Free Press, 2004), 259–66.

[10] S. Rajak, 'The Tito–Khrushchev correspondence, 1954', *Cold War International History Project Bulletin* 12 and 13 (2001), 315–24.

[11] S. Khrushchev (ed.), *Memoirs of Nikita Khrushchev*, vol. 3: *Statesman (1953–1964)* (University Park, Pa: Pennsylvania State University Press, 2007), 420–25, 727–44.

leading the charge against the Stalinist old guard, Khrushchev opened two fronts, combining de-Stalinization and 'peaceful coexistence'. At the Twentieth Congress of the CPSU in February 1956, he brought together his courageous denunciation of Stalin's crimes in the famous 'secret report' and the revival of the notion of 'peaceful coexistence', which Stalin had dropped at the end of the 1920s.

In both cases, Khrushchev revealed his political and intellectual limitations. On the one hand, his emphasis on Stalin's paranoid personality was an attempt to push into the past the more despotic and terroristic aspects of Stalin's regime, and not to reform the Soviet system. The 'secret report' condemned Stalin with the intention of distinguishing him from the system, in order to protect the socialist model. On the other hand, Khrushchev had no intention of reviewing the founding concepts of Soviet policy. The possibility of avoiding a new war was not entrusted to a revision of the Leninist theory of imperialism and a modern analysis of the global reality, but rather to a shift in the balance of power in favour of the Soviet Union and the communist movement. Such a vision no longer emphasized the expectation of war, but nor did it rule it out. These limitations would emerge more clearly in the long term, but were evident from the beginning.[12] In the immediate term, the impact of Khrushchev's decisions was in any event devastating, and exposed the fragility of Soviet international hegemony.

There was more than one unexpected consequence. The iconoclastic attack on Stalin generated hopes of liberalization in Central and Eastern Europe going further than would be acceptable to Moscow, while it triggered a crisis of trust amongst communists around the world on a much more serious scale than had ever occurred in the past. Only three years earlier, Stalin's death had marked the high point of the personality cult, with organized mourning by millions of communists on an incomparably grander scale than at Lenin's funeral. Now the fall of the Stalin myth was shaking the foundations of the symbolic edifice of international communism, and imposed the arduous task of defending the standing of the founding figure of the Soviet state, if its original legitimacy was to be defended. But in the meantime, the Soviet Union's authority and prestige was at risk. Many communists, at the time and then in their memories, experienced 1956 as an *annus terribilis*, although more in Europe than elsewhere.[13] But they did not realize that the decisions and events of the year had revealed failings that would be difficult to put right. The Cold War provided them with an alibi and an environment suited to rationalizing the impact of 1956, by using the presence and image of imperialism as the mainstay for holding together the 'socialist camp'. However, the Soviet myth, the expansionist power of the movement, and the unity of international communism emerged from it irredeemably damaged.

---

[12] A. Rossi (A. Tasca), *Autopsie du stalinisme: avec le texte intégral du rapport Khrouchtchev* (Paris: Pierre Horay, 1957).

[13] E. J. Hobsbawm, *Interesting Times: A Twentieth-Century Life* (London: Allen Lane, 2002), 230; G. Napolitano, *Dal PCI al socialismo europeo: un'autobiografia politica* (Rome: Laterza, 2005), 39–43; R. Martelli, *1956 communiste: le glas d'une espérance* (Paris: La Dispute, 2006).

The bomb Khrushchev primed in February exploded in June 1956. On 4 June the *New York Times* published the full text of the 'secret report' without receiving any official denial. Shortly afterwards, a workers' revolt broke out in Poznan in Poland, where on 28 June more than fifty demonstrators were massacred by the police. The memory of the crisis in East Germany three years earlier was obvious and not very reassuring. It now became difficult to think of that crisis as merely an episode linked to the fragility of the German communist regime immediately after Stalin's death. The leaderships of international communism reacted in different ways to this chain of events that put at risk both the stability of the Soviet bloc and the loyalty of millions of activists who until recently had been fed the Stalin myth. None of them was particularly enthusiastic about Khrushchev's iconoclastic decision, still less about his management of the 'secret report', which entered the public domain through an American newspaper. Some did not conceal their own links to the main features of Stalin's legacy. This was the position of Mao Zedong, who publicly declared that he only accepted part of Khrushchev's criticisms, limited his own criticism to Stalin's policy on the peasantry and his flawed management of relations with the 'socialist camp'. Confidentially Mao did not hold back his recriminations against Stalin for underrating Chinese revolutionaries at the end of the Second World War. Concerned that someone might draw parallels between the Stalinist dictatorship and his own, he asserted that '70 per cent' of Stalin's policies were correct.[14]

Others accepted the idea of an explicit de-Stalinization with more or less good grace, perhaps suggesting a few minor changes. Amongst these was Togliatti, who, having spent a few months in silence in spite of being aware of Khrushchev's denunciation, decided to intervene after the publication of the 'secret report' in June 1956. He attempted to provide a historically plausible explanation of Stalin's regime using the theory of 'bureaucratic degeneration', which smacked of Trotskyism and corrected Khrushchev's weak argument on the basis of personality—an embarrassing approach for a Marxist. The Italian leader thus implied criticism of Khrushchev over the way he carried out the de-Stalinization, but did not oppose it. Very probably he would have preferred a silent de-Stalinization, which would have been Malenkov's approach. But now he had to deal with the situation Khrushchev had imposed. Togliatti took the opportunity to launch the idea of 'polycentrism', which aimed to discard the old centralized model without compromising the unity of the international communist movement. Indeed, greater flexibility and regional organization might have strengthened it. Khrushchev remonstrated with Togliatti about the theory of 'bureaucratic degeneration', which he saw as a pretext that could be used by their enemies, particularly in Central and Eastern Europe; but he avoided the matter of polycentrism, which demonstrated a new tolerance in Moscow towards the revival of the 'national roads' for communist

---

[14] R. Macfarquhar, *The Origins of the Cultural Revolution*, vol. 1: *Contradictions among the People 1956–1957* (New York: Columbia University Press, 1974), 43–8. More recently, see L. M. Lüthi, *The Sino-Soviet Split: Cold War in the Communist World* (Princeton, N.J.: Princeton University Press, 2008), 49–52.

parties.[15] Togliatti's formula alluded to the need to recognize the increasing differences between communists and to eliminate the single model of socialism. But that was not how things would go.

The differences that had emerged between the leaders of international communism would increase. The launch of 'peaceful coexistence' was in fact the political and ideological motive for another division between moderates and radicals in international communism, which would have decisive implications for relations between states, this time the USSR and China, although this would emerge only after 1956. For a time, the crisis in Central and Eastern Europe brought everyone together. When it came to taking significant political decisions, all leaders of international communism spoke with one voice and adopted the Soviet language, revealing their identification with Stalin's imperial legacy. No one dreamt of abandoning their membership of the 'socialist camp' as it had been forged in the first decade of the Cold War. They were even involved in decisions taken by Moscow before the Polish and Hungarian crises, and exercised their influence over the outcome, although it is difficult to establish to what extent. In Poland, the response of the communist establishment to the workers' insubordination was to recall Gomułka to the position of party secretary, now that his persecution and arrest under the Stalinist regime constituted a motive for approval. On 19 October 1956 a Soviet delegation led by Khrushchev went unannounced to Warsaw to obtain from Gomułka the necessary assurances of loyalty to the Warsaw Pact, giving the impression of having had his appointment forced on them rather than having wanted it.[16] The possibility of using force had not been entirely ruled out. Immediately after the meetings in Warsaw, the Soviet leadership convened delegates from Bulgaria, Czechoslovakia, the German Democratic Republic, Romania, Hungary, and China for consultations in Moscow.[17]

Khrushchev thus decided to involve the forces of international communism in power, sending out the message that these forces were no longer only being asked to ratify decisions taken at the centre, as had happened under Stalin. At the meeting of the Presidium on 24 October in the presence of Eastern European delegates, Khrushchev made clear his intention to change things. He invited them 'to understand that we don't live as we did at the time of the KI [Comintern]', that operating through 'command' would have meant 'creating chaos', and that they needed to avoid disagreements between 'brother parties' if they did not want to end up with disagreements 'between nations'.[18] So the consultations took on

---

[15] M. L. Righi (ed.), *Quel terribile '56: i verbali della direzione comunista tra il XX Congresso del Pcus e l'VIII Congresso del PCI* (Rome: Editori Riuniti, 1996), 138–42; A. Agosti, *Palmiro Togliatti* (Turin: Utet, 1996), 443.

[16] S. Khrushchev (ed.), *Memoirs of Nikita Khrushchev*, vol. 2: *Reformer (1945–1964)* (University Park, Pa.: Pennsylvania State University Press, 2006), 223–4.

[17] *Prezidium TsK KPSS 1954–1964. Chernovye protokol'nye zapisi zasedanii. Stenogrammy. Postanovleniya* (3 vols, Moscow: Rosspen, 2003–8) (hereinafter *Prezidium*), vol. 1, doc. 76, p. 174. For developments in Poland from June to Oct. 1956, see P. Machcewicz, *Rebellious Satellite: Poland 1956* (Stanford, Calif.: Stanford University Press, 2009), 158–70.

[18] C. Békés, M. Byrne, and J. M. Rainer (eds), *The 1956 Hungarian Revolution: A History in Documents* (Budapest: Central European University Press, 2002), doc. 27, p. 226.

a special character, tied into Moscow's innermost decision-making processes. The Soviets had decided to rule out a military solution.[19] Instructed by Mao, Liu Shaoqi and Deng Xiaoping, the secretary of the CCP, supported the decision to avoid intervention in Poland.[20] Their opinion was a counterweight to the more bellicose intentions of some European leaders, such as Ulbricht.[21] The Chinese delegates played a more important role than the others, partly because they had recently established relations with the Poles, based on their common interest in defending a relative margin of independence from Moscow.[22]

Just as the situation in Poland was coming back under control, a massive protest movement got under way on 23 October in Hungary, where the regime was in crisis.[23] Order appeared to have been restored by the immediate intervention by Soviet troops already stationed in the country to repress the movement, which was decided by an overwhelming majority of the CPSU's ruling group, including Khrushchev.[24] But the crisis was not over, and Rákosi's replacement by another Stalinist, Ernő Gerő, which had occurred in July at Moscow's behest, proved to be a useless cosmetic exercise. On the advice of the Soviet envoys, Mikoyan and Suslov, Imre Nagy was recalled to a significant institutional role. Having lived for a long time in the Soviet Union before the war as a Comintern official, Nagy became a minister in the first postwar governments, but had been marginalized during the final years of Stalin's life only to return to the highest ranks in 1953. He was again removed from office in 1955 by Rákosi under the accusation of 'nationalism'. Appointed head of government, Nagy proved to be the only establishment personality associated with a promise of liberalization and also with popular following.[25] The replacement of Gerő with János Kádár as leader of the party appeared to consolidate the changes at the top. But the attempt to replicate the Polish model for managing the crisis did not succeed, because Moscow was from the beginning more inclined to the military option, the mass movement was much larger and Nagy, unlike Gomułka, was sensitive to the demands of the popular protest. The withdrawal of Soviet forces from Budapest on 30 October and Moscow's declaration the following day, which was based on respect for the sovereignty of socialist states and the principle of non-interference in their domestic affairs, proved only to be a truce. The Anglo-French intervention in Suez, the last spasm of European colonialism, raised the spectre of an international plot by the imperialist powers. Nagy's announcement of an end to the Communist Party's monopoly provoked

---

[19] *Prezidium*, vol. 1, doc. 77, p. 175.   [20] Ibid. doc. 79, pp. 178–9.

[21] Lüthi, *The Sino-Soviet Split*, 56.

[22] M. A. Kuo, *Contending with Contradictions: China's Policy toward Soviet Eastern Europe and the Origins of the Sino-Soviet Split, 1953–1960* (Lanham, Md.: Lexington Books, 2001), 87–95.

[23] C. Gati, *Failed Illusions: Moscow, Washington, Budapest, and the 1956 Hungarian Revolt* (Stanford, Calif.: Stanford University Press, 2006); P. Lendvai, *One Day That Shook the Communist World: The 1956 Hungarian Uprising and Its Legacy* (Princeton, N.J.: Princeton University Press, 2008); M. Kramer, 'The Soviet Union and the 1956 crises in Hungary and Poland: reassessments and new findings', *Journal of Contemporary History* 33.2 (1998).

[24] *Prezidium*, vol. 1, doc. 78, pp. 176–7; Békés et al., *The 1956 Hungarian Revolution*, doc. 25, pp. 217–18.

[25] J. M. Rainer, *Imre Nagy: A Biography* (London: I. B. Tauris, 2009).

further apprehension, even though it was merely an acknowledgement of the democratic revival that was already occurring.[26] In a few days, he had passed from 'national communism' to an unprecedented form of reformist communism.

The leaders of international communism did all they could to make clear Nagy's unreliability and the incompatibility of the Hungarian Revolution with the very nature of the 'socialist camp'. As occurred with Poland, the Chinese exerted the greatest influence, but on the other side. The Chinese delegation in Moscow was not consulted over Hungary before 30 October. But on the same day, Pavel Yudin, the Soviet ambassador in Peking, reported to the Presidium that the Chinese had expressed their concern over the possible Hungarian defection from the 'socialist camp' and their distrust of Nagy.[27] Liu asked the Soviets to keep their troops in Hungary and thus withdraw the declaration they had just made a few hours earlier.[28] On 30 October, Togliatti also sent a telegram to Khrushchev declaring his concern that the Hungarian government might be slipping in a 'reactionary direction'.[29] In other words, the Hungarian crisis was fulfilling the Bolshevik and Stalinist fear of a counter-revolutionary link between the enemy within and the enemy without, not only at the centre of the empire but also between the principal partners in the movement. Both Mao and Togliatti adopted language diametrically opposed to that of Nagy, who instead defined the protest as a national and democratic movement. Although Togliatti's influence was not on a par with Mao's, the joint pressure from the two most important leaders of the international communist movement in Europe and Asia certainly did not help the search for a compromise. Khrushchev shared Togliatti's pessimistic analysis and disavowal of Nagy in his reply sent on 31 October.[30] On the same day the Soviet leader met with the Chinese delegation, although they do not appear to have reached a final decision.[31] Under the increasing impression that socialist Hungary was on the edge of the precipice and that the new leadership in Moscow risked losing the consent of the Soviet elites themselves, as it was based on the imperial role of the Soviet Union, Khrushchev overturned the fragile compromise after just twenty-four hours. He told the Presidium that the moderate position of the previous day had to be re-examined, the Soviet troops could not be withdrawn, and the abandonment of Hungary would favour the 'imperialist' offensive.[32]

The decision to invade Hungary was finally taken on 1 November, driven by fear that this was a contagion that could affect other countries in Central and Eastern Europe, the impact of the Anglo-French intervention in Suez, and the conviction that the Soviet Union's security was at stake.[33] Nagy's declaration of Hungarian

---

[26] Gati, *Failed Illusions*, 188–9.

[27] *Prezidium*, vol. 1, doc. 82, p. 187; Békés et al. *The 1956 Hungarian Revolution*, doc. 49, p. 299.

[28] *Prezidium*, vol. 1, doc. 82, p. 188.

[29] *Sovetskii Soyuz i vengerskii krizis 1956 goda: dokumenty* (Moscow: Rosspen, 1998), doc. 123, pp. 476–7.

[30] Ibid. doc. 128, pp. 485–6.   [31] *Memoirs of Nikita Khrushchev*, vol. 3, p. 430.

[32] *Prezidium*, vol. 1, doc. 82, p. 191; Békés et al., *The 1956 Hungarian Revolution*, doc. 53, p. 307.

[33] *Prezidium*, vol. 1, doc. 83, pp. 193–5; Békés et al., *The 1956 Hungarian Revolution*, p. 202; *Memoirs of Nikita Khrushchev*, vol. 3, p. 651.

neutrality, which heralded the country's exit from the Warsaw Pact, provided further incendiary material, but was made when the Soviet decision had already been made and represented a vain attempt to launch an international appeal at the first signs of a mobilization of the Red Army.[34] Diffident about the conduct of the Eastern European allies, the Soviets preferred to avoid the involvement of the Warsaw Pact. But for two days, after having notified the Chinese delegation, they carried out tense consultations with the aim of preventing its members from distancing themselves from a decision that had already been made and would lead, all evidence concurred, to a bloodbath. Predictably, Gomułka was the only one to resist. The other leaders provided their support.[35] On 2 November Khrushchev met Tito, whom Moscow considered Nagy's main supporter. The Yugoslav leader gave his approval, perhaps fearing the potential threat of the Red Army on the Yugoslav border, but above all the contagion of Hungarian democratization.[36] The suppression of the Hungarian Revolution, which began on 4 November 1956, lived up to the worst predictions. The popular resistance could only be broken through the deployment of devastating violence, which demonstrated the communist regime's social isolation and the brutal face of Soviet rule. On the other side of the Iron Curtain, the rhetoric of the Eisenhower administration, which was based on the doctrine of rollback, did not come up with a credible response to the crisis.[37]

The Soviet invasion of Hungary was greeted by the main communist leaders as the necessary defence of a supreme good—the Soviet Union's military conquests in Europe. The crude political realism that informed the logic of the Cold War was the main justification for the Soviet invasion. Before the invasion, Togliatti warned his comrades: 'you stay with your own side even when it's making a mistake.'[38] Only after the event did he acknowledge the popular nature of the protest in Hungary, but he believed that domestic and foreign enemies had transformed it into an anti-communist rising. In reality this logic, which was applied in other similar circumstances, was not a creation of the Cold War but went back to an earlier period. Its origin was to be found in the political primacy of safeguarding the socialist state in the 'international civil war', which asserted itself before the Second World War. Now bipolar antagonism led to the identification of this legacy with the integrity of the entire state-political 'camp', thus keeping it intact in a different historical period. From this point of view, there was a close connection between the 1930s and the second half of the 1950s, although the size of the state system and communism's mass following were incomparably greater than they had been before the war. The interdependence between the politics of the Soviet state and the destiny of the communist movement had become more complex, but this did not mean that it had become weaker.

---

[34] Békés et al., *The 1956 Hungarian Revolution*, 212.
[35] Ibid. docs. 63, 69, 75; *Memoirs of Nikita Khrushchev*, vol. 3, pp. 431, 651–2.
[36] Békés et al., *The 1956 Hungarian Revolution*, doc. 76, p. 352; *Memoirs of Nikita Khrushchev*, vol. 3, pp. 653–6.
[37] Gati, *Failed Illusions*, 218–19.   [38] Righi, *Quel terribile '56*, 221.

However, the Western communist ruling groups needed to deal with the disobedience of considerable sections of their parties. In Italy, many rebelled against the idea that the popular protest in Hungary was being branded as a counter-revolution. One important leader, the head of the trade unions Giuseppe Di Vittorio, broke with the conformism of the ruling group and declared that he was convinced that only democratization could save the socialist system. In his telegram to Khrushchev on 30 October, Togliatti presented himself as the centrist balancing point between the dissidents and hardliners, and revealed his concerns over a split in the PCI. After the invasion, he managed to impose his decision to align himself with unconditional and disciplined support for the Soviet position on the ruling group, and forced Di Vittorio into silence. But in the following months the party lost a significant number of its members, which was only offset by the enormous size of its membership; in particular it suffered a dramatic loss of its intellectual energies.[39] In France, the leadership was more unified and compact, and thus avoided the blow suffered by the Italian party. Never sympathetic to the idea of 'national roads', Thorez had no difficulty in supporting the Soviet use of force, in spite of protests from intellectuals.[40] The Western parties conserved their working-class and territorial strongholds, but protests amongst intellectuals heralded a decline in their influence over 'fellow-travellers' and a loss of their monopoly over Marxist doctrine. This phenomenon was evident, for example, in radical left-wing circles in Britain, even though communists would maintain for some time their role as a small but active force.[41]

Despite the violence of the repression, the new regime led by Kádár took a few months to destroy the popular opposition and achieve an authoritarian normalization in Hungary. Nagy's personal tragedy dragged on much longer, following a failed Yugoslav attempt to offer him protection and his forced deportation to Romania. The Soviets had to face up to the impossibility of breaking his will and the inappropriateness of a public trial, given his tenacious refusal to support Kádár and admit his own 'errors'. The most significant moment was probably represented by the letters Nagy sent to Tito, Gomułka, and Togliatti in early 1957, in which he demanded unsuccessfully that his side of the argument be listened to, pointing out that Hungary's popular and national insurrection was of a socialist kind. In his letter to Togliatti, Nagy asked to be tried by a commission made up of representatives from the various communist parties, and not a tribunal.[42] Firmly loyal to the Soviet Union, Togliatti did not respond to the Hungarian leader's appeal. Nagy's fate would recall the Stalinist purges of ten years earlier. Following a summary trial, he was executed on 16 June 1958. By that time, the echo of the Hungarian tragedy was no longer heard. Overall, the dissent caused by the invasion of Hungary

[39] G. Gozzini and R. Martinelli, *Storia del Partito comunista italiano*, vol. 7: *Dall'attentato a Togliatti all'VIII Congresso* (Turin: Einaudi, 1998), 588ff.

[40] S. Courtois and M. Lazar, *Histoire du parti communiste français* (Paris: PUF, 2000), 295.

[41] J. Callaghan, *Cold War, Crisis and Conflict: The History of the Communist Party of Great Britain, 1951–68* (London: Lawrence & Wishart, 2003), 69–78.

[42] Lendvai, *One Day That Shook the Communist World*, 223; *Corriere della sera* (27 Sept. 2006), 16–17.

was a significant and unprecedented event in the world of European communism. Nothing similar had occurred since the beginning of the Stalinist era. The dissidents of twenty years earlier had been isolated and were few in number, although very active in publicizing their political and historical views. Now the diaspora of intellectuals and also activists had opened a significant breach in the principle of loyalty to the Soviet Union, in spite of the Cold War.

The culmination of the crisis in Hungary in October and November 1956 demonstrated that the empire created by Stalin could only be defended by repression, and that the post-Stalinist ruling groups and leaders of international communism were willing employ force to sustain it. It only took a few days for the paradigm of 'international civil war' to recover its centrality in communist discourse and influence decisions. Far more than the year of de-Stalinization, 1956 was the culmination of a cycle of civil conflicts that had been affecting Central and Eastern Europe for the decade that followed the war. Far more than a transition to a new image of international communism, it proved to be the moment of its identification with a conservative and repressive role. While the bugbear of imperialism could still be persuasive for many, the same could not be said of the appeal to violence as an antidote for the counter-revolution in Europe, which was no longer tainted with fascism and was, in its Western half, constructing a new basis for a civil, democratic, and cooperative state and neutralizing the conflicts of the past. The authoritarian normalization in Hungary and the creation of the European Community in 1957 symbolized the divergent trajectories of a divided Europe. Although the stark contrast between the continuing civil conflict in the East and the commencement of peaceful integration in the West was contained within the climate of the Cold War, its significance would emerge in the long term. In the communist world, a hostile attitude towards European integration was firmed up at the time and would prove lasting as well, with few exceptions. The European Community was accused of threatening aggression and being an insidious pole of attraction, an instrument for consolidating the influence of American power and destabilizing Central and Eastern Europe.[43] The syndrome created by the Marshall Plan had never been overcome.

The price paid by the communist movement was much higher than it seemed to the ruling groups. The fall of the myth of Stalin opened up a vacuum at the centre of imperial authority. The attempt to imagine a return to a legendary golden age of Lenin and thus preserve the foundations of revolutionary legacy appeared improvised, contradictory, and voluntarist. The liberating effect of the anti-Stalinist denunciation was largely reversed by the blood spilt in Budapest. The rebellion in Central and Eastern Europe revealed the deficit of legitimacy affecting the communist regimes installed after the Second World War. The acceleration of events demonstrated that the leaders of the USSR did not have the resources to deal with sudden, lacerating crises, except through methods of repression inherited from

---

[43] R. B. Day, *Cold War Capitalism: The View from Moscow 1945–1975* (Armonk, N.Y.: M. E. Sharpe, 1995), 156–8; V. Zubok, 'The Soviet Union and European integration from Stalin to Gorbachev', *Journal of European Integration History* 2 (1996).

Stalin. The credibility of the new post-Stalinist course was seriously shaken. In the Soviet Union, the intellectual generation that had experienced the liberalization encountered its first frustrations, even though most of its exponents continued to believe in the possibility of an anti-Stalinist communism based on the cult of Lenin, the need for moral redemption, and the civic function of reviving the national memory.[44] In Central and Eastern Europe, the violent repression left a wound and a profound but invisible trace, the sign of an insurmountable obstacle to national sovereignty, a persistent gap between the rulers and the ruled, and an alternation between instability and attempts at reform.[45] In Western Europe, the possibility of presenting Soviet communism as an alternative and a hope was now definitively compromised.[46] The entrenchment of the Western parties had the effect of increasing their political isolation and their separation from European socialism. Intellectual dissent with and disillusionment towards the communist parties turned out to be a process and not a passing episode. Some were immediately disenchanted, while others turned their backs on the parties in the conviction that only in this way could they recover the 'humanistic potential' of communism.[47] François Fejtő spoke for everyone when he invited Marxists 'to examine their consciences carefully' while wondering if 'our understanding and our consciousness of the world we live in haven't been left far behind reality'.[48] As though this were not enough, the consent around the decision to repress the Hungarian Revolution was not sufficient to maintain the unity of international communism.

THE END OF COMMUNIST UNITY

After the Hungarian crisis, the symbolically most significant move by the Soviet ruling group at international level was the decision to convene a conference of world communism. The initiative had been in the offing for some time. On the eve of the Twentieth Congress, the Presidium (Politburo) of the CPSU decided to suppress the Cominform. Mikoyan and Khrushchev wanted to create 'regional clusters' of communist parties giving life to a new system of contacts and they consulted the leaders of the socialist countries, as well as Togliatti and Thorez.[49] The dissolution of the Cominform was made public on 18 April. This provision went almost unobserved, given that the body had now existed for years only on paper and its disappearance would not evoke any regrets. But Stalin's successors

---

[44] V. Zubok, *Zhivago's Children: The Last Russian Intelligentsia* (Cambridge, Mass.: Harvard University Press, 2009), 87, 130–1.

[45] C. Békés, 'East Central Europe, 1953–1956', in Leffler and Westad, *The Cambridge History of the Cold War*, vol. 1: *Origins*, 352.

[46] T. Judt, *Postwar: A History of Europe since 1945* (New York: Penguin Press, 2005), 321–3.

[47] E. P. Thompson, *The Poverty of Theory and other essays* (London: Merlin Press, 1978).

[48] F. Fejtö, *La tragédie hongroise: ou, Une révolution socialiste anti-soviétique (1956)* (Paris: Pierre Horay, 1996), 286. See also F. Fejtö and M. Serra, *Il passeggero del secolo: guerre, rivoluzioni, Europe* (Palermo: Sellerio, 2001), 254–60.

[49] *Prezidium*, vol. 1, doc. 34, pp. 106–7.

proposed to launch a new era in relations between the Soviet Union and the communist movement. Khrushchev was toying with the idea of reorganizing the movement. In a letter addressed to Rákosi and other leaders of the 'socialist camp' in June 1956, which referred to meetings with Tito, Khrushchev wrote that while the Yugoslav blandly spoke of 'regular meetings' the Soviets did not think it inappropriate in principle to create 'an organization for international relations' between communist parties.[50]

In this light, it is significant that Khrushchev's first missions were to China and Yugoslavia, in 1954 and 1955 respectively. It is not clear whether Khrushchev's hyperactive behaviour was always following a precise plan, but it is not difficult to see that the emergence of his leadership amongst Stalin's successors was founded on a strategy of reuniting the 'socialist camp', and aimed to remedy the consequences of Stalin's policies. It was not just a diplomatic move. Khrushchev considered the break with Tito in 1948 to be one of Stalin's mistakes, and it was his ambition to bring Yugoslavia back into the 'socialist camp' and the international communist movement.[51] The attempt to resume relations with the Yugoslavs arose from the need to neutralize their potentially centrifugal influence on the countries in the European bloc, and to limit their autonomy in relation to the countries in neither bloc by extending Soviet influence into the Mediterranean. The alliance with China had an even more central strategic significance. After the Korean war, Stalin's successors invested a great deal in their relations with Peking. The Soviet economic and technological aid programme in China, which started in May 1953, was 'the Marshall Plan of the Soviet Union', destined to lay the foundations for the modernization of Chinese society and the state, which were definitively moulded around the Soviet model in industry, the institutions, and administrative and cultural practices.[52] From Moscow's point of view, this effort constituted a fundamental tool in the consolidation of the 'socialist community', given the insubordination that was surfacing in Central and Eastern Europe. The Soviets banked on the Chinese acknowledgement of the Soviet Union's centrality, and in exchange offered a genuine 'special relationship'. The Chinese felt that they had contributed decisively to saving the 'socialist camp' during the crises of 1956. Khrushchev worked to dissipate the inherited misunderstandings with Peking, but also to consolidate the political and economic interdependence between the USSR and China. In particular, he relaunched the idea of a division of labour between Moscow and Peking in the management of the communist movement, which assigned to the Chinese the task of guiding the Asian and African parties.[53]

Khrushchev held the role of the international communist movement dear, as it was a substantial part of his optimistic faith in the imminent triumph of communism on a global scale. His behaviour during the most frenzied days of the crises

---

[50] Békés et al., *The 1956 Hungarian Revolution*, doc. 14, p. 141.   [51] Ibid. 539.

[52] O. A. Westad, *The Global Cold War: Third World Interventions and the Making of Our Times* (Cambridge: Cambridge University Press, 2005), 69; T. P. Bernstein and H.-Y. Li (eds), *China Learns from the Soviet Union, 1949–Present* (Lanham, Md.: Lexington Books, 2010).

[53] *Memoirs of Nikita Khrushchev*, vol. 3, p. 424.

in Poland and Hungary showed that he was willing to involve leaders of the communist movement in ways that would have been unthinkable under Stalin. The invasion of Hungary only increased the need for this. From Khrushchev's point of view, it was a matter of both showing the world that international communism was united against Western reaction and capitalizing on the consensus amongst the communist ruling groups over the decision to invade, bringing them together after the divisions created during 1956. At the domestic level, the elimination of the Stalinist old guard, branded as the 'anti-party group' in June 1957, made it possible for him to present himself as an unchallenged leader and act with greater self-assurance when it came to relaunching an ideology free from Stalin's imperial mysteries.[54] However, it would prove an arduous task to adequately reconcile the different visions of the main players on the communist global stage.

Tito was not willing to resume Yugoslavia's membership of the 'socialist camp', especially after having witnessed the invasion of Hungary. In a speech delivered in Pula on 11 November 1956, he defined the invasion as a 'lesser evil' after having agreed to the Soviet use of force, but was critical of Moscow's inability to prevent the crisis and the Stalinist instincts of the ruling groups in Eastern Europe.[55] The Yugoslavs kept firmly to the route they had taken following the rift with Stalin, when they reinvented their identity, evading the logic of the blocs and proposing the creation of a decentralized model of the socialist economy. Tito had obtained a guarantee of Western protection against the Soviet Union's military threat without joining NATO, and wished to follow the Finnish neutralist model.[56] After his meeting with Nasser and Sukarno in June 1956, he gradually developed a network of relations with movements and governments emerging from the process of decolonization, which in a few years would constitute the bulwark of Yugoslav sovereignty. Belgrade rejected the idea that socialism had to identify itself with a territory or state.[57]

Mao Zedong, on the other hand, demanded that China have a role as the Soviet Union's privileged partner, while acknowledging the latter as the centre of world communism, as Liu Shaoqi expressed it during his stay in Moscow at the end of October, though he did not miss the opportunity to criticize the manner in which the crises in Poland and Hungary were managed. Unlike the Yugoslavs, the Chinese set themselves up as the guardians of Marxist-Leninist orthodoxy and largely rejected the denunciation of Stalinism. During his journey to the Soviet Union and Europe in January 1957, Zhou Enlai brought Chinese pressure to bear on the Polish communists and advised Gomułka against forming an overly close relationship with Tito, after the Polish and Yugoslav leaders had agreed special

---

[54] Taubman, *Khrushchev*, 317–24.

[55] Békés et al., *The 1956 Hungarian Revolution*, doc. 96, p. 425.

[56] G. Swain, *Tito: A Biography* (London: I. B. Tauris, 2010), 101–2; R. Kullaa, *Non-Alignment and Its Origins in Cold War Europe: Yugoslavia, Finland, and the Soviet Challenge* (London: I. B. Tauris, 2011).

[57] S. Rajak, 'The Cold War in the Balkans, 1945–1956', in Leffler and Westad, *The Cambridge History of the Cold War*, vol. 1: *Origins*, 214–15; J. R. Lampe, *Yugoslavia as History: Twice There Was a Country* (Cambridge: Cambridge University Press, 1996), 262–7.

bilateral relations between the communist parties.[58] In Budapest, Zhou met Kádár to offer him Peking's support for the normalization of Hungary and took the opportunity to criticize Tito, wondering whether the Yugoslav leader could 'really be considered a socialist'.[59] In his report to Mao on the trip, however, Zhou did not concentrate on the Yugoslavs, instead emphasizing the failings of the Soviet leadership in dealing with the problems of the 'socialist camp' and the communist movement. Zhou's journey marked an evident increase in Chinese influence.[60]

The Chinese were the ones to propose a conference on international communism in January 1957, after talks with the Soviets.[61] Initially it appeared that the initiative would be restricted to the parties in power, but the project was more ambitious. On meeting a delegation from the PCI, Khrushchev advocated the launch of an international magazine and argued that they needed 'to think about a conference': it was not a question of reviving the Comintern or the Cominform, but it was necessary to keep in mind that 'the social democrats have their International, and the Western powers have NATO'.[62] The Soviet leader was aiming at legitimization of the new leadership in the USSR and the full involvement of Tito. The second objective was only in part achieved. Despite the meeting between the Soviet and Yugoslav leaders which took place in Romania at the beginning of August, the Yugoslavs rejected the Soviet plan to include them in the 'socialist camp'.[63] Perhaps for this reason, the conference was divided into two parts. The first meeting of parties in power took place in Moscow from 14 to 16 November 1957, and the second gathered the delegates from seventy communist parties, including the Yugoslav one. The secrecy that surrounded the proceedings recalled the old conspiratorial ways, and weakened the renewal in the eyes of world public opinion. But the most important thing for the organizers was to establish order and create a new atmosphere in the movement's relations. The public document approved by the restricted conference was a declaration put together by the Soviets and agreed by the Chinese. In the 'socialist camp', the document exalted the principles of sovereignty and non-interference, but also the 'fraternal and reciprocal assistance' in the name of 'internationalism', an obvious reference to the Hungarian precedent and the bond that it placed on all communist states. In world politics, it pointed to the alternative between war and 'peaceful coexistence', admitted the possibility

---

[58] Kuo, *Contending with Contradictions*, 116–17.

[59] Békés et al., *The 1956 Hungarian Revolution*, doc. 109, p. 502.

[60] Z. Shen and Y. Xia, 'Zhou Enlai's shuttle diplomacy in 1957 and its effects', *Cold War History* 10.4 (2010); 'The emerging disputes between Beijing and Moscow: ten newly available Chinese documents, 1956–1958', *Cold War International History Project Bulletin* 6 and 7 (1995–5), doc. 3, pp. 153–54.

[61] *Prezidium*, vol. 1, doc. 101, pp. 224, 991; Z. Shen and Y. Xia, 'Hidden currents during the honeymoon: Mao, Khrushchev, and the 1957 Moscow Conference', *Journal of Cold War Studies* 11.4 (2009).

[62] Archives of the Hoover Institution, Dmitrii A. Volkogonov papers, box 24, reel 16, Conversation between Khrushchev, Suslov, Ponomarev, Longo, Spano, 22 Jan. 1957.

[63] *Prezidium*, vol. 1, doc. 133, pp. 274, 1017; V. Mićunović, *Moscow Diary* (New York: Doubleday, 1980).

of 'different roads' to socialism, and made provision for the scenario of a peaceful transition as well as that of revolutionary violence.[64]

The proceedings of the restricted meeting were dominated by Mao's proposal to acknowledge formally the 'leading role' of the USSR, with the argument that the other 'camp' also had its leading country—a move that could reflect their role play with the Soviet leaders, and in any case was not disagreeable to them. The Chinese leader managed to overcome the resistance of Gomułka, who was concerned at the obvious restrictions this placed on Polish sovereignty. The 'leading role' of the Soviet Union was acknowledged by all delegates. The objective of relaunching the symbolic unity of international communism around the Soviet Union had been fully achieved, but the enlarged meeting showed that reality was not that simple. Suslov's report presented an analysis that was widely shared, as it was based on the Declaration and the enduring theory of the 'two camps'. His dichotomous concept of the world was the same as the one Zhdanov had argued for, ten years earlier, with the sole difference that the progress of decolonization made it possible to enrol many countries outside Europe in the anti-imperialist ranks. Using a tradition that belonged to thirty years earlier, Suslov rejected the theories of 'organized capitalism' and reasserted his faith in the future crisis of capitalism. The novelty was to be found in the idea that, in spite of imperialism's immutability, 'the states of the socialist camp do not need wars to conserve and reinforce their own positions'. Suslov announced the global transition from capitalism to socialism under the aegis of the USSR and its policy of 'peaceful coexistence'.[65]

However, the Soviets' political proposal proved to be controversial precisely because of the stated positions of their main partner. Mao Zedong did in fact emphasize the centrality of the USSR, but also expressed serious reservations about 'peaceful coexistence' as the platform for the communist movement. In the speech he gave on 18 November, which would leave its mark, the Chinese leader argued that the 'east wind' had more force than the 'west wind', and that the balance of power had shifted decisively in favour of the 'forces of socialism'. The break-up of the European empires and the launch of the Soviet Union's Sputnik were clear evidence of this. Mao went out on a limb with a forecast of economic development that was even more optimistic than the Soviet one, claiming that in fifteen years' time the USSR would overtake the United States, and China would overtake Great Britain. His idea that the imperialist powers were only 'paper tigers' did not, however, induce him to embrace the prospect of a peaceful victory; quite the contrary, his calculations included an apocalypse. For Mao, a thermonuclear world war that could destroy a third or even half of humanity was all part of the possible. To his way of thinking, it would not destroy human civilization, but would wipe

---

[64] *Prezidium*, vol. 1, docs. 137, 138, 139, pp. 279–81, 1022; vol. 2, doc. 138, pp. 720–30. For two reconstructions of the 1957 conference, concentrating respectively on the role of the Chinese and of the Italians, see Shen and Xia, 'Hidden currents during the honeymoon', and C. Spagnolo, *Sul Memoriale di Yalta: Togliatti e la crisi del movimento comunista internazionale (1956–1964)* (Rome: Carocci, 2007), 180ff.

[65] SAPMO, SED, DY 30 J IV 2/201, b. 489; APCI, mf 252, b. 99.

imperialism from the face of this earth. 'All the world,' Mao declared, 'will become socialist.'[66]

Khrushchev recalled that Mao's speech was followed by a 'deathly silence', leaving many of those present in a state of shock.[67] In reality, Mao's prestige was such that no one openly challenged his views. But everyone knew very well that the question raised by the Chinese leader had been a decisive one for some years. Before 1956, Malenkov's prediction that a thermonuclear war would cause the end of 'civilization' had only been taken up properly by Togliatti.[68] But at the Twentieth Congress, Khrushchev had appropriated his rival's argument as the basis for the policy of 'peaceful coexistence'. Mao was therefore supporting a position linked to Stalinist orthodoxy and implicitly critical of the new Soviet leadership. His main objective was not purely doctrinaire. He contested 'peaceful coexistence' and its link with the scenario of a 'peaceful road' to socialism. This dissent arose from a specific interpretation in revolutionary mode of the 'spirit of Bandung', which assigned a primacy to the anti-colonial and anti-imperialist struggle of the 'oppressed nations' over the coexistence between peoples.[69] During the drafting of the conference Declaration, the Chinese had forced the Soviets into a compromise that lessened the emphasis on the 'peaceful road' and insisted on the scenario of revolutionary violence.[70] The compromise was reached by leaving open the possibility of both 'roads', which all communists would share without difficulty. But the difference of language and emphasis remained clear.

Mao presented himself as the coherent heir to the doctrine of the inevitability of war, defined militant anti-imperialism as the compass of international communism, and alluded to the revolutionary primacy now attained by the non-Western world. The vocabulary used in the principal European leaders' speeches did not conform to the Maoist one. 'Peaceful coexistence' constituted a necessary guarantee, although an insufficient one, in both Western and Eastern Europe for opening up room to manoeuvre in national politics, which had up till then been closed down by the Cold War. The admissibility of an atomic holocaust which would primarily strike at the European continent was irreconcilable with the need to consolidate their pacifist credentials and influence public opinion. Gomułka asked for the Declaration's anti-imperialist rhetoric to be toned down. Togliatti exhorted communists to develop the peace movement and build mass parties. Other leaders of European communism, such as Ulbricht and Thorez, were more reserved. But the agreement between the USSR and some of the main European parties implied a significant discordance with the Chinese.[71]

---

[66] M. Schoenhals, 'Mao Zedong: speeches at the 1957 Moscow Conference', *Journal of Communist Studies* 2.2 (1986).

[67] *Memoirs of Nikita Khrushchev*, vol. 3, p. 436.   [68] Agosti, *Palmiro Togliatti*, 417.

[69] C. Jian, 'Bridging revolution and decolonization: The "Bandung discourse" in China's early Cold War experience', in C. E. Goscha and C. F. Ostermann (eds), *Connecting Histories: Decolonization and the Cold War in Southeast Asia, 1945–1962* (Stanford, Calif./ Washington, D.C.: Stanford University Press/Woodrow Wilson Center Press, 2009).

[70] Shen and Xia, 'Hidden currents during the honeymoon', 89–94.

[71] SAPMO, Sed, DY 30 J IV 2/201, b. 1131; APCI, mf 252, b. 99.

The inconsistencies of the Moscow conference were therefore very serious, in spite of the apparent success in rewriting the ritual of communist unity following the destruction of the Stalin myth. There was a partnership between the Chinese and the Soviets, but there was also a dualism. The two main players in international communism were in agreement over the monocratic and compact structure of the 'socialist camp'. Both excluded the idea of a structure that made it similar to the Western bloc. Following the Hungarian crisis, the scenario of a polycentric organization became improbable, and Togliatti did not suggest it again but fell back on the vague concept of 'unity in diversity'.[72] The conference did not record a choice between centralism and polycentrism. The need for a centre invested with the role of command over the two peripheries of states and parties in the world communist movement was accepted by everyone, with more or less autonomist slants. However, Moscow and Peking diverged on their strategic visions and their political proposals. It was not just a matter of their greater or lesser nostalgia for Stalin; there was also the question of war and peace, which amounted to the central theme in defining the political role of the communist movement. The Chinese spoke of a possible choice between coexistence and world revolution, and between the interests of the Soviet Union and those of the movement. Mao argued that China and Asia were the new engine of world revolution, now that he was strengthened by the internal consolidation of his own regime and the possibility of relaunching the link between revolution and decolonization following Stalin's death. His support for the 'guiding role' of the Soviet Union absolved him of his duty to his main ally and was in line with the movement's centralist thinking, but it was not a blank cheque—indeed, it implied an attempt to influence the Soviets.

After the conference, on 17 December, Suslov criticized the Yugoslavs in the central committee of the CPSU for their rejection of the very notion of a 'socialist camp', and expressed his satisfaction that Gomułka and Togliatti had put aside their reluctance to accept the leading role of the Soviet Union. He made no reference to Mao's speech.[73] Very probably, the Soviets thought that the differences could be absorbed and glossed over. However, the aim of asserting a new leadership over international communism implied a political and syncretic capacity that they lacked. They did not renounce their claim to be the repository of the true doctrine, while condemning the unorthodox decisions of the Yugoslavs as 'revisionism' and the Chinese criticisms as 'dogmatism'. The Soviet state was an agent of modernization and secularization, and at the same time took on the mantle of ideological and doctrinal arbiter. Its primacy was clear, despite the rhetoric about establishing parity between the parties. But the splitting of the conference into two parts demonstrated the difficulties in reconciling the conflicting definitions of the Soviet Union's interests, inter-state relations in the 'socialist camp', and the different trends affecting the movement around the world. Even the Soviet

---

[72] J. Haslam, 'I dilemmi della destalinizzazione: Togliatti, il XX Congresso del PCUS e le sue conseguenze', in R. Gualtieri, C. Spagnolo, and E. Taviani (eds), *Togliatti nel suo tempo* (Rome: Carocci, 2007).
[73] RGANI, fo. 2, op. 1, d. 279.

agencies reflected this dichotomy. The international department of the CPSU 'for links with foreign parties', which was created in 1953 under the direction of Boris Ponomarev, was kept separate from the department that dealt with relations between parties in power in the 'socialist camp', under the direction of Yurii Andropov.[74] On the other hand; the positions of the ruling group of the Soviet Union did not abound with coherence. Unlike Stalin, Khrushchev did not believe that a third world war would lead to the end of capitalism and the advent of communism. But he believed that a gradual shift in the 'balance of power' towards the Soviet Union required the exercise of the nuclear threat and the assumption of the subsequent risks.[75] After all, he had not proclaimed the end of the doctrine of the inevitability of war, but merely argued that it was not inevitable. This formula was also a means for keeping the leadership of anti-Western forces around the world, while mediating the differences between European and Asian communists.

However, the potential conflict that emerged from Mao Zedong's ultra-radical positions presented a serious risk to relations between Moscow and Peking. The 'special relationship' between the two communist powers did not remove differences between the hinterlands in the revolutionary legacy arising from the Second World War. Revolutionary anti-imperialism represented the identity of the Chinese regime, and was inscribed in China's 'national memory' in a way that was not true of Russia. Peking had strengthened its alliance with Moscow and increased its material dependency on it, but was shaking off the political subservience that had typified the Stalin years. The acknowledgement of the Soviet Union's centrality did not mean unconditional support for the Soviet leadership's new course, suspected of political and ideological inadequacies. It was principally a means for exercising influence. Mao decided to follow a road different from that of Khrushchev's de-Stalinization. The Chinese thaw, which was promoted by the 'hundred flowers' campaign along the lines of the Soviet one, did not last long. The Chinese leader tightened up the regime once more, purged the critics whom he had encouraged, and prepared for the 'Great Leap Forward', which aimed to revive the modernizing campaign, the mass violence, and the social earthquake of Stalin's 'revolution from above' thirty years earlier. During 1957, Mao confirmed his mainly positive assessment of Stalin to the point that his arguments were quoted by Molotov and Khrushchev's other Stalinist opponents.[76] Although Mao joined the condemnation of the 'anti-party group', dispelling Khrushchev's fears that his adversaries might

---

[74] *Otdel TsK KPSS po svyazyam s inostrannimi kompartiyami 1953–1957: Annotirovannii spravochnik* (Moscow: Rosspen, 1999).

[75] J. Haslam, *Russia's Cold War: From the October Revolution to the Fall of the Wall* (New Haven, Conn.: Yale University Press, 2011), 179; V. Mastny, 'Imagining war in Europe: Soviet strategic planning', in V. Mastny, S. G. Holtsmark, and A. Wenger (eds), *War Plans and Alliances in the Cold War: Threat Perceptions in the East and West* (London: Routledge, 2006), 20.

[76] R. Macfarquhar, T. Cheek, and E. Wu, *The Secret Speeches of Chairman Mao: From the Hundred Flowers to the Great Leap Forward* (Cambridge, Mass.: Harvard University Press, 1989), 173; *Molotov, Malenkov, Kaganovich. 1957. Stenogramma iyun'skogo plenuma TsK KPSS i drugie dokumenty* (Moscow: Mezhdunarodnyi Fond 'Demokratiya', 1998), 70, 128.

find support in Peking, his assessment of Stalin would remain decidedly different from the one established by the 'secret report'.[77]

The crisis in Taiwan and the escalating tension with the United States in the summer and autumn of 1958 provided the external context for a revolutionary mobilization that in Mao's opinion would develop both in Chinese society and in international politics.[78] The meeting with Khrushchev from 31 July to 3 August 1958 was the first occasion on which Mao openly expressed his unhappiness with the Soviet Union's 'great-power chauvinism' to the Soviet leader, and his pretext was the question of Soviet technical assistance. The Chinese leader even took up his case against Stalin, accusing him of not having trusted in the potential of the Chinese Revolution, and of having believed that the Chinese People's Republic was 'another Yugoslavia'. He referred to the continuity in Soviet behaviour, but at the same time confirmed his own frosty assessment of de-Stalinization, forcing the Soviet leader to admit that 'if we speak of Stalin's accomplishments, then we too are part of them'. Khrushchev therefore found himself accused of two things: arrogance and revisionism.[79] Mao's operational linkage between the rejection of any kind of 'coexistence' with the imperialist enemy and the relaunch of a radical 'socialist offensive' in the country was clear.[80] However, Mao did not stop there. He harboured the ambition to influence the development of the communist world as a whole and place Peking at its head.

The Soviets did not immediately perceive the implicit challenge in the policy directions of the Chinese People's Republic. Their irritation with the way the Chinese criticized them and then presented them with the Taiwan crisis as a fait accompli was considerable but manageable. After all, the basis for the alliance had been confirmed at the meeting between Mao and Khrushchev in the summer of 1958. The Chinese leader had even expressed his gratitude for the existence of Soviet nuclear missiles, which, to his way of thinking, guaranteed the survival of the Chinese People's Republic.[81] However, when Khrushchev went to Peking for the tenth anniversary of the Revolution at the start of October 1959, his hopes of forging an agreement were frustrated. His trip to the United States the previous month had had the unequivocal significance of a relaunch of 'peaceful coexistence', in spite of the second Berlin crisis which had been provoked by Moscow in order to achieve recognition for East Germany and arrest the rush of transfers from East to West with a diplomatic agreement.[82] For the Chinese this constituted a confirmation of their worst fears, particularly as Moscow had adopted a position of neutrality in the conflict between India and China over Tibet. The Soviet reluctance to

[77] Lüthi, *The Sino-Soviet Split*, 73–4.

[78] C. Jian, *Mao's China and the Cold War* (Chapel Hill, NC: University of North Carolina Press, 2001), 172–5.

[79] V. Zubok, 'The Mao–Khrushchev conversations, 31 July–3 August 1958 and 2 October 1959', *Cold War International History Project Bulletin* 12 and 13 (2001), doc. 1, pp. 250–60.

[80] R. Macfarquhar, *The Origins of the Cultural Revolution*, vol. 2: *The Great Leap Forward* (New York: Columbia University Press, 1983), 96–8.

[81] Zubok, 'The Mao–Khrushchev conversations', doc. 1, p. 260.

[82] A. Fursenko and T. Naftali, *Khrushchev's Cold War: The Inside Story of an American Adversary* (New York: Norton, 2006), 229–40.

share its own nuclear technology with China did not improve the situation.[83] The talks between the two leaders, which took place on 2 October 1959, appeared to be less litigious than the ones held the year before, but Khrushchev did not succeed in persuading Mao of the reasons for dialogue with Eisenhower and the need for the 'socialist camp' to maintain good relations with India.[84] Khrushchev reported to the ruling group of the CPSU that the overall impression was negative, but insisted that it was in their interests to avoid a 'dispute' and an 'aggravation' in relations.[85] Shortly afterwards, Suslov expressed behind closed doors for the first time a criticism of Mao's foreign and domestic policies, accusing him of evading the necessary definition of 'a single line' for foreign policy in the 'socialist camp', underestimating the risks of war, and having set up a regime similar to that of Stalin in his later years.[86] In his turn, Mao argued that the alliance with Moscow had come to a dead end and that China had to set itself the target of gaining the support of the other communist parties. In a note written in December 1959, he accused Khrushchev and the Soviet ruling group of not understanding Marxism-Leninism and fearing both imperialism and Chinese communism. 'In the long term,' Mao prophesied, 'China will be isolated on one side, but on the other it will have the support of many communist parties, many countries and many peoples.'[87] The failure of the 'Great Leap Forward', which was turning out to be a horrific famine, helped to embitter the Maoist regime and its misunderstandings with the Soviet Union.[88]

The escalating disagreement between the two sides continued without interruption into the early months of 1960, particularly after the shooting down of an American spy plane at the beginning of March created an incident between Moscow and Washington. Fearing a revival of the Chinese condemnation of 'peaceful coexistence', Khrushchev decided to take the initiative. On 2 June he sent a letter to the parties in the 'socialist camp' proposing a meeting on the 'international situation' to be held in Bucharest at the end of the month.[89] At the time of the meeting, the Soviets circulated a document accusing the Chinese of having ignored the policy decisions adopted by the communist movement three years earlier in Moscow. Khrushchev declared that another war was not necessary to ensure the triumph of socialism, and accused the Chinese leadership of adventurism and nostalgia for Stalin. Taken by surprise, the Chinese delegation led by Peng Zhen found itself in isolation except for support of the Albanians.[90] In July, the Soviet

---

[83] Haslam, *Russia's Cold War*, 192; J. Chang and J. Halliday, *Mao: The Unknown History* (London: Jonathan Cape, 2005), 478–9.

[84] Zubok, 'The Mao–Khrushchev conversations', 263–72.

[85] *Prezidium*, vol. 1, doc. 202, p. 389.

[86] 'A new "cult of personality": Suslov's secret report on Mao, Khrushchev, and Sino-Soviet Tensions, December 1959', *Cold War International History Project Bulletin* 8 and 9 (1996–7), 248.

[87] D. Wolff, *"One Finger's Worth of Historical Events": New Russian and Chinese Evidence on the Sino-Soviet Alliance and Split, 1948–1959*, Cold War International History Project working paper no. 30 (Washington, D.C.: Woodrow Wilson Center, 2000), doc. 25, pp. 72–4.

[88] Macfarquhar, *The Origins of the Cultural Revolution*, vol. 2, pp. 264–5.

[89] *Prezidium*, vol. 3, doc. 218.1, pp. 128–30.

[90] SAPMO, Sed, DY 30 J IV 2/201, b. 613; Chang and Halliday, *Mao: The Unknown History*, 484.

Union unilaterally withdrew its technicians and drastically reduced its economic assistance to China. In September, the meeting between the two delegations led by Suslov and Deng ended in a clash rather than in a reconciliation. Suslov scolded the Chinese for their opposition to dialogue with Washington which led them 'to confuse matters of principle with the diplomacy of struggle'. Deng reproached the Soviets for having 'transferred ideological differences to the sphere of international relations between states'.[91] The Chinese leader had understood an essential point. The overlap between state relations and party relations, and the mixture of egalitarian principles and hierarchical traditions, were becoming structural features of the 'socialist camp' and weakening its governability.[92] The pressure Moscow brought to bear aimed at reconciliation, which it could only conceive as submission, would prove to be a blunt weapon and a counterproductive one.

The new world conference of communist parties which met in Moscow in November could not contain the Chinese dissent. In his opening report on 10 November 1960, Khrushchev relaunched 'peaceful coexistence' as a form of international 'class struggle' and pointed to the growth of the 'socialist camp' as the new foundation of world politics, which would be capable of weakening and thwarting American hegemony. It was now well established in Khrushchev's political discourse that war no longer constituted a necessary historical transition, and that to think otherwise was to show a lack of faith in the inevitable triumph of communism. The Soviet leader avoided any polemical points directed at China and addressed his criticisms to the 'national communism' of the Yugoslavs. But Deng Xiaoping ignored Khrushchev's speech. He put forward the Maoist polemic against the 'overestimation' of the enemy, branded the idea of war bringing about the end of humanity as a 'capitulation', described 'peaceful coexistence' as a mere truce before the impending revolutionary struggle, and rejected the notion of a 'peaceful road' to socialism out of hand. On 23 and 24 November, Khrushchev and Deng argued out the questions of war and Stalin in front of all the delegates, and revealed opposing interpretations of the 1957 Declaration. Deng went so far as to accuse Khrushchev of criticizing Stalin in order to refer to Mao.[93] It was the first time since the mid-1920s that a leader of a communist party had openly opposed Moscow at an official event, albeit not a public one. Deng, who was protected by Zhou Enlai and was moulded by his experience of France and the Soviet Union during the 1920s, asserted himself in the most important tribune of international communism and demonstrated the compactness of the Maoist ruling group. The immediate effect was to create a split. With the exception of the Albanians, all the delegates from European communist parties sided with Moscow. The Asian communist parties were much more cautious, with the exception of the Indian delegation. The united appearance of the communist movement was saved

---

[91] C. Jian, 'Deng Xiaoping, Mao's "continuous revolution", and the path toward the Sino-Soviet split: a rejoinder', *Cold War International History Project Bulletin* 10 (1998),173.

[92] Z. Shen and D. Li, *After Leaning to One Side: China and Its Allies in the Cold War* (Washington, DC/Stanford, Calif.: Woodrow Wilson Center Press/Stanford University Press, 2011), 166.

[93] SAPMO, Sed, DY 30 J IV 2/201, b. 625; APCI, URSS, mf 0474, 2885–2941.

through a diplomatic meeting between Khrushchev and Liu Shaoqi, which took place on 30 November following mediation from Ho Chi Minh.[94] The conference's final declaration was a carbon copy of the one approved three years earlier.[95]

Reporting to the Central Committee of the CPSU on 18 January 1961, Suslov remarked on the danger to the movement's unity and attributed its avoidance to the USSR. He accused the Chinese of causing 'confusion' over changes in the international situation. The nature of imperialism was unchanged, but progress and the increasing homogeneity of the 'socialist camp' made it possible to look to the future with optimism and to 'safeguard humanity from the catastrophe of a thermonuclear war'. Under aegis of the 'socialist camp', the new impetus of decolonization could create 'a new kind of state', a state founded on 'national democracy' similar to the 'people's democracy' born out of the defeat of fascism. Equally possible was the 'peaceful transition' to socialism in the capitalist countries. The scenarios for armed struggle could not be precluded, but neither were they to be considered necessary. According to Suslov, this was theoretical and political baggage acquired by the communist movement, which the Chinese would have to accept whether they like it or not.[96] The Soviets could not forego triumphal rhetoric about the growth in the communist party delegations—increased from sixty-four to eighty-one compared with three years earlier, thanks to the birth of new post-colonial states—and the movement's unity.[97] In reality, communists had not increased a great deal in number during the fifteen years that had passed since the end of the war, nor had they overcome the gaps in their territorial expansion. In the 'socialist camp', communists constituted an elite of over 30 million people (approximately one third in the Soviet Union, half in China, and the remainder in other countries within the 'camp'). Outside it, their number did not exceed 5 million (with three-quarters concentrated in Italy, France, India, Indonesia, and Japan). Whatever the geopolitical consistency of the movement, the real problem was that its unity was seriously at risk. The Yugoslavs had not taken part in the conference. The Chinese positions involved a strategy that would be difficult to reconcile with the Soviet one. The Soviet leaders showed a tendency to believe in their own propaganda, which created a vicious circle of self-delusion.

Moscow once again concentrated its attention on Europe, now at the height of the second Berlin crisis, which culminated with the construction of the Wall on 13 August 1961—a drastic solution to the German question favoured more by the East Germans than the Soviets, but elevated by all European communists to an ideological frontier between irreconcilable identities, and a symbol of the Cold War.[98] Khrushchev's final decision, taken after a prolonged confrontation with Ulbricht, was influenced by the polemic with Mao and the need to avoid risky

---

[94] *Memoirs of Nikita Khrushchev*, vol. 3, p. 502.
[95] *Dokumenty soveshchanii predstaviteley kommunisticheskikh i rabochikh partii, Moskva, nojabr' 1960 goda* (Moscow: Gosudarstvennoe izdatel'stvo politicheskoy literatury, 1960).
[96] RGANI, fo. 2, op. 1, d. 510.   [97] *Prezidium*, vol. 3, doc. 222, pp. 134–8.
[98] B. Ludwig, 'Le mur de Berlin, dernier rempart de l'antifascisme et ultime frontière du communisme en Europe', in S. Coeuré and S. Dullin (eds), *Frontières du communisme: mythologies et réalités de la division de l'Europe de la Révolution d'Octobre au mur de Berlin* (Paris: La Découverte, 2007).

disagreement with his European allies.[99] However, the increasing conflict with the Americans did not soften the tensions between Moscow and Peking. The apparent unanimity within European communism was not sufficient to safeguard the movement's unity. Khrushchev's resumption of de-Stalinization at the Twenty-Second Congress of the Soviet Party in November 1961 simply added fuel to the fire. Relations between Tirana and Moscow, which had seriously deteriorated after the previous year's conference, were broken off definitively. From February to May 1962, the Soviets and the Chinese confidentially exchanged mutual accusations of compromising the prospects of the communist movement. Moscow decided to make the other communist parties aware of the correspondence with Peking.[100]

The Chinese leaders did not back off, even though they had to deal with the disastrous consequences of the famine their policy had provoked in the countryside—comparable with the Soviet one in the 1930s, but with three or four times the number of victims.[101] The theory that Khrushchev's 'revisionism' was threatening the future of international communism became common currency in Chinese political discourse. The emergence within the Chinese ruling group of leaders critical of Mao's policies, following the failure of the 'Great Leap Forward' and gathered around Liu Shaoqi and Deng Xiaoping, produced no changes in Peking's foreign policy. After a period of silence, Mao took the stage in August and September 1962. He established a link between the permanent risk of a resurgence of the bourgeois 'classes' in socialist societies and his critique of Soviet 'revisionism'. In an obvious analogy with Stalin at the end of the 1920s, Mao justified his 'class' approach to the rural question and employed a revolutionary rhetoric in international politics, while ignoring the risks of China's isolation. In this radical relaunch, he went so far as to identify China's four principal enemies as Kennedy, Nehru, Tito, and Khrushchev.[102] The Soviet Union became a negative example of everything revolutionaries must avoid after taking power. Consequently, its historical mission could be considered over and was now to be taken on by genuine revolutionaries. Zhou declared in the same circumstances: 'the centre of world revolution has shifted from Moscow to Peking.'[103] The conflict between Moscow and Peking thus revealed a divergence between two visions of communism's global role: the prospect of competition between two poles based on 'peaceful coexistence' or an anti-imperialist guerrilla war in the world's periphery. The challenge to imperialism was an essential part of both viewpoints. The Third World thus

[99] H. M. Harrison, *Driving the Soviets Up the Wall: Soviet–East German Relations, 1953–1961* (Princeton, N.J.: Princeton University Press, 2003).

[100] *Prezidium*, vol. 3, doc. 246.2.1, pp. 257–8; docs 246.3, 246.3.1, pp. 258–78.

[101] J.-L. Margolin, 'Cina: una lunga marcia nella notte', in S. N. Courtois, N. Werth, et al., *Il libro nero del comunismo: crimini, terrore, repressione* (Milan: Mondadori, 1998), 455–66.

[102] Macfarquhar, *The Origins of the Cultural Revolution*, vol. 3; R. Macfarquhar, *The Coming of the Cataclysm, 1961–1966* (New York: Columbia University Press, 1997), 277, 290.

[103] Y. Kuisong, *Changes in Mao Zedong's Attitude toward the Indochina War, 1949–1973*, Cold War International History Project working paper no. 24 (Washington D.C.: Woodrow Wilson Center, 2002), 23.

became not only the principal theatre of the Cold War but also the place where the unity of international communism came to an end.

EXPANSION IN THE THIRD WORLD AND THE RIFT BETWEEN THE SOVIET UNION AND CHINA

Communism continued to be a predominantly Eurocentric movement after the war, and had few offshoots beyond the Eurasian borders of the Soviet Union. The Soviet victory in the war and the new anti-colonial drive in the Third World contributed to the spread of the anti-imperialist message, which had always been linked to the Russian Revolution, and the successful myth of Stalinist modernization. The allure of Marxism and the USSR was a powerful influence on intellectual and national elites, who were inclined to radicalize their political visions in countries that had emancipated themselves from European colonialism. The most significant personalities of this kind included Asian leaders such as the Indian Jawāharlāl Nehru, who was inspired by the British Labour politician Harold Laski and attracted by the model of central planning, and the Indonesian Sukarno, who was attracted to the idea of combining nationalism, Islam, and communism. In the Arab world and Africa too, the Soviet model was widely viewed as a suitable solution for the problems of economic backwardness. The authoritarian nature of the principal regimes emerging from decolonization, with the notable exception of India, and the dramatic problems concerning development meant that the model promised many more possibilities than it had in Europe. Where the creation of a nation required the support of a sufficiently strong state, state-building along Soviet lines appeared a promising instrument for development and authoritarian integration in post-colonial countries.[104]

At the same time, the power of the Soviet Union could be seen as a guarantee against colonialism's parting shots and support for a process of autarkic modernization free from economic dependency on a capitalist metropolis. However, this did not work in favour of communists outside Europe when Stalin was in power, nor did it produce a commitment from the Soviet Union to support anti-imperialist nationalism. Moscow did not play an active part in the early examples of decolonization or in the anti-colonial rebellions that developed in Southeast Asia. Stalin considered the revolutionary prospects of national liberation movements outside Europe to be peripheral, and of little significance in terms of the Soviet Union's interests. The Chinese Revolution decisively modified the presence of communism in the non-Western world, but only after the end of the Stalinist era. In the wake of the Chinese Revolution and the growth in anti-colonial movements, Stalin's

---

[104] Westad, *The Global Cold War*, 95.

successors realized that the Soviet Union and international communism could no longer divide their fate from that of the 'global south'.[105]

The Viet Minh at Dien Bien Phu in the spring of 1954 played a role in determining this change of policy. With huge military backing from the People's Republic of China and strongly encouraged by Mao to seek total victory, Vietnamese communists brought American-backed French domination in Indochina to an end after four years of war.[106] The other symbolically crucial event was the conference of Third World countries held in Indonesia at Bandung in April 1955. Although the tendency to avoid identification with either of the two blocs—which was typical of the more important countries represented at Bandung—was incompatible with the logic of the Cold War, the emergence of new players on the world stage, who were products of the anti-colonial struggle, appeared to promise some kind of convergence with the communist world. The Chinese delegates at the conference insisted on the common denominator of a colonial past. This vision meant it was credible that agreements could be made on the basis of development prospects and the condemnation of Western imperialism.[107] Unlike Washington, which feared its radical and anti-Western consequences, Moscow perceived Bandung's legacy as an opportunity. The front that was opening up appeared undeniably favourable in the bipolar context, given the evident imbalance between the widespread perception of the United States as the heir to the Western imperial powers and the perception of the Soviet Union as an anti-imperialist, socialist, and modernizing force.

The policy towards the Third World became a substantial part of a new strategy for the Soviet Union, alongside de-Stalinization and 'peaceful coexistence'. Europe continued to be seen as the theatre for a 'war of position' which was a priority in terms of security for the 'socialist community' and Soviet influence. The fate of that confrontation was now linked to the 'war of movement' that was starting in the Third World. Khrushchev proposed to revive the anti-colonialist impetus going back to the Bolshevik Revolution, believing that countries outside Europe constituted the principal terrain on which to challenge Western capitalism. Soviet policy was directed at the post-colonial nationalist leaderships, of which the alliance with the Egyptian leader Nasser was particularly important after the Suez crisis, even more than the militant vanguards of international communism. For the first time, the USSR was committing considerable economic, technical, and military resources in non-socialist countries. In some cases, this once again produced the classic contradiction between the interests of the Soviet state and those of the various national communist parties, which had already emerged during the 1920s in Europe but also in Turkey and China. For example, Moscow's attempt to influence Iran led it to reduce its financial aid to Tudeh, which was fighting against the dictatorship of Reza Pahlavi following the coup in August 1953.[108] Next it was

[105] M. P. Bradley, 'Decolonization, the global South, and the Cold War, 1919–1962', in M. P. Leffler and O. A. Westad (eds), *The Cambridge History of the Cold War*, vol. 1: *Origins* (Cambridge: Cambridge University Press, 2010), 474–5.

[106] Jian, *Mao's China and the Cold War*, 135–7.

[107] Westad, *The Global Cold War*, 99–103.   [108] *Prezidium*, vol. 1, doc. 59, p. 144.

the turn of Egyptian communists to experience the consequences of Soviet foreign policy. Their ferocious repression by the Nasser regime provoked formal protests, but did not impede the establishment of increasingly close relations between Moscow and Cairo.[109] Khrushchev's policy was motivated by considerable optimism over the possibilities for combining the interests of the 'socialist camp' and those of the anti-imperialist revolution under the aegis of socialist modernization. The spread of the Soviet myth in significant sectors of the political and intellectual nationalist elites appeared to make up for the blow suffered in Europe during the Hungarian crisis. The launch of the first artificial satellite in October 1957, which Mao extolled at the conference on world communism, created the impression of the Soviet Union taking the lead in scientific and technological progress, and this impression was particularly strong in the Third World. Khrushchev was persuaded that the progressive alliance with nationalism outside Europe was a natural event and a historical necessity that would lead to the triumph of the Soviet system and of communism over the ruins of European colonialism.

The Cuban Revolution in January 1959 only strengthened this conviction, even though the handful of nationalist guerrillas who took power under Fidel Castro's leadership were alien to the communist world and it took more than a year for the new regime to seek close relations with the Soviet Union under the threat of an American intervention. The birth of a revolutionary regime at the heart of the United States' sphere of influence seemed to confirm the universalist aspirations implicit in the wager on the global south.[110] Soviet ambition to extend the frontier of its presence outside Europe to the decolonization of Africa, by supporting the Congo of Patrice Lumumba in 1960–61, quickly proved to be a failure. However, the international department of the CPSU believed there were promising possibilities for the Soviet Union's influence in some West African countries such as Ghana, Guinea, and Mali, even after the fall and assassination of Lumumba.[111] The opening of a new university in Moscow for the technical and political training of militants from African and Asian countries, which was named after Lumumba, was an eloquent signal of Soviet Third Worldism, and involved an ambitious programme for preparing cadres and specialists.[112] A new expression appeared in communist vocabulary: 'national democratic state', which was used to indicate the road of non-capitalist development in post-colonial countries. The American response, by which President John F. Kennedy aimed to relaunch the containment of communism by taking up the challenge of development and progress, confirmed the new

---

[109] T. Y. Ismael and R. El-sa'id, *The Communist Movement in Egypt* (Syracuse, N.Y.: Syracuse University Press, 1990), 119–21.

[110] *Memoirs of Nikita Khrushchev*, vol. 3, p. 322.

[111] S. Mazov, *A Distant Front in the Cold War: The USSR in West Africa and the Congo, 1956–1964* (Stanford, Calif./Washington, D.C.: Stanford University Press/Woodrow Wilson Center, 2010); *SSSR i Afrika, 1918–1960: dokumentirovannaya istoriya vzaimootnoshchenii* (Moscow: Institut Vseobshchei Istorii, 2002), 250 ff.

[112] Mazov, *A Distant Front in the Cold War*, 232–3.

centrality of the Third World as a place where both antagonists in the Cold War felt that the future would be decided.[113]

At the beginning of the 1960s, the interaction between the 'socialist camp' and the rest of the world appeared much more intense, varied, and potentially outgoing than it had been at the time of Stalin's death. Khrushchev's policy did, however, present serious problems. The Soviet Union took up and drove forward the challenge from the post-colonial world on multiple fronts that were largely favourable to its clash with the United States, while bringing the communist movement within a possible hegemonic context. But its modus operandi was not very different from that of the past: a massive deployment of organizational and financial resources subject to a rigid chain of command and an inflexible concept of the Soviet Union's state interests. The Soviet model was conceived as a ready-made instrument to be exported, rather than adapted to very different situations because of social, cultural, and historical reasons. The bipolar approach in any case privileged the East–West conflict in international politics, as demonstrated by the second Berlin crisis.[114] The conflict with China laid bare the limitations of Soviet hegemonic capacity not only in Europe but also in the non-Western world, in spite of the resources directed towards the construction of China's state and the modernization of its economy. The Sino-Soviet alliance proved inadequate for the management of the new phase of the movement in the Third World, and was indeed destabilized by its repercussions, given that the Chinese were irritated by the Soviet Union's great power politics, distrustful of agreements with nationalist elites, and inclined to follow a substantially different strategy.

At the same time, crisis in the Sino-Soviet alliance was producing its inevitable repercussions on the communist presence in the Third World, just at the moment when decolonization was at its height. The spread of guerrilla experiences inspired by the example set by Castro in Latin America and Vietnam in Southeast Asia was seen by Moscow as a reality that presented many opportunities but also had to be kept under control, whereas the Chinese were increasingly eager to establish their own influence. Following the conference of communist parties in November 1960, a bitter rivalry developed between Moscow and Peking to gain the support of communists outside Europe. The emerging scenario was one of a dramatic split that would weaken the movement just where its expansion appeared to be most promising. The idea of coordinated action between the two communist powers destined to gain one success after another and oust the West from the post-colonial world was replaced within a few years by the prospect of a challenge from within the movement. The Soviets were obliged to combine the secularized image of modernization—seen as the only choice for the development of countries outside Europe—with an appeal to a hallowed unity around the Kremlin and a more militant commitment to the Third World. However, the challenge from China was an extremely hard blow.

---

[113] F. Romero, *Storia della Guerra Fredda: l'ultimo conflitto per l'Europa* (Turin: Einaudi, 2009), 137; M. Mazower, *Governing the World: The History of an Idea* (New York: Penguin Press, 2012), 258ff.
[114] Haslam, *Russia's Cold War*, 211.

The case of Vietnam threw light on the disagreements between Moscow and Peking, and helped to exacerbate them. Although he was preaching a gradualist strategy, aimed at positioning the Vietnamese Revolution in a global context, Ho Chi Minh had never renounced the possibility of destabilizing the structure set in place by the Geneva Peace Conference of 1954—a division of the country similar to that of the Korean peninsula, between the communist north and the pro-Western south. In the framework of the Sino-Soviet alliance, Moscow had largely delegated relations with Vietnam to Peking, entrusting the peaceful reunification of the country mainly to diplomacy.[115] Although the Chinese supported the Vietnamese with military equipment and political rhetoric, they were cautious about the idea of an armed insurrection in the south of the country, because they feared American intervention.[116] These apparently concordant policies concealed tendential differences. The Soviets preferred to work for a consolidation of the regime in the north through material assistance, whereas the Chinese feared the premature failure of a struggle they considered strategic, and a risk to their own security. For a few years, the communist regime was absorbed with agrarian reforms and political re-education campaigns, which involved violence and repression, just as they had in China. But in 1959, Hanoi decided to support the armed rebellion by the Vietcong in the south.[117] The two communist powers were confronted with a fait accompli. Civil war broke out in Laos towards the end of 1960, not long after the Vietnamese armed struggle. Khrushchev launched his public advocacy of the Vietnamese and Algerian causes, which he defined as just wars at the beginning of 1961, but he saw them as part of the Cold War and his vision of the 'two camps'.[118] Mao, on the other hand, perceived the events in Indochina as a good reason for pursuing his anti-imperialist strategy in place of 'peaceful coexistence'.

The cards in Chinese hands were anything but insignificant. The Maoist message spoke more directly than any other to the communists of the non-Western world, reviving the old and evocative idea of a capitalist metropolis encircled by a revolutionary countryside. The political model of Maoism, forged in the 1930s and 1940s, was the original source of inspiration for revolutionary movements outside Europe—a variant of the Bolshevik model that was equally disciplined but less elitist, as it was suited to the conditions of permanent guerrilla warfare in pre-modern society.[119] The radicalization of China's foreign policy, which Mao put forward in 1962, might have been brought about by the failure of the 'Great Leap Forward'.[120] However, it followed a precise logic, which had been clearly formed

[115] M. Olsen, *Soviet–Vietnam Relations and the Role of China, 1949–64: Changing Alliances* (London: Routledge, 2006), 70–71, 80–82. See also I. V. Gaiduk, *Confronting Vietnam: Soviet Policy towards the Indochina Conflict, 1954–1963* (Stanford, Calif.: Stanford University Press, 2003).

[116] Q. Zhai, *China and the Vietnam Wars, 1950–1975* (Chapel Hill, N.C.: University of North Carolina Press, 2000), 82–3.

[117] W. J. Duiker, *Ho Chi Minh: A Life* (New York: Hyperion, 2000), 512–13.

[118] Fursenko and Naftali, *Khrushchev's Cold War*, 336.

[119] R. J. Alexander, *International Maoism in the Developing World* (Westport, Conn.: Praeger, 1999).

[120] N. Jun, *1962: The Eve of the Left Turn in China's Foreign Policy*, Cold War International History Project working paper no. 48 (Washington, D.C.: Woodrow Wilson Center, 2005).

for some time and which challenged 'peaceful coexistence' and the idea of economic competition between the 'two systems' on a basis that was as cultural as it was political. By this stage, Mao had redefined the connection between revolution and decolonization, developing theories that were only embryonic in his speech on the 'two winds' back in 1957. The Chinese leader abandoned the theory of the 'two camps', which had been formulated by Stalin and continued by his successors, and replaced it with his vision of anti-imperialist revolution in the non-Western world, which explicitly shifted the leadership role to Peking. He was now using Marxist language to divide the world along different lines from those established by the Soviet tradition, countering the interests of the developed North with those of the Afro-Asiatic and Latin American South. The treacherous accusation that the Soviet Union had pulled back from its original revolutionary impulse, and was to all intents and purposes another member of the developed world dedicated to its own imperial interests and insensitive to the problems of the Third World, constituted a point of no return.

The Cuban crisis of October 1962 marked a turning point for the Cold War, and equally for international communism. The Cuban Revolutionary regime now constituted a bridgehead for the 'socialist camp' inside the United States' most immediate sphere of interest. The failed American attempt to invade the island and suppress the revolution had pushed Castro into the arms of the Soviet Union. Leaders of a group of revolutionaries much younger than the other protagonists of international communism, and little more than 30 years old, Castro and Ernesto Che Guevara could boast personal charisma and an aura of romanticism that no one else could. Even though their conversion to Marxism and communism was very recent, the Cubans' anti-imperialist fervour was not inferior to that of the Vietnamese—further confirmation of the potential for recruitment in the Third World.[121] The Soviet decision to install nuclear missiles on the island arose from a particular political and ideological context. During 1962, Castro had intensified his proclamations of faith in Marxism. The idea of defending the Cuban Revolution played a decisive role.[122] But the question did not only concern Cuba. In the general conquest of the Third World, the Cuban developments coincided with other phenomena that induced considerable optimism, such as the escalation of the Vietnamese struggle in the south of the country, the victory of the supporters of independence in the Algerian War and the presidency of Ben Bella, and Nasser's decision to define the Egyptian state as socialist and his internationalist intervention in Yemen, with Moscow's support.[123] In Khrushchev's view, the placing of nuclear arms on Cuba could only emphasize the centrality of the Soviet Union in what appeared to be an increasing wave of anti-imperialism in various communist and nationalist guises. The intention of preventing and containing the

[121] V. Skierka, *Fidel* (Rome: Fandango, 2003), 156–64.

[122] Gaddis, *We Now Know*, 263.

[123] J. Ferris, 'Soviet support for Egypt's intervention in Yemen, 1962–63', *Journal of Cold War Studies* 10.4 (2008).

influence of the Chinese, who were also active in Cuba, was clear. Conscious of the Soviet inferiority in relation to the United States, Khrushchev believed that precisely for this reason it was necessary to develop a strategy that aimed to exploit every opportunity to keep Washington on the ropes and modify the balance of power. Thus he launched a new and dangerous 'war of nerves' in Cuba, following the one triggered in Berlin a year earlier. However, this adventure would have harmful consequences. The defeat suffered during the confrontation with Kennedy would leave a poisoned legacy.[124]

The political and military elites in the Soviet Union would not forgive Khrushchev the humiliation they suffered and the damage to the prestige of the Soviet superpower, but this only became clear two years later. In the short term, it was Soviet internationalism that suffered the severest blow. The outcome of the crisis caused a serious conflict between the Soviets and the Cubans. Having conceived the deployment of the weapons not only as a deterrent against a possible American invasion but also as a consecration of their vanguard role in the world revolution, the Cubans felt betrayed by the negotiations Khrushchev entered into with Kennedy without their knowledge. Relations between Castro and the Soviet envoy Mikoyan experienced moments of extreme tension in November 1962, when it became clear that Moscow would not leave tactical nuclear weapons on the island.[125] Khrushchev did not exclude the possibility of a rift with the Cubans. Immediately after Mikoyan's return to Moscow, Khrushchev accused Castro of having talked rashly of a possible nuclear conflict, lamented his unpredictability, and declared to the Presidium: 'doing business with the Cubans was dangerous. They are the same kind of allies as the Albanians and Chinese.'[126] Thus the conflictual dynamic that had already emerged at the end of the Second World War in Stalin's relations with Tito and Mao were now emerging once more, albeit in completely different circumstances. This time the rift never occurred. In the spring of 1963 Castro met Khrushchev in Moscow and obtained new economic and military assistance. The two leaders clarified their positions on the missile crisis.[127] But the damage to the Soviet Union's militant image was irreparable. The Chinese did not hesitate to define Khrushchev's behaviour as evidence of the primacy of the logic of power over a coherent internationalist policy. No less aberrant did they find Soviet neutrality in the new border conflict between India and China, which broke out during the Cuban crisis.[128]

---

[124] Haslam, *Russia's Cold War*, 199–209; Fursenko and Naftali, *Khrushchev's Cold War*, ch. 9; A. Fursenko and T. Naftali, *'One Hell of a Gamble': Khrushchev, Castro, and Kennedy, 1958–1964* (New York: Norton, 1998).

[125] S. Mikoyan, *The Soviet Cuban Missile Crisis: Castro, Mikoyan, Kennedy, Khrushchev, and the Missiles of November*, ed. S. Savranskaya (Washington, DC/Stanford, Calif.: Woodrow Wilson Center Press/Stanford University Press, 2012).

[126] *Prezidium*, vol. 3, doc. 275.0.1, p. 408. [127] Ibid. vol. 1, doc. 293, pp. 720–1.

[128] S. Radchenko, *Two Suns in the Heavens: The Sino-Soviet Struggle for Supremacy, 1962–1967* (Washington, DC/Stanford, Calif.: Woodrow Wilson Center Press/Stanford University Press, 2009), 30–4.

The consequences were felt immediately. In November 1962, Khrushchev, speaking to the Plenum of the CPSU, vented his irritation at the 'demagogic' use the Chinese were making of the Cuban crisis and accused them of being anti-imperialists only in words.[129] Immediately afterwards, Peking publicly attacked Tito and Togliatti, accusing them of 'revisionism', and receiving from both leaders diplomatic replies that nevertheless firmly rejected the Chinese ideological positions. Thus Mao burnt his bridges with two possible mediators in the controversy between China and the Soviet Union, demonstrating all his intransigence.[130] But neither party was willing to leave space for a serious attempt at finding a compromise. Moscow's position was subject to rigid limitation of an ideological and imperial nature. The Soviets did not lose the opportunity to isolate the Chinese from the other parties, and bolstering the centrality of their own role. Peking, from a more aggressive and defiant position, no longer aimed to influence the Soviet Union. Mao was preparing to give his own line to the international communist movement, without being too concerned about finding allies amongst European communists, which he considered oblivious to the anti-imperialist struggle. From the end of 1962, the two sides traded accusations of nationalism and betraying internationalism, which culminated in an exchange of letters in the first half of 1963. The Soviets kept the other communist parties informed.[131] On 30 March 1963, the CPSU pedantically reasserted the primacy of its own doctrinal role, although without attacking the Chinese directly. Mao's response was delayed, but only in order to increase the level of conflict. On 14 June, the CCP made a public appeal to the international communist movement that called on the parties to remain united but repeated its most intransigent positions on the international class struggle and criticized Moscow. The Soviet reaction was fierce and immediate, although not public.[132]

At this stage, the chances of restoring relations were largely compromised. Each side was only concerned with blaming the other for the split. A meeting between delegations that took place in Moscow in July 1963 turned out to be a dialogue of the deaf. Suslov and Deng engaged in an inconclusive review of their recriminations. The Chinese leader accused Khrushchev of having seriously weakened the communist movement with his denunciation of Stalin and his pursuit of the interests of the Soviet superpower rather than those of world revolution. Suslov rejected the personal attacks on Khrushchev, and reminded the Chinese of Soviet economic and military aid.[133] Right in the middle of the proceedings, on 14 July, the Soviets published their reply to the Chinese documents, making public the ideological dispute between the two sides for the first time. The document did not contain anything new. Its most significant feature was something else. It was in fact published the day before they opened negotiations in Moscow with the Americans and British over banning nuclear tests (with the exception of underground tests), which

---

[129] RGANI, fo. 2, op. 1, d. 632.　　　[130] APCI, Minutes, 1 Feb. 1963.
[131] *Prezidium*, vol. 3, doc. 283, pp. 446–51.
[132] Lüthi, *The Sino-Soviet Split*, 242–3; Radchenko, *Two Suns in the Heavens*, 56–60.
[133] Jian, 'Deng Xiaoping, Mao's 'continuous revolution', and the path toward the Sino-Soviet split'.

had, with Khrushchev's personal involvement, been on course since the Cuban crisis. This was the final blow to the talks with the Chinese, which ended in a climate of mutual frostiness. On 5 August 1963, the first nuclear non-proliferation treaty was signed.[134]

The timing of the Sino-Soviet rift and the conclusion of the first accord between the Soviet Union and the USA on the question of nuclear armaments appears to be symbolic. The nuclear question went to the heart of the conflict between Moscow and Peking, but also of the differences between European communism and Asian communism, which emerged in 1957. Mao's attacks on Tito and Togliatti were based on the accusation of their having revised Marxist-Leninist analysis of war and peace, and were clearly aimed at Khrushchev. Shortly before the meeting between the delegations from the two parties, Khrushchev spoke sarcastically of the Chinese in front of the CPSU Central Committee, accusing them of wanting to build 'a wonderful future on the ruins of the old world destroyed by thermonuclear war', and wondering whether they had consulted the 'working class in the countries where imperialism still rules' about this.[135] Moscow had made its mind up. Immediately after the end of the talks with the Chinese and the conclusion of the treaty with the West, Khrushchev commented triumphantly that the time had come to 'cross swords with the Chinese'.[136] The failure of the attempt to maintain the unity of the 'socialist camp' occurred at the most pivotal moment of 'peaceful coexistence': Moscow's signing of the main agreement with the Western powers since the time of Yalta. It would be difficult to imagine a circumstance more symbolic of the latent tension between the interests of the Soviet state and world revolution. Nearly half a century after the October Revolution, this duplicity revealed an explosive contradiction.

From the Soviet point of view, the presence of communist China on the international scene had been transformed within a few years from a strength to an obstacle and a restriction on the Soviet Union's freedom of action. The political conflict between the two sides was unrelenting during the year that followed the failure of the talks in July 1963. Khrushchev's visit to Yugoslavia in August and September 1963 marked not only a rapprochement with Tito but also a reappraisal of socialist self-management which in Chinese eyes was yet more evidence of revisionism.[137] On 10 September Khrushchev exhorted Suslov, Ponomarev, and Andropov to intensify their work on persuading the communist movement to expose the irrationalism of the Chinese. The Soviet leader was seriously concerned about the threat to relations between the Soviet Union and the Third World, which could be 'subverted' by Chinese activism. He declared that counteracting China's Third World policy was the 'number one' task of the Soviet Union's foreign policy.[138] In December 1963, Ponomarev raised the alarm over China's increasing influence in the whole of the post-colonial world, including Africa.[139]

---

[134] Lüthi, *The Sino-Soviet Split*, 260–8; Fursenko and Naftali, *Khrushchev's Cold War*, 525–8.
[135] RGANI, fo. 2, op. 1, d. 658.   [136] *Prezidium*, vol. 1, doc. 295, p. 734.
[137] Swain, *Tito*, 136–8; *Prezidium*, vol. 1, doc. 297, p. 736.
[138] Ibid. doc. 299, pp. 757–60.   [139] RGANI, fo. 2, op. 1, d. 665.

The situation in Asia, where the communist forces were much more signifi-cant than anywhere else outside Europe, appeared to be largely favourable to the Chinese. The two communist regimes in Korea and Vietnam seemed to be in their orbit. Kim's regime in North Korea was decisively in favour of Peking, and rejected Khrushchev's de-Stalinization and the critique of the 'personality cult'.[140] The Chinese presence had always been strong in North Vietnam, although Vietnamese communists safeguarded their struggle by refusing to take sides. Peking and Hanoi shared the guardianship of the other parties in Southeast Asia, particularly in Cambodia and Laos, but also in Burma, Malaysia, and Thailand.[141] Chinese influence increased considerably in the second half of 1963, when the Vietnamese reacted against the rapprochement between the Soviet Union and the United States after the Cuban missile crisis and the nuclear non-proliferation agreement.[142] Mao once again put forward his vision of Southeast Asia as the main front in the anti-imperialist struggle. At a meeting with Vietnamese, Indonesian, and Laotian communist leaders in September 1963, Zhou Enlai claimed that China was the hinterland of the future revolution in Southeast Asia.[143] In January 1964, the trip to Moscow and Peking by a Vietnamese delegation led by Le Duan proved to be decidedly more worthwhile for bilateral relations with the Chinese. While the Soviet Union's actual implementation of 'peaceful coexistence' was a cause for dis-sent, the fight against 'revisionism' and the prospect of a militant struggle against imperialism found Mao and Le Duan in agreement.[144] Of the Asian communist parties not in power, the most important—the Indonesian one—was wholly in the Maoist orbit and constituted the principal chorus for the revolutionary argu-ment that contrasted the global south against the interests of the imperialist north. Having recovered from the suppression of the 1948 rising, the ICP had grown spectacularly since the mid-1950s under Aidit's leadership, thanks to Sukarno's tolerance. With more than 2 million members, it was for Peking what the French Communist Party was for Moscow. At the time, Indonesian communism provided perhaps the principal example of the combination of communism and national-ism in the Third World.[145] Even in India, where the Communist Party maintained a pro-Soviet majority, which supported Nehru, there was a polarization between two factions towards the end of 1963 which quickly led to the breakaway of the

---

[140] B. Schaefer, 'Weathering the Sino-Soviet conflict: the GDR and North Korea, 1949–1989', *Cold War International History Project Bulletin* 14 and 15 (2003–4), 29–31; B. Szalontai, 'You have no political line of your own: Kim Il Sung and the Soviets, 1953–1964', *Cold War International History Project Bulletin* 14 and 15 (2003–4), 96–8.

[141] B. Kiernan, *How Pol Pot Came to Power: Colonialism, Nationalism, and Communism in Cambodia, 1930–1975*, 2nd edn (New Haven, Conn.: Yale University Press, 2004), 220–22.

[142] W. J. Duiker, *The Communist Road to Power in Vietnam*, 2nd edn (Boulder, Colo.: Westview Press, 1996), 241–5.

[143] Jian, *Mao's China and the Cold War*, 208.

[144] Kuisong, *Changes in Mao Zedong's Attitude toward the Indochina War, 1949–1973*, 28.

[145] R. Mortimer, *Indonesian Communism under Sukarno: Ideology and Politics, 1959–1965* (Ithaca, N.Y.: Cornell University Press, 1974); O. Törnquist, *Dilemmas of Third World Communism: The Destruction of the PKI in Indonesia* (London: Zed Books, 1984).

sizeable and intransigent pro-Chinese one.[146] At the end of 1963 and the start of 1964, Zhou Enlai's long journey to numerous Asian and African countries confirmed Soviet apprehensions. It looked as though there could be a collapse of Soviet influence in Asia.[147]

In February 1964, Moscow abandoned its previous caution. A formal report read by Suslov to the Central Committee of the CPSU accused the Chinese of betraying 'the general line of the international communist movement', and once again denounced the 'terrible concept' expressed by Mao at the Moscow Conference in 1957—the possibility of 'resolving the contradictions between socialism and capitalism' by means of a thermonuclear war. The Soviet ideologue denounced China's overt attempt to divide the Soviet Union and European communists from the anti-imperialist nationalism of the Third World.[148] Putting aside any reservations they might have had up till then, the Soviet Union started to put pressure on communist parties to convene another world conference. The aim was obvious. But the Soviet proposal for a meeting between the main parties to organize the conference was returned to sender by the Chinese. Although they had previously been in favour of a new conference in order to weaken the authority of the CPSU, the Chinese now sensed the danger of an excommunication and kept their distance. Neither Khrushchev nor Mao appeared to want a compromise. In early June, the CPSU made public a harsh and wordy letter to the CCP that repeated the proposal for a world conference.[149] Supported by the main parties in Eastern Europe and the French communists, the Soviet sent out a circular on 31 July to open the procedure for a conference of world communism.[150] In early October the preparatory commission was convened.[151] Opposition from the Koreans, Vietnamese, and Romanians, the perplexities expressed by the Italians, and above all the dismissal of Khrushchev prevented the procedure from going any further. However, attempts at mediation and appeals to safeguard the unity of international communism fell on deaf ears. The communist parties followed the impulses triggered by the conflict between the two socialist powers and their priority interests. While the Europeans found that 'peaceful coexistence' reassured their survival, the Asians felt that wool was being pulled over their eyes and considered it a threat to the anti-imperialist struggle. The scenario of a split at the heart of the communist movement was now clear for all to see.

Of the movement's leaders, Togliatti was most acutely aware of the dangers. He had declared loyalty to Moscow and supported the idea of 'peaceful coexistence' without reservations, but he resisted the proposed excommunication of China, fearing a ruinous split in the 'socialist camp'. This caused tension with Suslov, a bitter polemic with Thorez, and a rapprochement with Tito.[152] In August

---

[146] R. Mallick, *Indian Communism: Opposition, Collaboration and Institutionalization* (Delhi: Oxford University Press, 1994), 58–69.

[147] Radchenko, *Two Suns in the Heavens*, 74–81. [148] RGANI, fo. 2, op. 1, d. 720.

[149] *Prezidium*, vol. 3, doc. 311, pp. 678–94. [150] APCI, URSS, 1964, mf 0520, 2649–65.

[151] *Prezidium*, vol. 3, doc. 319, pp. 750–67.

[152] M. Galeazzi, *Togliatti e Tito: tra identità nazionale e internazionalismo* (Rome: Carocci, 2005), 246.

1964, shortly before his sudden death, Togliatti wrote a long memorandum in Yalta which would prove to be his political testament.[153] The 'Yalta Memorial' was marked by realistic pessimism and an urgent appeal for the unity of the communist movement, which sounded like ill-concealed irritation with Khrushchev's leadership. The Italian leader made clear his concern at the dramatic risks associated with the split between Moscow and Peking which, in his opinion, undermined 'the very principles of socialism'. By now a protagonist of the past, he was unable to understand its origins and suggest a solution. Putting aside his theory of polycentrism, Togliatti now preached the more cautious slogan of 'unity in diversity', which aimed to acknowledge that the 'forms of transition' to socialism could no longer be ascribed to past experiences. The 'Memorial' expressed a wish for a less hierarchical and more integrated system capable of creating a new relationship between states and parties, and yearned for a return to 'Leninist standards'. In reality, the scenario of a flexible and more structured 'socialist camp', more similar in this to the workings of the Western system, was not credible. Such a scenario had never emerged since Stalin's death, but had only been imagined and then buried in the Hungarian crisis. A polycentric 'socialist camp' seemed incompatible with the mentality and practice of Soviet leadership, but this was also true of the Chinese, as demonstrated by the way they conducted the conflict. The largely unaltered nature of the Soviet Union's state system of command rendered this unworkable, and this system had been reproduced throughout the other socialist states, along with the political culture that sustained it.

Khrushchev had attempted to respond to the need which emerged after Stalin's death to review the strategies, objectives, and role of the Soviet Union and international communism. But his response was weak and inadequate. The idea of a peaceful affirmation of the 'socialist camp' was a wager on winning the economic rivalry in a naively quantitative manner, which was even more simplistic than the visions of a communist future back in the days of 'war communism'.[154] This ignored the fact that the formidable postwar development of capitalism had lessened expectations of another great depression and created a consensus in consumer society, seriously undermining the efficacy of the Soviet economic challenge. Still more importantly, the idea of competition between the 'two systems' did not prevent state power, rather than the state economy, from remaining at the heart of Soviet strategy. Khrushchev's vision of the 'balance of power' was still linked to the concept of 'two camps', with the sole aim of enlarging and consolidating the 'socialist camp'. Ten years after Stalin's death, the de facto diversity within the system of communist states and the movement had not produced a more complex structure. The Soviet exercise of power had translated into the deployment of force and command from above. Even in its relations with political and ideological partners, Moscow continued to be intolerant of diversity and horrified by a lack of uniformity. In spite of the rhetoric of equal dignity, Soviet political culture perceived unity of the movement solely as uniformity, orthodoxy, and discipline. In

---

[153] Spagnolo, *Sul Memoriale di Yalta.*   [154] Graziosi, *L'URSS dal trionfo al degrado*, 255.

other words, Moscow was not capable of bringing about any profound innovation, but was capable of provoking discord and conflict.

As had occurred with the break between Stalin and Tito, loyalty to the Soviet Union found its limitations when it came into conflict with the new revolutionary regime. The analogy was very clear, and more perspicacious observers could not fail to infer an unfavourable prognosis for the future of international communism.[155] The Sino-Soviet alliance had experienced moments of high tension from the very beginning, but it had been sustained by the Korean War and support for the anti-imperialist guerrilla wars in Indochina, as well as Moscow's economic aid. The foundations of the alliance suffered a heavy blow from the moment Stalin's successors definitively opted for 'peaceful coexistence'. Mao engaged in a long confrontation and nurtured his ambition to compensate for the disorientation of Stalin's successors. His radical decisions were certainly influenced by the need to shore up his own dictatorial regime through the well-tested orchestration of the enemy without.[156] But there was also a very definite cultural and ideological background. The Chinese leader was not entirely wrong in considering himself to be more loyal to the kernel of the communist tradition. Although critical of Stalin's lack of revolutionary coherence, Mao followed the Stalinist legacy, as he was unconcerned about the potential consequences of atomic weapons and anchored to the theory of inevitable war. At the same time, he set himself up as the main heir of the radical tendencies that emerged from the war and led to the Yugoslav and Chinese revolutions. In his vision of a Chinese model, which differed from the 'revisionist' one—whether in the Soviet or Yugoslav version—the international element was no less important than the national element. His idea for the communist movement was to relaunch a radical mass movement on an anti-imperialist basis. It seems likely that he believed that only the cataclysm of a new world war would be able to recreate the unity of international communism.

The nemesis of communist pacifism was to cause a split in the movement, superimposed on the conflict between state and national interests. But the question of atomic warfare gauged the persistence of profound cultural frameworks. The denunciation of a threat to world civilization contained the implicit acknowledgement of the unity of humankind, and potentially announced that the dichotomous perception of social and international relations had run its course. In this sense, the post-Stalinist version of 'peaceful coexistence' was not at all banal and might have suggested the need for a cultural reform of the relationship between war and politics, which even in the West was having difficulty in getting off the ground.[157] However, none of the protagonists wished to abandon the Leninist doctrine of imperialism, considered the key to understanding the contemporary world

---

[155] R. Loewenthal, *World Communism: The Disintegration of a Secular Faith* (New York: Oxford University Press, 1964).

[156] Jian, *Mao's China and the Cold War.*

[157] K. Osgood, 'The perils of coexistence: peace and propaganda in Eisenhower's foreign policy', in K. Larres and K. Osgood (eds), *The Cold War After Stalin's Death: A Missed Opportunity for Peace?* (Lanham, Md.: Rowman & Littlefield, 2006).

in Moscow as it was in Peking, and in Belgrade as it was in Rome. The ruling groups of international communism continued to be influenced in the long term by the memory of the seminal catastrophe, the First World War, and the impossibility of declaring the 'international civil war' over, after the Second World War. The difference was between those who believed it was possible to contain and weaken imperialism because of the power of the Soviet Union and the growth in the 'socialist camp', and those who could not believe in that possibility and experienced this policy as a retreat.

Both visions underestimated the endurance and dynamism of the Western system. The memory of the catastrophe and the great depression of the 1930s stopped them from seeing that capitalism had redefined itself and was undergoing a new expansion. Communists seemed to be incapable of understanding how, unlike in the interwar period, the rise of the 'socialist camp' itself, its reality and its mythologies, had contributed to triggering and then stabilizing a massive process of transnational reorganization in the West. This process was based on the Atlantic Alliance and its global dimension after the Korean War, but also structured through new economic interdependence, the consensual nature of American hegemony, the creation of European democratic welfare states, the end of the old colonial empires, European integration, and from the early 1960s the idea that a combination of challenge and dialogue, containment and conflict management was the winning card in bipolar rivalry.[158] The notion of global interdependence was interpreted by communists mainly in terms of geopolitics, revolutionary prospects, and the 'balance of power', which presupposed the false idea of besieging a static and declining West incapable of modifying its own inheritance and imperial identity.

THE LIMITS UPON SOVIET INFLUENCE

Khrushchev left the stage on 14 October 1964, the victim of plotters who blamed him for the muddle created by his contradictory initiatives in domestic and international politics, from the hare-brained attempts to reorganize the party-state along productivist lines to the Cuban missile crisis.[159] He left a more pacified and less despotic Soviet Union than the one he had inherited, an 'external empire' that had experienced thaw and repression, and a world caught between Cold War and détente. The balance sheet for his leadership was as controversial as the future prospects of Soviet system and empire, whose foundations remained those laid by Stalin. Undoubtedly the unity of international communism and the 'socialist camp' appeared to be seriously compromised. Khrushchev's dismissal and the accusation that he had brought the world to the edge of atomic warfare coincided with the explosion of the first Chinese atomic bomb, which happened two days later. It is difficult to avoid the symbolism of this coincidence. During the following

---

[158] Romero, *Storia della Guerra Fredda*, 118–19, 164 ff.
[159] *Nikita Khrushchev 1964: stenogrammy plenuma TsK KPSS i drugie dokumenty* (Moscow: Mezhdunarodnyi Fond 'Demokratiya', 2007).

years, international communism had to remain divided into two contrasting alliances, which heralded its disintegration. At the same time, the conflict between the Soviet Union and China decisively affected power politics and created geopolitical confrontation, which started with Peking's claims over Soviet territories from Lake Baikal to Vladivostok.[160]

The foreign-policy reasons for Khrushchev's dismissal included above all the repercussions of the Cuban missile crisis, but the Chinese question did not pass unnoticed. He was mainly accused of having damaged the 'international prestige of our state' with his 'adventurism' in Cuba, but amongst the charges against him was also that of having worsened relations with Mao.[161] The politico-ideological clash between Moscow and Peking had reached such a pitch that Krushchev's successors could say nothing more, even if they had wanted to. It was not necessarily the case that they shared the same views on the Chinese question. Some of them probably had the same opinion of Stalin as the Chinese did, but they could not go back on the official declarations of the previous years, nor could they risk divisions after having successfully plotted against Khrushchev. They were all certainly convinced that Mao's disobedience was outrageous and should have been censured, but their assessments of the chances of resolving the problem must have been varied and full of doubts. However, the most influential of the new oligarchs thought that the removal of Khrushchev would make it possible to re-establish friendly relations between the Soviet Union and China.

The main protagonists of the palace coup against Khrushchev, Leonid Brezhnev and Aleksey Kosygin, met a Chinese delegation led by Zhou Enlai on 8 November. The meeting was to sound out each other's opinions, and an opportunity for the Chinese to clarify that the disagreement was not simply a personal matter between Khrushchev and Mao.[162] The new Soviet leaders still tried to use the fall of Khrushchev to make an attempt at reconciliation. They were encouraged in this by Gomułka, and warned in vain by Tito that their efforts would come to nothing.[163] At the Plenum of the Central Committee in November, Brezhnev rejected the argument that the fall of Khrushchev was Peking's victory over 'revisionism', but declared that they needed to take steps 'to normalize Sino-Soviet relations'.[164] The escalation of America's military intervention in Vietnam, which occurred in early 1965, marked a turning point, but it did not live up to the new leaders' expectations nor those of the Maoist ruling group. Both parties, in different ways, aimed to establish a strong influence over Vietnam on an anti-American basis. Khrushchev's successors thought that forming a common front over the Vietnamese cause would restore unity. The Chinese thought that the time had come for them to assert their leadership in the anti-imperialist struggle. Neither of these scenarios would be realized.

---

[160] Lüthi, *The Sino-Soviet Split*, 276.
[161] *Nikita Khrushchev 1964*, section 2, doc. 7, pp. 198–9.
[162] Ibid. section 3, doc. 32, pp. 348–56.   [163] Ibid. doc. 18, p. 311, doc. 34, p. 361.
[164] Ibid. doc. 36, p. 413.

In February 1965, Kosygin went on a mission to Vietnam and China. On 11 February he met Mao in Peking and insisted on re-establishing good relations in the name of unity for the communist movement and the struggle against their common enemy, America. However, Mao displayed no willingness to come to an agreement with the new Soviet leadership. Provocatively, he asked Kosygin to withdraw the main documents in Moscow's anti-Chinese polemic, and rejected the invitation to take part in the conference of parties in the 'socialist camp' which had already been called for March to express support for the Vietnamese struggle.[165] Mao allowed Soviet military aid for Vietnam to cross Chinese territory, but rejected any form of political cooperation. His implacable hostility discouraged further conciliatory approaches from the new leaders of the Soviet Union. Their idea that American intervention in Vietnam required a strong response was separate from their hope of opening a way to recover Peking as part of a renewed anti-imperialist drive. The meeting of communist parties in Moscow in March 1965, which the Soviets wanted as the run-up to a new conference of world communism, now sounded more a challenge than a reconciliation. The attempt to get round the obstacle through a meeting between Brezhnev and the Indonesian leader Aidit, who had greeted the fall of Khrushchev as a victory for Marxism-Leninism but refused to take part in the Moscow meeting, was not successful.[166] On the other hand, Peking continued in its efforts to create an 'anti-imperialist bloc' made up of Asian communist parties in opposition to 'peaceful coexistence' and alliances with nationalists in the Third World.[167]

However, the Maoist plan to establish Chinese influence over the war in Vietnam also proved to be unrealistic. Although the Vietnamese accepted military support from the two communist colossi, they clung on to the autonomy they had established long before. Their worst nightmare was a repetition of the international accord that divided the country in 1954. Once the rift between Moscow and Peking became public, the ideological closeness of the Vietnamese to the Chinese was quite evident, but Hanoi adopted a shrewd strategy of receiving Chinese military aid without breaking off relations with the Soviet Union. Once the American intervention came, the People's Republic of China was in the frontline supporting North Vietnam and preparing for a possible extension of the war to its own territory. However, an exclusive alliance with Peking was never considered by Ho Chi Minh or other influential members of the Vietnamese ruling group, such as Pham Van Dong and Le Duan, the party's general secretary, both aware that this would have damaged their cause.[168] In his talks with Mao in May and June of 1965, Ho

---

[165] An account of the conversation between Kosygin and Mao on 11 Feb. 1965 was published in an appendix to Radchenko, *Two Suns in the Heavens*, 227–34.

[166] K. N. Brutents, *Tridtsat' let na staroy ploshadi* (Moscow: Mezhdunarodnye otnosheniya, 1998), 262–3.

[167] L. M. Lüthi, 'Twenty-four Soviet-bloc documents on Vietnam and the Sino-Soviet split, 1964–1966', *Cold War International History Project Bulletin* 16 (2008), doc. 3, p. 373.

[168] Duiker, *Ho Chi Minh*, 537–8; Olsen, *Soviet–Vietnam Relations and the Role of China, 1949–64*, 130–2; C. Marangé, *Le communisme vietnamien (1919–1991): construction d'un état-nation entre Moscou et Pékin* (Paris: Presses de la Fondation Nationale des Sciences Politiques, 2012), 327–31.

made it clear that, unlike what had happened in the first Indochinese war, the Vietnamese were determined to maintain their autonomy even when it came to strategic and military planning.[169] In the autumn of the same year, Mao unsuccessfully exhorted Ho to form a common front against Soviet 'revisionism',[170] and Zhou failed to convince Pham Van Dong to renounce Soviet aid.[171]

Chinese pressure on Hanoi to break with Moscow would continue for a long time without achieving anything. Peking's argument that there was a risk of being 'sold' to protect Soviet interests was not unfounded. But the idea of relying solely on Chinese assistance seemed unrealistic, and provoked suspicions that the Chinese wanted to set up a permanent guerrilla war to safeguard Peking's security interests instead of a war with real possibilities of success, which could only be achieved with Soviet technology. For the Vietnamese this was a matter of realism, but they were also putting forward a revolutionary vision that did not wholly correspond to the ultra-radical Chinese one. In April 1966, Le Duan explained to Deng that the Vietnamese struggle was 'a moral obligation' for international communism, but revolutionaries, including the Chinese, should be attempting to influence and attract the 'reformist movement in the world'—which in his view meant the forces and countries that harboured a genuinely anti-imperialist spirit outside the communist movement.[172] The latent tension between the Chinese and Vietnamese strategies would soon emerge: while the former aimed at a long guerrilla war of attrition against the United States, waged without compromise, the latter followed a more essentially military inspiration, but one that did not exclude the use of diplomacy and engagement in peace negotiations.[173] Thus this ended up as a more serious disagreement, brought about by Mao Sino-centrism and Vietnamese intolerance of any Chinese attempt to dominate Indochina. Despite its massive assistance in military resources and other material aid, Chinese influence in Vietnam would decline after reaching its height from 1963 to 1965.[174] Having been contained by the Vietnamese, Chinese influence in Southeast Asia suffered a terrible blow with the destruction of the Communist Party in Indonesia. The communist attempt to take power in September 1965, encouraged by Peking, was crushed by mass repression organized by General Suharto, which massacred half a million activists. Aidit was arrested and shot two months later. The destruction of the Indonesian Communist Party deprived China of its most important ally in the movement.[175]

---

[169] Jian, *Mao's China and the Cold War*, 219.

[170] Lüthi, 'Twenty-four Soviet-bloc documents on Vietnam and the Sino-Soviet split', docs 14 and 15, pp. 385–6.

[171] O. A. Westad, C. Jian, S. Tønnesson, N. V. Tung, and J. Hershberg (eds), *77 Conversations between Chinese and Foreign Leaders on the War in Indochina, 1964–1977*, Cold War International History Project working paper no. 22 (Washington, D.C.: Woodrow Wilson Center 1998), doc. 14, p. 87.

[172] Ibid. doc. 18, p. 95.

[173] Zhai, *China and the Vietnam Wars, 1950–1975*, 168–79.

[174] Jian, *Mao's China and the Cold War*, 230–3.

[175] Mortimer, *Indonesian Communism under Sukarno*, 375–94.

The scenario of the Soviet threat in the north and American military presence in the southeast drove Mao to radicalize his own apocalyptic vision in the domestic context.[176] The Cultural Revolution, which was triggered in the summer of 1966 with radical slogans that fomented an anti-bureaucratic rebellion, appeared to propose a mass mobilization which contrasted with the Soviet Union's inertia. This was a frontal attack on Moscow's 'hegemonism'. The siege of the Soviet embassy by red guards in Peking represented one of the more sensational rituals to put across the message of the Cultural Revolution. The Soviet Union was branded as a 'social imperialist' country, governed by a 'new class' of bureaucrats who constituted the principal threat to the Chinese Revolution and world revolution. In the Maoist version, the primacy of politics generated phenomena even more radical than what had happened in the Stalinist period, and included the use of terror by means of mass ideological mobilization. Unlike Stalinism, Maoism attacked social and institutional hierarchies, opening the way to a wave of anarchism that threatened to subvert the very foundations of the state.[177]

However, the similarities between the two phenomena appear more significant than the differences. As had occurred in the Soviet Union before the war, the social earthquake provoked by militarized mobilization in the countryside was followed by cruel score-settling destined to strike at the state apparatus, the educated urban classes, and society as a whole. In less than twenty years, a third wave of civil strife swept away the very foundations of social life, following on the revolutionary era and the construction of socialism. Created in the 1950s, the Chinese camps replicated the Soviet Gulag. The result would be the consolidation of the dictatorship and the re-establishment of even more rigid hierarchies.[178] Mao's extreme plan—to reinforce his own position as the supreme leader by using as his expedient the slogan 'Fire at the headquarters'—worked perfectly. Pragmatic leaders like Liu and Deng were purged and disappeared into the detention camps, while the star of Lin Biao, the head of the army, continued to rise. He was the one who came up with the Maoist gospel, the *Little Red Book*, which consisted of quotations by President Mao.

Despite obvious differences, the Chinese Cultural Revolution eventually followed the same logic as the Soviet tragedy during the Stalinist period. It also had an important international implication, as it reflected the failure to challenge the Soviet Union for revolutionary hegemony of the communist movement in the Third World. Behind the radical relaunch of Mao as a revolutionary leader lay a retreat and a crisis. Just when it was claiming to offer an alternative model of socialism, the Maoist regime turned in on itself in a destructive spiral and ceased to engage in a genuine policy on revolutionary movements. Maoist ideology would

---

[176] Macfarquhar, *The Origins of the Cultural Revolution*, vol. 3, 364, 377.

[177] R. MacFarquhar and M. Schoenhals, *Mao's Last Revolution* (Cambridge, Mass.: Harvard University Press, 2006).

[178] For a comparison between Stalinism and Maoism, see D. Priestland, *Stalinism and the Politics of Mobilization: Ideas, Power, and Terror in Inter-war Russia* (Oxford: Oxford University Press, 2007), 416–29. On the mechanisms of repression during the Chinese Cultural Revolution, see Margolin, 'Cina: una lunga marcia nella notte', 468ff.

undergo changing fortunes and influence guerrilla movements in some regions of India such as West Bengal, as well as in Nepal, Southeast Asia—particularly the Philippines—and Peru.[179] But the People's Republic of China quickly lost its leading role in Third World revolution, which it had claimed and pursued by way of various scenarios for the global south. The Maoist challenge did not therefore manage to construct an alternative pole to the Soviet Union and European communism. The most important conflict China lost was precisely the one over influencing Vietnam, which went back to the early 1960s.

The radicalism of the Cultural Revolution and Chinese intransigence in relation to any negotiated solution of the conflict worsened the cooling relations between Hanoi and Peking, and created new opportunities for Moscow. Soviet economic and military support was probably decisive in allowing North Vietnam to resist and respond to America's military intervention. When the Vietnamese decided to start negotiations with the United States, Moscow came out as the more reasonable party. The Soviet Union carried out an intermediary role between the belligerent parties at the peace negotiations starting in the spring of 1968, which aimed to avoid the use of atomic weapons.[180] Soviet politics combined a search for greater domestic stability through increased repression to head off the aspirations for change created by de-Stalinization, and the aim of achieving strategic parity with the United States through détente and avoiding too many adventures like the nuclear crises in Berlin and Cuba. Détente with Washington came to be seen as a process of stabilizing the bipolar world order that reflected the Soviet Union's vital interests, because it would have favoured its definitive rise to the rank of superpower. The Soviets entertained the idea of the Vietnam War leading to a decisive defeat of the United States and a consequent weakening of the entire Western system. The idea would prove to be a fatal delusion, but would endure partly because it helped them to ignore the debilitating effects of the Sino-Soviet split.

America's mirror-image perception of Vietnam as the new frontier for the global containment of communism led to the opposing symbolic image, which emphasized its expansionist potential and minimized its limitations. Even after commencement of the peace negotiations, Vietnam was therefore an important factor in how the Cold War was represented, no less so than in power politics. In the West, Vietnamese communists were erroneously perceived as no more than Soviet and Chinese pawns since the Stalinist era, particularly after the communists took power in China. The idea that Indochina constituted a decisive theatre against the expansion of communism was a constant determining factor for all American presidential administrations. Washington understood the seriousness of the Sino-Soviet conflict, but this did not affect their belief that blocking the advance of communism in Southeast Asia, and avoiding the 'domino effect' remained a

---

[179] Alexander, *International Maoism in the Developing World* .
[180] I. V. Gaiduk, *The Soviet Union and the Vietnam War* (Chicago: Ivan R. Dee, 1996), 149–55.

vital imperative for defending the 'credibility' of the United States.[181] Although the monolithic image of international communism was no longer sustainable, Western assessments were linked to the idea that it had a unitary strategy. This prevented the West from understanding the full extent of international communism's lack of unity and its tendency to fragment.

Paradoxically, it was Vietnam that showed up the limitations of communist policy in the Third World. The Soviet Union's concern for the Vietnamese arrived late and primarily emerged as a result of the conflict with China. After the failure of Khrushchev's successors to re-establish an alliance with China, competition between the two communist powers was unrelenting. Moscow's massive material assistance to Hanoi sustained a strategy of attrition to test out positions of strength with the American enemy. The Soviets thus managed to establish their pre-eminence and restrict Chinese influence. But their influence in Vietnam would remain much less that it was thought to be in the West, even in the final stage of the war.[182] Whereas the American war created an enormous international sensation, the Vietnamese successfully built their resistance on the basis of anti-imperialist nationalism. Within a few years, it was clear that the United States could not win the war, in spite of disparity between the forces in the field and the massive bombing of Hanoi. Although lacking the Cubans' internationalist inspiration, the Vietnamese became the principal symbol of militant Third Worldism. Shortly before he died, Che Guevara used his romantic rhetoric to consecrate their revolutionary example by launching his famous appeal to create 'two, three, many Vietnams' to defeat imperialism. At the time this appeal touched sensitive chords everywhere and permeated the revolutionary imagination of youth in Latin America and Asia, but also in Europe. The victorious Tet offensive in January 1968 placed the Vietnamese myth at the centre of Third World discourse, far beyond the confines of the communist movement.[183] Leaving aside the mythology, however, Vietnam would remain an isolated example, despite delusions of being able to replicate it in various revolutionary movements outside Europe. The Vietnam War caused a crisis and protests in the United States and Europe, but international communism had lost its sense of a united challenge to the West in the post-colonial world.

Neither of the two communist powers demonstrated the ability to impose their guardianship on the principal protagonists of revolutionary anti-imperialism. In different ways, both Ho Chi Minh and Castro were aware that the future of their respective revolutions was linked to the need and the possibility of setting themselves a mission and creating a mythology separate from the cumbersome presence of the Soviet Union and China. Unlike the Vietnamese, Castro kept his distance from the Chinese advances, although other Cuban leaders were more inclined

---

[181] F. Logevall, 'The Indochina Wars and the Cold War, 1945–1975', in Leffler and Westad, *The Cambridge History of the Cold War*, vol. 2: *Crises and Détente* (Cambridge: Cambridge University Press, 2010), 281–304; Romero, *Storia della Guerra Fredda*, 178, 182–3.

[182] Gaiduk, *The Soviet Union and the Vietnam War*, 247.

[183] Westad, *The Global Cold War*, 192.

towards Maoism, starting with Guevara himself, who had shown himself to be strongly in agreement with the Chinese leader on the peasant based revolution in the Third World since their first meeting back in November 1960.[184] Even at the height of the argument with the Soviets over the missile crisis, the Cuban leadership chose to adopt a neutral position in the conflict between the Soviet Union and China. The subsequent rapprochement with Moscow obliged Castro to denounce Chinese 'sectarianism' in January 1964. However, the Cubans shared the concerns of the Vietnamese and many other communists over the danger of an irreparable split within the communist movement. Immediately after the fall of Khrushchev, they hoped for a reconciliation between Moscow and Peking in order to relaunch the world revolution, and offered to act as mediators between the two parties. First Carlos Rafael Rodríguez and then Guevara were sent to Peking. In February 1965 Guevara met Liu Shaoqi and Deng Xiaoping. Cuban efforts at mediation therefore took place in parallel with attempts by Khrushchev's successors on the Kosygin mission. With the Cubans as with the Soviets, Mao left no room for hope. Shortly afterwards, Fidel and Raul Castro publicly attacked the Maoist ideology.[185]

From that moment on, Castro increasingly downgraded relations with China, but avoided too close an embrace with the Soviet Union. The Soviets and their European partners provided as much operational assistance with economic development as they did training for technical and political cadres, with the aim of turning Cuba into an example for Latin American revolutionaries of how socialism could be built there. However, relations between Havana and Moscow were difficult for a long time, given that the Cubans fomented guerrilla movements without consideration for the restrictions of 'peaceful coexistence'. They were firmly convinced that the export of the revolution was the only serious deterrent against a possible American attack, and that their own model, which contrasted openly with the communist orthodox parties, was the only truly effective one in the context of endemic violence affecting the continent. The Cuban attempt to promote guerrilla warfare was frenetic, particularly in Venezuela but also in Guatemala, Colombia, Bolivia, and Argentina, and could rely on the hopes of peasants' revolutions ignited throughout Latin America by their own model. However, the theory and practice of armed violence developed by Guevara attracted and recruited new revolutionary vanguards, but did not bridge the gap between these and the peasant masses. The Cuban strategy only produced failures, facilitating a generalized violent reaction from anti-insurrectionary and reactionary forces, supported by the United States, as in the military *coup d'état* of 1964 in Brazil.[186]

---

[184] 'Sino-Cuban relations and the Cuban Missile Crisis, 1960–62: new Chinese evidence', *Cold War International History Project Bulletin* 17 and 18 (2012), doc. 3, p. 53.

[185] Y. Cheng, 'Sino-Cuban relations during the early years of the Castro regime, 1959–1966', *Journal of Cold War Studies* 9.3 (2007), 78–114. For a historical account based on PCI sources, see O. Pappagallo, *Il PCI e la rivoluzione cubana: la 'via latino-americana al socialismo' tra Moscow and Pechino (1959–1965)* (Rome: Carocci, 2009).

[186] H. Brands, *Latin America's Cold War* (Cambridge, Mass.: Harvard University Press, 2010), 59–66.

For a few years, lack of success and sullen Soviet hostility did nothing to cool Cuban ardour. In November 1964, at a secret conference of Latin-American communists, Castro clashed with the majority of delegates, influenced by Moscow, who rejected the pressure and interference coming from Cuba. The Latin American communist parties were experiencing serious internal divisions, but everywhere the pro-Cuban tendencies found themselves in the minority and were expelled. It was precisely the Soviet containment of their actions in Latin America that caused the Cuban leaders to assess the possibility of extending their revolutionary ambitions to other hotspots of anti-imperialist activity in the Third World, particularly Africa.[187] They organized a Tri-Continental Conference in Havana in January 1966 with the intention of engaging in an internationalist mission in opposition to Maoism, but also averse to any 'peaceful transition' and distinct from Soviet interests.[188] The tensions with Moscow did not go away. In June 1967 Kosygin and Castro exchanged harsh accusations, but avoided a split. The Soviets continued to brand the Cubans' strategy as 'adventurism', while the latter felt that the Soviet Union had neglected its task of protecting Cuba after the missile crisis. Castro attacked the Latin American communist parties, which he accused of having lost their revolutionary nature, and defended Guevara's decision to fight in Bolivia, which in his opinion was a laboratory for the creation of new popular parties.[189] A few months later, Guevara took on the mantle of a legendary figure, even though the failure of his revolutionary missions in Congo and Bolivia, where he died in October 1967, were probably also the product of his increasing distance from Castro.[190] From that time on, the Cubans' revolutionary drive in Latin America would recede considerably.

The conflict between the two socialist powers was at the same time indirectly favouring Yugoslavia's containment of the Soviet Union. With the birth of the non-aligned movement at the Belgrade Conference of September 1961, Tito developed a policy of relations that would not only create a protective network around Yugoslavia but also restrict the influence of the Soviet Union and the 'socialist camp' in the post-colonial world and particularly in the Mediterranean.[191] The fall of some of the most important nationalist regimes supported by the Soviet Union in 1965 and 1966—not without meddling by the United States—took on the significance of a setback. The almost simultaneous disappearance of Sukarno in Indonesia, Ben Bella in Algeria, and Nkrumah in Ghana weakened the system of alliances the Soviet Union had built up. The optimistic claim that there was a

[187] P. Gleijeses, *Conflicting Missions: Havana, Washington, and Africa, 1959-1976* (Chapel Hill, N.C.: University of North Carolina Press, 2002), 28–9, 98.

[188] Alexander, *International Maoism in the Developing World*, 42–4.

[189] 'A mystery wrapped in a riddle and kept in a sphinx: new evidence on Soviet Premier Alexei Kosygin's trip to Cuba, June 1967, and the turn in relations between Cuba and the Soviet bloc, 1967–68', *Cold War International History Project Bulletin* 17/18 (2012), doc. 2, p. 796.

[190] Skierka, *Fidel*, 224–37; J. L. Anderson, *Che Guevara: A Revolutionary Life* (New York: Grove Press, 1997).

[191] R. Allison, *The Soviet Union and the Strategy of Non-Alignment in the Third World* (Cambridge: Cambridge University Press, 1988), 22ff.

natural concurrence between the interests of the 'socialist camp' and the interests of the post-colonial countries had proved to be fundamentally flawed and superficial. None of the pro-Soviet nationalist regimes in Asia and Africa, before their demise around the middle of the decade, had actually initiated a transition coherent with that idea, nor had they provoked a 'domino effect' in their geopolitical area.[192] India maintained its pro-Soviet orientation, but had also contributed to bringing the tensions between Moscow and Peking to a head.

Only Egypt appeared to be fulfilling the expectations of a genuine strategic influence, which was principally implemented in Syria and Yemen, in a manner that justified Moscow's investment of material resources. Khrushchev's visit in May 1964 had sealed a strategic alliance with Nasser's regime, which would continue into the second half of the decade.[193] In his report to the Politburo, the Soviet leader claimed that the Egyptians were following a progressive policy perfectly in line with Soviet interests, criticized the Syrian communist Bakdash for having expressed his disagreement with 'Arab unity', and attacked the 'dogmas' of many communists on nationalism and religion. Once again Chinese competition touched a raw nerve. Khrushchev liked to remark that the Arab leaders 'do not understand the Chinese positions, while they agree with ours'.[194] It took some time for communists in Arab countries to accept reluctantly the idea that the Nasser regime represented a 'revolutionary democracy' that aimed to create a non-capitalist type of development. In early 1965 the Egyptian communist movement was dissolved and incorporated into Nasser's regime.[195]

Khrushchev's successors maintained the same strategic aims in the region, but made greater use of power politics. The humiliation Israel inflicted on Egypt in the Six Day War in June 1967 caused Moscow to consolidate its military presence in the Mediterranean and its links with the Arab world, now extended to the Baathist regimes founded on nationalist socialism in Syria and Iraq. The progress achieved would prove to be short-lived. The idea of a combination of nationalism and communism in the Arab world along Indonesian lines would never become a reality. The tendency to indulge and support the increasing pro-Palestinian and anti-Israeli radicalism did not bring appreciable results in terms of influence. The Soviet military presence, which was the first massive intervention outside the 'socialist camp', did not have lasting effects and proved to be counterproductive. After Nasser's death and Sadat's rise to power in 1970, the Soviet Union lost a decisive ally, Egypt, in a very short time, demonstrating the limitations of a strategic policy that was not supported by sufficient economic, political, and diplomatic resources.[196] It was a lesson that the Soviet leaders were unable to learn.

[192] M. E. Latham, 'The Cold War in the Third World, 1963–1975', in Leffler and Westad, *The Cambridge History of the Cold War*, vol. 2: *Crises and Détente*, 272–3.

[193] *Memoirs of Nikita Khrushchev*, vol. 3, pp. 831–54.

[194] *Prezidium*, vol. 1, doc. 310, p. 823.

[195] Ismael and El-Sa'id, *The Communist Movement in Egypt*, 121ff.; R. Ginat, *Egypt's Incomplete Revolution: Lutfi Al-Khuli and Nasser's Socialism in the 1960s* (London: Frank Cass, 1997); J. Franzen, *Red Star over Iraq: Iraqi Communism Before Saddam* (London: Hurst, 2011), 151–3.

[196] Y. Ro'i and B. Morozov, *The Soviet Union and the June 1967 Six Day War* (Stanford, Calif./Washington, D.C.: Stanford University Press/Woodrow Wilson Center, 2008).

Khrushchev's challenge in the global south by means of an alliance between the Soviet Union and the post-colonial national regimes, and between communism and anti-imperialist nationalism, was almost destroyed within a decade. The 'socialist camp' had lost its cohesion precisely because of the impact of decolonization. The split between Moscow and Peking compromised the chances of expansion. Relations between the Soviet Union and China had plummeted into a state of permanent tension, and generated a mutual policy of containment. Though the challenge from China for control of the communist movement outside Europe and the leadership of world revolution did not achieve its aims, the consequences of the conflict between the Soviet Union and China were very serious. The Maoist scenario of encirclement of the capitalist metropolis presupposed a hegemony China was not capable of exercising in the post-colonial world, where nationalism maintained its evident primacy over communism. The tendency of the Chinese to claim a revolutionary birthright, an ideological centrality, and a strategic supremacy—similar to their Soviet antagonist's modus operandi—compromised their attempts to increase their influence. But China affected the Soviet Union's principal strategic decisions. Competition with Peking was a thorn in Moscow's flesh throughout the 1960s. It exacerbated the latent contradictions in de-Stalinization and the policy of 'peaceful coexistence'. It forced the Soviets to make every effort to maintain their leadership of the movement. It restricted their freedom of action in bipolar relations and forced them to adopt militant policies in the Third World.[197]

To some extent, the Soviet Union found itself 'a prisoner of international communism', after having been its mistress.[198] But the problem was not only the restrictions imposed on Soviet policy by the conflict with China. The impossibility of any reconciliation, and thus of restoring the unity of international communism, left a more profound mark. The very notion of international communism was worn out, and no longer expressed the profile of a strong political player. The increasing differentiation between various communist forces and experiences revealed cultural and political fragmentation much more than a plurality capable of following a common mission. Soviet authority had suffered one blow after another since Stalin's death. But no authority could replace that of the Soviet Union. At the end of the 1960s, neither of the competing variants of post-Stalinist communism, Soviet or Chinese, exerted an attraction and influence comparable with those of international communism even in the preceding decade. This simple truth was laid bare by the impact of 1968.

---

[197] J. Friedman, 'Soviet policy in the developing world and the Chinese challenge in the 1960s', *Cold War History* 10.2 (2010).

[198] A. B. Ulam, *The Communists: The Story of Power and Lost Illusions 1948–1991* (New York: Scribner, 1992), 173.

6

Time of Crisis (1968–1991)

Faced with the increasing danger that socialism is dislodged from one of the countries in the socialist community, we cannot, comrades, lock ourselves up in our own national apartments. This would be a betrayal of the interests of communism. Communism develops and exists only as an international movement. All its victories and all its conquests were due to this.

Leonid Brezhnev, 14 July 1968

To my mind, Stalin is still alive. The main tendency in today's world is revolution.... There's the possibility that the great powers start a world war. But no one dares start it, because of a few atomic bombs.

Mao Zedong to Le Duan, 11 May 1970

Socialism means the elimination of poverty. Pauperism is not socialism, and still less is it communism.

Deng Xiaoping, 30 June 1984

It is now impossible to examine global development solely from the point of view of the struggle between two opposing social systems.

Mikhail Gorbachev, 4 November 1987

1968 AND THE PRAGUE SPRING

Long described as the spectacular year in which revolution came to the West, 1968 was instead a historical transition towards the crisis of communism. The Soviet myth, which had occupied a key space in both the European and non-European imagination for about half a century, played any part in the first global movement of the post-war period.[1] This transition was obscured by the existence of replacement mythologies, starting with the Third Worldist one. Having resulted from the impact of decolonization and bringing together various cultural trends in a motley composition of rebellious yearnings, aversion to the Cold War, and moral condemnation of colonialism, Third Worldism became a mobilizing ideology

[1] C. Fink, P. Gassert, and D. Junker (eds), *1968: The World Transformed* (Cambridge: Cambridge University Press, 1998).

in the West just at the time that international communism was showing its first cracks. Its good luck was assisted by the tendency of the United States to support military and paramilitary dictatorships in the Third World; America sacrificed its progressive and liberal role in order to contain communism. The American policy on intervention in the Third World created a space for protest that embraced a much wider section of public opinion beyond those under the influence of the communist movement. A wave of political protest such as the one triggered by the American war in Vietnam would have been inconceivable at the time of the Korean War.[2] This did not mean that international communism was close to victory, but rather that the Cold War was losing its psychological grip on the new generations in Europe and elsewhere.[3] Vietnam was more important as a symbol of student protest in European and American universities than as a means by which communist-inspired movements could assert themselves. In reality, the Third Worldist mobilization indirectly marked the collapse of the pillar sustaining Soviet mythologies—the loss of the revolutionary state's centrality as represented by the USSR.

Many of the followers of the 'New Left' in Europe were in search of a new homeland, deluding themselves that the Cuban or Chinese Revolution could give rise to a socialism freed of the shackles of bureaucracy and technocratic tendencies, which were by then the hallmark of Soviet socialism. It was a delusion that replicated the mechanisms of the prewar Soviet myths. Old and new advocates of the European radical left, such as Sartre and Foucault, were fascinated by the Maoist Cultural Revolution, or rather by what they thought it represented.[4] Just as had occurred many years earlier under Stalin, intellectual blindness generated by political faith and the idea of seeing one's own dreams realized closed their eyes to the violence and mass repression that Mao was seeking a few years after the mass slaughter his regime had inflicted on rural China. Like every case of history repeating itself, the myth of the Cultural Revolution portrayed in the West was that of events as tragic as they were farcical, because they demonstrated an inability to learn from the past, but also because they occurred in the 1960s, when a dynamic, consumerist and welfare-based capitalism was offering much less fertile ground for the eschatological fantasies of 'a world turned upside down'. It was no coincidence that, unlike the Soviet mythology of the past, the Maoist one had few converts and ran out of steam within a few years.

As Tony Judt observed, Marxism was a 'secular religion' of the time, but only for those tendencies that could keep themselves distinct from Soviet orthodoxy.[5] Marxist thinkers most in vogue were the outsiders of communist history, such as Luxemburg, Lukács, and Gramsci. Conceived as a response to the ossification of

[2] O. A. Westad, *The Global Cold War: Third World Interventions and the Making of Our Times* (Cambridge: Cambridge University Press, 2005), 190–2.

[3] F. Romero, *Storia della Guerra Fredda: l'ultimo conflitto per l'Europa* (Turin: Einaudi, 2009), 172–3, 196.

[4] R. Wolin, *The Wind from the East: French Intellectuals, the Cultural Revolution, and the Legacy of the 1960s* (Princeton, N.J.: Princeton University Press, 2010).

[5] T. Judt, *Postwar: A History of Europe since 1945* (New York: Penguin Press, 2005), 401.

Marxism-Leninism, the relaunch of Marxism amongst Western European intellectuals implied a perceived deficit of credibility in the centre of the 'socialist camp'. The critique of the Western establishment in radical and libertarian cultures was not oriented towards international communism, principally because it was perceived as a mirror-image establishment that was even more exclusive and hierarchical, but also because it did not possess a vocabulary capable of reliably describing the complexity of a world no longer defined solely by the Cold War. Political protest ended up challenging the communist world by reviving the anti-bureaucratic theories of dissidents more or less inspired by sources of a Trotskyist or socialist stamp, such as the ex-Yugoslavian leader Djilas, author (while he was in Tito's prisons) of a pamphlet attacking the new technocratic communist class, or the philosopher of the Frankfurt school, Herbert Marcuse, who criticized Soviet Marxism and the 'totalitarianism' of advanced industrial societies, both capitalist and communist.[6] Such theories would display a breadth and a staying power inversely proportional to their immediate fortune, but the forcefulness of the protest that motivated them would last and reconnect with the anti-totalitarian concepts of liberal origin. In Central and Eastern Europe, the countercultures of the 1960s remained underground but did not follow very different trajectories. The idea of a return to Leninist purity aimed at uniting communism and freedom, which was widespread amongst intellectuals, provoked anti-authoritarian criticism of the official world for being the remaining Stalinist legacy that was still clinging on.

The spontaneous mass libertarian campaign that shook the European capitals in 1968 crossed the Iron Curtain and manifested itself in different ways in Paris and Rome just as in Belgrade, Warsaw, and Prague. This mobilization, which lacked clear objectives, was based on generic anti-authoritarian slogans, tended towards hyper-ideological language, and generated violent and anarchical repercussions. However, it did give rise to a protest from below against the Cold War order, and brought on stage a youth culture largely freed from the identities that had regimented Europe for two decades.[7] Starting with feminism, the new movements broke with tradition and the established forms of the European left. For the first time since the 1920s, young European revolutionaries no longer belonged to the communist movement, even when they called themselves Marxists.[8] The case of Giangiacomo Feltrinelli—the multimillionaire bibliophile and publisher of Pasternak's *Doctor Zhivago* in spite of Soviet censorship, who shifted from his communist identity to that of neo-revolutionary romanticism and further to the extreme choice of terrorism—was very much the exception and not the rule.[9] To communist eyes, the rebellious students appeared to be naive romantics or

---

[6] M. Djilas, *The New Class: An Analysis of the Communist System* (New York: Praeger, 1957); H. Marcuse, *Soviet Marxism: A Critical Analysis* (New York: Columbia University Press, 1958).

[7] J. Suri, *Power and Protest: Global Revolution and the Rise of Détente* (Cambridge, Mass.: Harvard University Press, 2003).

[8] G. Eley, *Forging Democracy: The History of the Left in Europe, 1850–2000* (Oxford: Oxford University Press, 2002), 350–3, 378–81.

[9] C. Feltrinelli, *Senior Service* (Milan: Feltrinelli, 1999).

theatrical revolutionaries—in any event, outside the main revolutionary tradition of the century. 'It almost seemed', Hobsbawm recalled, 'that although using the same vocabulary, we were not speaking the same language.'[10] The responses from the communist world were vacillating and contradictory. The main Western communist parties took up the ideological challenge, and managed, at least in part, to reabsorb the movement and sometimes even profited in terms of their consensus. The Soviet Union and the communist regimes in the East thought they could profit from the disorder provoked by the movements in Western societies. Their intelligence services got to work infiltrating groups more inclined to political violence, with the intention of destabilizing the European democratic states. There was no lack of osmosis between Western activists disillusioned by their parties' 'revisionism', groupings inspired by Third World guerrilla movements, and training networks provided by regimes in Eastern Europe.[11] But overall, the movements of 1968 were beyond the control of historical communism.

In the communist world, the protest expressed itself through aspirations and the need for freedom which referred back to their experience of being separated from the rest of Europe and to the legacy of Sovietization as a civil conflict that had never really been pacified. The new page of anti-totalitarian insubordination and imperial repression which was written in 1968 recreated a cyclical pattern of criticism, recalling the dramatic precedent of 1953–6. The destinies of the European world were seemingly more and more divergent. While in Western Europe young people were challenging the ruling classes, demanding new rights and calling for the imagination to take power, in Central and Eastern Europe they were still fighting unsuccessfully for basic human and civil rights. In reality, the division in Europe had lessened. The communist regimes' promises of economic competition with the West had opened up comparisons on the basis of prosperity and social expectations, which started to unwittingly erode the culture of sacrifice.[12] The previous generation's demands for freedom were relaunched in the new language of youth counter-cultures, revealing a circulation of ideas that had not existed in the past. The myths of Western mass culture, along a spectrum that ran from Marilyn Monroe to Bob Dylan, forced a breach in the youthful imaginations of Eastern Europe and the Soviet Union, having already overwhelmed communists in the West.[13] On the other hand, the symbolic message that emanated from the Berlin Wall was that of a separate world that was closing in on itself and thus exposing its inner fragility and its cultural isolation. Precisely because of this, 1968 was not just

[10] E. J. Hobsbawm, *Interesting Times: A Twentieth-Century Life* (London: Allen Lane, 2002), 277.

[11] C. Andrew and V. Mitrokhin, *The Mitrokhin Archive: The KGB in Europe and the West* (London: Allen Lane The Penguin Press, 1999); G. Fasanella and A. Franceschini, *Che cosa sono le BR: le radici, la storia, il presente* (Milan: Rizzoli, 2004).

[12] E. S. Rosenberg, 'Consumer capitalism and the end of the Cold War', in M. P. Leffler and O. A. Westad (eds), *The Cambridge History of the Cold War*, vol. 3: *Endings* (Cambridge: Cambridge University Press, 2010), 497.

[13] V. Zubok, *Zhivago's Children: The Last Russian Intelligentsia* (Cambridge, Mass.: Harvard University Press, 2009), 318; S. Gundle, *I comunisti italiani tra Hollywood e Mosca: la sfida della cultura di massa (1943–1991)* (Florence: Giunti, 1995), 235ff.

further evidence of a lack of national legitimacy in the communist regimes set up in Central and Eastern Europe; it was also an early sign of the decline in the allure of historical communism, particularly when it came to the generations born after the Second World War.

In six months, the Prague Spring and its repression determined the fate of European communism forever. Unlike the events of 1956, the original impulse came from within the establishment. The transition from Antonín Novotný to Alexander Dubček in December 1967 was not the result of popular pressure or a spontaneous uprising, but came with Moscow's blessing as an attempt to side-line an unpopular figure even by Soviet standards and introduce minor reforms to the economic system. But the new leadership almost immediately opened the way to political reform, which in a few months was already revealing the reactive potential that existed in society. Matured over the long season of hopes and frustrations that started with repercussions from de-Stalinization and the repressions in Central and Eastern Europe, what emerged in Prague was nothing less than a project of far-reaching reforms. The interaction between the commencement of radical reforms—the first of which was the abolition of censorship—and a reawakening of society that put the party's monopoly of power at risk, very soon produced a reaction. The Soviets and various communist leaders in Eastern Europe loudly demanded an end to a process considered dangerously contagious.[14]

The Czechoslovak question was internationalized at a meeting of representatives of the European socialist countries, with the exception of the Romanians, held in Dresden on 23 March 1968. Dubček tried in vain to present the reforms as a revival of the party's 'leading role' and an attempt at 'socialist democracy' that would be useful to the communist movement. He was subjected to a continuous barrage of criticisms and accusations. Brezhnev declared that the Soviet Union could not remain indifferent to the risks of losing control and of a 'counter-revolution' for reasons of 'an internationalist nature' and 'security for socialist countries'. The harshest tones came from Gomułka and Ulbricht, who raised the spectre of 'counter-revolution' as an imperialist plot.[15] The crisis from then on became deeper and deeper, without the ways in which the question was posed undergoing substantial changes. The Soviet ruling group held closely to the view that Czechoslovakia was a breeding ground for destabilization fomented by the West, which had to be defused. The 'hawks' of Eastern Europe, in East Germany, Poland, and Bulgaria, contributed to the fear of a possible defection from the Warsaw Pact. Concern over a Czechoslovak contagion grew not only in Eastern and Central Europe, but also in the Soviet Union. The ruling group formed around Dubček carried through the reforms in spite of increasing intimidation to make them reverse the changes, but they did seek mediation which had no real chance of success. In his talks

---

[14] M. Kramer, 'The Czechoslovak Crisis and the Brezhnev Doctrine', in Fink et al., *1968: The World Transformed*, 111–74.

[15] S. Karner et al., *Prager Frühling: Das internationale Krisenjahr 1968. Dokumente* (Vienna: Böhlau, 2008), doc. 75, pp. 411–506: J. Navrátil (ed.), *The Prague Spring 1968* (Budapest: Central European University Press, 2006), doc. 14, pp. 64–72.

with Brezhnev on 4–5 May, Dubček defended his decision to provide a political response to economic and social problems but fatally accepted the minefield proposed by the Soviets, that of combating the 'anti-socialist forces' even in the name of his allies' interests and of those of the 'world communist movement'.[16] At his meeting with the four most loyal leaders three days later, Brezhnev stated that his mind was made up: the Czechoslovak question would have to be resolved in the context of the 'ideological struggle between imperialism and socialism'. Gomułka made a personal attack on Dubček and declared that being a member of the leadership of KSČ was not enough to consider oneself a communist: the dividing line beyond which lay revisionism could always be crossed by anyone.[17]

The decisive moment was the meeting of five member-states of the Warsaw Pact held without the Czechoslovaks in Warsaw on 14–15 July. Gomułka used the tried and tested formula of bourgeois social-democratic degeneration to interpret the events in Czechoslovakia, and set them in the context of the new interaction between the two Europes, while acknowledging that the Iron Curtain had lost some of its efficacy. In his opinion, the 'counter-revolution' in Europe 'was unthinkable according to all the classical models', including the Hungarian one in 1956, but it was manifesting itself all the same in Prague in a new 'peaceful way'. The main point that had to be understood was the external influence of the capitalist world, which unlike in the past was mainly counting on the prospects of reform and 'democratic socialism', and deploying unheard-of resources in mass communications. This was even more serious, Gomułka made clear, because the communist movement was threatened by centrifugal forces and mistaken concepts ('We have got the lot: revisionism, anarchism, nationalism—all tendencies that exist within the international communist movement'). This may have been the new scenario, but the response of the communist leaders repeated the methods and instruments invariably adopted to maintain a monopoly of force. Gomułka's report assigned a central role to the integrity of the Warsaw Pact. Even Kádár, the dove in the group, came on side, although he earned a bitter scolding from Ulbricht for having neglected the international 'psychological war' and for talk of 'revisionist' forces similar to the Yugoslav model rather than 'counter-revolutionary' ones. For his part, Brezhnev declared that Czechoslovakia was leaving the 'socialist camp', and branded the 'spring' as a threat to 'socialist positions' in Europe and the world.[18]

The consensus reached amongst the five allies produced a 'letter from Warsaw' to the Czech leadership which sounded like an ultimatum and heralded the use of outside force. The letter was made known to 'fraternal parties' and made public on 20 July.[19] At the same time, Moscow declared itself opposed to the French initiative to urgently convene a conference of European communist parties to avoid

---

[16] Ibid. doc. 28, pp. 114–25.

[17] Karner et al., *Prager Frühling*, doc. 77, pp. 514, 554; Navrátil, *The Prague Spring 1968*, doc. 31.

[18] Karner et al., *Prager Frühling*, doc. 82, pp. 576–654; Navrátil, *The Prague Spring 1968*, doc. 52, pp. 212–33.

[19] *Chekhoslovatskii krizis 1967–1969gg. v dokumentakh TsK KPSS* (Moscow: Rosspen, 2010), doc. 58, p. 128, doc. 61, pp. 136–7, doc. 62, pp. 138–9.

the crisis spiralling out of control, and even Dubček failed to support it.[20] The Bratislava Declaration signed on 3 August by the leaders of the socialist countries, including Czechoslovakia, appeared to be a truce, but its emphasis on internationalist responsibilities in defence of the 'socialist community' did not bode well. At the Politburo of 6 August it was agreed 'to implement' the positions expressed in the declaration.[21] On 13 August the CPSU sent all the communist parties a statement that emphasized the declaration, but particularly stressed the fact that 'anti-socialist forces' had not yet been eradicated by the Czech leadership.[22] Three days later Brezhnev sent Dubček a threatening letter, which was followed by a stormy telephone conversation.[23] The final decision to invade was taken immediately afterwards. The other key figure—no less important than Brezhnev— was the chief of the KGB, Andropov, who back in 1956 had influenced Soviet decision-making whilst he was ambassador in Budapest.[24]

The option of armed intervention prevailed even though the consensus of the communist movement—outside the rhetoric coming from the Kremlin—was in no way comparable to the consensus in October–November 1956. The Soviets and their allies were quite aware of this. From April the East Germans considered the Romanians and, above all, the Italians to be amongst those who were using the events in Czechoslovakia 'to justify their own non-Marxist opinions'.[25] Longo, the leader of the PCI, met Dubček in early May to express his support for the reforms.[26] Tito had already notified Brezhnev of his own support for the Prague Spring.[27] At the Warsaw meeting in July, Brezhnev complained of the 'mistaken interpretations' of events in Czechoslovakia held in the French, Italian, and British parties.[28] Immediately afterwards, he expressed his concerns to the central committee of the CPSU over the widespread 'doubts' and antagonism to the initiatives coming from the 'five' (Warsaw Pact members)—with the Yugoslavs the first amongst the doubters.[29] The pressure from Moscow to garner support for the 'Warsaw letter' was unsuccessful. On 23 July the leader of the PCF, Waldeck Rochet, rejected the Soviet request and denounced the 'letter' as interference in the domestic affairs of the Czechoslovak party.[30] Although the Italian communists proved to be more diplomatic than the French, there was no question of their support for the use of force. Equally predictable was the hostility of the Chinese, who condemned the 'bourgeois' nature of the Prague Spring, but were

---

[20] Karner et al., *Prager Frühling*, doc. 165, p. 1252; *Chekhoslovatskii krizis*, doc. 64, pp. 144–5; Navrátil, *The Prague Spring 1968*, doc. 58, pp. 261–3.

[21] *Chekhoslovatskii krizis*, doc. 72, pp. 160–1.   [22] Ibid. doc. 76, pp. 170–3.

[23] Ibid. doc. 77, pp. 174–5.

[24] V. Zubok, *A Failed Empire: The Soviet Union from Stalin to Gorbachev* (Chapel Hill, N.C.: University of North Carolina Press, 2007), 208.

[25] Karner et al., *Prager Frühling*, doc. 162, p. 1218.

[26] Navrátil, *The Prague Spring 1968*, doc. 29, pp. 126–8.   [27] Ibid. doc. 32, p. 144.

[28] Karner, *Prager Frühling*, doc. 82, p. 626.

[29] Navrátil, *The Prague Spring 1968*, doc. 56, pp. 256–7.

[30] Navrátil, *The Prague Spring 1968*, doc. 59, p. 264.

ready to accuse Moscow of both ineptitude and imperialism.[31] At the beginning of August, the Bulgarian leader Todor Zhivkov expressed his concerns over the ability of the 'socialist camp' to hold together, and observed: 'China has broken away and the same is true of Albania, and the situation is only a little better in the case of Cuba, Romania and Yugoslavia'. 'Revisionism' had been established in the Western parties: the Italian one was no longer 'a genuine Marxist-Leninist party' and the French one was 'under the influence of Zionism'. This situation governed by centrifugal forces induced Zhivkov to consider it even more important 'to bring Czechoslovakia back onto the road to socialism'.[32] They came to similar conclusions in Moscow. The Soviet leaders and their closest allies decided to invade Czechoslovakia without the support of the main communist parties outside the 'socialist camp', as they believed that the use of force was justified by higher interests. But this was tantamount to exposing the fragmentation of the international communist movement. Ultimately, the leaders of the 'socialist camp' were involved as members of the Warsaw Pact and not as exponents of the movement.[33] The practical consequences were not significant. The nuance did, however, appear symbolic of a shift in Moscow's outlook from the legitimizing viewpoint of a political movement to that of an alliance of states that had been brought about by the conflict with Peking. This did not mean soft-pedalling the ideological doctrine of the 'socialist camp', but rather its codification and explicit use in the power politics of the Soviet Union.

The Soviet decision to replicate armed intervention in an Eastern European country in the summer of 1968 was taken in less dramatic circumstances that those of 1956. The reforming group led by Dubček had shown its will to be inflexible when it came to the implementation of the reforms, and was not going to be intimidated by threats from the Soviets and other members of the Warsaw Pact. With hindsight, Dubček would justify his decision not to become another Kádár or even end up like Gomułka, who had been transformed from the man who stood up for national defence in 1956 into a counter-reformist hawk.[34] But the change was occurring peacefully and did not herald a break with the system of Soviet alliances. In spite of this, Moscow was equally fearful of such an outcome, and was finding support from within the Czechoslovak party. As in 1956, the bogey of counter-revolution combined with an external enemy, involving democratization along with a break with the 'socialist camp', was the real leitmotiv of repression. Unlike in the past, the Soviet troops were not alone when they invaded Czechoslovakia during the night of 21 August 1968, but accompanied by troops from the other Warsaw Pact members with the exception of Romania. The

[31] O. A. Westad, C. Jian, S. Tønnesson, N. V Tung, and J. Hershberg (eds), *77 Conversations Between Chinese and Foreign Leaders on the War in Indochina*, Cold War International History Project, working paper no. 22 (Washington, D.C.: Woodrow Wilson Center, 1998), doc. 34, p. 128.

[32] Navrátil, *The Prague Spring 1968*, doc. 69, pp. 317–18.

[33] V. Mastny, 'The Warsaw Pact as history', in V. Mastny and M. Byrne (eds), *A Cardboard Castle? An Inside History of the Warsaw Pact, 1955–1991* (Budapest: Central European University Press, 2005), 36.

[34] Ibid. doc. 67, pp. 304–5.

reforming leaders were humiliated and taken to Moscow, where they were forced to sign a protocol that amounted to an act of submission. In exchange, they were allowed to remain in power for a few more months, but the Prague Spring had been terminated together with the promise of 'socialism with a human face'. Shortly afterwards, Brezhnev announced the doctrine that would bear his name, which was based on the principle of interdependence between the domestic institutions and the foreign policy of the 'socialist camp'. The interests of the Soviet state became openly identified with the defence of the 'socialist community' against the threat of destabilization.[35]

In the short term, it appeared that the Soviet Union's decision to take repressive action had been successful. The danger of contagion in Eastern Europe had been averted. The 'Brezhnev Doctrine' asserted the concept of restricted sovereignty under the auspices of most of the regimes in the 'socialist camp'. Western reactions to the invasion were harsher in their rhetoric than in their substance, leaving the way open to international détente. The negative reactions within the communist movement had already been accounted for. Moscow implemented a well worked-out strategy. The break with Peking, which denounced the imperial behaviour of the Soviet Union, was entirely expected. Even the opposition of Belgrade to the theory and practice of restricted sovereignty, which contained the spectre of a Soviet threat for Yugoslavia, was largely to be expected. The Soviets concentrated their efforts on dealing with the critical stance of the Western communist parties. The PCF and the PCI, as well as a group of minor parties—British, Norwegian, and Belgian—had publicly expressed their disapproval and started a dynamic that could have created a Western communist entity. There was a febrile series of meetings during the months that followed August 1968. Soviet pressure produced a result. The French soon took a few steps back and withdrew their more serious criticisms. They accepted the interpretation of the Czechoslovak 1968 as a 'counter-revolution' more or less the same as Hungary in 1956. The Italians turned out to be the harder nut to crack, and held firm to their link with the Prague Spring, without however dramatizing the situation—in fact they attempted a diplomatic reconciliation. Everyone acknowledged the normalization of Czechoslovakia, which would remove Dubček and replace him with Gustáv Husák in April 1969. Neither the French nor the Italians came to see the invasion of Czechoslovakia as an event that questioned their loyalty to the Soviet Union, although the ways in which they interpreted its significance would take different paths. The PCF went back to cultivating its own demand for a national tradition together with pro-Soviet internationalism, and this was bolstered by the replacement of Rochet by Georges Marchais in June 1969. The PCI, on the other hand, accentuated the idea of 'unity in diversity', in the conviction that this formula best served the interests of not just the national party but also the international movement.[36] Ultimately the Soviets could content themselves in the knowledge that

---

[35] Kramer, 'The Czechoslovak Crisis and the Brezhnev Doctrine'; M. J. Ouimet, *The Rise and Fall of the Brezhnev Doctrine in Soviet Foreign Policy* (Chapel Hill, N.C.: University of North Carolina Press, 2003).

[36] M. Bracke, *Which Socialism, Whose Détente?* (Budapest: Central European University Press, 2007).

things could have gone worse. Their link with European communism remained strong and sustained through traditional financial and organizational channels. Their financial donations, which for some time had clearly treated the PCF and the PCI preferentially, were not suspended and would constitute a powerful instrument for asserting their influence over the decade that followed.[37]

Nevertheless, the apparent success of Soviet force in Czechoslovakia would be short-lived and the product of a myopic policy. In the long term, the legacy of the 1968 would be devastating. In one of the meetings of the 'five' preparing the invasion, Gomułka declared that the European communist parties had a special responsibility because 'we are the force that gives prominence to socialism and represents socialism to the world. We are the ones who represent it, and not China, Cuba or Korea.'[38] The Polish leader thus unwittingly revealed a profound truth, whose meaning was the opposite of what he had intended. Central and Eastern Europe did not just constitute the Soviet Union's sphere of influence. The 'people's democracies' were an integral part of the socialist model, and in many ways the most advanced one. But their image in Europe had been compromised in 1956 and could not be considered rehabilitated by the timid economic reforms introduced principally in Kádár's Hungary or by the austere regime in the Prussian tradition that Ulbricht had established in East Germany.[39] In light of the technological and economic resources at the disposal of the East European countries, the possibility that their limited integration into Comecon would allow them to sustain the competition between the 'two systems' seemed problematic, at the very least. In the following years, the growing use of the expression 'real existing socialism', as a self-definition used to counter the protests within and outside the movement, would increasingly sound like an implicit admission that the challenge of the communist utopia had become much less ambitious, even in its material version. At the same time, the precedent of Sovietization constituted a burden because of the instability it brought, and because of its associations with oppression and lack of popularity, which had been underscored by the events of 1968.

However much it was repressed or sacrificed on the altar of coexistence in the European and Western conscience, the question became a millstone. The reality of Asian or Cuban communism engaged more easily with youthful imagination or was more functional to anti-imperialist discourse, but the cumbersome presence of 'real socialism' in Europe and its inability to reform itself had to count more in the course of time. The 'Third Worldist' revolutionary movements did not make up for the collapse of the Soviet myth in Europe after 1956, and still less after 1968. The

---

[37] V. Riva, *Oro da Mosca: i finanziamenti sovietici al PCI dalla Rivoluzione d'ottobre al crollo dell'URSS* (Milan: Mondadori, 1999), esp. docs 48, 51, 61, 79, 89, 91, 105, 116, 129, 141, 147; D. Volkogonov, *The Rise and Fall of the Soviet Empire: Political Leaders from Lenin to Gorbachev* (London: HarperCollins, 1998), 341.

[38] Karner et al., *Prager Frühling*, doc. 82, p. 592.

[39] F. Fejtö, *Storia delle democrazie popolari* (2 vols, Milan: Bompiani, 1977), vol. 2, pp. 145–8; J. Connelly, 'The paradox of East German Communism: from non-Stalinism to neo-Stalinism?' in V. Tismaneanu (ed.), *Stalinism Revisited: The Establishment of Communist Regimes in East-Central Europe* (Budapest: Central European University Press, 2009), 188–93.

suppression of the Prague Spring was a fatal blow for the feelings of a generation that had had hopes for de-Stalinization and a better form of socialism, even in the Soviet Union.[40] The hopes of reform did not die in the anti-conformist and intellectual milieu in Eastern Europe, but doubts that Prague might be the end of the line, rather than the starting point for substantial political change, began to multiply and firm themselves up. Much more than Gomułka's unconscious prophecy, Dubček's conscious one at his first meeting with Brezhnev after the invasion hit the target: 'As a communist who shares a large part of the responsibility for future events, I'm certain that not only in Czechoslovakia but also in Europe and in the entire communist movement this act will cause us to suffer our greatest defeat and will lead to a collapse and profound split in the ranks of the communist parties.'[41] What Dubček could not have seen was that international communism not only ran the risk of more splits, but was already experiencing a profound crisis which reached the point of no return in August 1968.

THE BREAK-UP OF THE MOVEMENT

As with the aftermath of Hungarian invasion, the convening of a world conference of communist parties for June 1969 appeared to be moving towards decreeing the end of the crisis in Czechoslovakia and the rediscovered unity of the communist movement, or rather what was left of it. In reality, the third conference of world communism had a long and difficult history behind it—one that had gone through various postponements. Both Khrushchev and his successors had attempted in vain to involve the Chinese and obtain an act of submission. No concrete results came of such attempts. Following the talks in Moscow in March 1965, a series of meetings of parties loyal to the USSR demonstrated that the Soviets were determined to gather together all the available forces, which were numerically higher, in order to show that they had emerged as the winners in the conflict with Peking. In October 1966, the Soviets formally proposed that a new world conference should be convened, and set up a series of consultations. The conference of communist parties on European security held in Karlovy Vary in 1967 emphasized the decision of Moscow and the Warsaw Pact to adopt a policy of international détente. Communist party delegates meeting in Budapest in February–March 1968, before the crisis in Czechoslovakia broke out, established that the world conference should be held before the end of that year, even in the absence of delegations from Vietnam, Korea, and Cuba, as well as China and the other Asian parties under its influence. At the beginning of April, Brezhnev declared before the Plenum of the Central Committee of the CPSU that Mao's isolation was now complete and that any reservations about the agenda were negligible—for example

[40] Zubok, *Zhivago's Children*, 294–6; R. D. English, *Russia and the Idea of the West: Gorbachev, Intellectuals, and the End of the Cold War* (New York: Columbia University Press, 2000), 110–15.
[41] Karner et al., *Prager Frühling*, doc. 106, p. 800; Navrátil, *The Prague Spring 1968*, doc. 116, p. 467.

the concerns of the PCI and the CPGB about avoiding too much insistence on divisions within the movement.[42] The invasion of Czechoslovakia caused the date to slip further. The significance of the world conference was thus unexpectedly emphasized by the concurrence of the authoritarian normalization in Prague and the sudden escalation of the conflict between Moscow and Peking in March 1969, with armed clashes on the Ussuri river. The episode marked a step change from the political and ideological conflict to a power struggle between the two giants of global communism. From that moment, the mutual sense of being under threat drove both to seek a diplomatic rapport with their common enemy, America.[43] The border clashes between the Soviet Union and China marked a new phase in the history of the Cold War, and turned the third conference of world communism into the chosen venue for ratifying the schism.

The Soviets emphasized the theme of anti-imperialism, with the obvious aim of reacting to the Maoist polemic and re-establishing their authority on the subject. But Brezhnev set out a clear continuity with the policy orientations decided upon at the time of Khrushchev. 'Peaceful coexistence', economic and international 'balance of power', and the possibility of avoiding nuclear war were identified as the essential elements for a communist. The harsh criticisms of the Chinese, who were accused of underestimating the dangers of war and having divided the movement, followed a well-known script. The alignment with Moscow was massive. The line-up of over seventy parties revealed the Chinese challenge for the leadership of the movement to be a fiasco. Czechoslovakia was reduced to a question now resolved, thanks to the internationalist solidarity of the other countries in the 'socialist camp'. The only discordant note amongst the Eastern Europeans was Ceauşescu's speech, which reasserted Romanian autonomy. Of the most important parties, only the PCI raised the 'Czechoslovak question'. The leader of the Italian delegation, Enrico Berlinguer, spoke of a crisis of internationalism and reasserted his disapproval of the Soviet invasion. The PCI violated the ritual unanimity with its refusal to sign the final document in its entirety.[44] The Soviets were willing, however, to accept this compromise. Unsurprisingly, Brezhnev expressed his satisfaction to the Plenum of the Central Committee of the CPSU, adopting the usual triumphalist rhetoric. He interpreted the conference as an expression of the broad approval for the normalization of Czechoslovakia and a censure of China's positions. He did not stint in his criticisms of the Italian communists and in his praise of the French ones, but in his eyes the most important thing was the presence of the Western delegations, which made it clear that the invasion of Czechoslovakia had not created new heresies.[45] Such a balance was self-serving, at the very least. The ritual unity obscured the reality. Leaving aside China and

[42] RGANI, fo. 2, op. 3, d. 95.
[43] S. Radchenko, 'The Sino-Soviet split', in M. P. Leffler and O. A. Westad (eds), *The Cambridge History of the Cold War*, vol. 2: *Crises and Détente* (Cambridge: Cambridge University Press, 2010), 367.
[44] APCI, Fondo Paolo Bufalini, b. 53, fasc. 49 and 50.
[45] RGANI, fo. 2, op. 3, d. 159.

Albania, Yugoslavia, North Vietnam, North Korea, and most of the Asian parties had not taken part in the proceedings. Even the Cubans did not send a delegation, but only an observer. Although Castro had publicly approved the invasion of Czechoslovakia and expressed contempt for Dubček's 'revisionism', he had also provoked the Soviets by asking them if they would have behaved in the same manner in the event of an American intervention in Cuba.[46] Compared with the previous post-Stalinist conferences, the overall tenor was one of fragmentation. That is without taking into account the dwindling memberships outside the 'socialist camp', principally because of the destruction of the Indonesian Communist Party, but evidently linked to the damage caused by the Sino-Soviet conflict. The conference of 1969 would be the last gathering of world communism.

At the time, Western intellectuals and analysts had observed that international communism was running out of vitality. An involved observer such as the Marxist historian Eric Hobsbawm wrote that the international communist movement had 'on the whole ceased to exist as such', and that it was by then difficult to understand 'the immense strength its members drew upon knowing they were soldiers in a unique international army' in the not too distant past.[47] From a very different viewpoint, a non-Marxist political scientist such as Alexander Dallin noted that 'international communism' was now just a myth, which had become even more elusive during the Vietnam War because of the fragmentation and diversity that had emerged in the movement.[48] These observations were largely ignored in the more widespread Western views and suppressed by the ruling groups of the communist parties. However, such interpretations were circulating not only amongst European and American intellectuals but also amongst the communist political elites—even on the other side of the Iron Curtain and in Moscow. The view from the centre of the empire could actually be more cogent and realistic than in Western communist circles. In 1972 Anatoly Chernyaev, one of the key officials in the international department of the CPSU under the direction of Ponomarev, noted in his personal diary that the celebratory articles on the third conference of world communism only asserted 'ancient banalities' and that no one knew 'what to do with the [communist] movement', while its 'old message' was simply out of touch.[49] Representative of those recruited in the Khrushchev era and now disenchanted, Chernyaev was not merely expressing a personal judgement; he was expressing the doubt, widely held in his generation, that the movement was in decline, at least in the form it had taken up till then. The end of communist unity no longer appeared to be the cause of the decline, but rather the most evident and

---

[46] P. Gleijeses, *Conflicting Missions: Havana, Washington, and Africa, 1959–1976* (Chapel Hill, N.C.: University of North Carolina Press, 2002), 220; J. G. Blight and P. Brenner, *Sad and Luminous Days: Cuba's Struggle with the Superpowers after the Missile Crisis* (Lanham: Rowman & Littlefield, 2002), 215–45.

[47] E. J. Hobsbawm, *Revolutionaries* (London: Quartet, 1975), 7.

[48] Archives of the Hoover Institution, Alexander Dallin papers, Stanford (Cal.), box 12 (n.d.) and 52 (May 1970).

[49] A. Chernyaev, *Sovmestnii iskhod: dnevnik dvukh epokh 1972–1991* (Moscow: Rosspen, 2008), 19.

devastating outcome. This doubt did not, however, penetrate the ranks of Soviet and Eastern European decision-makers.

1968 turned out to be a historical crossroads. The Czechoslovakian crisis revealed the Soviet Union's inability to exercise its hegemony rather than control over its European sphere of interest, while the same verdict was expressed by the split in the 'socialist camp' outside Europe. The protest from below against the Cold War was affecting the system of 'developed socialism'[50]—but not only that system. The attrition of Soviet authority was revealing the loss of communism's legitimacy. A generation had grown up in Europe, which in the West was challenging the principle of authority and the postwar social model, but without resorting to the alternative model once represented by the communist world, while in the East the expectations triggered by de-Stalinization were turning into disillusionment and people were increasingly looking to the other half of the continent for their only hope for the future. The revolutionaries of Western Europe and the reformers of Central and Eastern Europe were defeated, but at the end of the decade Soviet communism appeared to have lost all its progressive significance. The global uprising of 1968 did not play into the hands of international communism in Europe or anywhere else, except a few isolated exceptions. Quite the contrary, it accelerated its decline.

A quarter of a century after the Second World War, the communist world was a picture of substantial social and institutional homogeneity. The Soviet template had been copied through the direct intervention of advisers from Moscow, the training of political and administrative cadres in other parties, and the application and transference of knowledge and practices, not only along a route from the centre to the periphery but also in the opposite direction. Sovietized Eastern and Central Europe was a pool of technological resources at the service of a backward imperial centre, which contributed to the integration of the bloc.[51] Except in its backwardness, socialism in China did not provide a very different picture, in spite of the ambitions of its leaders, the mobilization of the Cultural Revolution, and the breaking of links with the Soviet Union. The particularities of the Asian revolutions and even the Cuban one were largely typified by monocratic state structures, collectivist social engineering, and command economies. The regimes in China, North Vietnam, North Korea, and Cuba shared more similarities than differences, which could be traced back to a model created in the Soviet Union and exported to Eastern and Central Europe, in terms of not only the institutions and economy but also the language and political and social practices.[52] The diversity in Eastern

---

[50] Suri, *Power and Protest.*

[51] A. Jersild, 'The Soviet state as imperial scavenger: "catch up and surpass" in the transnational socialist bloc, 1950–1960', *American Historical Review* 116.1 (2011).

[52] For the situation in China, see T. P. Bernstein, 'Introduction', and in particular K. Hanbing, 'The transplantation and entrenchment of the Soviet economic model in China', in T. P. Bernstein and H.-Y. Li (eds), *China Learns from the Soviet Union, 1949–Present* (Lanham, Md.: Lexington Books, 2010); for an overview, see A. Brown, *The Rise and Fall of Communism* (New York: HarperCollins, 2009), chs. 16 and 18; R. Service, *Comrades! A History of World Communism* (London: Macmillan, 2007), ch. 30.

and Central Europe was latent but never came to light. After 1956, the relatively liberal period of Gomułka's Poland soon came to an end, whereas 'Kadarism' never set an example to be followed.[53] The promise to develop production of consumer products remained a dead letter, when compared to the advances of Western capitalism. Moscow's semi-colonial exploitation of the 'external empire' had given way to an increasing transfer of resources from the centre to the periphery, but this increased dependency on the Soviet Union. After 1968 there came a new phase of homogenization in the name of 'real socialism', which was destined to head off any idea of reform. The only regime that was independent of Moscow was the dynastic and nationalist one of Nicolae Ceauşescu, Georghiu-Dej's successor, who came to power in Romania in 1965.[54] The only anomaly remained Yugoslavia, but its model of self-management and decentralization had proved inefficient and did not distinguish itself enough from the Soviet one to even remotely excite the hopes of the Prague Spring, In any case, Soviet repression in Czechoslovakia had halted reforms not only in the Warsaw Pact countries but in Yugoslavia as well. Although he had condemned the invasion, after 1969 Tito increased internal discipline, restricted debate to socialist experimentation, and opened up space for nationalist tendencies.[55]

However, the diversities created by the Second World War and the postwar period were also affecting the movement. The structural homogeneity of communist systems no longer corresponded to political and ideological unity. The import and adaption of the Soviet model provided no guarantee of cohesion, as was demonstrated unequivocally by Maoist China. The dualism between the Soviets and Chinese had brought about a fracture in the 'socialist camp', and not its plural organization. Moreover, the fracture in the system of socialist states was not simply producing two opposing camps amongst the parties, but rather autonomous and fragmentary dynamics. The political panorama now offered by communist parties, where they represented a reasonably significant force, was much more varied than would be suggested by a mere polarization between Moscow and Peking. The communist movement contained different experiences, varying from armed struggle to regional government, or from mass campaigns to national government. Parties with a 'governmental' vocation abounded in Europe. In Finland, the Communist Party returned to government twenty years after its exclusion.[56] In France and Italy, communists were the principal opposition party and maintained their territorial strongholds. The PCI had established lasting hegemony in the prosperous 'red regions' in Central Italy on the basis of efficient and reformist governments. More than the PCF, the PCI had become an integral part of the modernization

[53] R. Gough, *A Good Comrade: János Kádár, Communism, and Hungary* (London: I. B. Tauris, 2006).

[54] V. Tismaneanu, *Stalinism for All Seasons: A Political History of Romanian Communism* (Berkeley: University of California Press, 2003), 192ff.

[55] G. Swain, *Tito: A Biography* (London: I. B. Tauris, 2010), 165ff.; D. Priestland, *The Red Flag: A History of Communism* (New York: Grove Press, 2009), 403–24.

[56] D. Sassoon, *One Hundred Years of Socialism: The West European Left in the Twentieth Century* (London: I. B. Tauris, 1996), 319.

of the country, even though Italian communists, like the French, held on to their anti-consumerist mentality and clung to the expectation of a 'general crisis' of capitalism.[57]

Outside Europe, the paths taken by communists differed greatly. In Latin America, the example of Cuban militant activism was experiencing setbacks, while the practice of a 'peaceful road' to socialism was making an appearance. In Chile, the communists were taking part in the popular-front alliance that won the elections in September 1970, bringing the socialist Salvador Allende to power on the basis of a programme of nationalizations and causing concern in the United States. Allende established an ambiguous alliance with Cuba, but the model adopted by Unidad Popular was not a Castrist one.[58] In Southeast Asia, on the other hand, the destruction of the Communist Party in Indonesia and the victorious struggle of the Vietnamese party favoured the adoption of guerrilla warfare. In Cambodia, the movement of the Khmer Rouge intensified the armed struggle after the American intervention in the spring of 1970, even escaping the full control of their Chinese patrons and cooperating with the Vietnamese in a manner that also engendered conflict.[59] In India, following the failed insurrections in the late 1940s, the practice of the 'peaceful road' began to prevail, albeit very gradually. In spite of the divisions between the pro-Soviets and the pro-Chinese, communists maintained their mass followings, although on a regional basis and without any significant influence in the Indian parliament. After a brief democratic experience in government in the state of Kerala back in 1957–9, the communists established themselves in the late 1960s as the leading party in popular-front regional governments in Kerala and West Bengal. They carried out agrarian reforms and assisted in the suppression of armed rebellions in the countryside led by 'Naxalite' Maoists.[60] Elsewhere the situations were fairly varied, to say the least. In South Africa, the Communist Party was linked to African nationalism and at the flank of the African National Congress took part in the clandestine armed struggle against the racist apartheid regime.[61] In the Arab world, communists supported nationalist regimes allied to the Soviet Union, but in a permanently subordinate role. Following the incorporation of the communist movement in the Nasserite regime in Egypt, the Ba'athist regimes in Syria and Iraq also coopted the communist parties into 'national

---

[57] R. Gualtieri (ed.), *Il PCI nell'Italia repubblicana* (Rome: Carocci, 2001), pt 4; S. Courtois and M. Lazar, *Histoire du parti communiste français* (Paris: PUF, 2000), 325; C. Guiat, *The French and Italian Communist Parties: Comrades and Culture* (London: Frank Cass, 2003).

[58] J. Haslam, *The Nixon Administration and the Death of Allende's Chile: A Case of Assisted Suicide* (London: Verso, 2005), 55.

[59] B. Kiernan, *How Pol Pot Came to Power: Colonialism, Nationalism, and Communism in Cambodia, 1930–1975*, 2nd edn (New Haven, Conn.: Yale University Press, 2004), 297–322.

[60] R. Mallick, *Indian Communism: Opposition, Collaboration and Institutionalization* (New Delhi: Oxford University Press, 1994), 130–2, 143–7; T. J. Nossiter, *Marxist State Governments in India: Politics, Economics and Society* (London: Pinter, 1988).

[61] S. Onslow, 'The Cold War in southern Africa: white power, black nationalism and external intervention', in S. Onslow (ed.), *The Cold War in Southern Africa: White Power, Black Liberation* (London: Routledge, 2009), 13.

fronts'.[62] Uniquely in the Arab world, the Marxist-Leninist Party seized power in South Yemen by armed struggle in June 1969, after years of civil war, and started a process of Sovietization with the intention of promoting revolutionary politics in the region.[63]

In such circumstances, it was impossible to speak of 'models' of communism, as had occurred in the past for the German Bolshevized model or the French, Italian, and Yugoslav anti-fascist models, or the Chinese anti-imperialist model. The legalism of the main Western parties jarred with the guerrilla movements of the Third World. The struggles for citizens' rights were incongruous in the eyes of militant anti-imperialists. The idea of nation took on different meanings and interpretations, not only in Europe but also in the various realities of the post-colonial world. The only constant was that both in the West and in the Third World, the example set by the Soviet Union and the European communist regimes was ceasing to be a motivation; indeed, it was experienced as a straitjacket. Mao's Cultural Revolution had not gained many converts, but it had made a considerable contribution to demolishing the image of the Soviet Union. At the same time, the radical impact of the Cultural Revolution was not just that of an internationalist and Third-Worldist message. China's break with the 'socialist community' and particularly the threat of war that followed the clashes on the river Ussuri created the imperative of defending Chinese identity from Soviet 'social imperialism', defined not so much by ideology as by patriotism and territory.[64] More generally, Asian communism underwent an increasing, although still barely noticeable, nationalistic metamorphosis— the nurturing of 'imagined communities' based on territory and cultural legacies imbued with Marxism-Leninism. The resumption of these legacies provided the Asian communists with a shared language superimposed on Marxism that increasingly distinguished them from the Soviets and Western communists.[65] This very process had implications for further fragmentation and conflict. The increasing 'nationalization' of the Asian communist parties would soon lead them into conflict with each other.

In Europe, the Italian and French parties limited the damage caused by the Soviet invasion of Czechoslovakia, but this had been possible because, unlike in 1956, they had kept their distance from the USSR. The Prague Spring and its repression had left its mark, but it was difficult to assess its consequences in the long term. It was certainly true that Western communists had kept intact their mass membership and following, but the glue that could keep them together was no longer the same, nor was it clear that a replacement could be found. It seemed

---

[62] T. Y. Ismael, *The Rise and Fall of the Communist Party of Iraq* (Cambridge Cambridge: University Press, 2008), 166ff.; R. Gallissot, 'Libération nationale et communisme dans le monde arabe', in *Le siècle des communismes* (Paris: Éditions ouvrières, Éditions de l'Atelier, 2004).

[63] F. Halliday, *Revolution and Foreign Policy: The Case of South Yemen 1967–1987* (Cambridge: Cambridge University Press, 1990).

[64] R. MacFarquhar and M. Schoenhals, *Mao's Last Revolution* (Cambridge, Mass.: Harvard University Press, 2006), 312–13.

[65] O. A. Westad, 'Introduction', in Westad et al., *77 Conversations between Chinese and Foreign Leaders on the War in Indochina*.

that the Western communists' search for legitimacy was interminable, given that they were committed to demonstrating their respect for legality and establishing their national credentials while at the same time defending their revolutionary credibility against protesters of the 'new left', and maintaining their international links with the 'socialist camp' while distancing themselves from its most unacceptable features. The criticisms made against the Soviet Union during the months that followed the events of August 1968 were counterbalanced by the renewal of the anti-American campaign in support of Vietnam, a crucial factor in the policies of Rochet and Longo.[66] Anti-Americanism had never been a simple corollary for pro-Sovietism, but it now became a discourse that made up for the decline of the Soviet myth and reinforced the credibility of the communist parties' Third Worldism against the challenge of the 'new left'. In the case of the PCI, Third Worldism was not only a tool for ideological campaigns but also a policy pursued with the intention of bridging the gap between the 'socialist camp' and the post-colonial world. Whereas the French communists had failed to understand the significance of decolonization in time—obstructed by their nationalism at the time of the war in Algeria—the Italians built up a network of relations, particularly in the Mediterranean, following the Yugoslav example but with the aim of creating the alliances between communists and nationalists that Moscow appealed to but often failed to implement.[67] At the end of the 1960s, however, the moderate Third Worldism of the PCI was subordinated to other priorities. The policy decisions of the strongest Western communist party had to be principally concerned with the Europeanist agenda and the renegotiation of its relationship with the Soviet Union.

These were not the only dilemmas for the Italian and French parties. They were being affected by mass culture and the consumer society, which eroded the 'separate societies' created under the shield of the Cold War.[68] In the West, communist activists had largely lost their spirit of sacrifice and the cult of organization. Their practices were becoming increasingly disparate according to the national context, but everywhere communist party membership was no longer necessarily a lifestyle choice. Even the era of activism, including information-gathering for Soviet intelligence which many had carried out for ideological reasons during the Stalinist era, had long been a thing of the past. The search for approval amongst the younger generation exposed the parties to the allurements and tensions of mass culture. Western communists found themselves under pressure from a twin challenge: one demanding that they conform to consumerism and the other that they join the anti-conformist counterculture, both of which enhanced individualism.[69]

[66] A. Brogi, *Confronting America: The Cold War between the United States and the Communists in France and Italy* (Chapel Hill, N.C.: University of North Carolina Press, 2011), 306–8; A. Höbel, *Il PCI di Luigi Longo* (Naples: Edizioni scientifiche italiane, 2011).

[67] M. Galeazzi, *Il PCI e il movimento dei paesi non allineati 1955–1975* (Milan: FrancoAngeli, 2011).

[68] Gundle, *I comunisti italiani tra Hollywood e Mosca.*

[69] Brogi, *Confronting America*, p. 285.

Communist adaptation to the various social, national, and geopolitical contexts in Europe and beyond was almost never a sign of vitality. In the past, they had been capable of successfully adopting and cultivating identities and language that differed from those that belonged to their tradition, as had occurred with anti-fascism and pacifism, in spite of the contradictions this generated at the heart of their political culture. This capacity no longer existed. All communists continued to use the same vocabulary when they spoke of class and nation, war and peace, revolution and counter-revolution, and even when they exchanged amongst themselves their ferocious accusation of revisionism and degeneration. But the persistence of their 'language community' became a symptom of dogmatic rigidity and a fossilization of the imagination. At the same time, communists were subjected to or accepted all kinds of contamination, which arose from national circumstances, democratic contexts, and the unconscious adoption of cultural legacies and attitudes. The polymorphic nature of international communism concealed the erosion of the movement's cultural structures and idioms.

The practical and symbolic link with the Soviet Union was no longer sufficient to weave together the unity the movement needed. Almost all communist parties continued to proclaim their membership of the movement, their loyalty to the Soviet Union, and their faith in the 'superiority' of the socialist system over the capitalist one. It was precisely the constituent link to the Soviet state, which went back to their origins, that ultimately prevented the challenge of the Chinese from gathering sufficient adherents. China's defection from the 'socialist camp' demonstrated that an individual communist state could challenge Moscow and break away in the name of its own interests and self-defence, but could not replace the Soviet leadership of the movement with its own, even in the Third World. However, the Soviet Union found itself at the centre of forces that were undergoing contraction and fragmentation, while its authority no longer went unchallenged. Even if Moscow continued to recite the rituals of unity and to distribute aid throughout the world, except to pro-Chinese forces, blind loyalty to the leading state was now a memory lost in the past. The Chinese breakaway revealed the limitations of Soviet hegemony. The world system of communist states had gone forever. The notion of international communism as an actor in world politics had been lost.

THE GLOBAL SUPERPOWER

After the invasion of Czechoslovakia and the clashes on the Chinese border, the Soviet Union opted definitively for détente with the United States. The Soviet elites gave their consent to the plan for imperial stability and power politics much more than they did to any idea of reform or to ideological campaigns. Consequently the transition from oligarchy to personal leadership proved to be much less effortful than had occurred after Stalin's death. Brezhnev, the member of the post-Khrushchev oligarchy who emerged in pole position, asserted his leadership by marginalizing those who were most inclined to follow the path of economic reforms or to relaunch the Soviet Union's ideological and revolutionary profile. The suppression of the Prague Spring was a decisive step, opening the way to an era in which the very idea of reform became taboo in the Soviet Union.[70] Brezhnev was representative of the third generation of Soviet officials, who had had no experience of the Revolution and Civil War and had little memory of them, but had been moulded by Stalin's 'revolution from above', had risen to prominence thanks to the purges of 1936–8, and had strengthened their positions in the Second World War. Like Khrushchev, he was convinced that international détente was an advantageous terrain and a process made possible by the irresistible change in the balance of power in favour of the 'socialist camp'. But he counted more on power politics than on dreams of winning the economic race. In Moscow's view, détente continued to exclude the possibility of changes in Soviet concepts of international politics, which were primarily governed by their perception of a hostile and aggressive capitalist West. But now the interests of the Soviet Union became identified with the attainment of a global status on a par with that of the Americans, and with the recognition of its European sphere of influence.

The opening move in détente was supported by a new generation of *mezhdunarodniki*, experts in international politics who constituted a political and intellectual group, some of whom cut their teeth during the preparation of the review of the communist movement, 'Questions of Peace and Socialism', in 1960s Prague.[71] This group, which was curious and relatively well-informed about the West, would remain on the margins of the political decision-making process. In many ways, Brezhnev's policy was just a variant of the indissoluble mix of ideology and realism that was Stalin's legacy, and was interpreted as such by the regime's strongmen, such as Andropov and the foreign minister, Andrei Gromyko. At the height of détente in June 1972, Chernyaev, an exponent of *mezhdunarodniki*, wrote that 'the self-representation of ideological power (part of the international communist movement) still remains an element in our actual strength'.[72] He thus recorded the persistence of a way of thinking in the ruling group and the Soviet elites. His clear conviction that it was possible to wind up and then re-establish in a different way the historical legacy of 'ideological power' constituted an archetype of the ideas on the reform of communism, which would long remain an underlying theme in the USSR, although invisible from abroad.

From the Soviet viewpoint, the early 1970s confirmed the promises of the détente strategy. The two-way dialogue with the Nixon administration and the launch of Ostpolitik by the social democratic leader in West Germany, Willy Brandt, were considered by Moscow to be a twin opportunity to seek stability

---

[70] A. Graziosi, *L'URSS dal trionfo al degrado: storia dell'Unione sovietica, 1945–1991* (Bologna: il Mulino, 2008), 359–60.

[71] G. A. Arbatov, *Chelovek sistemy* (Moscow: Vagrius, 2002), 119–24; K. N. Brutents, *Tridtsat' let na staroy ploshadi* (Moscow: Mezhdunarodnye otnosheniya, 1998), 119ff.; G. K. Shakhnazarov, *S vozhdiami i bez nikh* (Moscow: Vagrius, 2001), 86ff.; English, *Russia and the Idea of the West*, 147–53.

[72] Chernyaev, *Sovmestnii iskhod*, 19.

and consolidate the international standing of the USSR. The harsh repression of the workers' revolts in Poland in 1970, which led to the Gomułka's replacement by Edward Gierek, was dismissed without too many repercussions abroad. In the GDR, the replacement of Ulbricht, the last leader in Eastern Europe to take power under Stalin, by Erich Honecker opened the way to détente between the two Germanies without any relaxation of the German regime in the east. In 1972 bipartisan talks led to the first agreement with the United States on restricting nuclear weapons. A broad agreement on the policy of détente was now formed in the Politburo, although consent could not have been unconditional.[73] The link between authoritarian normalization in Czechoslovakia and international détente therefore became a conservative paradigm for Moscow, and was to be applied to Eastern and Central Europe. Brezhnev made clear his conviction that the suppression of the Prague Spring was a decisive premise for détente.[74]

In this context, the only discordant note appeared to be the startling rapprochement between China and the United States which resulted from Nixon's visit to Peking in February 1972, bringing to an end two decades of bitter conflict between the two countries and clearly revealing its anti-Soviet intentions.[75] Moscow had not been sufficiently aware of the possibility that Chinese hostility might translate into a successful bid to establish relations with the United States. It was difficult to insert this event into the prospect of a shift in the 'balance of power' in favour of the Soviet bloc. However, the Soviets believed that their strategy was sufficiently promising to deal with the Sino-American rapprochement, and underestimated the consequences of their own country's isolation. The scenario of a European security conference, an *a posteriori* recognition of the 'sphere of influence', and parity in their nuclear arsenals with the United States remained the central issues, while there were signs of instability and crisis in the Western system when the dollar lost its dominant position. In 1973 and 1974 the American withdrawal from Vietnam, the shock of the oil crisis for the Western economies following the Yom Kippur War in the Middle East, the Watergate scandal, and the fall of Richard Nixon produced the perception of a winning strategy capable of actually projecting the Soviet Union into the role of global power, which it had never been. For the Soviets, the 'war of position' with the capitalist West was suddenly developing fast and promising some very optimistic scenarios.

The long-awaited crisis of the Western economies had finally occurred, and was rounded off by a crisis in the leadership of the hegemonic Western power. The old theory of a 'collapse' of capitalism might have been naive, but the conviction that the capitalist system was unable to resolve its internal contradictions now seemed to have been confirmed.[76] To a more or less self-evident degree, this conviction

---

[73] J. Haslam, *Russia's Cold War: From the October Revolution to the Fall of the Wall* (New Haven, Conn.: Yale University Press, 2011), 263–64.

[74] APCI, Fondo Berlinguer, Movimento operaio internazionale, fasc. 109.

[75] C. Jian, *Mao's China and the Cold War* (Chapel Hill, N.C.: University of North Carolina Press, 2001), 273–6.

[76] R. B. Day, *Cold War Capitalism: The View from Moscow 1945–1975* (Armonk, N.Y.: M. E. Sharpe, 1995), 265–76.

was harboured not only by Moscow but by all communists, including Western ones. However, this was much more cultural stubbornness than a realistic reading of the Western world. Still less did it represent a basis for formulating a political strategy for the communist movement. The view of the Western crisis belonged to a tradition of apocalyptic expectations, to which the fate of the global revolution had been entrusted. This conferred a paradoxical centrality on the Soviet Union, as a rising world power and deterrent to imperialism, just when the role of the Soviet myth had been lost forever and international communism was evidently in decline. The prospect of the Soviet Union as a world power had been inscribed in Stalinist political culture, and had been embryonic in the Cominform's declaration of the 'two camps' and the production of the first Soviet atomic bomb. Stalin's successors had consolidated this vocation for creating a bipolar world, but Soviet globalism was more a project than a reality even at the time of Khrushchev's fall. A decade later, it appeared to be a reality, at least in terms of the strategic balance it had achieved with the United States. In this challenge, the basis for Soviet power suffered no less than in the past from a considerable fragility and structural imbalances, particularly economic and technological ones, which were hidden but not resolved by the inflow of dollars resulting from the oil crisis.[77] The gap between the Soviet Union and the United States had not been overcome, but this was not at all clear to contemporaries. More visible, but ignored by the majority, was the fact that the Soviet Union's global project was reaching fulfilment—at least in appearance—when it no longer had the support of a cohesive and confident communist movement and still had not resolved the problem of how to stabilize its empire in the heart of Europe. In this sense, Brezhnev's power politics amounted to a hazardous attempt to respond to the decline of Soviet authority, as well as a misconceived authoritarian solution to the turbulence in the European sphere of influence.

The Vietnam War maintained hopes and expectations. At the beginning of the 1970s, the idea of relaunching a more active communist policy in the Third World was making headway, driven by various forces. The conviction that they had more cards to play in post-colonial societies than the United States had—the model of anti-capitalist development, the moulding of social relations through state intervention, the possibility of competing with the imperialist West even in terms of strength—had never really disappeared in Moscow, and was encouraged by the imminent debacle in Indochina and the rapprochement between Peking and Washington. The request to embrace more fully the internationalist and revolutionary message which seemed to be coming from Vietnam became a leitmotiv of some of Moscow's allies, particularly the Cubans. The prospect of an authoritarian stabilization in Europe led to a reassessment of the global south as the main terrain for the mutual encirclement of capitalism and communism. This trajectory was supported by the increasing radicalization of Third Worldist leaders and intellectuals, who now rejected the generation of Bandung. Activity in the Third World

---

[77] Graziosi, *L'URSS dal trionfo al degrado*, 409–10.

occupied an increasing part of the workload of CPSU's international department. However Moscow's tactics were different from in the past. The season of alliances with anti-imperialist nationalism was over. The lesson they drew from the defeats suffered during the 1960s was to engage with groups with a Marxist or communist affiliation, which they now saw as more reliable and suitable partners to sustain the modernizing mission which continued to inspire the Soviet Union's activities. This was much more a decision based on reliability and loyalty rather than a return to ideological roots.[78]

As the Vietnam War came to a close with a communist victory after the American withdrawal, a new terrain for possible intervention opened up in Africa following the fall of the Salazar dictatorship in Portugal and the collapse of the last European colonial empire in April 1974. This event had consequences outside Europe, given that a Civil War broke out in Angola between the Marxist and the nationalist wings of the liberation movement, and in Europe, given the strong influence of the Communist Party over the power established by the military in Lisbon through the 'Carnation Revolution'. Significantly, Moscow was more cautious in Europe than in Africa. The tendency of Portuguese communists, led by Álvaro Cunhal, to take over sections of power within the new regime with brusque methods was not impeded, but neither was it encouraged. The Soviets' objective was principally to create problems for NATO in the same way in which, from their point of view, Westerners had created problems for the Warsaw Pact six years earlier in Prague. But any ideas of installing a late 'people's democracy' in Portugal was a game not worth the candle, given the risk of compromising détente and given the precedent in Chile, where a few months earlier Allende's government had been overthrown by a reactionary coup led by General Pinochet with American complicity.[79] In Europe, the rules of the bipolar game did not allow for a change of regime in the opposing camp. The Soviets showed no sign of wanting to break these rules. Moscow was even less active in Lisbon that other Eastern European countries. In June 1975, Brezhnev told Gierek that the Soviet Union had no need of bases in Portugal.[80]

Things were somewhat different outside Europe. Paying for a weakness that went back to the interwar years, communists had not played a significant role in the decolonization of Africa. Guevara's failed revolutionary mission to Congo had felt like a harsh blow of reality. But the Cubans had not discontinued their presence in the continent, and when the Civil War in Angola broke out, they sent military aid in support of the Angolan Popular Movement of Liberation, the MPLA, led by the Marxist intellectual Agostinho Neto, who had been in contact with Castro for some time. The turning point came with the South African invasion of Angola and

---

[78] Westad, *The Global Cold War*, 202–6; Priestland, *The Red Flag*, 469–70; A. Dobrynin, *In Confidence: Moscow's Ambassador to America's Six Cold War Presidents (1962–1986)* (New York: Times Books, 1995), 362; C. Andrew and V. Mitrokhin, *The World Was Going Our Way: The KGB and the Battle for the Third World* (New York: Basic Books, 2005).
[79] Haslam, *The Nixon Administration and the Death of Allende's Chile*, 158–221.
[80] Chernyaev, *Sovmestnii iskhod*, 153.

the dispatch of Cuban troops in October and November 1975. Having observed the Cuban intervention with scepticism, the Soviet Union decided to hesitate no longer and came out in support of the MPLA. Angola was therefore the first terrain for international conflict that reflected the new situation in the Cold War, given that the anti-communist liberation movements were in effect supported by the United States and China. The anti-imperialist motivations for the Soviet–Cuban interventions were reinforced and made credible by the presence on the other side of the South African racist regime. The military defeat inflicted by the Cubans on South Africa led to a crisis in the apartheid regime.[81] At the same time, however, the intervention appeared to be an expansionist policy on behalf of the 'socialist camp' and a challenge to American influence in part of the world that had not been involved in Soviet interests. The final victory of the MPLA and the Cuban troops in March 1976 meant the creation of a Marxist-Leninist regime in Africa and a success for the Soviet Union on a new chessboard of the Cold War.[82]

The rise of the Soviet Union's power had given it two faces, one within and one outside Europe, and each was supposed to promise success. The Soviet Union's European policy culminated in the Helsinki Security and Cooperation Agreements in August 1975. For the Soviets, the final act of the CSCE constituted the high-point of bipolar détente, the acknowledgement of its own sphere of influence which had been lacking for thirty years, and the arrival point for the Eurocentric tradition in the Soviet Union's foreign policy.[83] In this light, there was little concern over the question of human rights which had been adopted amongst the Helsinki principles, and their implications for the status quo. Moscow believed that it had the processes of interpenetration with the world economy under control, and was not too concerned about the increasing indebtedness of Eastern European countries to Western Europe. The old Marshall Plan syndrome was in the past, thanks to the growth in the Soviet Union's power. The 'Carnation Revolution' in Portugal appeared to be creating new possibilities in Southern Europe, where the strongest Western communist parties were active.

In the eyes of Moscow and its allies, the balance of power with the West was shifting in their favour.[84] This justified the renewed challenges outside Europe. For Brezhnev's ruling group, international détente and the challenge for influence in the world outside Europe constituted two closely interlinked features of the same policy and were not alternatives. Once they had achieved strategic parity with the United States, and the West had recognized their sphere of influence in Europe, the contest could be resumed on a more realistic basis. It is not clear whether this second attempt by the Soviet Union to expand into the Third World, after the failure a decade earlier, was the product of a strategic plan or the result of opportunistic decisions and dynamics not wholly under their control. Moscow

---

[81] Onslow, *The Cold War in Southern Africa*, 16–17.
[82] Westad, *The Global Cold War*, 228–41; Gleijeses, *Conflicting Missions*, 259–72, 305–8, 339–46.
[83] S. Savranskaya and W. Taubman, 'Soviet foreign policy, 1962–1975', in Leffler and Westad, *The Cambridge History of the Cold War*, vol. 2: *Crises and Détente*, 154–5.
[84] Haslam, *Russia's Cold War*, 298.

had certainly never considered that the game was over. The first Soviet–Cuban intervention in Africa followed the final victory of the Vietnamese communists with the capture of Saigon in April 1975. Relations between Hanoi and Moscow had become very close during the first half of the decade, in spite of the lack of Vietnamese enthusiasm for détente.[85] United communist Vietnam was in every sense an important ally of the Soviet Union. The triumph of Vietnamese communists was probably decisive in persuading Moscow to take a series of very demanding steps that would have far-reaching consequences. The Vietnamese themselves suggested the anti-imperialist relaunch, demanding a role for their long struggle in the promotion of world revolution and exposing the weakness of the United States.[86] In this sense, the victory in Angola took on a much more general significance and was seen by Moscow as the demonstration that the decision to open a front in Africa would win through.[87]

This logic became much more evident when the Cubans and Soviets launched their second African intervention in the Horn of Africa, a year and a half after the Angolan one. Rather than supporting a liberation struggle, the Soviet Union and Cuba undertook to shore up the military dictatorship of Haile Menghistu, which was established in Ethiopia during the uncertain transition after Haile Selassie's fall from power and proclaimed itself socialist while triggering full-scale Red Terror. Yet again the idea came from Castro, who was convinced that the most important revolution since Cuba was taking place in Ethiopia, and that the intervention to defend the new regime in the war with Somalia provided an opportunity to remove American influence from the continent.[88] The Politburo accepted the Cuban appeal with some reluctance, partly because of concerns over Menghistu's cruel methods, and attempted to find a negotiated settlement between the two African countries. But the setbacks suffered by the Ethiopians and the pressure to assist them coming from pro-Soviet regimes in African countries convinced Moscow that it had to take action. The intervention of Cuban and South Yemeni troops was coordinated by the massive dispatch of Soviet military personnel in the final months of 1977. This contributed decisively to the internationalization of the conflict and the Ethiopian victory in March 1978. Thus in a few years, the 'socialist camp' had achieved two important successes in Africa, and appeared to be creating the prospect of a socialist transformation of the continent through military intervention. In this sense, the intervention in the Horn of Africa constituted the endorsement of the Soviet Union as a great power with a global range. For Moscow, this signified a second kind of legitimacy, which compounded and rebalanced the final act of Helsinki

[85] S. J. Morris, *The Soviet–Chinese–Vietnamese Triangle in the 1970s: The View from Moscow*, Cold War International History Project working paper no. 25 (Washington, D.C.: Woodrow Wilson Center, 1999).

[86] B. Schaefer, 'Communist vanguard contest in East Asia during the 1960s and 1970s', in T. Vu and W. Wongsurawat (eds), *Dynamics of the Cold War in Asia: Ideology, Identity and Culture* (London: Palgrave Macmillan, 2010), 122–3.

[87] Andrew and Mitrokhin, *The World Was Going Our Way*, 95.

[88] P. Gleijeses, 'Cuba and the Cold War, 1959–1980', in Leffler and Westad, *The Cambridge History of the Cold War*, vol. 2: *Crises and Détente*, 344–5.

and was destined to relaunch the fate of socialism around the world.[89] The interdependence of states on the contemporary stage was no longer denied by the Soviets, but it was not only perceived through the lens of détente. The interaction between bipolar antagonism and local conflicts around the world outside Europe constituted the most important strategic scenario.

The intervention in the Horn of Africa was perceived in Moscow both as a step forward in promoting a socialist perspective in one of the main countries on the continent and as a response to the emerging alliance between Washington and Peking. The schism between the Soviet Union and China was still having its consequences. The Chinese strategy in challenging the hegemony of the great powers had for some time identified the Soviet Union as the principal enemy. The ambition to compete with the Soviet Union as the revolutionary vanguard in the Third World had moderated since the Cultural Revolution, but Mao had not abandoned the aim of obstructing the Soviets in any way he could, given his prediction of increasing disorder around the globe and an imminent war of global proportions. Peking had mobilized against the Soviet–Cuban intervention in Africa and had reacted to the realignment of North Vietnam with Moscow by supporting the Khmer Rouge in Cambodia. In appearance, the almost simultaneous victory of the Vietnamese and Cambodian communists in April 1975, which was completed by the victory of the Laotians in December, constituted a triumph for the communist movement in Indochina after thirty years of armed struggle. Reality was very different. The tension between the pro-Soviet Vietnamese and the Maoist Khmer Rouge was superimposed on the increasing contrast between Hanoi's internationalism in Indochina and Cambodia's nationalism. The potential conflict between the Khmers and the Vietnamese, which had already become apparent during the common struggle against the Americans, emerged more clearly immediately after the fall of Phnom Penh and Saigon. The Khmers' anti-Vietnamese ethnic hatred was one of the motives for the sudden mass deportations and terror aimed at transforming Cambodian society, along with populist and anti-intellectual class hatred. Their ideal was not to support the Vietnamese revolution. They were following the example of the Chinese Cultural Revolution, but in a more extreme form, a unique mix of communism, anti-colonialism, ultra-nationalism, and racism.[90] Their leader, Pol Pot, who had been a member of the PCF in the early 1950s, worked underground in Cambodia and Vietnam for many years, and visited Peking when the Cultural Revolution started, believed fanatically that any other social or human experiment enacted by communist regimes was imperfect and incomplete.[91] Within a few years, the Khmer Rouge had perpetrated a genocide

---

[89] Westad, *The Global Cold War*, 276–9.

[90] B. Kiernan, 'External and indigenous sources of Khmer Rouge ideology', in O. A. Westad and S. Quinn-Judge (eds), *The Third Indochina War: Conflict between China, Vietnam, and Cambodia, 1972–79* (London: Routledge, 2006), 187–206.

[91] D. Chandler, *Brother Number One: A Political Biography of Pol Pot* (Boulder, Colo.: Westview Press, 1992).

which dwarfed many of the previous ones in the century by exterminating about one fifth of the Cambodian population.[92]

Mao's death in 1976 would radically change China's domestic policy, but not the anti-Soviet strategy in foreign policy. Having re-emerged from the disgrace he had fallen into during the Cultural Revolution and having been recalled to Peking by Zhou Enlai before Mao's death, Deng Xiaoping prevailed in the struggle for succession against the radicals of the so-called 'gang of four'. Now a 70-year-old, he imposed a pragmatic agenda of modernization, and dumped Mao's 'permanent revolution' and dreams of leading world communism.[93] In the history of communism, Deng was a figure much closer to Malenkov than to Khrushchev. He set in motion a prudent and selective de-Maoization, which avoided sensational announcements in secret or in public. China's internationalist aid to Asian communists, already in decline during Mao's latter years, was drastically reduced. The doctrine of the inevitability of war was put aside, though its demise was never declared. The policy towards the two superpowers revealed more continuity than change. The new leader's first significant undertaking on the international stage was to enter into an alliance with the United States in December 1978, bringing to a conclusion the rapprochement that had been going on for some years.[94]

The Chinese policy against the 'hegemonism' of the Soviet Union actually became significantly harsher with support for the Pol Pot regime in Cambodia. Relations between Peking and Hanoi suffered an irreversible deterioration. At the end of 1978, following three years of low-level conflict, Vietnam invaded Cambodia, bringing the Pol Pot regime to an end in a matter of days. This was the first armed conflict between two communist states, linked to the Soviet Union and China respectively. Immediately afterwards, a Chinese punitive expedition against Vietnam decreed the break-up of Asian communism. The Vietnamese prepared for a long war with China, which they considered to be dominated by 'reactionary circles', just as the Chinese had judged the Soviet Union in the past.[95] A genuine war was only avoided by Deng's decision to withdraw his own troops rapidly, but the outcome of the third Indochinese war had definitively fragmented communism in Asia.[96]

[92] J.-L. Margolin, 'Cambogia: nel paese del crimine sconcertante', in S. Courtois, N. Werth, et al., *Il libro nero del comunismo: crimini, terrore, repressione* (Milan: Mondadori, 1998); B. Kiernan, *The Pol Pot Regime: Race, Power, and Genocide in Cambodia under the Khmer Rouge, 1975–1979*, 2nd edn (New Haven, Conn.: Yale University Press, 2002).

[93] E. Vogel, *Deng Xiaoping and the Transformation of China* (Cambridge, Mass.: Harvard University Press, 2011); R. Baum, *Burying Mao: Chinese Politics in the Era of Deng Xiaoping* (Princeton, N.J.: Princeton University Press, 1996).

[94] C. Jian, 'China and the Cold War after Mao', in Leffler and Westad, *The Cambridge History of the Cold War*, vol. 3: *Endings* (Cambridge: Cambridge University Press, 2010), 188–90.

[95] 'Le Duan and the break with China', *Cold War International History Project Bulletin* 12 and 13 (2001), 273–88.

[96] C. E. Goscha, 'Vietnam, the Third Indochina War and the meltdown of Asian internationalism', in Westad and Quinn-Judge, *The Third Indochina War*.

Following the revolutionary victories in Vietnam, Cambodia, and Laos, the paradox was that Southeast Asia did not become the theatre for a triumph of international communism, but rather for conflict between communist regimes that shifted from the political and ideological to the military. The construction of revolutionary experiences and language imbued with Marxism over decades of relations between Chinese and Indochinese communists proved to be a fragile and superficial structure. The national 'imagined communities' definitively asserted themselves amongst Asian communists and buried the legacy of the 'international community'.[97] The construction of the state and its burgeoning militarized bureaucracy produced social engineering and ethnic cleansing that increased the gravity of the conflicts in spite of the regimes' apparent homogeneity. The question was not only confined to Asian communism. Back in the 1960s the rift between Moscow and Peking had brought to light contradictions and compromised the fate of the movement. Now the very credibility of communism as the antagonist of Western capitalism was being demolished. If communist states could produce opposing alliances and go to war, even allying themselves with the ancient enemy, then communism had lost its original mission and its *raison d'être*. The end of communist unity did not only produce heresies; it undermined the entire ideological and political architecture. Ten years earlier it had been legitimate to raise serious questions about the fate of international communism. Now the questions had to be extended to the very survival of twentieth-century communism.

The Soviet leadership was far from understanding such problems. Seen from Moscow, the shattered unity of the communist movement represented a crime of *lèse-majesté* and an open wound, but it could be repaired and even reintegrated due to the Soviet Union's global profile. Expansionism in Africa appears with hindsight to have been a move on the chessboard of the global Cold War and an attempt to raise the fortunes of Soviet-led communism, rebalancing the conflicts in the Asian theatre. The alliance with Cuba now took on a strategic significance and influenced the search for new prospects in the Third World. Following the coup against Allende in Chile and the establishment of military dictatorships in Argentina and Uruguay, characterized by anti-communism which removed all possibility of 'peaceful transitions', the Sandinista Revolution in July 1979 in Nicaragua was seen by Moscow as confirmation that the game was still on outside Europe and could be relaunched.[98] For the Soviets, the power struggle with the United States would create new opportunities. In reality, the interventions in Africa were a contingent success which did not open wide horizons to the Soviet presence and the communist movement in the Third World, and still less made the Soviet Union's model attractive. The decision to back groups that proclaimed their faith in Marxism-Leninism, rather than seeking understandings with nationalist forces, was probably the result of the persistent competition from the Chinese, even though this had lost incisiveness.

---

[97] B. Anderson, *Imagined Communities: Reflections on the Origin and Spread of Nationalism* (London: Verso, 2006), 155–62.
[98] Brutents, *Tridtsat' let na staroy ploshadi*, 349; H. Brands, *Latin America's Cold War* (Cambridge, Mass.: Harvard University Press, 2010), 195–6.

In any case, it demonstrated a restricted horizon and thinking based exclusively on uniformity and conformism, instead of a plan to establish alliances. The idea that Vietnam represented a model to be replicated by mixing Marxism and nationalism while responding to Moscow's interests proved to be fallacious.

The ideological polarization that had occurred in the Third World over the previous decade had brought about an escalation in violence and given rise to the replacement of many nationalist governments by military dictatorships and radical Marxist-Leninist regimes. In spite of this, the increasing use of force by the two superpowers and the gradual decline of non-alignment did not reabsorb countries outside Europe into the logic of a bipolar world. The Soviets believed they could profit from divisions in the Non-Aligned Movement, in which the Cubans opposed the Yugoslavs and promoted radical agendas. But they did not realize that the radicalism that had emerged in the Third World a decade earlier had run its course, and that a selection of allies based on faith in Marxism-Leninism was limiting and not expansionist. The primacy of power politics as a revolutionizing force caused Brezhnev's Soviet Union to accentuate the tendency to impose a rigid model. The export of the model amounted to building state structures from scratch, including the political and ideological education of the ruling classes. The case of Ethiopia was typical.[99] However, the representation of pro-Soviet regimes in Africa as the new frontier of international communism seemed credible only to Moscow and its closest allies, such as the Cubans and the East Germans. The intervention in the Horn of Africa did not enhance the image of Soviet communism. On the other hand, it had many more consequences for bipolar relations. The idea of keeping the challenges in the Third World separate from bilateral relations with the United States proved to be entirely fanciful, as some of the sharper *mezhdunarodniki*, to whom the leadership was deaf, had feared.[100] The logic of power led simultaneously to decisions that destabilized détente and created the conditions leading to the Soviet empire overreaching itself, without the benefits of an authentic increase in credibility.

Shortly afterwards, the invasion of Afghanistan was decided upon in Moscow on the basis of the same logic that had inspired the intervention in Africa. The communist regime installed in the country in April 1978 with a coup carried out without the knowledge of the Soviets, which was weak and divided into competing factions, risked being swept away by the Civil War started a year later with an insurrection by Islamic guerrillas. Initially the Politburo rejected the option of sending in the Red Army. Kosygin and Kirilenko in particular were opposed, and argued that military intervention in Afghanistan risked ending up in a war similar to the one in Vietnam. But the reasonable argument was put to one side. Once again, Andropov played a central role, arguing that without Soviet intervention the USSR would lose its geopolitical influence over Afghanistan and compromise the prospects of the Afghan Revolution. The Politburo reversed its decision in

---

[99] Westad, *The Global Cold War*, 280.
[100] Arbatov, *Chelovek sistemy*, 284; Dobrynin, *In Confidence*, 405.

December 1979, and the invasion was carried out by the end of the month.[101] The Soviet leaders believed that the invasion of Afghanistan was a necessary move in the context of the global Cold War. In their opinion, the increasing bitterness of bipolar relations would inevitably escalate interventions in the Third World, as one of the principal spokesmen of the CPSU's international department, Vadim Zagladin, confessed to Italian communists in February 1980.[102] The result would create a Soviet Vietnam, destined to aggravate the Cold War once more, usher in new waves of violence, and cause the Soviet Union's image to plummet in the world outside Europe.

EUROCOMMUNISM

The fragmentation of international communism had continued unabated in Europe too. By the mid-1970s, the highpoint of détente and Brezhnev's power politics, did not live up to Moscow's optimistic scenarios, but coincided with the emergence of more dissent amongst Western communists. The idea of political and cultural reform had survived the suppression of the Prague Spring, The hopes of 'socialism with a human face' had been severely dented, but were still there. Its banner was taken up by the Western communist parties, albeit with hesitancy and diplomacy. The conformism of Italian and French communists was more striking than their proclamation of autonomy. In spite of their fundamental loyalty, Western communists were seen by Moscow to be overcome by legalistic scruples and inclined to distance themselves when it was expedient. This was the case, for example, when it came to the censure and repression of dissident intellectuals in the Soviet Union. Western communists had in fact neglected them, and manifested cautious reservations only after the persecution of Dubček's communist followers. The international *causes célèbres* concerning the Soviet regime's persecution of Andrei Sakharov and Aleksandr Solzhenitsyn in 1973 provoked some lukewarm hairsplitting, which was enough to cause irritation and concern in Moscow. Chernyaev noted in his diary the tendency of Western communism to see the Soviet Union 'only as a subjective reality' and avoid 'at all costs identifying with Soviet and Eastern European communism'.[103]

The repression and persecution of dissident intellectuals that had started in the Soviet Union around the middle of the 1960s was now taking on international proportions. Political and intellectual dissent represented a movement that had put on the agenda the question of freedom of thought in the Soviet Union and Eastern Europe. Western communists could not ignore it, although they did not go so far as to make it a central question in their relations with Moscow. Their

---

[101] Westad, *The Global Cold War*, 316–22; Andrew and Mitrokhin, *The World Was Going Our Way*, 398–400.

[102] APCI, Estero, 1980, mf 8003, 394–408.

[103] Chernyaev, *Sovmestnii iskhod*, 68. For the role of dissident intellectuals in the USSR, see Zubok, *Zhivago's Children*, 302–10.

sensitivity on this point was selective and reticent, and was primarily a generic plea for freedom of expression rather than an attempt to understand the profound reasons for dissent.[104] However, the problem Chernyaev referred to was serious. The close link between Moscow and Western communists was becoming weaker, and the image of the Soviet Union no longer exercised such an attraction even amongst their ranks. They did not seem perfectly reliable at the very time when the Soviet strategy of détente appeared to be having success and the Western world was undergoing a crisis in its economy and in its leadership. The heirs of Togliatti and Thorez promoted mass mobilizations but also demanded governmental responsibility, while evading Soviet influence. Their real problem was that of facing up to the decline of the Soviet image. The main protagonist was the PCI.

The only party to benefit from the long-term repercussions of 1968 in terms of the considerable increase in its consensus, the PCI developed its own political strategy in the first half of the decade. Its leader, Berlinguer, followed the legacy of Togliatti by capitalizing on the grass roots of a mass party in a democracy logjammed by the arithmetic of the Cold War. But he moved away from Togliatti to propose a 'historic compromise' with the Catholics, embrace European integration, and concentrate on creating a profile for Western communism that was freed from the tight links with the 'socialist camp'. Concerned by the precedent in Chile, Berlinguer aimed to form a coalition government with moderate forces, while rejecting the old strategies of popular fronts and exploiting the space created by European détente. At the same time, he wished to draw up a list of principles and a distinctive political agenda for Western communists by endorsing the values of democracy and pluralism, the idea of 'moving beyond the blocs' while acknowledging their existence, following the example of the German Ostpolitik, and the concept of Europe as a political entity and a new international player. The Italian communists' first attempt at getting these ideas accepted ended in failure. The majority of delegates turned a deaf ear at the conference of Western communist parties held in Brussels in January 1974. Only the French and Spanish moved towards the PCI's position.[105]

However, Berlinguer continued down his own path and attached great importance to forming an alliance with the PCF, the only partner with a mass following amongst a group of parties that were either tiny or illegal. His strategy did not only aim to establish national legitimacy for the PCI; he also wanted to reverse the minority and sectarian nature of the communist parties in most of Western Europe, faced with the strength and consensus enjoyed by social democratic parties, and thus to influence possible change in Central and Eastern Europe. He thought that the Western crisis and the problems afflicting American hegemony provided an opportunity to occupy a political space within which to revive the primacy of anti-fascism over anti-communism, which in his opinion had been lost because of the Cold War. The most revealing feature of Berlinguer's ideas was

---

[104] V. Lomellini, *L'appuntamento mancato: la sinistra italiana and il dissenso nei regimi comunisti (1968–1989)* (Florence: Le Monnier, 2010).
[105] A. Rubbi, *Il mondo di Berlinguer* (Rome: Napoleone, 1994), 34.

the link he established between European détente and the possibility of political change inspired by the precedent of the Prague Spring, which overturned Brezhnev's axiom about the link between détente and the authoritarian normalization of the bloc. The Italian leader presented himself as the communist exponent most conscious of the need to provide a response to the political problems that had built up over time and the failure of the 'socialist camp' to attract consensus after 1968.[106]

However, the PCI was struggling to find authentic interlocutors for this project. Amongst the main political players, the only similar positions were those of the League of Communists of Yugoslavia. In early 1975, Berlinguer and Tito agreed that supporting 'the existence of a communist movement united by a shared ideology and separate from the rest' would only respond to 'a limited range of possibilities'. Both expressed their negative assessment of the Portuguese communists and the support they were guaranteed by the Soviets, which risked compromising détente.[107] The alliance between Italian and Yugoslavian communists would remain solid, particularly when it came to their relations with anti-imperialist movements outside Europe. On the other hand, the Yugoslavs were not the ideal partners for building an alliance with a Europeanist vocation. Neither were the Japanese communists, the only non-European party inclined to be inspired by the Italians. The responses to the 'Carnation Revolution' demonstrated that Western communists were more in disagreement than in agreement. In the spring of 1975, Berlinguer publicly criticized the Portuguese communists. He shared the concerns of the general secretary of the Spanish Communist Party, Santiago Carrillo, that Cunhal was following the same tactic adopted by Eastern European communists in the 'people's democracies' at the end of the Second World War, thus irreparably damaging any attempt at innovation.[108] Their positions on Portugal were not dissimilar from those of the European socialist parties. Marchais, on the other hand, positioned himself on the opposing side and defended Cunhal's behaviour. Consequently, the prospect of a Western communist grouping proved to be hardly practicable and lacking solid political foundations. In spite of this, a series of bilateral meetings between the PCI, the PCF, and the PCE in 1975 and 1976 gave rise to 'Eurocommunism'. Rather than a movement with a specific programme, Eurocommunism was an alliance that distanced itself from the Soviet model and acknowledged the value of Western democracy.[109] Eurocommunist political discourse introduced a novelty in recent communist tradition, because Berlinguer, Marchais, and Carrillo explicitly enunciated a moderate critique of the Soviet model, which was only implicit in Dubček's discourse.

This was a necessary condition, but not sufficient to gain consensus in the West, particularly given the ambiguities that emerged in the Portuguese crisis. It was

---

[106] S. Pons, *Berlinguer e la fine del comunismo* (Turin: Einaudi, 2006).
[107] APCI, Estero, 1975, mf 204 (29 Mar. 1975).
[108] APCI, Fondo Berlinguer, serie Movimento Operaio Internazionale, fasc. 125.
[109] S. Pons, 'The rise and fall of Eurocommunism', in Leffler and Westad, *The Cambridge History of the Cold War*, vol. 3: *Endings*, 50–4.

enough, however, to provoke concerns in Moscow. The Soviets had expressed their unhappiness with developments amongst Western communists on several occasions. They were suspicious of the Italians' Europeanist leanings, which they found incomprehensible and likely to cause another split. They had accepted the Brussels Conference, but on condition that it was a step towards a fourth conference of world communism, which had been planned during 1973 with the aim of revisiting the excommunication of the Chinese.[110] They had supported Cunhal as an example of orthodox communism. Paradoxically, their view was shared by the American secretary of State, Henry Kissinger, who feared a 'domino effect' spreading communism in Southern Europe and a subsequent threat to the American system of alliances at least as much as the Soviets desired it in their most intimate dreams.[111] But both sides feared that the status quo guaranteed by détente could be upset in Europe by the political actions of forces outside the control of the great powers. In this context, the attention shifted rapidly from Portugal to Italy. Whereas the Portuguese Revolution was moving towards moderate political solutions by the end of 1975, precluding the policies supported by the PCP, the PCI was putting itself forward for a leading role in government as a result of its visible increase in electoral support, which was confirmed by the general election in June 1976—when it obtained almost 35 per cent of the vote though remaining by a narrow margin the second party in Italy. Washington interpreted this as a threat to NATO, and Moscow perceived it as an unpredictable scenario that could create more problems than advantages.

This particular headache was more serious for the Soviets than it was for the Americans: the possibility of the principal Western communist party entering government could not only undermine the status quo guaranteed by détente in terms of bipolar relations, but also the Soviet leadership of European communism. To be more precise, the PCI in power would upset the delicate balance established in Helsinki and would also constitute a source of destabilization in Eastern Europe, particularly if the experience of government took it even further out of the Soviet orbit, as was quite likely. In reality, the Soviet ruling group lacked a shared vision and even a decision-making process to deal with the matter. Tired and ill, Brezhnev displayed little interest in the activities of the CPSU's international department. Portrayed by the Western press as an *éminence grise* and secret manipulator of revolutionary movements around the world, Ponomarev had now been marginalized from politics and was seen even by his subordinates as an old, obtuse, and inveterate bureaucrat of the Comintern era. Consequently, Moscow was largely in a state of torpor and lacked a genuine policy for the communist movement. The ruling bodies of the CPSU did not even discuss the joint declaration by Berlinguer and Marchais after their meeting in November 1975, which ratified the creation of the Eurocommunist Alliance.[112] It was the loyal Soviet allies, such as the East

---

[110] APCI, Estero, 1973, mf 048, 621–9.

[111] M. Del Pero, *Henry Kissinger e l'ascesa dei neoconservatori: alle origini della politica estera americana* (Rome: Laterza, 2006), 88–94.

[112] Chernyaev, *Sovmestnii iskhod*, 188, 204.

Germans, who felt the need to make clear that Helsinki had represented a point of arrival and not of departure, and that the détente did not mean an end to antagonism between the superpowers.

Thus a strategy on how to contain Eurocommunism only emerged in a confused manner. As in the past, the instrument for sorting these things out was another conference of communist parties, this time restricted to European ones. The Italians themselves were asking for one, principally to avoid another world conference being convened. The Soviets and East Germans took over the initiative after Helsinki. Their aims were somewhat vague. It was a matter of counterbalancing the diplomatic message of détente with an ideological message that reaffirmed the class content and united the restless world of European communism. The main purpose of the conference was to bring the Eurocommunists back into the fold, while acknowledging the right to debate but also respecting the unitary rituals of the communist tradition.[113] After a great deal of pressure from the promoters, the French and Italian communists decided to participate in the hope of influencing the other parties. Tito's presence, almost twenty years after the previous Yugoslavian participation in an assembly of international communism, gave the event even greater significance.

The conference of European communists took place in Berlin at the end of June 1976. Berlinguer was the principal player, especially given the media coverage in the West. For the first time, he used the term 'Eurocommunism' before an international audience of communists, and insisted on the pluralist nature of the movement. Marchais did not do the same, preferring to emphasize the usual theme of autonomy for the parties. All the same, the monolithic image of the movement was affected. In accordance with a strategy agreed just before the proceedings, Brezhnev and Suslov avoided all polemic and chose to emphasize the role of the Soviet Union, reminding European communists that only Moscow could guarantee a global profile for the movement.[114] The Soviet delegation considered the conference to be a success.[115] But this time, it had become admissible within the movement to express ideas that differed from the orthodoxy, rather than disagreements on singles issues.[116] The ruling group of the Soviet Union had not understood all the consequences of such a transition. The day after the Berlin Conference a paradox began to become clear. The Eurocommunist Alliance was not garnering support amongst the smaller Western parties, which were mainly under the direct control of the 'socialist camp'. Eurocommunism was exercising an influence that was more intellectual than political, as in Great Britain, where it was linked to the discovery of Gramsci's thought.[117] It was, however, getting a sympathetic and not overly disguised response in Eastern Europe, particularly in Budapest and Warsaw, where it presented itself as a political project that could

---

[113] Ibid. 234–8.
[114] A. Chernyaev, *Moya zhizn' i moe vremya* (Moscow: Mezhdunarodnye otnosheniya, 1995), 345.
[115] Shakhnazarov, *S vozhdiami i bez nikh*, 272.   [116] Chernyaev, *Sovmestnii iskhod*, 239.
[117] G. Andrews, *Endgames and New Times: The Final Years of British Communism 1964–1991* (London: Lawrence & Wishart, 2004), 159–66.

open up a margin of autonomy.[118] At the same time, the two main Western parties appeared to be on the rise precisely because they had been distancing themselves from the Soviet Union. The PCI took another step closer to government—de facto supporting a parliamentary majority through the abstruse mechanism of abstention in the summer of 1976—while the PCF established the basis for an alliance with the socialists in the next French election.

For the Soviet leaders, this was an undesirable scenario and they were persuaded that the containment of Eurocommunism at the Berlin Conference was not sufficient. Moscow's strategy took another turn at the end of the summer of 1976, once the Politburo had discussed the outcome of the Berlin Conference. Suslov and Andropov insisted on the need to react against yet another manifestation of 'revisionism' in communist history.[119] The problem was exacerbated when Jimmy Carter won the American election in November 1976, and installed a democratic administration that was much more sensitive to the human rights issue than the previous one and therefore much less reassuring for the Soviets. The conservative détente guaranteed by Kissinger was at risk. Consequently, the Politburo found it easier to take the idea that détente was the product of Western weakness to its logical conclusion. This view was governing Soviet behaviour in the Third World, but also meant that there was a limit to the price to be paid in Europe. Authoritarian stabilization was now accompanied by tighter ideological control over the communist movement and counter-propaganda on the question of human rights. At the same time, Moscow had started to modernize its theatre missiles without too much concern for Western reactions, possibly in an attempt to initimidate Western Europe.[120] In this political context, 'hawks' like Andropov, Suslov, and Dmitriy Ustinov were relaxed about their decisions, while the leadership of Brezhnev was weakened by his precarious physical condition.[121]

At the beginning of 1977, the Soviets sought in vain to prevent the first public meeting between the three Eurocommunist leaders, which in their opinion put at risk the movement's unity in Europe.[122] The tension between Moscow and the Eurocommunists reached its height in the immediate wake of the meeting between Berlinguer, Carrillo, and Marchais held in Madrid on 3 March 1977. The *casus belli* was provided by Carrillo's pamphlet, which attempted to suggest a political line for Eurocommunism, but actually revealed the vagueness of Eurocommunist ideas and was little more than an anachronistic ideological polemic. In spite of this or precisely because of this, the Soviets branded it as a revisionist manifesto.[123] Moscow reacted more angrily than it appeared to do in public, and did all it could to foment splits inside the Eurocommunist parties. The KGB orchestrated a campaign to discredit Berlinguer and weaken his leadership.[124] All the same, Berlinguer

---

[118] S. Segre, *A chi fa paura l'eurocomunismo?* (Rimini: Guaraldi, 1977).
[119] Chernyaev, *Moya zhizn' i moe vremya*, 349. [120] Haslam, *Russia's Cold War*, 303–4.
[121] Zubok, *A Failed Empire*, 251, 254–5.
[122] APCF, Fondo Gaston Plissonier, 264 J 17 (14 Feb. 1977).
[123] Chernyaev, *Sovmestnii iskhod*, 278–9.
[124] C. Andrew and V. Mitrokhin, *L'archivio Mitrokhin: le attività segrete del KGB in occidente* (Milan: Rizzoli, 2000), 372.

went to Moscow in November 1977 for the sixtieth anniversary of the Revolution to declare that democracy was 'a universal value'. His meeting with Brezhnev was frosty. The Soviets asked the Italian communists to renounce their own political positions and serve the interests of Moscow by starting a campaign against NATO, which would obviously destroy their chances of getting into government.[125] At this stage, détente was no longer an understanding between two partners, as it had been until the previous year, though with differences concerning static and dynamic interpretations. In Moscow, Eurocommunism was no longer seen simply as a risky destabilizing factor, but also as a damaging heresy in the imminent scenario of renewed antagonism between the two blocs.

The behind-the-scenes clash between the Soviets and the Italians continued over successive months and culminated in talks held in Moscow in October 1978. On this occasion, Berlinguer defended Eurocommunism from the accusation of being a movement that furthered the interests of the enemy and divided Western communism from the 'socialist camp'. He posed a question that embraced the whole of the previous decade when he expressed his concern that 'in the moment in which the crisis of capitalism is deepening and the need for socialism is increasing, there is sadly no great attraction to the socialist ideal'. But his dialogue with Suslov, Ponomarev, and Brezhnev was a dialogue of the deaf. Suslov branded the Eurocommunists' plea for freedom of expression for the dissidents as an inadmissible request to 'return to a society divided into classes'. Brezhnev accused the PCI of giving in to NATO's 'aggressive plans' with its governmental strategy.[126] The very fact that Western communists acknowledged that there was a problem of human rights in the Soviet Union and the bloc countries, albeit in a prudent and selective manner, made them suspected of treachery and submission to anti-Sovietism. Moscow considered the criticisms expressed by Western communists even more unacceptable at a time when tensions with the United States were on the increase and after the success of the Cuban–Soviet international campaign in the Horn of Africa. The main spectre was the alliance between the United States and China, which the Soviet leaders considered a 'new Munich', revealing the depth of their ancient insecurities. They perceived the legacy of the Prague Spring and Eurocommunism to be a weakening of the anti-Western front and a threat to destabilize the 'socialist community'. Thus the Soviet offensive against Eurocommunism implied a call to order against any centrifugal force in Europe.

To some degree, the Soviet counteroffensive was successful, especially because the Eurocommunist alliance was divided and imaginary. The Madrid meeting had actually marked the start of its decline. The agreement between the two major parties had always been limited when it came to strategic matters, particularly on Europe, given that the French communists rejected the idea of political integration, while the Italians had embraced it. The Carter administration's cautious openness towards Eurocommunism was soon withdrawn and was seen, with an

---

[125] APCI, Fondo Berlinguer, serie Movimento Operaio Internazionale, fasc. 151.
[126] S. Pons, 'Meetings between the Italian Communist Party and the Communist Party of the Soviet Union, Moscow and Rome, 1978–80', *Cold War History* 3.1 (2002).

outlook similar to Kissinger's, as more of a problem for the Western alliances than an opportunity to weaken the Soviet Union.[127] The internal difficulties did the rest.[128] In June 1977 the PCE obtained a result of less than 10 per cent, which was well below expectations at the first free election after the fall of Franco. The PCF was still able to recruit activists, but its electoral following was stagnating around one fifth of the electorate, while its competition with the socialists ended in a split and a defeat for the left in March 1978. The PCI maintained enviable grass roots, but was affected by the attrition of its shared national responsibilities without ever managing to take part in government, having to return to opposition in January 1979. In a climate poisoned by the assassination of the principal political leader in Italy, the Christian democrat Aldo Moro, by terrorists in the Red Brigades, the mainstay of Eurocommunism failed in its governmental ambition and had to diminish its international profile, although it did continue to have considerable support within the country. At the start of the second half of the decade, the communist parties in Southern Europe appeared to have genuine electoral strength capable of taking on the socialist parties. But by the end of the decade, the gap between them was once more considerable and in favour of the reformist left, except in Italy. Eurocommunism had run its course.

For Moscow, the failure of Eurocommunism favoured unity amongst the communist parties in the face of imminent international tensions. During 1979, an international crisis was caused by the Soviet deployment of new missiles in the European theatre. NATO's reaction and its decision to install a similar system in Western Europe over the following years marked the end of détente. The Soviet decision to invade Afghanistan was taken shortly afterwards as a result of the situation in the country, but also in the hope that some Western countries might break ranks. The long-held hopes of putting a wedge between the United States and Western Europe had a significant role in this decision.[129] This scenario only strengthened the resolve of Soviet leaders to demand conformity amongst the communist parties, in accordance with a reflex action that was as old as the Cold War. Moscow called them into line, even if this demonstrated a shrinking and indeed insignificant consensus. On 26 February 1980, the leaders of the Eastern and Central European parties, excluding Ceauşescu, met in Moscow to express their support for Soviet policy and prepare a conference that would be expanded to include the Western parties.[130] Now close to death, Tito criticized the military intervention in Afghanistan in a letter to Brezhnev, which opened a new front of protest from the non-aligned countries.[131] The PCI condemned the invasion, together with some minor parties such as the Spanish, British, and Japanese ones.

---

[127] I. Wall, 'L'amministrazione Carter e l'eurocomunismo', *Ricerche di storia politica* 9.2 (2006).

[128] A. Agosti, *Bandiere rosse: un profilo storico dei comunismi europei* (Rome: Editori Riuniti, 1999), 278ff.

[129] Haslam, *Russia's Cold War*, 326–7.

[130] C. Békés, 'Why was there no "second Cold War" in Europe? Hungary and the Soviet invasion of Afghanistan in 1979. Documents from the Hungarian archives', *Cold War International History Project Bulletin* 14 and 15 (2003–4), doc. 5, pp. 211–14.

[131] Ibid. docs 7 and 8, pp. 215–17.

This caused more tension between the Soviets and the Italians. For the International Department of the CPSU, the PCI was a thorn in their side: it was now the only mass communist party in the West and had re-established relations with China, which had not lost the opportunity provided by Afghanistan to denounce yet again the threat posed by the Soviet Union's plans for 'world hegemony'. The funding for the PCI was brusquely suspended, and diverted to factions wishing to break away.[132] The Italians did not take part in the conference of European communists held in Paris in May 1980 at the behest of the Poles and the French to express support for the Soviet war in Afghanistan. Following the same path taken by Tito three years earlier, Berlinguer went to Peking to meet Deng Xiaoping and Hu Yaobang. The communist conference in Paris was reduced to a grotesque masquerade of orthodoxy, which evoked the threat of imperialism and a new world war just when the Soviet Union was venturing on an imperial war of its own in a country outside Europe. The possibility of convening another world conference to react against the PCI's positions was considered, but even the Soviet leaders were sceptical of such a move.[133]

The fact that it had halted the centrifugal forces was not an indicator of a degree of success for Moscow. Western European communism, with the exception of Italy, was reduced to a small troop of tiny parties that were easy to control but lacked any influence, whereas Eastern European communism resembled the periphery of a militarized empire, not entirely different from thirty years earlier. People in Moscow were aware of their country's isolation as a 'military superpower', the lack of any grand plan for international communism, and the sense of an ethical and cultural crisis even more than an economic one, but the Soviet leaders were not.[134] The different trajectories of the PCI and the PCF demonstrated that the chances of a communist party's survival as a mass party in the West were inversely proportional to its closeness to Moscow and the 'socialist camp'. The PCI was condemned to opposition in Italy's 'logjammed democracy' and seemed to be gripped by an increasing identity crisis, but it resisted the challenge from the socialist leader Bettino Craxi and maintained the support of one third of the electorate. The PCF attained its aim of entering government thanks to the victory of the left that took François Mitterrand to the presidency in May 1981, but it was now in a support role and had undergone drastic electoral decline.[135] Only the Italian communists had adopted practices and language that were anathema to the Soviet tradition, and had abandoned conspicuous elements of the communist tradition. Berlinguer's refusal to approve the invasion of Afghanistan on the basis of a principle 'of class' was one example. Concepts developed by the Western European left had made inroads on the PCI's culture, particularly those of Brandt and Olof Palme, such as the crisis of the bipolar order, the interdependence of European security, and the problem of the North–South relationship in the world.[136] The

---

[132] Riva, *Oro da Mosca*, docs 152, 153, 157.   [133] Chernyaev, *Sovmestnii iskhod*, 407.
[134] Chernyaev's numerous reflections on this subject between 1978 and 1980 are very instructive: see ibid. 339, 377, 386–7, 423.
[135] Agosti, *Bandiere rosse*, 305, 313.
[136] Pons, *Berlinguer e la fine del comunismo*, 182–3.

cultural change in Italian communism did not seem to have had any influence on other parties outside the national context. The defeat of Eurocommunism was thus part of a wider crisis that promised difficult times for all communists. As a political movement, Eurocommunism was a failure. Its main result was to bury international communism in Europe as well.[137]

THE CRISIS OF LEGITIMACY

Moscow's success in re-establishing discipline over European communism was hazardous, and concealed dramatic problems in Central and Eastern Europe. A chronic economic and social crisis now afflicted 'real socialism', revealing that its centralized and stagnant economies—impervious to reform and less equipped than the Western ones to undertake the post-Fordist transformation—were the main victims of the world crisis in the 1970s.[138] The ungovernability of the 'external empire' became startlingly topical in the summer of 1980, when the workers of Danzig and other Polish industrial cities resumed protests and strikes, as they had done on more than one occasion during the previous decade. This time, however, their spontaneous movement found an unprecedented form of organization, that of the independent trade union Solidarność. For the first time in a Soviet-type society an institution had been born that was emancipated from state control—and was *de facto* structured as an alternative power. The anti-communist resistance had in the past presented the features of hot-headed rebellion, unthinking alienation, and intellectual dissent. Now it assumed those of a mass movement hardened by suffering but peaceful, and became an opposition with a vast social base. Solidarność did not aim to create a political party, but it could boast an indisputable social consensus. Its Catholic inspiration, heightened by the popularity of the Polish pope, John Paul II, gave it a national character and threw light on the discredited communist regime. The establishment's response in Warsaw and Moscow was a dual one, following a model that went back to 1956. In Poland, the replacement of Gierek by Stanisław Kania was an attempt to follow a reformist course and set up a dialogue with the unionized workers. In the Soviet Union, a secret crisis committee under Suslov's direction was appointed to organize yet another repressive solution.[139] On 18 September 1980, Brezhnev addressed the Politburo and defined the events in Poland as 'another form of intervention by the class enemy'.[140]

---

[137] Chernyaev, *Moya zhizn' i moe vremya*, 268; S. Pons, 'The rise and fall of Eurocommunism', in Leffler and Westad, *The Cambridge History of the Cold War*, vol. 3: *Endings*, 60–3.

[138] C. S. Maier, *Il crollo: la crisi del comunismo e la fine della Germania Est* (Bologna: Il Mulino, 1999), 136–37, 149–54.

[139] M. Kramer, *Soviet Deliberations during the Polish Crisis, 1980–1981*, Cold War International History Project, special working paper no. 1 (Washington, D.C.: Woodrow Wilson Center, 1999); Ouimet, *The Rise and Fall of the Brezhnev Doctrine in Soviet Foreign Policy*, 136.

[140] Chernyaev, *Sovmestnii iskhod*, 418.

Moscow applied the same kind of intimidation to Kania that it had used against Dubček. Unlike the Czechoslovak leader, Kania lacked a genuine reforming vision and above all the confidence to oversee transition. The Polish Communist Party was visibly fragmenting—demonstrating amongst other things that the progressive growth of the ranks of the political elite in power since the end of the Second World War had followed a logic all of its own, which had nothing to do with social consensus. For Moscow, the only real alternatives were another armed intervention or repression implemented by the Polish establishment. As in 1968, the leaders of the Warsaw Pact were involved in the decision-making process. Their conservative vision was wholly intact and obstinately linked to the paradigm of 'counter-revolution'. The leader of the 'hawks' was Honecker, who at the meeting of spokespeople for the Pact held in Moscow on 5 December 1980 called for drastic measures and attacked the moderation of Kania. Concern over the possible contagion of the Solidarność example outside Poland was expressed by everyone, including Kádár.[141] The Polish crisis was therefore seen as a threat to the very existence of the 'socialist community'. The analogies with 1968 ended there. Poland in 1980–81 experienced no attempt at reform, only a search for an impossible balance, given the strength of the social opposition, the weakness of the Communist Party, and the harshness of external pressure.

The duration of the crisis was, above all, the result of uncertainties in Moscow. The Politburo was aware that this time the risk of a mass revolt against any intervention by the Red Army was much higher than in previous crises in Eastern Europe.[142] The Soviet decision was to avoid military intervention from outside, pushing the regime into using the police to resolve the problem. In the spring of 1981 the pressure coming from the Politburo and Warsaw Pact intensified once more. Honecker even took the initiative, requesting that the Soviets convene the talks that took place in Moscow on 16 May 1981. On this occasion, the East German leader delivered a tirade against Kania, now accused of having turned a blind eye to the 'counter-revolution'.[143] The pressure from the Soviet Union and its principal allies became increasingly intimidating. The resistance of the Polish leadership was not overcome for another six months, after Kania had been removed from office and the main offices of state and the party had been concentrated in the hands of General Wojciech Jaruzelski. There followed a 'phoney war' in Poland, largely manipulated by Moscow.[144] At the Plenum of the Central Committee of the CPSU held in November, Suslov announced that the Soviet Union would use its 'political influence' around the world 'to prevent the escalation of imperialist interference in Polish affairs', which would permit the final reckoning within the country against the 'anti-socialist forces'.[145] In spite of Solidarność's moderation,

---

[141] A. Paczkowski and M. Byrne (eds), *From Solidarity to Martial Law: The Polish Crisis of 1980–1981. A Documentary History* (Budapest: Central European University Press, 2007), doc. 22, pp. 141–61.

[142] Mastny, *The Warsaw Pact as History*, 50.

[143] Paczkowski and Byrne, *From Solidarity to Martial Law*, doc. 49, pp. 280–93.

[144] F. Fejtö, *La fine delle democrazie popolari: l'Europa orientale dopo la rivoluzione del 1989* (Milan: Mondadori, 1994), 131.

[145] RGANI, fo. 2, op. 3, d. 568.

Jaruzelski declared martial law on 13 December 1981, and the oppositionists were arrested without any blood being spilled. The most catastrophic scenario had been avoided, but the Polish crisis had left its indelible mark on the reality and image of 'real socialism'.

Jaruzelski's *coup d'état* had perhaps saved Poland from a worse fate. But in every other way, the balance sheet was showing a loss. The Cold War justifications for the creation of a military dictatorship in the centre of Europe did not seem very credible. On the other hand, the discredit to the regimes that originated out of Sovietization was clear to all. Moreover, the option of strong-arm police methods was an admission of the difficulties in applying the letter of the 'Brezhnev doctrine'. In their confidential debates, members of the Politburo acknowledged that Moscow could no longer allow itself the same freedom of action it had had in the past without running serious risks. Andropov went so far as to acknowledge that a military intervention would be a catastrophe, and that the Soviet Union would not be able to carry it through 'even if Poland fell under the control of Solidarność'.[146] The day after 13 December, they breathed a sigh of relief in communist ruling circles, but the bravado of previous military interventions was not there. One of the signs of shaky confidence within the Soviet ruling group was the absence of rhetoric linking the actions that had weakened the 'counter-revolution' in Poland with the interests of the international communist movement. Although there was hardly any need, the sham of international communism was now being confirmed again and again.

Having vainly hoped for reform from above, the PCI condemned Jaruzelski's coup and referred to it as a demonstration of a decline that was affecting the whole Soviet world. In a famous television interview, Berlinguer declared that Soviet-type societies had lost their 'ability to evolve'. Although the PCI's reaction had been predictable, Soviet leaders were uncertain for over a month about the counter-measures they should take. The proposal put forward by Ponomarev with Suslov's backing was to issue an excommunication, but this was rejected by the Politburo. Andropov argued that they had to do everything they could to avoid a rift. Brezhnev thought that an 'arraignment' was not advisable.[147] Eventually Moscow reacted by censuring Italian communists through an editorial in *Pravda* which was frosty and bureaucratic, but avoided passing its final verdict. However, the decision to make a public statement attacking the party was unprecedented in relations between the Soviet Union and Western communists. Relations with the PCI became cool, though they were not broken off.[148] The rift between the two sides rounded off a process of fragmentation. Whereas China after Mao and Yugoslavia after Tito continued on their own nationalistic paths, the only large communist party in the West was on a collision course with Moscow. The Politburo had decided in April 1981 to revive the initiative of a fourth conference of world communism, which had first been aired eight years earlier, but the project

[146] Kramer, *Soviet Deliberations during the Polish Crisis*, doc. 21, p. 165.
[147] Chernyaev, *Sovmestnii iskhod*, 471–2.
[148] Pons, *Berlinguer e la fine del comunismo*, 215ff.

still did not get off the ground.[149] The problem on the agenda, identified by the brightest officials at the International Department of the CPSU, was the crisis in the communist movement, but Ponomarev ignored its very existence.[150]

However, the Polish crisis was also a defeat for the ideas of reforming communism, which were now defended publicly only by the PCI. The hopes of finding an heir to 'socialism with a human face' in Poland were misplaced. Italian communists hoped they were the vanguard, but they were actually the exception, linked to a specific national context—the 'logjammed democracy' and the legacy of the mass party created after the war. Italian communism was not in danger of collapse, as French communism was, because its grass roots and its profile as a national and democratic force were much more solid. But its fate was subject to worrying questions and dilemmas following the demise of Eurocommunism. The resilience of the PCI could not be taken for granted. Its ability to mount effective campaigns was still significant, when it came to the pacifist movements which emerged as a reaction to the NATO's decision to deploy missiles in Europe; but there were no political outcomes from them. Its reformist practice in local government was contradicted by its cultural baggage, which meant rejecting reformism in the name of a communist moral 'diversity' and putting forward a largely apocalyptic view of where capitalist societies were going. Berlinguer and the ruling group of the PCI did not want to make the final break with the Soviet Union, because they still hoped that they could bring influence to bear and were counting on a revival of détente, but also because such a move would have compromised the party's identity and conjured up the spectre of 'social democratization'. So they turned their back on international communism without seeking out a new family and a different alliance on the European left. In spite of its Europeanist ideology, the PCI was an isolated force, entrusting its own fate to expectations of a future reform of communism.[151]

The most noticeable feature of the Soviet Union and the regimes in Eastern Europe was, however, their stasis and paralysis. Without any mechanisms for changes in leadership, the communist states were ruled by old men who had been promoted under Stalin and had impeded access to power by the generation of the thaw. Their view of the future was pessimistic. Their parameters for judging the world were fixed and immutable; their perceptions of reality hazy and stereotypical. Their capacity to confront the crisis or even acknowledge it was almost non-existent. In international politics, Moscow and its most loyal allies perceived the presidency of Ronald Reagan, who was elected in 1980 with a promise to adopt a more confrontational approach and relaunch American prestige, as purely and simply a threat of war. They deluded themselves that the European pacifist movements, which were huge in Germany and Italy, constituted a rerun of the 1950s and were a political tool for the Soviet bloc. But the scenarios and allegiances of the Cold War were no longer the same. The leaderships of communist countries

---

[149] Chernyaev, *Sovmestnii iskhod*, 453.   [150] Ibid. 479, 482.
[151] Pons, *Berlinguer e la fine del comunismo*, 247ff.

seemed to be incapable of understanding the cultural and political changes taking place in the West, which on the one hand demonstrated the increasing neoconservative hegemony and made possible a renewed consolidation of transatlantic relations, and on the other hand cut off the link between the communist world and Western pacifist sentiments. Only Italian communism managed to maintain its grip on the new wave of pacifism. Across Europe, pacifist movements were assembling disparate cultural frameworks—socialists, grass-roots activists, environmentalists, and feminists—in which the pro-Soviet components were negligible.[152] The conflict between Atlanticism and pacifism had become a reality within the Western community, which communism of Soviet observance could no longer influence as it had done in the past.

With the death of Brezhnev in November 1982, the reaction to decline was entrusted to the regime's strongman, Andropov, who had long thought that energetic intervention was necessary. During his brief period in power, he aimed to increase efficiency and pragmatism, but his foreign policy was still anchored to the idea that the challenge in the Third World was advantageous for the 'socialist camp' and that the problems encountered by Soviet-type societies in Europe were attributable to outside attempts at destabilization.[153] Ten years younger than Brezhnev but seriously ill, Andropov died little more than a year after his appointment without having achieved anything significant. He was replaced by another gerontocrat, the characterless Konstantin Chernenko, who in turn would only last a year. A whole generation in the Soviet Union was being swallowed up—the generation that was the bridge to the Stalinist era, had seen the high point of international communism and lived through its fragmentation; that had built Soviet global power and experienced its decline.

In the decade between 1968 and the late 1970s, the heights to which the Soviet Union had risen as a superpower, the defeat of the United States in Vietnam, the Third Worldist ideologies, and capitalism's economic crisis had produced a gigantic misconception in the way international communism viewed itself and Western perceptions. In the communist world, conformists, radicals, and reformers all shared the idea that there was now a historical opportunity to advance the position of socialism against American imperialism, even though they differed over the means and policies most suited to translating this into practice. The Soviets saw the approaching triumph of a strategy that privileged the politics of power as a response to global geostrategic changes and to increasing economic and cultural internationalization. They believed that they were putting forward their own variant of global politics in opposition to the tendency towards interdependence that was being asserted in the West. In their eyes, the legacy of communist internationalism was now part of the rivalry for world power, and this rivalry was working in favour of the 'socialist camp', in spite of the defections, insubordinations, and failed promises of prosperity. Moscow's main allies in Europe, the East Germans,

[152] Eley, *Forging Democracy*, 419–20; Sassoon, *One Hundred Years of Socialism*, 715–17.
[153] Haslam, *Russia's Cold War*, 338.

helped to sustain this vision, which rendered indispensable the role of gendarme fulfilled by the communist establishments. Outside Europe, the Cubans were putting themselves forward as the secular arm of the new internationalist mission. Of the Western communists, only the Italians criticized the Soviet Union's imperial vocation but they did not deny that its role as a great power was essential to safeguard the fate of the cause that was born with the October Revolution. All this ended up creating illusions even amongst the communists who were most conscious of the movement's decline and the serious dilemmas facing Soviet-type societies. Those who hoped the system could be reformed accepted that Soviet communism was a backward form of socialism, but not that it constituted a totalitarian model in decay. The conviction that Soviet-type societies at least provided an example of anti-consumerism and harboured a potential for renewal was difficult to shake off. This was even truer of the idea that the Soviet Union carried out the necessary role of counterweight to American imperialism, irrespective of its attraction as a social model.[154] Indeed, the persistence of anti-Americanism helped to defend an identity that was in crisis and to counterbalance the decline of Soviet myths.

Even the adversaries of communism were largely of the opinion that they were up against a force with a potential for expansion. Ironically, this perception was to some extent the result of the Soviet Union's tenacious self-promotion as a superpower with a role in the bipolar context and in the Third World. Elected on a wave of discontent with détente, seen as a repeat of appeasement, President Reagan did not restrict himself to relaunching the United States' role as the bulwark against totalitarianism, but branded the Soviet Union an 'evil empire', the source of terrorist or subversive movement on a planetary scale. The turn towards neoconservatism in the West was based on a twin vision of Soviet communism. On the one hand, it emphasized the difficulties of 'real existing socialism' and the structural fragility of the Soviet economy; on the other, it fostered the image of a pervasive power capable of threatening Western liberties.[155] But the success of the neoconservatives was in itself proof of communism's lack of influence. Not by chance, they did not even take up the challenge of an 'alternative modernity' but were only concerned with declaring Western supremacy and putting the communist economies on the ropes. The Polish crisis demonstrated that the scenario of a 'Finlandization' and pro-Soviet neutralism of Western Europe—feared in the West since the start of the Cold War and seen as a possible consequence of Soviet theatre missiles[156]—was much less likely than an erosion of communist domination of Central and Eastern Europe. The threat posed by the Soviet Union to the West now appeared much more circumscribed, although still serious. It was not the possibility of an expansion of communism into Europe or anywhere else, but the risk that the decay and

---

[154] Hobsbawm, *Interesting Times*, 308–9.
[155] Romero, *Storia della Guerra Fredda*, 284–5, 293–4; A. Gleason, *Totalitarianism: The Inner History of the Cold War* (Oxford: Oxford University Press, 1995), 196–7; D. S. Foglesong, *The American Mission and the 'Evil Empire': The Crusade for a 'Free Russia' since 1881* (Cambridge: Cambridge University Press, 2007), 174–85.
[156] Del Pero, *Henry Kissinger e l'ascesa dei neoconservatori*, 131–5.

overexposed nature of the empire might lead the Soviet gerontocracy to highly pessimistic conclusions and desperate solutions to defend their own chances of success in the Cold War. The truth is that the representation and deceits of the 1970s concealed a crisis that was much more serious than the one being experienced by the West at the time.

The Soviet Union as a great power was compared with the United States, even though its economic and technological base was much inferior. But the prospect of a shift in the balance of power in favour of the 'socialist camp', which was central to Brezhnev's political discourse, had proved to be without foundation. In a bipolar world, the Soviet Union had always been kept separate from the principal centres of economic and geopolitical power—Western Europe and Japan—but now its isolation was aggravated by the creation of an alliance between the United States and China for anti-Soviet reasons. The consequences of this alliance were immediately revealed in the wake of the thirty-year war in Indochina, which, in accordance with the crude logic of the Cold War, saw Washington embrace Chinese positions and denounce Vietnam as the aggressor while remaining silent over the atrocities committed by the Khmer Rouge.[157] But the problems of the Soviet Union were not only in the Far East. The triumphant Islamic Revolution in Iran at the beginning of 1979, in spite of Moscow's and the Iranian communists' initial hopes, was no less anti-Soviet than anti-American, and rejected both ideologies of modernization proposed by the great powers.[158] The struggle of the Afghan mujahideen against the Soviet invasion became the principal cause of the Islamic internationalism invoked by the Iranian Revolution. The war promoted anti-Soviet hostility around the Islamic world that was on a par with that of the Chinese, attracting action in support of the Afghan resistance in Arab capitals, as well as Peking and Washington.[159] Even relations with India, the non-communist country in which there had been continuous Soviet influence over the previous two decades, were cooled considerably. The communist hegemony in important states such as Kerala and West Bengal, which would last for more than twenty years, did not produce significant consequences at national and international level.[160] To complete the panorama, Moscow was marginalized in the Middle East. Its decision to support the more intransigent positions in the Arab world after the Yom Kippur War had turned out to be a fiasco. The loss of the alliance with Egypt could not be made up for by relations with other Arab countries. The accords between Egypt and Israel in September 1978, under the aegis of the United States, set the seal on the

[157] C. Menétrey-Monchau, 'The changing post-war US strategy in Indochina', in Westad and Quinn-Judge, *The Third Indochina War*, 79–81.

[158] M. Behrooz, *Rebels with a Cause: The Failure of the Left in Iran* (London: I. B. Tauris, 1999), 99–105, 124–30.

[159] A. Saikal, 'Islamism, the Iranian Revolution, and the Soviet invasion of Afghanistan', in Leffler and Westad, *The Cambridge History of the Cold War*, vol. 3: *Endings*, 129–31.

[160] V. Mastny, 'The Soviet Union's partnership with India', *Journal of Cold War Studies* 12.3 (2010), 50–90; S. Basu and A. Majumder, 'Dilemmas of parliamentary communism: the rise and fall of the Left in West Bengal', *Critical Asian Studies* 45.2 (2013), 167–200.

Soviet Union's exclusion from the region.[161] Even a traditional ally such as the Iraqi Ba'athist Party, under Saddam Hussein's leadership, implemented yet another suppression of local communists and launched the foolhardy war against Khomeini's Iran, which appeared to be much more in the interests of Washington than those of Moscow.[162] It was a picture of loss of influence and an empire that had overstretched itself—the opposite of a possible Soviet expansion in various geostrategic directions, feared by Brzezinski and exaggerated by the Reagan administration.[163]

The Soviet Union of the 1980s, as Odd Arne Westad has observed, interacted less and less with the rest of the planet.[164] Its leaders did not seem to understand the gradual transformation of the bipolar order into a multipolar one. As this change took place, the significance of the communist movement centred around the Soviet state and the attraction of the Soviet model appeared increasingly ill-defined. In Europe this phenomenon had been clearly visible for some time, and the hopes of reversing the direction of travel were based on no firm evidence. The idea that the simultaneous defeat of the Americans in Vietnam and the 'Carnation Revolution' in Portugal could open the way to a new radicalization of politics was one of the many delusions of communist history. The idea that a 'general crisis of capitalism' would produce new forms of fascism and consequently revive anti-fascism was startlingly disproved by the fall of all the right-wing dictatorships in Southern Europe. The transitions to democracy in Portugal, Greece, and Spain did not favour the communists, whether orthodox or reforming, but rather Socialist reformists, which demonstrated the role and influence of the European Community. The only dictatorships left on the old continent were communist ones, and this constituted an obvious delegitimizing factor, which compounded the unexpected consequences of Helsinki. Contrary to what the Soviet leaders had expected, the question of human rights, which was secured in the final act of the conference, would not remain a dead letter and was not relegated to the opposing rhetorics of the Cold War, but instead acquired centrality in international public opinion, contributing to the defence of dissidents and compromising the credibility of regimes.[165] Jaruzelski's coup in Poland came to symbolize the continuity of police states and the repressive nature of communist regimes.

At the same time, the record of pro-Soviet internationalism and the alliances established outside Europe was hardly brilliant, as the most observant commentators noted at the time.[166] The only success it could boast of was the defeat inflicted

[161] Brutents, *Tridtsat' let na staroy ploshadi*, 370; A. Shlaim, *The Iron Wall: Israel and the Arab World* (London: Penguin, 2000), 321–2.

[162] Ismael, *The Rise and Fall of the Communist Party of Iraq*, 196–7; J. Franzen, *Red Star over Iraq: Iraqi Communism Before Saddam* (London: Hurst, 2011), 240.

[163] M. P. Leffler, *For the Soul of Mankind: The United States, the Soviet Union, and the Cold War* (New York: Hill and Wang, 2007), 295, 323–4, 336–7.

[164] O. A. Westad, 'How the Cold War crumbled', in S. Pons and F. Romero (eds), *Reinterpreting the End of the Cold War: Issues, Interpretations, Periodizations* (London: Frank Cass, 2005).

[165] D. C. Thomas, *The Helsinki Effect: International Norms, Human Rights, and the Demise of Communism* (Princeton, N.J.: Princeton University Press, 2001); R. Foot, 'The Cold War and human rights', in Leffler and Westad, *The Cambridge History of the Cold War*, vol. 3: *Endings*.

[166] Archives of the Hoover Institution, Alexander Dallin papers, Stanford (Calif.), box 14.

on the South African racist regime, which had been inspired and carried through by the Cubans. But the African Marxist-Leninist regimes in Angola, Mozambique, and Ethiopia only created problems for the Soviet Union, given their fierce internal divisions and ethnic conflicts, which were multiplied rather than resolved by socialist and statist policies. The situation in South Yemen was no better. None of the new experiences inspired by Soviet socialism could constitute a basis for spreading the anti-imperialist struggle, still less present an attractive example. In the Arab world, the model of the party-state and the command economy had left its mark on the shape of the regimes, but this did not produce any identification with the 'socialist camp', even where it was strongest, as in Algeria. Serious doubts about the validity and outcomes of the policy commitments in the Third World were raised by officials in charge of foreign policy even before the invasion of Afghanistan, but the Soviet leadership did not seem disposed or even able to modify its direction.[167] Instead of constituting a targeted short-term intervention, as Moscow's plans had originally intended, Afghanistan made their worst nightmares come true. The Soviet Union found itself bogged down in a full-scale war, of a kind it had not fought since the Second World War—a war that swallowed up human and material resources and which typified the substantial failure of the interventionist policies outside Europe. The Soviets had believed that the use of huge military power provided a shortcut to asserting their credibility and resolving the problems of the regimes they supported, thus making the same mistake as the United States in Vietnam but with consequences that were much more destructive to their destiny.[168]

The global context seemed to have been utterly reversed since ten years earlier, when the Western crisis had aroused fanciful ambitions and justified improbable calculations. The United States had recovered their leadership. The transatlantic alliance with Western Europe had been strengthened partly because of the deployment of Soviet missiles in theatre. Brandt's Ostpolitik had favoured new forms of interdependence between the two Europes, placing the Eastern European states in a position of minority and material dependency, and had lowered cultural and communications barriers by encouraging East European citizens to perceive the distance that separated the regimes' propaganda from the reality of the West. In this sense, European détente was a serious challenge to the division of the continent.[169] The end of bipolar détente could not mean the restoration of the old social and cultural separation behind the 'Iron Curtain'. The underestimation of the degree of autonomy in Western European politics—from de Gaulle to Brandt and on to Mitterrand and Kohl—and the idea of using European détente as a channel for Soviet influence were two of the main entries in the interminable list of strategic errors made by Brezhnev's ruling group. Long depicted by communist

---

[167] Brutents, *Tridtsat' let na staroy ploshadi*, 308; Westad, *The Global Cold War*, 284–5.

[168] M. E. Latham, 'The Cold War in the Third World, 1963–1975', in Leffler and Westad, *The Cambridge History of the Cold War*, vol. 2: *Crises and Détente*, 278–9.

[169] J. M. Hanhimäki, 'Détente in Europe, 1962–1975', in Leffler and Westad, *The Cambridge History of the Cold War*, vol. 2: *Crises and Détente*, 216–18.

propaganda as the base for a military threat, the Europe of integration had become, on the contrary, a civic and political pole of attraction capable of influencing the other half of the divided continent.[170]

Precisely because of European détente, the chasm between the stagnant societies of the Soviet bloc and the social and technological change taking place in Western societies was increasingly visible. The authoritarian modernization of the preceding decades had created a relative complexity within Soviet-type societies, which however lacked outlets both in its oligarchic political system and in its seized-up economic mechanisms. The preponderance of the military-industrial complex was a deadweight that inhibited reforms and prevented the application of mass-production technologies.[171] The promise of catching up with and overtaking the advanced capitalist countries in mass consumption had proved to be the most unrealistic and counterproductive of the ambitions held by Stalin's successors and nourished by their own propaganda. More than any other dream for the future, this promise could be questioned in the light of reality; populations experienced disaffection, particularly when the gap between the Soviet bloc and Western consumerism could no longer be hidden.[172] While the capitalist West was overcoming its economic crisis through a dynamic transformation and an information revolution, Soviet communism could not follow the same path for political, economic, and ideological reasons. It was therefore entering a crisis whose outcome was unpredictable, while remaining shackled to a variant of industrial civilization that for decades had been seen as in the vanguard and was now revealed as being in the rearguard, an appendage with an extremely uncertain future.[173]

Moreover, the new capitalist dynamism was affecting not only the metropolis but also the world's periphery, increasing the diversity and undermining the very concept of the Third World, which had sustained the hopes of an anti-imperialist revolution after the Second World War. As far as models of modernity are concerned, the most significant process to emerge outside Europe was not the installation of Marxist-Leninist regimes in a few African states that were destined to plunge into ethnic conflicts and famines, but the economic take-off of a few Asian countries, such as South Korea, Taiwan, and Malaysia. From the moment Deng's China launched its market reforms, redefined the notion of socialism as the development of productive forces, and ended its separation by opening itself to the world in the early 1980s, the image of the Soviet model took a definitive blow to its foundations. This was the extreme nemesis of the Chinese split from the 'socialist camp'. It was precisely the rejection of economic competition with the West that was at the heart of the Maoist challenge to the Soviet Union. Now that competition had failed and a decisive factor in the delegitimization of the Soviet system

[170] Romero, *Storia della Guerra Fredda*, 222, 280, 298.
[171] V. Zaslavsky, *Storia del sistema sovietico: l'ascesa, la stabilità, il crollo* (Rome: La Nuova Italia Scientifica, 1995), 206–14.
[172] Rosenberg, 'Consumer capitalism and the end of the Cold War', 508.
[173] D. Reynolds, 'Science, technology, and the Cold War', in Leffler and Westad, *The Cambridge History of the Cold War*, vol. 3: *Endings*, 396–8.

was revealed, the Chinese challenge was completely overturned, and contributed to burying the whole idea of anti-capitalist modernity.[174]

The Soviet Union's isolation was only one aspect of the marginalization of its political culture and the model that had distinguished its role in the history of the twentieth century. In the Western and European world, the decline of Soviet myths and communist culture had been taking place for some time, and accelerated after 1968. But now it was associated with an even larger landslide, which decreed the decline of revolutionary culture and the 'withdrawal from the state'.[175] The more ideological components of the 1968 experience were rapidly dissolving to leave space for a libertarian anti-authoritarianism, a distrust in radical political transformations, a rediscovery of the value of individual choice, and an attempt to redefine politics in terms of new postmodern identities. While the generation of rebellious students and intellectuals had mainly challenged historical communism from neo-Marxist positions, now the same Western revolutionary tradition seemed to have been swallowed up. The popular metaphor that praised chaos, which Mao constantly repeated right up to the end of his life ('Great is the confusion under the sky, so the situation is excellent'), was perhaps the last revolutionary slogan to echo around Europe. The political culture of reformism, which communists had always opposed and the 'new left' despised, turned out to have more stamina. The link between democracy and prosperity seemed to ensure that Western society had moral superiority even before it had political and economic primacy.

In this climate the new anti-communism of European intellectuals was born, and incorporated many of the protagonists of the protests ten years earlier, particularly in France.[176] Strong criticism of the totalitarian nature of communism rapidly emerged in public discourse. The myths of Third Worldism were replaced by reactions against violations of human rights and the repression of dissent in Eastern Europe. The monumental moral outrage expressed by Solzhenitsyn in his *Gulag Archipelago* found a much wider public willing to embrace it than in the past—even the recent past. The impact of red terrorism in Europe and its message of death and desperation, bloated with Marxist metaphors and more than a little suspected of murky affiliations with some communist regimes, was disastrous for what was left of revolutionary rhetoric.[177] The revelations of the genocide carried out by the Khmer Rouge in their extermination camps revealed a dystopia worse than any Orwellian nightmare, and suggested that the communist regimes could replicate ad infinitum the crimes that had punctuated their history. The immense

---

[174] O. A. Westad, 'The Great Transformation: China in the Long 1970s', in N. Ferguson, C. S. Maier, E. Manela, and D. J. Sargent (eds), *The Shock of the Global: The 1970s in Perspective* (Cambridge, Mass.: Harvard University Press, 2010); Y. Sun, *The Chinese Reassessment of Socialism 1976–1992* (Princeton, N.J.: Princeton University Press, 1995); Jian, 'China and the Cold War after Mao'.

[175] Judt, *Postwar*, 561.

[176] J.-W. Mueller, 'The Cold War and the intellectual history of the late twentieth century', in Leffler and Westad, *The Cambridge History of the Cold War*, vol. 3: *Endings*, 5–8.

[177] A. Orsini, *Anatomia delle Brigate rosse: le radici ideologiche del terrorismo rivoluzionario* (Soveria Mannelli: Rubbettino, 2009).

tragedy of a little country like Cambodia contributed to the refusal of Western consciences to continue repressing the memory of the Gulag and the massacres of the Chinese Cultural Revolution.[178]

Unlike what happened during the first decades of the Cold War, communists were no longer in possession of the instruments of counter-mobilization and even language to oppose their critics and adversaries. This was also largely true of Western communists. Classist and progressive discourse sounded antiquated. Their vision of modernity, which was industrialist and catastrophist, seemed incongruous and obsolete even to the new postmodern apocalyptic cultures inspired by pacifism or ecology. The anathema of anti-Sovietism as a synonym of anti-progress and as an instrument to discredit and intimidate had now lost all efficacy. Anti-Americanism maintained its grip, but it revealed profound contradictions, as it was addressed to a public that no longer rejected American culture and civilization as a whole—not even the intellectuals.[179] The anti-American discourse of the communist tradition no longer reflected the image of an 'alternative modernity', only a dated and anti-modern mentality. Even behind what had once been called the 'Iron Curtain', anti-Western propaganda felt empty and nonsensical, denouncing a capitalism that no longer existed and celebrating a socialism that almost no one wanted. The communists' political culture was linked to dogmas and stereotypes that no longer reflected the reality of the societies they governed and did not speak to the great majority of the world, including its periphery. The legacy of communist state-building revealed an indissoluble link to a catastrophist tradition that went back to the First and the Second World War. This was the last message to come out of Vietnam, where the heroic image of the liberation struggle had given way to a harsh regime that produced desperate refugees. Even more than other communist states, the Vietnamese state had been forged by the experience of war over thirty years, and confirmed the centrality of this experience in the history of communism.[180] But that legacy did not express a political culture capable of providing responses to the experience of decline.

Was there a remedy to this crisis? Were any forces capable of generating genuine change? Could the system be reformed? Such questions had provoked political and intellectual debate in Europe and the United States, and also amongst dissidents, and produced contrasting opinions which were more or less in support of either dialogue or intransigence on the Western side. But very few were inclined to place complete faith in the possibility of reforming communism. Forces of change existed in some communist parties and within the establishment, but they were weak, scattered, and isolated. The Prague Spring continued to represent the foundation myth of reforming communism, but its suppression had left a trail

---

[178] Margolin, 'Cambogia: nel paese del crimine sconcertante', 543.

[179] A. Brogi, *Confronting America: The Cold War between the United States and the Communists in France and Italy* (Chapel Hill, N.C.: University of North Carolina Press, 2011), 388.

[180] S. Quinn-Judge, 'Through a glass darkly: reading the history of the Vietnamese Communist Party 1945–1975', in M. P. Bradley and M. B. Young (eds), *Making Sense of the Vietnam Wars: Local, National, and Transnational Perspectives* (New York: Oxford University Press, 2008), 111–34.

of frustration and disillusionment.[181] It was not even clear what reforming communists wanted, other than to revive some vague archetype of socialist humanism. One of the protagonists of post-communist disillusionment, Adam Michnik, wrote in 1978 that the 'revisionism' produced in his generation from the latent conflict between 'humanistic phraseology' and 'totalitarian practices' amounted to an irresolvable ambiguity.[182] Whatever the term meant, the reform of communism required an 'invention of tradition' that would be highly problematic to achieve, because it could undermine the original identity itself.

The problems left by Sovietization and the end of communist unity just kept increasing as the challenge from Western competition became more arduous and hopeless. The Soviet imperial model in Central and Eastern Europe had never been rehabilitated, and had in fact propagated its effects over the long term under the weight of economic failure and violent repressive measures by the police state. The communist regimes in Eastern Europe not only lacked national legitimacy but also constituted a source of permanent disrepute. At the same time, international communism had ceased to exist as an actor on the global political stage, having restricted itself to a ritual make-believe to connote pro-Soviet orthodoxy. The concept of 'two camps' had lost all efficacy. The very prospect of an 'alternative modernity' had been battered to death. Chinese communism was identified with a form of nationalism which, as such, was unable to hegemonize a separate grouping and could at the most suggest a means for survival to other communist regimes in Asia. Soviet communism had placed its trust in a global state power, thus compounding a massive imperial overstretch with the loss of a universalist tradition. This was the main question facing the last leader of the Soviet Union, Mikhail Gorbachev.

REFORM AND COLLAPSE

Elected in March 1985 with a mandate to halt the decline, Gorbachev would go down in history for his attempt at radical reform and its spectacular failure, culminating within a few years with the end of the 'external empire' and the dissolution of the Soviet Union. A little over 50 years old, he was not only the protagonist of a rejuvenation of the Soviet ruling group that had been postponed for far too long but also the representative of the generation moulded by the ideas of change during the Khrushchev era. Experience of foreign affairs was not his strong point, but international politics quickly became the mainstay of his attempts at reform. Under his leadership, the legacy of 'peaceful coexistence' and de-Stalinization was transformed into the idea of ending the Cold War and restructuring the Soviet Union. Lacking a clear project for reform, Gorbachev had a twin approach that he followed in a pragmatic manner: he aimed to free up resources for the economy

---

[181] M. Gorbachev and Z. Mlynář, *Conversations with Gorbachev: On Perestroika, the Prague Spring, and the Crossroads of Socialism* (New York: Columbia University Press, 2002), 57–66.

[182] A. Michnik, *Letters from Prison and Other Essays* (Berkeley: University of California Press, 1985), 157–8.

through international détente, and to regain credibility and dynamism through internal liberalization. Within a few years, he would attack the main Soviet categories of the Cold War: the idea of 'two camps', the perceived threat of the Western world, the classist interpretation of international relations and the philosophies of military security that had dominated the 'long postwar era'. His 'new thinking' arose as much from an accumulation of generational ideas that had never found expression in the Soviet decision-making process as it did from the increasing perception that the inertia in the system needed radical responses.[183]

Whatever the balance between the two motivations, the 'new thinking' contradicted basic elements of the Soviet identity by acknowledging global interdependence and erasing the image of the enemy inherited from the perceived 'international civil war'.[184] One of its implications was the abandonment of the residual ideas of world revolution and the defence of the 'socialist community' at any cost. But this did not mean also erasing the universalism linked to the legacy of the October Revolution. Gorbachev even proposed a relaunch of the politics and ideals of communism.[185] He behaved right up to the end not only as the leader of a great power that was revising its own concepts of security but also as the representative of a state that believed in its universal mission. Universalism constituted an essential element of Gorbachev's culture, which was linked to the myth of Lenin and the distinctive humanistic rhetoric of Soviet discourse. In this sense, his plan was an attempt to build a new legitimacy. However, his 'socialist idealism' suffered from the contradictions within reforming communism and increased their tension to its highest level.[186] This tradition had never clearly defined the consequences and shape of the reform, which required a profound change in identity and put the compatibilities within the system at risk. Gorbachev reproduced this aporia in the heart of the communist world.

Initially, Gorbachev proposed to regain the initiative for the Soviet Union in foreign policy and in relations with the communist movement. His attempt to thaw bipolar relations and the withdrawal from Afghanistan were the most important elements of this move. The latter meant ending a bloody and senseless military intervention, eliminating a source of international conflict, and removing a millstone from relations with the most important Third World countries.[187] At the same time, two of Gorbachev's early decisions were to replace the indestructible Ponomarev with Anatoly Dobrynin as head of the Foreign Section of the CPSU and to heal relations with the PCI, acknowledging retrospectively the importance of Eurocommunism.[188] His conviction, which he expressed for example in May

---

[183] A. Brown, *The Gorbachev Factor* (Oxford: Oxford University Press, 1996); A. Brown, *Seven Years That Changed the World: Perestroika in Perspective* (Oxford: Oxford University Press, 2007).

[184] R. Jervis, 'Identity and the Cold War', in Leffler and Westad, *The Cambridge History of the Cold War*, vol. 2: *Crises and Détente*, 42.

[185] Gorbachev and Mlynář, *Conversations with Gorbachev*, 137–9.

[186] S. Kotkin, *Armageddon Averted: The Soviet Collapse 1970–2000* (Oxford: Oxford University Press, 2001), 176–8.

[187] Westad, *The Global Cold War*, 366–7.

[188] Chernyaev, *Sovmestnii iskhod*, 666; A. Chernyaev, *Shest' let s Gorbachevym: po dnevnikovym zapisam* (Moscow: Kul'tura, 1993), 19.

1986, was that other political forces, such as social democrats and ecologists, had 'found their place in contemporary developments' but communists had 'yet to redefine theirs'.[189]

However, Gorbachev and his assistants would arrive at much more radical conclusions over the next two years. The 'new thinking' led them to declare the concept of 'peaceful coexistence' defunct in that it was based on a classist interpretation of international relations, while numerous elements alien to the communist tradition, mainly adaptations from the European social democratic left, entered Gorbachev's political discourse.[190] His judgement of the communist movement became harsher to the point of being dismissive. In March 1988 Gorbachev expressed a disconsolate evaluation of the state of the movement, complaining that many parties 'do not understand or do not want to understand' the basic concepts of the 'new thinking'.[191] Following a conversation with the leader of the PCI, Alessandro Natta, Gorbachev reported to the Politburo that he agreed with the Italians over the 'serious and dangerous backwardness of the concepts of many communist parties...in particular the ones that are most loyal to us'.[192] A few months later, in July, his close associate on foreign policy, Chernyaev, wrote in a confidential note that the communist movement 'that we are traditionally used to seeing as such, does not in fact exist'. In light of his merciless historical analysis, which dated the crisis of international communism back to the 1920s, Chernyaev concluded that defining a role for the communist movement was now an unworkable plan. This conclusion arose from the inherent development of the 'new thinking'. From the moment that the latter had abandoned the theory of 'peaceful coexistence', the solution to 'global problems' could not be the task of a revolutionary movement. So after years of mere stagnant 'conservation', the time had come to wind up the international communist movement as a 'political entity'.[193]

In other words, Gorbachev's ruling group acknowledged the end of international communism, which had occurred some time earlier, and ascertained that reformed communism was incompatible with that whole notion. He consequently ended the tradition of the 'second centre' of Soviet foreign policy, removing the powers and functions of the international department of the CPSU and transferring them to the Ministry of Foreign Affairs.[194] This measure was part of the diminution of the party's role within the Soviet state, which was central to Gorbachev's domestic reforms. But it was above all an indicator of the end of 'ideological power'. The interaction between the Soviet state and the communist movement lost all meaning. The notion of 'international communist movement' disappeared from Gorbachev's vocabulary and the pages of Chernyaev's diary. The view of the global south was substantially modified, resulting in the Soviet Union's withdrawal from

---

[189] *V Politburo TsK KPSS...Po zapisami Anatoliya Chernyaeva, Vadima Medvedeva, Georgiya Shakhnazarova (1985–1991)* (Moscow: Al'pina Biznes Buks, 2006), 43.

[190] Brown, *The Gorbachev Factor*, 175, 248.

[191] Fond Gorbacheva, fo. 2, op. 1, k. 1110.   [192] *V Politburo TsK KPSS*, 312.

[193] Fond Gorbacheva, fo. 2, op. 1, k. 1163.

[194] Interviews with A. S. Grachev and V. A. Medvedev, Archives of the Hoover Institution, The Hoover Institution and the Gorbachev Foundation Project, b. 1.15 and b. 2.10.

the world outside Europe in the conviction that Soviet interventions had exposed the country to risks, but above all contributed to the delegitimization of socialism, because of the gratuitous violence and economic failure experienced everywhere.[195] Soviet reformers thus left their Khrushchevian baggage behind them and adopted entirely new perspectives, concepts, and language.

However, this transition did not involve a break with universalism, but rather an attempt to shift the foundations and create a new legitimacy based on the sensational impact of Gorbachev's initiative on ending the Cold War, which found partners in dialogue in Reagan and Shultz, who were able to drop their extremist approach of the first half of the decade.[196] On the eve of his speech to the UN in December 1988, Gorbachev showed himself to be fully aware of what was at stake in the link between perestroika in the Soviet Union and 'perestroika in relations throughout the world'.[197] His recurring argument was that the only alternative was the decline of the Soviet Union in world affairs, an event to be avoided not only because of national interests but also because it would put at risk the destiny of socialism itself. Gorbachev was quite evidently contradictory in his approach to the socialist countries, arguing both that change had to mature autonomously in the satellite states and that it was necessary and urgent.[198] But the abandonment of the idea of the leading state and the repeated declarations of non-intervention in the affairs of other communist states in Central and Eastern Europe did not mean at all that he had given up on the socialist mission. In a note to Gorbachev written in early 1989, Chernyaev insisted on the task of defining a socialist humanitarian model.[199]

The reaction of communist parties to Gorbachev's reforming message was extremely defensive and conservative, fully confirming the pessimistic and dismissive analysis coming from Moscow. Conscious of the fact that what remained of international communism was hostile to Soviet reformers, Gorbachev produced the last and definitive rift in an already fragmented movement. In the habit of perceiving restricted sovereignty as a protective umbrella for their regimes, the communist establishments of Central and Eastern Europe found the drive for liberalization and the professed renunciation of force as a mortal threat. This was particularly the case with the East Germans and the Czechoslovaks, but none of the parties in power in Europe espoused Gorbachev's cause, not even Kádár and Tito's successors in Yugoslavia. Of the more important Western parties, the only one to support the Soviet Union's radical reforms was the PCI. The legacy of Eurocommunism, represented by Italian communism, became one of the sources of inspiration to which Gorbachev explicitly referred in formulating his own ideas. The partnership with the PCI was founded on the acknowledgement that reformed communism

---

[195] Westad, *The Global Cold War*, 384–5.
[196] Leffler, *For the Soul of Mankind*, 448–50, 462–3.   [197] *V Politburo TsK KPSS*, 420.
[198] Interviews with V. A. Medvedev, Archives of the Hoover Institution, The Hoover Institution and the Gorbachev Foundation Project, b. 2.10. Medvedev was responsible for the CPSU's section on socialist countries until 1989.
[199] Fond Gorbacheva, fo. 2, op. 1, k. 19411.

had to direct its ideas and actions at the left in the West.[200] However, the opposing alliance was numerous, impervious, and hostile, even if made up of minority and increasingly discredited parties. When Marchais declared in December 1988 that perestroika only concerned the Soviet Union, he expressed an opinion that was certainly shared by most of the remnants of European communism, from Cunhal to Honecker.[201] Outside Europe, things were going no differently, irrespective of whether there were alliances with the Soviet Union. When Castro openly rejected the ideas of perestroika at his meeting with Gorbachev in April 1989, he gave voice to widely held views.[202] Certainly, the ideas of reforming communism had never had much success outside Europe, but Gorbachev's ruling group did not appear to have any remaining illusions about international communism. In May 1989 Chernyaev noted that one of Gorbachev's merits was to have made clear the irreversible 'fragmentation' of ancient and recent sacred cows, including the 'myths' of the international communist movement, the socialist model in Central and Eastern Europe, and the role of communist parties in Western Europe.[203]

China went in the opposite direction to Gorbachev's Soviet Union. Deng Xiaoping accepted the Soviet proposal to re-establish diplomatic relations but forcefully rejected the ideas of reform, after having imposed severe restrictions on any arguments in favour of socialist humanism and having dismissed the most liberal leading politician of the post-Mao period, Hu Yaobang. Gorbachev's trip to Peking in May 1989 took on the significance of a historical watershed that went far beyond the resumption of relations between the two socialist powers. It contributed indirectly to incentivizing the student-led campaign for democracy, which was crushed in the bloody massacre in Tiananmen Square on 3–4 June 1989. Taking place under the eyes of millions of viewers around the world, the tragedy permitted the survival of the Chinese regime, but also reminded world opinion of the repressive nature of communist regimes.[204] During the following months, Soviet perestroika and Chinese repression constituted the two opposing models for the destiny of Central and Eastern Europe. While the 'Peking Spring' had met a tragic fate, it was yet to be seen whether a new European 'spring' was in the offing and whether it would experience a different outcome.

The symbols of the Iron Curtain were still in place, and the 'Brezhnev Doctrine' had not been officially repudiated. The birth in Poland of a legal opposition around the political and symbolic force of Solidarność, its electoral victory in June, and the creation in August of the first government since the war led by a non-communist, Tadeusz Mazowiecki, constituted a stunning sequence of events that undermined

---

[200] S. Pons, 'L'invenzione del "post-comunismo": Gorbacev e il Partito comunista italiano', *Ricerche di storia politica* 11.1 (2008).

[201] Courtois and Lazar, *Histoire du parti communiste français*, 408; M.-P. Rey, 'La gauche française face à la perestroika', *Communisme* 76 and 77 (2003–4).

[202] V. Skierka, *Fidel* (Rome: Fandango, 2003), 343–6.

[203] Chernyaev, *Sovmestnii iskhod*, 793.

[204] Vogel, *Deng Xiaoping and the Transformation of China*, 616–39; Baum, *Burying Mao*, 275ff.

the old relationship with the Soviet bloc. It was not certain whether this was a precursor to a more generalized phenomenon and, should this have happened, what Moscow's reaction would be. Greeted favourably by Gorbachev, the Polish events appeared to prefigure a gradualist path that would take some time to spread and deepen the extent of the changes. Instead, a sudden acceleration took place from the moment in which the border between Hungary and Austria was opened in September, allowing a mass exodus of East Germans. The spontaneous mass demonstrations in Leipzig were repeated and spread like wildfire. At this stage, yet another crisis in Eastern Europe was facing a dramatic fork in the road. The solution necessarily had to pass through Moscow, but this time the outcome was completely different. Gorbachev looked on without lifting a finger as the German regime started rapidly to break up, and offered no hope of an attempt at a repressive response. Ultimately, he showed himself ready to pay the price of change even when he understood that the price would be much higher than expected.[205]

The decision to renounce the use of force thus became the premise for radical change of the kind that had not been possible since the Prague Spring.[206] The idea of following the same repressive model adopted in Tiananmen was certainly considered by Honecker, but it could not be enacted. Deprived of Soviet military support, the East German regime was literally incapable of survival. On 9 November, the announcement of the opening of the frontier led within a few hours to the fall of the Berlin Wall. What followed was the most classic of domino effects, which the world's great powers, from Moscow to Washington, could only watch from the sidelines. Unlike revolutions of the past, the media played a decisive role, amplifying the message, multiplying the circulation of news and images, and determining the vertiginous speed of events. Within a few weeks, all the communist regimes imploded and the Eastern Europeans freed themselves through a succession of 'velvet revolutions' in Budapest, Prague, Sofia, and finally, the only violent event, in Bucharest. This stunning concatenation was not a foregone conclusion. The Cold War and the communist regimes could have precipitated an enormous catastrophe. Not only were the events magnificent but also the manner in which they occurred. In spite of the radical outcomes, 1989 was a peaceful change that is not easy to place in the history of European revolutions.[207]

The peaceful collapse of the communist regimes originated over time from the inexorable slippage of the establishment's authority and the loss of confidence amongst the political elites themselves.[208] However inclined to defend their power as an end in itself, which was perceived as guaranteeing the 'socialist nature' of the system, the communist leaderships could not easily ignore the fact that their *raison*

[205] M. Kramer, 'Gorbachev and the demise of East European Communism', in Pons and Romero, *Reinterpreting the End of the Cold War*.

[206] J. Lévesque, *The Enigma of 1989: The USSR and the Liberation of Eastern Europe* (Berkeley: University of California Press, 1997), 76, 84, 180.

[207] Maier, *Il crollo*, 200; J. Lévesque, 'The East European Revolutions of 1989', in Leffler and Westad, *The Cambridge History of the Cold War*, vol. 3: *Endings*, 311–32.

[208] S. Kotkin, *Uncivil Society: 1989 and the Implosion of the Communist Establishment*, with a contribution by J. T. Gross (New York: Modern Library, 2009), 142–3.

d'être was wavering. Aggravated by Gorbachev's message of reform, the crisis of legitimacy paralysed the existing potential for a violent reaction from above. The conservative establishment was not wrong in denouncing the destabilizing effects of political change, but it did not possess any real strategies to oppose that change. It is therefore difficult to overestimate the role played by Gorbachev's decisions in dispiriting and neutralizing the communist regimes' capacity for active and violent resistance, thus contributing to their collapse.[209] After the fall of the Berlin Wall and the communist regimes in Central and Eastern Europe, Gorbachev repudiated the iron link between the geopolitical conquests of the Second World War and the Soviet Union's imperial profile bequeathed by Stalin, and rejected the accusation of having 'lost' Eastern Europe. He therefore brought to an end the concept of power that had led to the tragedies of 1953, 1956, 1968, and 1981. In the sources of this radical overturning of the paradigms of communist history, it is probably impossible to distinguish between the invention of a humanistic tradition belonging more to the rhetoric of the communist discourse, on the one hand, and an understanding of the adversaries' motivations in their Wilsonian form, on the other. In any event, the ideal of humanitarian socialism induced Gorbachev to reject the option of market authoritarianism, which was chosen by China. His programme for bringing the Cold War to an end was carried to its logical conclusion. Gorbachev accepted the reunification of Germany within NATO, which took place in July 1990, not only because the geopolitical retreat of the USSR and its economic crisis weakened his negotiating position but because that event constituted the final chapter of the Cold War.

However, the end of the communist regimes in Europe and the end of the Cold War did not assist the reform of the Soviet Union, which actually underwent a marked regression.[210] The high point of the application of the 'new thinking' was also the moment at which its limitations and contradictions started to emerge. The expectations of the Soviet reformers of a new arrangement for Europe and a 'second Helsinki' that would involve the Soviet Union proved unrealistic. The scenario that emerged from Europe's liberation from the consequences of the Second World War was the marginalization of the Soviet Union. Gorbachev had contributed decisively to the liquidation of the European communist establishment and had entered into close relations with the principal European and American leaders irrespective of their political credos, but this had not created any new alliances. He was forced to acknowledge Europe as a genuine pole of attraction. He deluded himself, however, that the new post-communist states in Eastern and Central Europe would conserve a socialist orientation or at least act as a conduit to involve the Soviet Union in a future European structure. Instead, the prospect was a process of European unification that aimed to establish a border between the countries of the former Soviet sphere of interest and Moscow.[211] In March 1990 Chernyaev sent

---

[209] Interview with A. Chernyaev, Archives of the Hoover Institution, The Hoover Institution and the Gorbachev Foundation Project, b. 1.12; A. Bennett, 'The guns that didn't smoke: ideas and the Soviet non-use of force in 1989', *Journal of Cold War Studies* 7.2 (2005).

[210] Chernyaev, *Sovmestnii iskhod*, 894–6.

[211] Lévesque, *The Enigma of 1989*, 162–5, 210–11.

Gorbachev a note arguing that the principal objective was to shift the centre of gravity in relations with Eastern and Central Europe from the communist parties to the new governmental forces.[212] But the model for change that established itself in Eastern and Central Europe was to exclude any 'socialist' perspective, including that of perestroika. Soviet reforming communism found itself isolated, in spite of the change brought about by the USSR's international role.

The success in bringing the Cold War to an end did not provide the Soviet Union with any results that could enhance its international status. At the same time, the political inspiration that had sustained Gorbachev's foreign policy proved to be inadequate or counterproductive for his domestic policy. After 1989, the interaction between reforms in foreign policy and domestic reforms could no longer be conceived as a gradual process, whereas it was precisely the rapid end to the Cold War that exposed the absence of a coherent programme of reform. Liberalization aroused political and intellectual forces that were increasingly radical and impatient with Gorbachev's compromises. Intransigent sentiments hostile to the ruling group of reformers became open inside the CPSU, and became an obstacle to reform rather than its instrument. The political structure that aimed to shift the centre of gravity of power from the party to the state, in order to create a new source of legitimacy in the presidency of the USSR, was complicated, and weakened the authority of his power.[213] In the absence of an authentic adoption of the market, the political reforms were a factor aggravating the dramatic economic crisis afflicting the country. The panorama of the crisis was rounded off by the arousal of nationalist forces, which in the Ukraine and elsewhere drew inspiration from the events of 1989.[214] The end of the Cold War deprived a largely unchanged system of its external enemy, the glue that kept it together, while the country was in a state of increasing confusion and collapse, without any alternative solution appearing on the horizon.

In November 1990, on the eve of the anniversary of the Revolution, Gorbachev confided in Chernyaev: 'With all that made it significant, October divided the world. The current revolution unites it and leads it to the gates of an era of a great and effective shared civilization.'[215] In reality, Gorbachev's 'revolution' was over by that stage and it had failed. It would not leave a reformed USSR or a 'shared civilization'. The idea that, once the Cold War was over, the destructive side of the political and economic reforms would give way to the construction of a democratic Soviet state based on law and integrated into a new world order was the last delusion of Gorbachev's reformers.[216] And yet no one could ignore the impact of those reforms. Without the 'new thinking' it would be difficult to see how the end of the Soviet Union could have come about so peacefully. The 'tiredness of empire'

---

[212] Fond Gorbacheva, fo. 2, op. 1, k. 8219.
[213] Chernyaev, *Shest' let s Gorbachevym*, 240–1.
[214] M. Kramer, 'The collapse of East European Communism and the repercussions within the Soviet Union', *Journal of Cold War History* 5.4 (2003); 6.4 (2004); 7.1 (2005).
[215] Chernyaev, *Shest' let s Gorbachevym*, 379.
[216] Fond Gorbacheva, fo. 2, op. 1, k. 19402.

that distinguished the Soviet ruling classes in decline did not in itself constitute a reassuring condition. Gorbachev understood that going down the 'Chinese route' could have meant a tragedy of incalculable proportions for Europe and the Soviet Union. The organizers of the coup in August 1991 sought in vain to obtain from him the authority for the use of force. The Chinese example remained for most Soviet communists, who were against perestroika, a reactionary ideal that they could not follow even though they considered their leader a traitor. At the end of 1991, at the time of the dissolution of the Soviet Union, Gorbachev left the scene as a defeated politician. Nevertheless there was an undeniable fact about this defeat: also leaving the political scene were the most illiberal options capable of producing catastrophic consequences, which his policies had made impossible. Gorbachev's political initiative had neither changed the system nor renewed communism. In spite of this, he had made its defence at any cost a senseless objective.

The alternative between creating a new legitimacy or dying had been misleading. Gorbachev did not have the means to transform communism. Both conservatives and reformers were swept away by the fall of the Wall and the break-up of the Soviet Union.[217] Dubček withdrew to private life after having been symbolically replaced by the liberal and non-communist dissident intellectual Václav Havel. The heirs to Berlinguer improvised their 'post-communist' search for integration on the European democratic left. Gorbachev abandoned the political scene and never returned, maintaining his prestige abroad which was of no use in his own country. The idea of reformed communism only demolished the old identity, which was unserviceable and had run its course, but failed to create a new one. The search for an alternative within the history of communism amongst the myths of Lenin or Bukharin had in vain engaged exponents of 'socialism with a human face'. The self-narrative of communism, even in its reforming variants, had never been able since 1956 to define a credible past to build a future, and remained stuck with iconoclastic denunciations without fully healing the mutilated memories going back to the Stalinist era. The counter-memories of the Hungarian Revolution and the Prague Spring now constituted a political symbolism that implied liquidation, not reform.[218] Communist reformers in Europe felt they had been justified by the advent of Gorbachev, and had exchanged perestroika for the demonstration that the Soviet system could be reformed. But their reform would prove to be wishful thinking.

By rejecting the legacy of Sovietization and acknowledging that the regimes in Central and Eastern Europe could not be defended with force, Gorbachev decreed the end of the communist experience in the autumn of 1989. The link between the 'velvet revolutions' and the dissolution of the USSR was not automatic, but it was

---

[217] S. Pons, 'Western communists, Mikhail Gorbachev and the 1989 revolutions', *Contemporary European History* 18.3 (2009).

[218] H. Wydra, *Communism and the Emergence of Democracy* (Cambridge: Cambridge University Press, 2007), 242–3. For an account by a communist historian who supported reform, see G. Boffa, *Memorie dal comunismo: storia confidenziale di quarant'anni che hanno cambiato il volto dell'Europa* (Florence: Ponte alle Grazie, 1998).

evident. The effects of exporting Stalinism were never exclusive to the regimes of Eastern Europe and to their national discredit. The creation of an imperial space in Central and Eastern Europe had established a close interdependence between the Soviet regime and the others, founding a dominion but also a channel of mutual influence. The reality of European communism in power meant too much for Soviet communism. The process of delegitimization that had prepared the way for the collapse of the Eastern European regimes affected the Soviet Union as well, given that the loss of the 'external empire' required a redefinition of identity that was out of reach for the Soviet elite. In the context of the imperial breakdown, the implosion of the CPSU was similar to the experience of European party-states two years earlier, even though it met with general indifference and the absence of any grass-roots mobilization.[219]

Gorbachev's attempt to remove the rift between the global dimension of the Soviet superpower and communism's ability to provide a credible universalist message had failed. Depository for the principal revolutionary mission of the century, the Soviet Union had been transformed during the 'long postwar period' into a gigantic bulwark of resistance to the processes of economic and cultural globalization driven by the West. Gorbachev's reforms weakened that role without building a credible and sustainable alternative. His relaunch of the universalist message did not revitalize anything; it rather revealed communism's lack of significance as a player in the modern world. The decline of international communism which had emerged in the 1960s was thus the premise and the harbinger of a profound crisis destined to create all kinds of problems. Fundamentally it was a crisis of legitimacy of communism's states, movement, and political culture. The reformers' response to this crisis was not only inadequate but also ended up triggering final outcomes. Once the justification of the Cold War had passed, the European and Soviet communist world collapsed and broke up almost instantly.

---

[219] M. Kramer, 'The reform of the Soviet system and the demise of the Soviet state', *Slavic Review* 18.3 (2004).

Epilogue
The End of Soviet and European Communism in World History

It is clear to all that the communist movement, as we were traditionally in the habit of seeing it, does not actually exist, above all as an international force.

Anatoly Chernyaev, 26 July 1988

The fall of the Soviet Union was not inevitable. It was Gorbachev who unwittingly brought it about. His ideal of 'socialism with a human face' led him to introduce reforms that were incompatible with the system, and that triggered self-dissolution.[1] The reforming drive arose from an attempt to redefine a mission that allowed the Soviet Union and communism to re-enter the dynamics of the global world, after having been relegated to its margins. He excluded the possibility of entrenching himself in imperial pride, power rivalry, and the totalitarian tradition. Going down that path might have extended the survival of the Soviet state for a certain period, but it would not have confronted the roots of the crisis of legitimacy. Gorbachev and his ruling group went in the opposite direction, to the point of denying the split between socialism and democracy brought about by Leninism. Their failure laid bare the insurmountable contradictions inherent in the attempt to reform Soviet communism, and the impossibility of relegitimizing it as a universalist project.

The 'Chinese road' of Deng Xiaoping, which was rejected by the Soviet reformers, was configured as a reinvention of the totalitarian tradition. Post-Maoist China had come to terms with the limitations of the Soviet model and gone down the path of market authoritarianism, definitively renouncing its ambition to replace the USSR as the leader of international communism. By the time of the fall of the Soviet Union, the country had experienced a decade of considerable economic expansion and had preserved the single-party system while forcefully repressing any demands for liberalization. The pragmatic rediscovery of nationalism as an instrument of state cohesion represented an effective response to the decline of Maoist ideology, which came in the wake of the anti-colonial revolution.[2] China's

---

[1] S. Kotkin, *Armageddon Averted: The Soviet Collapse 1970–2000* (Oxford: Oxford University Press, 2001), 178.

[2] S. Zhao, *A Nation-State by Construction: Dynamics of Modern Chinese Nationalism* (Stanford, Calif.: Stanford University Press, 2004), 208–18, 261–5.

access to globalization was planned without any ambition to develop a universalist message, which was not necessary in the light of China's own history. While the Soviet Union was collapsing, together with the order created by the Cold War, to give way to a post-Soviet neo-statist and neo-capitalist Russia, the communist tradition of state power shifted to China, underwent a metamorphosis oriented towards a realist concept of national interests, and jettisoned the fundamental principles during the country's rise in the post-bipolar world. At the same time, the repercussions of Soviet collapse consolidated the tendency for the Chinese regime to oppose all political liberalization for an entire era.

The survival of the Chinese communist state was not an exception. The main communist regimes outside Europe have stayed in place after the end of European and Soviet communism, following the route of international economic integration, as in Vietnam, or autarky, as in Cuba and North Korea. In these countries, communism discovered a founding principle in anti-imperialist nationalism, similar to what had occurred in China. In Europe, on the other hand, the national legacies had contributed to the implosion of the regimes or propelled them into ethnic conflicts and civil wars, as in the case of Yugoslavia. The inheritance of communist state-building survived where it had overseen the construction of 'national communities', and collapsed where it was founded on the pre-existing body of a nation or had favoured its consolidation within an imperial structure, as in the USSR. These processes laid bare the limitations of the communist experience rather than its achievements. The 'building of socialism' on the principle of territoriality implied from the very beginning the idea that the nineteenth-century nation-state was a remnant of the past, as well as an artificial edifice. The Bolsheviks appropriated the state as a transformational force and instrument of modernity, but they separated it from the nation. To their eyes, the concept of nationality was not linked to political sovereignty. Signs of crisis in the nation-state that emerged in the First World War in Europe were interpreted as a terminal phase, which was then confirmed and ratified by the defeat of fascist nationalism. With the Second World War, the example of Soviet patriotism encouraged communist states and parties to make use of nationalism as a supplementary and auxiliary force, or as an ally in the Third World. But ultimately, the persuasion that anti-capitalist modernity would make it obsolete remained unaltered.

The project of Soviet state power was based on the assumption that the future belonged to a state formation that differed from the nation-state: a new player capable of imposing itself on the global world by combining the principal of territoriality with the invention of an 'international community' made up of parties and states, and based on an exclusive system of relations between the centre and the periphery. However, the monocratic nature of the Soviet empire obstructed the creation of a community with a transnational destiny. Whereas the nation-states of Western Europe were disposing of their militarist and imperial past, transforming their nature into a cooperative one, and giving life to new forms of supranationalism, the project of the power-state hit a crisis, undermined by contradictions at the political, economic, and cultural base of its power and by its global ambitions. It was tugged in different directions by state interests and the prospects of the movement, the need for absolute unity, and increasing diversity and fractures in the 'socialist camp'. The belated attempt to reform this base led to the final collapse. With the exception of the Cuban regime, only in Asia did communist regimes keep themselves in power by linking themselves to a 'national mission' and jettisoning internationalism. But if reforming communism brought about the dissolution of the Soviet state and the end of the original identity, nationalist communism emptied the identity of all meaning that could relate to the revolutionary mission. In both cases, the communism of the twentieth century came to the end of the line, leaving a statist imprint and an industrial archaeology, but exposing above all the far-reaching dismemberment of its culture and the failure of its universalist project.

The rise and fall of communism thus took place in a few decades. In the first twenty years of their existence, the revolutionary state and the communist movement had moulded the first political network of global dimensions, but with meagre and uncertain results, and with a Eurocentric structure. It was the victory over the Nazi global project that sanctioned the rise of the Soviet Union to world power and legitimized the communist global project. A few years after the Second World War, the Soviet Union was at the centre of a system of states spread over a vast area stretching from Prague to Peking, and a network of parties developed in the rest of the world. The complex matrix of states and communist parties—interwoven with mass mobilization, recruitment, pedagogy, social transformation, and armed struggle—became impressive. International communism was configured as a formidable global factor, because of its ideological, symbolic, political, and power-based challenge to the West. The Chinese Revolution established a connection between decolonization and world revolution. The impact of communism on the non-Western world was the main trigger for intervention by the superpowers on a planetary scale and for the depiction of this as a clash between two antithetical versions of modernity, which aimed to define the variety of choices made by post-colonial entities.

The Western vision of an international order inspired by the principles of liberalism, open society, and the market had been around for some time, but its translation into American hegemony and its principal transnational and multilateral instruments and connections were forged in the contest with the communist challenge. In this sense, the direct contribution of communism to the Cold War was much more significant than its indirect contribution to bringing about a reform of capitalism.[3] The decisive impetus for the creation of democratic welfare came out of the Second World War and the destruction of Nazism, which highlighted the role of communism. The very presence of the USSR justified the prevention of uncontrollable social conflicts in the West. But social democratic, liberal, and Christian forces engaged in the reform of capitalism after the war were more damaged than favoured by the existence of communism as a model and a movement.

[3] For the theory of communism's indirect contribution to the reform of capitalism, see E. J. Hobsbawm, *The Age of Extremes: The Short 20th Century 1914–1991* (London: Michael Joseph, 1994).

It was the combination of power politics, warfare, and universalist mission that invoked the connotations of international communism as an alternative player in world politics.

The connection between communism and global phenomena would very soon be broken. The original link between the revolutionary state and the world movement, and between the centre and the periphery, hid irresolvable flaws behind the monolithic facade offered to the outside world. Before the war, the imperatives of the state interest and development of the movement had already revealed the two faces of a necessary symbiosis and a recurring collision. The diversities generated by the war, with the birth of new communist states, amplified to the highest degree both aspects just at the time of apparent triumph. The limitations of Soviet power and the contradictions of international communism were definitively brought to light after Stalin's death, even though they were not brought into focus during the challenge for world power. Public opinion and the main governmental forces in the West stubbornly internalized the idea of their enemy's unity and cohesion. The obsession of the communist plot would soften in the course of time, but was never wholly removed, as with the tendency to extend the definition of 'communism' indiscriminately to include any radical or even reformist entity. The perception that the USSR had never resolved its inherited dualism between state interests and world revolution hit the target. However, in the game of smoke and mirrors of the Cold War, the representation of the ideological and political strength of communism, together with the power of the Soviet Union, was for a long time overemphasized, whereas the contradictions that were gnawing away at it generally passed unobserved, unmentioned, or underestimated. Fear of the 'domino effect' lay behind some of the most disastrous actions taken by the West in the Third World, contributing to and increasing the immense human, civil, and material costs of the bipolar conflict.

In reality, the Soviet state proved incapable of exercising genuine hegemony. Even after Stalin's death, the Soviet political elites continued to perceive their state not only as an agent of modernization and secularization but also as a monopolistic power in terms of legitimacy and doctrine. However, the authority of the Soviet Union was badly affected both by the consequences of the 'revolution from above' in Central and Eastern Europe and by the independent revolutions in Yugoslavia and China. Instead of constituting the theatre for a united relaunch of the movement under the leadership of the USSR, the encounter with the post-colonial world brought the unity of international communism to an end. Not even the discipline of the Cold War could hold the 'socialist camp' together. Thus the political, cultural, and symbolic erosion of communism did not follow but preceded the self-evident crisis of its economic system. The processes of de legitimization were caught up in internal and international dynamics, in line with a clear phenomenology of how state systems fell apart in the last century.[4] In the case of communism,

---

[4] P. Macry, *Gli ultimi giorni: stati che crollano nell'Europa del Novecento* (Bologna: il Mulino, 2009), 146–8.

however, the international element that was essential for building legitimacy was equally decisive when the crisis spiralled out of control.

The monocratic profile of the Soviet Union could not compete with the American ability to diversify its instruments of power, and to combine military force with economic dynamism, governance of the Western system, and cultural influence, as well as security and democracy. It was the 'polyhedric and composite nature' of the hegemonic challenge of the West that resolved the bipolar antagonism.[5] Although already evident at the end of the Second World War, it took time for the full effects of this imbalance to be felt. The communist project remained credible until the shadow of the Second World War slowly faded, albeit unevenly and at different times in Europe, Asia, and the post-colonial world. The regimes of Central and Eastern Europe experienced their first crisis about ten years after the end of the war. The prospect of revolution and the myth of an 'alternative modernity' proved to be more lasting in the non-European world, where the historic problem of backwardness combined with the recent memory of Western colonial domination and, still more, with the reality of armed struggles and civil wars. Nevertheless, a quarter of a century after the Second World War, international communism no longer represented a player in global politics. It increasingly looked like a divided movement, fragmented and bereft of a unitary purpose, a synonym for dogmatism and imperial conservatism, a model incapable of responding to elementary demands of freedom and progress, a power inclined to replicate ad infinitum the use of violence, and a force that had irredeemably lost its revolutionary impetus. The more it became clear that the 'international civil war' was not the only mark of the postwar period, the less international communism appeared to have any cards to play.

The distance between myth and the reality then presented its bill. The very existence of Soviet communism and the 'socialist camp' had in the past represented a dilemma for the West, but from the 1960s onwards the situation was inexorably reversed, just at the time when the Soviet Union's global aspirations were beginning to show. The result was that the Western international order put the Soviet communist one on the ropes, not only forcing it into an imperial overstretch but above all relegating it to the margins, an alternative of a past that had turned out to be a blind alley. In the last quarter of the century, the global networks no longer belonged to the communist world, but to international institutions and non-governmental organizations created in the Western world. The only existing 'international community' was founded on the transatlantic relationship between Europe and the United States, even though its relations with various key countries in the global south appeared to be uncertain and problematic. In the post-colonial world, the methods used by both the superpowers to affirm their respective version of modernity were not very different from the ones used by the European colonial empires.[6] But the revolutionary states had only produced devastation and no development. Only the world market appeared to open up a way out. Long

---

[5] F. Romero, *Storia della Guerra Fredda: l'ultimo conflitto per l'Europa* (Turin: Einaudi, 2009), 339.
[6] O. A. Westad, *The Global Cold War: Third World Interventions and the Making of Our Times* (Cambridge: Cambridge University Press, 2005), 397.

before the fateful two-year period of 1989–91, communism lost its image of an 'alternative modernity' and became resistant to Western globalization, without, however, enjoying the support of many of the forces that were rebelling against the Cold War.

The collapse of the communist states removed every unilinear and monocausal vision of history from the horizon of our times, marking the breakdown of a concept and experience of modernity centred on the mythologies of the new state, on organized messianism, and on the violent transformative force of power.[7] Communism had postulated a division of the world along class lines, a division that had to be healed by the revolutionary state, by its territorial system, and by its followers, in the name of ideals of justice that it claimed to monopolize as the exclusive interpreter of the profound course of history. Instead it was condemned to succumb in an increasingly unified world which was not necessarily producing uniformity, but which exalted diversity, pluralism, and multilateralism. The link between politics and war, social and cultural homogenization, militarism, and elitism proved not to be principles and instruments suited to a universal mission. The Cold War prolonged the duration of the communist systems. But the Clausewitzian structure of the communist project was not compatible with the global world in the long term. Long before the end of the century, its responses to the dilemmas of poverty, inequality, and development began to lose credibility, whereas it had never formulated responses to the problems of civil liberties, human rights, and environmental decay. Demands for political participation and a broadening of the democratic public sphere, gender issues, mass communications networks and cultures, identity systems based on communitarian or individualistic dimensions, ideologies with nationalistic or religious content, and new social, ethnic, and cultural conflicts took shape without the communist tradition being able have any significant voice in the matter.

After 1989–91, the Western transatlantic system consolidated itself and expanded for about a decade to incorporate the space previously occupied by Soviet communism, modelling the features of the new post-bipolar international system in its own image and semblance. The fall of the communist regimes fostered the illusion that this process was the logical product of a hegemony destined to establish itself firmly and last for a long time.[8] For a while, indeed, the supremacy of the United States continued along the multilateral paradigm that had been one of its essential strengths since the Second World War. Europe developed its original supranational architecture in its single currency, enlarged its borders to include the central and eastern part of the continent in the Union, and defined its role as a 'civil power'. Albeit paying a high price and experiencing an uncertain democratic transition, Russia was integrated into the world economy. At the end of the century, the

---

[7] F. Halliday, *Revolution and World Politics: The Rise and Fall of the Sixth Great Power* (Durham, NC: Duke University Press, 1999), 54.

[8] G. J. Ikenberry, 'The restructuring of the international system after the Cold War', in M. P. Leffler and O. A. Westad (eds), *The Cambridge History of the Cold War*, vol. 3: *Endings* (Cambridge: Cambridge University Press, 2010), 544–5.

short-lived paradoxes of the 'end of history' or the triumphalism of the victors of the Cold War did not define the principal political identities in the West; this was the work of much more meaningful attempts to consolidate a liberal world order and reinvent ideologies of progress based on a post-social-democratic version.

However, the process of expanding the multilateral features of the Western system into various parts of the world has encountered an increasing impasse since the start of the new century. The sustainability of a substantially unipolar system has become increasingly critical, precisely because of structural transformations, particularly in relation to economic growth in Asia, which had appeared to integrate and sustain the world order just after the Cold War. The threat of Islamic fundamentalism and international terrorism has divided the West. The United States' role of architrave has vacillated between imperial unilateralism, tending to deny the principal features of hegemony, and a new multilateralism, which has still to be thought out and defined. The loss of Europe's centrality in world affairs corresponds to a crisis in its unification project and widespread political disappointment. Economic recovery in Russia has coincided with the neo-authoritarian development of its political system. The rise of China poses serious questions about the future of a risky combination of a monocratic state and its role as the second world power. The dilemmas for an effective redefinition of American hegemony, the contradictions in humanitarian intervention, the tendency to reject any idea of governing the world economy, and the 'crisis of governance' in a world that is as plural and interdependent as it is unstable and dangerous appear to be asserting themselves in the long term.[9] The very notion of globalization has become more complex and difficult to decipher, throwing a different light on its distant and recent history from the one that lets us see a mere impulse exclusive to the liberal West.

None of this evokes regrets over communism's passing, except for the recriminations over lost power that every now and then resurface in Russia. Its memory divides Europeans, but the line of division does not pass through rejection and nostalgia, given that those who feel the latter sentiment have been reduced to a handful who are devoted to deploring the present. It passes between the national memories of those who experienced communism as a police regime imposed from outside, as in Central and Eastern Europe, and the ones of those who keep alive its role in society and in the processes of citizenship, as in Italy and France. It is between the appeal to condemn the communist past as a whole because of its criminal character and the invitation to distinguish historical analysis from moral judgement. It is between the risk of rehabilitating all adversaries of communism, including fascism, and the risk of indifference and unjustified selectivity towards totalitarianisms and their victims. Together with memories that are certainly tragic and bitter, the communist story appears to have left all posterity, not just the European one, with a profound sense of distrust for universalist projects, which

---

[9] M. Mazower, *Governing the World: The History of an Idea* (London: Penguin, 2012), 415ff.

finds its natural environment in the scenario of an economic and cultural globalization stripped of a political dimension.

And yet it is precisely the history of the communist global project and its crisis that leads us to rethink the complexity of the concept of globalization in the last century as a process that was not at all unilinear, monopolized by Western hegemony, or ascribable to a simple economic and financial dimension. The end of communism in Europe and Russia can hardly be understood without recourse to concepts of a political nature, such as the collapse of authority and the loss of legitimacy, which do not appear to be confined to single national realities, but reveal an international dimension and a world profile. The impact of globalization was devastating for communism in the final quarter of the century, because its *raison d'être* and identity were worn out and unserviceable. The extreme form of modernity identified in the century-long link between state and revolution, which founded the communist global project, lost its significance over time because it could not withstand the challenge from processes and movements oriented by increasing civil, democratic, individualistic, and anti-authoritarian influences and aspirations around the world. The death throes and disappearance of European and Soviet communism refer back, therefore, to signs of a global policy that emerged in the second half of the twentieth century. Those very signs are reappearing in our own times in the delegitimization of and protests against monocratic, oppressive, and hierarchical regimes and systems in South Africa, Serbia, the Ukraine, the former Soviet Union, Iran, Egypt, and the Arab world. Today we can see the end of communism in the twentieth century not only as the failure of a fallacious mythology and the fatal implosion of a totalitarian system, but also as a fundamental transition in world history that is taking place in front of our eyes.

References

ARCHIVES

Archive du Parti communiste français, Paris
Archives of the Hoover Institution, Stanford, California
Archivio del Partito comunista italiano, Rome
Arkhiv Vneshnei Politiki Rossiiskoy Federatsii, Moscow
Fond Gorbacheva, Moscow
Rossiiskii Gosudarstvennyi Arkhiv Noveishei Istorii, Moscow
Rossiiskii Gosudarstvennyi Arkhiv Sotsial'no-Politicheskoy Istorii, Moscow
Stiftung Archiv der Parteien und Massenorganisationen der DDR im Bundesarchiv, Berlin

BOOKS AND ARTICLES

1941 god. Moscow: Mezhdunarodnyi Fond 'Demokratiya', 1998.

Abrams, B. F., *The Struggle for the Soul of the Nation: Czech Culture and the Rise of Communism.* Lanham, Md.: Rowman & Littlefield, 2004.

Adibekov, G., *Kominform i poslevoennaya Evropa.* Moscow: Rossiya Molodaya, 1994.

Adibekov, G., et al. (eds), *Soveshchaniya Kominforma 1947/1948/1949.* Moscow: Rosspen, 1998.

Adibekov, G., et al. (eds), *Politburo TsK Rkp(b)–Vkp(b) i Evropa: resheniya 'Osoboy Papki' 1923–1939.* Moscow: Rosspen, 2001.

Adibekov, G. M., Shakhnazarova, E. N., and Shirinya, K. K., *Organizatsionnaya struktura Kominterna 1919–1943.* Moscow: Rosspen, 1997.

Adibekov, G. M., and Shirinya, K. K. (eds), *Politburo TsK Rkp(b)–Vkp(b) i Komintern 1919–1943: dokumenty.* Moscow: Rosspen, 2004.

Aga Rossi, E., and Zaslavsky, V., *Togliatti e Stalin: il PCI e la politica estera italiana negli archivi di Mosca,* 2nd edn. Bologna: il Mulino, 2007.

Agosti, A., *Palmiro Togliatti.* Turin: Utet, 1996.

Agosti, A., *Bandiere rosse: un profilo storico dei comunismi europei.* Rome: Editori Riuniti, 1999.

Agosti, A., 'La famiglia politica comunista negli anni Venti: spunti per una storia comparativa'. In A. Agosti, *Il partito mondiale della rivoluzione: saggi sul comunismo e l'Internazionale.* Milan: Unicopli, 2009.

Alexander, R. J., *International Maoism in the Developing World.* Westport, Conn.: Praeger, 1999.

Allison, R., *The Soviet Union and the Strategy of Non-Alignment in the Third World.* Cambridge: Cambridge University Press, 1988.

Amendola, G., *Lettere a Milano.* Rome: Editori Riuniti, 1973.

Amendola, G., *Una scelta di vita.* Milan: Rizzoli, 1976.

'A mystery wrapped in a riddle and kept in a sphinx: new evidence on Soviet Premier Alexei Kosygin's trip to Cuba, June 1967, and the turn in relations between Cuba and the Soviet Bloc, 1967–68', *Cold War International History Project Bulletin* 17–18, 2012.

Anderson, B., *Imagined Communities: Reflections on the Origin and Spread of Nationalism.* London: Verso, 2006.

Anderson, J. L., *Che Guevara: A Revolutionary Life*. New York: Grove Press, 1997.

Andreucci, F., *Falce e martello: identità e linguaggi dei comunisti italiani tra stalinismo e guerra fredda*. Bologna: Bononia University Press, 2005.

Andrew, C., and Mitrokhin, V., *The Mitrokhin Archive: The KGB in Europe and the West*. London: Penguin, 1999. Translated into Italian as *L'archivio Mitrokhin: le attività segrete del KGB in occidente* (Milan: Rizzoli, 2000).

Andrew, C., and Mitrokhin, V., *The World Was Going Our Way: The KGB and the Battle for the Third World*. New York: Basic Books, 2005.

Andrews, G., *Endgames and New Times: The Final Years of British Communism 1964–1991*. London: Lawrence & Wishart, 2004.

'A new "cult of personality": Suslov's secret report on Mao, Khrushchev, and Sino-Soviet tensions, December 1959', *Cold War International History Project Bulletin* 8–9, 1996–7.

Anikeev, A. S., *Kak Tito ot Stalina ushel: Yugoslaviya, SSSR i SShA v nachalnii period 'kholodnoy voiny' (1945–1957)*. Moscow: Is Ran, 2002.

Arbatov, G. A., *Chelovek sistemy*. Moscow: Vagrius, 2002.

Archivio Pietro Secchia 1945–1973. Milan: Feltrinelli, 1979.

Arendt, H., *On Revolution*. New York: Viking Press, 1963.

Banac, I., *With Stalin against Tito: Cominformist Splits in Yugoslav Communism*. Ithaca, N.Y.: Cornell University Press, 1988.

Basu, S., and Majumder, A., 'Dilemmas of parliamentary communism: the rise and fall of the Left in West Bengal'. *Critical Asian Studies* 45.2, 2013.

Bauer, O., *Zwischen zwei Weltkriegen? Die Krise der Weltwirtschaft, der Demokratie und des Sozialismus*. Prague: Prager, 1936. Translated into Italian as *Tra due guerre mondiali? La crisi dell'economia mondiale, della democrazia and del socialismo* (Turin: Einaudi, 1979).

Baum, R., *Burying Mao: Chinese Politics in the Era of Deng Xiaoping*. Princeton, N.J.: Princeton University Press, 1996.

Bayerlein, B. H., Peschanski, D., Narinsky, M. M., Studer, B., and Wolikow, S., *Moscou–Paris–Berlin: télégrammes chiffrés du Komintern (1939–1941)*. Paris: Tallandier, 2003.

Bayly, C., and Harper, T., *Forgotten Wars: Freedom and Revolution in Southeast Asia*. Cambridge, Mass.: Harvard University Press, 2006.

Becker, M., *Mariategui and Latin American Marxist Theory*. Athens: Ohio University Press, 1993.

Behrooz, M., *Rebels with a Cause: The Failure of the Left in Iran*. London: I. B. Tauris, 1999.

Békés, C., 'Soviet plans to establish the Cominform in early 1946: new evidence from the Hungarian archives'. *Cold War International History Project Bulletin* 10, 1998.

Békés, C., 'Why was there no "second Cold War" in Europe? Hungary and the Soviet invasion of Afghanistan in 1979: documents from the Hungarian Archives'. *Cold War International History Project Bulletin* 14–15, 2003–4.

Békés, C., 'East Central Europe, 1953–1956'. In M. P. Leffler and O. A. Westad (eds), *The Cambridge History of the Cold War*, vol. 1: *Origins*. Cambridge: Cambridge University Press, 2010.

Békés, C., Byrne, M., and Rainer, J. M. (eds), *The 1956 Hungarian Revolution: A History in Documents*. Budapest: Central European University Press, 2002.

Bellamy, B., *Absolute War: Soviet Russia in the Second World War*. London: Pan, 2010.

Bennett, A., 'The guns that didn't smoke: ideas and the Soviet non-use of force in 1989'. *Journal of Cold War Studies* 7. 2, 2005.

Benvenuti, F., *The Bolsheviks and the Red Army*. Cambridge: Cambridge University Press, 1988.

Berghahn, V. R., *America and the Intellectual Cold Wars in Europe*. Princeton, N.J.: Princeton University Press, 2001.

Bernstein, T. P., and Li, H.-Y. (eds), *China Learns from the Soviet Union, 1949–Present*. Lanham, Md.: Lexington Books, 2010.

Berti, G., *I primi dieci anni di vita del Pci: documenti inediti dell'archivio Angelo Tasca*. Milan: Feltrinelli, 1967.

Bettanin, F., *La fabbrica del mito: storia e politica nell'URSS staliniana*. Naples: Edizioni scientifiche italiane, 1996.

Bettanin, F., *Stalin e l'Europa: la formazione dell'impero esterno sovietico (1941–1953)*. Rome: Carocci, 2006.

Blight, J. G., and Brenner, P., *Sad and Luminous Days: Cuba's Struggle with the Superpowers after the Missile Crisis*. Lanham, Md.: Rowman & Littlefield, 2002.

Boffa, G., *Memorie dal comunismo: storia confidenziale di quarant'anni che hanno cambiato il volto all'Europa*. Florence: Ponte alle Grazie, 1998.

Borkenau, F., *The Communist International*. London: Faber and Faber, 1938.

Borkenau, F., *The Totalitarian Enemy*. London: Faber and Faber, 1940.

Bracke, M., *Which Socialism, Whose Détente?* Budapest: Central European University Press, 2007.

Bradley, M. P., 'Decolonization, the global South, and the Cold War, 1919–1962'. In M. P. Leffler and O. A. Westad (eds), *The Cambridge History of the Cold War*, vol. 1: *Origins*. Cambridge: Cambridge University Press, 2010.

Brandenberger, D., *National Bolshevism: Stalinist Mass Culture and the Formation of Modern Russian National Identity, 1931–1956*. Cambridge, Mass.: Harvard University Press, 2002.

Brands, H., *Latin America's Cold War*. Cambridge, Mass.: Harvard University Press, 2010.

Brogi, A., *A Question of Self-Esteem: The United States and the Cold War Choices in France and Italy, 1944–1958*. Westport, Conn.: Praeger, 2002.

Brogi, A., *Confronting America: The Cold War between the United States and the Communists in France and Italy*. Chapel Hill, N.C.: University of North Carolina Press, 2011.

Brown, A., *The Gorbachev Factor*. Oxford: Oxford University Press, 1996.

Brown, A., *Seven Years that Changed the World: Perestroika in Perspective*. Oxford: Oxford University Press, 2007.

Brown, A., *The Rise and Fall of Communism*. New York: HarperCollins, 2009.

Brutents, K. N., *Tridtsat' let na staroy ploshadi*. Moscow: Mezhdunarodnye otnosheniya, 1998.

Brzezinski, Z., *The Soviet Bloc: Unity and Conflict*. Cambridge, Mass.: Harvard University Press, 1967.

Buber-Neumann, M., *Under Two Dictators: Prisoner of Stalin and Hitler*. London: Pimlico, 2009.

Bukharin, N. I., *Put' k sotsializmu i raboche-krestyanskii soyuz* (1925). In *Izbrannie proizve-deniya*. Moscow: Politizdat, 1988.

Bukharin, N. I., *Problemy teorii i praktiki sotsializma*. Moscow: Izdatel'stvo politicheskoy literatury, 1989.

Buton, P., *Les lendemains qui déchantent: le Parti communiste français à la Libération*. Paris: Presses de la Fondation Nationale des Sciences Politiques, 1993.

Bystrova, N., *SSSR i formirovanie voenno-blokovogo protivostoyaniya v Evrope (1945–1955gg.)*. Moscow: Institut Rossiiskoy Istorii, 2005.

Caballero, M., *Latin America and the Comintern, 1919–1943*. Cambridge: Cambridge University Press, 2002.

Callaghan, J., *Cold War, Crisis and Conflict: The History of the Communist Party of Great Britain, 1951–68*. London: Lawrence & Wishart, 2003.

Carlton, D., *Churchill and the Soviet Union*. Manchester: Manchester University Press, 2000.

Carr, B., 'From Caribbean backwater to revolutionary opportunity: Cuba's evolving relationship with the Komintern, 1925–34'. In T. Rees and A. Thorpe (eds), *International Communism and the Communist International*. Manchester: Manchester University Press, 1998.

Carr, E. H., *A History of Soviet Russia*, vol. 1: *The Bolshevik Revolution 1917–1923*. London: Macmillan, 1950.

Carr, E. H., *A History of Soviet Russia: Socialism in One Country, 1924–1926*. London: Macmillan, 1958.

Carr, E. H., *The Interregnum, 1923–1924*. London: Macmillan, 1965.

Carr, E. H., *Il socialismo in un solo paese*, vol. 1: *La politica interna, 1924–1926*. Turin: Einaudi, 1968.

Carr, E. H., *The Twilight of the Comintern, 1930–1935*. London: Macmillan, 1982.

Carr, E. H., *The Comintern and the Spanish Civil War*. London: Macmillan, 1984.

Carr, E. H., *The Russian Revolution from Lenin to Stalin 1917–1929*, 2nd edn. London: Palgrave Macmillan, 2003.

Cattaruzza, M. (ed.), *La nazione in rosso: socialismo, comunismo e 'questione nazionale', 1889–1953*. Soveria Mannelli: Rubbettino, 2005.

Cattell, D., *Communism and the Spanish Civil War*. Berkeley: University of California Press, 1955.

Ceplair, L., *Anti-Communism in Twentieth Century America: A Critical History*. Santa Barbara, Calif.: ABC-Clio, 2011.

Cerchia, G., *Giorgio Amendola: un comunista nazionale*. Soveria Mannelli: Rubbettino, 2004.

Chandler, D. P., *Brother Number One: A Political Biography of Pol Pot*. Boulder, Colo.: Westview Press, 1992.

Chang, J., and Halliday, J., *Mao: The Unknown Story*. London: Jonathan Cape, 2005.

Chaqueri, C. (ed.), *The Left in Iran 1941–1957*. London: Merlin Press, 2011.

Chase, W. J., *Enemies within the Gates? The Comintern and the Stalinist Repression, 1934–1939*. New Haven, Conn.: Yale University Press, 2001.

Chekhoslovatskii krizis 1967-1969gg. v dokumentach TsK KPSS, Fond El'cina. Moscow: Rosspen, 2010.

Cheng, Y., 'Sino-Cuban relations during the early years of the Castro regime, 1959–1966'. *Journal of Cold War Studies* 9.3, 2007.

Chernyaev, A., *Shest' let s Gorbachevym: po dnevnikovym zapisam*. Moscow: Kul'tura, 1993.

Chernyaev, A., *Moya zhizn' i moe vremya*. Moscow: Mezhdunarodnye otnosheniya, 1995.

Chernyaev, A., *Sovmestnii iskhod: dnevnik dvukh epokh 1972–1991*. Moscow: Rosspen, 2008.

Chiarotto, F., *Operazione Gramsci: alla conquista degli intellettuali nell'Italia del dopoguerra*. Milan: Bruno Mondadori, 2010.

Chin, C. C., and Hack, K. (eds), *Dialogues with Chin Peng: New Light on the Malayan Communist Party*. Singapore: Singapore University Press, 2004.

Chowdhuri, S. R., *Leftism in India, 1917–1947*. London: Palgrave, 2007.

Chubaryan, A. O., and Pechatnov, V. O., 'Molotov "the liberal": Stalin's 1945 criticism of his deputy'. *Cold War History* 1.1, 2000, 129–40.

Clark, K., and Schlögel, K., 'Mutual perceptions and projections: Stalin's Russia in Nazi Germany—Nazi Germany in the Soviet Union'. In M. Geyer and S. Fitzpatrick (eds), *Beyond Totalitarianism: Stalinism and Nazism Compared*. Cambridge: Cambridge University Press, 2009.

Claudin, F., *La crisi del movimento comunista: dal Comintern al Cominform*. Milan: Feltrinelli, 1974.

Coeuré, S., *La grande lueur à l'Est: les Français et l'Union soviétique 1917–1939*. Paris: Seuil, 1999.

Cohen, S., *Bukharin and the Bolshevik Revolution: A Political Biography 1888–1938*. New York: Knopf, 1973. Translated into Italian as *Bukharin e la rivoluzione bolscevica: biografia politica 1888–1938* (Milan: Feltrinelli, 1975).

Connelly, J., 'The paradox of East German Communism: from non-Stalinism to neo-Stalinism?'. In V. Tismaneanu (ed.), *Stalinism Revisited: The Establishment of Communist Regimes in East-Central Europe*. Budapest: Central European University Press, 2009.

Courtois, S., *Le bolchévisme à la française*. Paris: Fayard, 2010.

Courtois, S., et al., *The Black Book of Communism: Crimes, Terror, Repression*. Cambridge, Mass.: Harvard University Press, 1999. Translated into Italian as *Il libro nero del comunismo: crimini, terrore, repressione* (Milan: Mondadori, 1998).

Courtois, S., and Lazar, M., *Histoire du Parti communiste français*. Paris: PUF, 2000.

Cox, R., 'Gramsci, hegemony and international relations: an essay in method'. In S. Gill (ed.), *Gramsci, Historical Materialism and International Relations*. Cambridge: Cambridge University Press, 1993.

Dallin, A., and Firsov, F. I. (eds), *Dimitrov and Stalin 1934–1943: Letters from the Soviet Archives*. New Haven, Conn.: Yale University Press, 2000.

Daniele C. (ed.), Gramsci a Roma, Togliatti a Mosca: il carteggio del 1926, with an essay by G. Vacca. Turin: Einaudi, 1999.

Daniele, C. (ed.), *Gramsci a Roma, Togliatti a Mosca: il carteggio del 1926*. Turin: Einaudi, 1999.

Daniels, R. V., *The Conscience of the Revolution: The Communist Opposition in the Soviet Union*. Cambridge, Mass.: Harvard University Press, 1960.

David-Fox, M., *Showcasing the Great Experiment: Cultural Diplomacy and Western Visitors to the Soviet Union, 1921–1941*. Oxford: Oxford University Press, 2012.

Davidson, A., et al., *South Africa and the Communist International: A Documentary History*. 2 vols. London: Frank Cass, 2003.

Davies, N., *White Eagle, Red Star: The Polish–Soviet War, 1919–1920*. London: Pimlico, 1972.

Davies, N., *Rising '44: The Battle for Warsaw*. London: Macmillan, 2003.

Day, R. B., *Cold War Capitalism: The View from Moscow 1945–1975*. Armonk, N.Y.: M. E. Sharpe, 1995.

Debo, R. K., *Revolution and Survival: The Foreign Policy of Soviet Russia 1917–1918*. Toronto: Toronto University Press, 1979.

Debo, R. K., *Survival and Consolidation: The Foreign Policy of Soviet Russia, 1918–1921*. Montreal: McGill-Queen's University Press, 1992.

Deery, P., and Del Pero, M., *Spiare e tradire: dietro le quinte della guerra fredda*. Milan: Feltrinelli, 2011.

De Felice, F., *Fascismo, democrazia, fronte popolare: il movimento comunista alla svolta del VII Congresso dell'Internazionale*. Bari: De Donato, 1973.

Del Pero, M., *Henry Kissinger e l'ascesa dei neoconservatori: alle origini della politica estera americana*. Rome: Laterza, 2006.

Derrick, J., *Africa's 'Agitators': Militant Anti-Colonialism in Africa and the West, 1918–1939*. New York: Columbia University Press, 2008.

Devyataya Konferentsiya Rkp(b). Sentjabr' 1920 goda. Protokoly. Moscow: Izdatel'stvo politicheskoy literatury, 1972.

Di Biagio, A., 'Moscow, the Comintern and the war scare, 1926–1928'. In S. Pons and A. Romano (eds), *Russia in the Age of Wars 1914–1945*. Milan: Feltrinelli, 2000.

Di Biagio, A., *Coesistenza e isolazionismo: Mosca, il Comintern e l'Europa di Versailles (1918–1928)*. Rome: Carocci, 2004.

Djilas, M., *The New Class: An Analysis of the Communist System*. New York: Praeger, 1957.

Djilas, M., *Conversations with Stalin*. London: Hart-Davis, 1962. Published in Italian as *Conversazioni con Stalin* (Milan: Feltrinelli, 1962).

Djilas, M., *Wartime*, 2nd edn. New York: Harcourt Brace, 1980.

Djilas, M., *Rise and Fall*. London: Macmillan, 1985.

Djilas, M., *Se la memoria non m'inganna: ricordi di un uomo scomodo 1943–1962*. Bologna: il Mulino, 1987.

Dimitrov, G., 'Voyna i rabochii klass kapitalisticheskikh stran'. *Kommunisticheskii Internatsional*, 1939.

Dimitrov, G., *Dnevnik 9 mart 1933–6 februari 1949*. Sofia: Universitetsko izdatel'stvo 'Sv. Kliment Okhridski', 1997.

Dimitrov, G., *Diario: gli anni di Mosca (1934–1945)*, ed. S. Pons. Turin: Einaudi, 2002.

Dimitrov, V., 'Revolution released: Stalin, the Bulgarian Communist Party and the establishment of the Cominform'. In F. Goriand and S. Pons (eds), *The Soviet Union and Europe in the Cold War, 1943–1953*. London: Macmillan, 1996.

Dimitrov, V., *Stalin's Cold War: Soviet Foreign Policy, Democracy and Communism in Bulgaria 1941–48*. Basingstoke: Palgrave Macmillan, 2008.

Diner, D., *Raccontare il Novecento: una storia politica*. Milan: Garzanti, 2001. Translated as *Cataclysms: A History of the Twentieth Century from Europe's Edge*. (Madison: University of Wisconsin Press, 2008).

'Direktivy I. V. Stalina V. M. Molotovu pered poezdkoy v Berlin v noyabre 1940 g'. *Novaya i noveishaya istoriya* 4, 1995.

Dobrynin, A., *In Confidence: Moscow's Ambassador to America's Six Cold War Presidents (1962–1986)*. New York: Times Books, 1995.

Dokumenty soveshchanii predstavitelei kommunisticheskikh i rabochikh partii, Moskva, noyabr' 1960 goda. Moscow: Gosudarstvennoe izdatel'stvo politicheskoy literatury, 1960.

Drabkin, J. S. (ed.), *Komintern i ideya mirovoy revoliutsii: dokumenty*. Moscow: Nauka, 1998.

Drew, A., *Discordant Comrades: Identities and Loyalties on the South African Left*. Aldershot: Ashgate, 2000.

Dreyfus, M., et al., *Le siècle des communismes*. Paris: Éditions ouvrières, 2000.

Duiker, W. J., *The Communist Road to Power in Vietnam*, 2nd edn. Boulder, Colo.: Westview Press, 1996.

Duiker, W. J., *Ho Chi Minh: A Life*. New York: Hyperion, 2000.

Dundovich, E., Gori, F., and Guercetti, E. (eds), *Reflections on the Gulag*. Milan: Feltrinelli, 2003.

Dvenadtsatii s'ezd Rkp(b) 17–25 aprel'ya 1923 goda: stenograficheskii otchet. Moscow: Gosudarstvennoe izdatel'stvo politicheskoy literatury, 1958.

Egorova, N. I., *The Iran Crisis of 1945–46: A View from the Russian Archives*. Washington, D.C.: Cold War International History Project, working paper 15, 1996.

Egorova, N. I., 'Nato i evropeiskaya bezopasnost': vospriiatie sovetskogo rukovodstva'. In *Stalin i kholodnaya voyna.* Moscow: Ivi Ran, 1998.

Egorova, N. I., 'La formation du bloc de l'Est comme frontière occidentale du système communiste (1947–1955)'. In S. Coeuré and S. Dullin (eds), *Frontières du communisme: mythologies et réalités de la division de l'Europe de la Révolution d'Octobre au mur de Berlin.* Paris: La Découverte, 2007.

Eley, G., *Forging Democracy: The History of the Left in Europe, 1850–2000.* Oxford: Oxford University Press, 2002.

Elorza, A., and Bizcarrondo, M., *Queridos camaradas: la Internacional comunista y España, 1919–1939.* Barcelona: Planeta, 1999.

Engerman, D. C., *Know Your Enemy: The Rise and Fall of America's Soviet Experts.* Oxford: Oxford University Press, 2009.

English, R. D., *Russia and the Idea of the West: Gorbachev, Intellectuals, and the End of the Cold War.* New York: Columbia University Press, 2000.

Epstein, C., *The Last Revolutionaries: German Communists and Their Century.* Cambridge, Mass.: Harvard University Press, 2003.

Exécutif élargi de l'Internationale communiste: compte rendu analytique de la session du 21 mars au 6 avril 1925. Paris: Librairie de l'Humanité, 1925.

Fasanella, G., and Franceschini, A., *Che cosa sono le BR: le radici, la storia, il presente.* Milan: Rizzoli, 2004.

Fejtö, F., *A History of the People's Democracies.* 2 vols. New York: Praeger, 1971. Translated into Italian as *Storia delle democrazie popolari* (2 vols. Milan: Bompiani, 1977).

Fejtö, F., *La fin des démocraties populaires: les chemins du post-communisme.* Paris: Séuil, 1992. Translated into Italian as *La fine delle democrazie popolari: l'Europa orientale dopo la rivoluzione del 1989* (Milan: Mondadori, 1994).

Fejtö, F., *La tragédie hongroise: ou, Une révolution socialiste anti-soviétique (1956).* Paris: Pierre Horay, 1996.

Fejtö, F., and Serra, M., *Le passager du siècle: guerres, révolutions, Europes.* Paris: Hachette, 1999. Translated into Italian as *Il passeggero del secolo: guerre, rivoluzioni, Europe* (Palermo: Sellerio, 2001).

Feltrinelli, C., *Senior Service.* Milan: Feltrinelli, 1999.

Ferris, J., 'Soviet support for Egypt's intervention in Yemen, 1962–63'. *Journal of Cold War Studies* 10.4, 2008.

Figes, O., *A People's Tragedy: The Russian Revolution 1891–1924.* London: Pimlico, 1997.

Fink, C., Gassert, P., and Junker, D. (eds), *1968: The World Transformed.* Cambridge: Cambridge University Press, 1998.

Firsov, F. I., *Sekretnye kody istorii Kominterna 1919–1943.* Moscow: Airo-XXI, 2007.

Flores, M., *L'immagine dell'URSS: l'occidente e la Russia di Stalin (1927–1956).* Milan: il Saggiatore, 1990.

Flores, M., and Gallerano, N., *Sul PCI: un'interpretazione storica.* Bologna: il Mulino, 1992.

Flores, M., and Gori, F. (eds), *Il mito dell'URSS: la cultura occidentale e l'Unione sovietica.* Milan: FrancoAngeli, 1990.

Foglesong, D. S., *The American Mission and the 'Evil Empire': The Crusade for a 'Free Russia' since 1881.* Cambridge: Cambridge University Press, 2007.

Foot, R., 'The Cold War and human rights'. In M. P. Leffler and O. A. Westad (eds), *The Cambridge History of the Cold War,* vol. 3: *Endings.* Cambridge: Cambridge University Press, 2010.

Frankel, J. (ed.), *Dark Times, Dire Decisions: Jews and Communism*. Oxford: Oxford University Press, 2004.

Franzen, J., *Red Star over Iraq: Iraqi Communism before Saddam*. London: Hurst, 2011.

Friedman, J., 'Soviet policy in the developing world and the Chinese challenge in the 1960s'.*Cold War History* 10.2, 2010.

Furet, F., *Marx and the French Revolution*. Chicago: University of Chicago Press, 1988.

Furet, F., *The Passing of an Illusion: The Idea of Communism in the Twentieth Century*. Chicago: The University of Chicago Press, 1999. Translated into Italian as *Il passato di un'illusione: l'idea comunista nel XX secolo* (Milan: Mondadori, 1995).

Fursenko, A., and Naftali, T., *'One Hell of a Gamble': Khrushchev, Castro, and Kennedy, 1958–1964*. New York: Norton, 1998.

Fursenko, A., and Naftali, T., *Khrushchev's Cold War: The Inside Story of an American Adversary*. New York: Norton, 2006.

Gaddis, J. L., *We Now Know: Rethinking Cold War History*. Oxford: Oxford University Press, 1997.

Gaddis, J. L., *George F. Kennan: An American Life*. New York: Penguin, 2011.

Gaiduk, I. V., *The Soviet Union and the Vietnam War*. Chicago: Ivan R. Dee, 1996.

Gaiduk, I. V., *Confronting Vietnam: Soviet Policy towards the Indochina Conflict, 1954–1963*. Stanford, Calif.: Stanford University Press, 2003.

Gaiduk, I. V., 'Soviet Cold War strategy and prospects of revolution in South and Southeast Asia'. In C. E. Goscha and C. F. Ostermann (eds), *Connecting Histories: Decolonization and the Cold War in Southeast Asia, 1945–1962*. Stanford, Calif./Washington, D.C.: Stanford University Press/Woodrow Wilson Center Press, 2009.

Galeazzi, M., *Togliatti e Tito: tra identità nazionale e internazionalismo*. Rome: Carocci, 2005.

Galeazzi, M., *Il PCI e il movimento dei paesi non allineati 1955–1975*. Milan: Franco Angeli, 2011.

Gallissot, R., 'Libération nationale et communisme dans le monde arabe'. In *Le siècle des communismes*. Paris: Éditions ouvrières, Éditions de l'Atelier, 2004.

Gati, C., *Failed Illusions: Moscow, Washington, Budapest, and the 1956 Hungarian Revolt*. Stanford, Calif.: Stanford University Press, 2006.

Gefter, M. Y., *Iz tekh i etikh let*. Moscow: Progress, 1991.

Gerolymatos, A., *Red Acropolis, Black Terror: The Greek Civil War and the Origins of Soviet–American Rivalry, 1943–1949*. New York: Basic Books, 2004.

Getzler, I., 'Ottobre 1917: il dibattito marxista sulla rivoluzione in Russia'. In *Storia del marxismo*, vol. 3.1: *Il marxismo nell'età della Terza Internazionale: dalla Rivoluzione d'ottobre alla crisi del '29*. Turin: Einaudi, 1981.

Getzler, I., *L'epopea di Kronstadt 1917–1921*. Turin: Einaudi, 1982.

Gibianskii, L. Y., 'Kak voznik Kominform: po novym arkhivnym materyalam'. *Novaya i noveishaya istoriya* 4, 1993.

Gibianskii, L. Y., 'Kominform v deistvii. 1947–1948 gg: po arkhivnym dokumentam'. *Novaya i noveishaya istoriya* 1–2, 1996.

Gibianskii, L. Y., 'The Soviet bloc and the initial stage of the Cold War: archival documents on Stalin's meetings with Communist leaders of Yugoslavia and Bulgaria, 1946–1948'. *Cold War International History Project Bulletin* 10, 1998.

Gide, A., *Retour de l'URSS*. Paris: Gallimard, 1936. Translated into Italian as *Ritorno dall'URSS seguito da Postille al mio ritorno dall'URSS (1936–1937)* (Turin: Bollati Boringhieri, 1988).

Ginat, R., *Egypt's Incomplete Revolution: Lutfi Al-Khuli and Nasser's Socialism in the 1960s*. London: Frank Cass, 1997.

Ginat, R., *A History of Egyptian Communism: Jews and Their Compatriots in Quest of Revolution*. Boulder, Colo.: Lynne Rienner, 2011.

Gleason, A., *Totalitarianism: The Inner History of the Cold War*. Oxford: Oxford University Press, 1995.

Gleijeses, P., *Conflicting Missions: Havana, Washington, and Africa, 1959–1976*. Chapel Hill N. C: University of North Carolina Press, 2002.

Gleijeses, P., 'Cuba and the Cold War, 1959–1980'. In M. P. Leffler and O. A. Westad (eds), *The Cambridge History of the Cold War*, vol. 2: *Crises and Détente*. Cambridge: Cambridge University Press, 2010.

Gorbachev, M., and Mlynář, Z., *Conversations with Gorbachev: On Perestroika, the Prague Spring, and the Crossroads of Socialism*. New York: Columbia University Press, 2002.

Gori, F., and Pons, S. (eds), *Dagli archivi di Mosca: l' URSS, il Cominform e il PCI (1943–1951)*. Rome: Carocci, 1998.

Gorlizki, Y., and Khlevniuk, O., *Cold Peace: Stalin and the Soviet Ruling Circle, 1945–1953*. Oxford: Oxford University Press, 2004.

Gorodetsky, G., *Grand Delusion: Stalin and the German Invasion of Russia*. New Haven, Conn.: Yale University Press, 1999.

Goscha, C. E., 'Vietnam, the Third Indochina War and the meltdown of Asian internationalism'. In O. A. Westad and S. Quinn-Judge (eds), *The Third Indochina War: Conflict between China, Vietnam, and Cambodia, 1972–79*. London: Routledge, 2006.

Gough, R., *A Good Comrade: János Kádár, Communism, and Hungary*. London: I. B. Tauris, 2006.

Gozzini, G., and Martinelli, R., *Storia del Partito comunista italiano*, vol. 7: *Dall'attentato a Togliatti all'VIII Congresso*. Turin: Einaudi, 1998.

Gramsci, A., *La costruzione del Partito comunista, 1923–1926*. Turin: Einaudi, 1971.

Graziosi, A., *L'URSS di Lenin e di Stalin: storia dell'Unione sovietica, 1914–1945*. Bologna: il Mulino, 2007.

Graziosi, A., *L'URSS dal trionfo al degrado: storia dell'Unione sovietica, 1945–1991*. Bologna: il Mulino, 2008.

Gromyko, A., *Memories*. London: Hutchinson, 1989. Published in Italian as *Memorie* (Milan: Rizzoli, 1989).

Gross, J. T., *Revolution from Abroad: The Soviet Conquest of Poland's Western Ukraine and Western Belorussia*. Princeton, N.J.: Princeton University Press, 1988.

Gross, J. T., 'War as revolution'. In N. M. Naimark and L. Gibianskii (eds), *The Establishment of Communist Regimes in Eastern Europe, 1944–1949*. Boulder, Colo.: Westview Press, 1997.

Gualtieri, R. (ed.), *Il PCI nell'Italia repubblicana*. Rome: Carocci, 2001.

Gualtieri, R., Spagnolo, C., and Taviani, E. (eds), *Togliatti nel suo tempo*. Rome: Carocci, 2007.

Guiat, C., *The French and Italian Communist Parties: Comrades and Culture*. London: Frank Cass, 2003.

Guiso, A., *La colomba e la spada: 'lotta per la pace' e antiamericanismo nella politica del Partito comunista italiano (1949–1954)*. Soveria Mannelli: Rubbettino, 2006.

Gundle, S., *Between Hollywood and Moscow: The Italian Communists and the Challenge of Mass Culture, 1943–1991*. Durham, N.C: Duke University Press, 2000. Translated into Italian as *I comunisti italiani tra Hollywood and Mosca: la sfida della cultura di massa (1943–1991)* (Florence: Giunti, 1995).

Gupta, D. N., *Communism and Nationalism in Colonial India, 1939–45*. New Delhi: Sage, 2008.

Gupta, S. D., *Comintern and the Destiny of Communism in India, 1919–1943*. Calcutta: Seribaan, 2006.

Gupta, S. K., *Stalin's Policy Towards India, 1946–1953*. New Delhi: South Asian Publishers, 1988.

Hájek, M., *Storia dell'Internazionale comunista (1921–1935): la politica del fronte unico*. Rome: Editori Riuniti, 1969.

Halliday, F., *Revolution and Foreign Policy: The Case of South Yemen 1967–1987*. Cambridge: Cambridge University Press, 1990.

Halliday, F., *Revolution and World Politics: The Rise and Fall of the Sixth Great Power*. Durham, N.C.: Duke University Press, 1999.

Hanbing, K., 'The transplantation and entrenchment of the Soviet economic model in China'. In T. P. Bernstein and H.-Y. Li (eds), *China Learns from the Soviet Union, 1949–Present*. Lanham, Md.: Lexington Books, 2010.

Hanhimäki, J. M., 'Détente in Europe, 1962–1975'. In M. P. Leffler and O. A. Westad (eds), *The Cambridge History of the Cold War*, vol. 2: *Crises and Détente*. Cambridge: Cambridge University Press, 2010.

Harrison, H. M., *Driving the Soviets up the Wall: Soviet–East German Relations, 1953–1961*. Princeton, N.J.: Princeton University Press, 2003.

Haslam, J., *The Soviet Union and the Threat from the East, 1933–1941: Moscow, Tokyo and the Prelude to the Pacific War*. London: Macmillan, 1992.

Haslam, J., 'Litvinov, Stalin, and the road not taken'. In G. Gorodetsky (ed.), *Soviet Foreign Policy 1917–1991*. London: Macmillan, 1994.

Haslam, J., *The Vices of Integrity: E. H. Carr, 1892–1982*. London: Verso, 1999.

Haslam, J., *The Nixon Administration and the Death of Allende's Chile: A Case of Assisted Suicide*. London: Verso, 2005.

Haslam J., 'I dilemmi della destalinizzazione: Togliatti, il XX Congresso del PCUS e le sue conseguenze'. In R. Gualtieri, C. Spagnolo, and E. Taviani (eds), *Togliatti nel suo tempo*. Rome: Carocci, 2007.

Haslam, J., *Russia's Cold War: From the October Revolution to the Fall of the Wall*. New Haven, Conn.: Yale University Press, 2011.

Haupt, G. (ed.), *Correspondance entre Lénine et Camille Huysmans, 1905–1914*. Paris: Mouton, 1963.

Haupt, G., *Lenin e la Seconda Internazionale*. Rome: Samonà e Savelli, 1969.

Haynes, J. E., Klehr H., and Vassiliev A., *Spies: The Rise and Fall of the KGB in America*. New Haven, Conn: Yale University Press, 2009.

Hedeler, W., and Vatlin, W. (eds), *Die Weltpartei aus Moskau: der Gründungskongress der Kommunistischen Internationale 1919. Protokoll und neue Dokumente*. Berlin: Akademie, 2008.

Heinzig, D., *The Soviet Union and Communist China 1945–1950: The Arduous Road to the Alliance*. Armonk, N.Y.: M. E. Sharpe, 2004.

Hellbeck, J., *Revolution on my Mind: Writing a Diary under Stalin*. Cambridge, Mass.: Harvard University Press, 2006.

Höbel, A., *Il PCI di Luigi Longo*. Naples: Edizioni scientifiche italiane, 2011.

Hobsbawm, E. J., *Revolutionaries*. London: Weidenfeld & Nicolson, 1972. Repr. in paperback, London: Quartet, 1975.

Hobsbawm, E. J., *The Age of Extremes: The Short 20th Century 1914–1991*. London: Michael Joseph, 1994.

Hobsbawm, E. J., *Interesting Times: A Twentieth-Century Life*. London: Allen Lane, 2002. Translated into Italian as *Anni interessanti: autobiografia di uno storico* (Milan: Rizzoli, 2002).

Hoffman, D. L., *Stalinist Values: The Cultural Norms of Soviet Modernity*. Ithaca, N.Y.: Cornell University Press, 2003.

Hollander, P., *Political Pilgrims: Travels of Western Intellectuals to the Soviet Union, China, and Cuba, 1928–1978*. New York: Oxford University Press, 1981. Translated into Italian as *Pellegrini politici: intellettuali occidentali in Unione Sovietica, Cina e Cuba* (Bologna: il Mulino, 1988).

Holloway, D., *Stalin and the Bomb: The Soviet Union and Atomic Energy, 1939–1956*. New Haven, Conn.: Yale University Press, 1994.

Holquist, P., *Making War, Forging Revolution: Russia's Continuum of Crisis, 1914–1921*. Cambridge, Mass.: Harvard University Press, 2002.

Hosking, G., 'The state and Russian national identity'. In L. Scales and O. Zimmer (eds), *Power and the Nation in European History*. Cambridge: Cambridge University Press, 2005.

Humbert-Droz, J., *Il contrasto tra l'Internazionale e il PCI 1922–1928: documenti inediti dell'archivio di Jules Humbert-Droz segretario dell'Internazionale comunista*. Milan: Feltrinelli, 1969.

Humbert-Droz, J., *L'Internazionale comunista tra Lenin e Stalin: memorie di un protagonista 1891–1941*. Milan: Feltrinelli, 1974.

Iatrides, J. O., 'Revolution or self-defense? Communist goals, strategy, and tactics in the Greek Civil War'. *Journal of Cold War Studies* 7.3, 2005.

Iazhborovskaia, I., 'The Gomułka alternative: the untravelled road'. In M. Naimark and L. Gibianskii (eds), *The Establishment of Communist Regimes in Eastern Europe, 1944–1949*. Boulder, Colo.: Westview Press, 1997.

Ikenberry, G. J., 'The restructuring of the international system after the Cold War'. In M. P. Leffler and O. A. Westad (eds), *The Cambridge History of the Cold War*, vol. 3: *Endings*. Cambridge: Cambridge University Press, 2010.

Ismael, T. Y., *The Communist Movement in the Arab World*. London: Routledge Curzon, 2005.

Ismael, T. Y., *The Rise and Fall of the Communist Party of Iraq*. Cambridge: Cambridge University Press, 2008.

Ismael, T. Y., and El-Sa'id, R., *The Communist Movement in Egypt*. Syracuse, N.Y.: Syracuse University Press, 1990.

Jacobson, J., *When the Soviet Union Entered World Politics*. Berkeley: University of California Press, 1994.

Jersild, A., 'The Soviet state as imperial scavenger: "catch up and surpass" in the transnational socialist bloc, 1950–1960'. *American Historical Review* 116.1, 2011.

Jervis, R., 'Identity and the Cold War'. In M. P. Leffler and O. A. Westad (eds), *The Cambridge History of the Cold War*, vol. 2: *Crises and Détente*. Cambridge: Cambridge University Press, 2010.

Jian, C., 'Deng Xiaoping, Mao's "continuous revolution", and the path toward the Sino-Soviet split: a rejoinder'. *Cold War International History Project Bulletin* 10, March 1998.

Jian, C., *Mao's China and the Cold War*. Chapel Hill N. C.: University of North Carolina Press, 2001.

Jian, C., 'Bridging revolution and decolonization: the "Bandung discourse" in China's early Cold War experience'. In C. E. Goscha and C. F. Ostermann (eds), *Connecting Histories: Decolonization and the Cold War in Southeast Asia, 1945–1962.* Stanford, Calif./Washington, D.C.: Stanford University Press/Woodrow Wilson Center Press, 2009.

Jian, C., 'China and the Cold War after Mao'. In M. P. Leffler and O. A. Westad (eds), *The Cambridge History of the Cold War*, vol. 3: *Endings.* Cambridge: Cambridge University Press, 2010.

Jones, W. D., *The Lost Debate: German Socialist Intellectuals and Totalitarianism.* Urbanail: University of Illinois Press, 1999.

Judt, T. (ed.), *Resistance and Revolution in Mediterranean Europe 1939–1948.* London: Routledge, 1989.

Judt, T., *Postwar: A History of Europe since 1945.* New York: Penguin Press, 2005.

Judt, T., 'Arthur Koestler, the exemplary intellectual'. In T. Judt, *Reappraisals: Reflections on the Forgotten Twentieth Century.* New York: Penguin Press, 2008.

Jun, N., *1962: The Eve of the Left Turn in China's Foreign Policy.* Washington, D.C.: Cold War International History Project, working paper 48, 2005.

Jun, N., 'The birth of the People's Republic of China and the road to the Korean War'. In M. P. Leffler and O. A. Westad (eds), *The Cambridge History of the Cold War*, vol. 1: *Origins.* Cambridge: Cambridge University Press, 2010.

Kak lomali Nep: stenogrammy plenumov TsK Vkp(b) 1928–1929. 5 vols. Moscow: Mezhdunarodnyi Fond 'Demokratiya', 2000.

Kardelj, E., *Memorie degli anni di ferro.* Rome: Editori Riuniti, 1980. Translated as *Reminiscences: The Struggle for Recognition and Independence. The New Yugoslavia, 1944–1957* (London: Blond & Briggs, 1982).

Karner, S., et al., *Prager Frühling: Das internationale Krisenjahr 1968.* Vienna: Böhlau, 2008.

Kemp, W. A., *Nationalism and Communism in Eastern Europe and the Soviet Union: A Basic Contradiction?* London: Macmillan, 1999.

Kenez, P., *Hungary from the Nazis to the Soviets: The Establishment of the Communist Regime in Hungary, 1944–1948.* New York: Cambridge University Press, 2006.

Kennan, G. F., 'The sources of Soviet conduct'. In F. J. Fleron, E. P. Hoffmann, and R. F. Laird (eds), *Classic Issues in Soviet Foreign Policy.* New York: de Gruyter, 1991.

Kershaw, I., *Hitler 1889–1936: Hubris.* London: Penguin, 2001.

Kershaw, I., *Fateful Choices: Ten Decisions that Changed the World 1940–1941.* London: Penguin, 2008.

Kersten, K., *The Establishment of Communist Rule in Poland, 1943–1948.* Berkeley, Calif.: University of California Press, 1991.

Khlevniuk, O., 'The reasons for the Great Terror: the foreign-political aspect'. In S. Pons and A. Romano (eds), *Russia in the Age of Wars 1914–1945.* Milan: Feltrinelli, 2000.

Khlevniuk, O., *Master of the House: Stalin and his Inner Circle.* New Haven, Conn.: Yale University Press, 2009.

Khrushchev, S. (ed.), *Memoirs of Nikita Khrushchev.* 3 vols. University Park, Pa.: Pennsylvania State University Press, 2004–7.

Kiernan, B., *The Pol Pot Regime: Race, Power, and Genocide in Cambodia under the Khmer Rouge, 1975–1979*, 2nd edn. New Haven, Conn.: Yale University Press, 2002.

Kiernan, B., *How Pol Pot Came to Power: Colonialism, Nationalism, and Communism in Cambodia, 1930–1975*, 2nd edn. New Haven, Conn.: Yale University Press, 2004.

Kiernan, B., 'External and indigenous sources of Khmer Rouge ideology'. In O. A. Westad and S. Quinn-Judge (eds), *The Third Indochina War: Conflict between China, Vietnam, and Cambodia, 1972–79*. London: Routledge, 2006.

Kissinger, H., *Diplomacy*. New York: Simon & Schuster, 1994.

Klehr, H., Haynes, J. E., and Anderson, K. M. (eds), *The Soviet World of American Communism*. New Haven, Conn: Yale University Press, 1998.

Knei-Paz, B., *The Social and Political Thought of Leon Trotsky*. Oxford: Clarendon Press, 2001.

Knight, N., *Rethinking Mao: Explorations in Mao Zedong's Thought*. Lanham, Md.: Lexington Books, 2007.

Koch, S., *Double Lives: Stalin, Willi Münzenberg, and the Seduction of the Intellectuals*. New York: Enigma Books, 2004.

Koestler, A., *Scum of the Earth*. London: Jonathan Cape, 1941. Traslated into Italian as *Schiuma della terra* (Bologna: il Mulino, 1989).

Koestler, A., *The Invisible Writing: The Second Volume of an Autobiography, 1932–40*. London: Collins, 1954. Translated into Italian as *La scrittura invisibile: autobiografia 1932–1940* (Bologna: il Mulino, 1991).

Komintern i Finlandiya, 1919–1943. Moscow: Nauka, 2003.

Komintern i grazhdanskaya voyna v Ispanii. Moscow: Nauka, 2001.

Komintern i Latinskaya Amerika: sbornik dokumentov. Moscow: Nauka, 1998.

Komintern protiv fashizma: dokumenty. Moscow: Nauka, 1999.

Kosats, G. G., *Krasny flag nad Blizhnim Vostokom? Kompartii Egipta, Palestiny, Sirii i Livana v 20–30-e gody*. Moscow: 2001.

Kotkin, S., *Armageddon Averted: The Soviet Collapse 1970–2000*. Oxford: Oxford University Press, 2001.

Kotkin, S., 'Modern times: the Soviet Union and the interwar conjuncture'. *Kritika: Explorations in Russian and Eurasian History* 1.2, 2001.

Kotkin, S., *Uncivil Society: 1989 and the Implosion of the Communist Establishment*. New York: Modern Library, 2009.

Kramer, M., 'Research note: documenting the early Soviet nuclear weapons program'. *Cold War International History Project Bulletin* 6–7, 1995–6.

Kramer, M., 'The Czechoslovak Crisis and the Brezhnev Doctrine'. In C. Fink, P. Gassert, and D. Junker (eds), *1968: The World Transformed*. Cambridge: Cambridge University Press, 1998.

Kramer, M., 'The Soviet Union and the 1956 crises in Hungary and Poland: reassessments and new findings'. *Journal of Contemporary History* 33.2, 1998.

Kramer, M., 'The early post-Stalin succession struggle and upheavals in East-Central Europe: internal-external linkages in Soviet policy making', *Journal of Cold War Studies* 1. 1–3, 1999.

Kramer, M., *Soviet Deliberations during the Polish Crisis, 1980–1981*. Washington, D.C.: Cold War International History Project, special working paper 1, 1999.

Kramer, M., 'The reform of the Soviet system and the demise of the Soviet state', *Slavic Review* 63.3, 2004.

Kramer, M., 'The collapse of East European communism and the repercussions within the Soviet Union', *Journal of Cold War History* 5. 4, 2003; 6.4, 2004; 7.1, 2005.

Kramer, M., 'Gorbachev and the demise of East European communism'. In S. Pons and F. Romero (eds), *Reinterpreting the End of the Cold War: Issues, Interpretations, Periodizations*. London: Frank Cass, 2005.

Kramer, M., 'Stalin, Soviet policy, and the consolidation of a communist bloc in Eastern Europe'. In V. Tismaneanu (ed.), *Stalinism Revisited: The Establishment of Communist Regimes in East-Central Europe*. Budapest: Central European University Press, 2009.

Kriegel, A., and Courtois, S., *Eugen Fried: le grand secret du PCF*. Paris: Éditions du Seuil, 1997.

Kuisong, Y., *Changes in Mao Zedong's Attitude toward the Indochina War, 1949–1973*. Washington, D.C.: Cold War International History Project, working paper 24, 2002.

Kullaa, R., *Non-Alignment and Its Origins in Cold War Europe: Yugoslavia, Finland, and the Soviet Challenge*. London: I. B. Tauris, 2011.

Kuo, M. A., *Contending with Contradictions: China's Policy toward Soviet Eastern Europe and the Origins of the Sino-Soviet Split, 1953–1960*. Lanham, Md.: Lexington Books, 2001.

Kuromiya, H., 'Stalin in the light of the Politburo transcripts'. In P. R. Gregory and N. M. Naimark (eds), *The Lost Politburo Transcripts: From Collective Rule to Stalin's Dictatorship*. New Haven, Conn.: Yale University Press, 2008.

Kynin G. P., and Laufer, J. (eds), *SSSR i Germanskii Vopros 1941–1949*. 3 vols. Moscow: Mezhdunarodnye otnosheniya, 1996–2003.

Lampe, J. R., *Yugoslavia as History: Twice There Was a Country*. Cambridge: Cambridge University Press, 1996.

Lankov, A., *From Stalin to Kim Il Sung: The Formation of North Korea 1945–1960*. London: Hurst, 2002.

Laporte, N., 'Presenting a crisis as an opportunity: the KPD and the Third Period, 1929–1933'. In M. Worley (ed.), *In Search of Revolution: International Communist Parties in the Third Period*. London: I. B. Tauris, 2004.

Laporte, N., Morgan, K., and Worley, M. (eds), *Bolshevism, Stalinism and the Comintern: Perspectives on Stalinization, 1917–53*. Basingstoke: Palgrave Macmillan, 2008.

Latham, M. E., 'The Cold War in the Third World, 1963–1975'. In M. P. Leffler and O. A. Westad (eds), *The Cambridge History of the Cold War*, vol. 2: *Crises and Détente*. Cambridge: Cambridge University Press, 2010.

Lazar, M., *Maisons rouges: les partis communistes français et italien de la Libération à nos jours*. Paris: Aubier, 1992.

Lazar, M., 'La strategia del PCF e del PCI dal 1944 al 1947: acquisizioni della ricerca e problemi irrisolti'. In E. Aga-Rossi and G. Quagliariello (eds), *L'altra faccia della luna: i rapporti tra PCI, PCF e Unione sovietica*. Bologna: il Mulino, 1997.

Lazar, M., *Le communisme: une passion française*. Paris: Perrin, 2005.

Lazitch, B., and Drachkovitch, M., *Lenin and the Comintern*. Stanford, Calif.: Hoover Institution Press, 1972.

Lebedeva, N. S. (ed.), *Katyn Mart' 1940 g.–sentyabr' 2000 g. Rasstrel. Sudby zhivykh. Ekho Katyni. Dokumenty*. Moscow: Ves' Mir, 2001.

Lebedeva, N. S., and Narinskii, M. M. (eds), *Komintern i Vtoraya Mirovaya Voyna*. 2 vols. Moscow: Pamyatniki Istoricheskoy Misly, 1994, 1998.

'Le Duan and the break with China'. *Cold War International History Project Bulletin* 12–13, 2001.

Leffler, M. P., *The Specter of Communism: The United States and the Origins of the Cold War, 1917–1953*. New York: Hill and Wang, 1994.

Leffler, M. P., *For the Soul of Mankind: The United States, the Soviet Union, and the Cold War*. New York: Hill and Wang, 2007.

Leffler, M. P., 'The emergence of an American grand strategy, 1945–1952'. In M. P. Leffler and O. A. Westad (eds), *The Cambridge History of the Cold War*, vol. 1: *Origins*. Cambridge: Cambridge University Press, 2010.

Lendvai, P., *One Day that Shook the Communist World: The 1956 Hungarian Uprising and Its Legacy*. Princeton, N.J.: Princeton University Press, 2008.

Lenin, V. I., *Polnoe sobranie sochinenii*, 5th edn. 55 vols. Moscow: Izdatel'stvo politicheskoy literatury, 1958–75.

Lévesque, J., *The Enigma of 1989: The USSR and the Liberation of Eastern Europe*. Berkeley, Calif.: University of California Press, 1997.

Lévesque, J., 'The East European revolutions of 1989'. In M. P. Leffler and O. A. Westad (eds), *The Cambridge History of the Cold War*, vol. 3: *Endings*. Cambridge: Cambridge University Press, 2010.

Lewin, M., *The Making of the Soviet System: Essays in the Social History of Inter-War Russia*. New York: New Press, 1994.

Lewin, M., *Lenin's Last Struggle*. Ann Arbor, MI: University of Michigan Press, 2005.

Lieven, D., *Empire: The Russian Empire and Its Rivals*. London: John Murray, 2000.

Loewenthal, R., *World Communism: The Disintegration of a Secular Faith*. New York: Oxford University Press, 1964.

Logevall, F., 'The Indochina Wars and the Cold War, 1945–1975'. In M. P. Leffler and O. A. Westad (eds), *The Cambridge History of the Cold War*, vol. 2: *Crises and Détente*. Cambridge: Cambridge University Press, 2010.

Lomellini, V., *L'appuntamento mancato: la sinistra italiana e il dissenso nei regimi comunisti (1968–1989)*. Florence: Le Monnier, 2010.

Loth, W., 'Stalin's plans for post-war Germany'. In F. Gori and S. Pons (eds), *The Soviet Union and Europe in the Cold War, 1943–1953*. London: Macmillan, 1996.

W. Loth, *Stalin's Unwanted Child: The Soviet Union, the German Question, and the Founding of the GDR*. New York: St. Martin's Press, 1998. Translated into Italian as *Figliastri di Stalin: Mosca, Berlino e la formazione della RDT* (Urbino: Quattro Venti, 1997).

Lubyanka: Stalin i VCK-GPU-OGPU-Nkvd. Yanvar' 1922–Dekabr' 1936. Moscow: Mezhdunarodnyi Fond 'Demokratiya', 2003.

Ludwig, B., 'Le mur de Berlin, dernier rempart de l'antifascisme et ultime frontière du communisme en Europe'. In S. Coeuré and Dullin (eds), *Frontières du communisme: mythologies et réalités de la division de l'Europe au mur de Berlin*. Paris: La Découverte, 2007.

Lukes, I., 'The Czech road to communism'. In N. M. Naimark and L. Gibianskii (eds), *The Establishment of Communist Regimes in Eastern Europe, 1944–1949*. Boulder, Colo.: Westview Press, 1997.

Lüthi, L. M., 'Twenty-four Soviet-bloc documents on Vietnam and the Sino-Soviet split, 1964–1966'. *Cold War International History Project Bulletin* 16, 2008.

Lüthi, L. M., *The Sino-Soviet Split: Cold War in the Communist World*. Princeton, N.J.: Princeton University Press, 2008.

MacFarquhar, R., *The Origins of the Cultural Revolution*, vol. 1: *Contradictions among the People 1956–1957*. New York: Columbia University Press, 1974.

MacFarquhar, R., *The Origins of the Cultural Revolution*, vol. 2: *The Great Leap Forward*. New York: Columbia University Press, 1983.

MacFarquhar, R., *The Coming of the Cataclysm, 1961–1966*. New York: Columbia University Press, 1997.

MacFarquhar, R., Cheek, T., and Wu, E. (eds), *The Secret Speeches of Chairman Mao: From the Hundred Flowers to the Great Leap Forward*. Cambridge, Mass.: Harvard University Press, 1989.

MacFarquhar, R., and Schoenhals, M., *Mao's Last Revolution*. Cambridge, Mass.: Harvard University Press, 2006.

Machcewicz, P., *Rebellious Satellite: Poland 1956*. Stanford, Calif.: Stanford University Press, 2009.

Mackay, D., *The Malayan Emergency 1948–60: The Domino that Stood*. London: Brassey's, 1997.

Macry, P., *Gli ultimi giorni: stati che crollano nell'Europa del Novecento*. Bologna: il Mulino, 2009.

Maier, C. S., 'I fondamenti politici del dopoguerra'. In P. Anderson et al. (eds), *Storia d'Europa*, vol.1: *L'Europa oggi*. Turin: Einaudi, 1993.

Maier, C. S., *Dissolution: The Crisis of Communism and the End of East Germany*. Princeton, N.J.: Princeton University Press, 1997. Translated into Italian as *Il crollo: la crisi del comunismo e la fine della Germania Est*. (Bologna: Il Mulino, 1999).

Maier, C. S., 'Who divided Germany?', *Diplomatic History* 3, 1998.

Maier, C. S., *Among Empires: American Ascendancy and Its Predecessors*. Cambridge, Mass.: Harvard University Press, 2006.

Majander, M., 'Post-Cold War historiography in Finland'. In T. B. Olesen (ed.), *The Cold War and the Nordic Countries*. Odense: University Press of South Denmark, 2004.

Major, P., *The Death of KPD: Communism and Anti-Communism in West Germany*. Oxford: Clarendon Press, 1997.

Malaka, T., *From Jail to Jail*. Athens: Ohio University Press, 1991.

Mallick, R., *Indian Communism: Opposition, Collaboration and Institutionalization*. New Delhi: Oxford University Press, 1994.

Mansourov, A. Y., 'Stalin, Mao, Kim, and China's decision to enter the Korean War, September 16–October 15, 1950: new evidence from the Russian archives'. *Cold War International History Project Bulletin* 6–7, 1995–6, 94–119.

Marangé, C., *Le communisme vietnamien (1919–1991): construction d'un état-nation entre Moscou et Pékin*. Paris: Presses de la Fondation Nationale des Sciences Politiques, 2012.

Marcuse, H., *Soviet Marxism: A Critical Analysis*. New York: Columbia University Press, 1958.

Margolin, J.-L., 'Cambodia: the country of disconcerting crimes', in S. Courtois et al., *The Black Book of Communism: Crimes, Terror, Repression*. Cambridge, Mass.: Harvard University Press, 1999. Translated into Italian as 'Cambogia: nel paese del crimine scon-certante' in S. Courtois, N. Werth, et al., *Il libro nero del comunismo: crimini, terrore, repressione* (Milan: Mondadori, 1998).

Margolin, J.-L., 'China: a long march into the night'. In S. Courtois et al., *The Black Book of Communism: Crimes, Terror, Repression*. Cambridge, Mass.: Harvard University Press, 1999. Translated into Italian as 'Cina: una lunga marcia nella notte', in S. Courtois, N. Werth, et al., Il libro nero del comunismo: crimini, terrore, repressione. (Milan: Mondadori, 1998).

Mark, E., *Revolution by Degrees: Stalin's National-Front Strategy for Europe, 1941–1947*. Cold War International History Project,working paper 31. Washington, D.C.: Woodrow Wilson Center, 2001.

Martelli, R., *1956 communiste: le glas d'une espérance*. Paris: La Dispute, 2006.

Martin, B. K., *Under the Loving Care of the Fatherly Leader: North Korea and the Kim Dynasty*. New York: St. Martin's Press, 2004.

Martin, T., *An Affirmative Action Empire: Nations and Nationalism in the Soviet Union, 1923–1939*. Ithaca, N.Y.: Cornell University Press, 2001.

Martinelli, R., *Storia del Partito comunista italiano*, vol. 6: *Il 'partito nuovo' dalla Liberazione al 18 aprile*. Turin: Einaudi, 1995.

Martinelli, R., and Righi, M. L. (eds), *La politica del Partito comunista italiano nel periodo costituente: i verbali della direzione tra il V e il VI Congresso, 1946–1948*. Rome: Editori Riuniti, 1992.

Martov, J., *Bolscevismo mondiale: la prima critica marxista del leninismo al potere (1919)*. Turin: Einaudi, 1980.

Mastny, V., *Russia's Road to the Cold War: Diplomacy, Warfare, and the Politics of Communism, 1941–1945*. New York: Columbia University Press, 1979.

Mastny, V., *The Cold War and Soviet Insecurity: The Stalin Years*. Oxford: Oxford University Press, 1996.

Mastny, V., 'Imagining war in Europe: Soviet strategic planning'. In V. Mastny, S. G. Holtsmark, and A. Wenger (eds), *War Plans and Alliances in the Cold War: Threat Perceptions in the East and West*. London: Routledge, 2006.

Mastny, V., 'The Warsaw Pact as history'. In V. Mastny and M. Byrne (eds), *A Cardboard Castle? An Inside History of the Warsaw Pact, 1955–1991*. Budapest: Central European University Press, 2005.

Mastny, V., 'The Soviet Union's partnership with India'. *Journal of Cold War Studies* 12.3, 2010.

Mastny, V., and Byrne, M. (eds), *A Cardboard Castle? An Inside History of the Warsaw Pact, 1955–1991*. Budapest: Central European University Press, 2005.

Mawdsley, E., *Thunder in the East: The Nazi–Soviet War 1941–1945*. London: Hodder Arnold, 2005.

Mayer, A. J., *Wilson vs Lenin: Political Origins of the New Diplomacy*. New York: World Publishing, 1964.

Mayer, A. J., *The Furies: Violence and Terror in the French and Russian Revolutions*. Princeton, N.J.: Princeton University Press, 2000.

Mazov, S., *A Distant Front in the Cold War: The USSR in West Africa and the Congo, 1956–1964*. Washington, DC/Stanford, Calif.: Woodrow Wilson Center Press/Stanford University Press, 2010.

Mazower, M., *Hitler's Empire: How the Nazis Ruled Europe*. New York: Penguin Press, 2008.

Mazower, M., *Governing the World: The History of an Idea*. London: Penguin, 2012.

Mazuy, R., *Croire plutôt que voir? Voyages en Russie soviétique*. Paris: Odile Jacob, 2002.

McDermott, K., and Agnew, J., *The Comintern: A History of International Communism from Lenin to Stalin*. Basingstoke: Macmillan, 1996.

McMeekin, S., *The Red Millionaire: A Political Biography of Willi Münzenberg, Moscow's Secret Propaganda Tsar in the West 1917–1940*. New Haven, Conn.: Yale University Press, 2003.

McVey, R., *The Rise of Indonesian Communism*. Ithaca, N.Y.: Cornell University Press, 1965.

Meijer, J. M. (ed.), *The Trotsky Papers 1917–1922*. The Hague: Mouton, 1964.

Menétrey-Monchau, C., 'The changing post-war US strategy in Indochina'. In O. A. Westad and S. Quinn-Judge (eds), *The Third Indochina War: Conflict between China, Vietnam, and Cambodia, 1972–79*. London: Routledge, 2006.

Mevius, M., *Agents of Moscow: The Hungarian Communist Party and the Origins of Socialist Patriotism, 1941–1953*. Oxford: Oxford University Press, 2005.

Michnik, A., *Letters from Prison and Other Essays*. Berkeley, Calif.: University of California Press, 1985.

Mićunović, V., *Moscow Diary*. New York: Doubleday, 1980.

Mikoyan, A., *Tak bylo: Razmyshleniya o minuvshem*. Moscow: Vagrius, 1999.

Mikoyan, S., *The Soviet Cuban Missile Crisis: Castro, Mikoyan, Kennedy, Khrushchev, and the Missiles of November*, ed. S. Savranskaya. Washington, DC/Stanford, Calif.: Woodrow Wilson Center Press/Stanford University Press, 2012.

Mitter, R., and Major, P. (eds), *Across the Blocs: Cold War Cultural and Social History*. London: Frank Cass, 2004.

Molotov, Malenkov, Kaganovich. 1957. Stenogramma iyun'skogo plenuma TsK KPSS i drugie dokumenty. Moscow: Mezhdunarodnyi Fond 'Demokratiya', 1998.

Morgan, K., *The Webbs and Soviet Communism*, vol. 2: *Bolshevism and the British Left*. London: Lawrence & Wishart, 2006.

Morgan, K., Flinn, A., and Cohen, G., *Communists and British Society 1920–1991*. London: Rivers Oram Press, 2007.

Morozova, I. Y., *The Comintern and Revolution in Mongolia*. Cambridge: White Horse Press, 2002.

Morris, S. J., *The Soviet–Chinese–Vietnamese Triangle in the 1970s: The View from Moscow*. Washington, D.C.: Cold War International History Project, working paper 25, 1999.

Mortimer, R., *Indonesian Communism under Sukarno: Ideology and Politics, 1959–1965*. Ithaca, N.Y.: Cornell University Press, 1974.

Mueller, J.-W., 'The Cold War and the intellectual history of the late twentieth century'. In M. P. Leffler and O. A. Westad (eds), *The Cambridge History of the Cold War*, vol. 3: *Endings*. Cambridge: Cambridge University Press, 2010.

Murashko, G. P., 'Fevral'skii krizis 1948g. v Chekhoslovakii i sovetskoe rukovodstvo. Po novym materyalam rossiiskikh arkhivov', *Novaya i noveishaya istoriya* 3, 1998.

Murashko, G. P., and Noskova, A. F., 'Sovetskii faktor v poslevoennoy Vostochnoy Evrope (1945–1948)'. In *Sovetskaya vneshnyaya politika v gody* 'Kholodnoy voyny' *(1945–1985): novoe prochtenie*. Moscow: Mezhdunarodnye otnosheniya, 1995.

Naimark, N. M., *The Russians in Germany: A History of the Soviet Zone of Occupation, 1945–1949*. Cambridge, Mass.: Harvard University Press, 1995.

Naimark, N. M., *Fires of Hatred: Ethnic Cleansing in the Twentieth Century*. Cambridge, Mass.: Harvard University Press, 2001.

Naimark, N. M., 'Stalin and Europe in the postwar period, 1945–53: issues and problems'. *Journal of Modern European History* 2.1, 2004.

Naimark, N. M., 'The Sovietization of Eastern Europe, 1944–1953'. In M. P. Leffler and O. A. Westad (eds), *The Cambridge History of the Cold War*, vol. 1: *Origins*. Cambridge: Cambridge University Press, 2010.

Naimark, N. M., and Gibianskii, L. (eds), *The Establishment of Communist Regimes in Eastern Europe, 1944–1949*. Boulder, Colo.: Westview Press, 1997.

Napolitano, G., *Dal PCI al socialismo europeo: un'autobiografia politica*. Rome: Laterza, 2005.

'Na poroge pervogo raskola v "sotsialisticheskom lagere": peregovory rukovodyashchikh deyatelei SSSR, Bolgarii i Jugoslavii, 1948g'. *Istoricheskii Arkhiv* 4, 1998.

Narinskii, M. M., 'The Soviet Union and the Berlin Crisis 1948–9'. In F. Gori and S. Pons (eds), *The Soviet Union and Europe in the Cold War, 1943–53*. London: Macmillan, 1996.

Narinsky, M. M., and Rojahn, J. (eds), *Centre and Periphery: The History of the Comintern in the Light of New Documents*. Amsterdam: International Institute of Social History, 1996.

Nation, R. C., *War on War: Lenin, the Zimmerwald Left, and the Origins of Communist Internationalism*. Durham, N.C. Duke University Press, 1989.

Nation, R. C., 'A Balkan union? Southeastern Europe in Soviet security policy, 1944–8'. In F. Gori and S. Pons (eds), *The Soviet Union and Europe in the Cold War, 1943–53*. London: Macmillan, 1996.

Navrátil, J. (ed.), *The Prague Spring 1968*. Budapest: Central European University Press, 2006.

Nevezhin, V. A., *Sindrom nastupatelnoy voiny: sovetskaya propaganda v preddverii 'sviashchennykh boyev' 1939–1941 gg*. Moscow: Airo-XX, 1997.

Nevezhin, V. A., *Zastol'nye rechi Stalina: dokumenty i materialy*. Moscow: Airo-XX, 2003.

'New evidence on Poland in the early Cold War'. *Cold War International History Project Bulletin* 11, 1998.

Nikita Khrushchev 1964: stenogrammy plenuma TsK KPSS i drugie dokumenty. Moscow: Mezhdunarodnyi Fond 'Demokratiya', 2007.

Nolte, E., *Der europäische Bürgerkrieg 1917–1945: Nationalsozialismus und Bolschewismus*, Berlin: Propyläen Verlag, 1987.

Nossiter, T. J., *Marxist State Governments in India: Politics, Economics and Society*. London: Pinter, 1988.

Novikov, N. V., *Vospominaniya diplomata: Zapiski 1938–1947*. Moscow: Izdatel'stvo politicheskoy literatury, 1989.

Olsen, M., *Soviet–Vietnam Relations and the Role of China, 1949–64: Changing Alliances*. London: Routledge, 2006.

Onslow, S., 'The Cold War in southern Africa: white power, black nationalism and external intervention'. In S. Onslow (ed.), *The Cold War in Southern Africa: White Power, Black Liberation*. London: Routledge, 2009.

Orsini, A., *Anatomia delle Brigate rosse: le radici ideologiche del terrorismo rivoluzionario*. Soveria Mannelli: Rubbettino, 2009.

Osgood, K., 'The perils of coexistence: peace and propaganda in Eisenhower's foreign policy'. In K. Larres and K. Osgood (eds), *The Cold War after Stalin's Death: A Missed Opportunity for Peace?* Lanham, Md.: Rowman & Littlefield, 2006.

Ostermann, C. (ed.), *Uprising in East Germany 1953*. Budapest: Central European University Press, 2001.

Otdel TsK KPSS po svyazyam s inostrannimi kompartiyami 1953–1957: Annotirovannii spravochnik. Moscow: Rosspen, 1999.

Ottanelli, F. M., *The Communist Party of the United States from Depression to World War II*. New Brunswick, N.J.: Rutgers University Press, 1991.

Ouimet, M. J., *The Rise and Fall of the Brezhnev Doctrine in Soviet Foreign Policy*. Chapel Hill, N.C.: University of North Carolina Press, 2003.

Overy, R., *The Dictators: Hitler's Germany, Stalin's Russia*. London: Penguin, 2005.

Paczkowski, A., 'Poland, the "enemy nation"'. In S. Courtois et al., *The Black Book of Communism: Crimes, Terror, Repression*. Cambridge, Mass.: Harvard University Press, 1999. Translated into Italian as 'Polonia, la "nazione nemica"', in S. Courtois, N. Werth, et al., *Il libro nero del comunismo: crimini, terrore, repressione* (Milan: Mondadori, 1998).

Paczkowski, A., and Byrne, M. (eds), *From Solidarity to Martial Law: The Polish Crisis of 1980-1981. A Documentary History*. Budapest: Central European University Press, 2007.

Pantsov, A., *Tainaya istoriya sovetsko-kitayskikh otnoshenii: bol'sheviki i kitayskaya revoliutsiya (1919–1927)*. Moscow: Muravey-Gayd, 2001.

Pantsov, A., *Mao Tseedun*. Moscow: Molodaya Gvardiya, 2012.

Papathanasiou, I., 'The Cominform and the Greek Civil War, 1947–49'. In P. Carabott and T. D. Sfikas (eds), *The Greek Civil War*. London: Ashgate, 2004.

Pappagallo, O., *Il PCI e la rivoluzione cubana: la 'via latino-americana al socialismo' tra Mosca e Pechino (1959–1965)*. Rome: Carocci, 2009.

Patenaude, B. M., *Trotsky: Downfall of a Revolutionary*. New York: HarperCollins, 2009.

Payne, S., *The Spanish Civil War, the Soviet Union, and Communism*. New Haven, Conn.: Yale University Press, 2004.

Pechatnov, V. O., *The Big Three after World War II: New Documents on Soviet Thinking about Post War Relations with the United States and Great Britain*. Cold War International History Project, working paper 13. Washington, D.C.: Woodrow Wilson Center, 1995.

Pechatnov, V. O., ' "Strel'ba cholostymi": sovetskaja propaganda na Zapad v nachale kholodnoy voyny, 1945–1947'. In *Stalin i kholodnaya voyna*. Moscow: Ivi Ran, 1998.

Pechatnov,V. O., 'The Soviet Union and the outside world, 1944–1953'. In M. P. Leffler and O. A. Westad (eds), *The Cambridge History of the Cold War*, vol. 1: *Origins*. Cambridge: Cambridge University Press, 2010.

Peng, C., *My Side of History*. Singapore: Media Masters, 2003.

Pennetier, C., and Pudal, B. (eds), *Autobiographies, autocritiques, aveux dans le monde communiste*. Paris: Belin, 2002.

Perović, J., 'The Tito–Stalin split: a reassessment in light of new evidence'. *Journal of Cold War Studies* 9.2, 2007.

Petersen, R. D., *Resistance and Rebellion: Lessons from Eastern Europe*. Cambridge: Cambridge University Press, 2001.

Piatnitskii, V. I., *Osip Piatnitskii i Komintern na vesakh istorii*. Minsk: Kharvest, 2004.

Pipes, R., *Russia under the Bolshevik Regime, 1919–1924*. New York: Alfred A. Knopf, 1993.

Pipes, R. (ed.), *The Unknown Lenin: From the Secret Archive*. New Haven, Conn.: Yale University Press, 1996.

Pipes, R., *Il regime bolscevico: dal terrore rosso alla morte di Lenin*. Milan: Mondadori, 1999.

Pis'ma I. V. Stalina V. M. Molotovu 1925–1936 gg: sbornik dokumentov. Moscow: Rossiya Molodaya, 1995.

Pleshakov, C., *Stalin's Folly: The Secret History of the German Invasion of Russia, June 1941*. London: Weidenfeld & Nicolson, 2005.

Polanyi, K., *Europe To-day*. London: Workers' Educational Trade Union Committee, 1937. Translated into Italian as *Europa 1937: guerre esterne e guerre civili* (Rome: Donzelli, 1995).

Pons, S., *Berlinguer e la fine del comunismo*. Turin: Einaudi, 2006.

Pons, S., 'Stalinismo, antifascismo e "guerra civile europea"'. In F. De Felice (ed.), *Antifascismi e resistenze*. Rome: La Nuova Italia Scientifica, 1997.

Pons, S., *L'impossibile egemonia: l'URSS, il PCI e le origini della guerra fredda (1943–1948)*. Rome: Carocci, 1999.

Pons, S., 'In the aftermath of the age of wars: Soviet security policy during World War Two'. In S. Pons and A. Romano (eds), *Russia in the Age of Wars 1914–1945*. Milan: Feltrinelli, 2000.

Pons, S., 'Stalin, Togliatti, and the origins of the Cold War in Europe'. *Journal of Cold War Studies* 3.2, 2001, 3–27.

Pons, S., 'Meetings between the Italian Communist Party and the Communist Party of the Soviet Union: Moscow and Rome, 1978–80'. *Cold War History* 3.1, 2002.

Pons, S., *Stalin and the Inevitable War*. London: Frank Cass, 2002.

Pons, S., 'L'invenzione del "post-comunismo": Gorbacev and il Partito comunista italiano'. *Ricerche di storia politica* 11.1, 2008, 21–36.

Pons, S., 'Western communists, Mikhail Gorbachev and the 1989 revolutions'. *Contemporary European History* 18.3, 2009, 349–62.

Pons, S., 'The rise and fall of Eurocommunism'. In M. P. Leffler and O. A. Westad (eds), *The Cambridge History of the Cold War*, vol. 3: *Endings*. Cambridge: Cambridge University Press, 2010.

Pons, S., 'Stalin and the European communists after World War Two (1943–1948)'. In M. Mazower, J. Reinisch, and D. Feldman (eds), *Post-War Reconstruction in Europe: International Perspectives, 1945–1949*. New York: Oxford University Press, 2011.

Pons, S., and Romero, F. (eds), *Reinterpreting the End of the Cold War: Issues, Interpretations, Periodizations*. London: Frank Cass, 2005.

Poretsky, E. K., *Our Own People: A Memoir of 'Ignace Reiss' and His Friends*. London: Oxford University Press, 1969.

'Poslednii vizit I. Broza Tito k I. V. Stalinu'. *Istoricheskii Arkhiv* 2, 1993.

Prazmowska, A. J., *Civil War in Poland, 1942–1948*. London: Macmillan, 2004.

Prezidium TsK KPSS 1954–1964. Chernovye protokol' nye zapisi zasedanii. Stenogrammy. Postanovleniya. 3 vols. Moscow: Rosspen, 2003–8.

Priestland, D., *Stalinism and the Politics of Mobilization: Ideas, Power, and Terror in Inter-war Russia*. Oxford: Oxford University Press, 2007.

Priestland, D., *The Red Flag: A History of Communism*. New York: Grove Press, 2009.

Procacci, G., 'La "lotta per la pace" nel socialismo internazionale alla vigilia della seconda guerra mondiale'. In *Storia del marxismo*, vol. 3, part 2. Turin: Einaudi, 1981.

Procacci, G., 'La coesistenza pacifica: appunti per la storia di un concetto'. In L. Sestan (ed.), *La politica estera della perestrojka: l'URSS di fronte al mondo da Breznev a Gorbaciov*. Rome: Editori Riuniti, 1988.

Procacci, G., et al. (eds), *The Cominform: Minutes of the Three Conferences 1947/1948/1949*. Milan: Feltrinelli, 1994.

Protokoll des III Kongresses der Kommunistischen Internationale (Moskau, 22 Juni bis 12 Juli 1921). Hamburg, 1921.

Protokoll des Vierten Kongresses der Kommunistischen Internationale: Petrograd–Moskau vom 5 November bis 5 Dezember 1922. Hamburg, 1923.

Protokoll: Erweiterte Exekutive der Kommunistischen Internationale. Moskau, 22 November–16 Dezember 1926. Hamburg/Berlin, 1927.

Pupo, R., *Trieste '45*. Rome: Laterza, 2010.

Pyatnadtsatii s'ezd Vkp(b). Dekabr' 1927 goda: stenograficheskii otchet. Moscow: Gosudarstvennoe izdatel'stvo politicheskoy literatury, 1961.

Quinn-Judge, S., *Ho Chi Minh: The Missing Years*. London: Hurst, 2003.

Quinn-Judge, S., 'Through a glass darkly: reading the history of the Vietnamese Communist Party 1945–1975'. In M. P. Bradley and M. B. Young (eds), *Making Sense of the Vietnam Wars: Local, National, and Transnational Perspectives*. New York: Oxford University Press, 2008.

Radchenko, S., *Two Suns in the Heaven: The Sino-Soviet Struggle for Supremacy, 1962–1967*. Washington, DC/Stanford, Calif.: Woodrow Wilson Center Press/Stanford University Press, 2009.

Radchenko, S., 'The Sino-Soviet split'. In M. P. Leffler and O. A. Westad (eds), *The Cambridge History of the Cold War*, vol. 2: *Crises and Détente*. Cambridge: Cambridge University Press, 2010.

Radchenko, S., and Wolff, D., 'To the summit via proxy-summits: new evidence from Soviet and Chinese archives on Mao's Long March to Moscow, 1949'. *Cold War International History Project Bulletin* 16, 2007–8.

Radek, K., *Vneshnyaya politika Sovetskoy Rossii*. Moscow: Gosudarstvennoe izdatel'stvo, 1923.

Radosh, R., Habeck, M. R., and Sevostianov, G. (eds), *Spain Betrayed: The Soviet Union in the Spanish Civil War*. New Haven, Conn.: Yale University Press, 2001.

Rainer, J. M., *Imre Nagy: A Biography*. London: I. B. Tauris, 2009.

Rajak, S., 'The Tito–Khrushchev correspondence, 1954'. *Cold War International History Project Bulletin* 12–13, 2001.

Rajak, S., 'The Cold War in the Balkans, 1945–1956'. In M. P. Leffler and O. A.Westad (eds), *The Cambridge History of the Cold War*, vol. 1: *Origins*. Cambridge: Cambridge University Press, 2010.

Ranzato, G., *L'eclissi della democrazia: la guerra civile spagnola e le sue origini 1931–1939*. Turin: Bollati Boringhieri, 2004.

Rapone, L., *La socialdemocrazia europea tra le due guerre: dall'organizzazione della pace alla resistenza al fascismo*. Rome: Carocci, 1999.

Rasshchirennii plenum Ispolnitel'nogo Komiteta Kommunisticheskogo Internatsionala 12–23 iunia 1923g. Otchet. Moscow, 1923.

Reale, E., *Nascita del Cominform*. Milan: Mondadori, 1958.

Rees,T., 'The highpoint of Comintern influence? The Communist Party and the Civil War in Spain'. In T. Rees and A. Thorpe (eds), *International Communism and the Communist International*. Manchester: Manchester University Press, 1998.

Reiman, M., *The Birth of Stalinism: The USSR on the Eve of the Second Revolution*. London: I. B. Tauris, 1987.

Rentola, K., 'The Soviet leadership and Finnish communism'. In J. Nevakivi (ed.), *Finnish–Soviet Relations 1944–1948*. Helsinki: Dept of Political History, University of Helsinki, 1994.

Rentola, K., 'Finnish Communism, O. W. Kuusinen, and their two native countries'. In T. Saarela and K. Rentola (eds), *Communism National and International*. Helsinki: SHS, 1998.

Rey, M.-P., 'La gauche française face à la perestroika'. *Communisme* 76–7, 2003–4.

Reynolds, D., 'Science, technology, and the Cold War'. In M. P. Leffler and O. A. Westad (eds), *The Cambridge History of the Cold War*, vol. 3: *Endings*. Cambridge: Cambridge University Press, 2010.

Riddell, J. (ed.), *To See the Dawn. Baku, 1920: First Congress of the Peoples of the East*. New York: Pathfinder, 1993.

Rieber, A. J., 'Civil wars in the Soviet Union'. *Kritika: Explorations in Russian and Eurasian History* 6.1, 2003, 129–62.

Righi, M. L. (ed.), *Quel terribile '56: i verbali della direzione comunista tra il XX Congresso del PCUS e l'VIII Congresso del PCI*. Rome: Editori Riuniti, 1996.

Riva, V., *Oro da Mosca: i finanziamenti sovietici al PCI dalla Rivoluzione d'ottobre al crollo dell'URSS*. Milan: Mondadori, 1999.

Rkp(b), *Vnutripartiinaya bor'ba v dvadtsatye gody: dokumenty i materialy 1923 g*. Moscow: Rosspen, 2004.

Roberts, G., *The Soviet Union and the Origins of the Second World War: Russo-German Relations and the Road to War, 1933–1941*. London: Macmillan, 1995.

Roberts, G., *Stalin's Wars: From World War to Cold War, 1939–1953*. New Haven, Conn.: Yale University Press, 2006.

Roger, P., *The American Enemy: The History of French Anti-Americanism*. Chicago: University of Chicago Press, 2005.

Ro'i, Y., and Morozov, B., *The Soviet Union and the June 1967 Six Day War*. Washington, DC/Stanford, Calif.: Woodrow Wilson Center Press/Stanford University Press, 2008.

Romero, F., *Storia della Guerra Fredda: l'ultimo conflitto per l'Europa*. Turin: Einaudi, 2009.

Rosenberg, A., *Geschichte des Bolschewismus von Marx bis zur Gegenwart*. Berlin: Rowohlt, 1932. Translated into Italian as *Storia del bolscevismo* (Florence: Sansoni, 1969).

Rosenberg, E. S., 'Consumer capitalism and the end of the Cold War'. In M. P. Leffler and O. A. Westad (eds), *The Cambridge History of the Cold War*, vol. 3: *Endings*. Cambridge: Cambridge University Press, 2010.

Rosenfeldt, N. E., *The 'Special' World: Stalin's Power Apparatus and the Soviet System's Secret Structures of Communication*. Copenhagen: Museum Tusculanum Press, University of Copenhagen, 2009.

Rossanda, R., *La ragazza del secolo scorso*. Turin: Einaudi, 2005.

Rossi, A. (Tasca, A.), *Autopsie du stalinisme: avec le texte intégral du rapport Khrouchtchev*. Paris: Pierre Horay, 1957.

Rossiya nepovskaya. Moscow: Novyi Khronograf, 2002.

Roy, S., *M. N. Roy: A Political Biography*. New Delhi: Orient Longman, 1997.

Rubbi, A., *Il mondo di Berlinguer*. Rome: Napoleone, 1994.

Russko-kitayskie otnosheniya v XX veke: materialy i dokumenty, ed. S. L. Tikhvinskii. 5 vols. Moscow: Pamyatniki Istoricheskoy Mysli, 2000.

Ryan, J. G., *Earl Browder: The Failure of American Communism*. Tuscaloosa: University of Alabama Press, 1997.

Rzheshevskii, O. A., 'Vizit A. Idena v Moskvu v dekabre 1941 g. Peregovory s I. V. Stalinym i V. M. Molotovym'. *Novaya i noveishaya istoriya* 2, 1994.

Rzheshevskii, O. A., *Stalin i Cherchill. Vstrechi. Besedy. Diskussii. Dokumenty, kommentarii 1941–1945*. Moscow: Nauka, 2004.

Saich, T., *The Origins of the First United Front in China: The Role of Sneevliet (Alias Maring)*. 2 vols. Leiden: E. J. Brill, 1991.

Saich, T. (ed.), *The Rise to Power of the Chinese Communist Party: Documents and Analysis*. Armonk, N.Y.: M. E. Sharpe, 1996.

Saikal, A., 'Islamism, the Iranian Revolution, and the Soviet invasion of Afghanistan'. In M. P. Leffler and O. A. Westad (eds), *The Cambridge History of the Cold War*, vol. 3: *Endings*. Cambridge: Cambridge University Press, 2010.

Samuel, R., *The Lost World of British Communism*. London: Verso, 2006.

Samuelson, L., 'Wartime perspectives and economic planning: Tukhachevsky and the military-industrial complex, 1925–1937'. In S. Pons and A. Romano (eds), *Russia in the Age of Wars, 1914–1945*. Milan: Feltrinelli, 2000.

Santamaria, Y., *Le pacifisme, une passion française*. Paris: Armand Colin, 2005.

Santamaria, Y., *Le parti de l'ennemi? Le Parti communiste français dans la lutte pour la paix (1947–1958)*. Paris: Armand Colin, 2006.

Sassoon, D., *One Hundred Years of Socialism: The West European Left in the Twentieth Century*. London: I. B. Tauris, 1996.

Savranskaya, S., and Taubman, W., 'Soviet foreign policy, 1962–1975'. In M. P. Leffler and O. A. Westad (eds), *The Cambridge History of the Cold War*, vol. 2: *Crises and Détente*. Cambridge: Cambridge University Press, 2010.

Schaefer, B., 'Weathering the Sino-Soviet conflict: the GDR and North Korea, 1949–1989'. *Cold War International History Project Bulletin* 14–15, 2003–4.

Schaefer B., 'Communist vanguard contest in East Asia during the 1960s and 1970s'. In T. Vu and W. Wongsurawat (eds), *Dynamics of the Cold War in Asia: Ideology, Identity and Culture*. London: Palgrave Macmillan, 2010.

Schoenhals, M., 'Mao Zedong: speeches at the 1957 Moscow conference'. *Journal of Communist Studies* 2.2, 1986.

Schram, S. R., *The Political Thought of Mao Tse-tung*. New York: Praeger, 1963. Translated into Italian as *Il pensiero politico di Mao Tse-Tung* (Florence: Vallecchi, 1971).

Schrecker, E., *Many Are the Crimes: McCarthyism in America*. Princeton, N.J.: Princeton University Press, 1998.

Segre, S., *A chi fa paura l'eurocomunismo?* Rimini: Guaraldi, 1977.

Selden, M., *China in Revolution: The Yenan Way Revisited*. Armonk, NY: M. E. Sharpe, 1995.

Selverstone, M. J., *Constructing the Monolith: The United States, Great Britain, and International Communism, 1945–1950*. Cambridge, Mass.: Harvard University Press, 2009.

Service, R., *Lenin: A Political Life*, vol. 2: *Worlds in Collision*. London: Macmillan, 1991.

Service, R., *Lenin: A Political Life*, vol. 3: *The Iron Ring*. London: Macmillan, 1995.

Service, R., *Comrades! A History of World Communism*. London: Macmillan, 2007.

Service, R., 'The way they talked then: the discourse of politics in the Soviet Party Politburo in the late 1920s'. In P. R. Gregory and N. M. Naimark (eds), *The Lost Politburo Transcripts: From Collective Rule to Stalin's Dictatorship*. New Haven, Conn.: Yale University Press, 2008.

Service, R., *Trotsky: A Biography*. London: Macmillan, 2009.

Seton-Watson, H., *From Lenin to Malenkov: The History of World Communism*. New York: Praeger, 1953.

Shakhnazarov, G. K., *S vozhdiami i bez nikh*. Moscow: Vagrius, 2001.

Shen, Z., and Li, D., *After Leaning to One Side: China and Its Allies in the Cold War*. Washington, DC/Stanford, Calif.: Woodrow Wilson Center Press/Stanford University Press, 2011.

Shen, Z., and Xia, Y., 'Hidden currents during the honeymoon: Mao, Khrushchev, and the 1957 Moscow conference'. *Journal of Cold War Studies* 11.4, 2009.

Shen, Z., and Xia, Y., 'Zhou Enlai's shuttle diplomacy in 1957 and its effects'. *Cold War History* 10.4, 2010.

Sheng, M. M., *Battling Western Imperialism: Mao, Stalin, and the United States*. Princeton, N.J.: Princeton University Press, 1997.

Shlaim, A., *The Iron Wall: Israel and the Arab World*. London: Penguin, 2000.

Simoncini, G., *The Communist Party of Poland 1918–1929: A Study in Political Ideology*. New York: Mellon Press, 1993.

Singer, W., 'Peasants and the peoples of the East: Indians and the rhetoric of the Komintern'. In T. Rees and A. Thorpe (eds), *International Communism and the Communist International*. Manchester: Manchester University Press, 1998.

'Sino-Cuban relations and the Cuban Missile Crisis, 1960–62: new Chinese evidence'. *Cold War International History Project Bulletin* 17–18, 2012.

Skierka, V., *Fidel*. Rome: Fandango, 2003.

Skocpol, T., *Social Revolutions in the Modern World*. Cambridge: Cambridge University Press, 1994.

Slezkine, Y., *The Jewish Century*. Princeton, N.J.: Princeton University Press, 2004.

Smith, J., *The Bolsheviks and the National Question 1917–1923*. London: Macmillan, 1999.

Smith, S. A., *A Road is Made: Communism in Shanghai, 1920–1927*. Honolulu: University of Hawai'i Press, 2000.

Snyder, T., *The Reconstruction of Nations: Poland, Ukraine, Lithuania, Belarus, 1569–1999*. New Haven, Conn.: Yale University Press, 2003.

Snyder, T., *Bloodlands: Europe Between Stalin and Hitler*. New York: Basic Books, 2010.

Soutou, G.-H., 'General de Gaulle and the Soviet Union, 1943–5: ideology or European equilibrium'. In F. Gori and S. Pons (eds), *The Soviet Union and Europe in the Cold War, 1943–53*. London: Macmillan, 1996.

Souvarine, B., *Staline: aperçu historique du bolchévisme*. Paris: Plon, 1935.

Sovetskii faktor v Vostochnoy Evrope 1944–1953: dokumenty. 2 vols. Moscow: Rosspen, 1999, 2002.

Sovetskii Soyuz i vengerskii krizis 1956 goda: dokumenty. Moscow: Rosspen, 1998.

Spagnolo, C., *Sul Memoriale di Yalta: Togliatti e la crisi del movimento comunista internazionale (1956–1964)*. Rome: Carocci, 2007.

Spenser, D., *The Impossible Triangle: Mexico, Soviet Russia, and the United States in the 1920s*. Durham, N.C. Duke University Press, 1999.

Spriano, P., *Storia del Partito comunista italiano*, vol. 1: *Da Bordiga a Gramsci*. Turin: Einaudi, 1967.

Spriano, P., *I comunisti europei e Stalin*. Turin: Einaudi, 1982. Translated as *Stalin and the European Communists* (London: Verso, 1985).

SSSR i Afrika, 1918–1960: dokumentirovannaya istoriya vzaimootnoshchenii. Moscow: Institut Vseobshchei Istorii, 2002.

SSSR-Polsha. Mekhanizmy podchineniya. 1944–1949 gg: sbornik dokumentov. Moscow: Airo-XX, 1995.

Stalin, I. V., *Sochineniya*. 13 vols. Moscow: Gosudarstvennoe izdatel'stvo politicheskoy literatury, 1946–51.

Stalin, J. V., *Works [Sochineniya]*, ed. R. McNeal. 3 vols. Stanford, Calif.: Hoover Institution, 1967.

'Stalin's conversations with Chinese leaders: talks with Mao Zedong, December 1949–January 1950, and with Zhou Enlai, August–September 1952'. *Cold War International History Project Bulletin* 6–7, 1995–6.

Stankova, M., *Georgi Dimitrov: A Biography*. New York: I. B. Tauris, 2010.

Stavrakis, P. J., *Moscow and Greek Communism, 1944–1949*. Ithaca, N.Y.: Cornell University Press, 1989.

Stenogrammy zasedanii Politburo TsK Rkp(b)–Vkp(b) 1923–1938gg. V trekh tomakh, vol. 1: *1923–1926gg.*; vol. 2:*1926–1927*; vol. 3: *1928–1938*. Moscow: Rosspen, 2007.

Stephanson, A., *Kennan and the Art of Foreign Policy*. Cambridge, Mass.: Harvard University Press, 1989.

Sternhell, Z., *Naissance de l'idéologie fasciste*. Paris: Fayard, 1989. Translated into Italian as *Nascita dell'ideologia fascista* (Milan: Baldini & Castoldi, 1993).

Stites, R., *Revolutionary Dreams: Utopian Vision and Experimental Life in the Russian Revolution*. Oxford: Oxford University Press, 1989.

Sto sorok besed s Molotovym. Iz dnevnika F. Chueva. Moscow: Terra-Terra, 1991.

Studer, B., 'Liquidate the errors or liquidate the person? Stalinist Party practices as techniques of the self'. In B. Studer and H. Haumann (eds), *Stalinist Subjects: Individual and System in the Soviet Union and the Comintern, 1929–1953*. Zurich: Chronos, 2006.

Sun, Y., *The Chinese Reassessment of Socialism 1976–1992*. Princeton, N.J.: Princeton University Press, 1995.

Suri, J., *Power and Protest: Global Revolution and the Rise of Détente*. Cambridge, Mass.: Harvard University Press, 2003.

Swain, G., 'The Comintern and southern Europe, 1938–1943'. In T. Judt (ed.), *Resistance and Revolution in Mediterranean Europe 1939–1948*. London: Routledge, 1989.

Swain, G., 'The Cominform: Tito's International?' *Historical Journal* 35.3, 1992, 641–63.

Swain, G., 'Tito and the twilight of the Komintern'. In T. Rees and A. Thorpe (eds), *International Communism and the Communist International*. Manchester: Manchester University Press, 1998.

Swain, G., *Tito: A Biography*. London: I. B. Tauris, 2010.

Swift, A., *The Road to Madiun: The Indonesian Communist Uprising of 1948*. Ithaca, N.Y.: Cornell University Press, 1989.

Szalontai, B., 'You have no political line of your own: Kim Il Sung and the Soviets, 1953–1964'. *Cold War International History Project Bulletin* 14–15, 2003–4.

Szlachta, B. (ed.), *Polish Perspectives on Communism: An Anthology*. Lanham, Md.: Lexington Books, 2004.

Taubman, W., *Khrushchev: The Man and His Era*. London: Free Press, 2004.

Teiwes, F. C., *The Formation of the Maoist Leadership*. London: Contemporary China Institute, 1994.

'The emerging disputes between Beijing and Moscow: ten newly available Chinese documents, 1956–1958'. *Cold War International History Project Bulletin* 6–7, 1995–6.

Thing, M., 'The signs of communism, signs of ambiguity: language and communism'. In T. Saarela and K. Rentola (eds), *Communism National and International*. Helsinki: SHS, 1998.

Thomas, D. C., *The Helsinki Effect: International Norms, Human Rights, and the Demise of Communism*. Princeton, N.J.: Princeton University Press, 2001.

Thompson, E. P., *The Poverty of Theory and Other Essays*. London: Merlin Press, 1978.

Thorpe, A., *The British Communist Party and Moscow, 1920–1943*. Manchester: Manchester University Press, 2000.

Tismaneanu, V., *Stalinism for All Seasons: A Political History of Romanian Communism*. Berkeley: University of California Press, 2003.

Tismaneanu, V. (ed.), *Stalinism Revisited: The Establishment of Communist Regimes in East-Central Europe*. Budapest: Central European University Press, 2009.

Togliatti, P., *Sul fascismo*, ed. G. Vacca. Rome: Laterza 2004.

Tökés, R. L., *Béla Kun and the Hungarian Soviet Republic: The Origins and Role of the Communist Party of Hungary in the Revolution of 1918–1919*. New York: Praeger, 1967.

Törnquist, O., *Dilemmas of Third World Communism: The Destruction of the PKI in Indonesia*. London: Zed Books, 1984.

Traverso, E., *A ferro e fuoco: la guerra civile europea 1914–1945*. Bologna: il Mulino, 2007.

Trinadtsatii s'ezd Rkp(b). Mai 1924 goda. Stenograficheskii otchet. Moscow: Gosudarstvennoe izdatel'stvo politicheskoy literatury, 1963.

Trotsky, L., *La crise du parti communiste français*. Paris: Librairie de l'Humanité, 1922.

Trotsky, L., *Towards Socialism or Capitalism?* London: Methuen, 1926. Repr. Abingdon: Routledge, 2012.

Trotsky, L., *My Life: An Attempt at Autobiography*. New York: Charles Scribner's Sons, 1930. Translated into Italian as *La mia vita* (Mondadori, Milan, 1930).

Trotsky, L., *The Revolution Betrayed*. New York: Doubleday, Doran, 1937.

Trotsky, L., *Scritti 1929–1936*. Milan: Mondadori, 1962.

Tucker, R. C., *Stalin in Power: The Revolution from Above, 1928–1941*. New York: Norton, 1990.

Tumarkin, N., *Lenin Lives! The Lenin Cult in Soviet Russia*. Cambridge, Mass.: Harvard University Press, 1997.

Ulam, A. B., *Titoism and the Cominform*. Cambridge, Mass.: Harvard University Press, 1952.

Ulam, A. B., *Expansion and Coexistence: The History of Soviet Foreign Policy, 1917–1967.* New York: Praeger, 1968. Translated into Italian as *Storia della politica estera sovietica* (1917–1967) (Milan: Rizzoli, 1968).

Ulam, A. B., *The Communists: The Story of Power and Lost Illusions 1948–1991.* New York: Scribner, 1992.

Ulunian, A. A., 'The Soviet Union and the Greek Question, 1946–53: problems and appraisals'. In F. Gori and S. Pons (eds), *The Soviet Union and Europe in the Cold War, 1943–53.* London: Macmillan, 1996.

Van Ree, E., *The Political Thought of Joseph Stalin: A Study in Twentieth-Century Revolutionary Patriotism.* London: Routledge Curzon, 2002.

Vatlin, A. Y., *Komintern: pervye desyat let.* Moscow: Rossiya Molodaya, 1993.

Vatlin, A., '"Class brothers unite"! The British General Strike and the formation of the "United Opposition"'. In P. R. Gregory and N. M. Naimark (eds), *The Lost Politburo Transcripts: From Collective Rule to Stalin's Dictatorship.* New Haven, Conn.: Yale University Press, 2008.

Vatlin, A. Y., *Komintern: idei, resheniya, sudby.* Moscow: Rosspen, 2009.

Vatlin, A. Y., and Tutochkina, J. T. (eds), *'Pravyi uklon' v KPG i stalinizatsiya Kominterna: stenogramma zasedaniya Prezidiuma EKKI po germanskomu voprosu 19 dekabrya 1928g.* Moscow: Airo-XX, 1996.

V Congrès de l'Internationale Communiste (17 juin–8 juillet 1924): compte rendu analytique. Paris: Librairie de l'Humanité, 1924.

VI Congrès de l'Internationale Communiste, 17 juillet–1er septembre 1928:compte rendu sténographique. Milan: Feltrinelli, 1967.

Vkp(b), *Komintern i natsional' no-revolyutsionnoe dvizhenie v Kitae: dokumenty,* vols I and II. Moscow: Institut Dalnego Vostoka Ran, 1994.

Vkp(b), *Komintern i Yaponiya 1917–1941.* Moscow: Rosspen, 2001.

Vkp(b), *Komintern i Kitay: dokumenty,* vol. 4, part 2. Moscow: Rosspen, 2003.

Vkp(b), *Komintern i Kitay: dokumenty,* vol. 5. Moscow: Rosspen, 2007.

Vkp(b), *Komintern i Koreya 1918–1941.* Moscow: Rosspen, 2007.

Vneshnyaya politika Sovetskogo Soyuza, 1946 god. Moscow: 1952.

Vogel, E., *Deng Xiaoping and the Transformation of China.* Cambridge, Mass.: Harvard University Press, 2011.

Volkogonov, D., *Triumf i tragediya: politicheskii portret I.V. Stalina.* Moscow: APN, 1989.

Volkogonov, D., *The Rise and Fall of the Soviet Empire: Political Leaders from Lenin to Gorbachev.* London: HarperCollins, 1998.

Volkov, V. K., and Gibianskii, L. Y. (eds), *Vostochnaya Evropa mezhdu Gitlerom i Stalinym 1939–1941 gg.* Moscow: Indrik, 1999.

Volokitina, T. V., Murashko, G. P., Noskova, A. F., and Pokivailova, T. A., *Moskva i vostochnaya Evropa: Stanovlenie politicheskikh rezhimov sovetskogo tipa 1949–1953. Ocherki istorii.* Moscow: Rosspen, 2002.

von Hagen, M., *Soldiers in the Proletarian Dictatorship: The Red Army and the Soviet Socialist State, 1917–1930.* Ithaca, N.Y.: Cornell University Press, 1990.

Vostochnaya Evropa v dokumentakh rossiiskikh arkhivov 1944–1953. 2 vols. Moscow/ Novosibirsk: Sibirskii Khronograf, 1997–8.

V Politburo TsK KPSS…Po zapisami Anatoliya Chernyaeva, Vadima Medvedeva, Georgiya Shakhnazarova (1985–1991). Moscow: Al'pina Biznes Buks, 2006.

Waddington, L., *Hitler's Crusade: Bolshevism and the Myth of the International Jewish Conspiracy.* London: I. B. Tauris, 2007.

Wall, I. M., *French Communism in the Era of Stalin: The Quest for Unity and Integration, 1945-1962*. Westport, Conn.: Greenwood Press, 1983.

Wall, I. M., 'L'amministrazione Carter e l'eurocomunismo'. *Ricerche di storia politica* 9.2, 2006, 181–96.

Weathersby, K., *Should We Fear This? Stalin and the Danger of War with America*. Washington, D.C.: Cold War International History Project, working paper 39, July 2002.

Webb, S., and Webb, B., *Soviet Communism: A New Civilization?* London: Longman, 1935.

Weber, H., *Die Wandlung des deutschen Kommunismus: die Stalinisierung der KPD in der Weimarer Republik*. Frankfurt am Main: Europäische Verlagsanstalt, 1969. Translated as *La trasformazione del comunismo tedesco: la stalinizzazione della KPD nella Repubblica di Weimar* (Milan: Feltrinelli, 1979).

Weiner, A., *Making Sense of War: The Second World War and the Fate of the Bolshevik Revolution*. Princeton, N.J.: Princeton University Press, 2001.

Weitz, E. D., *Creating German Communism, 1890–1990: From Popular Protests to Socialist State*. Princeton, N.J.: Princeton University Press, 1997.

Werth, A., *Russia at War: 1941–1945*. New York: Carroll & Graf, 1996.

Werth, N., 'A state against its people: violence, repression, and terror in the Soviet Union'. In S. Courtois et al., *The Black Book of Communism: Crimes, Terror, Repression*. Cambridge, Mass.: Harvard University Press, 1999. Translated into Italian as 'Uno stato contro il suo popolo: violenze, repressioni, terrori nell'Unione Sovietica', in S. Courtois, N. Werth, et al., *Il libro nero del comunismo: crimini, terrore, repressione* (Milan: Mondadori, 1998).

Westad, O. A. (ed.), *Brothers in Arms: The Rise and Fall of the Sino-Soviet Alliance*. Stanford, Calif./Washington, D.C.: Stanford University Press/Woodrow Wilson Center Press, 1998.

Westad, O. A., *Decisive Encounters: The Chinese Civil War, 1946–1950*. Stanford, Calif.: Stanford University Press, 2003.

Westad, O. A., 'How the Cold War crumbled'. In S. Pons and F. Romero (eds), *Reinterpreting the End of the Cold War: Issues, Interpretations, Periodizations*. London: Frank Cass, 2005.

Westad, O. A., *The Global Cold War: Third World Interventions and the Making of Our Times*. Cambridge: Cambridge University Press, 2005.

Westad, O. A., 'The Cold War and the international history of the twentieth century'. In M. P. Leffler and O. A. Westad (eds), *The Cambridge History of the Cold War*, vol. 1: *Origins*. Cambridge: Cambridge University Press, 2010.

Westad, O. A., 'The Great Transformation: China in the Long 1970s'. In N. Ferguson, C. S. Maier, E. Manela, and D. J. Sargent (eds), *The Shock of the Global: The 1970s in Perspective*. Cambridge, Mass.: Harvard University Press, 2010.

Westad, O. A., Jian, C., Tønnesson, S., Tung, N. V., and Hershberg, J. (eds), *77 Conversations between Chinese and Foreign Leaders on the War in Indochina, 1964–1977*. Washington, D.C.: Cold War International History Project, working paper 22, 1998.

Wilson, S., 'The Komintern and the Japanese Communist Party'. In T. Rees and A. Thorpe (eds), *International Communism and the Communist International*. Manchester: Manchester University Press, 1998.

Wolff, D., 'One Finger's Worth of Historical Events': New Russian and Chinese Evidence on the Sino-Soviet Alliance and Split, 1948–1959*. Washington, D.C.: Cold War International History Project, working paper 30, 2000.

Wolikow, S., *L'Internationale communiste (1919–1943): le Komintern ou le rêve déchu du parti mondial de la révolution*. Paris: Éditions de l'Atelier, 2010.

Wolin, R., *The Wind from the East: French Intellectuals, the Cultural Revolution, and the Legacy of the 1960s*. Princeton, N.J.: Princeton University Press, 2010.

Worley, M. (ed.), *In Search of Revolution: International Communist Parties in the Third Period*. London: I. B. Tauris, 2004.

Wydra, H., *Communism and the Emergence of Democracy*. Cambridge: Cambridge University Press, 2007.

XVII s'ezd vsesoyuznoy kommunisticheskoy partii (b) 26 janvarya–10 fevralya 1934 g.: stenograficheskii otchet. Moscow: Partizdat, 1934.

Zaslavsky, V., *Storia del sistema sovietico:l'ascesa, la stabilità, il crollo*. Rome: La Nuova Italia Scientifica, 1995.

Zaslavsky, V., 'L'apparato paramilitare comunista nell'Italia del dopoguerra (1945–1955)'. In V. Zaslavsky, *Lo stalinismo e la sinistra italiana: dal mito dell'URSS alla fine del comunismo*. Milan: Mondadori, 2004.

Zaslavsky, V., *Class Cleansing: The Massacre at Katyn*. Candor, N.Y.: Telos Press, 2008.

Zhai, Q., *China and the Vietnam Wars, 1950–1975*. Chapel Hill, N.C.: University of North Carolina Press, 2000.

Zhao, S., *A Nation-State by Construction: Dynamics of Modern Chinese Nationalism*. Stanford, Calif.: Stanford University Press, 2004.

Zubok, V., 'The Soviet Union and European integration from Stalin to Gorbachev'. *Journal of European Integration History* 2, 1996.

Zubok, V., 'The Mao–Khrushchev conversations, 31 July–3 August 1958 and 2 October 1959'. *Cold War International History Project Bulletin* 12–13, 2001.

Zubok, V., *A Failed Empire: The Soviet Union from Stalin to Gorbachev*. Chapel Hill N. C: University of North Carolina Press, 2007.

Zubok, V., *Zhivago's Children: The Last Russian Intelligentsia*. Cambridge, Mass.: Harvard University Press, 2009.

Zubok, V., and Pleshakov, C., *Inside the Kremlin's Cold War: From Stalin to Khrushchev*. Cambridge, Mass.: Harvard University Press, 1996.

Index